Paris Lopez

A Personal Journey

SECOND EDITION

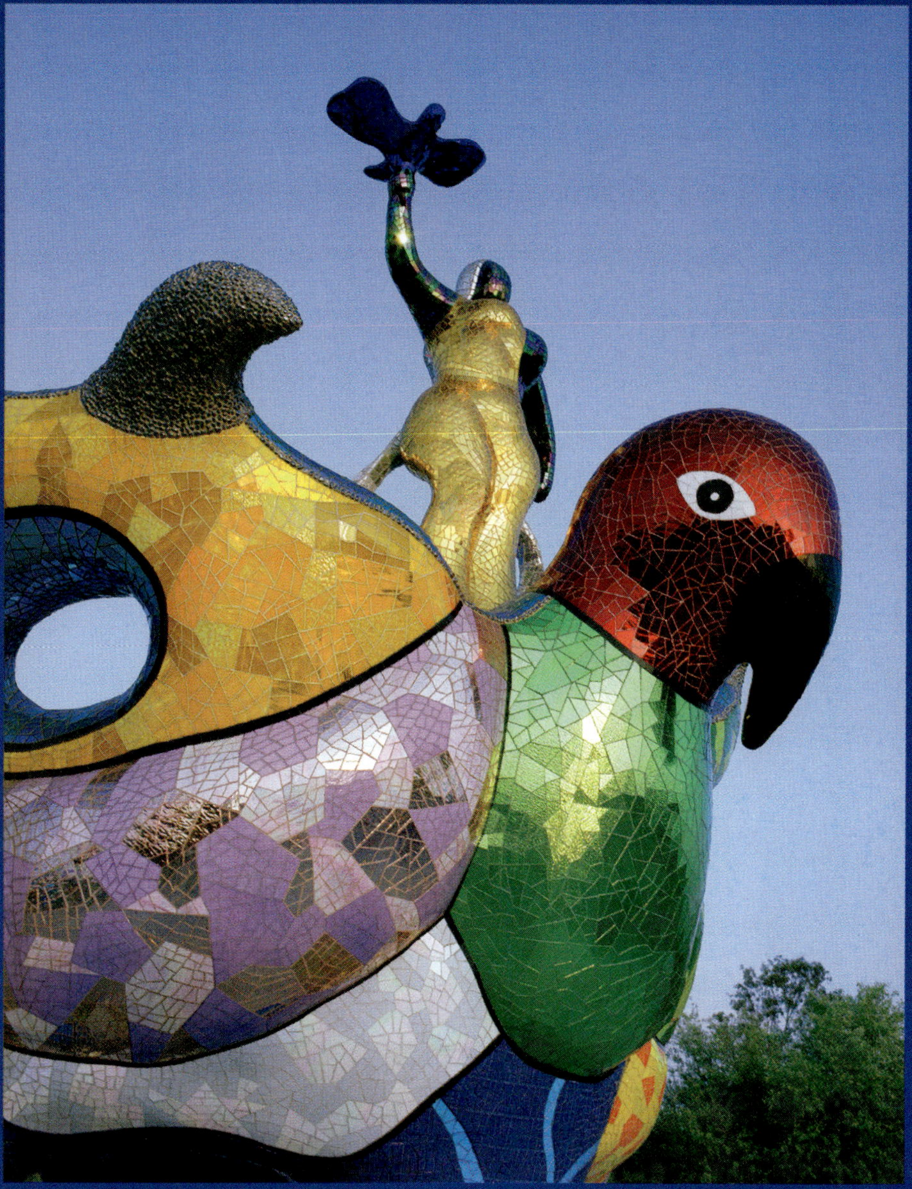

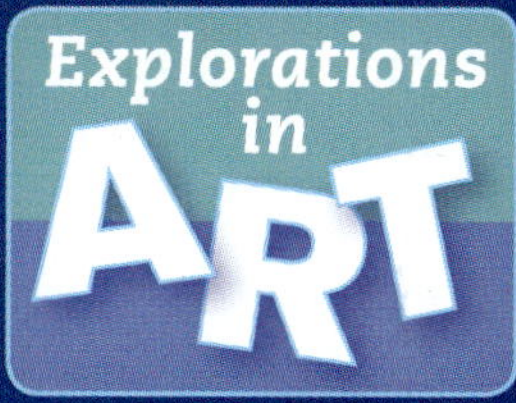

Davis Publications, Inc.
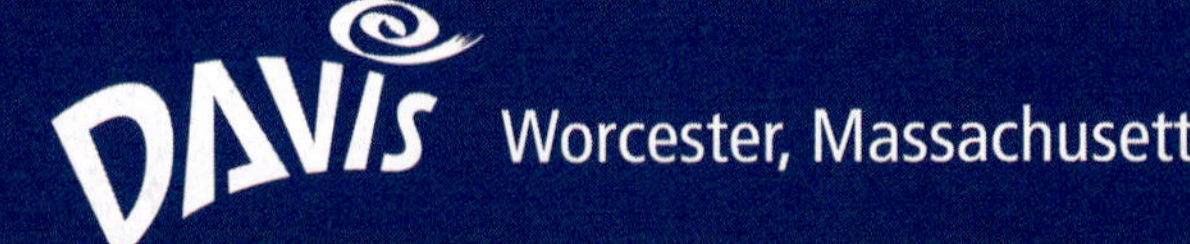

Worcester, Massachusetts

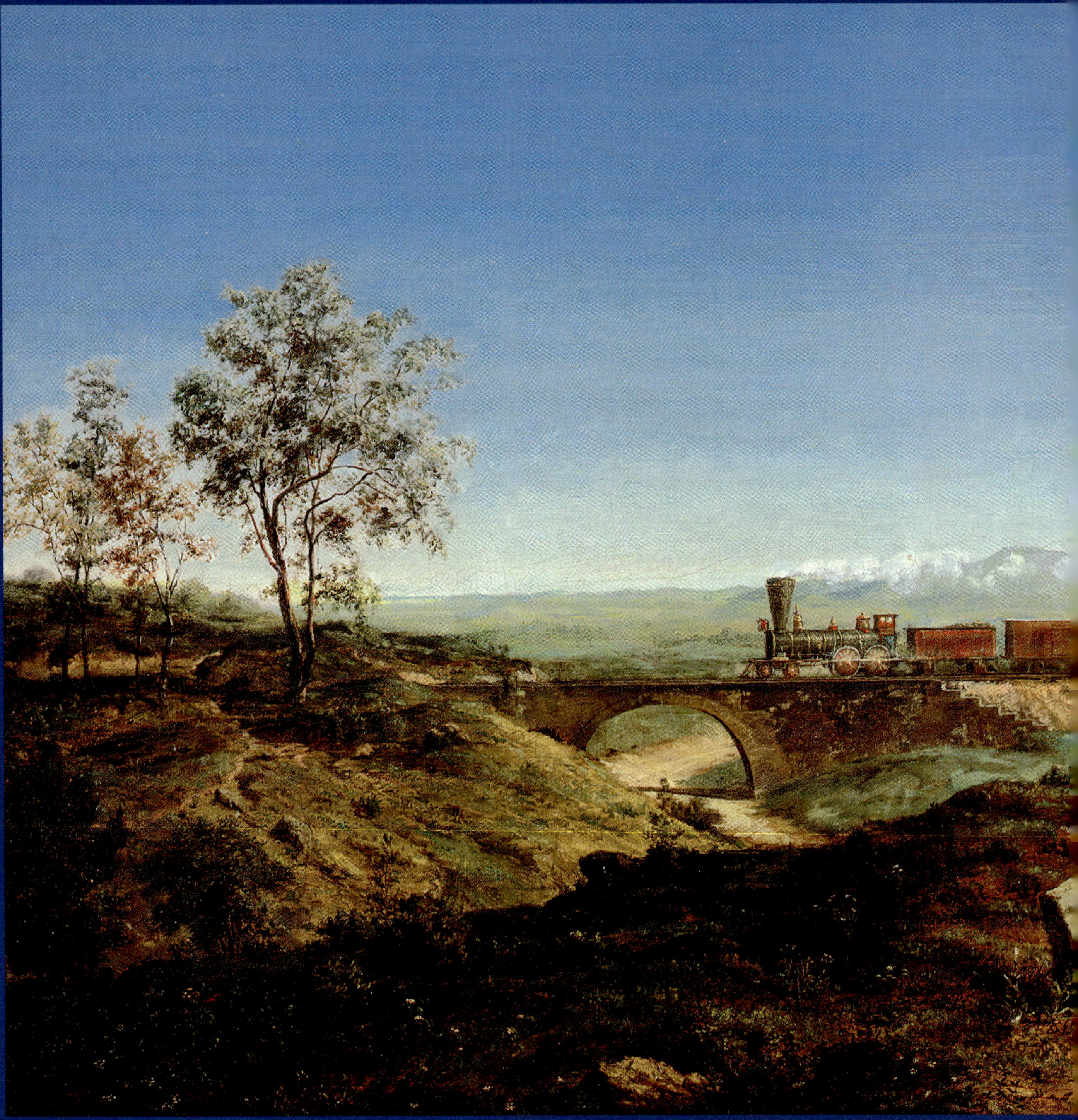

A Personal Journey

SECOND EDITION

Marilyn G. Stewart and Eldon Katter

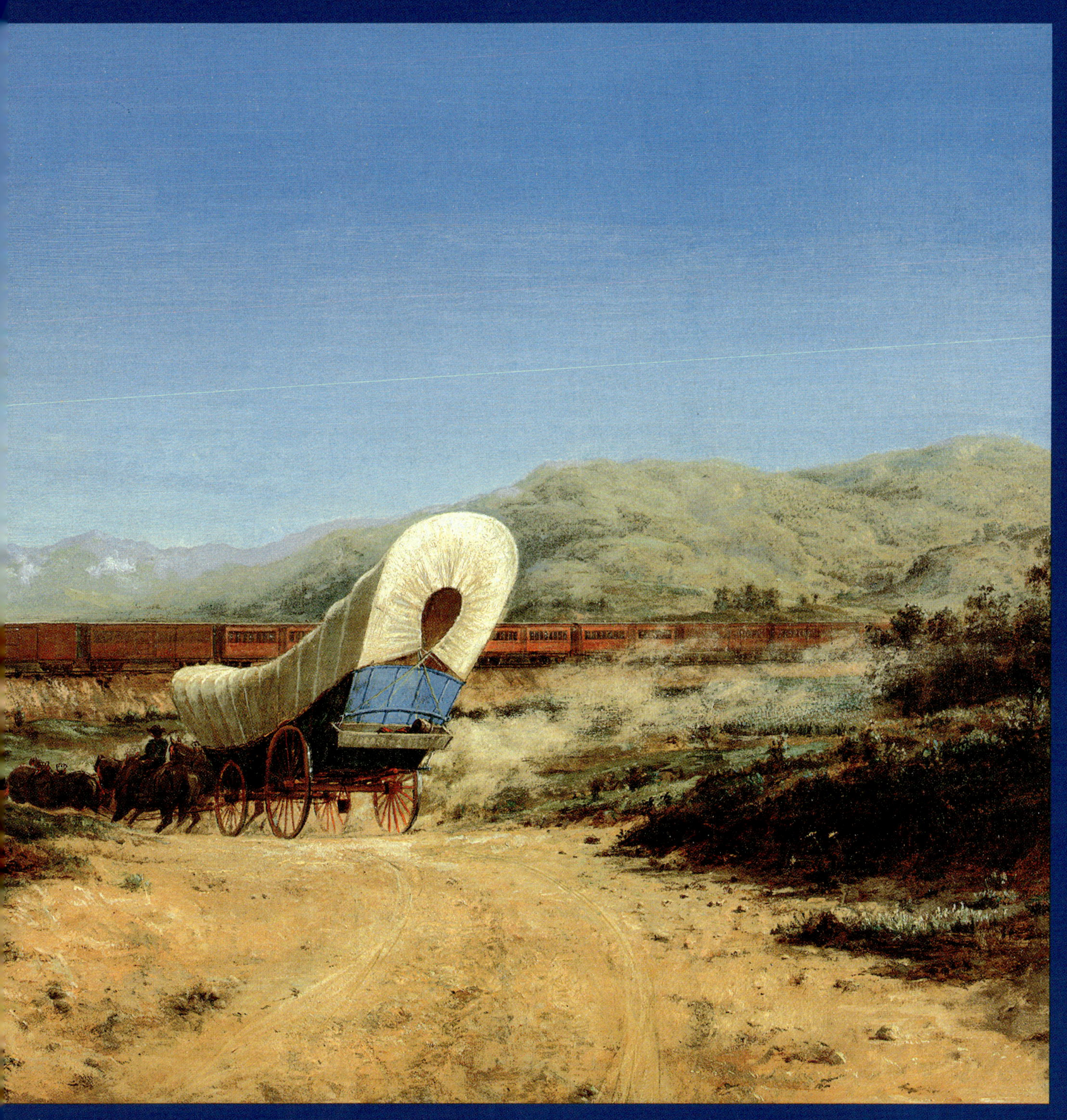

Reviewers

Donna Andrich
Houston, Texas

Jaci Hanson
Art Education Consultant
Winter Haven, Florida

BettyAnn Plishker
Fairfax County Public Schools
Annandale, Virginia

Sharon Warwick
National Consultant
Denton, Texas

Cindy Walker
Art Consultant
Chesterfield, Missouri

Educational Consultants

Monica Brown
Laurel Nokomis School
Nokomis, Florida

Ted Coe
Garfield School
Boise, Idaho

Anita Cook
Thomas Prince School
Princeton, Massachusetts

Mary Coy
Spry Middle School
Webster, New York

Robin W. Cutler
Grafton Middle School
Grafton, Massachusetts

Dale Dinapoli
Archie R. Cole Junior High School
East Greenwich, Rhode Island

Wendy Dougherty
Northview Middle School
Indianapolis, Indiana

Judith Durgin
Merrimack Valley Middle School
Penacook, New Hampshire

Leah Dussault
Plymouth Middle School
Plymouth, Minnesota

Carolyn Freese
Yorkville Middle School
Yorkville, Illinois

Elaine Gale
Sarasota Middle School
Sarasota, Florida

Cathy Gersich
Fairhaven Middle School
Bellingham, Washington

Nancy Goan
Fred C. Wescott Junior High School
Westbrook, Maine

Rachel Grabek
Chocksett Middle School
Sterling, Massachusetts

Kerri Griffin
Springhouse Middle School
Allentown, Pennsylvania

Lizabeth Lippke Haven
Kamiakin Junior High School
Kirkland, Washington

Grace A. Herron
Hillside Junior High School
Boise, Idaho

Maryann Horton
Camels Hump Middle School
Richmond, Vermont

Robin Jackson
Advent Episcopal School
Birmingham, Alabama

Anne Jacques
Smith Middle School
Fort Hood, Texas

Alice S. W. Kepley
Penn View Christian School
Souderton, Pennsylvania

Nancy Kopp
The Art Workshop
Wyoming, Ohio

Bunki Kramer
Los Cerros Middle School
Danville, California

Patricia Laney
Fletcher-Johnson Education Center
Washington, D.C.

Marguerite Lawler-Rohner
Fred C. Wescott Junior High School
Westbrook, Maine

Karen Lintner
Mount Nittany Middle School
State College, Pennsylvania

Betsy Logan
Samford Middle School
Auburn, Alabama

Emily Lynn
Smith Middle School
Fort Hood, Texas

Sara Macaulay
Winsor School
Boston, Massachusetts

Patricia Mann
T.R. Smedberg Middle School
Sacramento, California

Deborah A. Meyers
Colony Middle School
Palmer, Alaska

Phyllis Mowery-Racz
Desert Sands Middle School
Phoenix, Arizona

Jennifer Ogden
Victor School
Victor, Montana

David A. Petit
Eagle Hill Middle School
Manlius, New York

Lorraine Pflaumer
Thomas Metcalf Laboratory School
Normal, Illinois

Sharon Piper
Islesboro Central School
Islesboro, Maine

Sandy Ray
Johnakin Middle School
Marion, South Carolina

Amy R. Richard
Daniel Boone Middle School
Birdsboro, Pennsylvania

Connie Richards
William Byrd Middle School
Vinton, Virginia

Sandra Richey
Sweetwater Middle School
Sweetwater, Texas

Susan Rushin
Pocono Mountain Intermediate School South
Swiftwater, Pennsylvania

Richard Shilalae
Holy Name Central Catholic Middle School
Worcester, Massachusetts

Roger Shule
Antioch Upper Grade School
Antioch, Illinois

Betsy Menson Sio
Jordan-Elbridge Middle School
Jordan, New York

Sharon Siswick
Islesboro Central School
Islesboro, Maine

Karen Skophammer
Manson Northwest Webster Community School
Barnum, Iowa

Evelyn Sonnichsen
Plymouth Middle School
Plymouth, Minnesota

Ann Titus
Central Middle School
Galveston, Texas

Shirley W. Whitesides
Asheville Middle School
Asheville, North Carolina

Program Authors

Marilyn G. Stewart
Eldon Katter

Writers

Judy Douglass
Tracy Ellen
Kaye Passmore
Cory Perewiznyk
Kathleen Walck
Nancy Walkup
Tara Young

Project Staff

President and Publisher
Wyatt Wade

Content Editor
Claire Mowbray Golding

Editor
Reba Libby

Product Manager
Barbara Place

Design
WGBH Design:
Tong-Mei Chan
Tyler Kemp-Benedict
Greta Merrick
Jonathan Rissmeyer
Douglass Scott
Michelle Vaira

With extremely helpful image guidance from Karl Cole, Curator of Images

Production
Chrysalis Publishing Group

Editorial Assistants
Photo Acquisitions
Jane McKeag
Abigail Reip
Donna Young

Illustrator
Susan Christy-Pallo

Photography
Tom Fiorelli

Manufacturing
Georgiana Rock

Library of Congress Control Number 2008931904

Printed in the United States of America

ISBN: 978-0-87192-883-2

1 2 3 4 5 6 7 8 9 RRD 15 14 13 12 11 10 09 08

Cover: Niki de Saint Phalle, *Queen Califia's Magical Circle*, Kit Carson Park, Escondido, California, 2002–2003 ©2008 NIKI CHARITABLE ART FOUNDATION, All rights reserved, Photo Credit: ©Philip Scholz-Rittermann Artist Rights Society (ARS), NY.

Title Page: Thomas Otter, *On the Road*, 1860. Oil on canvas, 22" x 45 ⅜" (55.8 x 115.3 cm). The Nelson-Atkins Museum of Art, Kansas City, Missouri (Purchase Nelson Trust).

A Letter from the Authors

Dear Student,

We are delighted that you'll be using *A Personal Journey* as your art textbook this year.

Our goal in writing this book was to offer you experiences in art that will matter to you today and remain part of your thinking well into the future.

We hope this textbook will inspire you to notice the art all around you. We also hope it will help you express your own ideas and feelings through art in its many forms—drawing, painting, sculpture, photography, printmaking, fiber arts, ceramics, graphic design, and their countless combinations.

You may wonder why we chose the book's unit titles. Each unit focuses on a "big idea" such as Nature, Messages, or Daily Life. These ideas have been important to people around the world throughout history. As you learn about them, we hope you'll begin to see that ideas like these connect you to people who may live far away, people you will never meet. These are the ideas that make us all human. These are the ideas that form the basis for the art people make, no matter when or where they live.

Enjoy your journey!

Marilyn G. Stewart Eldon Katter

Marilyn G. Stewart is Professor of Art Education, Kutztown University of Pennsylvania. She is co-author, with Eldon Katter, of *Explorations in Art 1–5*, author of *Thinking Through Aesthetics*, co-author, with Sydney Walker, of *Rethinking Curriculum in Art*, and series editor of the Art Education in Practice series, all published by Davis Publications. Her honors and awards include 1998 Eastern Region Higher Education Art Educator of the Year, 2006 Pennsylvania Art Educator of the Year, and 1997–98 Getty Education Institute for the Arts Visiting Scholar. A frequent speaker and consultant, she has conducted more than 160 staff development institutes, seminars, or workshops in over 25 states.

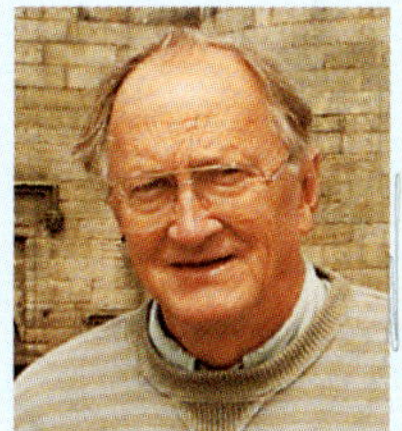

Eldon Katter is Emeritus Professor of Art Education at Kutztown University. He is co-author, with Marilyn Stewart, of *Explorations in Art 1–5*, former editor of *SchoolArts,* and former president of the National Art Education Association. He has taught art in elementary schools in Illinois and Massachusetts. As a Peace Corps volunteer in the 1960s, he taught art at a teacher training school in Harar, Ethiopia. He also worked for the Teacher Education in East Africa project in Kampala, Uganda.

An Introduction to Art

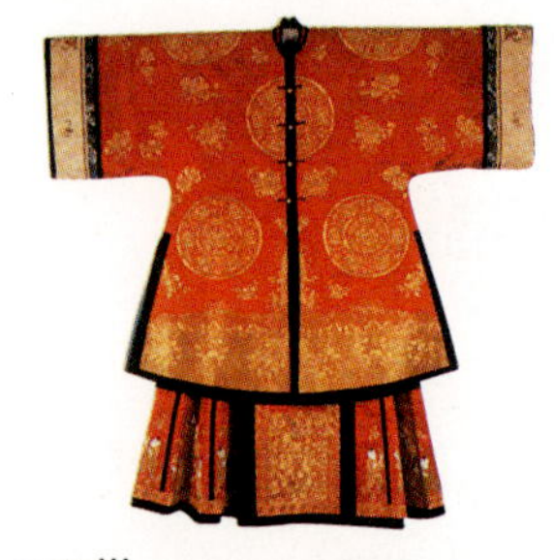

p. xviii

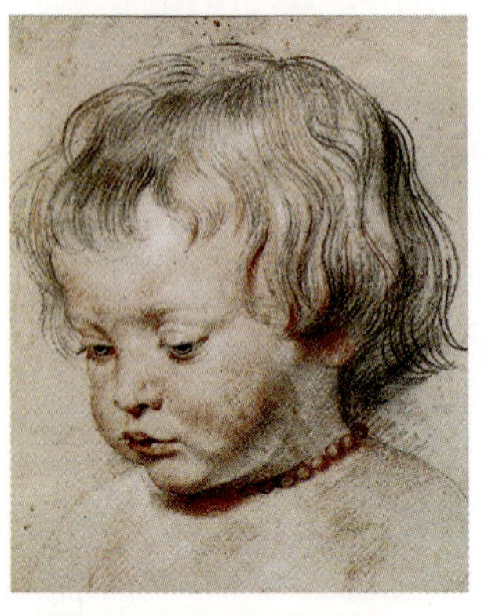

p. xx

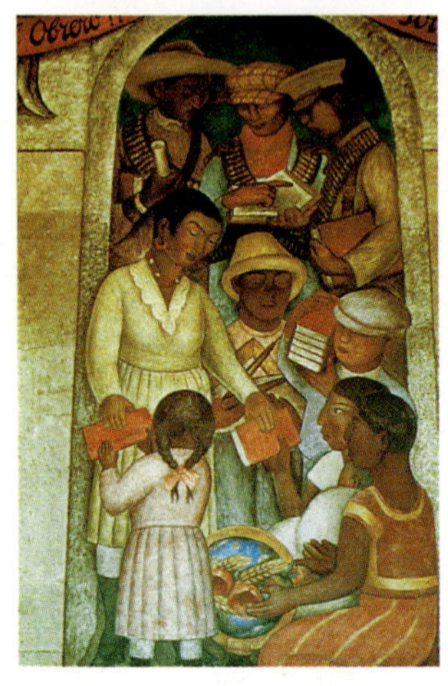

p. xx

Unit 1 Artists Are Storytellers

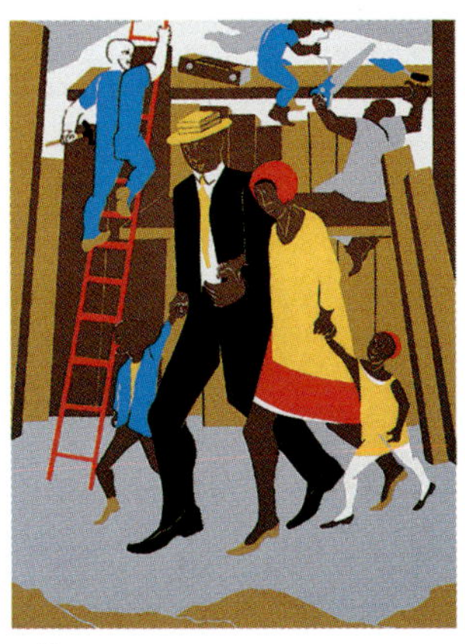

p. 2

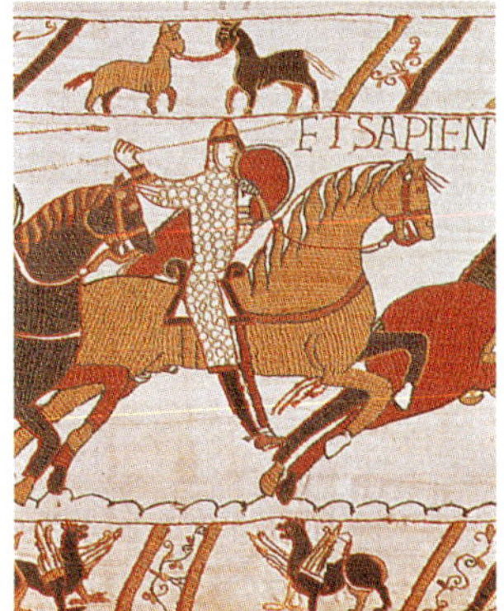

p. 16

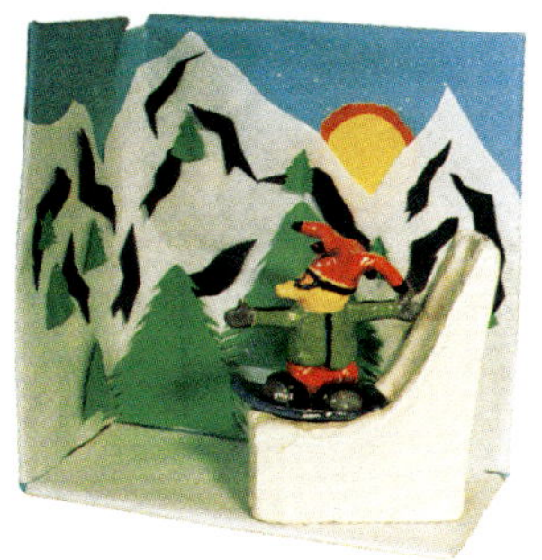

p. 27

Unit 1 Artists

Unit 2 Artists Are Recorders

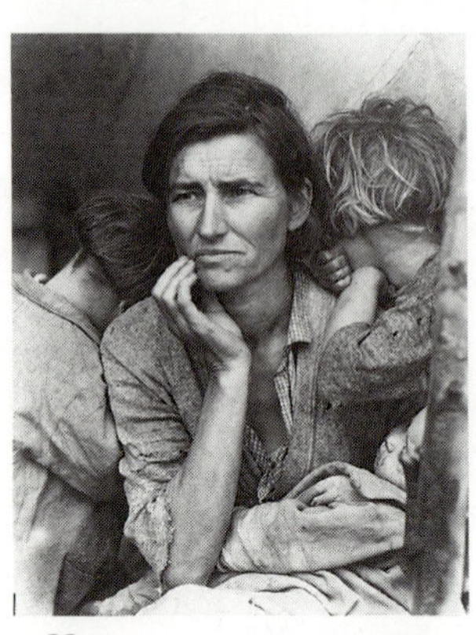
p. 32

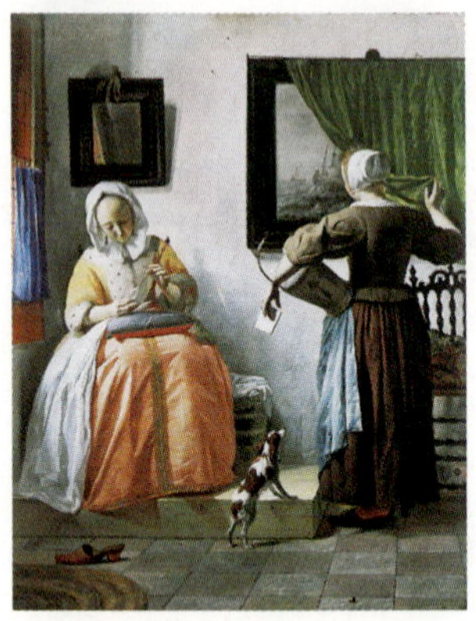
p. 46

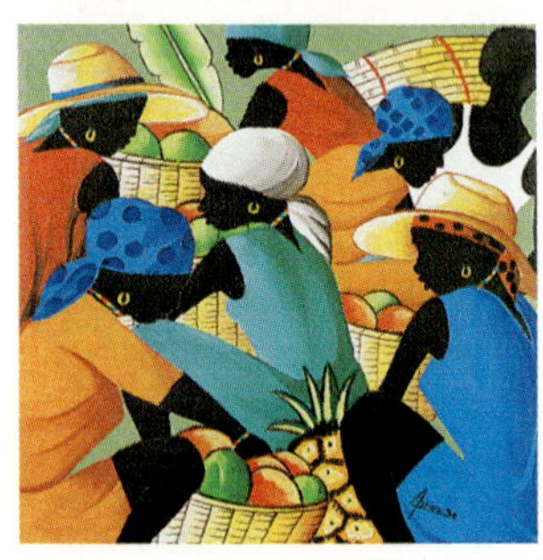
p. 53

Unit 2 Artists

Unit 3 Artists Are Designers

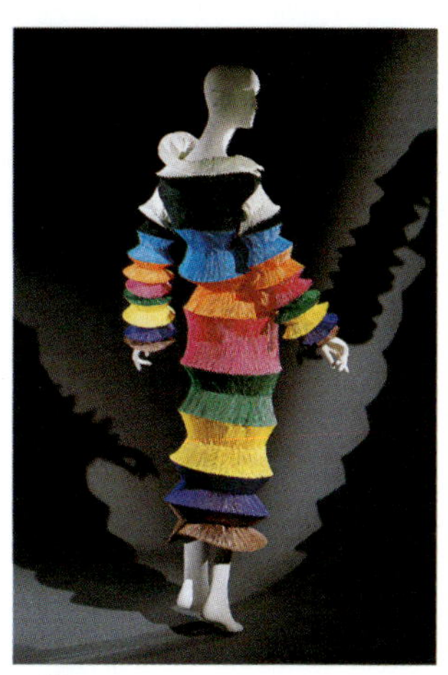
p. 62

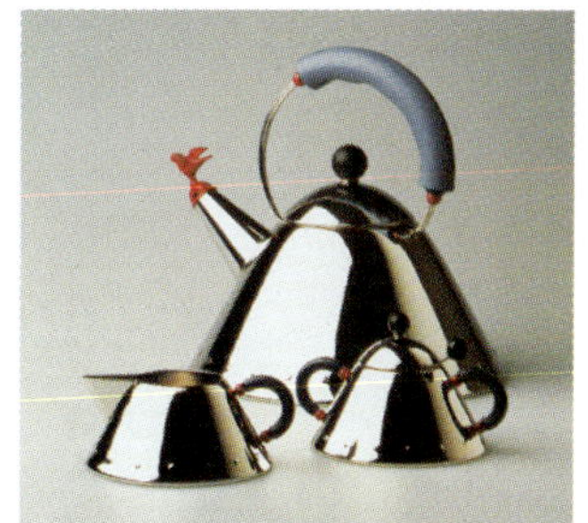
p. 78

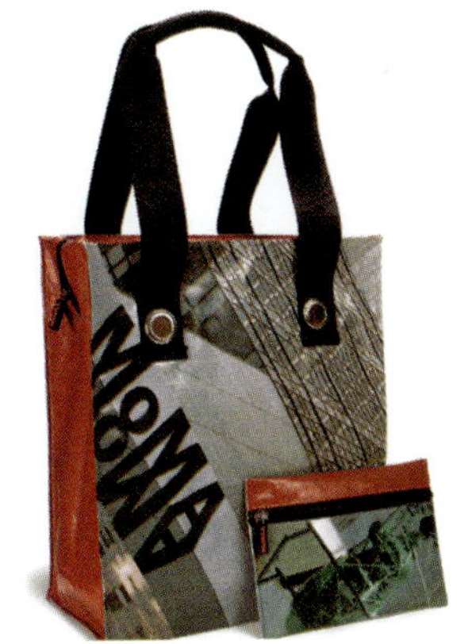

p. 85

Unit 3 Artists

Unit 4 Artists Are Teachers

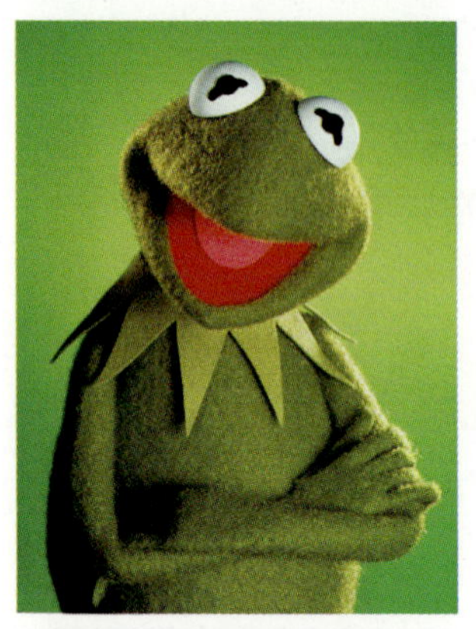
p. 94

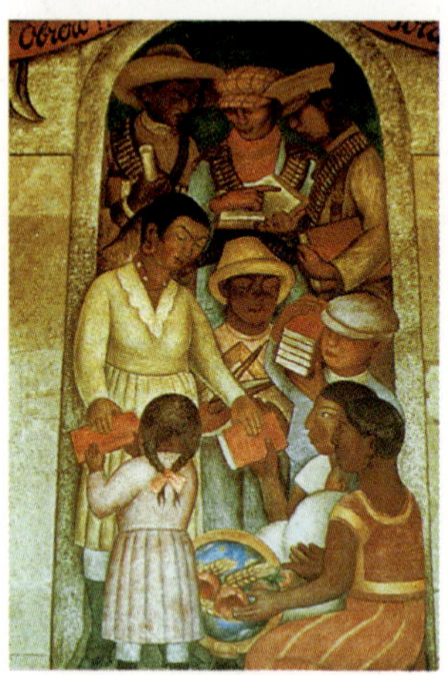
p. 107

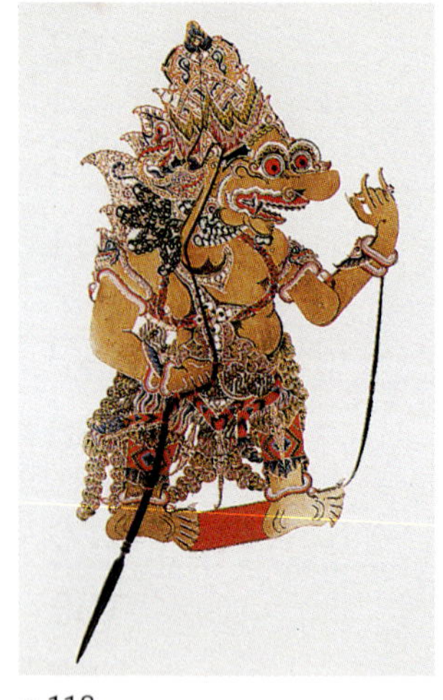
p. 118

Unit 4 Artists

Unit 5 Artists Are Naturalists

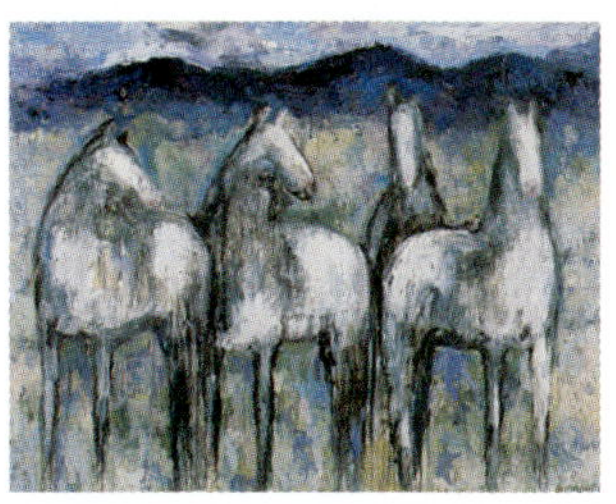
p. 125

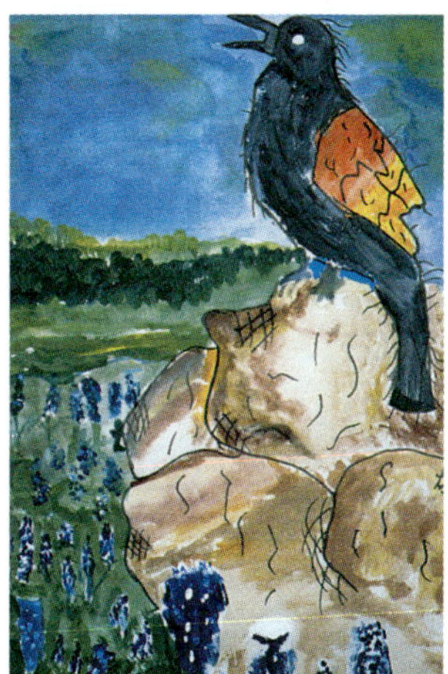
p. 135

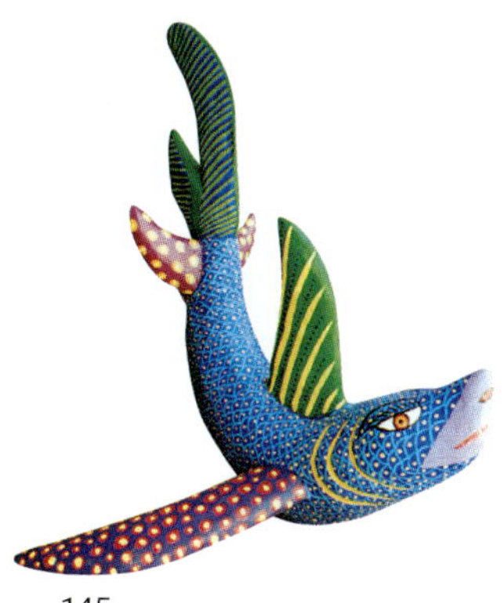
p. 145

Unit 5 Artists

Unit 6 Artists Are Messengers

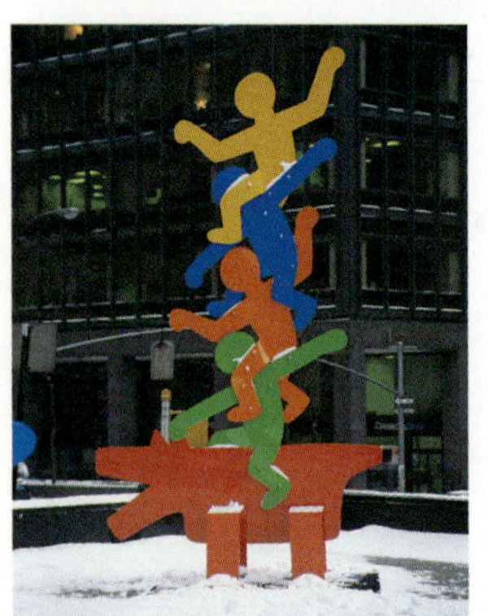
p.152

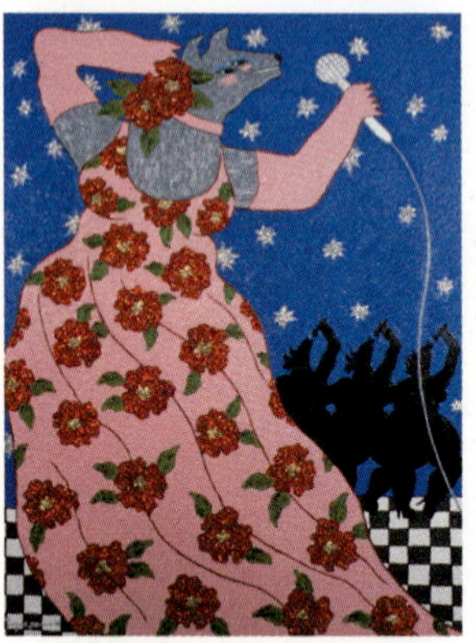
p. 168

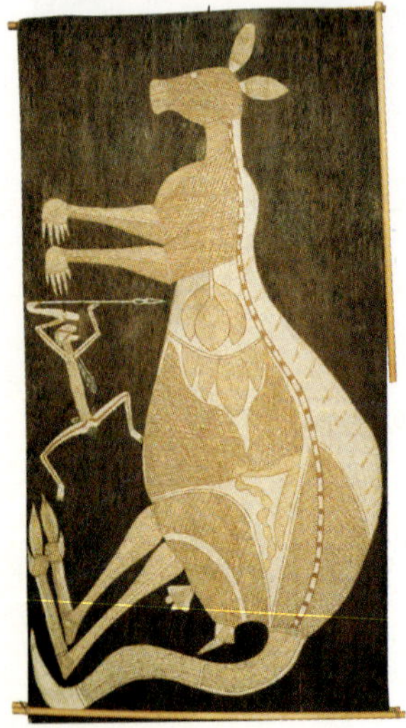
p. 171

Unit 7 Artists Are Inventors

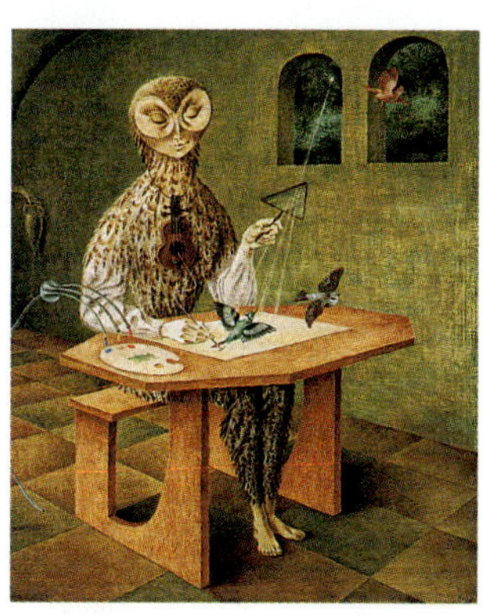
p. 183

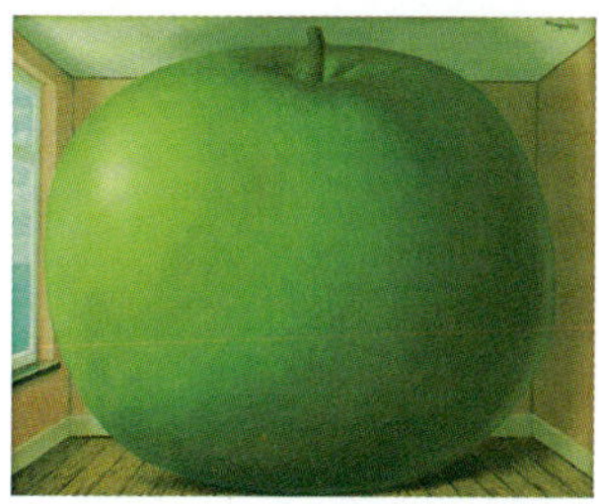
p. 196

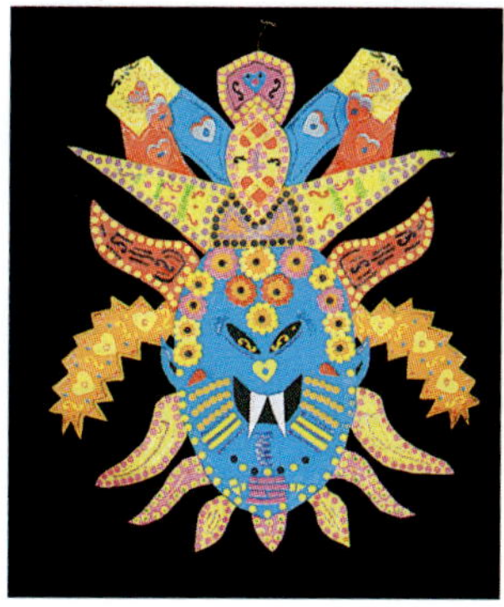
p. 203

Unit 8 Artists Are Planners

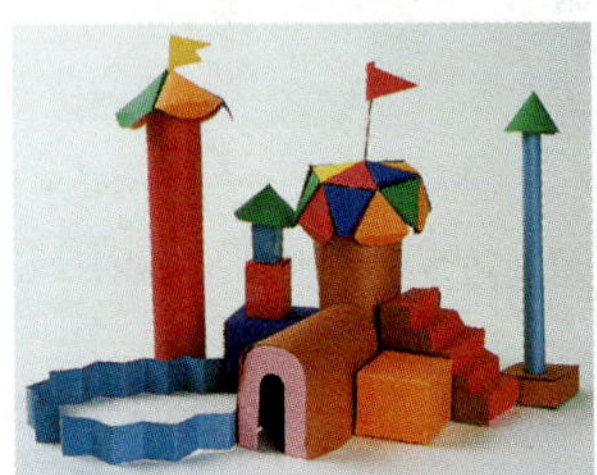
p. 221

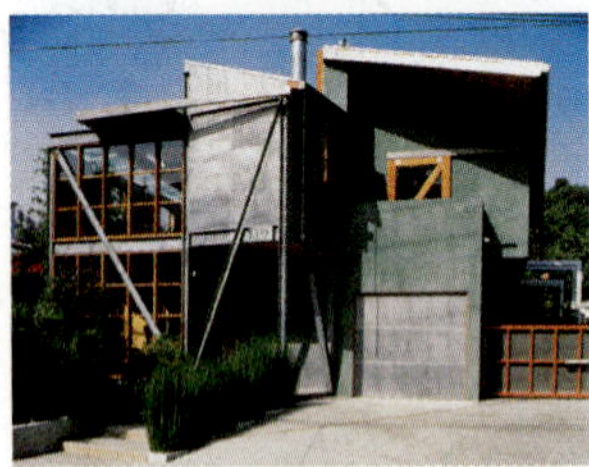
p. 228

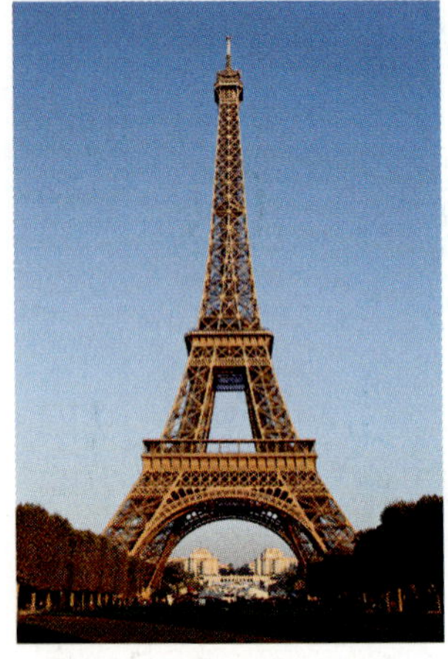
p. 235

Unit 8 Artists

Unit 9 Artists Are Pioneers

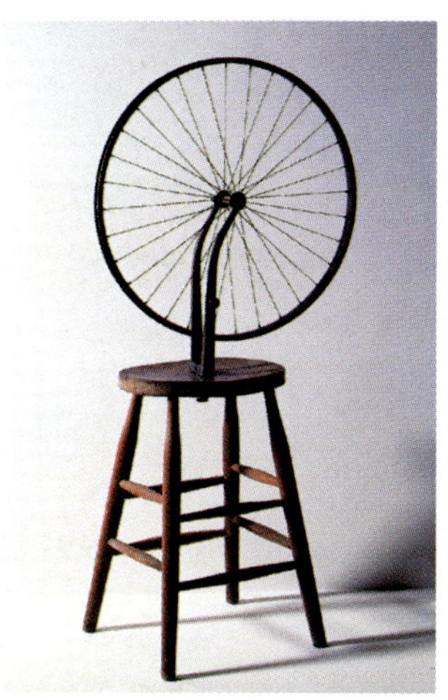
p. 246

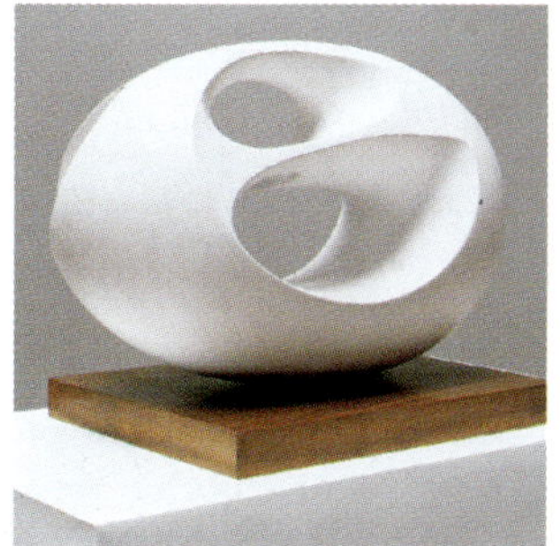
p. 256

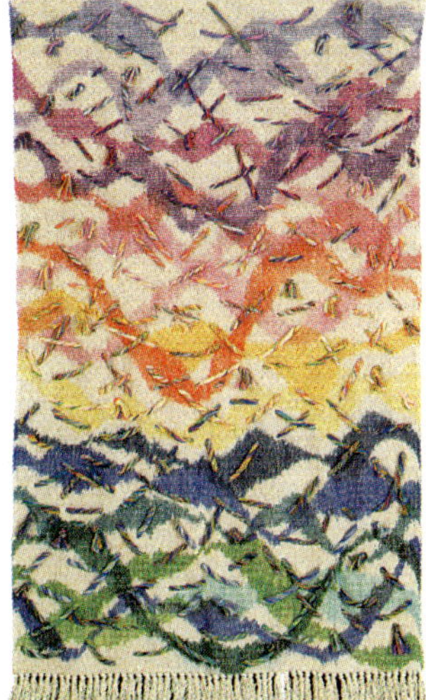
p. 269

Student Handbook

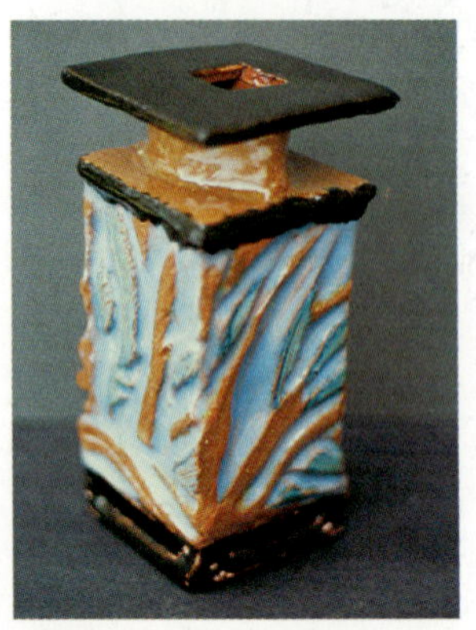
p. 277

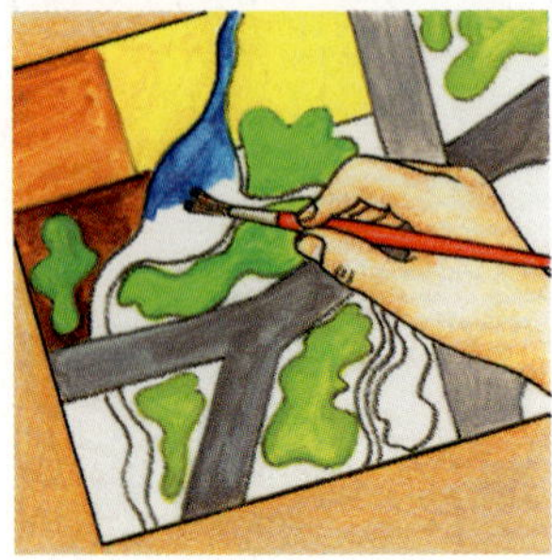
p. 301

Resources

An Introduction to Art

Art. It's a simple, three-letter word that you probably could spell when you were five years old. It's easy to define, too, isn't it? Art is... Well, wait a minute. What *is* art?

This section of your book has been created to introduce you to art. You may think you don't need an introduction—after all, you've probably seen a painting or two here or there over the years, and that's art, right? Right. But that's not all you need to know about art. Why do people make it? How do they use it? What about buildings or clay pots—are they artworks? What are artworks made of? What do they mean? These questions don't always have easy answers, but it's a great adventure to think about them. That's what this section—and the rest of this book—will help you do.

This section also introduces you to art's most basic building blocks—the elements of art and principles of design—through artworks that show them clearly. You'll learn about the steps to use when you look thoughtfully at a work of art. You'll also learn about the steps to use when creating your own artwork.

Come back to this section again and again, whenever you need to review art's most fundamental ideas. And keep asking yourself: What *is* art, and what is it *for*?

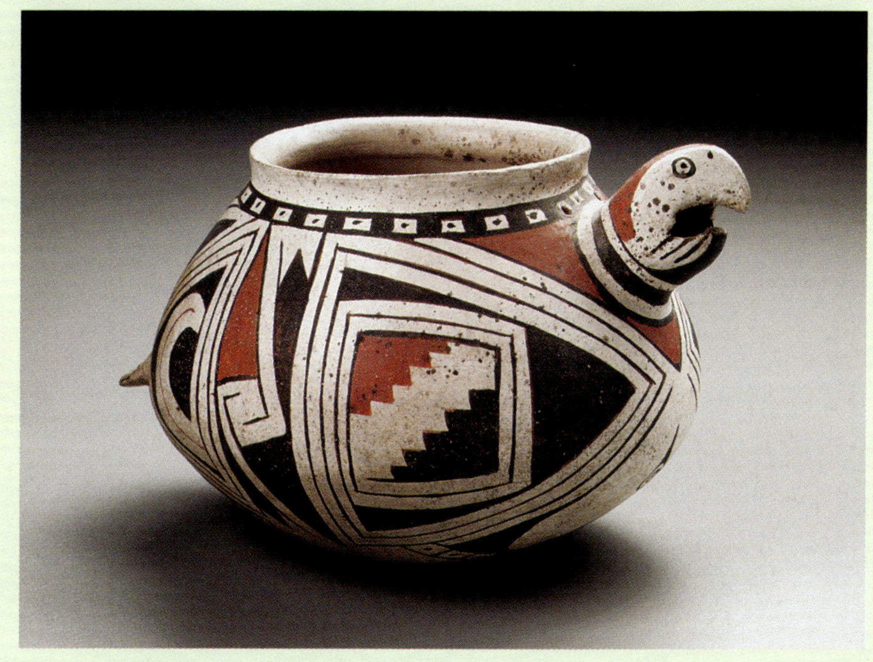

Mogollon (Casas Grandes style), *Macaw Bowl*, Tardio Period, 1300–1350.

What is art?

Architecture

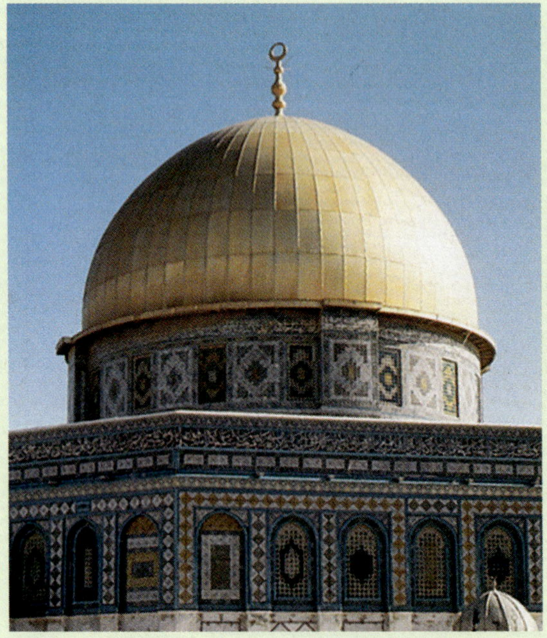

Dome of the Rock, late 7th century. Jerusalem, Israel.

Furniture

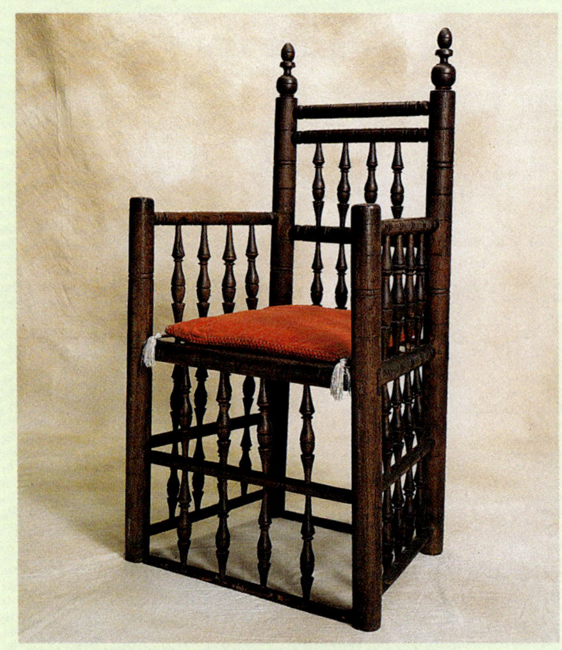

Massachusetts Bay Colony, *Bradford Chair*, 1630.

Clothing

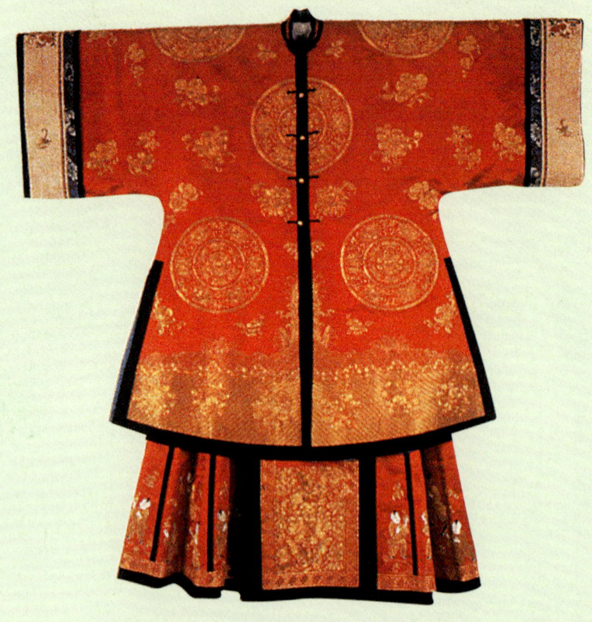

China, Qing dynasty, *Wedding Ensemble*, ca. 1860.

Photography

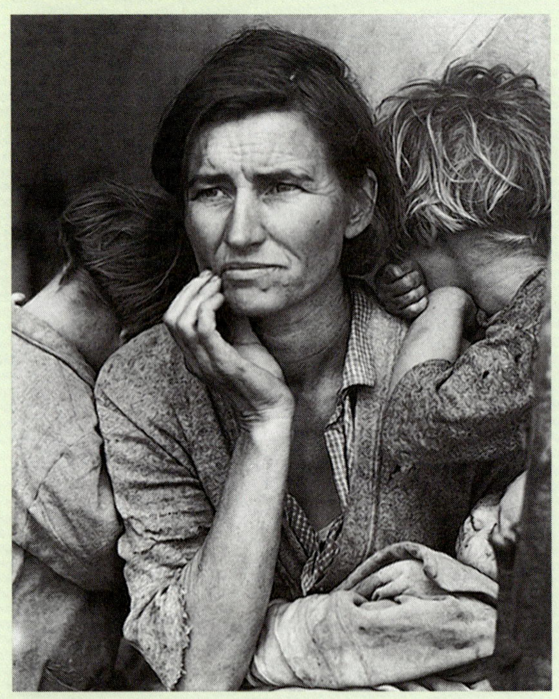

Dorothea Lange, *Migrant Mother, Nipomo, California,* 1936.

Painting

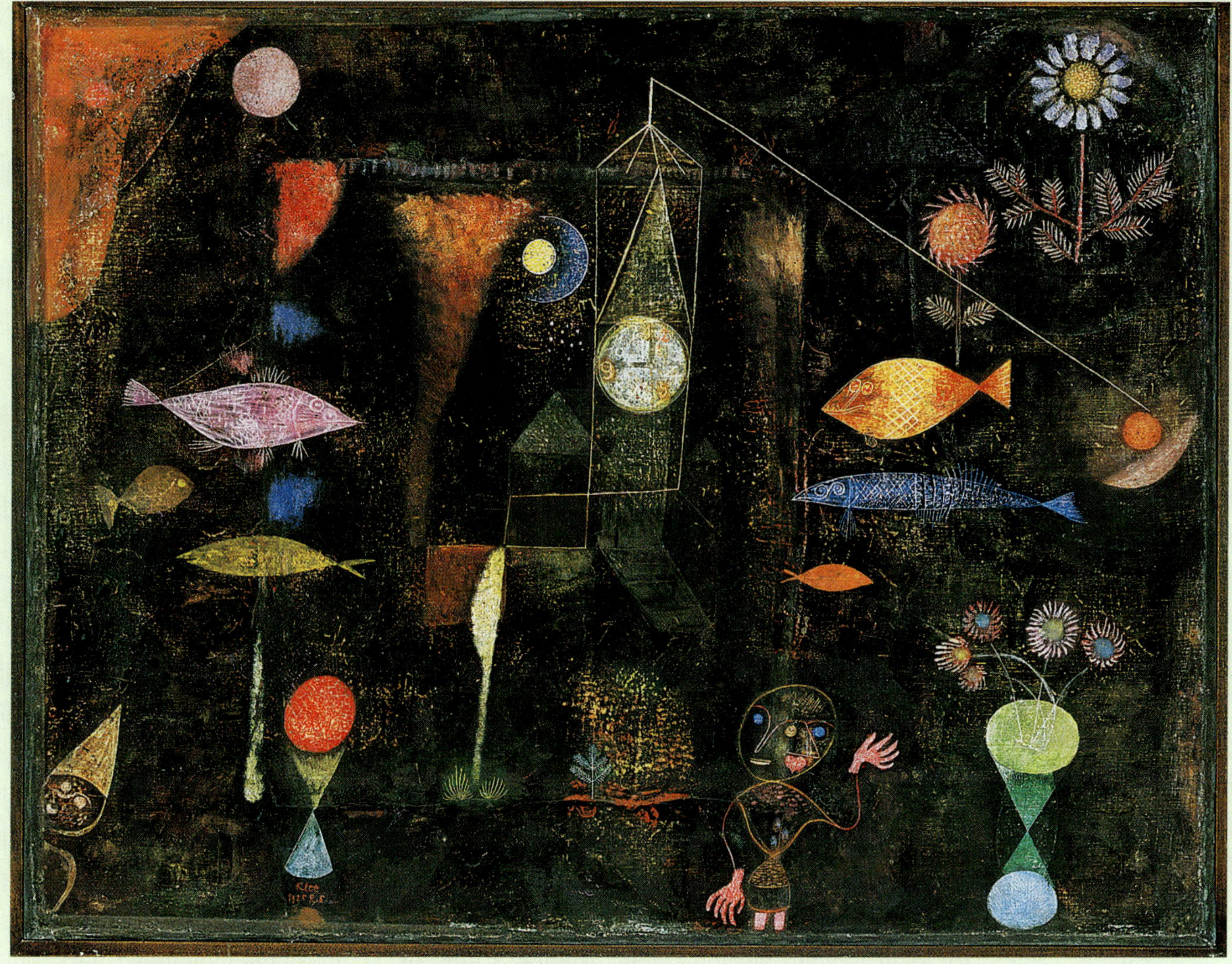

Paul Klee, *Fish Magic*, 1925.

Art can take many forms.

Look for examples of art in the world around you.

Why do people make art?

To express themselves

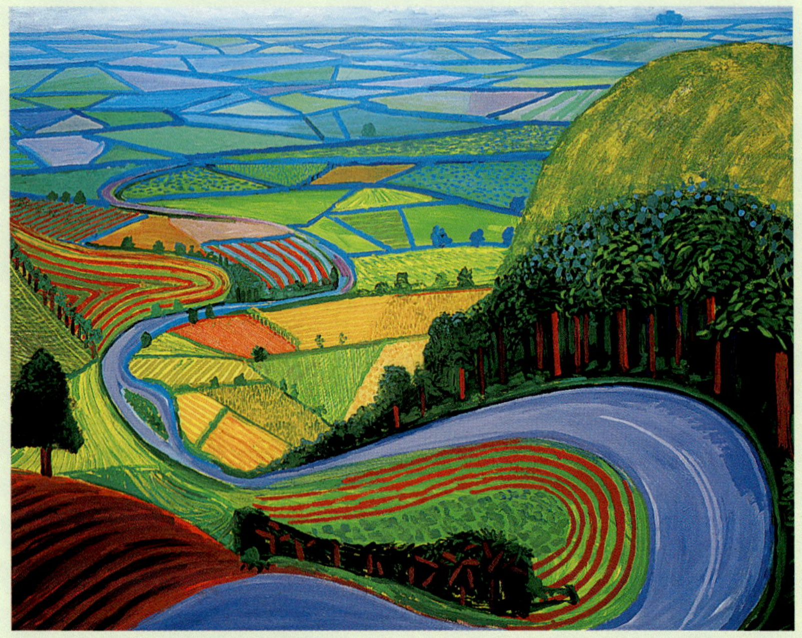

David Hockney, *Garrowby Hill*, 1998.

To tell a story

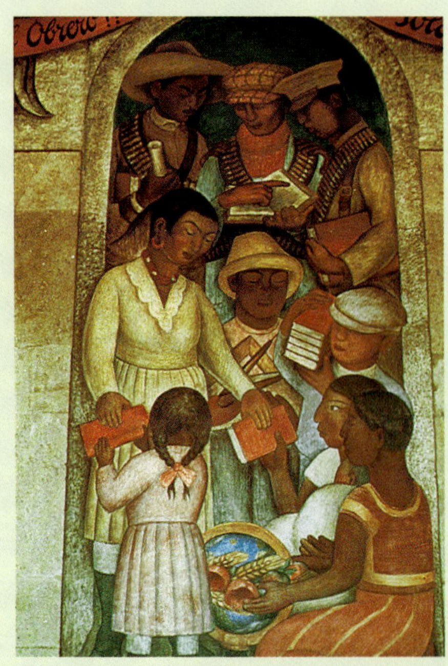

Diego Rivera, *Learning the ABC's (Alfabetizacion)*, 1923–28.

To share feelings

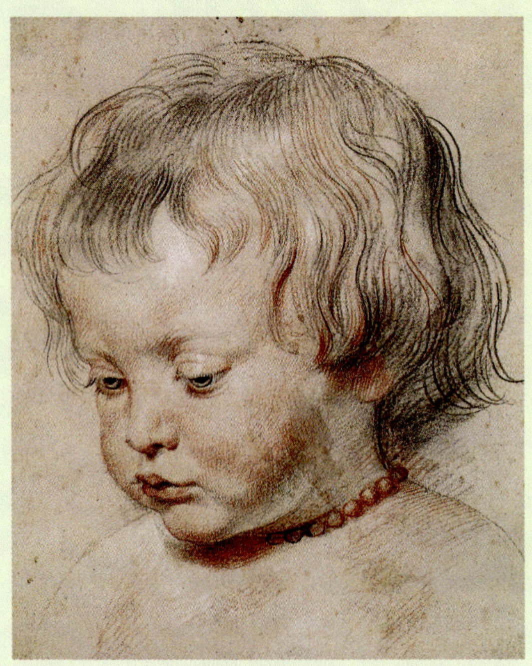

Peter Paul Rubens, *Portrait Study of His Son Nicolas*, 1621.

To make things look beautiful

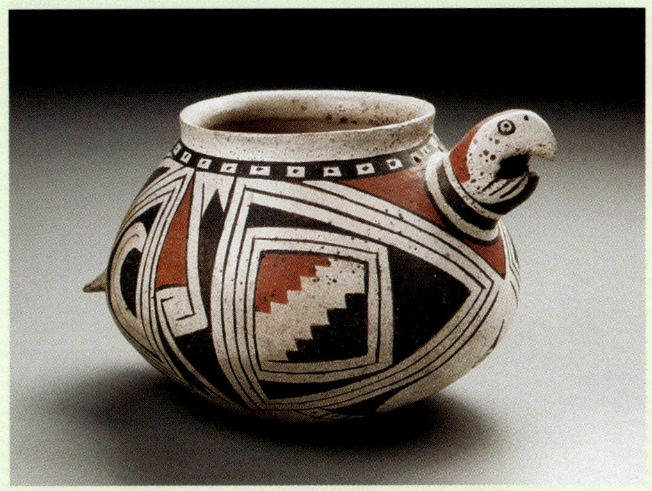

Mongollon (Casas Grandes style), *Macaw Bowl*, Tardio Period, 1300–1350.

To remember important people

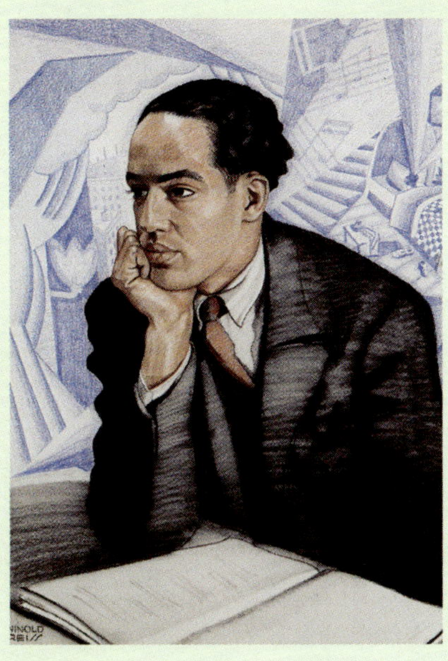

Winold Reiss, *Langston Hughes (1902–1967), Poet*, ca. 1925.

To remember special times

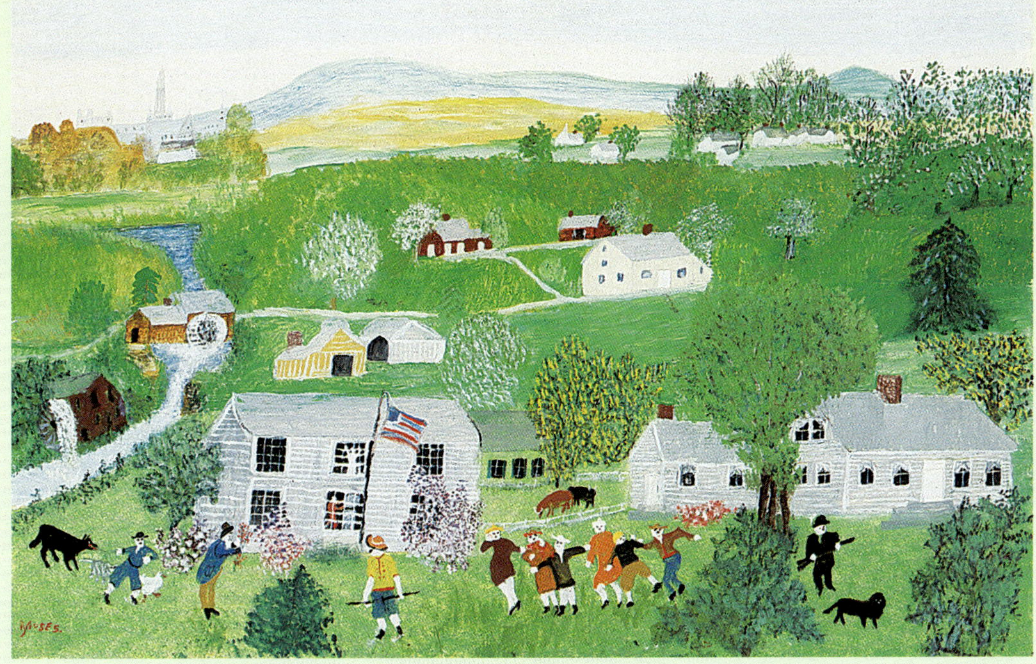

Anna Mary Robertson Moses, called Grandma Moses, *Summer Party*, 20th century.

What other reasons do people make art?

There are subjects and themes in art.

Subject: Members of the Peale family

Theme: The joy of family

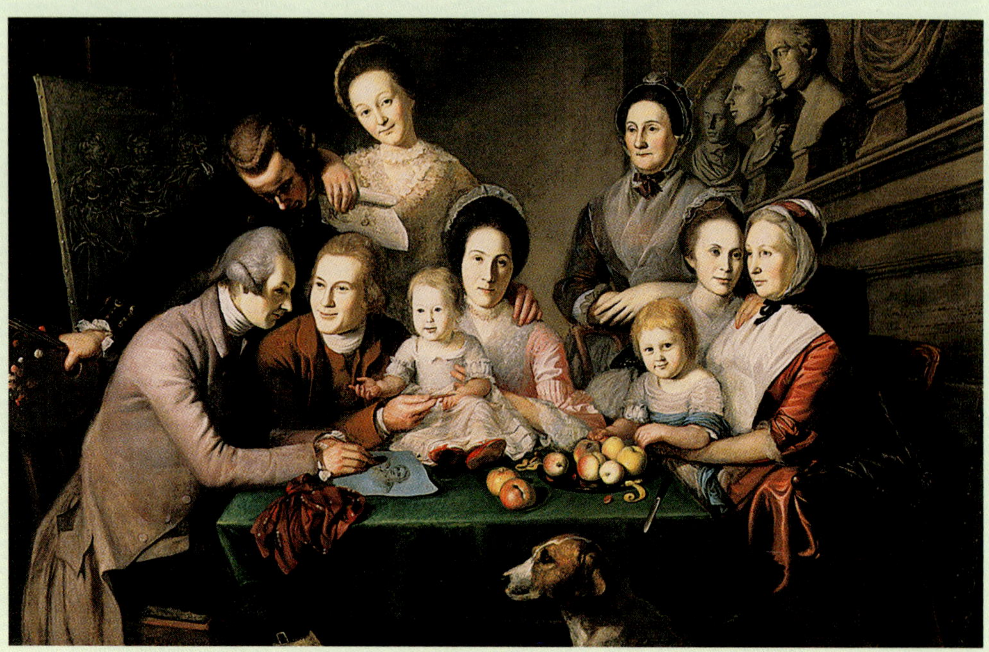

Charles Willson Peale, *The Peale Family*, ca. 1770–73 and 1880.

Subject: Lion

Theme: Strength and power

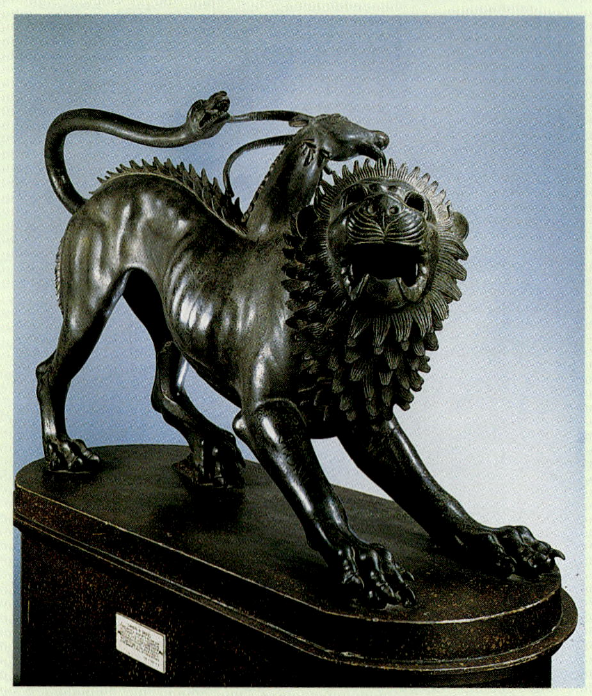

Etruscan, *Chimera of Arezzo*, 6th century BCE.

Subject: Soap box racing
Theme: Good times with friends

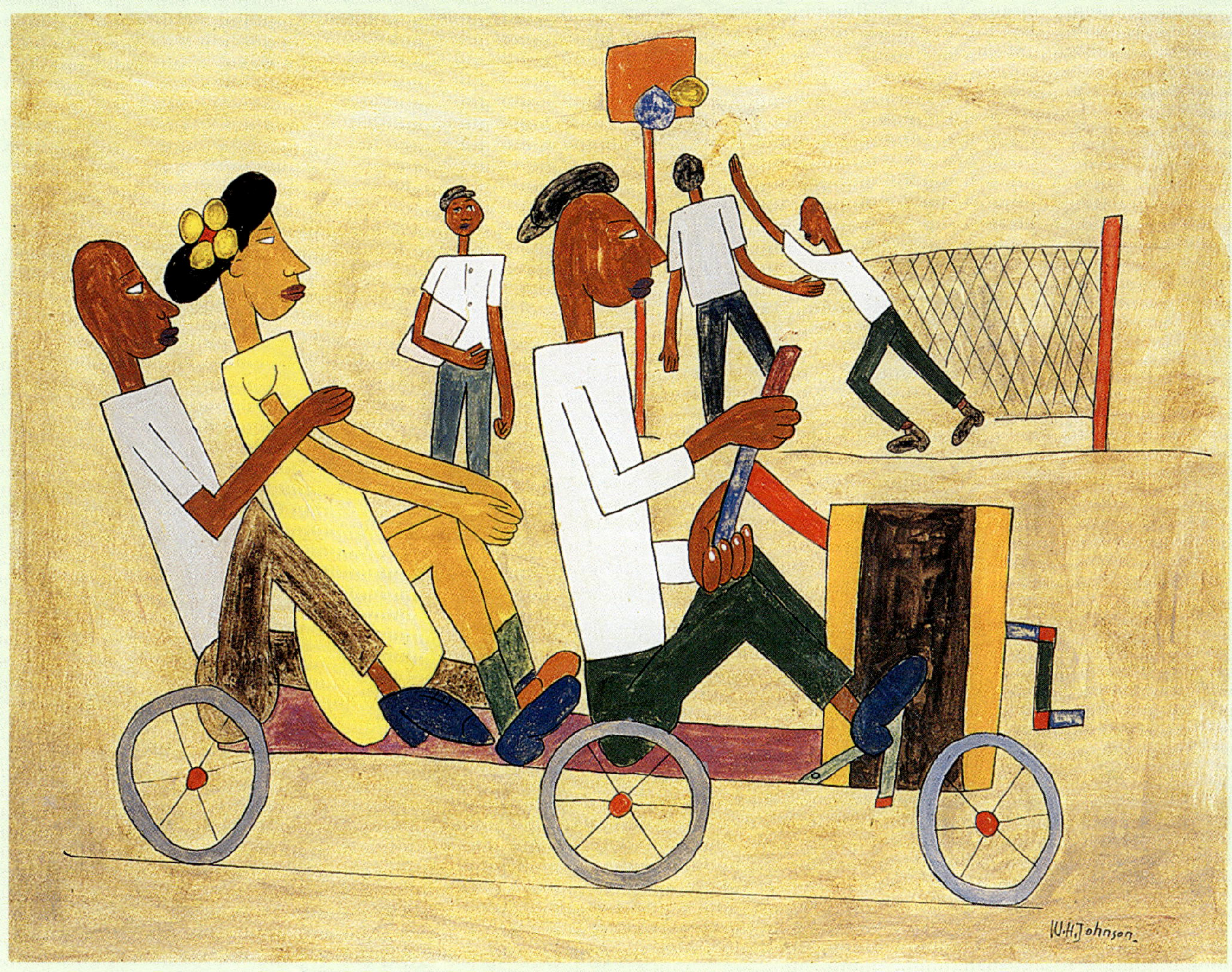

William H. Johnson, *Soap Box Racing*, ca. 1939–40.

Artists choose their art forms.

Sculpture

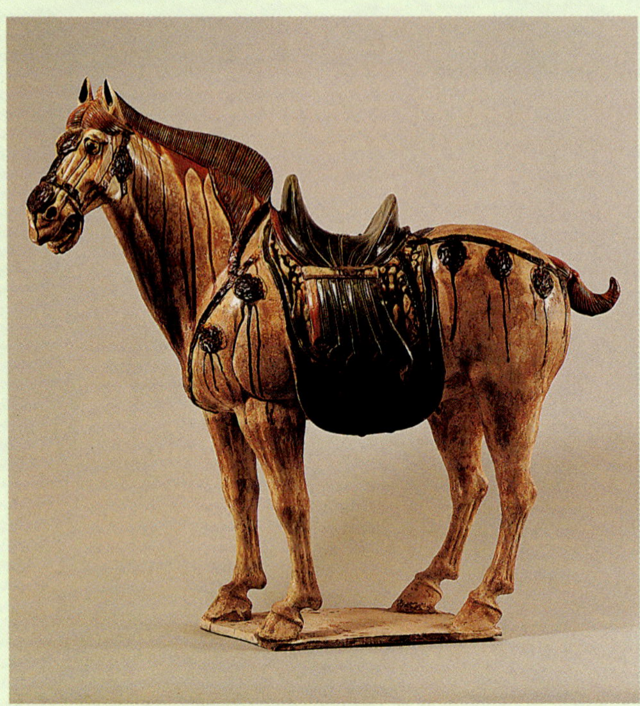

China, Tang dynasty, *Horse*, early 8th century.

Drawing

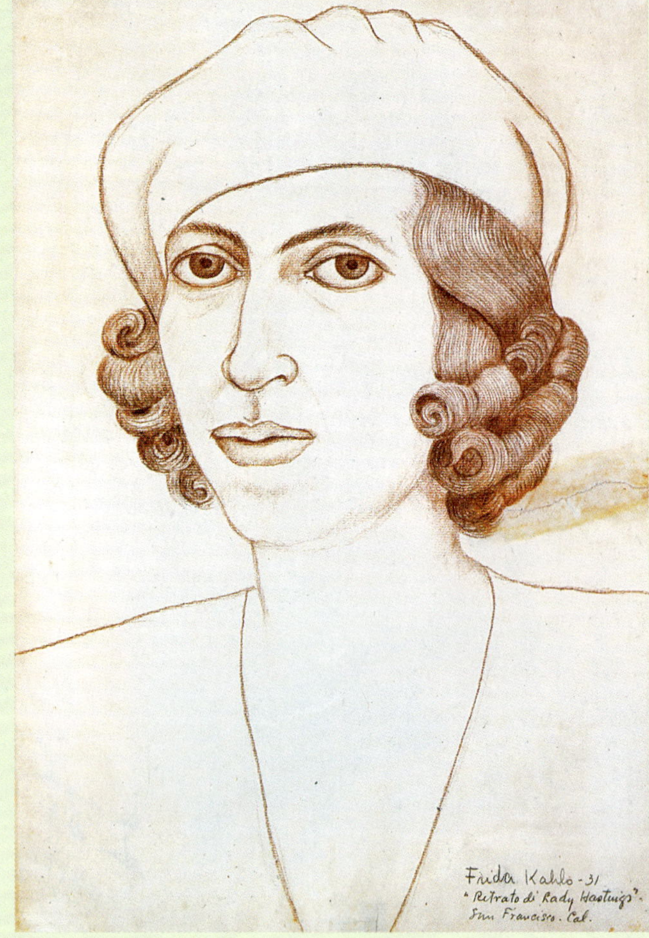

Frida Kahlo, *Portrait of Mrs. Christian Hastings*, 1931.

Collage

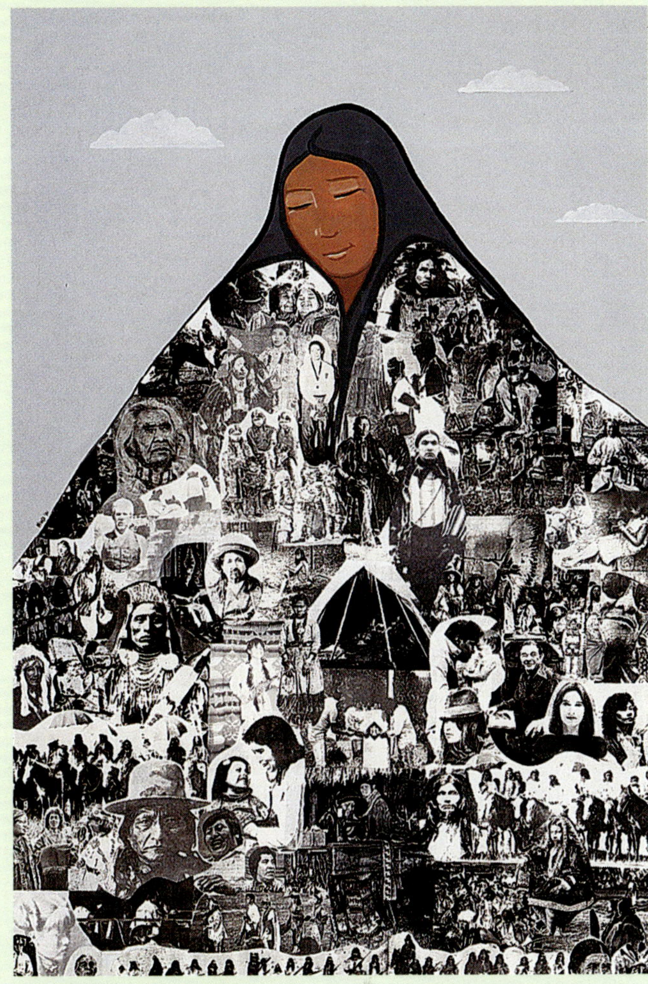

Warren Smith, *Cloak of Heritage*, 1991.

Photography

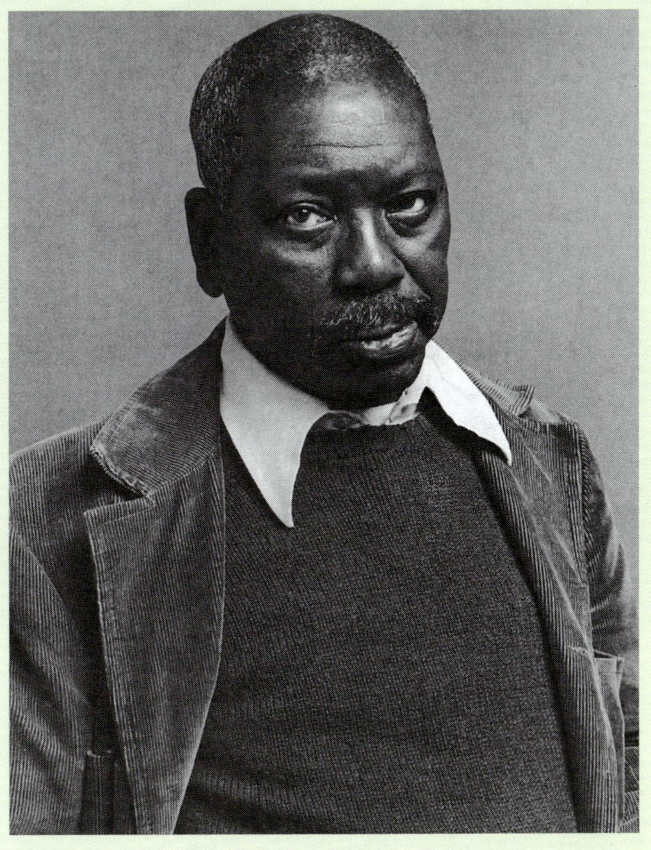

Marsha Burns, *Jacob Lawrence*.

What other art forms can you name?

Artists choose their media.

Oil Paint

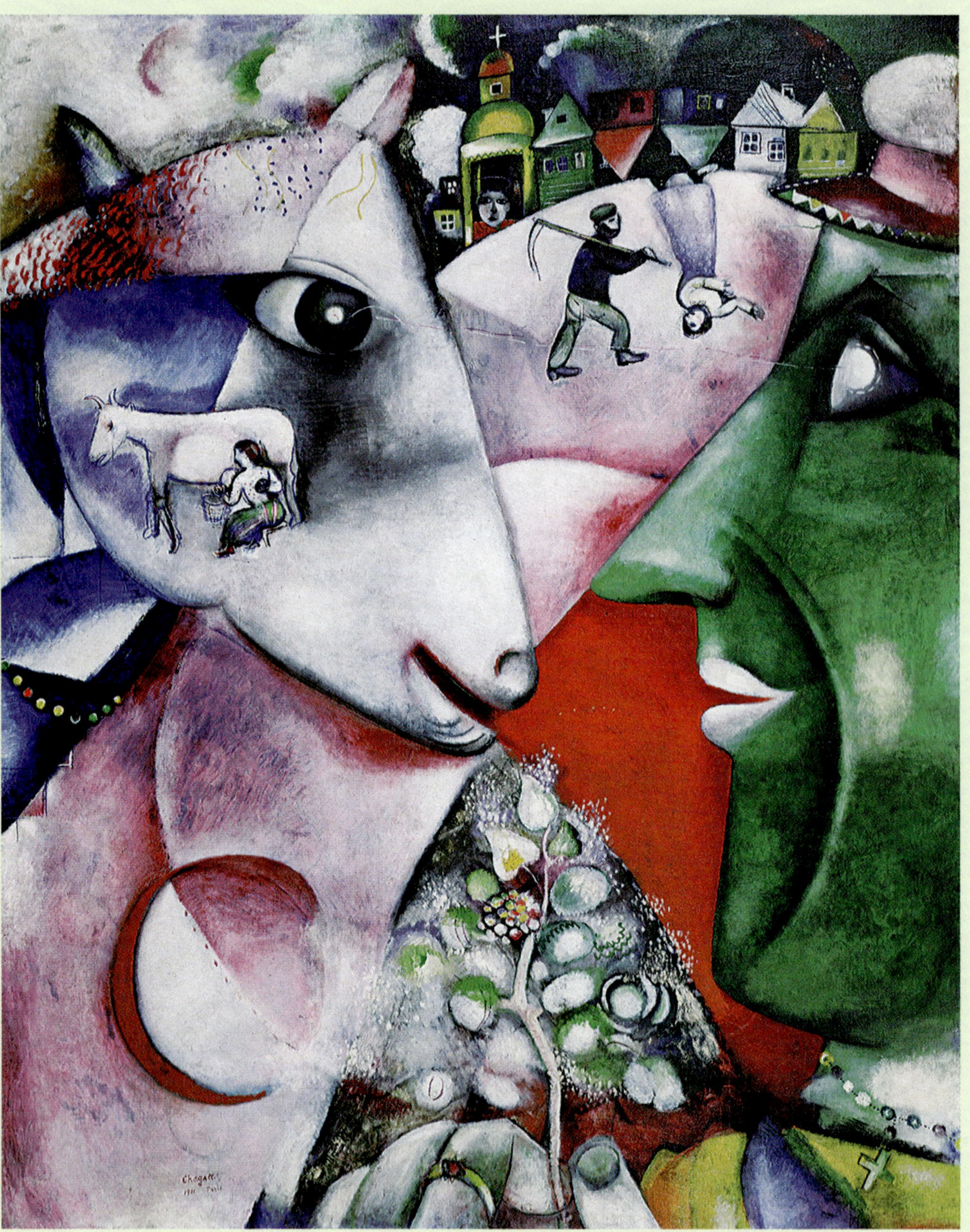

Marc Chagall, *I and the Village*, 1911.

Clay

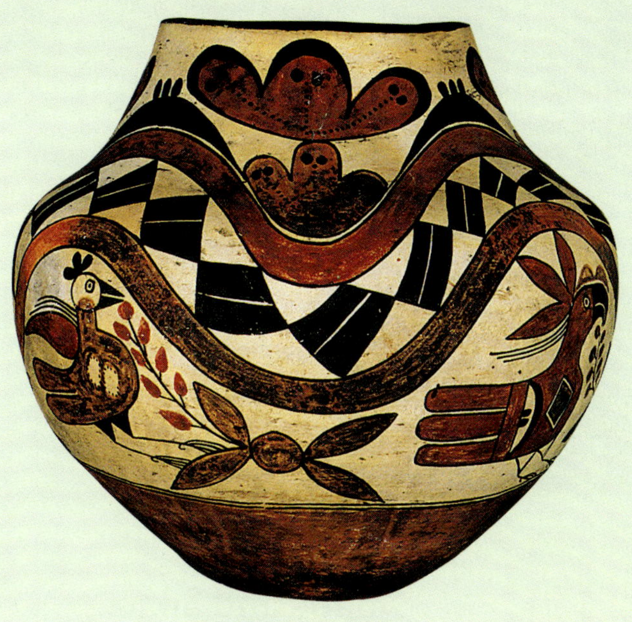

North American Indian, *Acoma Polychrome Jar.*

Glass

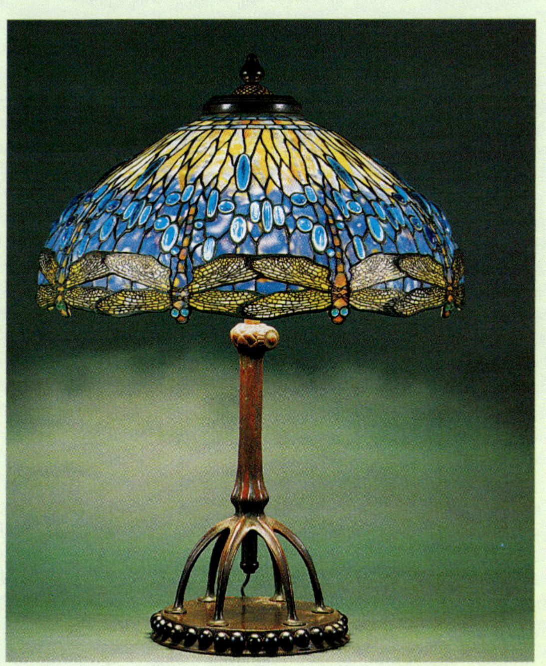

Louis Comfort Tiffany, *Dragonfly Lamp*, ca. 1900.

What other media can you name?

Art is a language.

The elements of art are the words of the language.

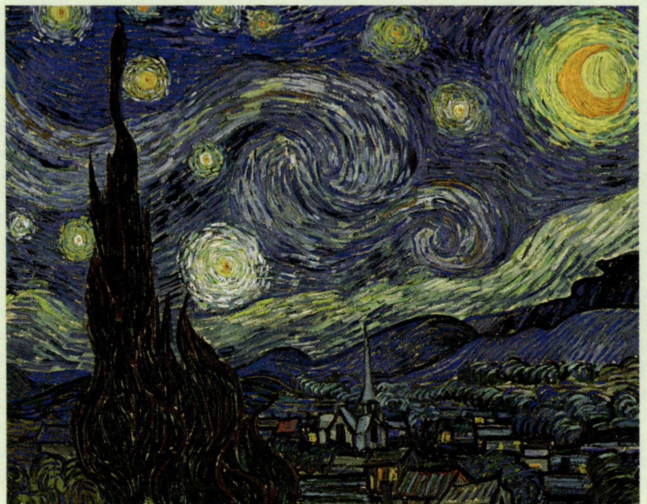

Vincent van Gogh, *The Starry Night*, 1889.

Color

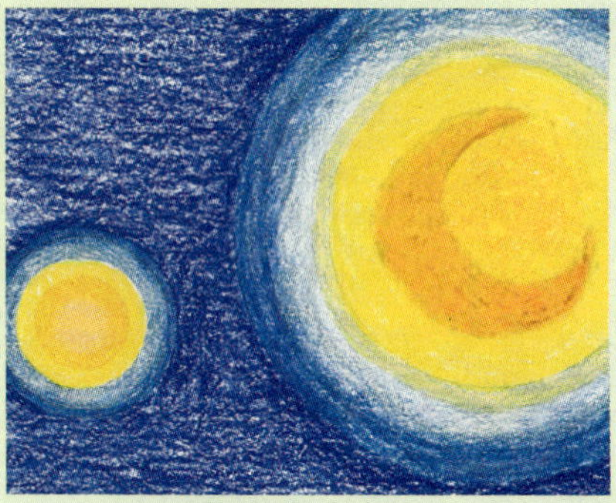

Line

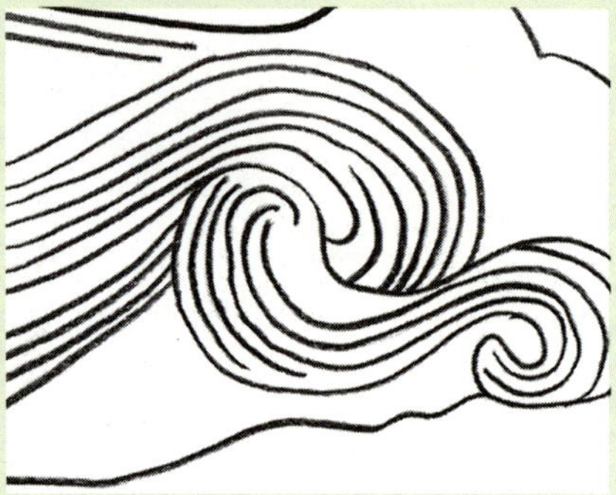

Shape and Space

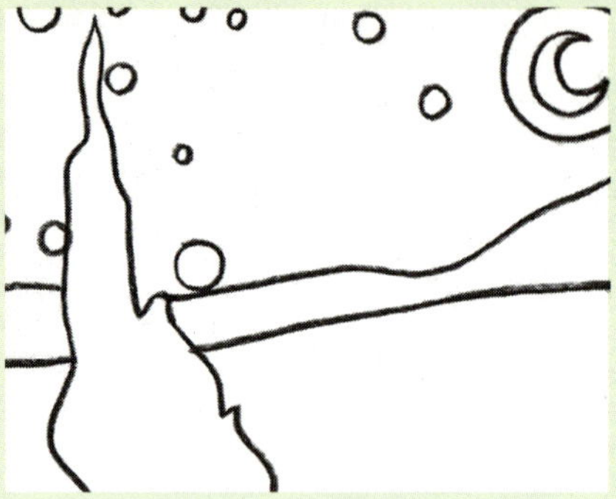

Form

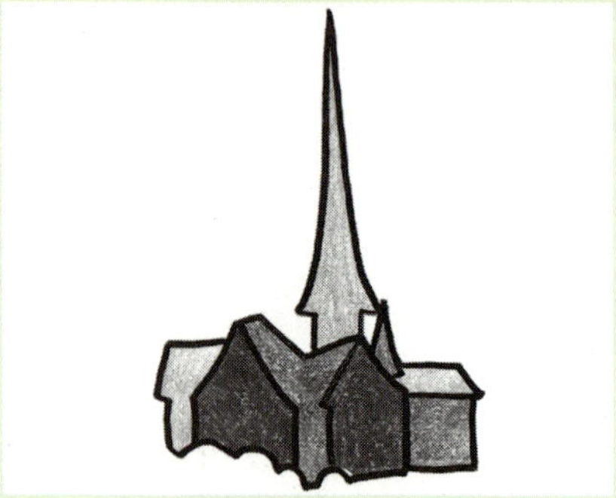

Texture

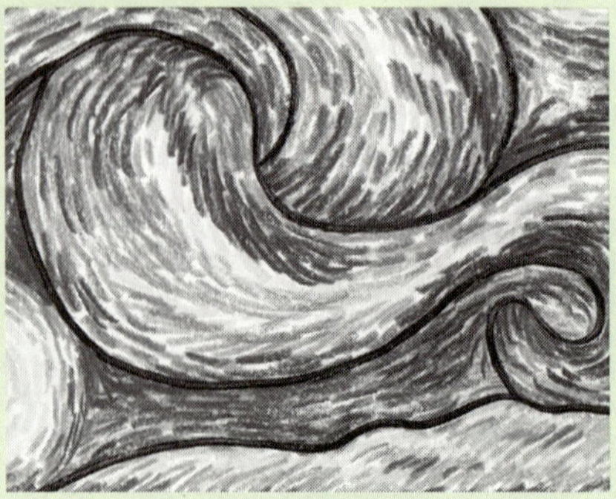

Value

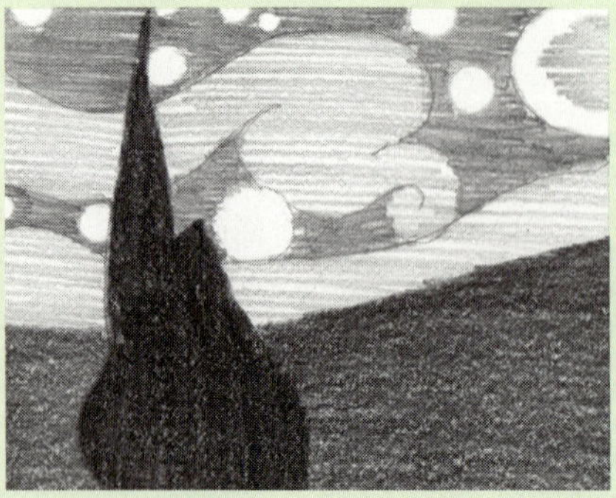

The elements of art are in everything that we see.

You can find the elements of art in all kinds of artworks.

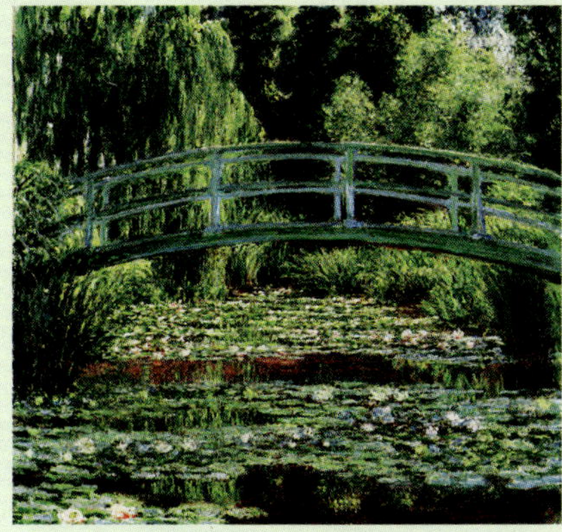

Claude Monet, *Japanese Footbridge and the Water Lily Pond, Giverny*, 1899.

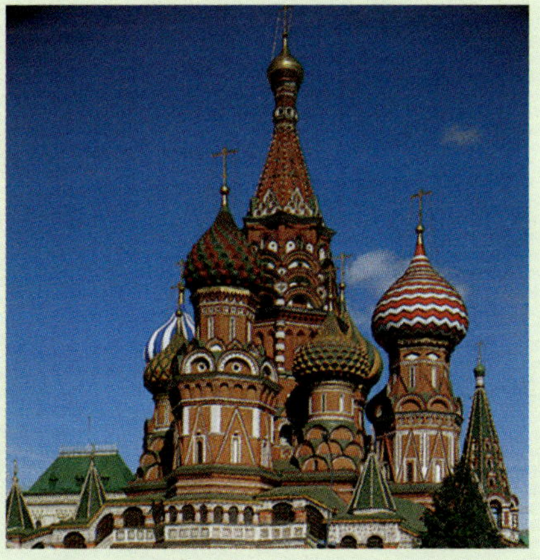

Cathedral of St. Basil, 1554–1566. Moscow.

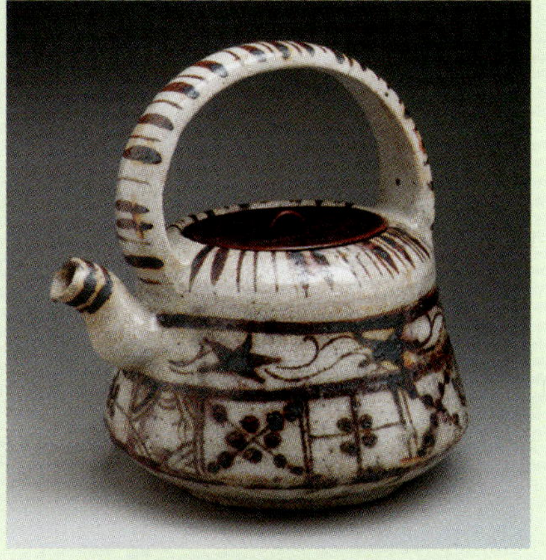

Japan, Momoyama period (1568–1615), *Ewer for Use in Tea Ceremony*, early 17th century.

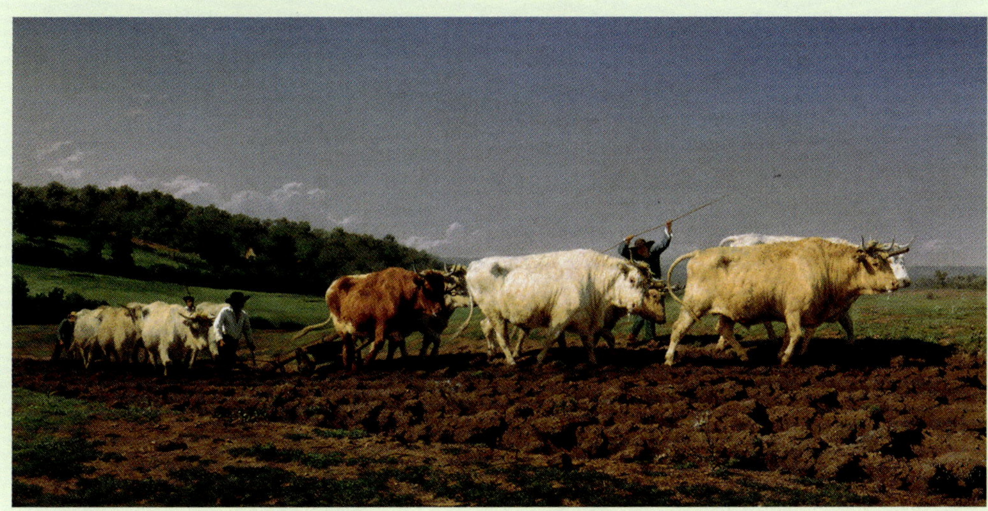

Rosa Bonheur, *Ploughing in the Nivernais*, 1849.

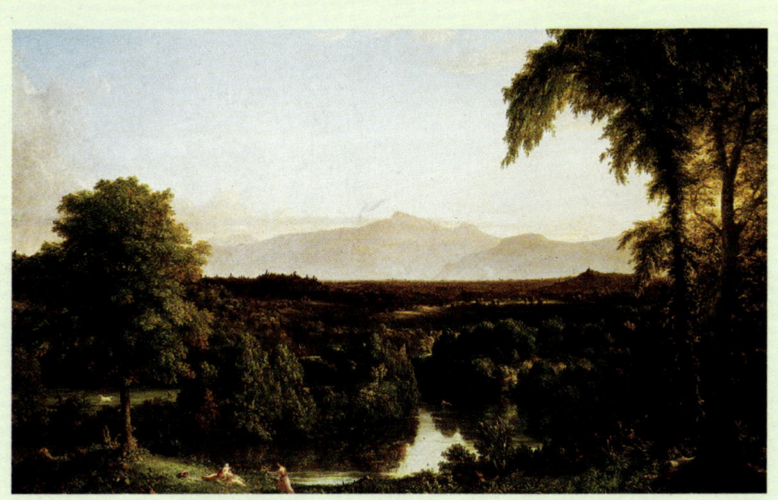

Thomas Cole, *View on the Catskill, Early Autumn*, 1837.

Artists organize these works using the principles of design.

Balance

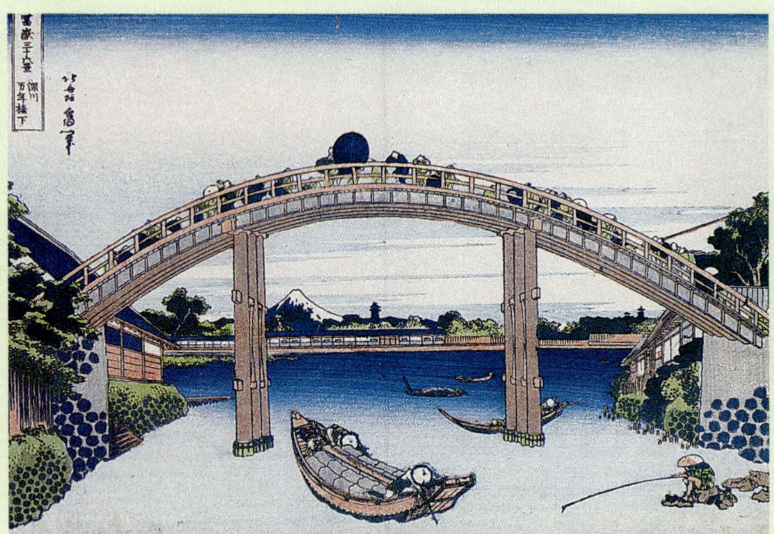

Sakino Hokusai IITSU, *Fukagawa Mannembashi*, from 36 Views of Mt. Fuji, 1830.

Pattern

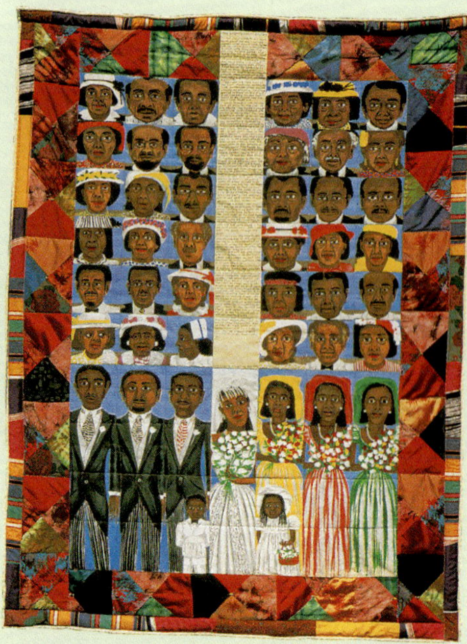

Faith Ringgold, *The Wedding Lover's Quilt No. 1*, 1986.

Proportion

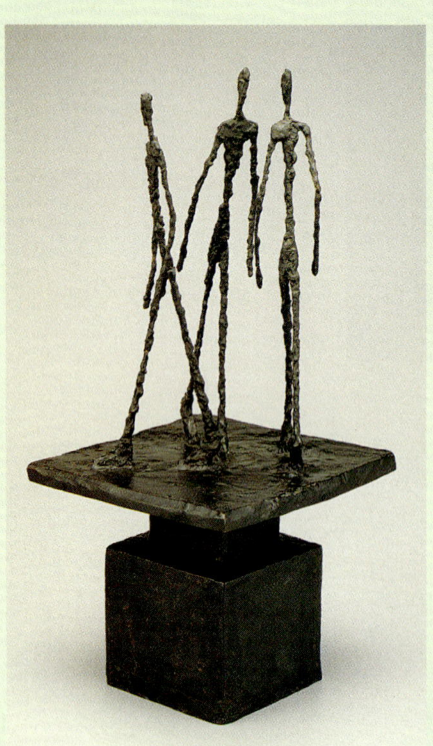

Alberto Giacometti, *Three Men Walking*, 1948–49.

Rhythm and Movement

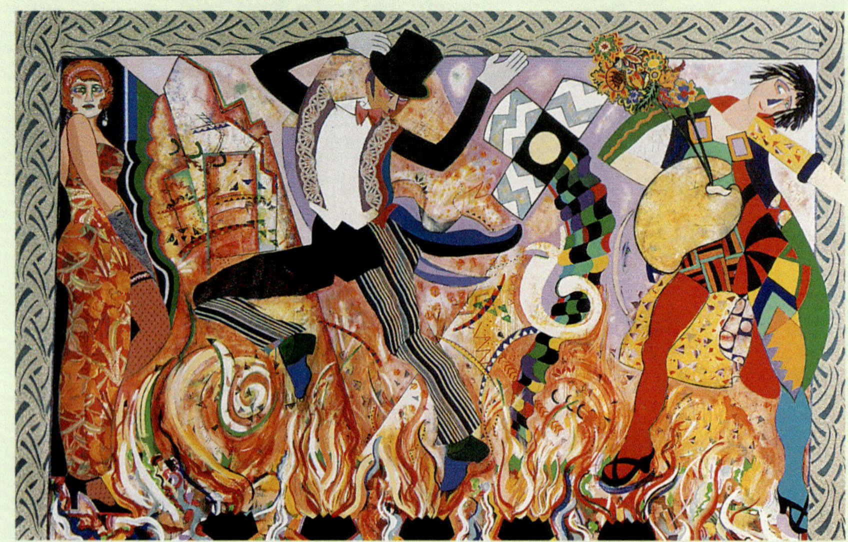

Miriam Schapiro, *Master of Ceremonies*, 1985.

Contrast

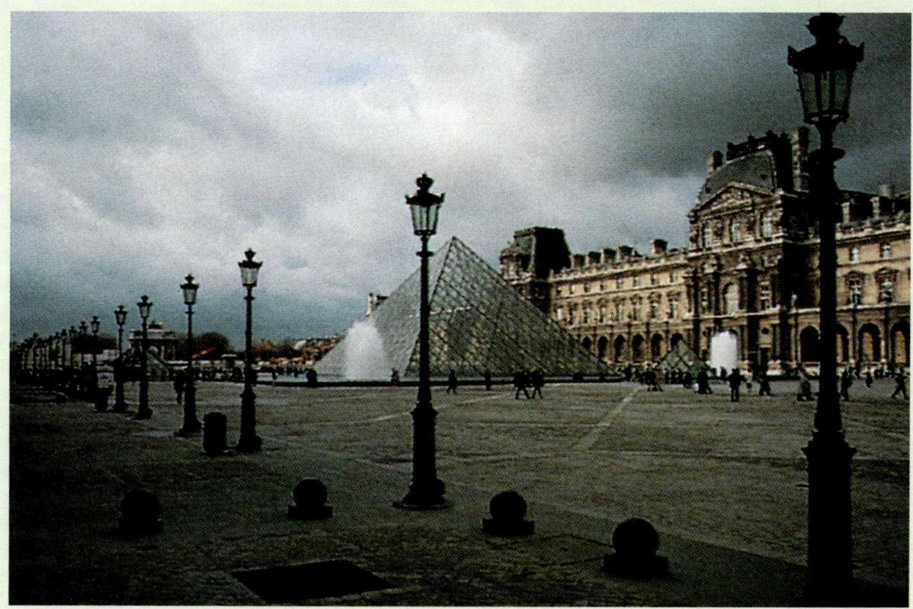

I. M. Pei, *Addition to the Louvre*, 1988.

Variety and Unity

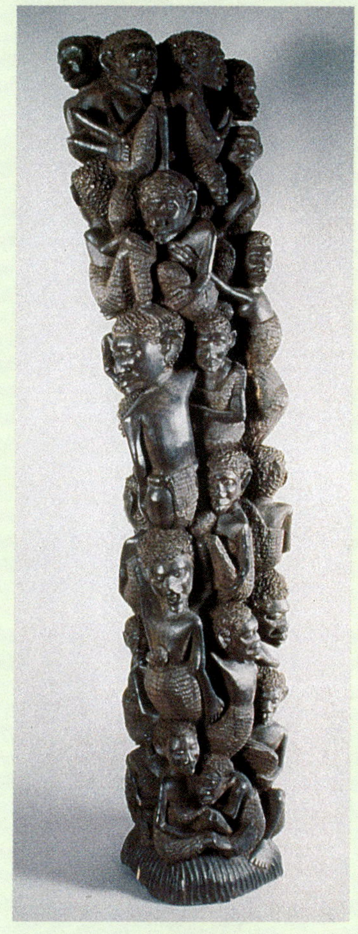

Makonde, Tanzania, *Family Group*, 20th century.

Emphasis

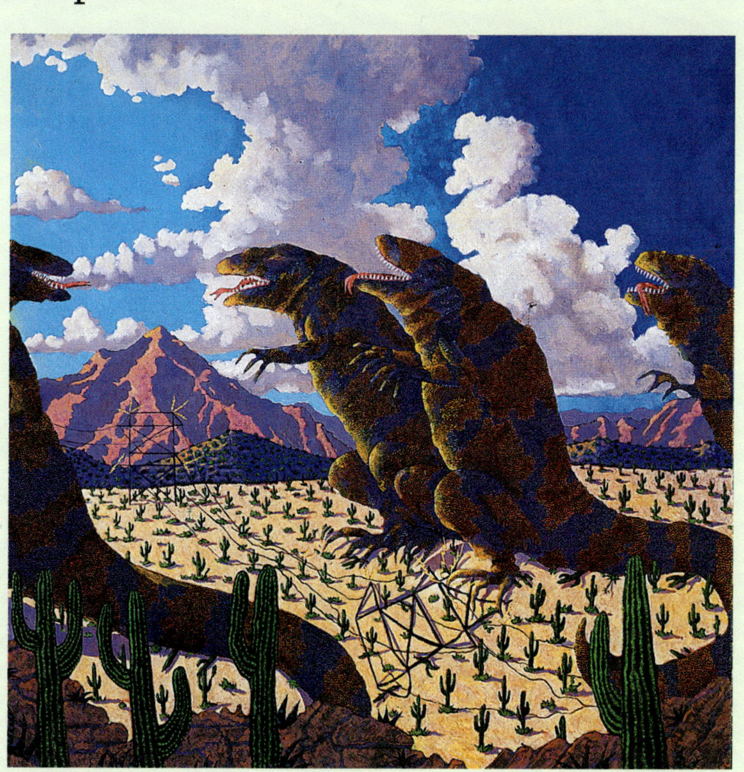

Anne Coe, *Migrating Mutants*, 1986.

Art Criticism

Learn to view artworks thoughtfully.

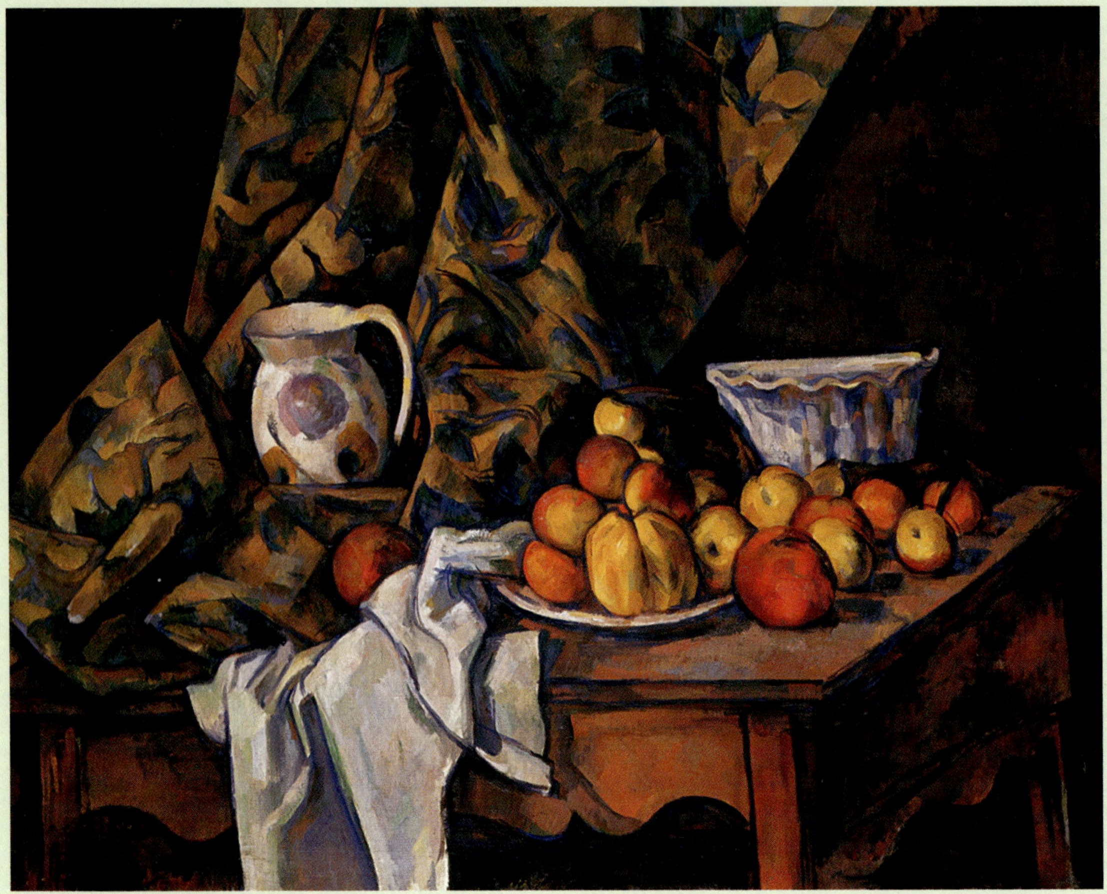

Paul Cézanne, *Still Life with Apples and Peaches*, c. 1905.

1. **Describe** what you see.
   What do you see in this painting?
2. **Analyze** the painting's organization.
   How did the artist organize the elements?
   How did Cézanne create the illusion of three dimensions?
3. **Interpret** what the artist's goals were in creating this artwork.
   What do you think Cézanne cared about in creating this painting?
   Explain your answer.
4. **Evaluate** the artwork. How effective is this painting
   in creating a balanced design?

A Five-Step Process

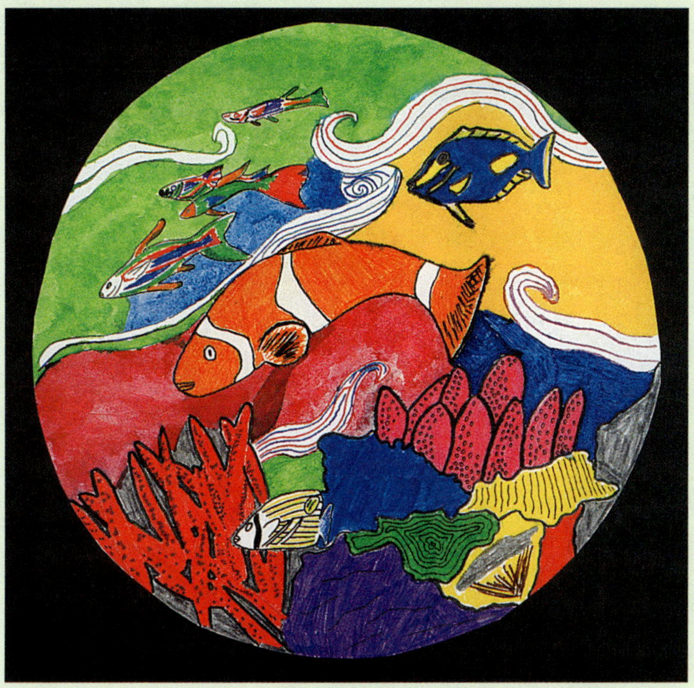

Keith Bush, *Deep Blue Sea*, 2000.

When you create an artwork, think about these steps.

Step 1 **Plan and Practice**

- What idea do you want to communicate?
- What subject and theme will you choose?
- What form and media will you use?

Step 2 **Begin to Create**

- Start your process.
- Be prepared to revise if necessary.

Step 3 **Revise**

- Do you need to change your initial plan?
- Do you need to make other adjustments?

Step 4 **Add Finishing Touches**

- What details will make a difference?

Step 5 **Share and Reflect**

- What can you learn from others?
- What did you learn about yourself as an artist?

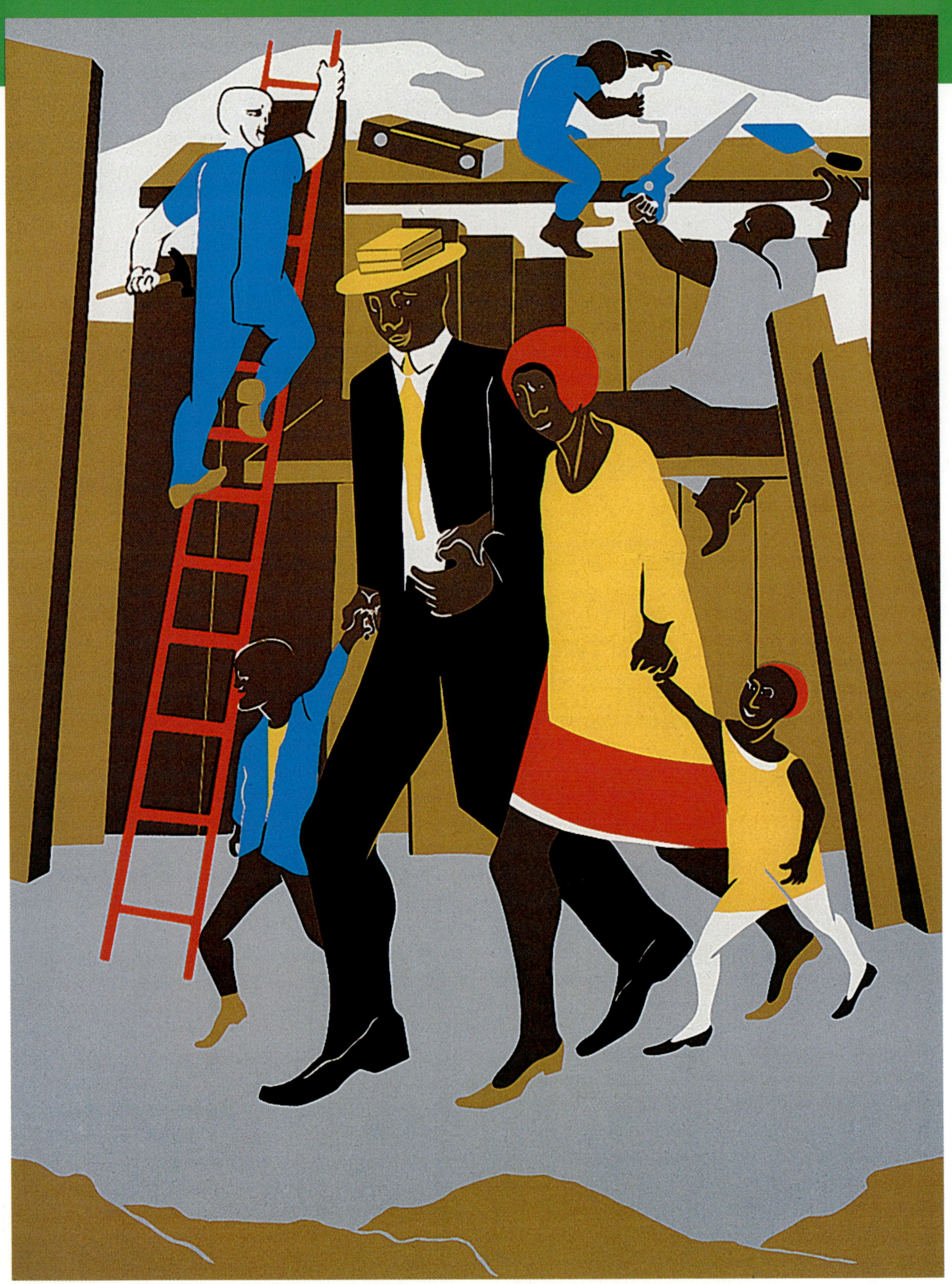

Jacob Lawrence, *The Builders*, 1974. See page 2

Art Is a Personal Journey

Have you ever been on a journey? You take little journeys all the time: you go to school, walk down the street, ride in a car or a bus. On any of these journeys you might see something new, something that changes your point of view.

As artists grow and change, their artwork changes. They find new materials to work with, explore new ideas, ask new questions. An artist's journey might lead anywhere.

In this book, you'll learn about many artists and their journeys. You'll find out how they think, what they like, and where their journeys have taken them. As you travel through these units, think about big or small journeys you have taken. How have they changed you? How can you show these changes through your art? How might the art around you change the way you see?

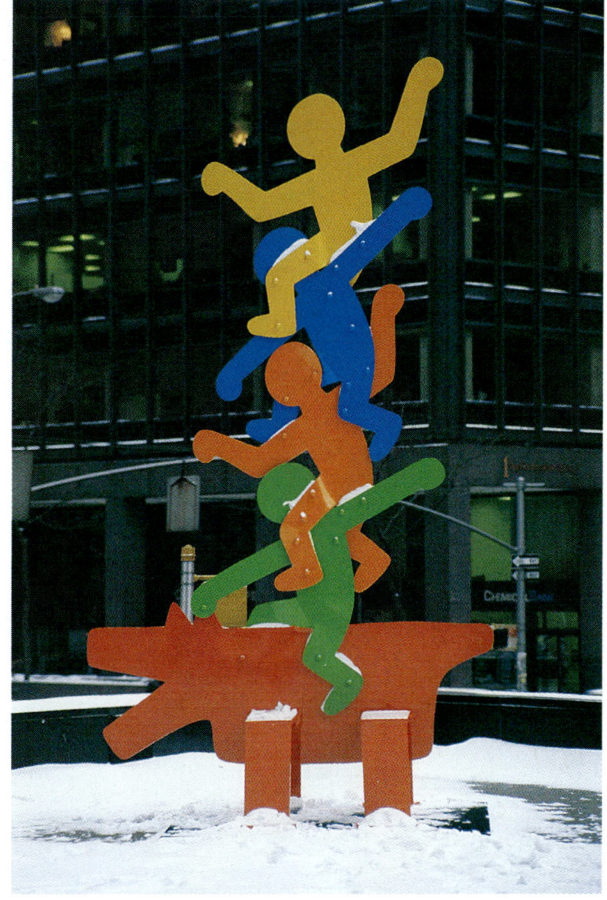

Keith Haring, *Untitled (Four Figures on Dog)*, 1985. See page 152.

Unit 1

Artists Are Storytellers

Fig. 1–1 **Jacob Lawrence sends a powerful message in this painting. How does it show that people can live and work together to build a better world?**

Jacob Lawrence, *The Builders*, 1974. Screenprint, 34" x 25 ¾" (86.4 x 65.4 cm). Courtesy of the Estate of Jacob Lawrence and the Francine Seders Gallery. Photo by Spike Mafford. Artists Rights Society (ARS), NY.

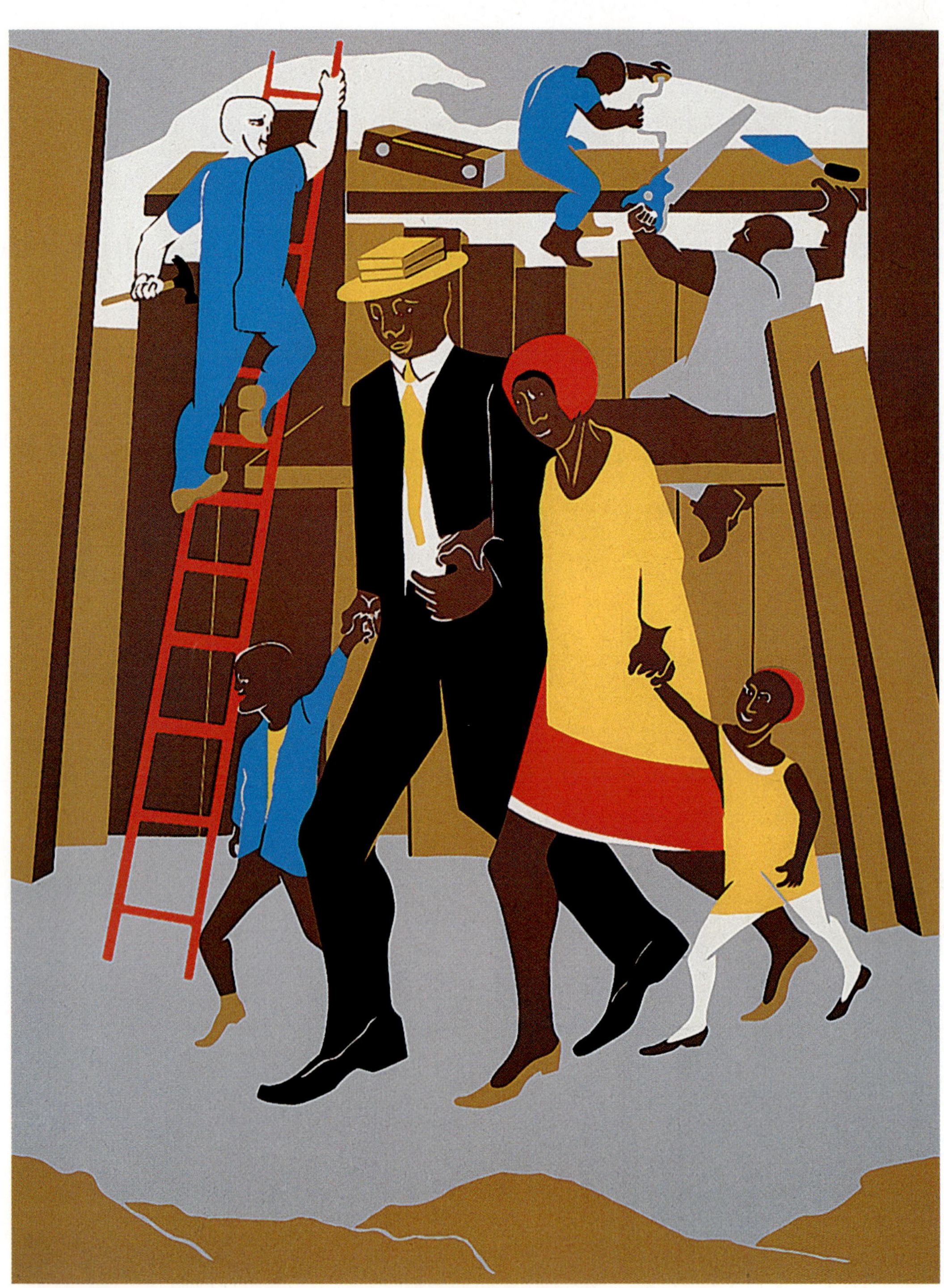

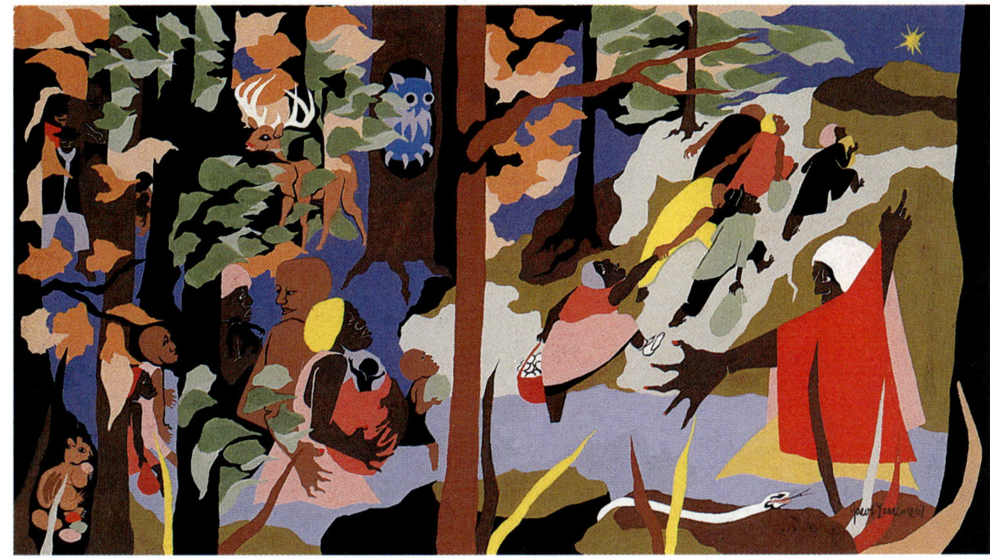

Fig. 1–2 **This image depicts the work of Harriet Tubman, who helped people escape from slavery. What details did the artist choose to show?**

Jacob Lawrence, *Through Forest, Through Rivers, Up Mountains*, 1967. Tempera, gouache and pencil on paper, 15 11/16" x 26 7/8" (40 x 60 cm). Hirshhorn Museum and Sculpture Garden, Smithsonian Institution. The Joseph H. Hirshhorn Bequest, 1981. Artists Rights Society (ARS), NY.

Think about a time when you couldn't wait to get to school to tell a friend about something that happened to you. Remember how you included important parts of the story? You probably chose details to make it interesting. If you shared your story more than once, you might have changed the way you told it to make it more exciting.

People have been sharing their stories for thousands of years. Stories take us to faraway lands, introduce us to fascinating characters, and show us how people lived in the past. When a storyteller tells a tale, we follow the words and create pictures in our mind.

In this unit, you will learn:

- How artists use their art to tell stories about what they have seen or experienced.
- How to create contour and gesture drawings.
- How to look at artwork to understand the stories that artists tell.

Finding a Story to Tell

When artist Jacob Lawrence created stories about things that happened in the past, he was following an ancient storytelling tradition. Much of what we know about the past has come in the form of stories, often told by older members of our family or community. Artists use visual stories to tell about the past. Look at the artworks by Lawrence on these pages. How can you find out more about the story these artworks tell?

Retelling History in Art

Good storytellers tell stories in a way that keeps the audience interested. Jacob Lawrence did this by working with brightly colored paint to create pleasing shapes and patterns for his characters and settings. If a story had too many parts to tell in one image, he created a series, or a related group, of several paintings. The artworks on these pages are paintings from the same

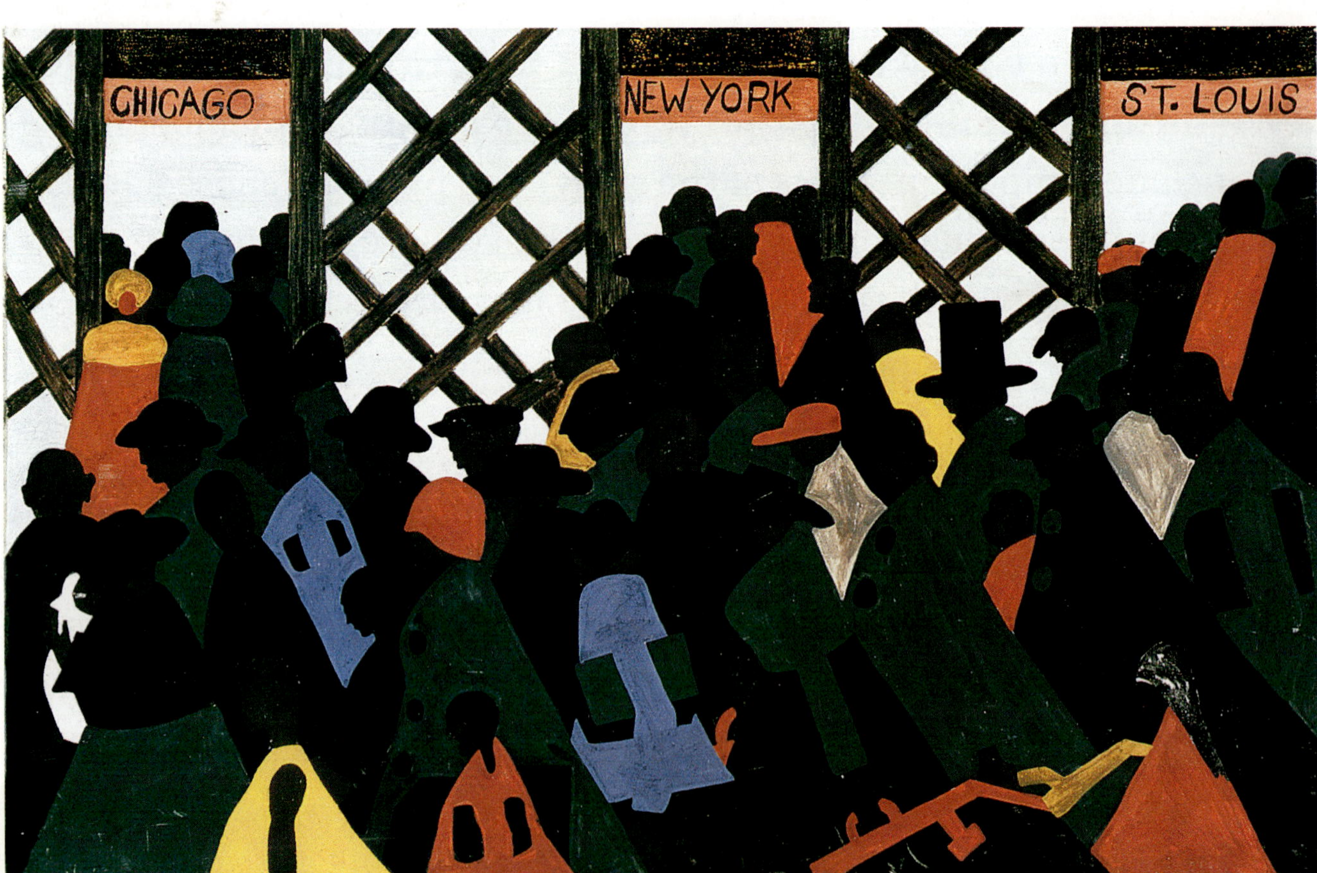

Fig. 1–3 **Lawrence told about African Americans moving from the rural South to the industrial North. How do details in this painting help to tell that story?**

Jacob Lawrence, *The Migration of the Negro*, 1940–41. Panel No. 1. Casein tempera on hard-board, 12" x 18" (30.5 x 45.7 cm). Acquired 1942, The Phillips Collection, Washington, DC. Artists Rights Society (ARS), NY.

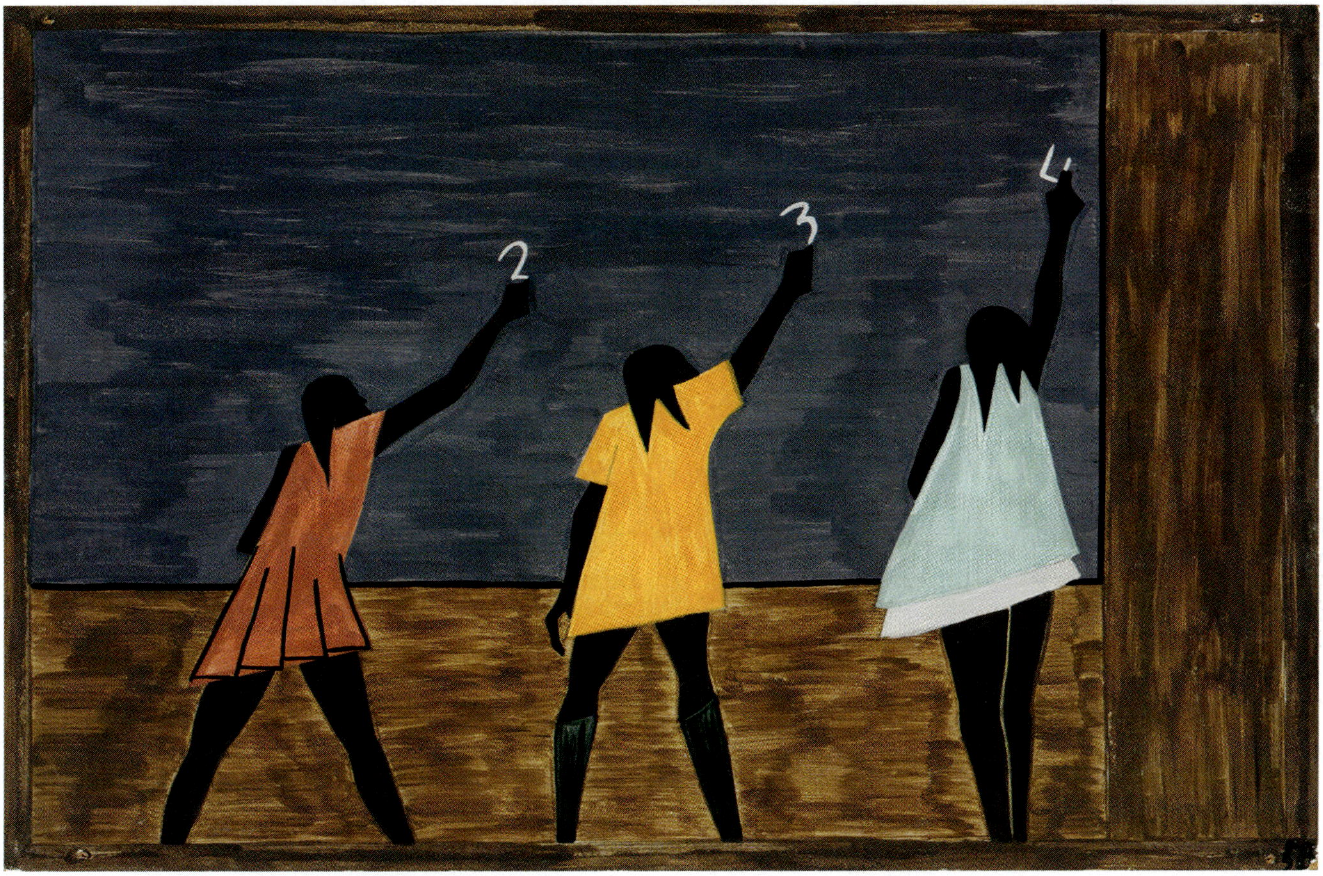

series. Lawrence decided what to show as the story continued and how to bring it to an interesting end. His paintings seem like little stages where action takes place, just as in a theater.

Fig. 1–4 **How does the title of the painting on this page help you understand the story the painting is trying to tell?**

Jacob Lawrence, *In the North the Negro Had Better Educational Facilities,* 1940–41. Panel 58 from the *Migration Series.* Tempera on gesso on composition board, 12" x 18" (30.5 x 45.7 cm). Gift of Mrs. David M. Levy. (28.1942.29) The Museum of Modern Art, New York, NY, U.S.A. Digital Image ©The Museum of Modern Art/Licensed by SCALA/Art Resource, NY.

Meet Jacob Lawrence

Lawrence grew up during the Great Depression in Harlem, a neighborhood in New York City. As a teenager, he enrolled in after-school art classes. Lawrence loved to visit the Metropolitan Museum of Art. He especially liked the artworks that told stories. The young artist spent many hours in the library. There, he read about the kingdoms of Africa and about heroic African Americans. He was always interested in people—what they cared about and what they accomplished. The more he learned, the more he wanted to find a way to tell others about their lives.

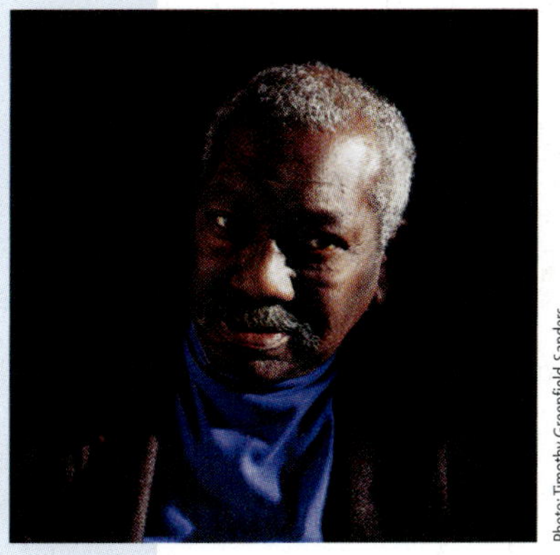

Photo: Timothy Greenfield-Sanders.

"I wanted to tell a story...so I did it in panels."

—Jacob Lawrence (1917–2000)

Stories for Different Purposes

Another reason for storytelling in art is to communicate a message. All over the world, stories are carved in stone or painted on the walls of public buildings, where many people can see them. Jacob Lawrence's brightly colored paintings pass on important messages about events in human history. Artists also tell stories to entertain an audience. Such stories may be scary or funny. The characters might be people, or they might be animals or objects brought to life by the artist.

Stories in Many Forms Artists use art forms such as drawing, printmaking, photography, and sculpture to tell stories. They may do so in a series of images or in a single image. A single image may show a complete story or only one scene, leaving the viewer to imagine what happened before and what will happen after. Stories are told in visual form in movies, such as in the cartoon on this page, on television, and in magazines and newspapers.

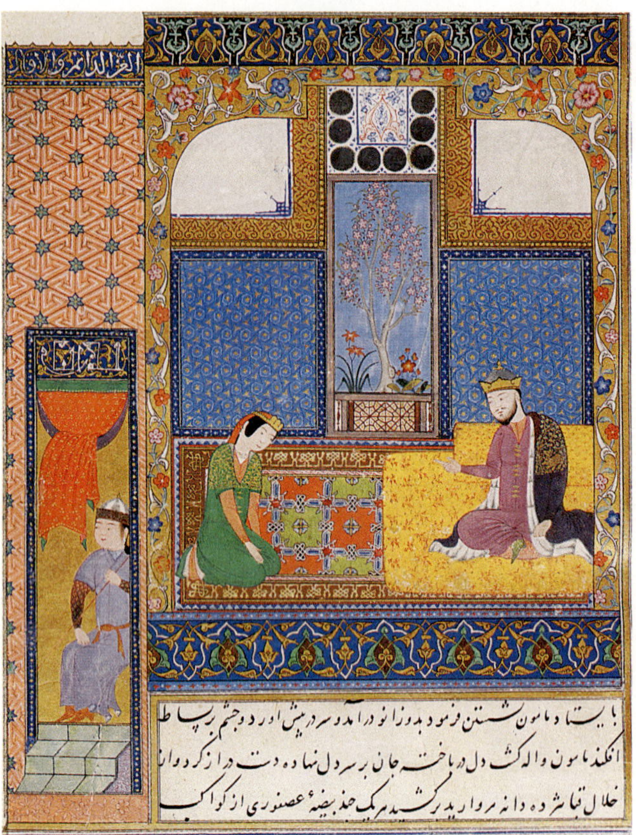

Fig. 1–5 **This small, detailed painting is called a miniature. What details might people find interesting?**

Persian (Herat School), *A Court Scene from the "Chahar Maqaleh,"* c. 1431. Ink, colors, and gold on paper. The Minneapolis Institute of Arts, Bequest of Margaret McMillan Weber in memory of her mother, Katherine Kittredge McMillan (51.37.30).

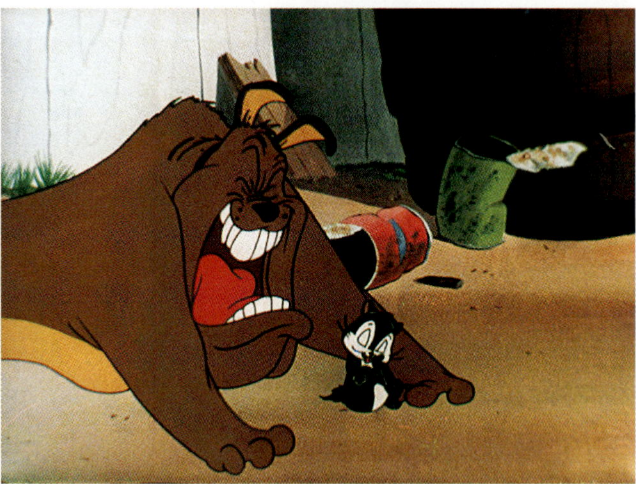

Fig. 1–6 **Movies are made of thousands of individual frames. What story details can you learn from this frame?**

Still from the Warner Bros. Cartoon "Feed the Kitty," 1952. Looney Tunes characters, names, and all related indicia are trademarks of Warner Bros. © 2001.

Studio Time

Story Illustration

You can create an illustration based on a familiar story or from a story you have imagined.

- How can you get across the main idea of the story in one picture? Who are the important characters in your story? What do you want people to notice first?
- Use light pencil lines to plan the main shapes and figures in your drawing.
- Use fine line marker or crayon to outline the main shapes and figures in your drawing.
- Consider ways to add texture and pattern to your illustration.
- Experiment with crayon rubbings over textured surfaces.

Reflect on how well your drawing captures the theme of your story.

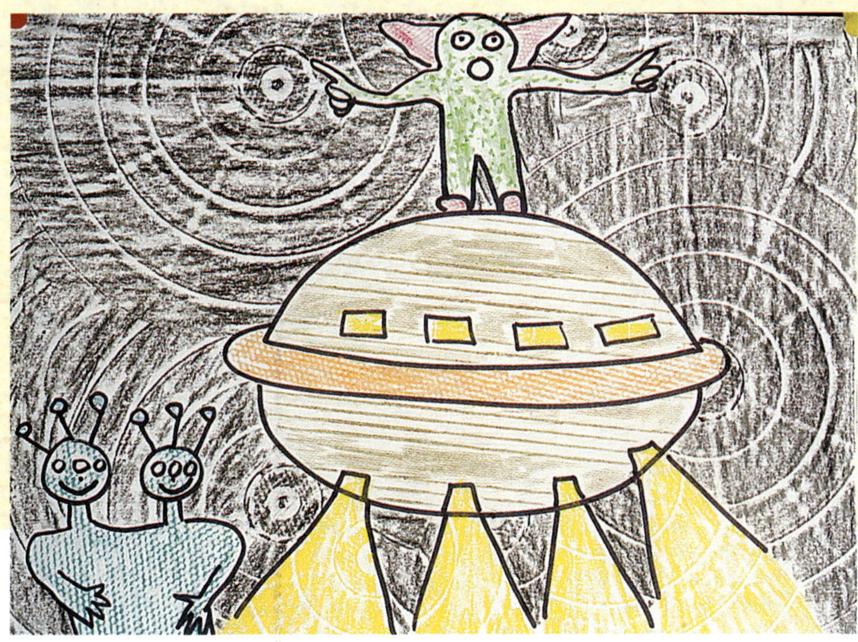

Fig. 1–7 Student artwork

Check Your Understanding

1. Name three different purposes that artists may have for creating storytelling artworks.

2. How does telling a story in images differ from telling a story in words? How is it the same?

3. What makes storytelling through artwork effective?

Contour and Gesture Drawing

For hundreds of years, artists have used two basic approaches to drawing: contour drawing and gesture drawing. A **contour drawing** shows the shape of an object or figure. It also includes interior details and is usually done slowly. A **gesture drawing** shows the movement or position of an object or figure. Gesture drawing is different from contour drawing because it is done quickly and without details.

Contour Drawing Making contour drawings can help you develop your ability to view and record the world around you. Continued practice will also improve your eye-hand coordination. You may use contour drawing to make a sketch for a print or painting or to create a finished drawing. You can also use contour and gesture drawings when you create visual stories.

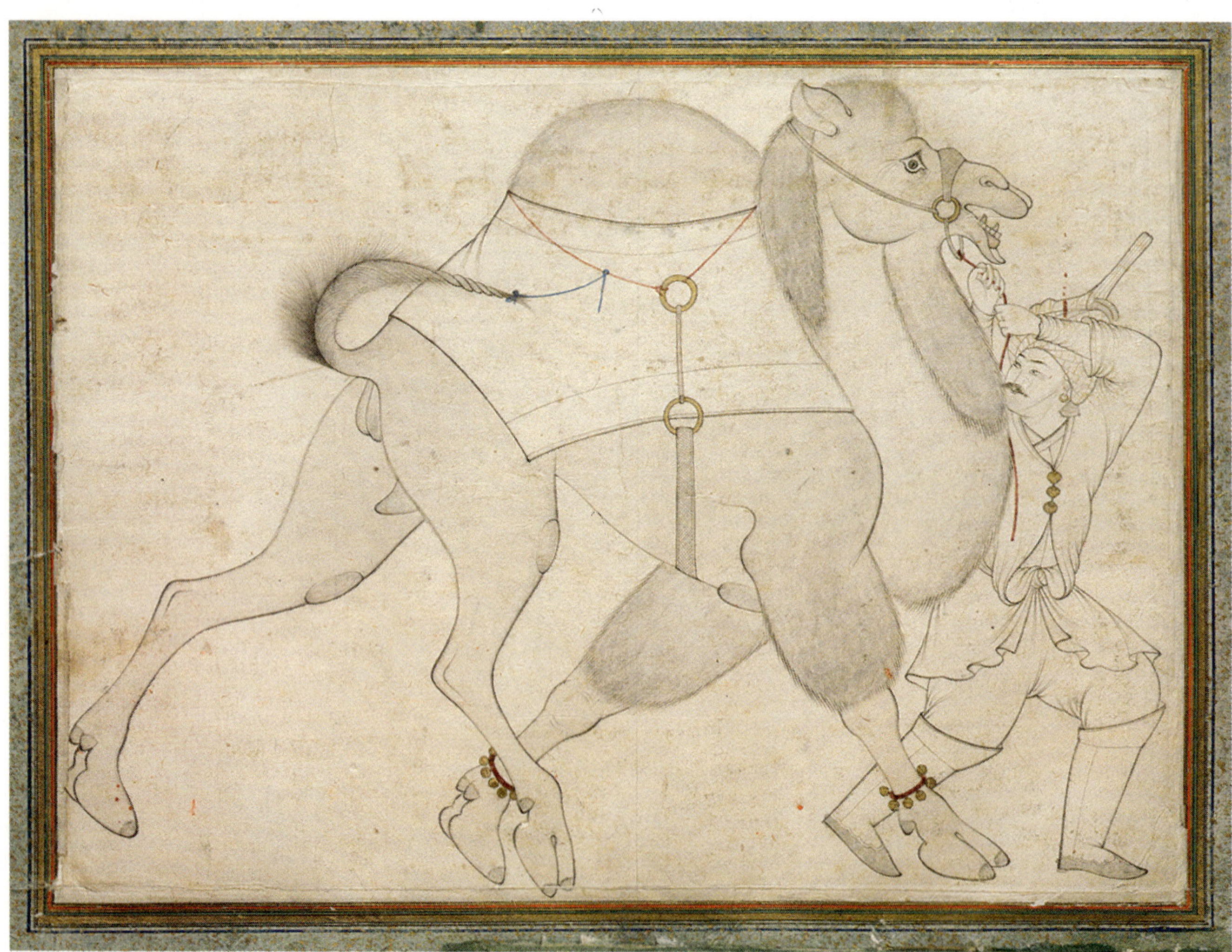

Fig. 1–8 **Is this image a contour drawing or a gesture drawing? How can you tell?**

Shaykh Muhammad (Iranian). *Camel and Groom*, c. 1545. Ink, gold, and colors on paper, 11 ¼" x 16" (28.5 x 40.6 cm). The Cleveland Museum of Art, purchase from the J.H. Wade Fund, 1944.489.

Observe Look again at the contour drawings on these pages. Notice the interior details that the artist chose to include. Think also about the details that the artist chose not to include.

Tools: A drawing tool with a sharp point, such as a pencil, marker, or ballpoint pen.

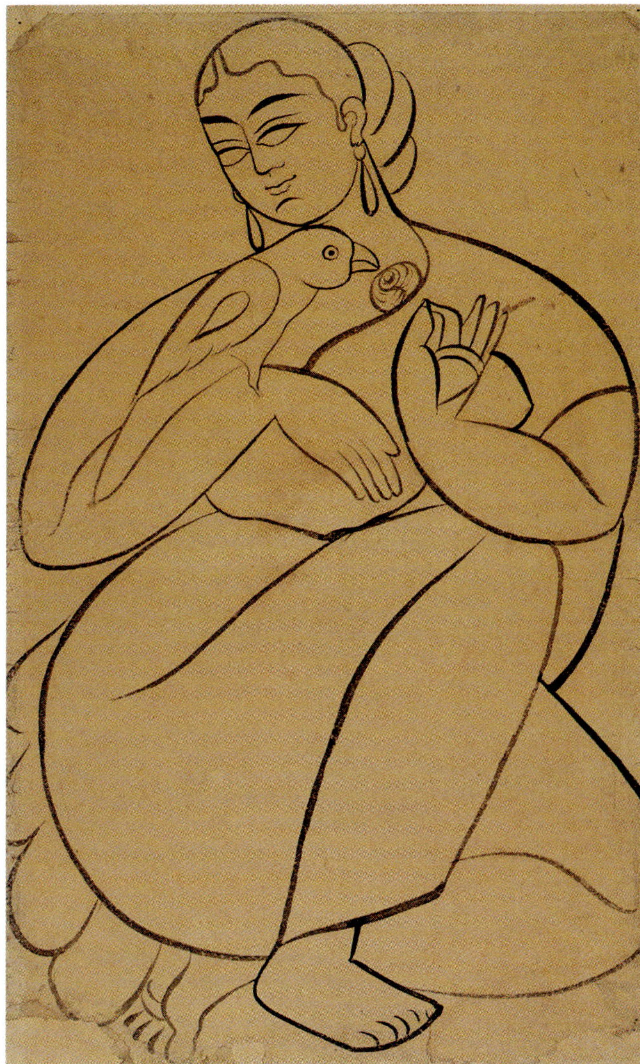

Fig. 1–9 **In this contour drawing, the artist used curved lines to create details in the subject. What are some details that the artist chose to include?**

India, West Bengal, Calcutta, *Souvenir Painting of a Woman with a Parrot*, c. 1875. Philadelphia Museum of Art: Stella Kramrisch Collection, 1994.

Practice: Contour Drawing

- Ask a classmate to sit in a relaxed pose for you. Make a contour drawing that captures the pose.
- Draw slowly and carefully. Imagine that your drawing tool is touching and slowly moving along each edge of your subject.
- Concentrate on the edges and interior details of your subject, such as pockets or buttons on a shirt.
- Keep your eyes on your subject. Look at your paper only when you begin to draw a new edge.

Gesture Drawing You can use gesture drawing as a way to quickly capture the main parts of a subject before something moves or changes. Most gesture drawings are thought of as sketches rather than as finished drawings. You may use them to help you plan a painting, sculpture, or print.

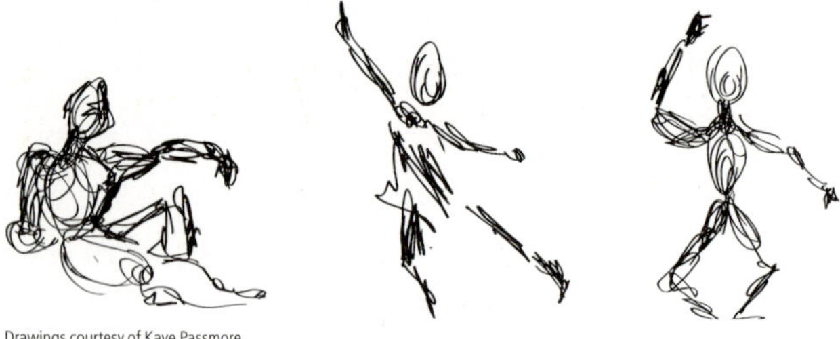

Drawings courtesy of Kaye Passmore.

Observe Look at the gesture drawings again. Think about how the artists used lines in various ways to show the movement or position of their subjects.

Tools: A wide, soft pencil, a crayon, or piece of chalk.

Practice: Gesture Drawing

- Ask a classmate to hold an action pose, such as throwing a ball or running.
- Draw quickly. You can add details later, if you want.
- Take in the action of the scene and the position of your subject.
- Use large, swift strokes to capture shapes, angles, and positions.

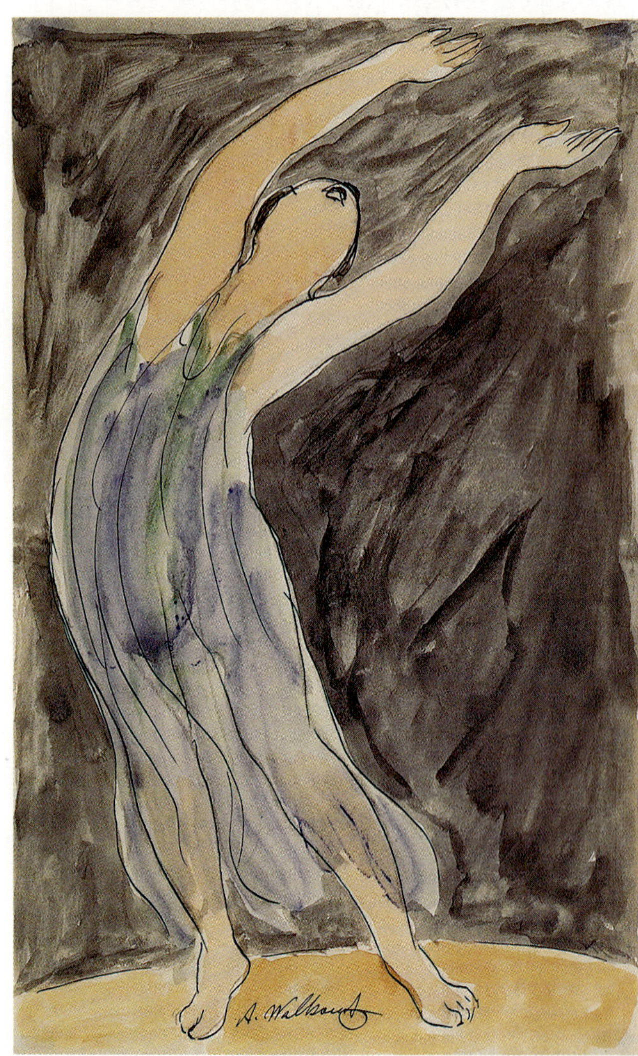

Fig. 1–10 **How does this gesture drawing capture the movement of the subject?**

Abraham Walkowitz, *Isadora Duncan*, c. 1920. Ink, watercolor on white wove paper 14" x 8 ½" (35.6 x 21.6 cm). Gift of Mr. and Mrs. Roy R. Neuberger. Mount Holyoke College Art Museum.

Check Your Understanding

1. Define contour drawing. Name two subjects that would make good contour drawings.

2. Why should the drawing tools used in contour drawing be different from those used in gesture drawing?

3. Name a situation in which you would use gesture drawing instead of contour drawing. Why would you use gesture drawing?

4. Why are gesture drawings thought of as sketches rather than finished drawings?

Studio Time

Character in Line

You can use your drawing skills to develop ideas for a character in a story.

- Base your drawing on observation.
- Use contour or gesture drawing techniques to record what you see.
- You may ask classmates to pose for you.
- Concentrate on line quality and proportion.

Reflect on the potential of your sketch for further character development.

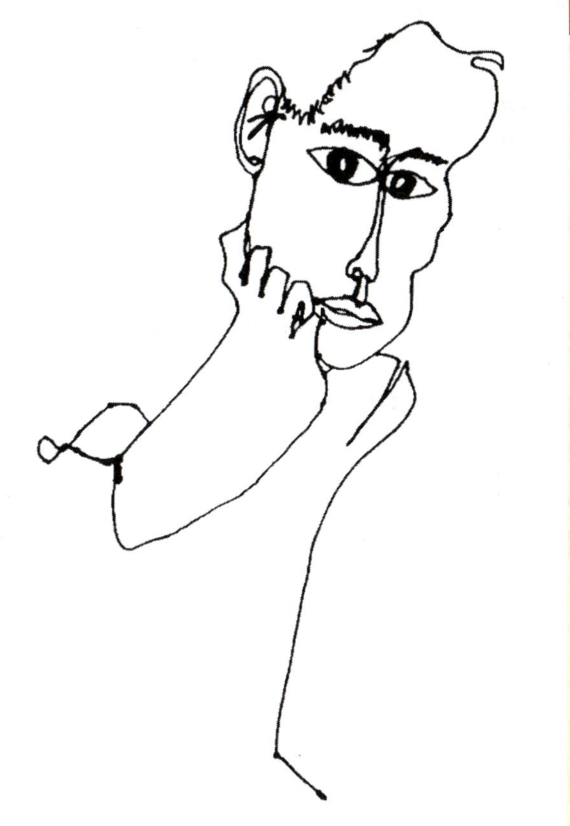

Fig. 1–11 Student artwork

Picture a Story

Studio Background

Have you ever thought about using only pictures to tell a story? What type of story would you tell? Would you use pictures to tell about something that happened in real life? Or would you create a visual story that tells about people and places from your imagination?

In this studio exploration, you will draw a series of pictures in frames that tell a story. Think of a story that you want to tell in pictures. How will you show the beginning, middle, and end of your story? How will you create pictures that look as though they belong together? Think about how to make your picture story interesting to viewers.

You Will Need

- 12 x 18 drawing paper
- smaller scrap paper for sketching
- pencil and eraser
- colored pencils
- rulers
- markers

Step 1 Plan and Practice

- Decide the story you want to tell.
- How many frames will you need to tell your story?
- Determine what scene you will show for the beginning, the middle parts, and end of your story.
- Which scenes will be close-up views? Which will show more background?
- Think about the mood you want to create in your series.

Things to Remember:

✓ Choose colors that best express the story's mood.

✓ Relate each scene to the story you want to tell, and sequence the scenes for the beginning to the end of your story.

✓ Make some scenes close-up views.

Inspiration from Our World

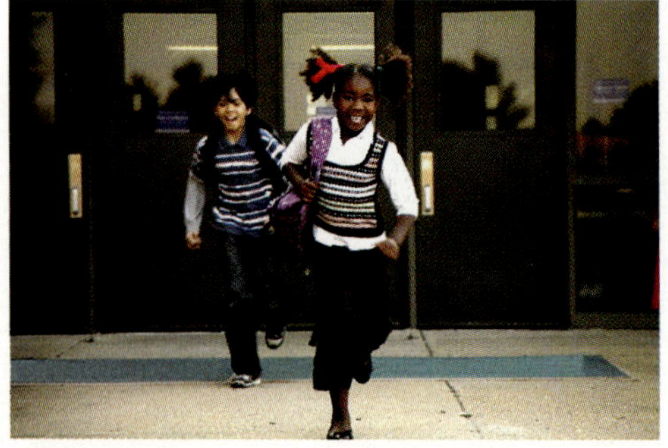

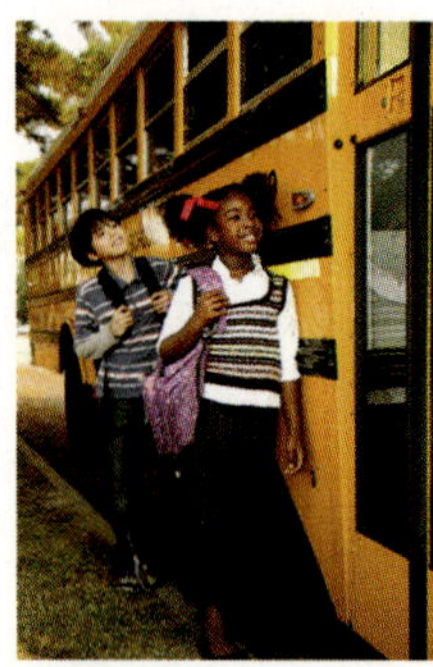

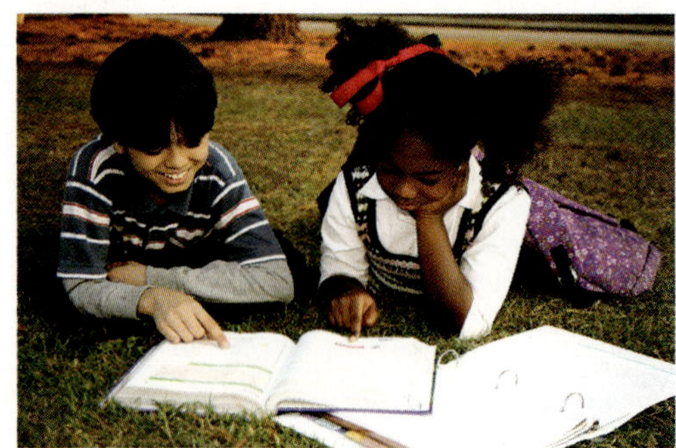

Inspiration from Art

When Jacob Lawrence decided to paint a series, he created the story's plot in pictures, sketching each scene with a pencil on sketch paper. After copying the sketches onto paper or board, Lawrence chose all the colors. He used one color at a time to paint the images. He painted the first color on all the boards. Then he added the second color, then the third, and so on, until he finished the images. By using many of the same colors in all the boards, he created a series of images that look as though they belong together. Lawrence used this system of working whenever he made a series of pictures.

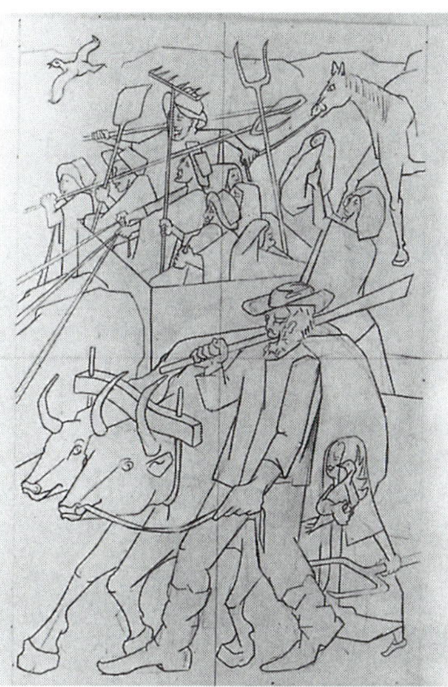

Fig. 1–12 **Notice the strong lines in this sketch. What details do you notice in the sketch?**

Jacob Lawrence, *In the Iowa Territory* (sketch), 1973. Casein gouache on paperboard, 31 ½" x 19 ½" (80 x 49.5 cm). Both images: Photo: Grace Carlsen. Courtesy of the University of Washington Art Slide Library. Artists Rights Society (ARS), NY.

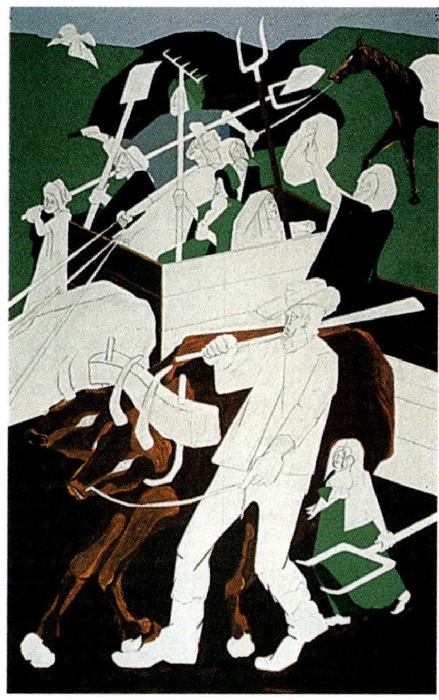

Fig. 1–13 **This image illustrates the artist's technique of painting a picture one color at a time. Why might he have chosen not to paint the people until later?**

Jacob Lawrence, *In the Iowa Territory* (unfinished), 1973. Casein gouache on paperboard, 31 ½" x 19 ½" (80 x 49.5 cm). Both images: Photo: Grace Carlsen. Courtesy of the University of Washington Art Slide Library. Artists Rights Society (ARS), NY.

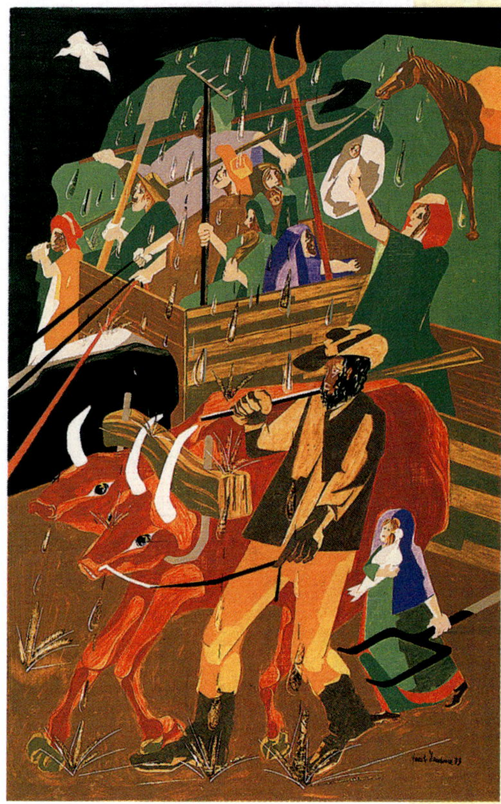

Fig. 1–14 **How is this finished artwork different from the sketch? How is it different from the unfinished painting?**

Jacob Lawrence, *In the Iowa Territory*, panel 2 from *George Washington Bush* series, 1973. Casein gouache on paperboard, 31 ½" x 19 ½" (80 x 49.5 cm). Washington State Historical Society, Tacoma. State Capital Museum Collection. Artists Rights Society (ARS), NY.

Step 2 **Begin to Create**

- Create a pencil sketch of each scene on scrap paper.
- Use ruler and pencil to divide your drawing paper into frames or sections.
- **Draw your scenes on each frame.**

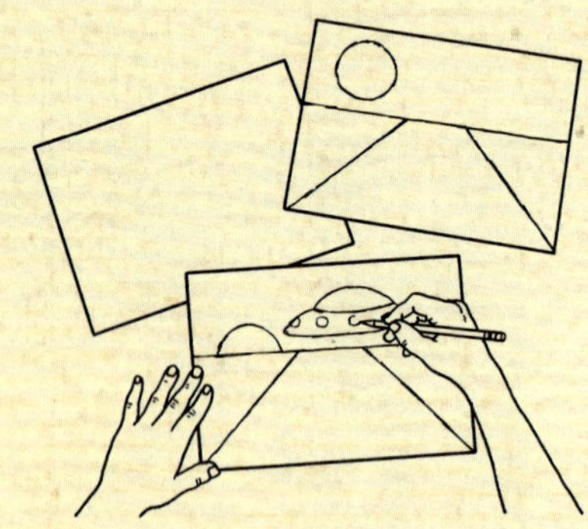

- How can you use shapes to express your ideas?
- How will you sequence your sketches from one frame to the next?
- **Carefully color each frame.** Will you finish each scene before moving to the next? Or will you use Jacob Lawrence's system of adding colors one at a time to the whole series?

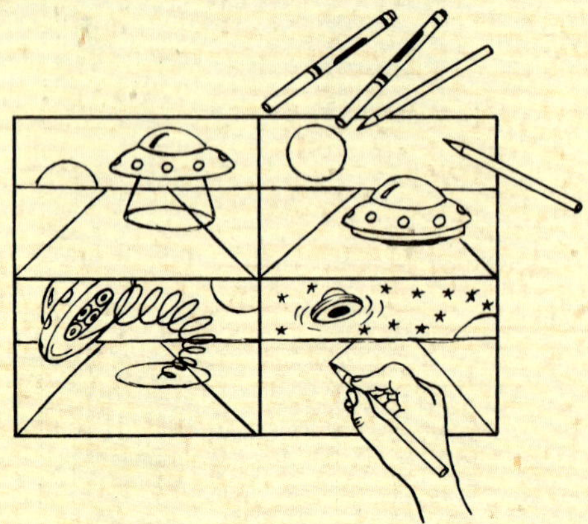

Step 3 **Revise**

Did you remember to:

✓ Choose colors that best express the story's mood?

✓ Relate each scene to the story you want to tell, and sequence the scenes of your story?

✓ Make some scenes close-up views?

Adjust your work if necessary. In your sketchbook, make a note of your revisions and why you made them.

Step 4 **Add Finishing Touches**

- Ensure that each frame develops the plot of the story. If you include a character, be sure that the character's age, clothing, and so forth, change if the plot develops over a long period of time. Add color and final details that help link the frames and make the story interesting. Be sure to sign the final frame in the series.

Step 5 **Share and Reflect**

- Discuss your work with your classmates. Take turns describing the stories you see in each other's work.
- Discuss how each artist used shape and color to tell a story.
- How many frames did each artist use to tell a story?
- How do certain details in the scenes make the story interesting?
- Explain to your classmates how each frame contributes to your story.

Art Criticism

Describe What do you recognize in each scene of the story?

Analyze How did the artist arrange the frames in the story sequence?

Interpret What do you think this story is about?

Evaluate What do you think the artist did especially well?

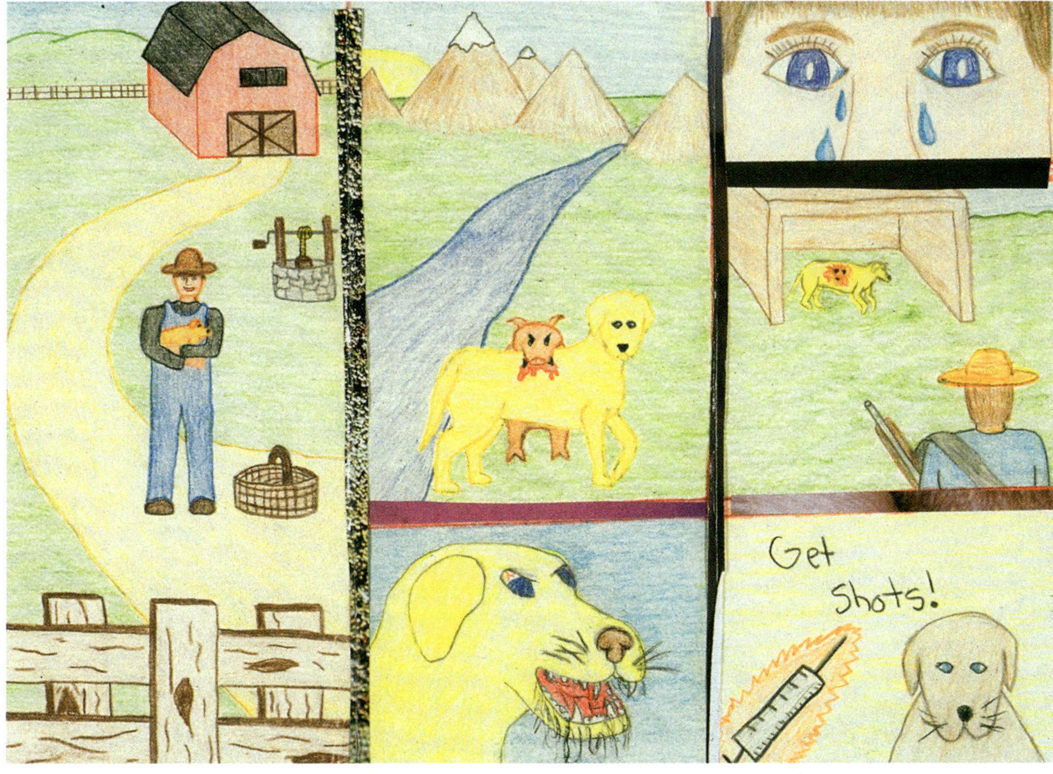

Fig. 1–15
Student artwork

A Tradition of Narrative Art

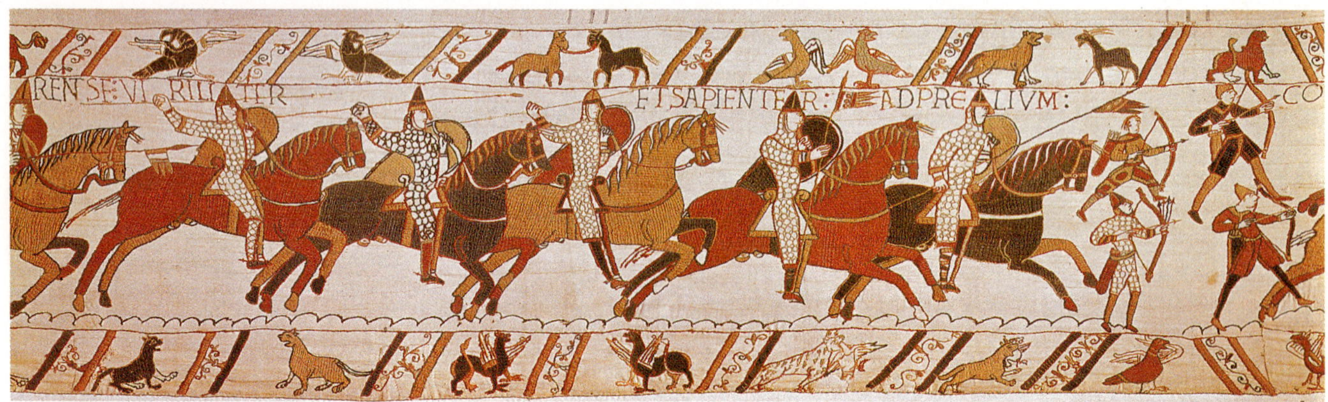

Art that tells a story is called narrative art. Throughout history, people have told stories with pictures. Long ago, people painted stories on cave walls. They carved stories in stone and made tapestries, artworks stitched or woven in cloth. In the Middle Ages, artists used needles and thread to embroider a story. This long tapestry, called the *Bayeux Tapestry*, told the story of a great battle. The battle scenes were arranged in a series of connected pictures, or frames.

Fig. 1–16 **This tapestry shows scenes in connected frames. This method eventually led to other ways of telling stories, such as the newspaper comic strip.**

English, *Bayeux Tapestry* (detail: *The Norman cavalry rushes into battle*), 11th century. Embroidered wool on linen, entire fabric: 20" x 230' (.51 x 70 m). Musée de la Tapisserie, Bayeux, France. Erich Lessing/Art Resource, New York. By Special permission of the City of Bayeux.

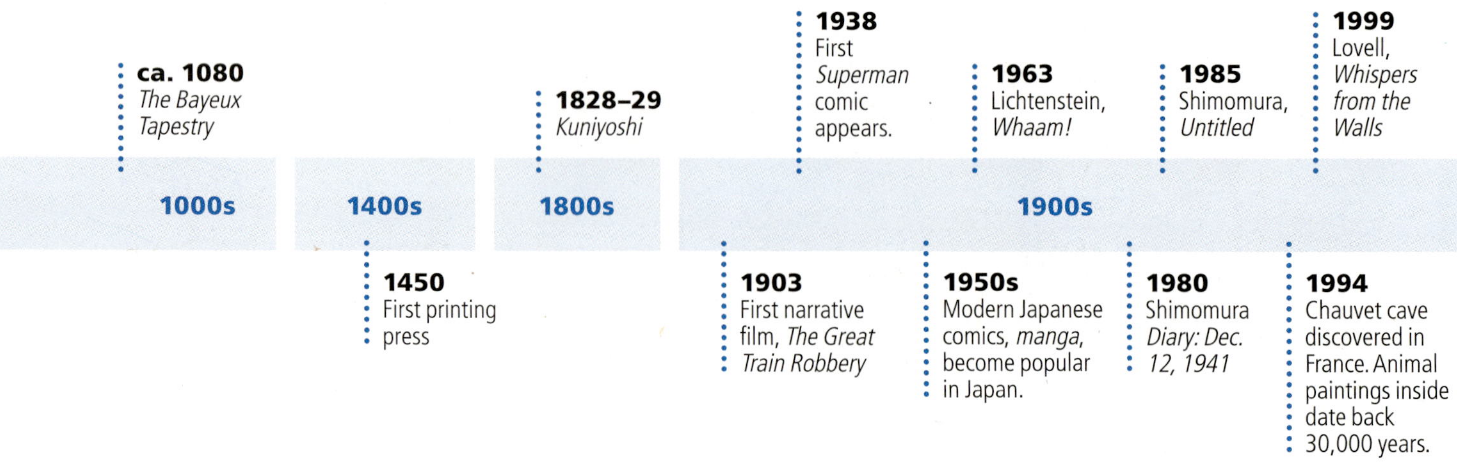

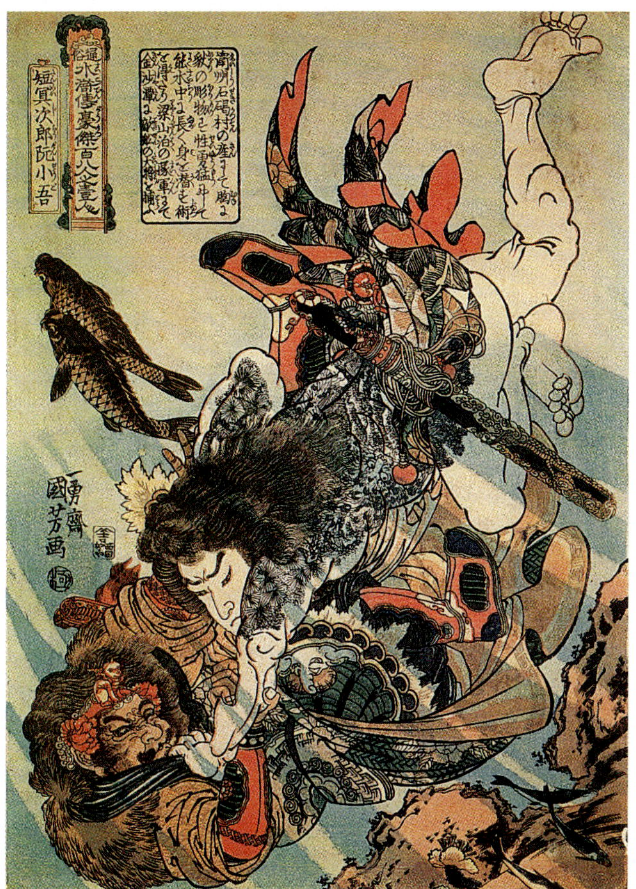

Fig. 1–17 **What is the largest shape in this artwork? Which figure is Tameijiro dan Shogo? Why do you think so?**

Utagawa Kuniyoshi, *Tameijiro dan Shogo Grapples with His Enemy under Water*, 1828–29. Folio from *The Heroes of Suikoden*. Woodcut on paper. Private Collection. Courtesy of Bridgeman Art Library.

Stories of the Past and the Popular

These visual stories help us connect to the past. In the 1800s, the Japanese printmaker Kuniyoshi created woodcuts to tell stories. **Woodcuts** are prints made by carving into a block of wood, inking the wood, and pressing paper against it.

The stories in Kuniyoshi's prints, such as the one shown on this page, were based on legends of great warriors. His images look like comic book superheroes.

In the 1900s, American artist Roy Lichtenstein created a series of storytelling paintings based on the images and style of comic-book art. His work is known as Pop Art, because it borrows from widely-popular images.

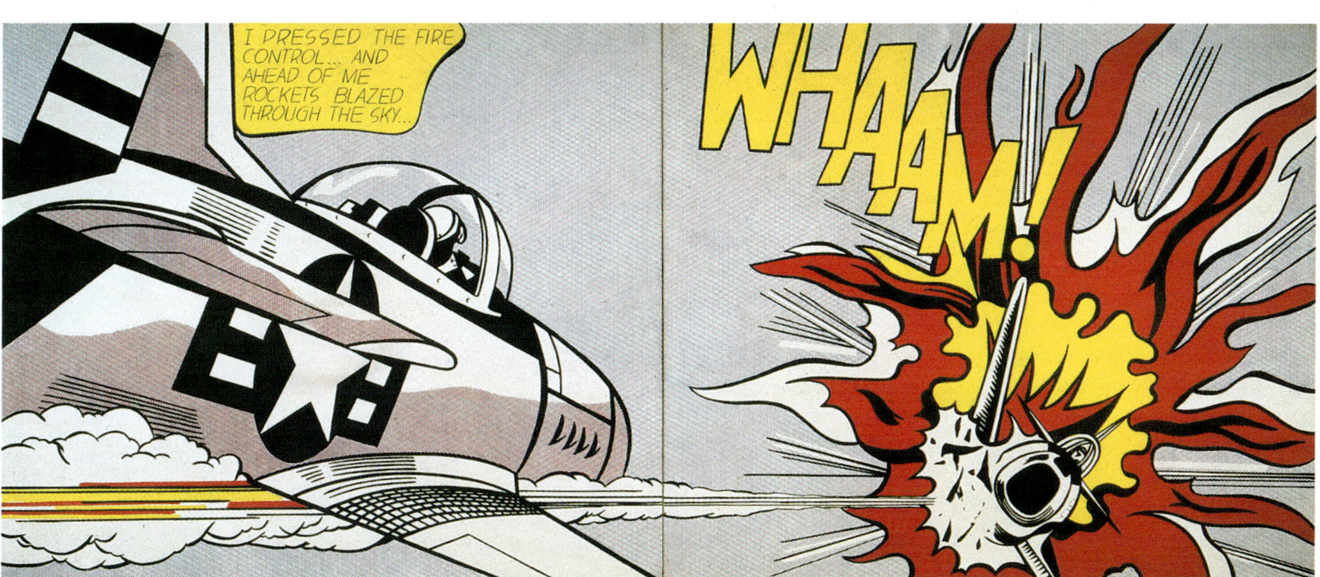

Fig. 1–18 **This artwork is two separate paintings placed side by side. In the first frame, the pilot takes aim. What happens in the second frame? Note the shapes in each canvas. How would you describe the differences?**

Roy Lichtenstein, *Whaam!* 1963. Acrylic and oil on two canvases, 67 ½" x 158 ¼" (170.2 x 402 cm). Courtesy of The Tate Gallery, London, England. © Tate London, 2001.

1.4 Continued

Stories in a Personal Style Artists sometimes tell stories that relate to their personal life. The stories may be based on their own experiences, on the lives of people or ancestors who are important to them, or on events from their time.

The paintings on this page by artist Roger Shimomura show some of the influences on his art. Shimomura has developed a style that is influenced by American comic books, Pop Art, and Japanese woodcut prints. His artwork *Untitled* is an example of his large, early canvases filled with the shapes of comic-book characters. Notice how he outlined the shapes of color in black. Shimomura's work shows not only the influence of such Pop artists as Roy Lichtenstein, but also the lines and details like those in Japanese woodcut prints.

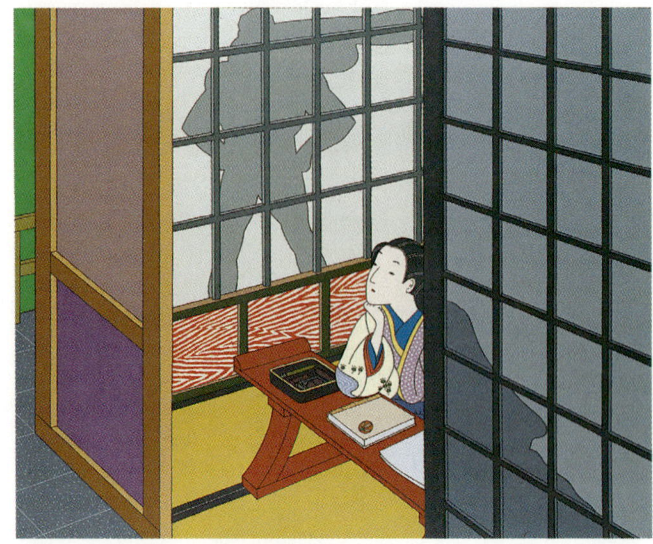

Fig. 1–20 **What does the woman seem to be doing? Who might the person behind the screen be? Why do you think so?**

Roger Shimomura, *Diary: Dec. 12, 1941*, 1980. Acrylic on canvas, 50 ¼" x 60" (127 x 152.4 cm). Smithsonian American Art Museum, Washington, DC/Art Resource, NY.

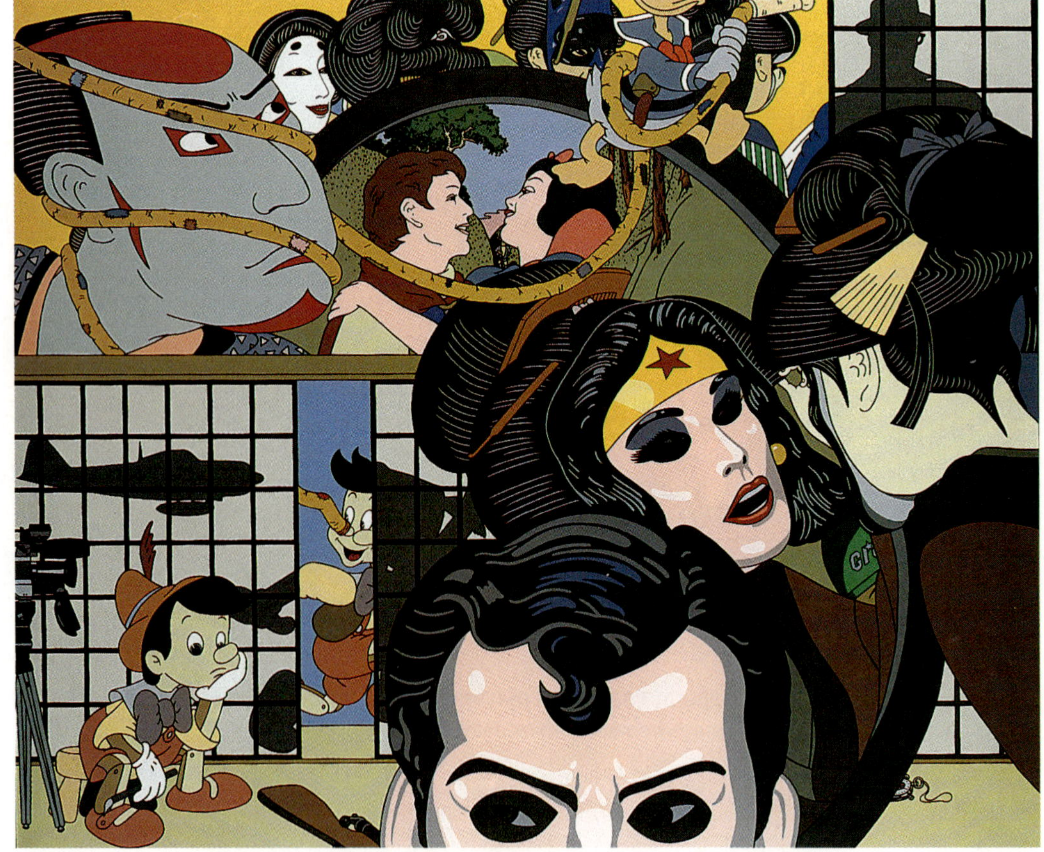

Fig. 1–19 **Look at the images within this painting. Which are familiar to you? From where do you know them?**

Roger Shimomura, *Untitled*, 1985. Acrylic on canvas, 60" x 72" (152.4 x 182.9 cm). Museum Purchase, Bumeta Adair Endowment Fund, Wichita Art Museum, Wichita, Kansas.

Meet Roger Shimomura

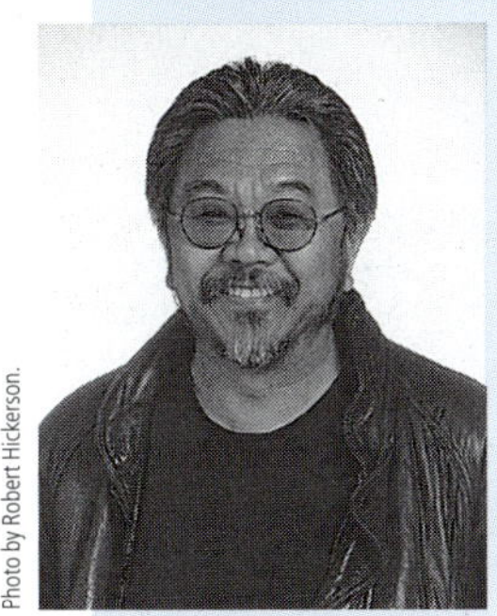

Photo by Robert Hickerson.

Roger Shimomura is a second-generation American of Japanese descent. In elementary school, Shimomura made many drawings of comic-book characters, such as Donald Duck and Mickey Mouse. As a teenager, he collected comic books. *Superman*, *Dick Tracy*, and *Wonder Woman* were his favorites. Many of his paintings, prints, and performance-art pieces deal with events in his early life as well as the social and political issues faced by Japanese Americans. Some of his artworks, such as *Diary*, are narratives based on diaries his immigrant grandmother wrote during her lifetime.

"Art was always my first love, and my family and teachers reinforced that I was good in art. My grandmother kept my drawings from first through sixth grade."

—Roger Shimomura (born 1939)

Check Your Understanding

1. What is narrative art?
2. What elements in Roy Lichtenstein's *Whaam!* make it similar to comic-book art?
3. Look back to the artwork of Jacob Lawrence in lesson 1.1. Why would his paintings be an example of narrative art?

Studio Time

A Story Collage

You can create a collage that tells a personal story.

- Look through old newspapers, catalogues, and magazines for photographs. Look for patterned papers in wallpaper sample books or gift wrapping scraps.
- When you find several images and patterned papers that relate to your story, cut them out and trim the edges of the shapes carefully.
- Move the images around and overlap them in different ways to develop your composition.
- Think about how you can create a center of interest to draw attention to your story.
- Glue the parts down neatly and carefully.

Reflect on how well your collage tells your story.

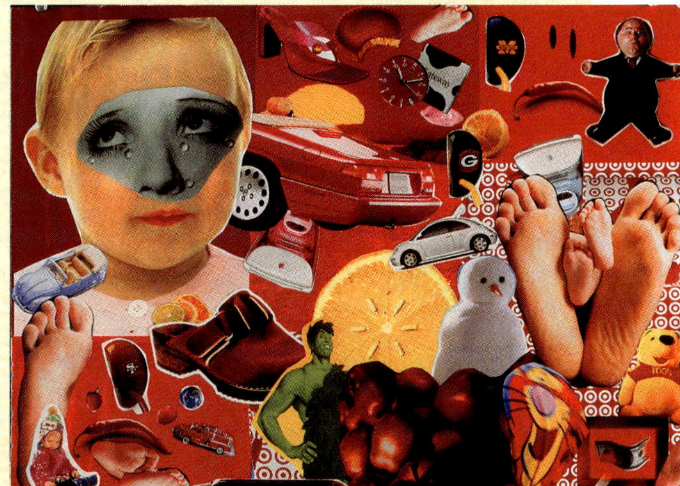

Fig. 1–21 Student artwork

Narrative Art from Dahomey

Stories in Memory of Kings In Dahomey, West Africa, the Fon royal court controlled the artists. Each artist belonged to a guild, which is a group of people in the same occupation. One Fon guild created life-size wood sculptures for the royal court. Another guild worked with metal. Still other guild artists decorated the palace walls with stories of historical events in bas-relief. A bas-relief is a sculpture in which parts of the design stand out from the background.

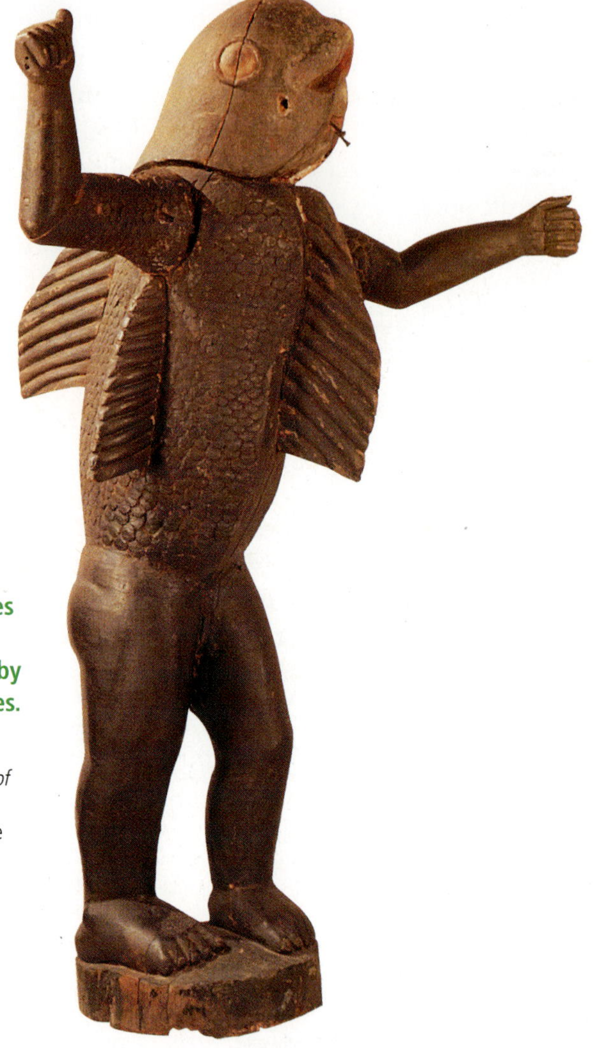

Fig. 1–22 **This wood sculpture relates to a story of a king's power and greatness. The sculpture was made by joining many different carved shapes. Which shapes were added?**

Africa, Benin, *Wooden Statue of Behanzin, King of Dahomey as the Figure of a Shark*, 19th century. Wood, height: 5' 2" (1.6m). Collection, Musée de l'homme, Paris, France.

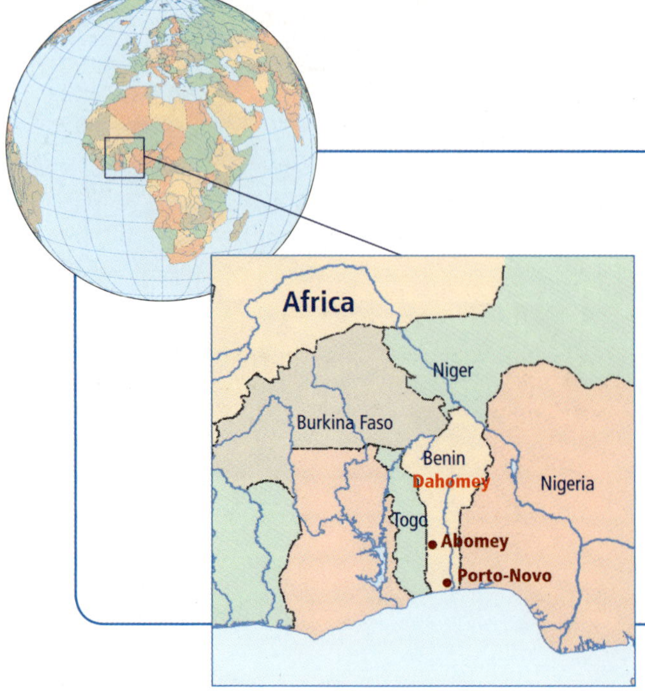

Social Studies Connection

In the late 1600s, the Fon people of West Africa formed the kingdom of **Dahomey**, which thrived for over 200 years. Abomey was the kingdom's capital city. In the late 1800s, the French began to colonize Dahomey, and it soon became part of French West Africa. It became an independent state in 1960, called the Republic of Benin. Some of the languages spoken in the Republic of Benin are French, Fon, and Yoruba.

Storytelling Banners in Appliqué

Upon taking office, a king received a gift of imported cloth. Artists stitched the cloth with images that told the stories of the king's power and great deeds. In the banner on page 22, the lion represents a Dahomey king of the 1800s. A **banner** is a piece of cloth with a design. The tailors cut a variety of symbolic shapes and hand-stitched them to a background cloth, a process known as **appliqué**.

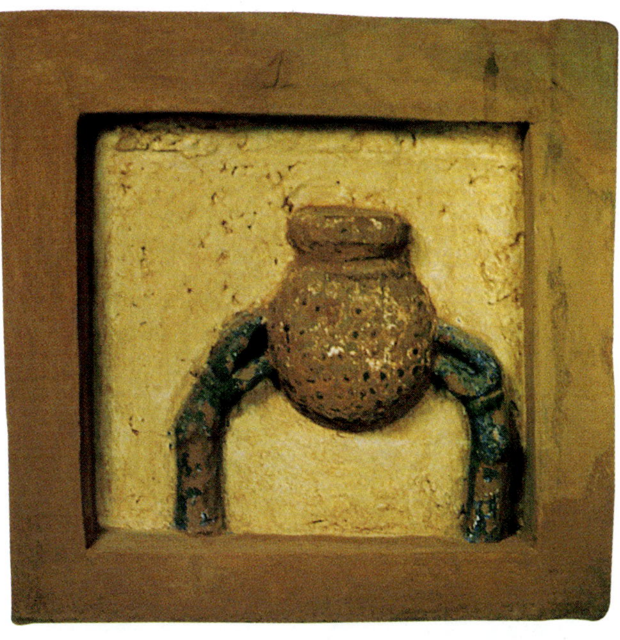

Fig. 1–23 **Bas-relief mud sculptures served as illustrations for storytellers who recited the history of the Dahomey kings. Why would the storytellers want to illustrate their stories?**

Africa, Benin, Abomey, *Earthen Relief #1*, after conservation in March 1996. Musée Historique d'Abomey. Photograph: Susan Middleton. ©The J. Paul Getty Trust.

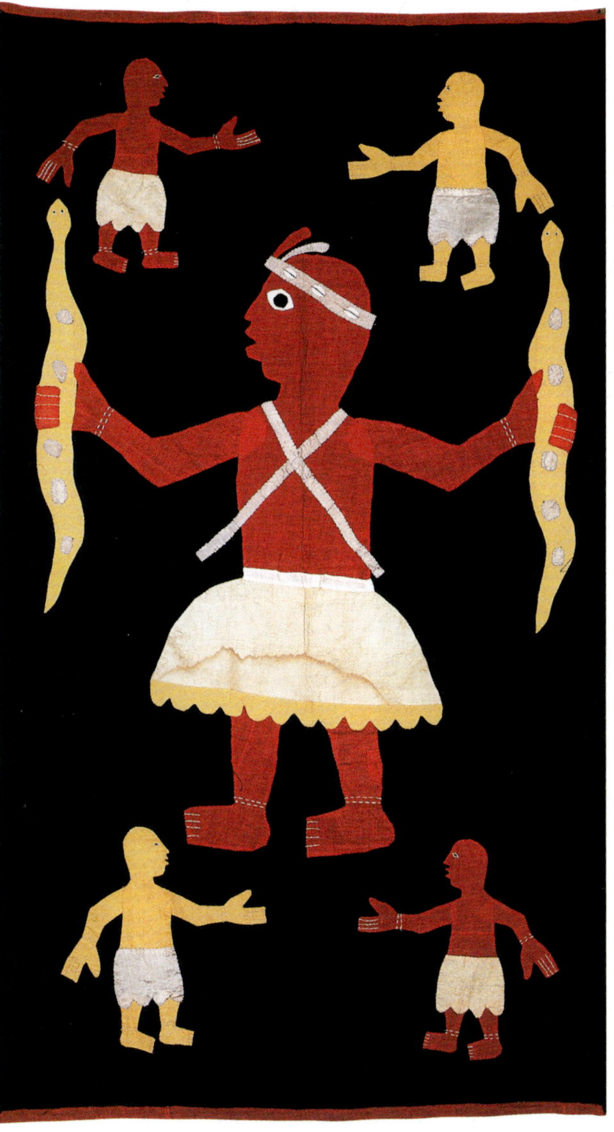

Fig. 1–24 **The shapes in this banner were cut from patterns and sewn to a background. Why do you think the artist made the central subject much larger than the others?**

Africa, Benin, Fon kingdom, *Wall Hanging Representing Da, A Symbol of Prosperity, in Human Form*, 19th–20th century. Appliquéd cloth, height 86 ⅝" (220cm) ©Musée de l'homme, Photo D. Ponsard. Musée de l'homme, Paris, France.

Visual Culture

Many towns and neighborhoods are decorated with banners. Sometimes we see banners hanging from light posts along the main streets in a community. Some people hang banners in front of their homes. These often change with the seasons or holidays. Look for banners in your community. What do the images and symbols mean to you?

Appliqué has continued in present day Benin. The memory of kings and their influence on Fon culture is still strong. However, stories about daily life, farming, and hunting are now also part of the subjects in appliquéd cloths.

A Family of Storytellers In creating appliquéd cloth, the Yemadje family of artists follow the basic Fon artistic principle of *nu ta do nu me*, which means "the highlighting of one thing by another." The artists highlight a background cloth with different colors of other cloth. Look at the banner on this page. What makes the shapes stand out against the background?

Creating Stories in Cloth The artists also follow the Fon principle of spreading the cutout patterns over the surface of the background cloth. The story's characters and images are pinned to the background. The shapes are hand-stitched to the background. Afterward, an artist decides the color and width of the cloth borders.

Meet Joseph Yemadje

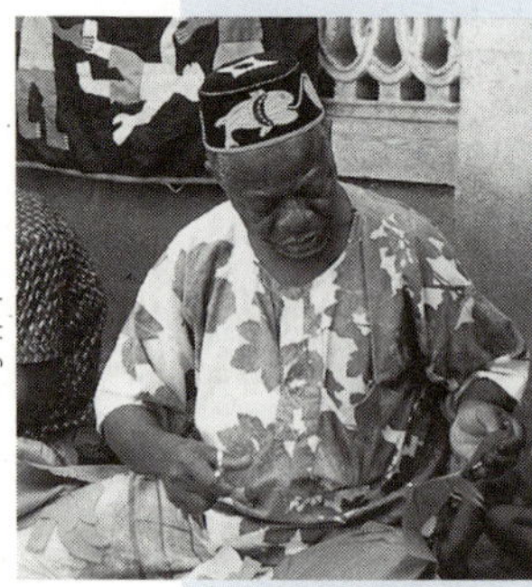

Detail of *Fon Men Making Appliqué Cloth.*

Joseph Yemadje and his family are descendants of the 1800s Fon royal court artists. They continue the storytelling tradition in appliqué workshops in Abomey and other Benin cities. For much of their work, the Yemadje artists use a pure form of appliqué with traditional royal colors and symbols. They also combine some of the traditional images with new ones, such as images from daily life.

"We divide the work. One uses patterns to cut the shapes. Another does the tacking. Someone else does the final stitching. Then an apprentice attaches the border."

—Yemadje family member

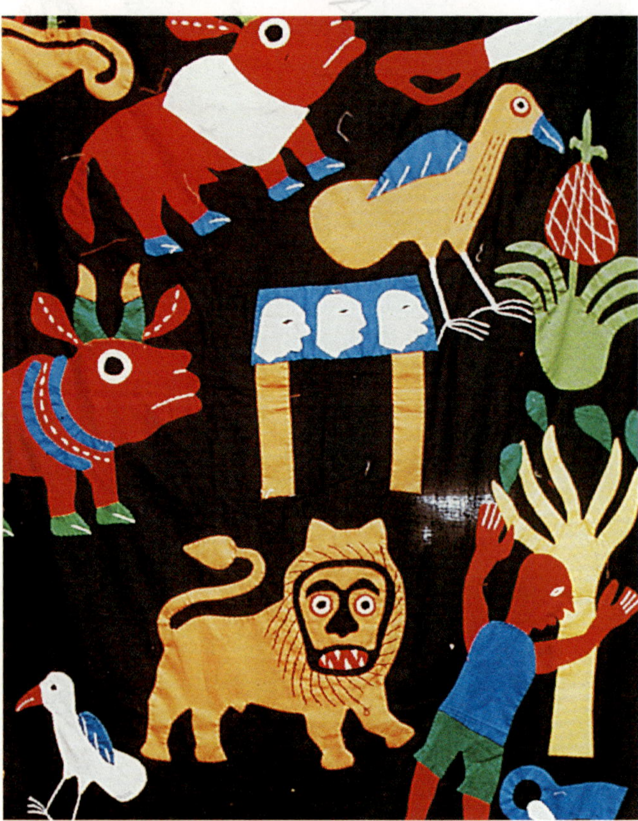

Fig. 1–25 **Compare and contrast this banner to the one shown on page 21. What differences do you see? How are the two banners alike?**

Africa, Benin, Abomey, *Fon Appliqué Cloth* (detail), c. 1971. Photograph by Eliot Elisofon. Image no. H FON 10.1 (7021) Eliot Elisofon Photographic Archives, National Museum of African Art, Smithsonian Institution.

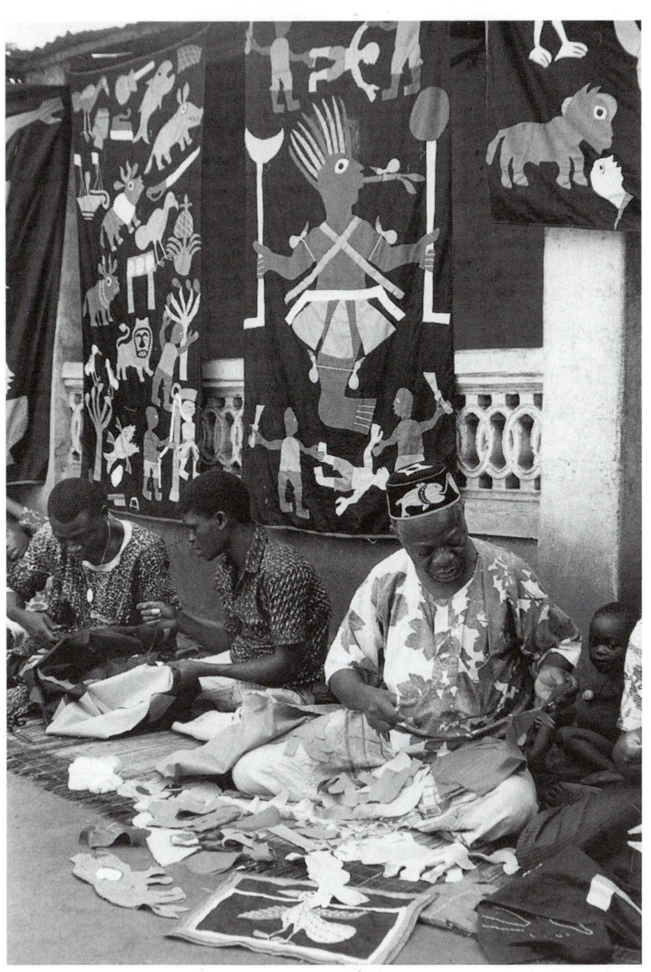

Check Your Understanding

1. What is the definition of bas-relief?
2. Compare and contrast the Dahomey banners to the banners or flags that people hang from their homes or in the streets of your community today.
3. In the region that was once Dahomey, how has the making of appliqué banners changed over the past 300 years?

Fig. 1–26 **Family members divide the work when they create banners. Some banners are made with new and different shapes created upon request.**

Benin, Abomey, *Fon Men Making Appliqué Cloth*, 1971. Photograph by Eliot Elisofon, March 1971. Image no. H2 FON 10.1EE 71. Eliot Elisofon Photographic Archives, National Museum of African Art, Smithsonian Institution.

Studio Time

Animal Banner

Choose an animal whose qualities you admire.

- Use the animal character to create a banner that tells part of your life story.
- If possible, use cloth, needle, and thread, and follow the traditional way of working with appliqué.
- You could also cut shapes from felt and then glue them to a background cloth, or you may make a cut-paper banner.

Reflect on how well the animal and shapes you chose tell your story.

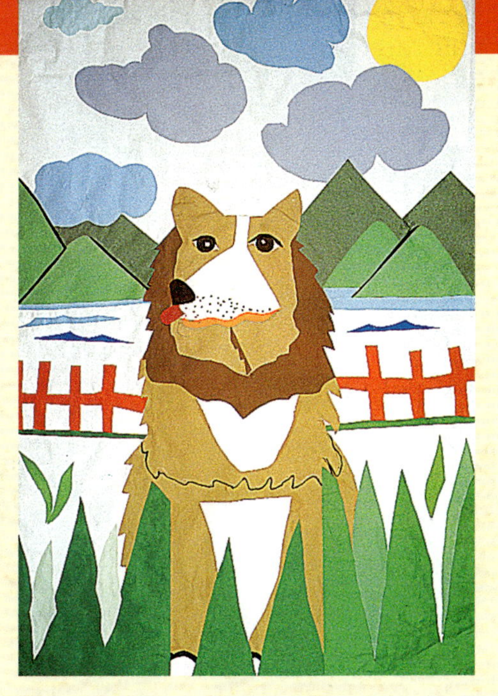

Fig. 1–27 Student artwork

A Story Under Construction

Studio Background

The superhero meets his or her enemy face-to-face. What happens next? For a storytelling artwork, artists first decide which special moment such as this in the story to show. Will it be from the story's beginning, middle, or end?

In this studio exploration, you will construct a scene that shows a special moment from a story. Think about a scene that is important to the plot of the story. What does the setting look like? Which characters are involved in the scene? Imagine stopping the action of the characters in that moment. What are they doing? How are they posed?

You Will Need

- prepared cardboard box
- colored construction paper
- cardboard scraps
- scissors
- white glue
- clay
- tools for creating surface textures

Step 1 Plan and Practice

- Decide what kind of story you want to show. Will your scene be of an imaginary or real moment?
- Think about the characters that will be in your scene.
- Make some simple sketches of the setting and of your characters to help guide you.

Things to Remember:

✓ Pick a moment that is important to the plot of the story.

✓ Include gestures in your characters' poses to show a frozen action.

✓ Include details and props to show the setting of the scene.

Inspiration from Our World

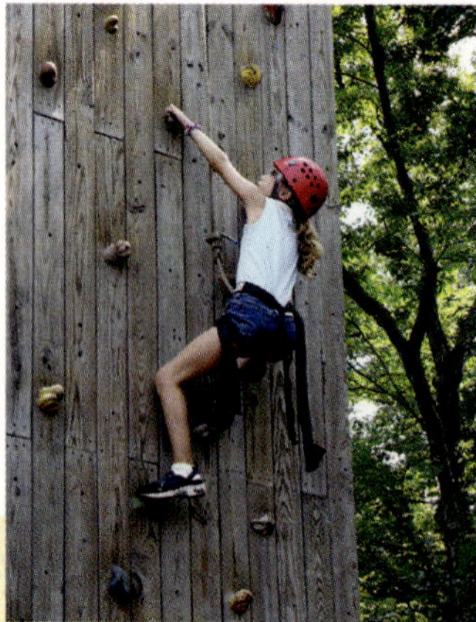

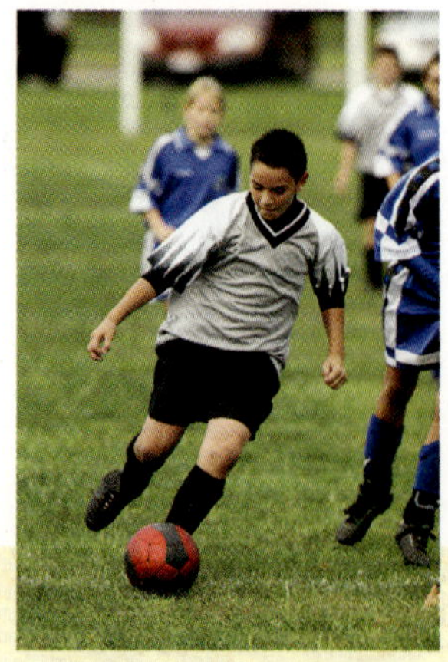

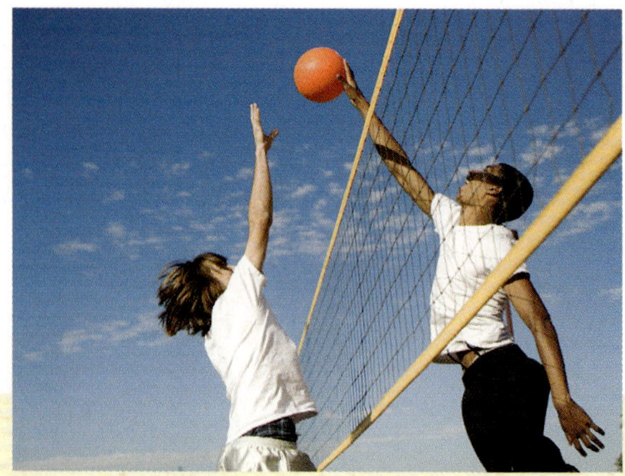

Inspiration from Art

Red Grooms and Viola Frey are two contemporary artists who have created storytelling sculptures. Both of their stories are about everyday life, but their journeys through telling the stories have been different.

In his stories, Grooms highlights the **setting**, or the time and place in which events occur. He often uses cardboard, wood, and foam core to build his scenes. He is best known for building exaggerated environments, such as city streets and subway cars that viewers can actually walk through. Frey focuses on characters and creates life-size clay figures. Her work is influenced by the Japanese porcelain figurines she played with as a child.

Grooms' and Frey's sculptures seem frozen in time, which helps to fire up viewers' imaginations. It's almost as if all you have to do is flip a switch and everything in the sculptures will start moving again and the stories will go on.

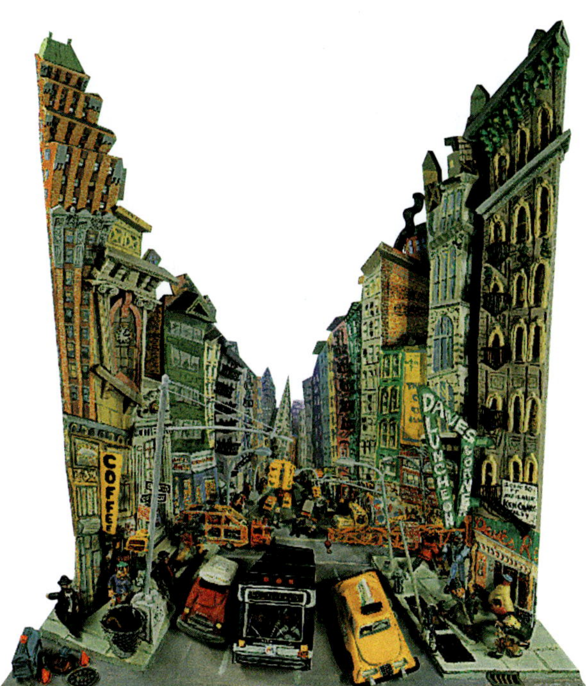

Fig. 1–28 **How do you think the feeling of this setting would change if the shapes were straight and regular?**

Red Grooms, *Looking Along Broadway towards Grace Church*, 1981. Mixed media, height: 71" (180.3 cm). ©The Cleveland Museum of Art, 2001. Gift of Agnes Gund in honor of Edward Henning, 1991.27. ©2001 Red Grooms/Artists Rights Society (ARS), New York.

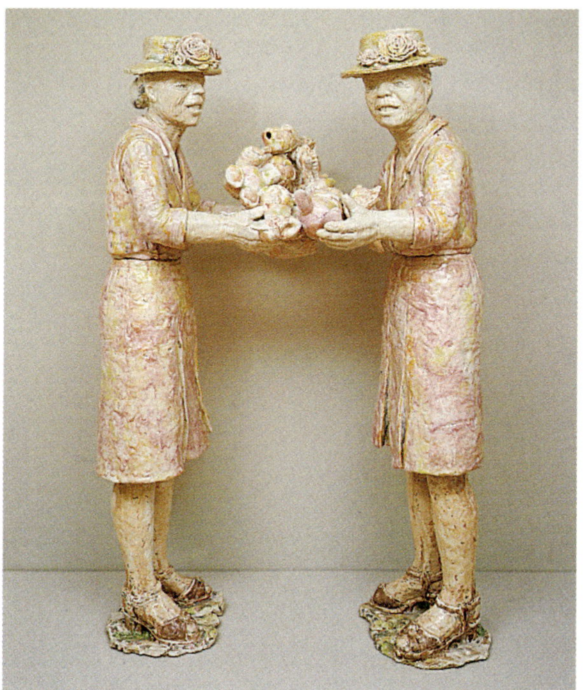

Fig. 1–29 **If these sculpted figures were characters in a play or movie, what might they be saying to each other?**

Viola Frey, *Double Grandmother*, 1978–79 VAGA. Glazed white clay, height: 61 ¼" (156 cm). The Minneapolis Institute of Arts, Gift of the Regis Corporation (81.29.1.2).

Step 2 Begin to Create

- **Create your background scene with the box and construction paper.** Think of ways to cut, fold, curl, or crumple construction paper to make colorful shapes and forms.

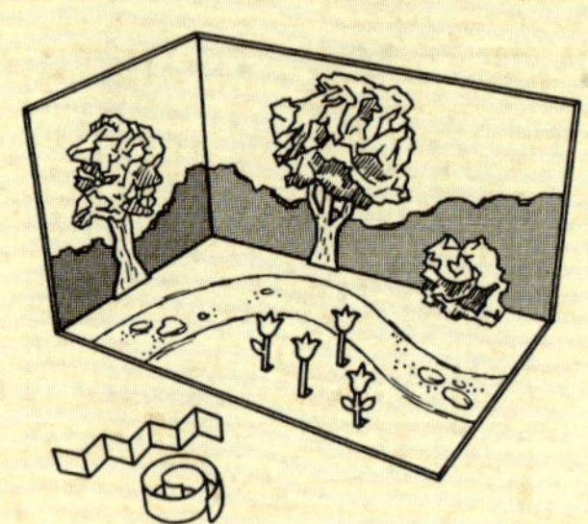

- Glue the details to the sides and floor of the box.
- **Make your characters out of a ball of clay.** Create a five-point star by pulling out a point for the head, each arm, and each leg.

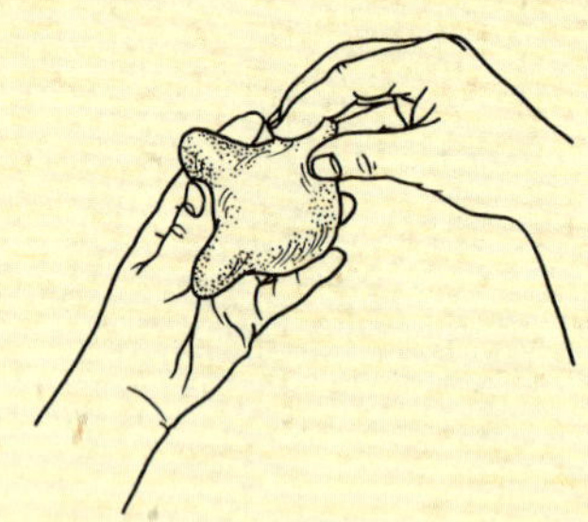

- **Model, or shape, the head and limbs by pinching and pulling the points.** Think about the pose you want each character to have.

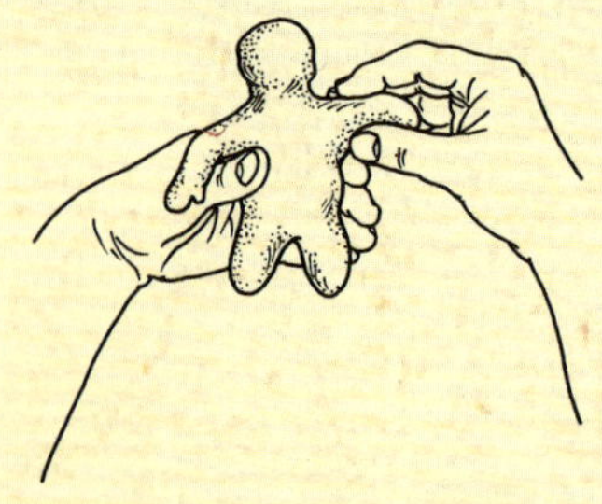

- **Add details, such as facial features, hair, and clothing patterns.** Will you press materials onto the figures? Or will you create details by pressing textures onto the surfaces?

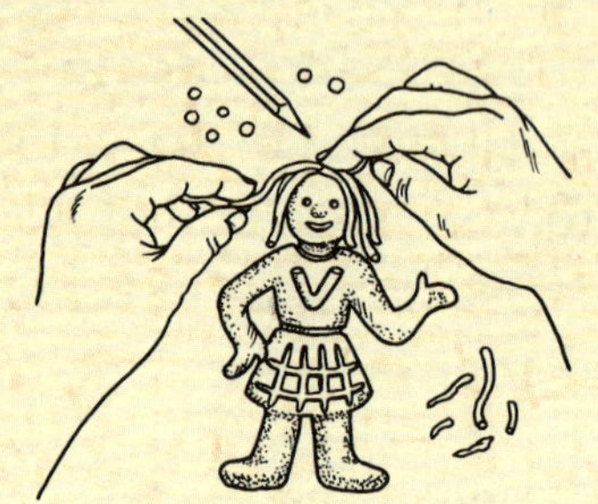

- Make props from clay, cardboard, or construction paper. Does your scene need furniture, trees, or cars? Do your characters need to hold special objects?

Step 3 Revise

Did you remember to:

✓ Pick a moment that is important to the plot of the story?

✓ Include gestures in your characters' poses to show a frozen action?

✓ Include details and props to show the setting of the scene?

Adjust your work if necessary. In your sketchbook, make a note of your revisions and why you made them.

Step 4 Add Finishing Touches

- Add whatever props are necessary. Then place the characters in the scene.

Step 5 **Share and Reflect**

- Discuss your completed sculpture with your classmates.
- Explain the part of your story your artwork tells.
- Describe how you used shapes and forms in your artwork.
- What was the biggest challenge for you in making your sculpture? How did you handle this challenge?
- What changes, if any, would you make in the process you used to create this artwork?

Art Criticism

Describe What is going on in this sculpture? Name all the things you see.

Analyze How has the artist created unity and variety in this sculpture?

Interpret How would you describe the feeling you get when you look at this sculpture?

Evaluate What features of this sculpture are especially pleasing to you? Why?

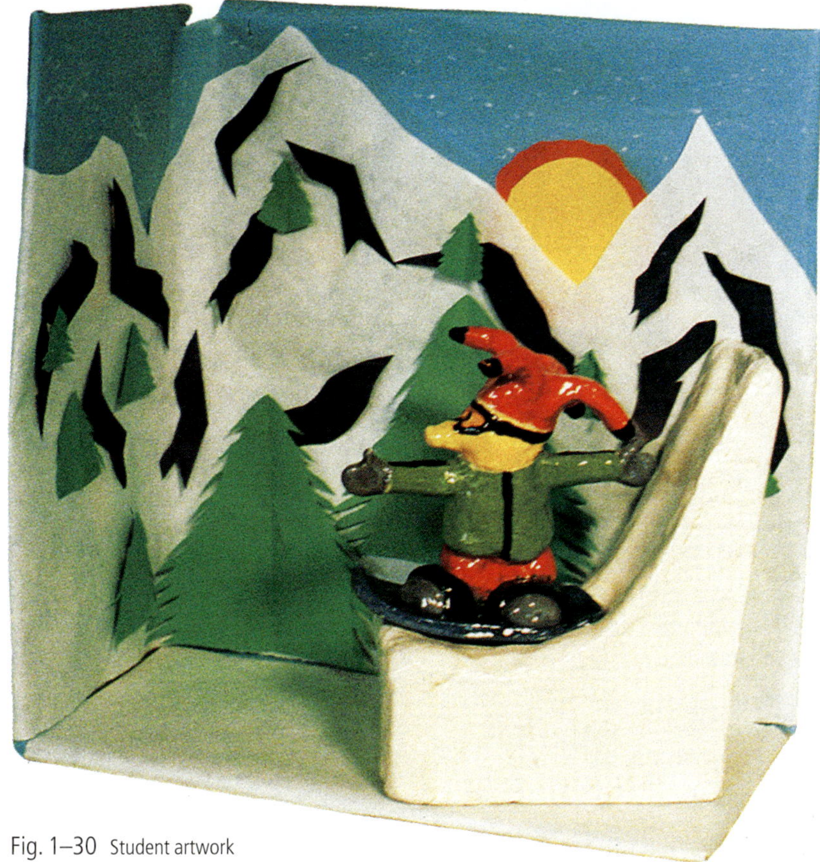

Fig. 1–30 Student artwork

Social Studies

In many cultures the traditions of storytelling appear in artifacts and artworks. For example, Fon tailors in West Africa made appliquéd banners about events from their culture's history and from their own lives. Harriet Powers, born a slave in the United States in 1837, made story quilts. Like the Fon, Powers used large, simple cutouts. Powers' use of contrasting foreground and background colors, balanced placement of figures across the background, and the addition of borders also reflect Fon techniques.

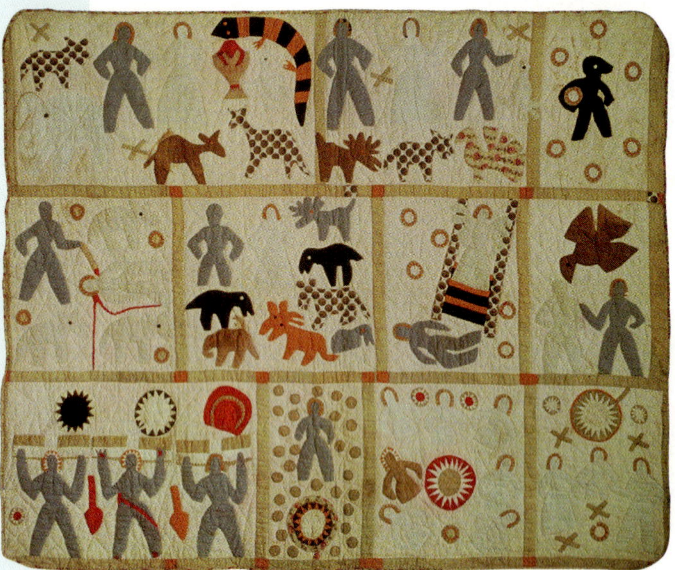

Fig. 1–31 **Each panel in this quilt tells a story from the Christian Bible. Why is appliqué a useful technique for telling stories in cloth?**

Harriet Powers, *Bible Quilt*, c. 1886. Pieced and appliquéd, plain and roller-printed cotton, 75" x 89 3/8" (191 x 227 cm). Smithsonian Museum of American History. Gift of Mr. and Mrs. H. M. Heckman.

Theater

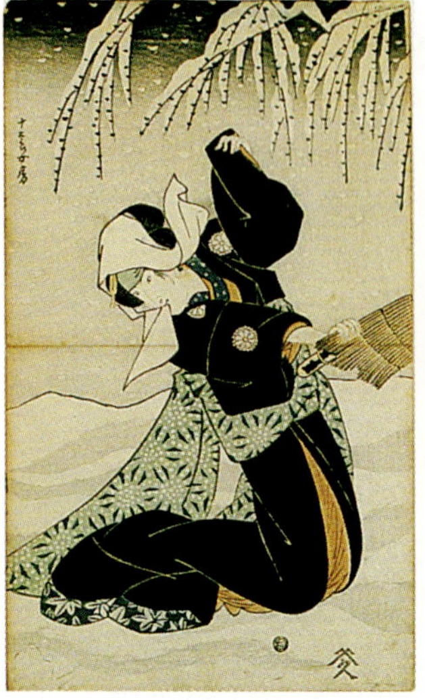

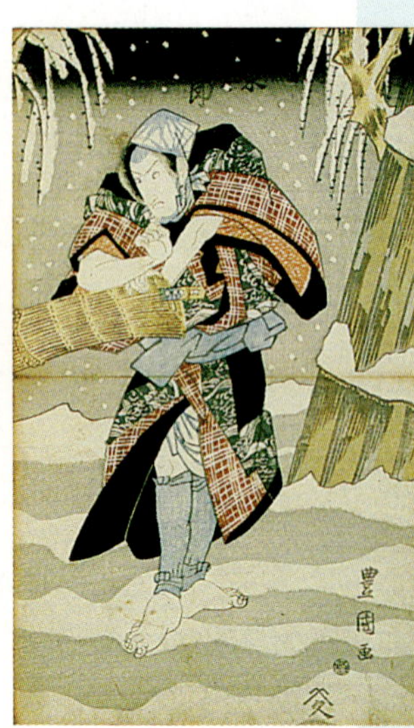

Fig. 1–32 **In traditional Kabuki theater, female roles are played by men. Male actors who play female characters are called *onnagata*. Why are these prints examples of narrative art?**

Utagawa Kunisada, *Scene from a Kabuki Play*, c. 1842. Published by Yamatoya Heikichi (Eikudo). Color woodblock print. Museum Collections, the Bayly Art Museum, University of Virginia.

Theater is an excellent way to experience the art of storytelling. The theater offers stories played out by live actors. Many cultures have developed unique forms of theater. In Japan, for example, the traditional dance-drama called *kabuki* has delighted audiences since about 1600. Kabuki performers act out dramatic stories of historical events and everyday life in an exaggerated style. Spectacular scenery, colorful costumes, and a large orchestra enhance the sensational tales.

Careers **Painters**

Many painters focus on and create narrative art—art that tells a story. Have you ever seen a painting that told a story? Did it make you want to know more about the artist? Painters develop their own individual style and may use different media and materials, such as oil, acrylic, or water-based paints. They may paint on canvas, paper, or wood. Many painters receive a master of fine arts degree from a school, while others are self-taught.

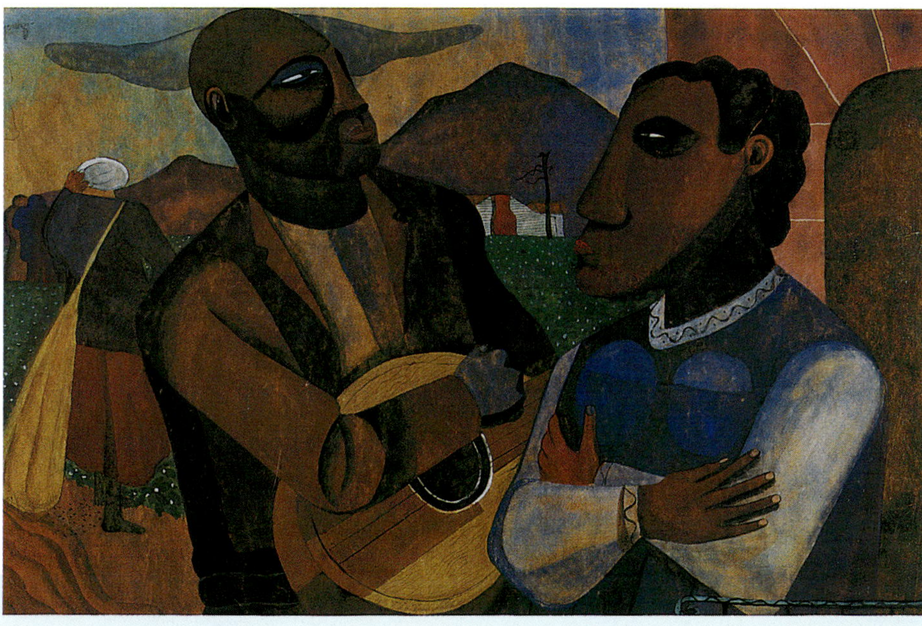

Fig. 1–33 **This artist is known for creating narrative artworks based on the lives of people he knew.**

Romare Bearden, *Serenade*, 1941. Gouache/Casein on Kraft paper, 30" x 47" (78 x 119 cm). ©Grant Hill/Licensed by Grant Hill.

Daily Life

You encounter different kinds of stories every day. Some obvious times are when you read a book or magazine, watch television or a movie, and when you surf the Internet. You also hear and tell stories when you listen to the radio, when you talk to your friends, and during class discussions. Think of the stories you hear and the stories you tell. Are they more fiction than fact? Are you more likely to tell or hear stories?

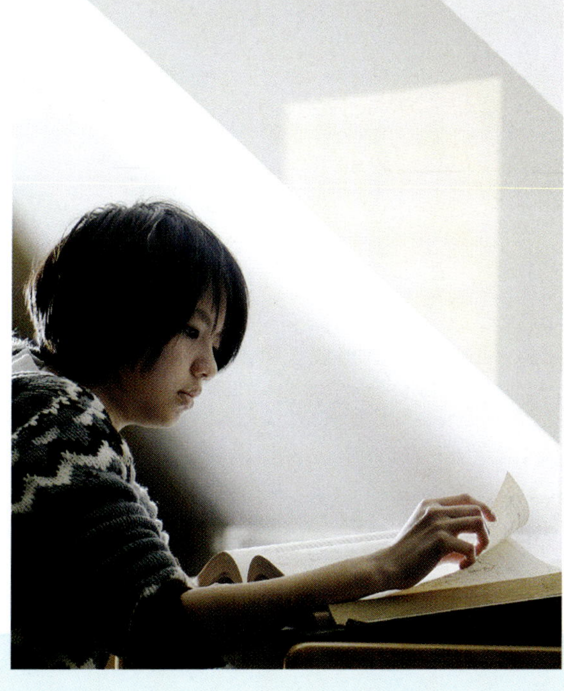

Fig. 1–34

Unit 1 Vocabulary and Content Review

Vocabulary Review

Match each art term below with its definition.

series

woodcuts

tapestries

gesture drawing

contour drawing

1. prints made by carving into a block of wood, inking the wood, and pressing paper against it
2. shows the shape of an object or figure
3. stitched cloths often containing a story
4. shows the movement or position of an object or figure
5. a group of related artworks

Aesthetic Thinking

How might the understanding of a visual story differ from person to person? Why is it important to learn about the artist and his or her culture when trying to understand a work of art?

Write About Art

Look carefully at the figures' hand gestures, body language, and facial expressions in this scene showing Trajan (on the far left) addressing his troops. Based on these observations, write an excerpt of what you imagine Trajan is saying.

Fig. 1–35 **This column celebrates how the emperor Trajan led his Roman soldiers to victory in battle.**

Apollodorus of Damascus, *Column of Trajan* (detail: Trajan addressing his troops), 113 CE. Located in Rome, Italy. Marble, column height: 128' (39 m); each band: 36" (91 cm). Photo courtesy Davis Art Slides.

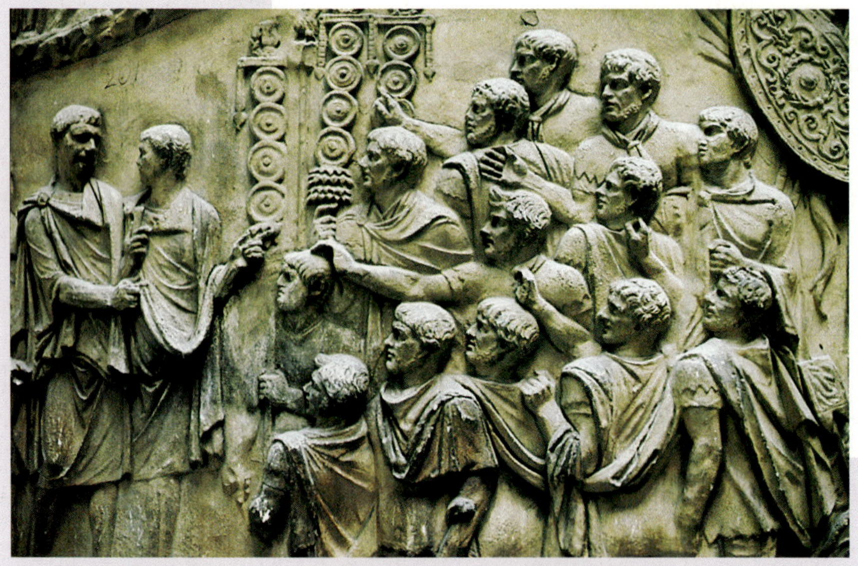

Art Criticism

Describe What do you see in this photograph of an outdoor sculpture garden?

Analyze How does the artist use pattern and texture to create visual interest?

Interpret The image of an eagle often appears in Niki de Saint Phalle's sculpture. What do you think it might symbolize?

Evaluate This sculpture is placed in a setting with other sculptures by the same artist. Do you think this sculpture garden tells a story? How would walking through it help you to answer this question?

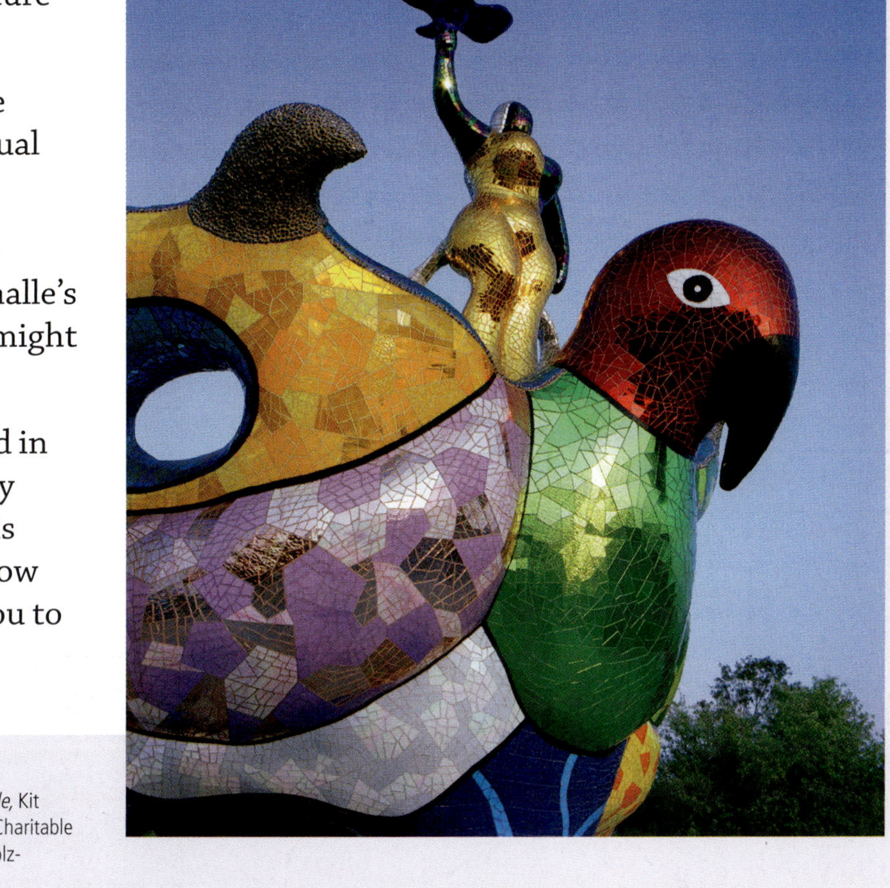

Fig. 1–36 Niki de Saint Phalle, *Queen Califia's Magical Circle,* Kit Carson Park, Escondido, California, 2002–2003 ©2008 Niki Charitable Art Foundation, All rights reserved, Photo Credit: ©Philip Scholz-Rittermann. Artists Rights Society (ARS), NY.

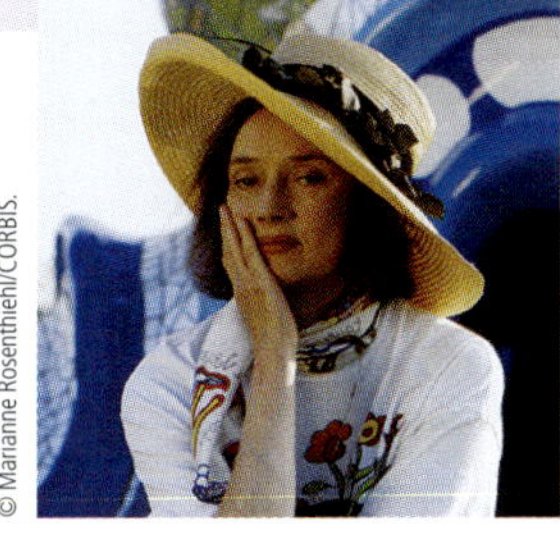

© Marianne Rosenstiehl/CORBIS.

Meet the Artist

Niki de Saint Phalle (1930–2002) lived in the United States as a child before returning to her native France. Though she worked in media ranging from painting to performance art, de Saint Phalle is best known for her large-scale papier-mâché and plaster sculptures of figures from mythology.

For Your Portfolio

Start a portfolio to keep track of your personal journey in art. Add samples of your artwork for each unit. Add an artwork you created during this unit. Use self-stick notes to label techniques and elements in your work that you learned in this unit.

For Your Sketchbook

Your sketchbook is a good place to explore new ideas about art. For this unit, explore different ways to tell stories with shapes, colors, and lines.

Unit 2

Artists Are Recorders

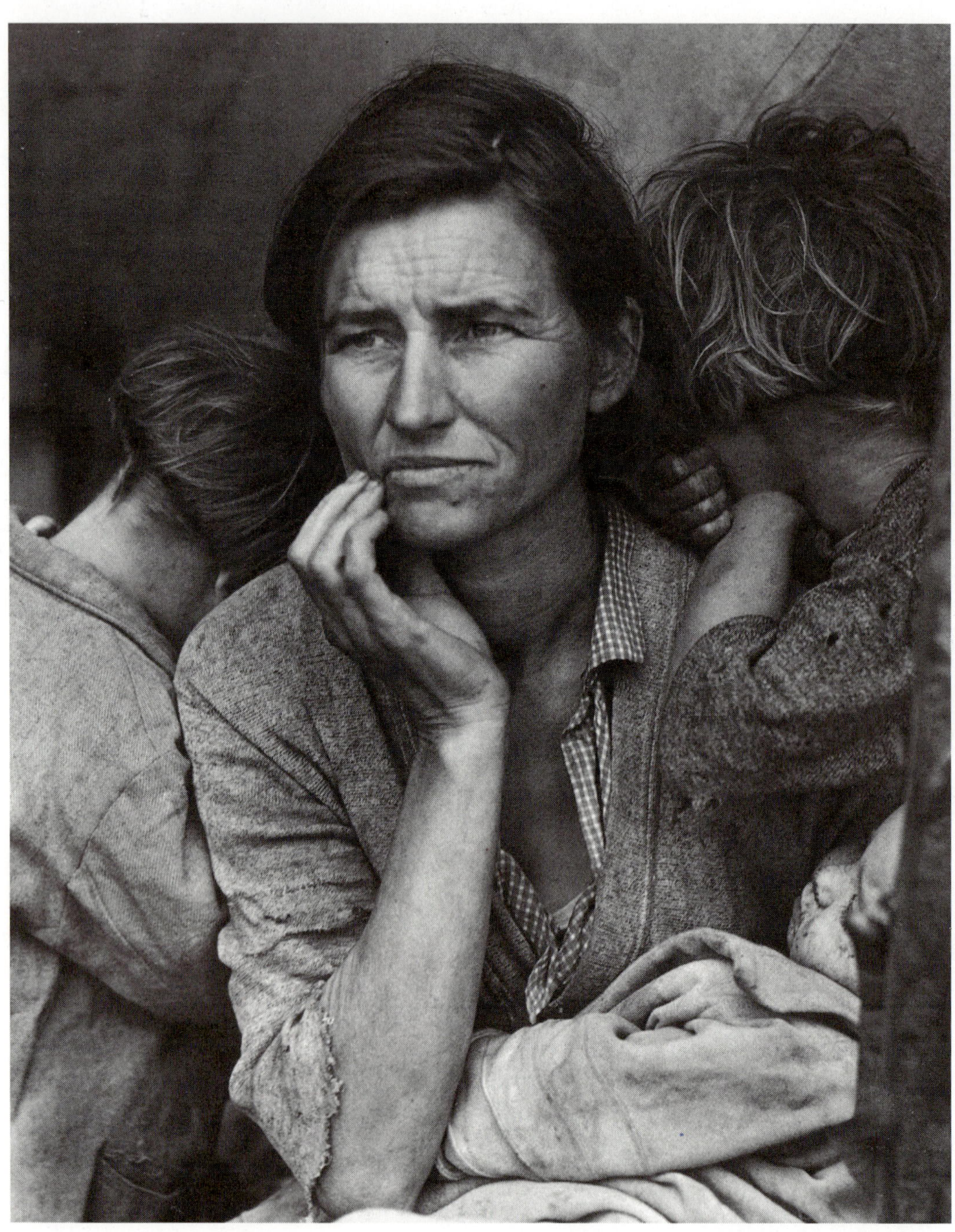

Fig. 2–1 **This photograph is a record of the struggles of many people during the Depression in the 1930s. What makes this such a powerful and enduring image?**

Dorothea Lange, *Migrant Mother, Nipomo, California,* 1936. Gelatin silver print. Reproduced from the Collections of the Library of Congress.

Many people worldwide keep diaries to track the events of their day-to-day life. Historians may use diaries to learn how people lived and what they thought about in the past. When individuals write in their diary, they do not usually think that someone in the future will use what they've written. They don't think of themselves as recorders of their time.

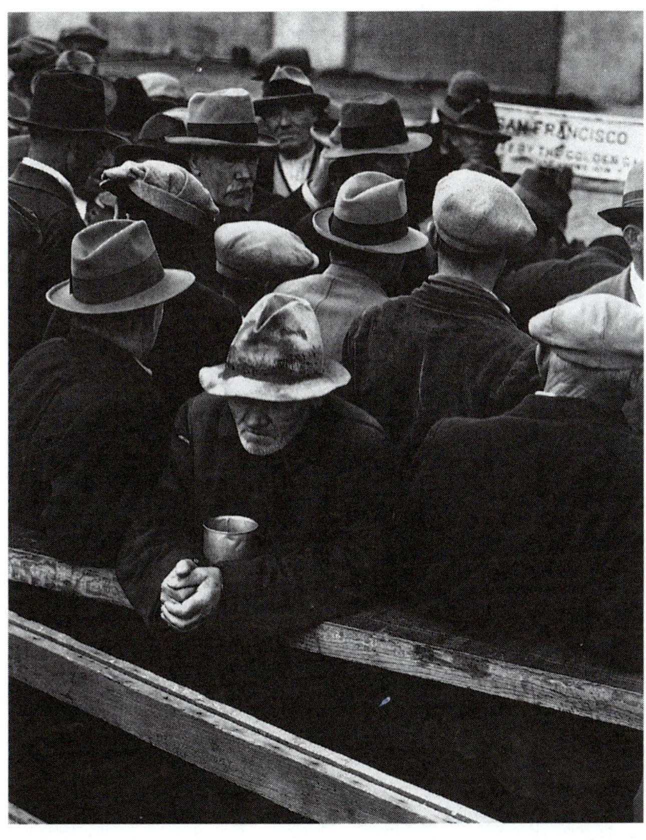

Fig. 2–2 **These men are waiting in line for a free meal. How did Lange use lights and darks to direct our attention?**

Dorothea Lange, *White Angel Breadline, San Francisco,* 1933. Gelatin silver print. © The Dorothea Lange Collection, Oakland Museum of California. City of Oakland. Gift of Paul S. Taylor.

Artworks, like diaries, also can tell us about times gone by. We can look at artworks for clues about how people lived and what they cared about. Although all artists don't create their artworks to be historical records, some are especially interested in documenting the people and events of their time.

In this unit, you will learn:

- How artists select and depict people, objects, and events of their daily life.
- How to create drawings and paintings using value and contrast.
- How to look at artworks as records of life in different times and places.

Recording Daily Life

The photographs on pages 32 and 33 and on these two pages are all artworks by Dorothea Lange. Lange was an important American artist whose photographs include records of the Great Depression, one of the most difficult times in our nation's history. Lange's compassion for the people she photographed allowed her to capture the strength and courage of the human spirit, even in the most challenging situations.

Selecting What to Show One of Dorothea Lange's great strengths as an artist was her selection of subject matter. Subject matter refers to the people, objects, and other things shown in an artwork.

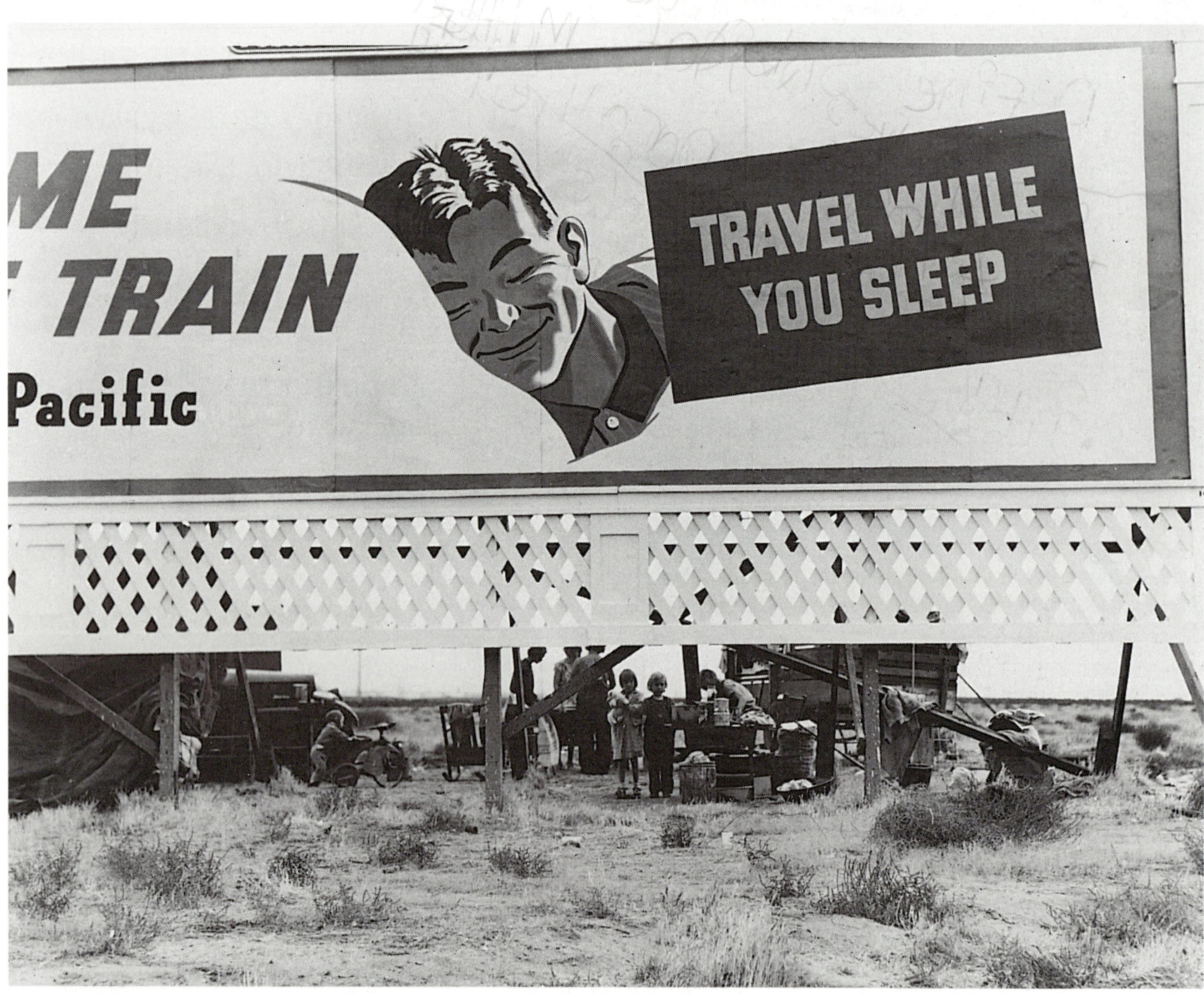

Fig. 2–3 **During the Depression, the families shown here lived beneath a giant billboard. Why do you think Lange photographed the families from a distance?**

Dorothea Lange, *Three Families, Fourteen Children on U.S. 99, San Joaquin Valley, California*, 1938. Gelatin silver print, 9 5/8" x 7 1/2" (24.5 x 19.1 cm). The St. Louis Art Museum. Purchase: Museum Shop Fund.

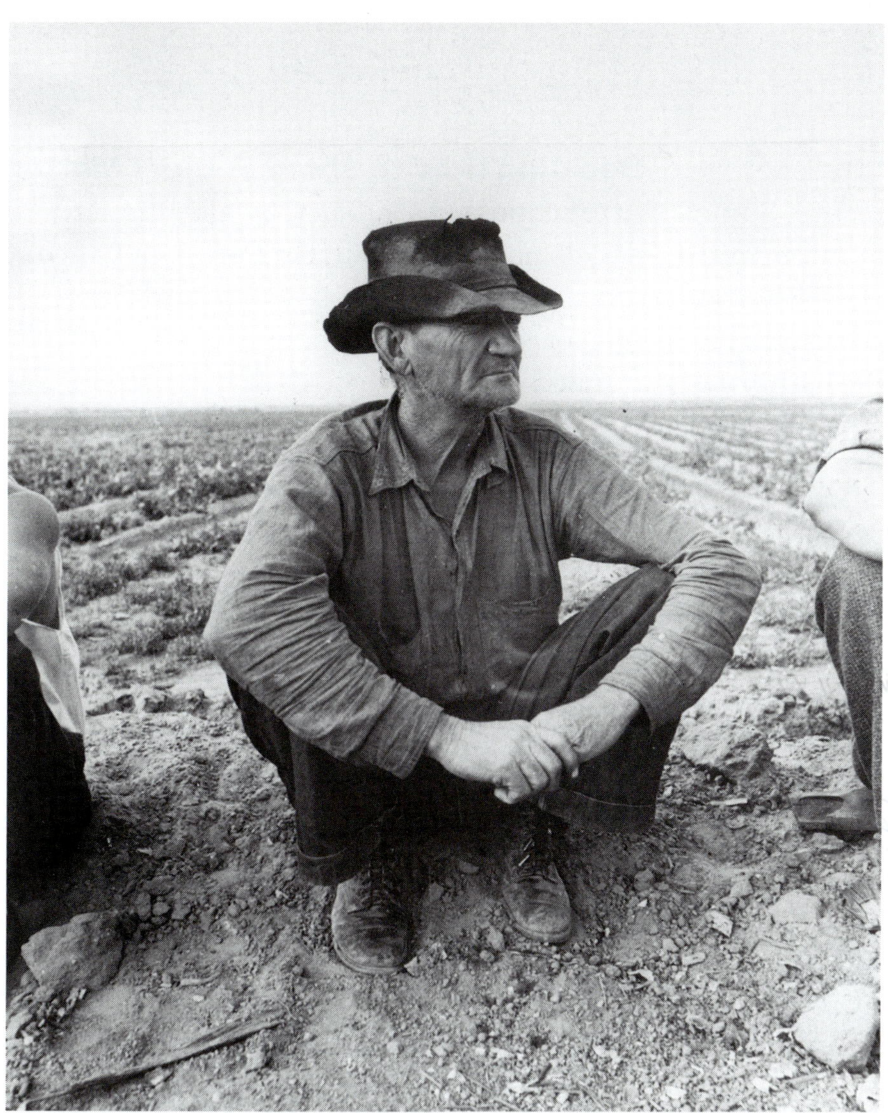

Fig. 2–4 **What does this image tell you about the life of a migrant agricultural worker?**

Dorothea Lange, *Migrant Agricultural Worker, Near Holtville, California.* Photograph, 1937, Snark/Art Resource, NY.

Meet Dorothea Lange

Dorothea Lange is known for her photographs of people who faced hardships. Lange was hired by the federal government to document the plight of rural Americans during the Great Depression and the dust bowl of the 1930s.

Lange traveled around the Midwest and West, which had been suffering severe drought. There she recorded the lives of families who were forced to leave their farms and travel all over the country in search of work.

Today her photographs are records of this time in America's history.

"Pick a theme and work it to exhaustion...the subject must be something you truly love or truly hate."

—Dorothea Lange (1895–1965)

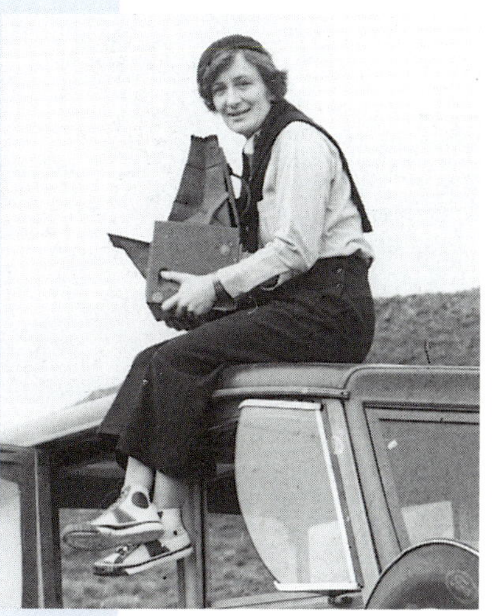

Choosing Subject Matter All artists must select what they want to record. Some artists focus on special events or important people. Others show ordinary people doing ordinary things, such as children playing in the rain (Fig. 2–5) or doing the laundry (Fig. 2–6).

How do artists who work without a camera remember what they have seen? Some artists train themselves to observe carefully. Other artists make some sketches on the spot. Later, they select what to show in their final artwork.

Deciding How to Show Subject Matter After choosing a subject, an artist must decide how to show it. As Dorothea Lange did, an artist may choose to record close-up views of just a few people or views of a faraway crowd.

Settings are also important. The addition of buildings, scenery, or objects helps put people and events into a recognizable world. To highlight certain features or draw attention to certain parts of an artwork, the artist can create contrast by experimenting with light and dark.

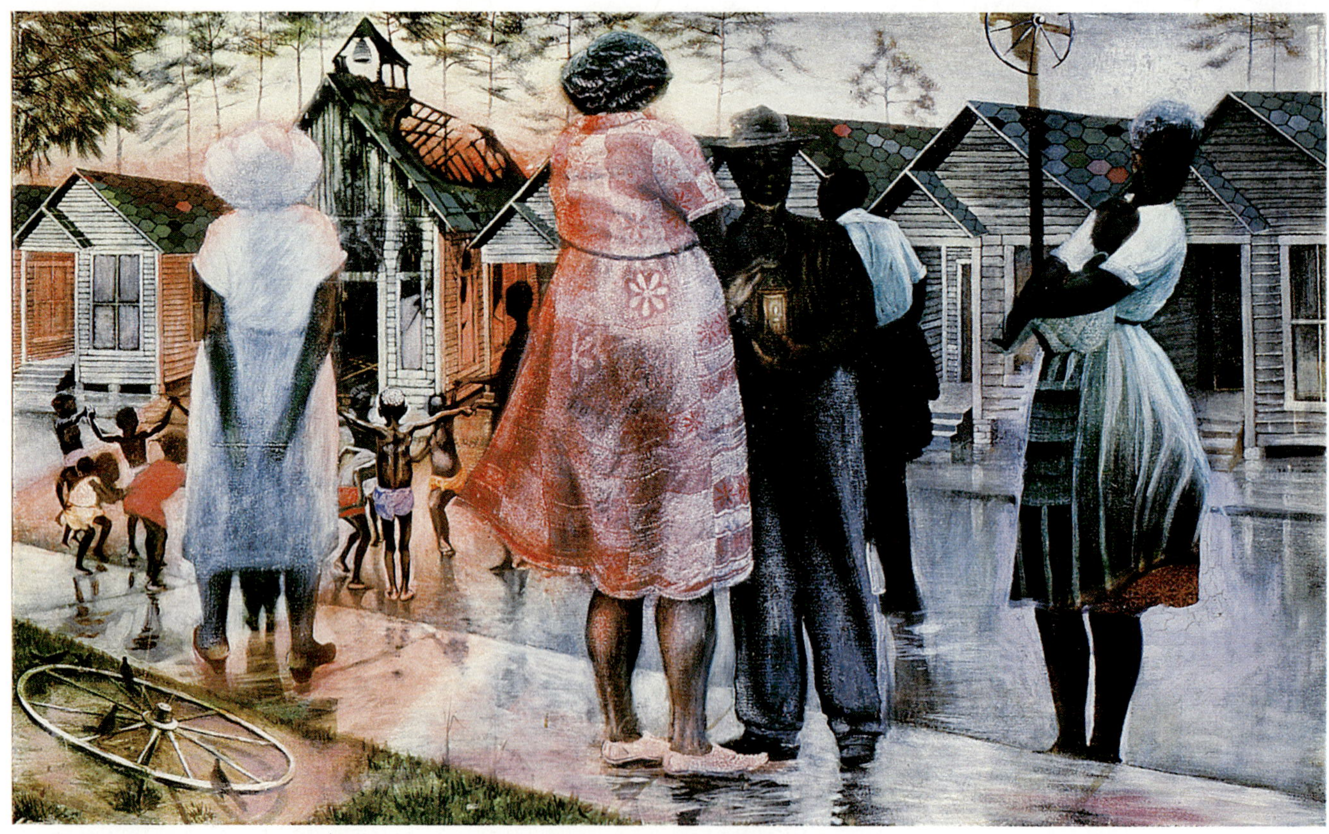

Fig. 2–5 **What ordinary events did the artist, John Biggers, choose to show in this painting?**

John Biggers, *Shotgun, Third Ward #1,* 1966. Oil on canvas, 30" x 48" (76.2 x 121.9 cm). Smithsonian American Art Museum, Washington, DC/Art Resource, New York.

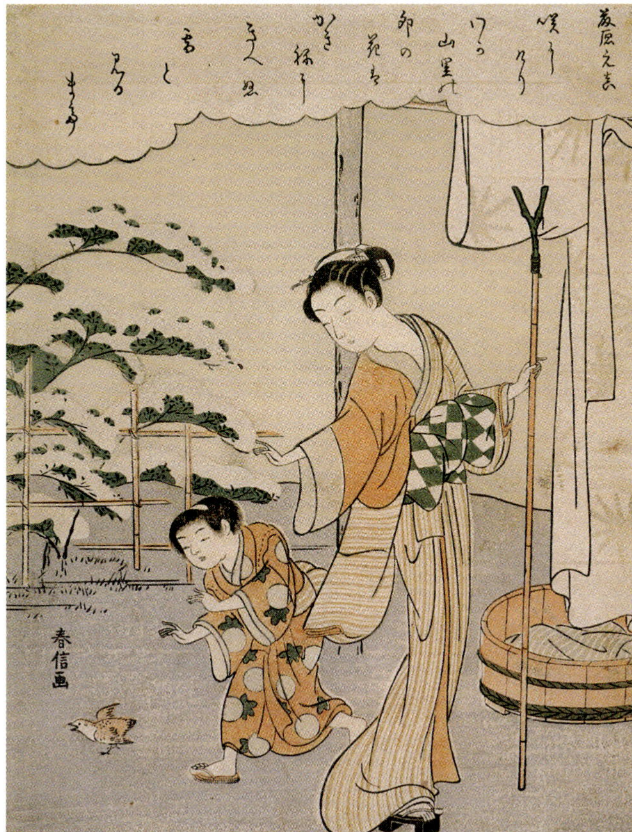

Fig. 2–6 **How does the setting make this a scene from daily life?**

Suzuki Harunobu, *Drying Clothes,* 1767–68. Color woodcut on paper, 11" x 8" (28 x 21 cm). Philadelphia Museum of Art.

Check Your Understanding

1. Why is setting important in artworks that record daily life?
2. Compare and contrast the Dorothea Lange photographs on pages 32 and 34. How are they similar? How are they different?
3. Select an artwork in this lesson and explain how the artist provided us with a record of that time and place.

Studio Time

Drawing Student Life

Draw a scene from a typical school day.

- What will you show? What students will you include? Observe the people you want to draw. Make sketches of them in your sketchbook to use in your final drawing.
- How will you organize your drawing? Remember to include background and objects that will show a typical school day. What details will you include?
- Experiment with pencil, marker, and charcoal to determine the type of line quality that will work best for your subject.

Reflect on how well your drawing shows a typical scene in your school.

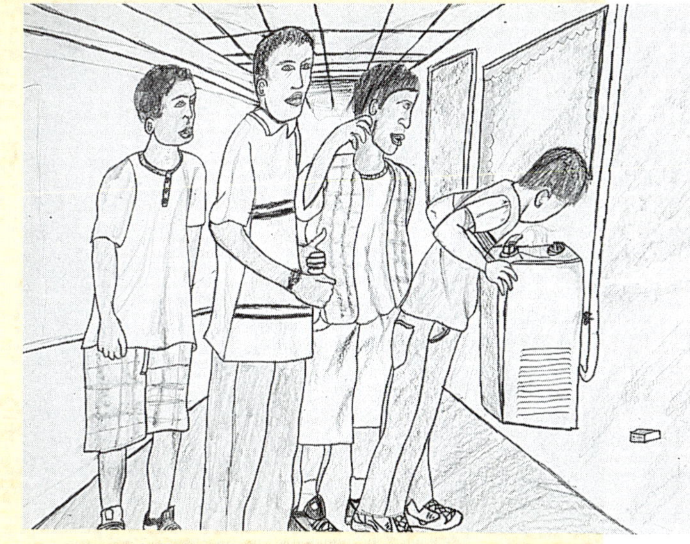

Fig. 2–7 Student artwork

Shading

Creating the Illusion of Form Have you ever noticed how some artists can draw objects, buildings, and people so that they look three-dimensional, even though they are drawing on a flat surface? One way that artists create the illusion of a three-dimensional form is through shading techniques.

Value refers to the lightness or darkness of a color. Artists use value, or various tones of a color, to create the illusion of three dimensions.

These two value scales show a range of values from white to black, and a range of values for the color purple.

In a black-and-white drawing, for example, black is the darkest value, and white is the lightest value. There are many values of gray between black and white. Every imaginable color has a darkest value, a lightest value, and a range of values in between.

Shading refers to the darkened areas, or shadows, on an object. Highlights refer to the area on a form that reflects the most light. Artists who are making a realistic drawing think about the actual or suggested light source to decide where to use shading, or darker values, and where to use highlights, or lighter values. Contrast is the use of strong differences between values.

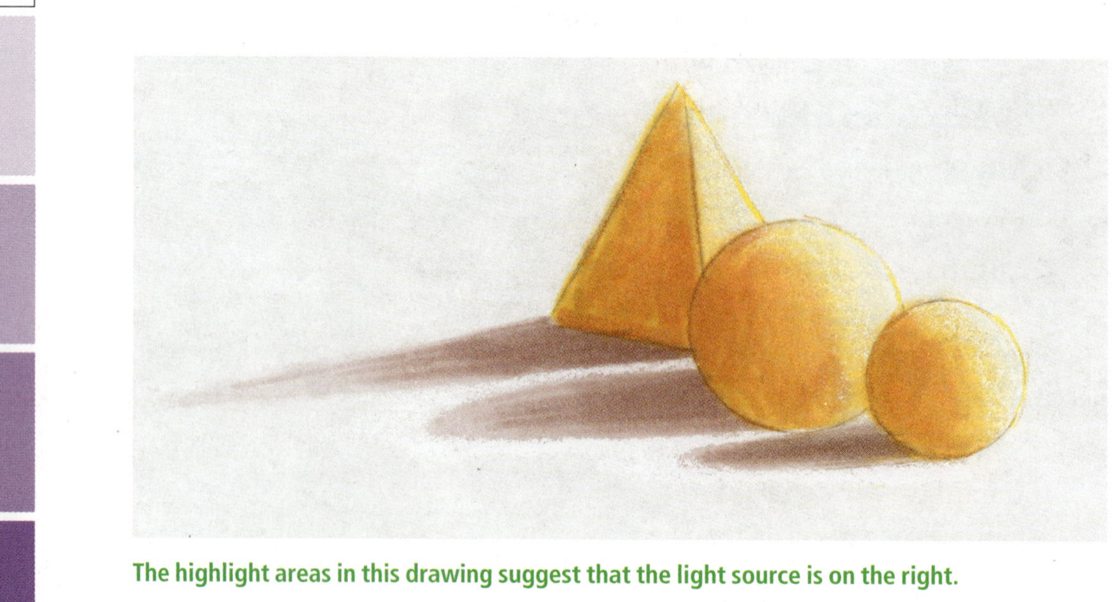

The highlight areas in this drawing suggest that the light source is on the right.

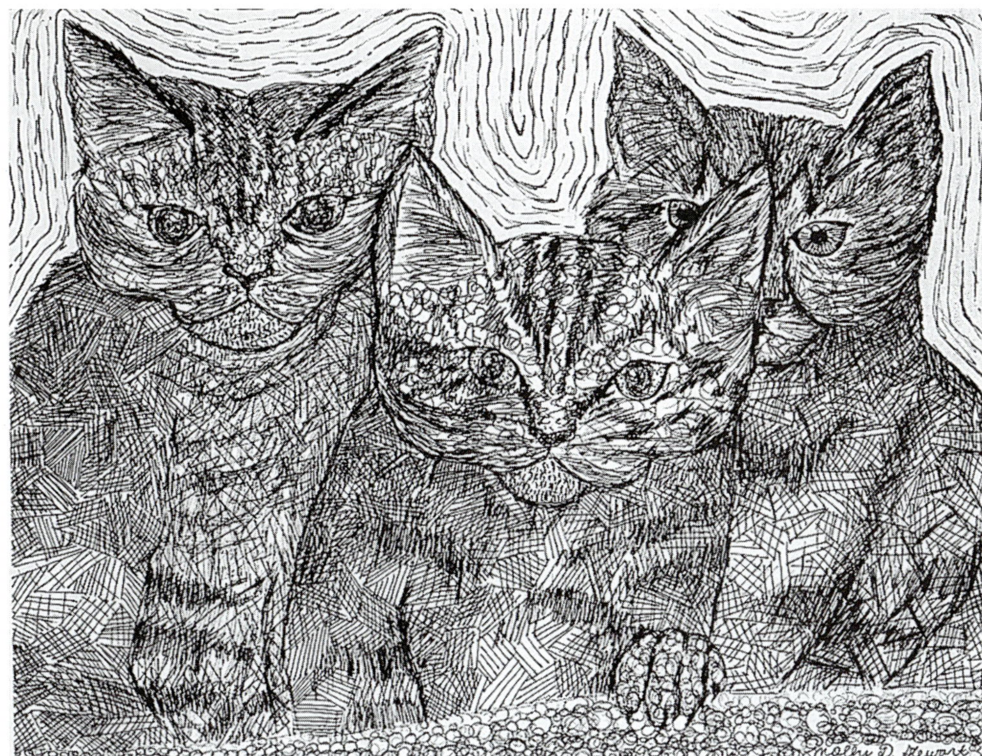

Fig. 2–8 Student artwork

Shading techniques, such as hatching, crosshatching, stippling, and blending, allow artists to create gradual changes between light and dark areas. Artists use different tools for different techniques. As an artist, you should learn which tools are best for which techniques and effects.

Hatching and Crosshatching

Hatching is created by using closely spaced, parallel lines. When the lines are placed close together, they create a dark area. When they are placed farther apart, they create a lighter area.

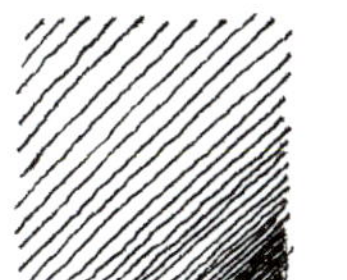

Crosshatching is created by using crossed parallel lines. Crosshatched lines go in two different directions. When crosshatching, an artist begins by creating hatched lines. Then the artist crosses them with another set of lines.

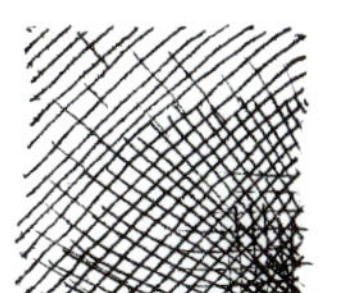

Observe Look for examples of hatching and crosshatching in Fig. 2–8. Notice how the artist created lighter and darker areas. The closer together the lines are, the darker the shading becomes.

Tools: Fine-tipped drawing tools, such as pencils, markers, and a pen and ink.

Practice: Hatching and Crosshatching

Practice using both hatching and crosshatching techniques to create shadows and highlights on an object.

- Try using different tools, such as pencils and markers. How does each tool change the effect?

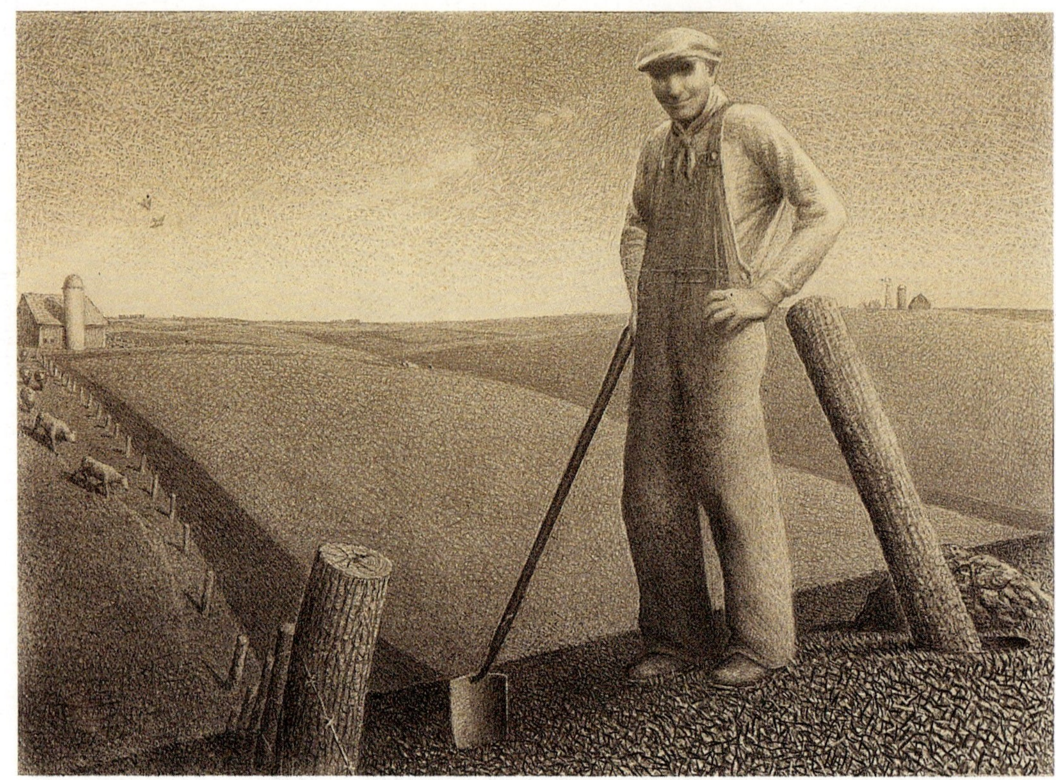

Fig. 2–9 **How does Grant Wood use stippling to create the illusion of three dimensions? Notice the smooth transition between the light and dark values.**

Grant Wood, *In The Spring*, 1939. Pencil on paper, 18" x 24" (45.7 x 61.0 cm). Courtesy of The Butler Institute of American Art, Youngstown, Ohio. ©Estate of Grant Wood/Licensed by VAGA, New York, NY.

Stippling

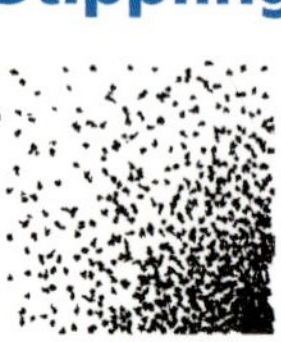

Stippling uses patterns of dots to create values and gradual changes in values.

Observe Find examples of light and dark values in Fig. 2–9. Notice how the closer the dots are, the darker the value.

Tools: Fine-tipped drawing tools, such as pencils, markers, and a pen and ink.

Practice: Stippling

- Begin with wide spaces between the dots.
- Then gradually add more dots.
- Now use the stipple technique to practice drawing an object.

Blending

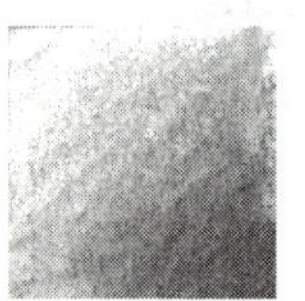

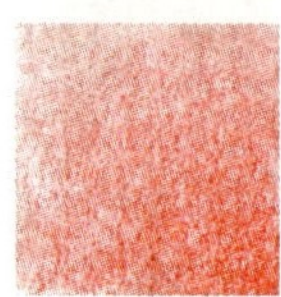

Blending is a shading technique in which you rub from dark to light to create a gradual change in value.

Observe Look at this example of blending.

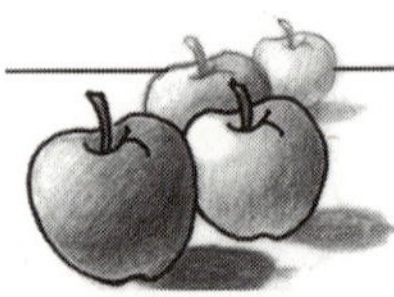

How do the techniques help to create the illusion of three-dimensional forms?

Tools: A soft drawing tool, such as a soft lead pencil, charcoal, or colored chalk.

Studio Time

Illusion of Three-Dimensional Forms

Create a drawing of an arrangement of interesting objects.

- Draw the arrangement using any one of the techniques described in this lesson. Remember that you will use these shading techniques to create the illusion of three-dimensional form.
- Choose the appropriate drawing tools for the techniques that you will use. Try to achieve a full range of value in your drawing.

Reflect on the range of values you were able to show in your drawing.

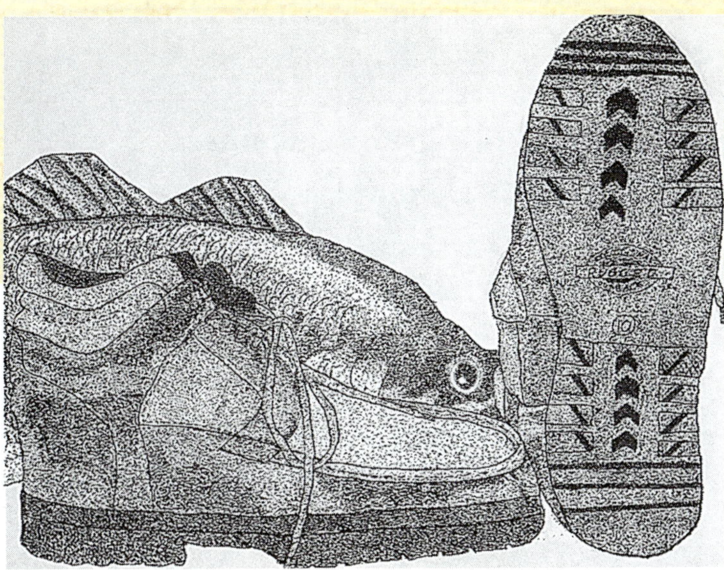

Fig. 2–10 Student artwork

Practice: Blending

- Using one tool at a time, create an area of color on drawing paper.
- Rub the area with your fingers, a tissue, or a cotton swab.
- Work from dark to light to show a gradual change in value.
- Then choose one of the tools and create a practice drawing of an object.
- Try using an eraser to create highlights.

Check Your Understanding

1. Explain how you would use each shading technique to create light and dark values.
2. Compare and contrast two paintings in this unit that have the illusion of three dimensions. How are the techniques that the artists used to create depth similar? How are they different?
3. Why does creating the illusion of form make artworks seem more realistic?

Recording My Daily Life

Studio Background

Dorothea Lange said that she lived a "visual life." As she went about her daily routine, she paid attention to what she saw happening around her. What do you see happening when you go out into the world each day?

In this studio exploration, you will create a drawing that records a scene from your daily life. When you leave your home, look around. Notice people's activities, gestures, and body positions. Be aware of settings—the objects, buildings, or scenery that you see. Think of ways to show these details in your drawing.

You Will Need

- sketch paper
- pencil
- eraser
- drawing paper

Step 1 Plan and Practice

- Brainstorm on paper or with a classmate a list of possible images from your daily life.
- Choose one that you can visualize well enough to draw.
- Will your drawing be horizontal or vertical?

Things to remember:

- ✓ Fill the page with your drawing.
- ✓ Use shading techniques to give the illusion of three dimensions.
- ✓ Pay attention to your light source and light and dark values. Where will you place shadows? Where will you place highlights?

Inspiration from Our World

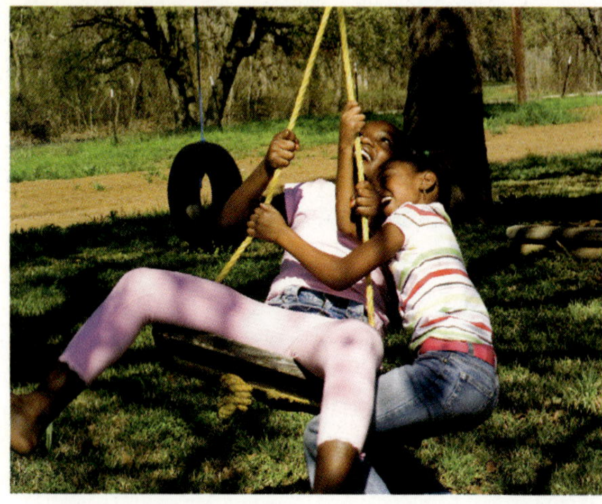

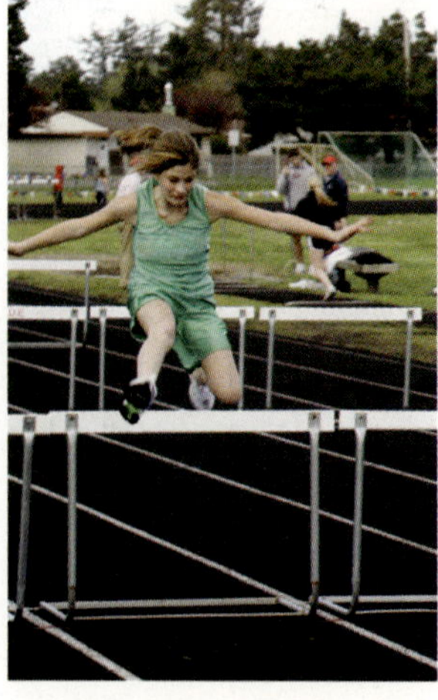

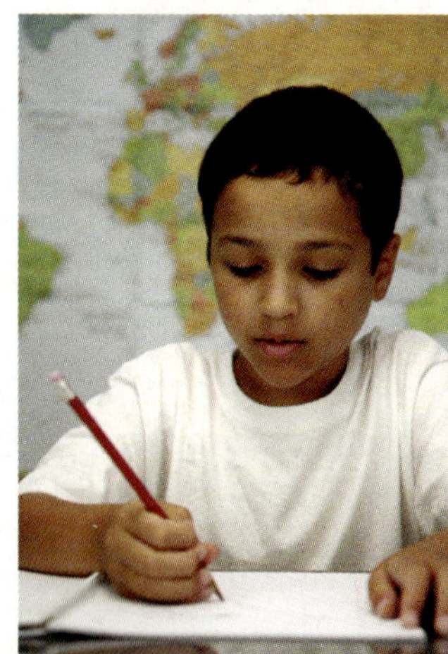

Inspiration from Art

Dorothea Lange was known for her "compassionate eye," and her ability to capture an image that could communicate the plight or hardships of others. She almost always had her camera with her, but she didn't photograph everything she saw. She carefully observed the world and selected scenes that she thought were important to record.

She often shot more than one photograph of a scene. Sometimes she stood back and shot from a distance, and then moved in for closer views. She chose those photographs that best captured the message that she was trying to convey. In the darkroom where she developed her film, she would decide how to crop, or frame, each image to eliminate some parts and emphasize others.

When Lange came upon Nettie Featherston and her three children **(Figs. 2–11 and 2–12)**, the strong and determined mother had just sold her car tires to buy food. Lange took six photographs, moving closer for each image.

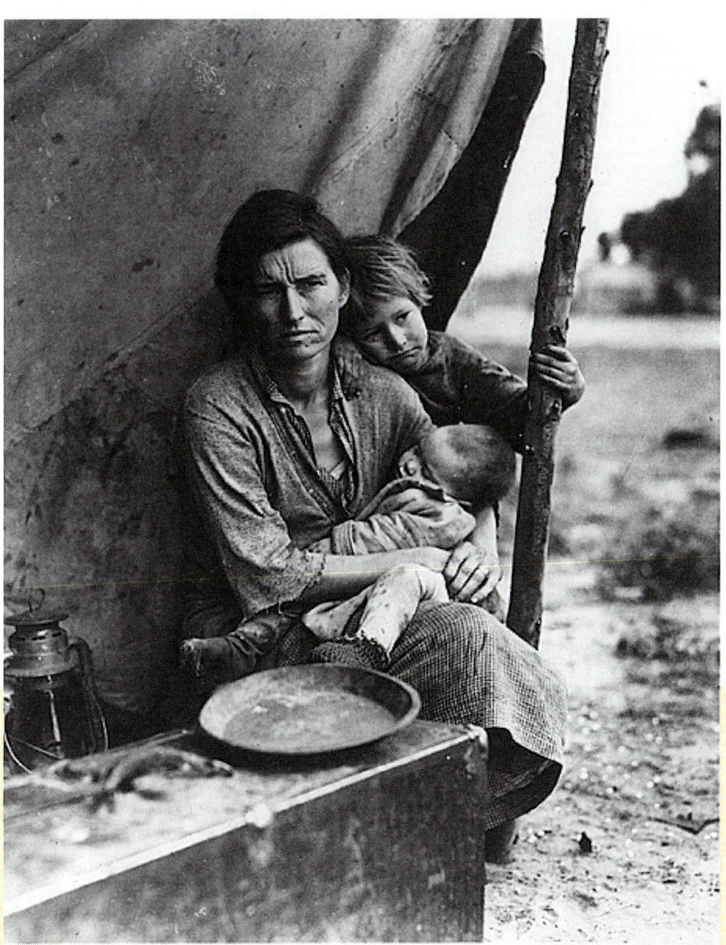

Fig. 2–11 **Compare this image with Fig. 2–12. Which photograph do you feel is more dramatic? Explain your answer.**

Dorothea Lange, *Migrant Agricultural Workers Family,* 1936. Gelatin silver print. Reproduced from the Collections of the Library of Congress.

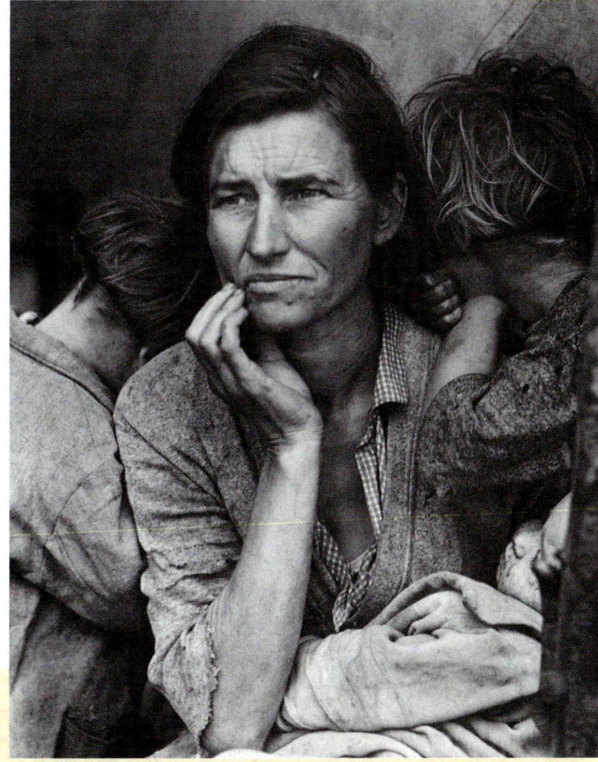

Fig. 2–12 Dorothea Lange, *Migrant Mother, Nipomo, California,* 1936. Gelatin silver print. Reproduced from the Collections of the Library of Congress.

Step 2 Begin to Create

- **Experiment with different sketches of your subject.** Then choose one that you want to refine using shading techniques.

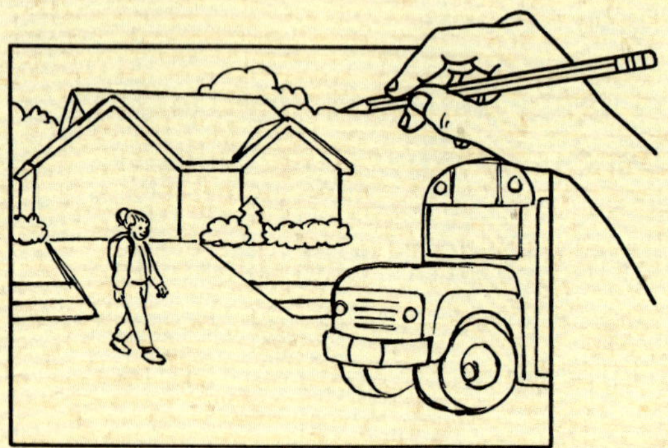

- Will you show lots of details, or will you focus on the overall shapes and forms?
- Decide whether you want to show your subject up close or from a distance.
- **Try using strips of paper to frame, or crop, your sketches.** Cropping to the outside edges of a sketch can give you a distance view. Cropping to a smaller part of a sketch can give you a close-up view.

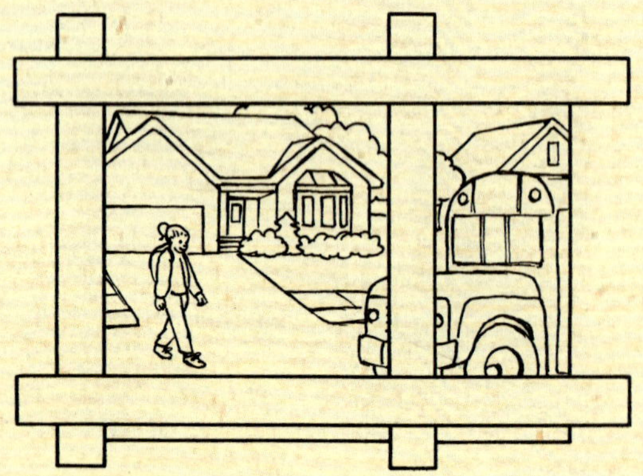

- Look at all of your sketches and cropping ideas before selecting an image for your final drawing.
- **As you work on your drawing, pay particular attention to value—light and dark areas.** Where will you place shadows? Where will you place highlights?

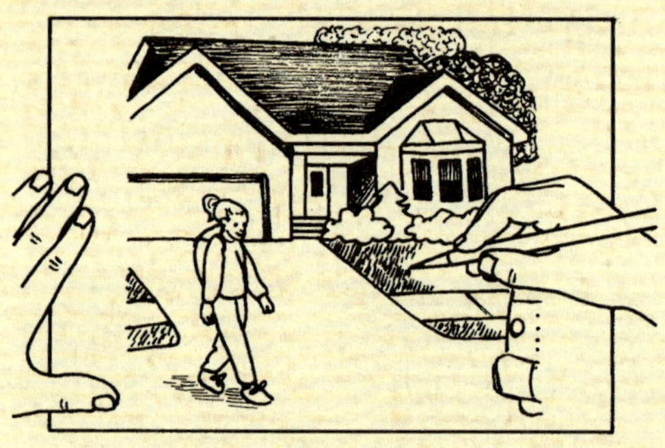

Step 3 Revise

Did you remember to:

✓ Fill the page with your drawing?

✓ Use shading techniques to give the illusion of three dimensions?

✓ Pay attention to your light source and light and dark values to show shadows and highlights?

Adjust your work if necessary. In your sketchbook, make a note of your revisions and why you made them.

Step 4 Add Finishing Touches

- If you want to give special attention to a part of your drawing, use contrast, or big differences in value, to help direct the viewer's attention.

Step 5 **Share and Reflect**

- Share your finished drawing, along with your original sketches, with a group of classmates.
- Talk about your subject matter, and why you chose to show it the way you did.
- Take turns telling why you chose a particular sketch.
- Make sure to talk about your decisions to include some parts or exclude other parts.
- Reflect on what you learned in this studio that you could apply to another art form, such as painting or photography.

Art Criticism

Describe Name as many things as you can identify in this artwork.

Analyze What shading techniques did the artist use? Where do you see light values? Where do you see dark values?

Interpret What did the artist choose to show in this artwork, and why?

Evaluate How effective is this artwork in creating the illusion of three dimensions?

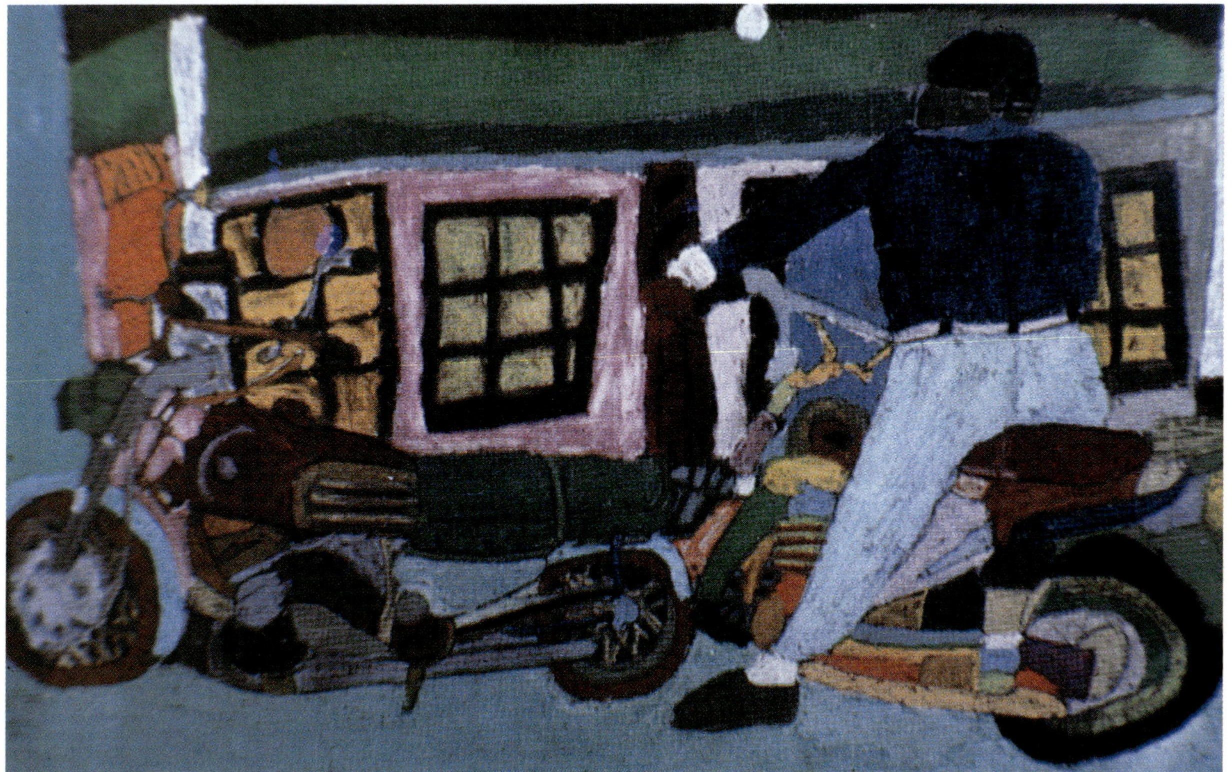

Fig. 2–13 Student artwork

Genre Scenes of Daily Life

We can learn a lot about the way people live, work, and play just by looking at artworks. Throughout history, artists have recorded the daily life activities of the people around them. Art historians call such artworks genre scenes. Genre scenes are scenes that show people doing ordinary activities at work and at play.

From artworks, we know about work in ancient Egypt and games in ancient Greece. We also have some idea of what the interior of people's homes looked like in Holland in the 1600s **(Fig. 2–14)**. Since the invention of photography in the late 1800s, some artists have also used cameras to record daily life.

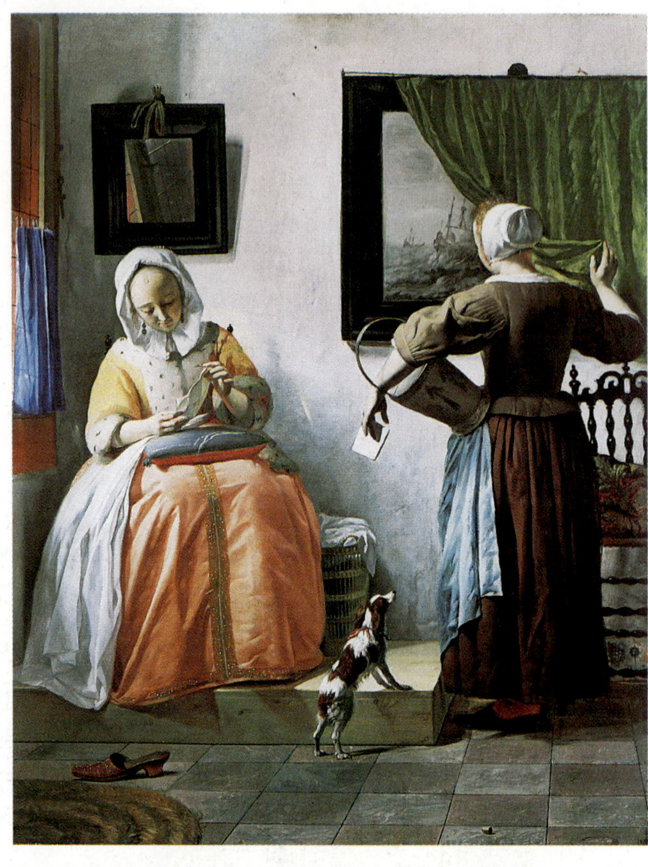

Fig. 2–14 **Where do you see examples of shading and highlights in this painting. Where is the light source?**

Gabriel Metsu, *The Letter Reader,* 1662–65. Oil on panel, 20 ½" x 16" (52.07 x 40.6 cm). Reproduced courtesy of the National Gallery of Ireland.

1600s–1700s

1662–65 Metsu, *The Letter Reader*

1704 The first issue of the *Boston News-letter,* America's first continuously published newspaper

1800s

1838 First permanent photographic image

1877 Thomas Edison invents the first machine to record sounds.

1896 The first motion picture shown in a movie theater

1900s

1915 VanDerZee, *Miss Suzie Porter*

1938 The first ballpoint pen

1951 The first videotape recorder

1995 Mark, *High School Prom*

1999 Lovell, *Whispers from the Walls*

Photographing Urban Life New York artist James VanDerZee looked at urban African American culture through the lens of a camera. His black-and-white photographs display a wide range of values, from dark to light **(Fig. 2–15)**. VanDerZee's photographs of daily life in Harlem span fifty years, from the early 1900s to the 1950s.

VanDerZee is, however, particularly known for his photographs of the Harlem Renaissance. The Harlem Renaissance refers to an era during the 1920s and 1930s in Harlem when there was a renewal of the creative and intellectual contributions of African Americans.

Contemporary Approaches Mary Ellen Mark is a contemporary photographer whose subject matter includes genre scenes of everyday life across society. Like Dorothea Lange, she is known for her ability to capture the human spirit of her subjects.

Mark's subject matter includes a wide variety of people, from the party goers in **Fig. 2–16** to people living in poverty in both urban and rural environments. Mark establishes trust with her subjects in order to capture them in their everyday lives, whether they are rodeo performers, carnival workers, or a homeless family living in a car.

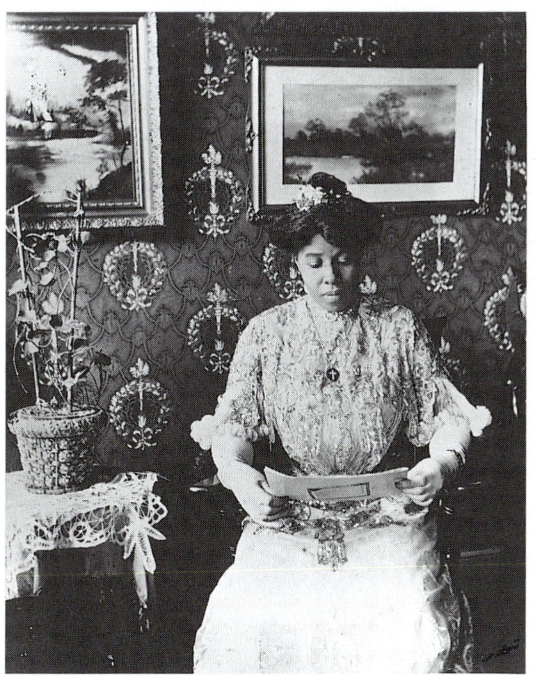

Fig. 2–15 **Where do you see a contrast in values? What is the center of interest?**

James VanDerZee, *Miss Suzie Porter, Harlem,* 1915. Gelatin silver print. © Donna Mussenden VanDerZee.

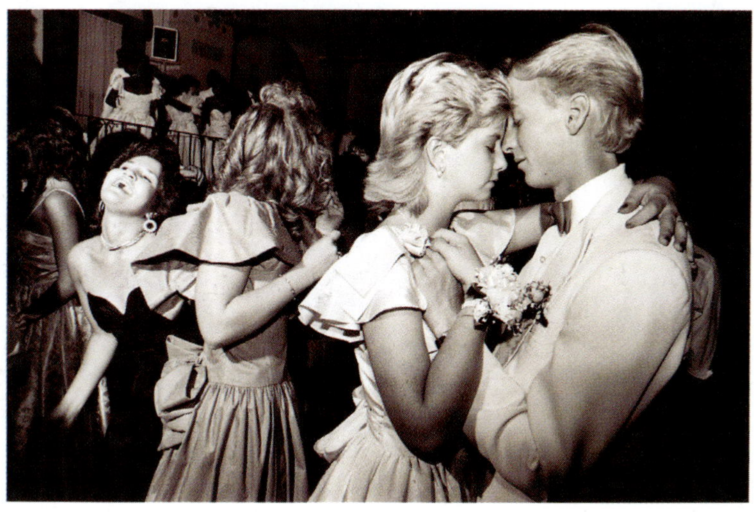

Fig. 2–16 **What makes this image look informal? Where do you see dark and light values?**

Mary Ellen Mark, *Gibbs Senior High School Prom, St. Petersburg, Florida,* 1986. Photograph, Mary Ellen Mark Library, New York. Published by CRIZMAC Art and Cultural Education Materials.

Installations as Temporary Records

Some artists use installation art to document daily life. Installation art is usually a temporary exhibit, large in scale, which includes both two- and three-dimensional objects.

Artists create installations with real objects in a section of a museum or gallery. Because installations are usually temporary, a photograph of the installation often becomes the permanent record of the artist's creation.

Figs. 2–17 and 2–18 show two different views of *Whispers from the Walls*, an installation created by Whitfield Lovell. Study Lovell's use of value in his charcoal drawings of people in Fig. 2–17.

Lovell's control of the dark and light values makes the people in his drawings seem like ghosts coming through the walls. He also uses carefully placed spotlights to create contrast between highlights and shadows.

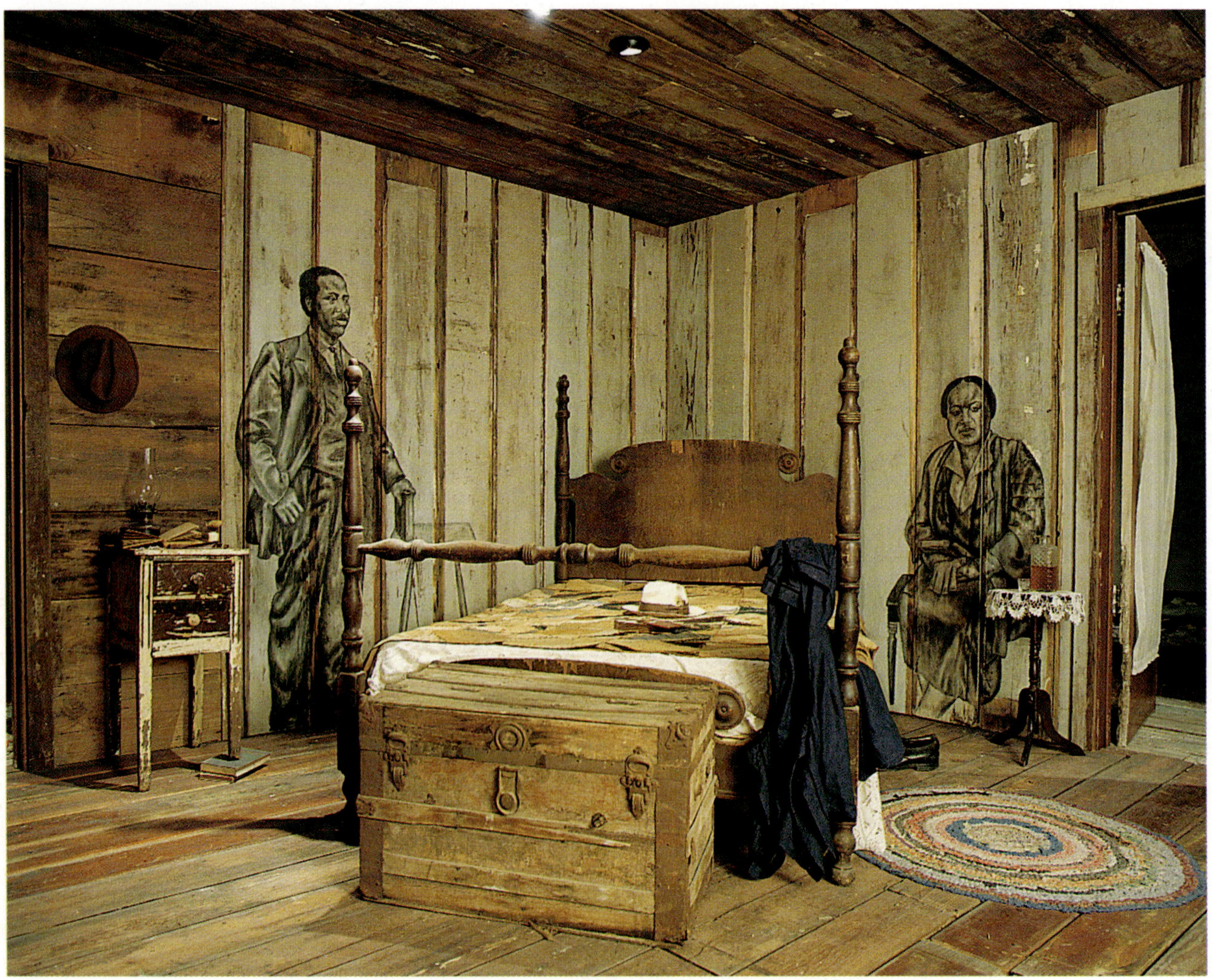

Fig. 2–17 **What catches your eye in this bedroom scene?**

Whitfield Lovell, *Whispers from the Walls* (bedroom installation view), 1999. Photo by Steve Dennie/University of North Texas Press. Courtesy DC Moore Gallery, New York.

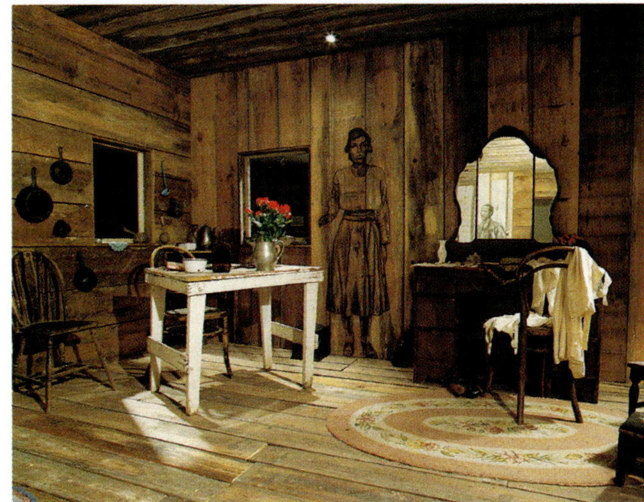

Fig. 2–18 **The artist installed this scene in a museum gallery. Why might he have been interested in controlling the lighting to create highlights and shadows?**

Whitfield Lovell, *Whispers from the Walls* (table and vanity installation view), 1999. Photo by Steve Dennie/University of North Texas Press. Courtesy of DC Moore Gallery, New York.

Meet Whitfield Lovell

Born in the Bronx, in New York City, Whitfield Lovell documents rural African American life of the past in his artworks. Lovell learned about photography from his father, an amateur photographer. His father also taught him to pay attention to the way shapes, values, and colors work together.

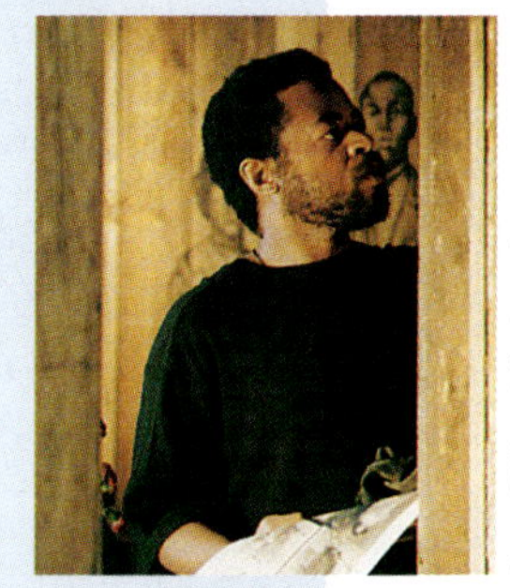

Courtesy DC Moore Gallery, New York.

Lovell likes to go to flea markets. There, he collects objects from the past to include in his installations.

"I enjoyed the fact that my father and I shared the trait of being particular about visual things."

— Whitfield Lovell (born 1959)

Check Your Understanding

1. What are genre scenes?
2. Compare and contrast the people and objects in *Whispers from the Walls* with the people and objects shown in *The Letter Reader* on page 46.
3. Why is photography a good way to document daily life?

Studio Time

Records of the Past

Make a drawing showing what daily life was like in the past.

- Use a family photograph or magazine cutout as inspiration.
- What people and objects will you include?
- What kind of background setting will you draw?
- You may choose to add color to your drawing when it is finished.

Reflect on ways your drawing shows the past.

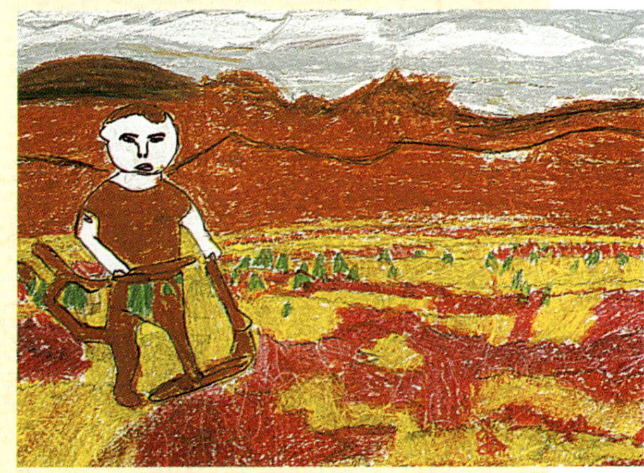

Fig. 2–19 Student artwork

Genre Paintings: Focus on Haiti

Daily Scenes in Haitian Art Haitian genre paintings, or scenes of daily life, are common subjects of Haitian art. They are among the most valued artworks by museums, galleries, and private collectors in the world. These paintings serve as records of daily life in Haiti. Look at the three paintings on these pages. What scenes from daily life do you see in each painting?

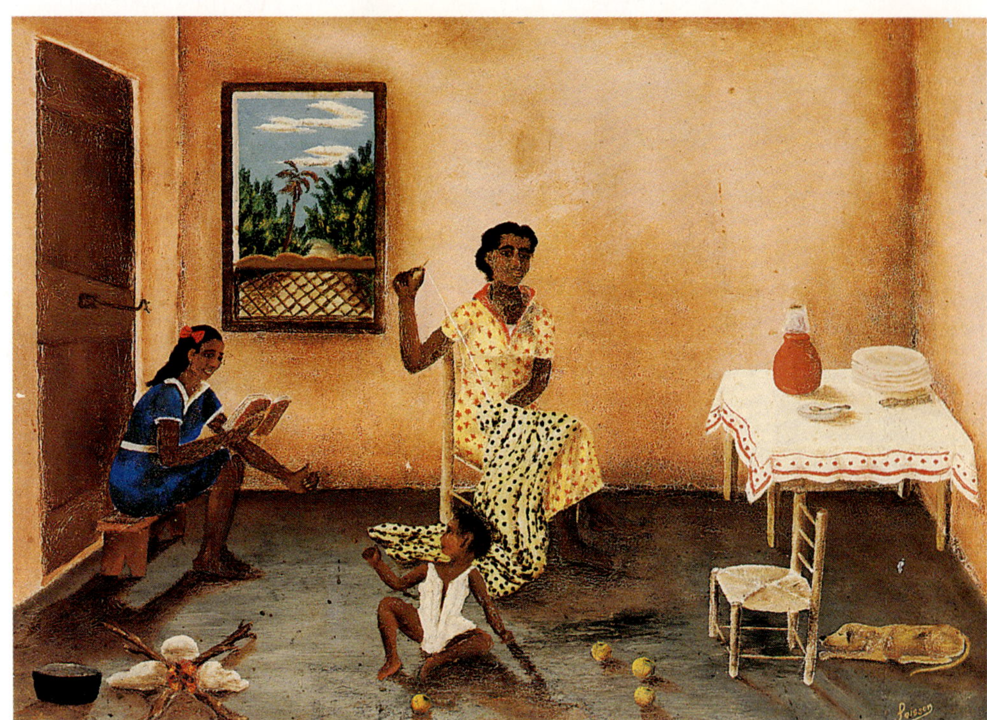

Fig. 2–20 **What does this picture show about daily life in this Haitian home?**

Louverture Poisson, *The Lesson,* ca. 1946–47. Oil on masonite, 14 5/8" x 20 1/4" (37 x 51.4 cm). Milwaukee Art Museum, Gift of Richard and Erna Flagg (M1979.229). Photography by Larry Sanders.

Social Studies Connection

Haiti is a small country in the Caribbean's West Indies. It covers the western third of the island of Hispaniola. Christopher Columbus started a Spanish colony there in 1492. Most of Haiti's people are descendents of Africans brought to the island as slaves in the 1500s. In 1697 Haiti became a French colony. The country has been independent since 1804. Today, most of the people are farmers who grow such crops as coffee, corn, sugar cane, and sisal.

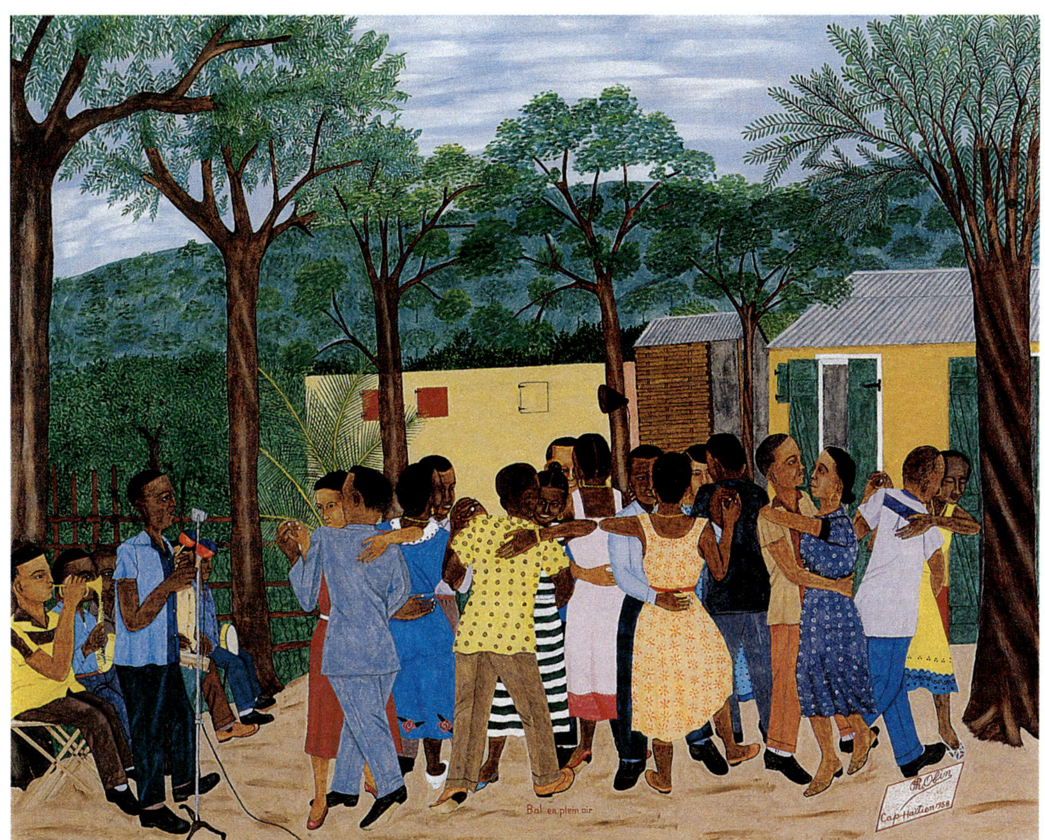

Fig. 2–21 **What lines, shapes, and colors are repeated to create visual rhythm in this Haitian daily life scene?**

Philomé Obin, *Bal en Plein Air (Outdoor Dance),* 1958. Oil on masonite, 24" x 29 ½" (61 x 75 cm). Milwaukee Art Museum, Gift of Richard and Erna Flagg (M1991.142). Photography by Larry Sanders.

Visual Rhythm Look at **Figs. 2–21** and **2–22**. Notice how each has a sense of movement and rhythm. Visual rhythm is created when an artist repeats an element, such as a color, line, or shape. What elements are repeated in **Figs. 2–22** and **2–24** to create a sense of visual rhythm?

Visual Culture

Look for examples of visual rhythm in signs, advertisements, and packaging. Remember that book covers are considered a form of packaging.

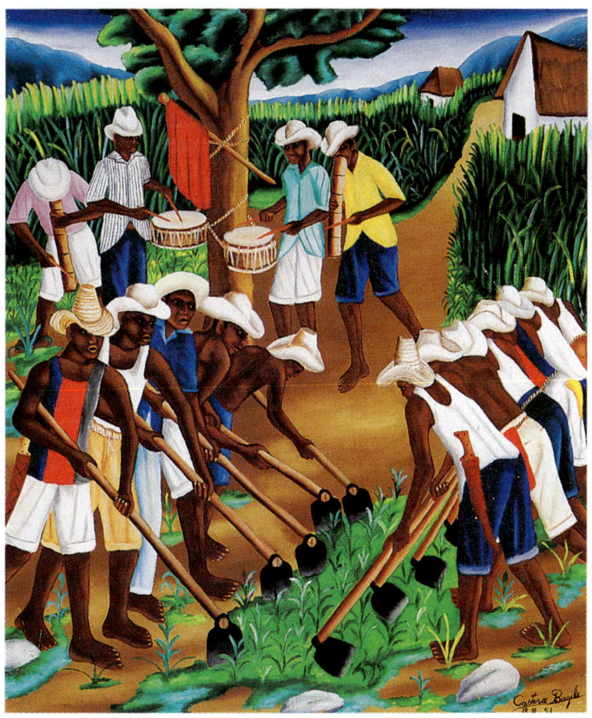

Fig. 2–22 ***Coumbite*** **is Haitian Creole for "communal activity." How did the artist place light and dark areas to give you a feeling of rhythmic movement? What else did the artist do to create a sense of rhythm and movement?**

Castera Bazile, *Coumbite Communal Fieldwork,* 1953. Oil on masonite, 24" x 19 ¼" (61 x 49 cm). Milwaukee Art Museum, Gift of Mr. and Mrs. Richard B. Flagg (M1991.106).

Viewing Genre Scenes as Records

Notice **Figs. 2–23** and **2–24** by Inatace Alphonse, a contemporary Haitian artist of genre scenes. First, look at each painting as a record of daily life in Haiti. What can you learn about life in Haiti by looking at these two paintings as records of Haitian life?

Identifying the Artist's Techniques

Next, look at each painting for examples of visual rhythm. Each of these two paintings captures the movement and action of the human figures on the canvas. Notice in **Fig. 2–23** how the artist captures the hustle and bustle of people going about their daily activities. Look for examples of repeated colors, shapes, and lines in each artwork. These repeated elements create a sense of visual rhythm and movement.

Finally, look for examples of shading and highlights. Alphonse uses bright colors with strong highlights and carefully blended values in both images. Find examples in each artwork of how this shading technique helps to create the illusion of three dimensions on a two-dimensional artwork.

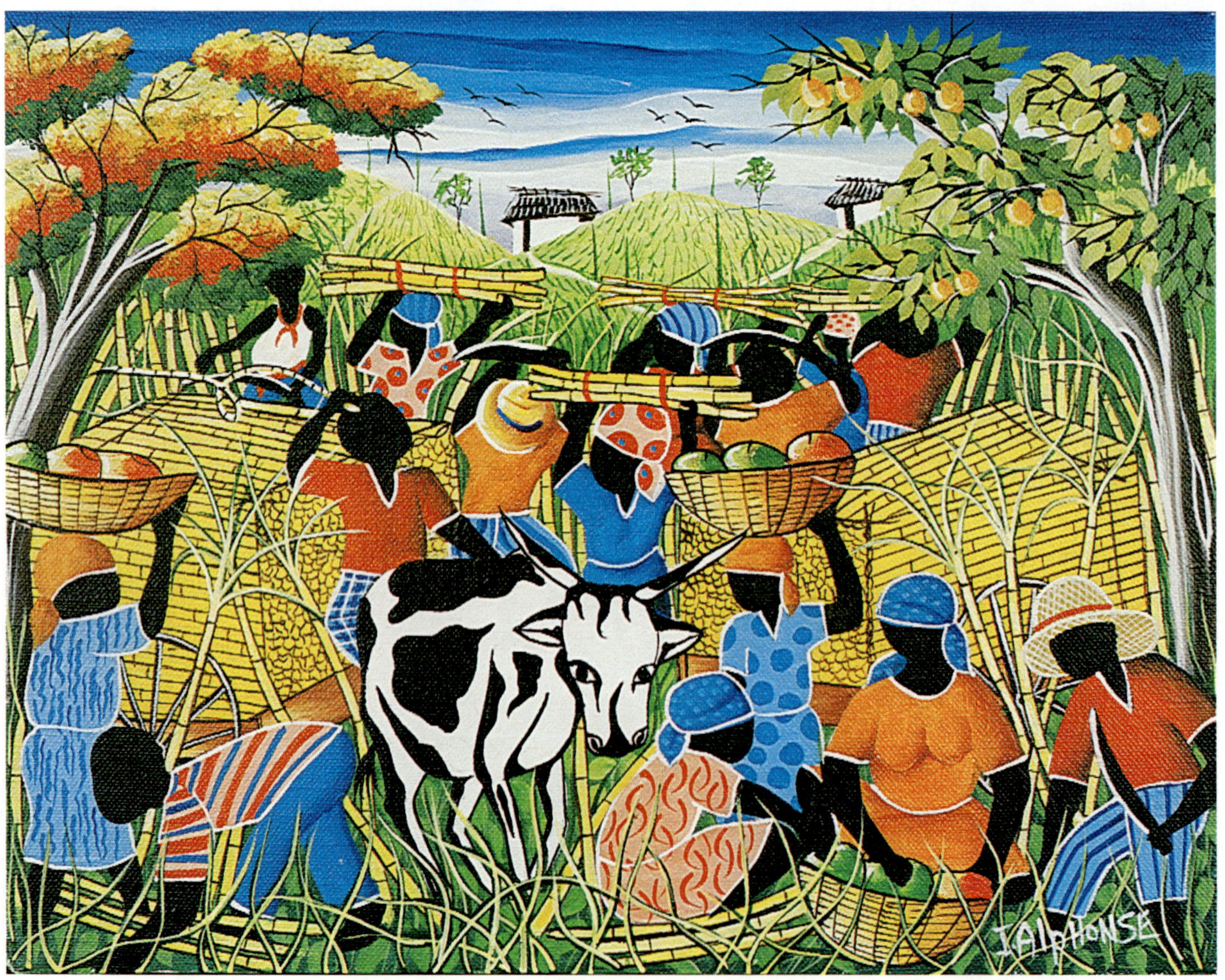

Fig. 2–23 **Compare and contrast this painting of communal workers with the one by Castera Bazile in Fig. 2–22. How is the sense of movement different in each work?**

Inatace Alphonse, *Harvest with Cows,* 1990s. Acrylic on canvas, 11" x 14" (28 x 35.6 cm). Courtesy of the artist. Reproduced with permission.

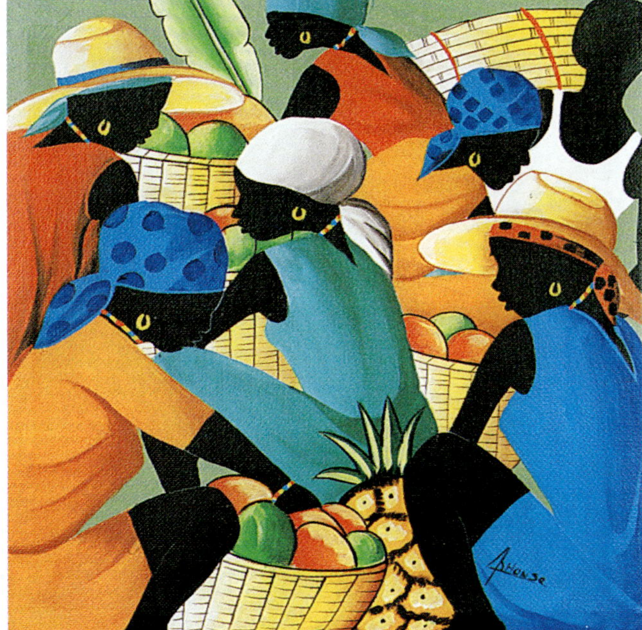

Fig. 2–24 **Note how the figures fill the canvas. How did the artist use dark and light values to give the figures three-dimensional form?**

Inatace Alphonse, *Market,* 1990s. Acrylic on canvas, 12" x 12" (31 x 31 cm). Courtesy of the artist. Reproduced with permission.

Check Your Understanding

1. Find and describe examples of how the Haitian painters featured in this lesson used dark and light values to create the illusion of three-dimensional forms.

2. Find examples of visual rhythm in the artworks of two different Haitian artists in this lesson. Compare and contrast how each artist created a sense of movement and rhythm.

3. Compare and contrast the artwork of Inatace Alphonse with the artworks of the earlier artists in this lesson. How did each artist document daily life differently?

Meet Inatace Alphonse

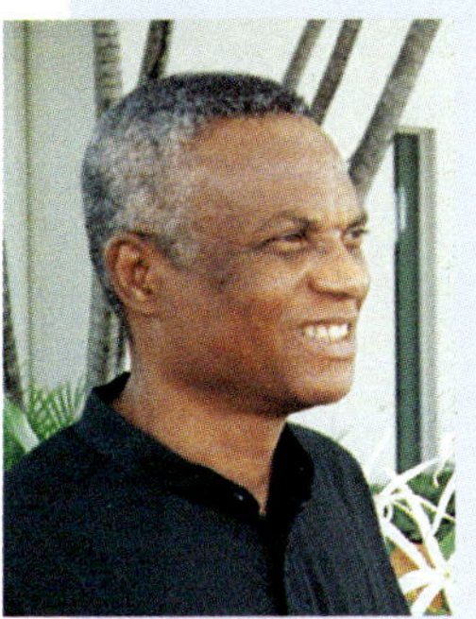

Courtesy of the artist and the Haitian Art Collection, Del Ray Beach, Florida.

Alphonse was born in Port-au-Prince, the capital of Haiti. Alphonse's paintings, valued by collectors around the world, demonstrate his talent for capturing the movement and action of the human figure on canvas. Alphonse's genre paintings of contemporary life in Haiti are known for their vibrant colors and visual rhythm.

"I paint the Haiti of my childhood, everyone working together to help each other."

— Inatace Alphonse (born 1943)

Studio Time

Record Your Daily Life

Paint a scene from your daily life.

- To begin, choose a scene, make sketches, and plan your composition in pencil.
- Use dark and light values to create the illusion of three dimensions.

Reflect on your color choices.

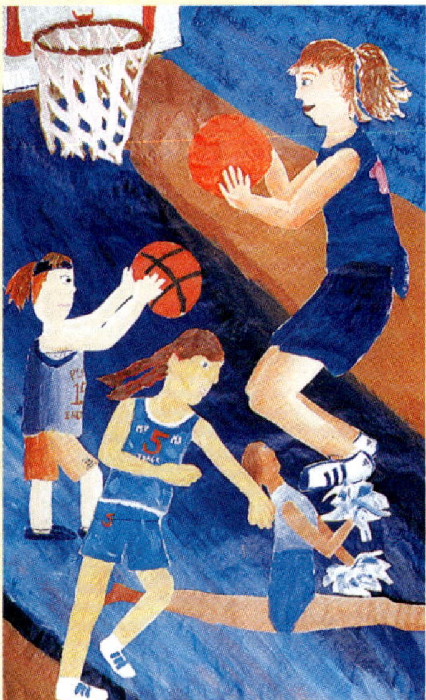

Fig. 2–25 Student artwork

The Objects of My Life

Studio Background

If someone found your book bag and emptied its contents, what clues to your life would those contents provide? We rarely think about objects as historical records, but archaeologists and historians often rely on them as they piece together evidence of how people once lived.

In this studio exploration, you will draw a still life that "says" something about you. A still life is an arrangement of objects that are not alive and cannot move. You will select and arrange objects that suggest who you are, how you live, and what you care about.

You could choose items from home and school, such as knickknacks, a favorite cup, a book, or photographs. You may want to choose natural objects, such as shells, rocks, and twigs. Open up your imagination and find things that really tell about you.

You Will Need

- drawing paper
- pencil and eraser
- markers, colored pencils, or pastels
- variety of objects
- flashlight or other light source (optional)

Step 1 Plan and Practice

- You may want to choose objects you have with you, such as a book bag, or your shoes, or objects from the classroom.
- Think about how you might want to organize the objects. Will one object be the center of interest?

Things to Remember:

- ✓ Focus on the main shapes and forms first.
- ✓ Use value and contrast to direct the attention of your viewer.
- ✓ Use shading techniques to give the illusion of three dimensions.

Inspiration from Our World

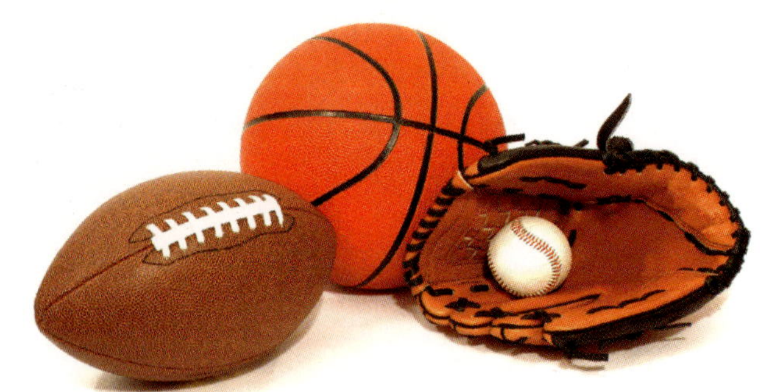

Inspiration from Art

Many artists choose to paint simple, ordinary objects from daily life. Pop artists of the 1960s often focused on everyday popular objects. These artists sometimes expressed a point of view about how daily life is surrounded by an ever-increasing assortment of products to buy and use. Artist James Rosenquist sometimes layered his still-life objects. In other paintings, he painted objects individually around the canvas. Why do you think this artist chose to paint something as ordinary as dishes in a dish drainer?

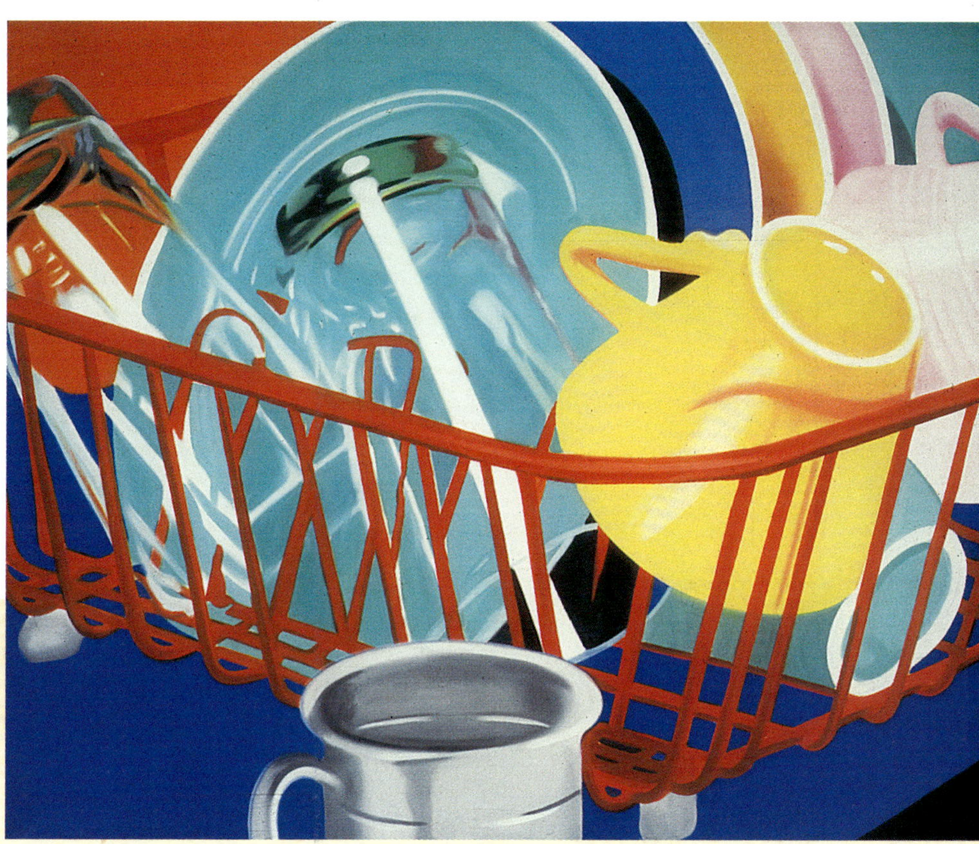

Fig. 2–26 **In this painting, how did the artist show which objects are closer and which objects are farther away?**

James Rosenquist, *Dishes,* 1964. Oil on canvas, 50" x 60" (127 x 152.4 cm). © James Rosenquist/Licensed by VAGA, New York, New York.

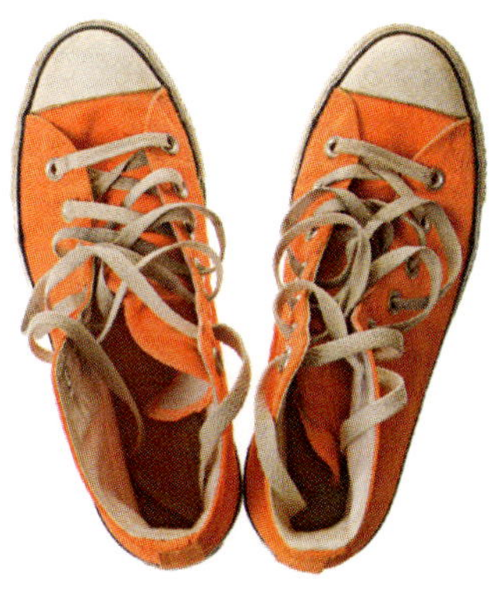

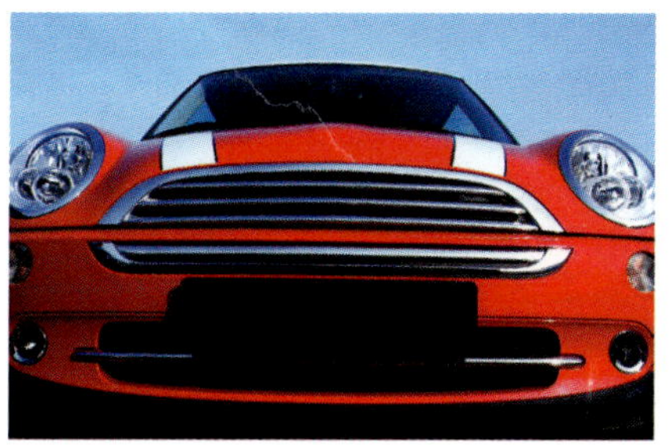

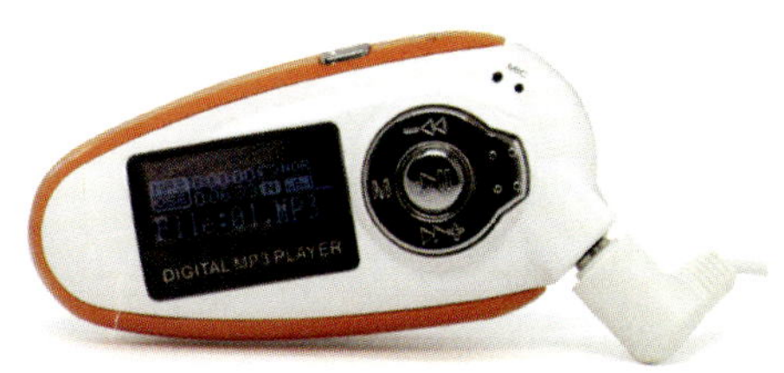

Step 2 Begin to Create

- Begin by arranging your objects. As you decide where to place them, think about the parts of the arrangement that you want to emphasize in your drawing.
- **Experiment with lighting.** Shine a light onto the arrangement from a particular direction, such as from above or one side. How can you use the light to create shadows and contrast?

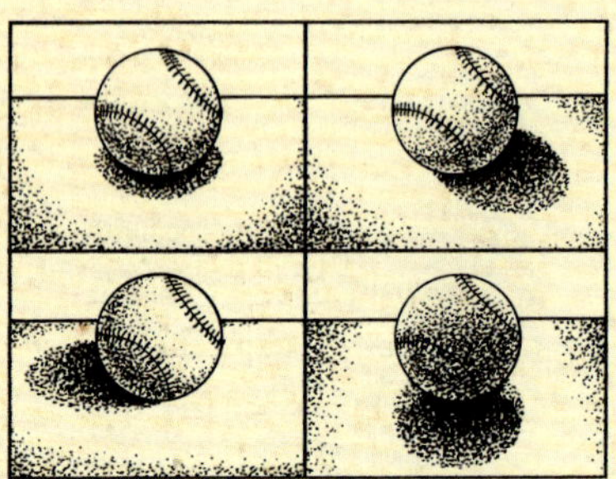

- **Create a pencil sketch** when you are satisfied with the arrangement and lighting.

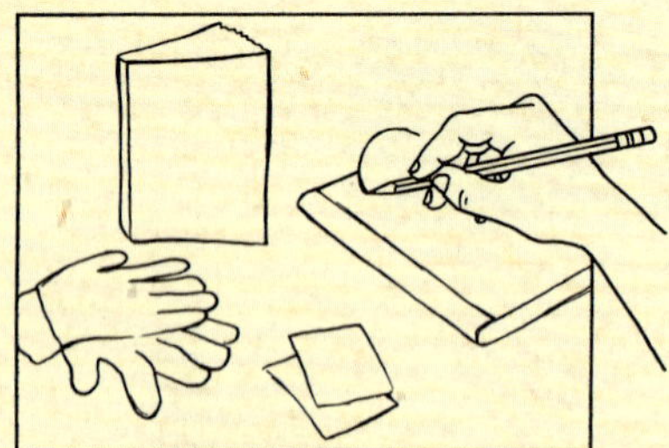

- Focus on the main shapes and forms first. Lightly sketch the outlines. Then add smaller shapes and forms as needed.
- Don't worry about details at this point, as you will focus on those later.
- Fill the paper with your sketch.

- **Next, add color and detail.** How can you use color to help emphasize the important parts of your drawing?

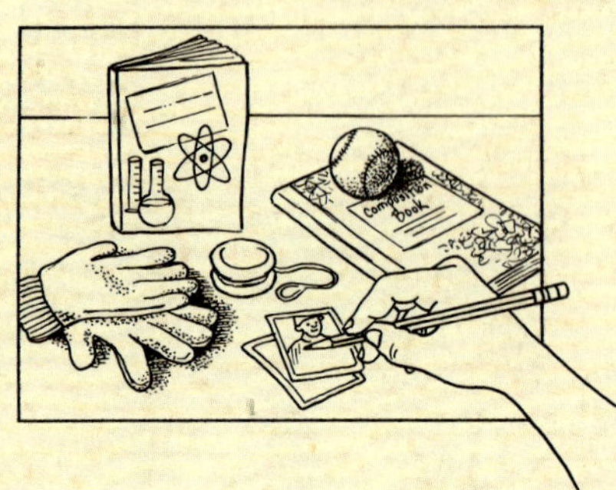

- How can you use value and contrast to direct your viewer's eye?
- Decide which details of each object you want to show. Will you include all of the details, or only the most obvious ones?

Step 3 Revise

Did you remember to:

✓ Focus on the main shapes and forms first?

✓ Use value and contrast to direct the attention of your viewer?

✓ Use shading techniques to give the illusion of three dimensions?

Adjust your work if necessary. In your sketchbook, make a note of your revisions and why you made them.

Step 4 Add Finishing Touches

- Are there any details of your objects that you want to add?
- Can additional shading techniques help to make your objects appear to be three-dimensional?

Step 5 **Share and Reflect**

- Share your finished drawing with one or more classmates.
- Talk about the objects in your drawing and how you decided to show them.
- What do the objects say about you? What do they say about the time in which you live?
- Describe the way you used value and contrast to direct the attention of your viewer.
- How would you change your artwork if you were to create another version?

Art Criticism

Describe What objects did the artist include? What details did the artist choose to show from each object?

Analyze Explain how the red fabric helps create unity. Find examples of different values that help to create the illusion of three dimensions.

Interpret Why do you think the artist chose each object? How would you describe what interests this artist?

Evaluate How effective is this artwork in showing three-dimensional forms? How effective was the artist in creating an interesting composition? Explain your answer.

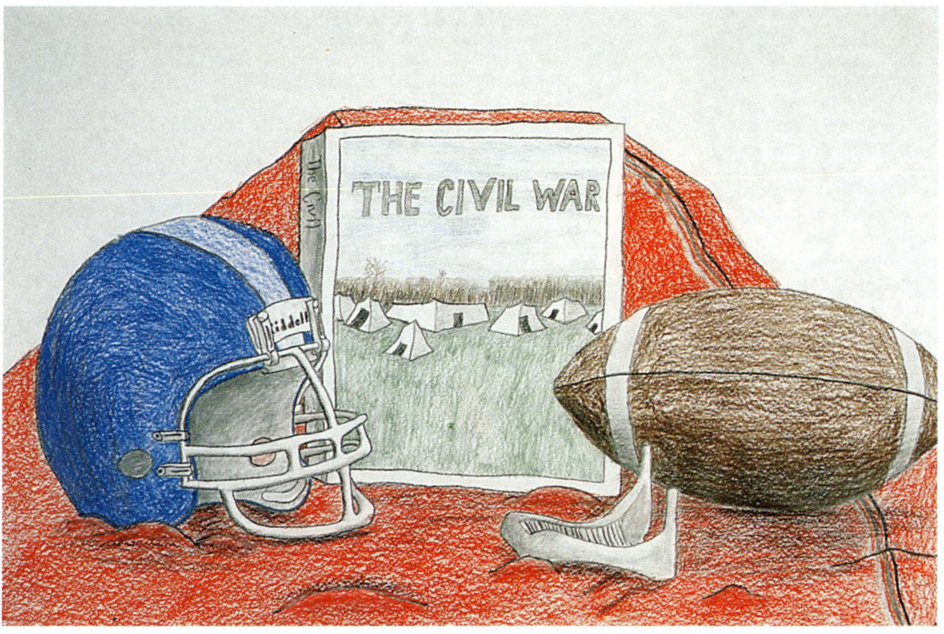

Fig. 2–27 Student artwork

Language Arts

Writing has long been a method for recording events, people, and beliefs. For the ancient Mesoamerican and South American people, writing was a way to record religious beliefs and keep track of time. These people created books, called codices, whose pages were made from bark paper or deerskin arranged like a folding screen. They used signs and pictures, rather than words, to record what was important to them.

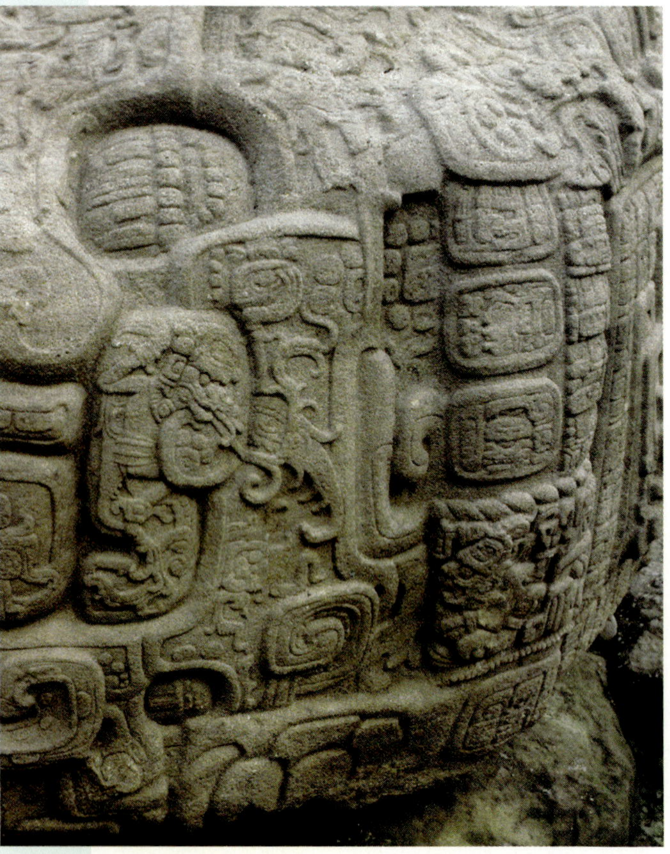

Fig. 2–28 **Ancient peoples also carved their writing on statues and architectural features.**

Pre-Columbian Guatemala, Zoomorph P from Quiriga, ca. 300–630. Courtesy Davis Art Images.

Music

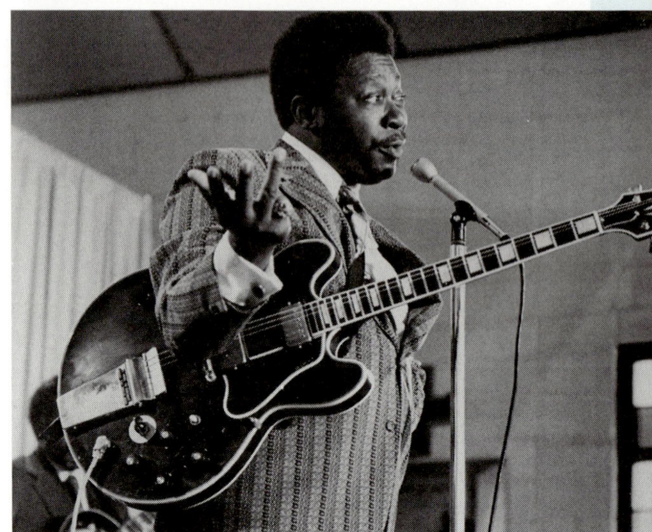

Fig. 2–29 **Blues guitarist B. B. King**
Rose Archive.

Music can also serve as a record of a specific time or place. Music often reflects a unique culture or time in history. For example, the blues are an African American musical invention.

Because the blues originated with African Americans, many of the origins of blues music can be traced back to African cultures. What do you think that people in the future may learn about your generation by listening to today's popular music for young people?

Careers Art Historians

Art historians are concerned with the history of art and its relationship to our culture. Art historians work like detectives, trying to find out as much as they can about artworks from the past. They ask questions like these: Who made this artwork? What is it made of? Who used it, and for what? What can we learn from it now? Art historians usually earn a graduate degree. Often, they become experts in a particular subject, style, culture, time period, art form, or medium.

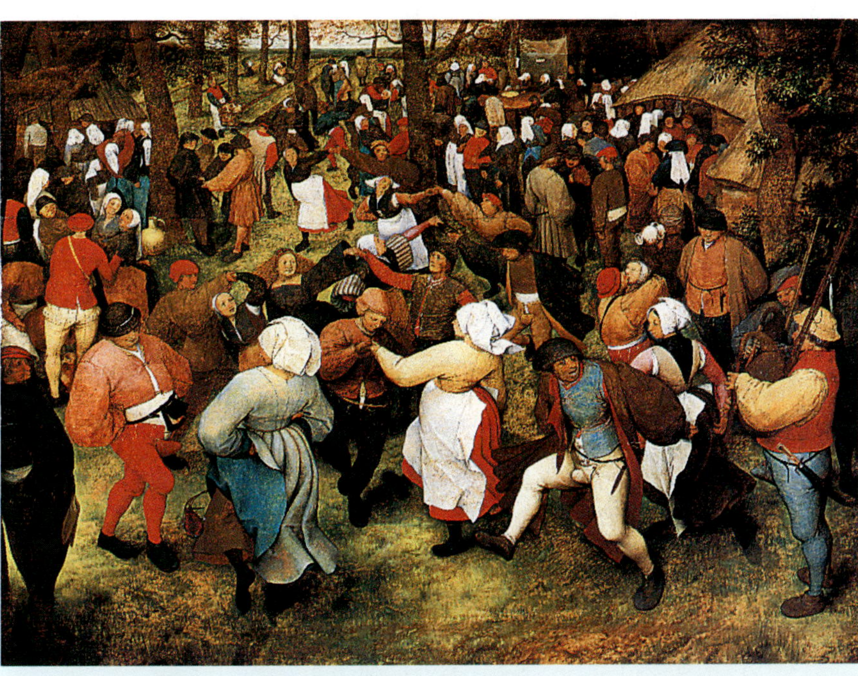

Fig. 2–30 **Compare this painting from the 1500s with the work of Inatace Alphonse (pages 52 and 53). What could an art historian learn from each artwork?**

Pieter Bruegel the Elder, *The Wedding Dance,* 1566. Oil on panel. City of Detroit Purchase, Detroit Institute of Arts. Photograph ©1984 The Detroit Institute of Arts.

Daily Life

People keep many kinds of records. What kinds of records of you do you think your school and family have? Your school probably has grade reports, text scores, school photos, and letters from your parents and teachers. Your parents may have your birth certificate, medical records, photographs, and special keepsakes from your childhood. What kinds of records do you keep for yourself?

Fig. 2–31 **Report card ca. 1954**
Rose Archive.

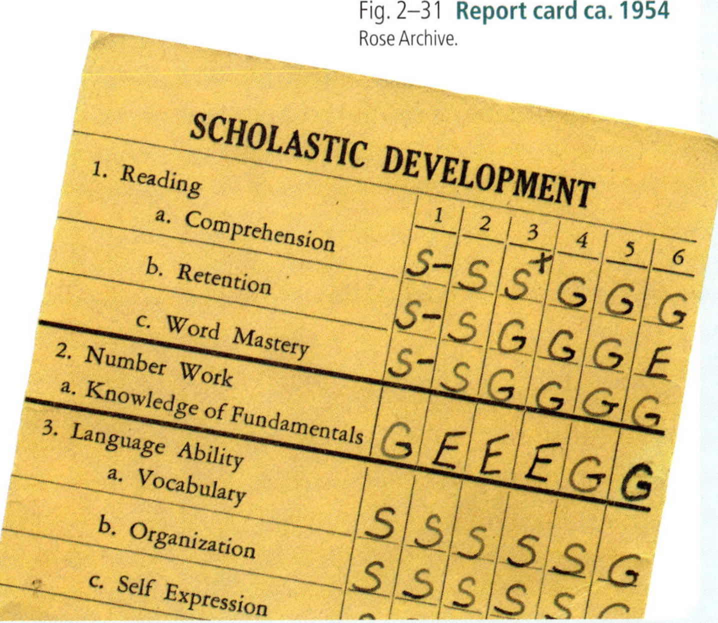

SCHOLASTIC DEVELOPMENT

	1	2	3	4	5	6
1. Reading						
a. Comprehension	S-	S	S	G	G	G
b. Retention	S-	S	G	G	G	E
c. Word Mastery	S-	S	G	G	G	G
2. Number Work						
a. Knowledge of Fundamentals	G	E	E	E	G	G
3. Language Ability						
a. Vocabulary	S	S	S	S	S	G
b. Organization	S	S	S	S	S	[illegible]
c. Self Expression	[illegible]					

Vocabulary Review

Match each art term below with its definition.

value
hatching
highlight
stippling
subject matter

1. a shading technique that uses patterns of dots
2. a shading technique that is created by using parallel lines
3. the area on a form that reflects the most light
4. the lightness or darkness of a color
5. the people, objects, and other things shown in an artwork

Aesthetic Thinking

What makes a photograph an artwork? What types of photographs would not be considered artworks?

For Your Portfolio

Review your artworks from this unit. Look for effective examples of shading to create the illusion of form, and repeated lines, colors, and shapes to create the sense of visual rhythm.

Write About Art

Discuss what elements the artist chose to show in this genre scene of life in rural Spain in the late 1700s. How did the artist use light and dark values to focus our attention?

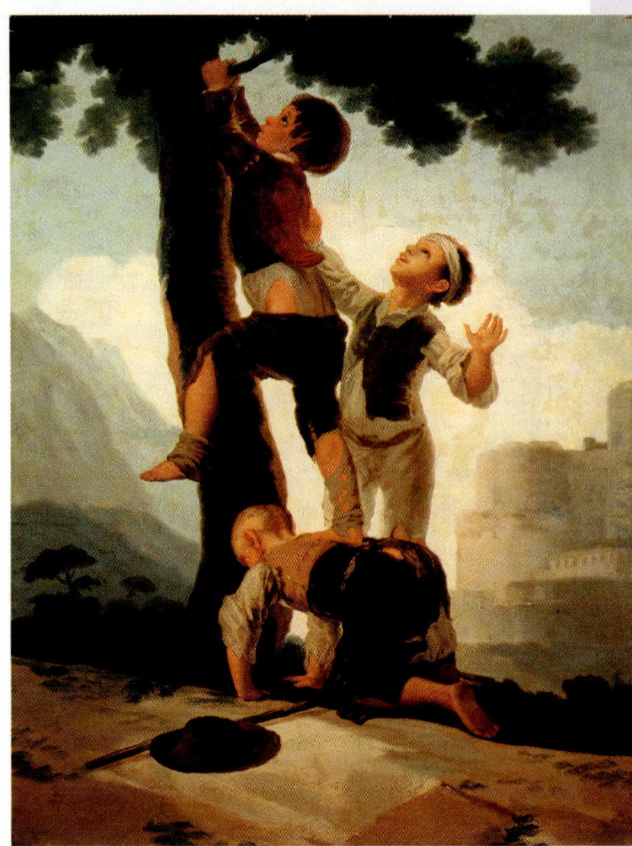

Fig. 2–32 Francisco Goya y Lucientes, *Boys Climbing a Tree*, 1792. Oil on canvas 55 ½" x 43 7⁄10" (141 x 111 cm). Museo del Prado, Madrid, Spain. Photo Credit: Scala/Art Resource, NY.

Art Criticism

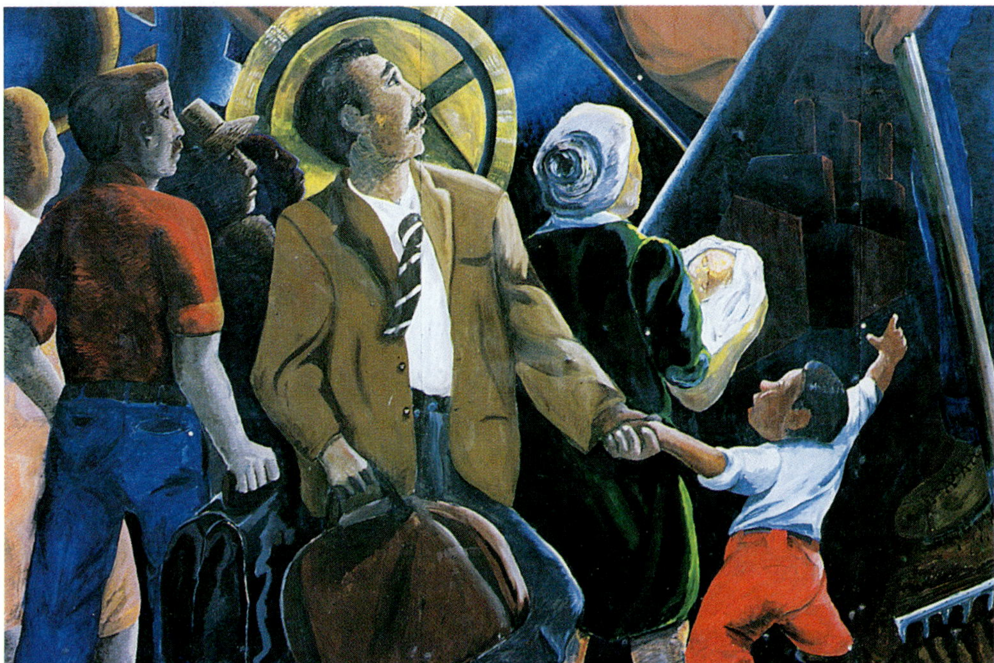

Fig. 2–33 Chicago Mural Group, *Latino and Asian-American History,* 1974. Left detail: *Hispanic Immigration* by Oscar Martínez. (912 West Sheridan, Chicago)

Describe What do you see in this mural?

Analyze How did the artist use highlights and shadows to create the illusion of form?

Interpret What ideas about daily life does this artwork communicate?

Evaluate Why (or why not) would you consider this a genre painting?

Meet the Artist

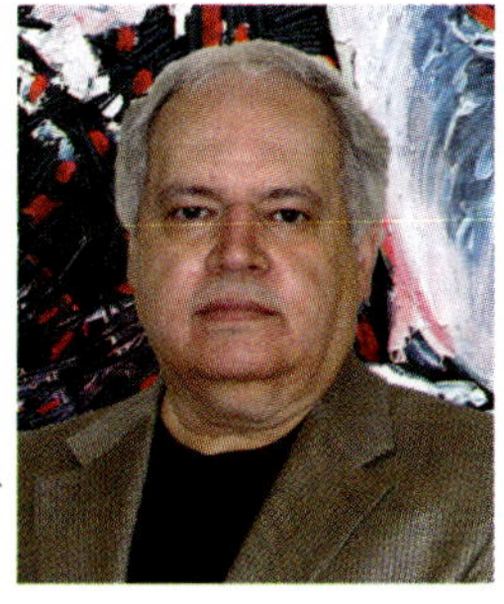

Izer Tuohey Martínez.

Oscar Martínez was born in Mayagüez, Puerto Rico. He lives in Chicago, Illinois, where he founded the Latin American Museum of Art.

"My artwork is about creating the appearance of stories and dramas that are based on reality, dreams, and the imagination."

— Oscar Martínez (born 1950)

For Your Sketchbook

Use your daily life to inspire future artworks. Keep a list of words and phrases, as well as sketches and photographs, that you find interesting or that inspire you.

Unit 3

Artists Are Designers

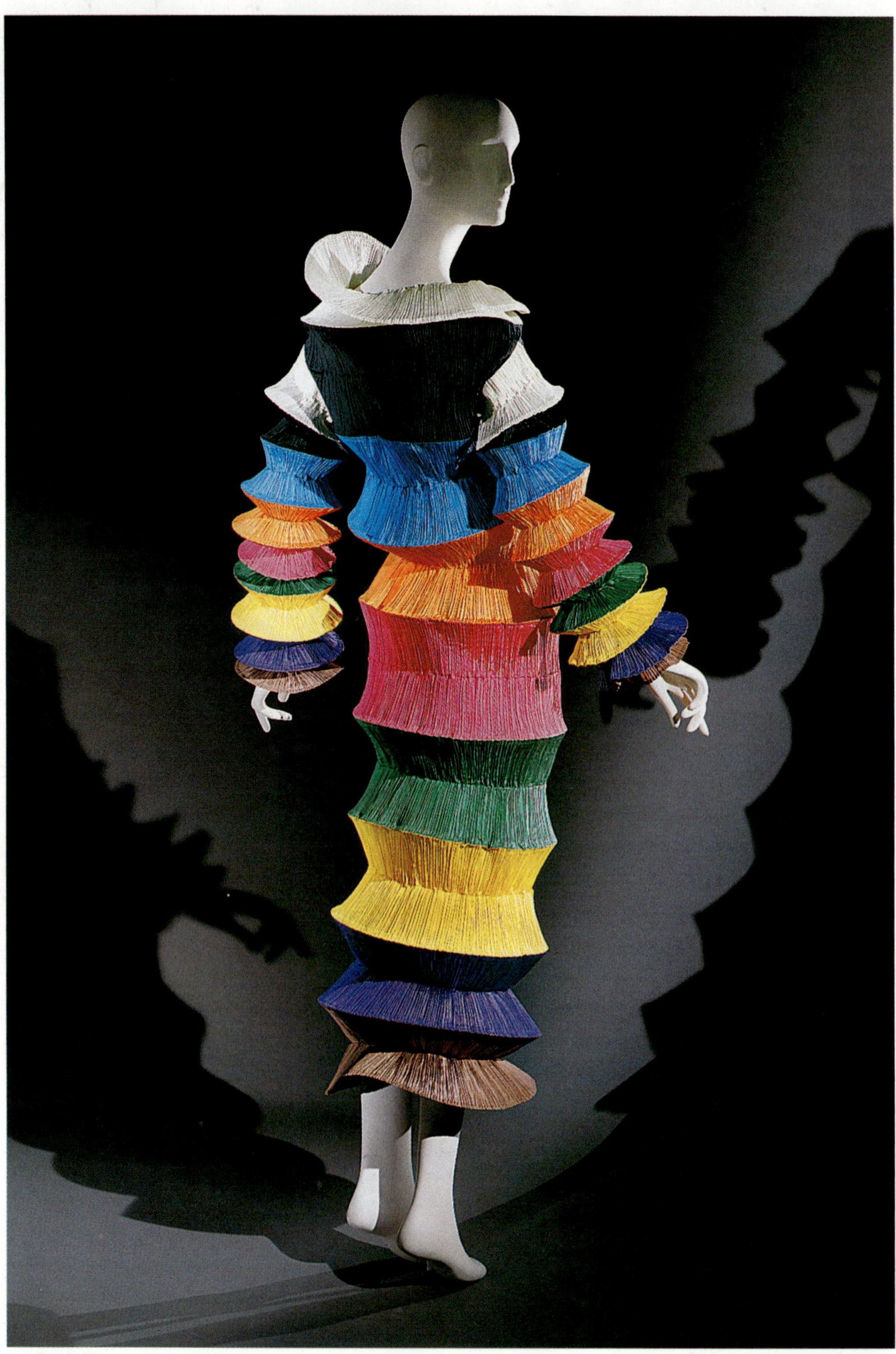

Fig. 3–1 **Issey Miyake thinks of new and creative ways to use fabrics. What familiar objects does this dress bring to mind?**

Issey Miyake, *Flying-Saucer Dress*, 1994. Heat-set polyester. Philadelphia Museum of Art: Gift of Issey Miyake. Photo by Lynn Rosenthal and Graydon Wood, 1997.

Have you considered that most things you see and use every day were once just ideas? Our school desks, cars, telephones, and toys are all products designed by artists who started with a problem and some ideas about how to solve it.

Designers think about how a product will be used and how it will look. For example, people want their clothes to keep them warm or cool, but they also want to have the right "look." Fashion designers plan the clothes and other items we wear. They may design in familiar styles or create designs that surprise and even shock.

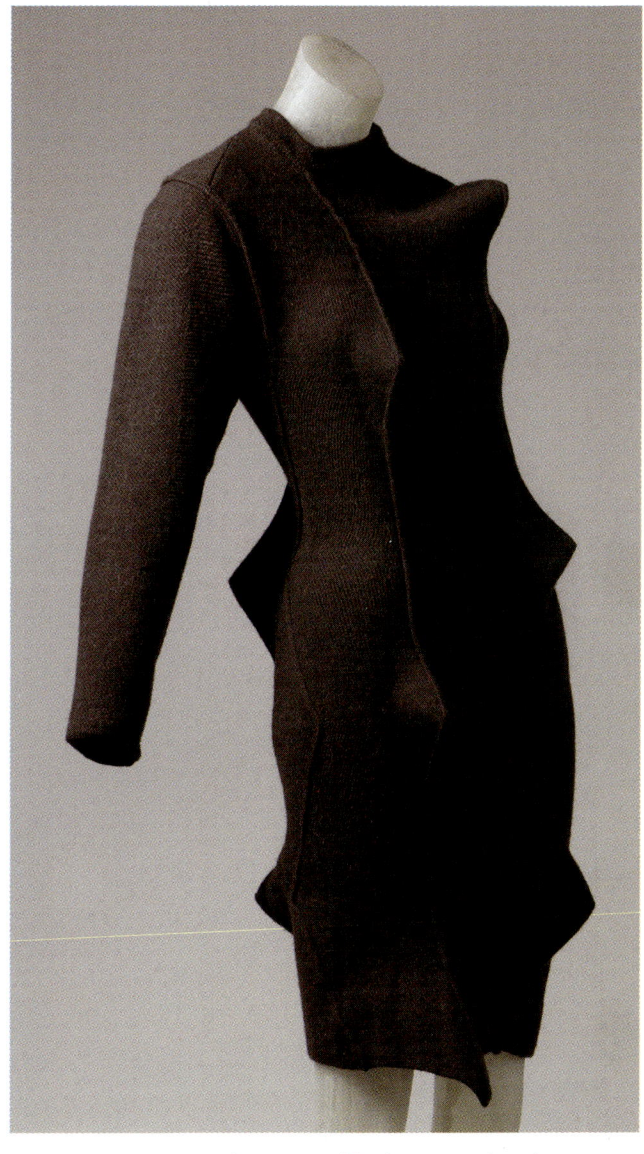

Fig. 3–2 **Compare and contrast this dress to other dresses you have seen. How is it the same? In what ways is it different?**

Issey Miyake, *Dress,* 1989. Brown wool knit. The Metropolitan Museum of Art. Gift of Muriel Kallis Newman, 2003 (2003.79.3) Image ©The Metropolitan Museum of Art.

In this unit, you will learn:

- How artists design the things we see and use.
- How to draw figures with human proportions.
- How art addresses the human need for well-designed objects and spaces.

Meeting Human Needs

Issey Miyake is a fashion designer who has traveled around the world, paying attention to the way people dress and the colors in the landscape. Like all designers, he starts with a problem to solve. To him, clothing should be beautiful, give pleasure to those who wear it and see it, and make people think about clothing in new ways. He creates clothing that not only covers the body, but also extends it, like a sculpture. How does the dress on page 62 resemble a sculpture?

Fashion as Art Miyake experiments with fabrics and ways to use them. He plays with the patterns created by crushing, pleating, twisting, shrinking, bleaching, and recycling textiles. Patterns are repetitions of lines, shapes, or colors. The colors of his fabrics may be bright and cheerful or soft, natural, and quiet. Miyake works with other creative people. He invites artists to plan fashion shows with him. He works with designers to research ideas and make new creations. Today, he uses the newest technologies for creating fabrics and designing clothing.

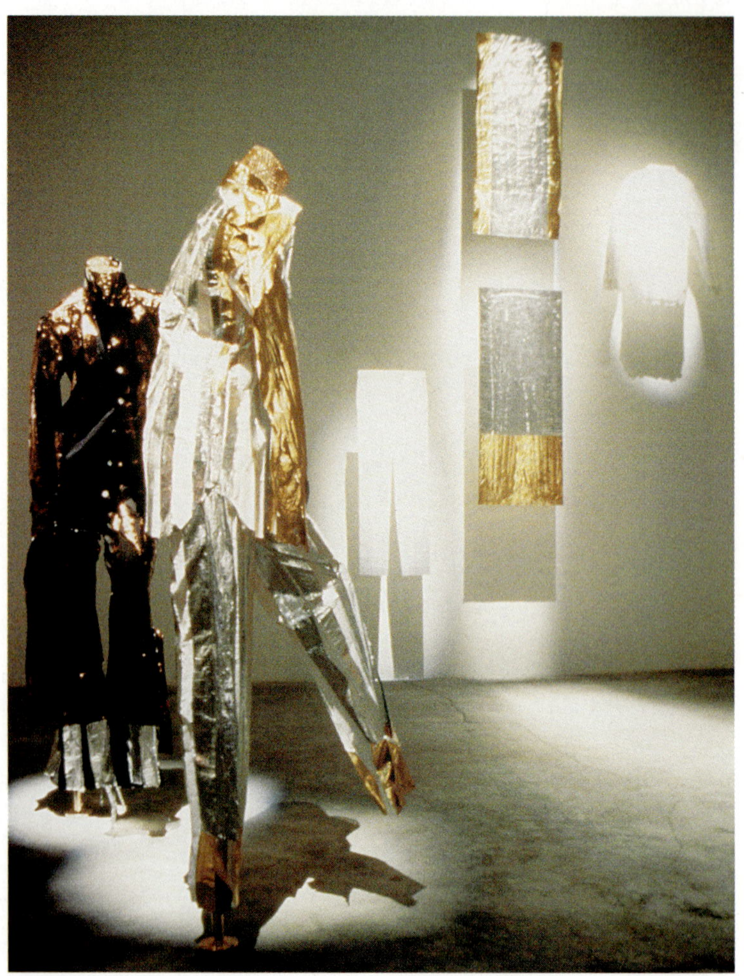

Fig. 3–3 **In these designs, Issey Miyake emphasizes the need to recycle. What materials do you think he used?**

Issey Miyake, *Laboratory Starburst*, 1999–2000. Photo by Yasuaki Yoshinaga. From "Issey Miyake, Making Things," 12 Nov. 1999–29 Feb. 2000. Ace Gallery, New York. © Issey Miyake, Inc.

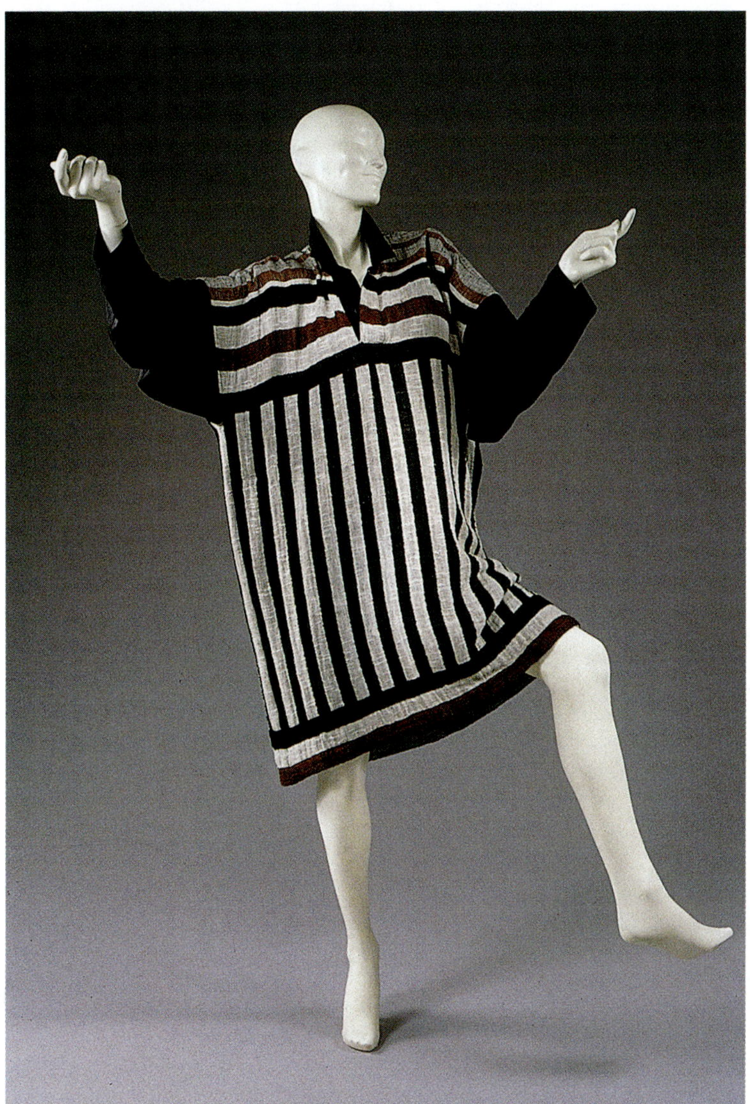

Fig. 3–4 **How did you respond to this dress when first looking at it? What about the dress made you have that response?**

Issey Miyake, *Shirt Dress*. Cincinnati Art Museum, Gift of Arlene C. Cooper, 1986.93.

Meet Issey Miyake

Issey Miyake was interested in clothing design at an early age. While studying graphic design in Tokyo, he showed his first collection of clothing. He is known for his creative use of materials and textiles in fashion design. Miyake brings together the worlds of art and fashion. His works are influenced by both Western and Eastern culture, and he uses both traditional and original designs. He is also inspired by nature, even though he experiments with technology to alter fabrics. His clothing designs not only cover the body, but also surprise and delight his audience.

"If you take T-shirts or pairs of jeans...people always know what to expect from them. I prefer to surprise people, to cause emotion."

— Issey Miyake (born 1938)

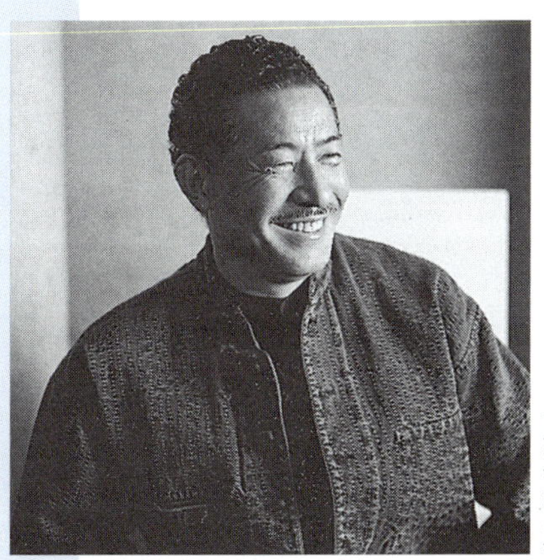

Photo © Yuriko Takagi.

3.1 Continued

Design Through Time People have always designed products to meet their special needs. Over the centuries, however, people have needed and wanted different things. The telephone on this page once inspired thoughts of a future world. Who could have known that people someday would want a flip-top cell phone?

People also care about the way useful objects look. Designers create products that both meet people's needs and are visually appealing. They pay attention to the form (how it looks) as well as the function (how it works) of their designs. Like function, form may change, depending on what appeals to people at different times.

Designers for Every Need Many kinds of designers fill our needs. Product designers plan items such as appliances and toys. The forklift **(Fig. 3–6)** pictured shows the work of an industrial designer. Fashion designers consider comfort and style. Interior designers improve the spaces where we live and play. Landscape designers plan with trees and walkways. Theater designers plan sets and lighting. Graphic designers plan advertisements and brochures. And Web designers create electronic ads and websites **(Fig. 3–7)**.

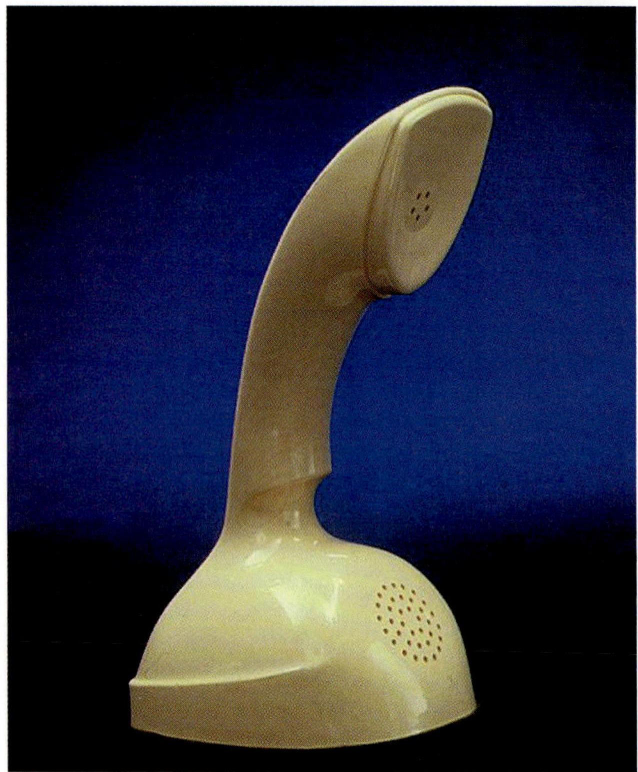

Fig. 3–5 **Compare and contrast this telephone to the ones you use. How are they alike? How are they different?**

Hugo Blomberg, Ralph Lysell, Gosta Thames, *Eriofon*, 1949. Plastic and Rubber. L.M. Ericsson Sweden.

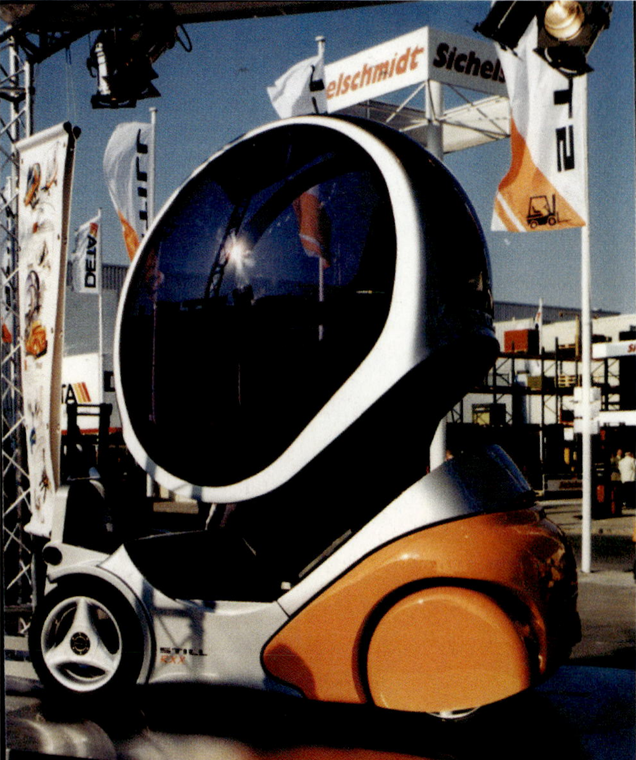

Fig. 3–6 **This forklift allows the driver to move up with the lift instead of looking up from ground level. Compare and contrast the look of this forklift with that of today's car.**

Courtesy of Teams Design.

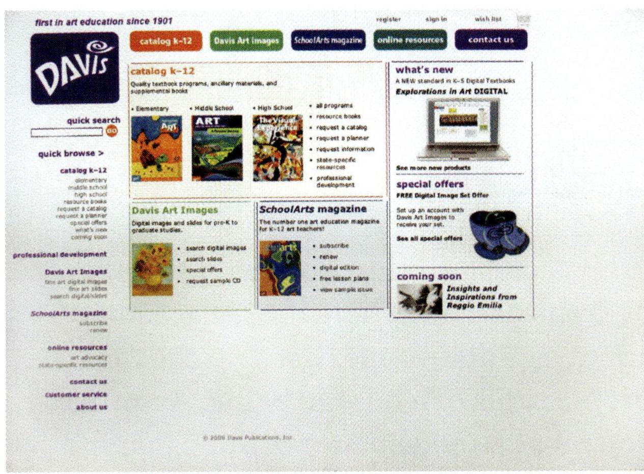

Fig. 3–7 **Why do you think the Web designer used different fonts and colors?**

Davis Publications, Worcester, MA www.davisart.com

Check Your Understanding

1. Describe Issey Miyake's approach to designing clothing.
2. Give examples of at least three different items that are designed by artists. Compare how these objects meet human needs.
3. Why must designers consider both form and function when designing items for our use?

Studio Time

Design for the Future

Plan for and draw several different views of a high-tech product for the future, such as a cell phone, clock, or computer.

- Use contour lines to show as many features as possible.
- Consider needs in communication, transportation, entertainment, the home, and so on.
- Think about efficiency. Who will use the product? How will it be used?

Reflect on how your design is an improvement over something that now exists.

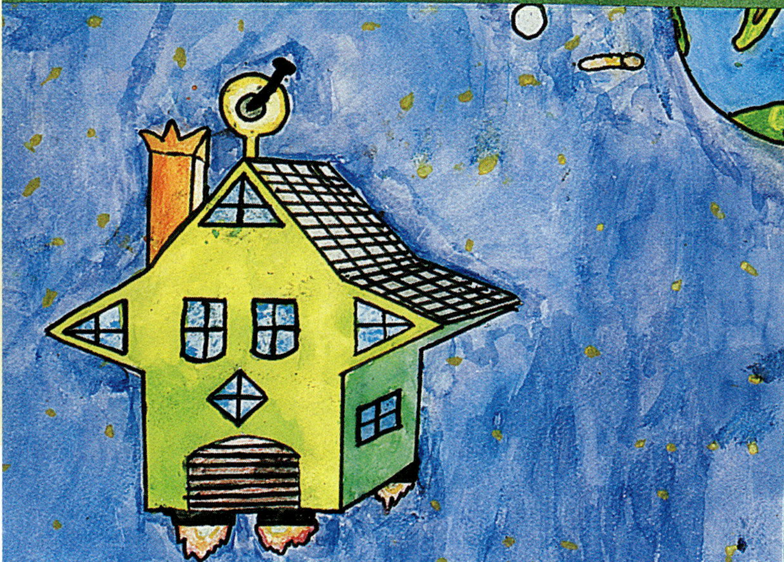

Fig. 3–8 Student artwork

Drawing Human Proportions

Take a look at the people around you. How do they differ from one another? Some may be tall, while others may be short. Some may have blond hair, while others may have black. What do they have in common? Most people are alike in their proportions. **Proportions** are the size relationship between one part of the body and another.

When creating items such as clothing or furniture, designers make decisions about size and shape based on the typical proportions of a human being. As an artist, you must also keep proportions in mind. Whether you are drawing a picture of a man, woman, or young child, the general rules of proportion will help make your drawing seem right.

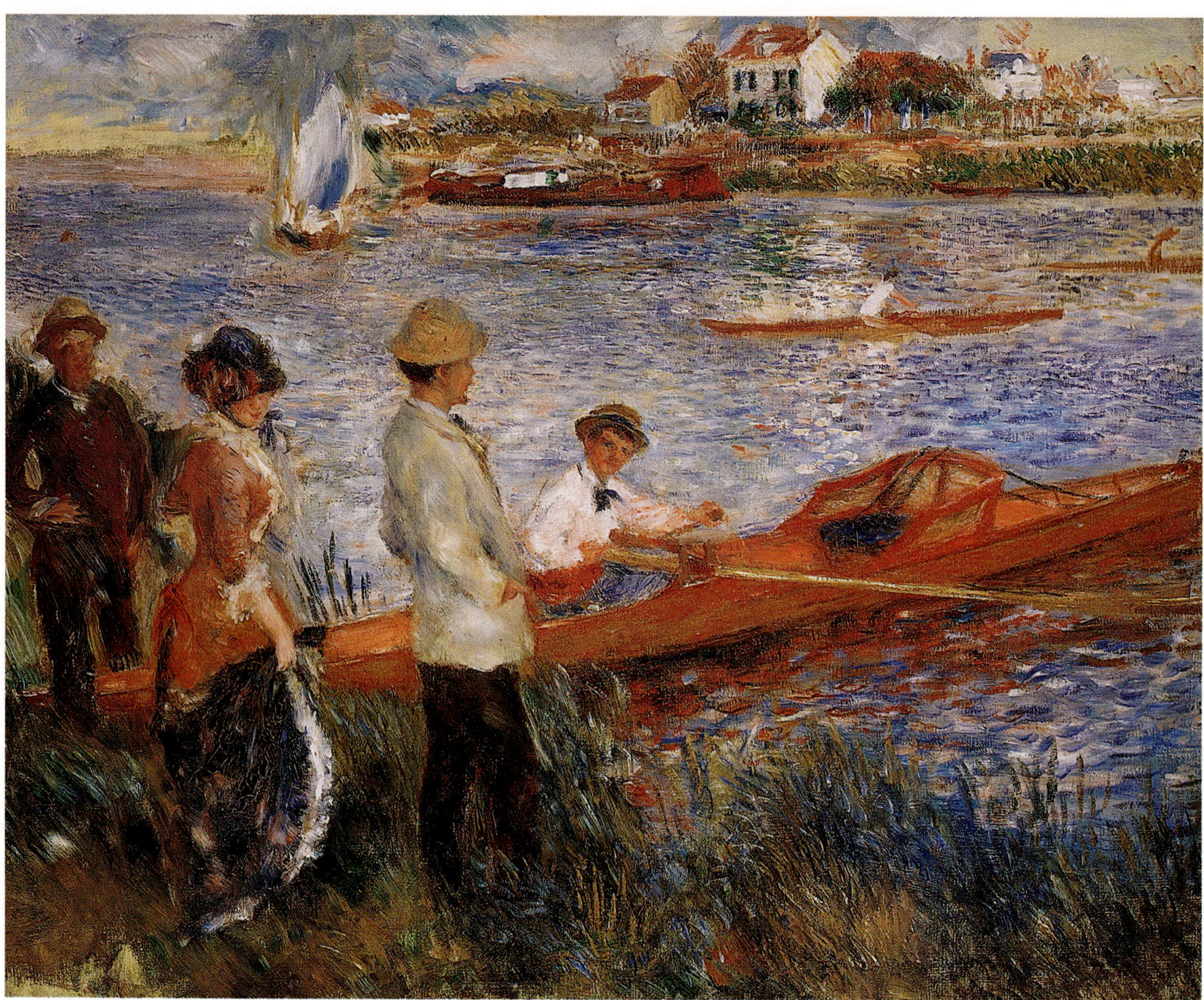

Fig. 3–9 **Look at the bodies and the faces of the people in this painting. What makes them look real? How could you tell if each person has correct proportions?**

Auguste Renoir *Oarsmen at Chatou*, 1879. Oil on canvas, 31 15/16" x 39 7/16" (81.2 x 100.2 cm). Gift of Sam A. Lewisohn. Image courtesy of the Board of Trustees, National Gallery of Art, Washington, DC.1951.1.2 (1062) PA.

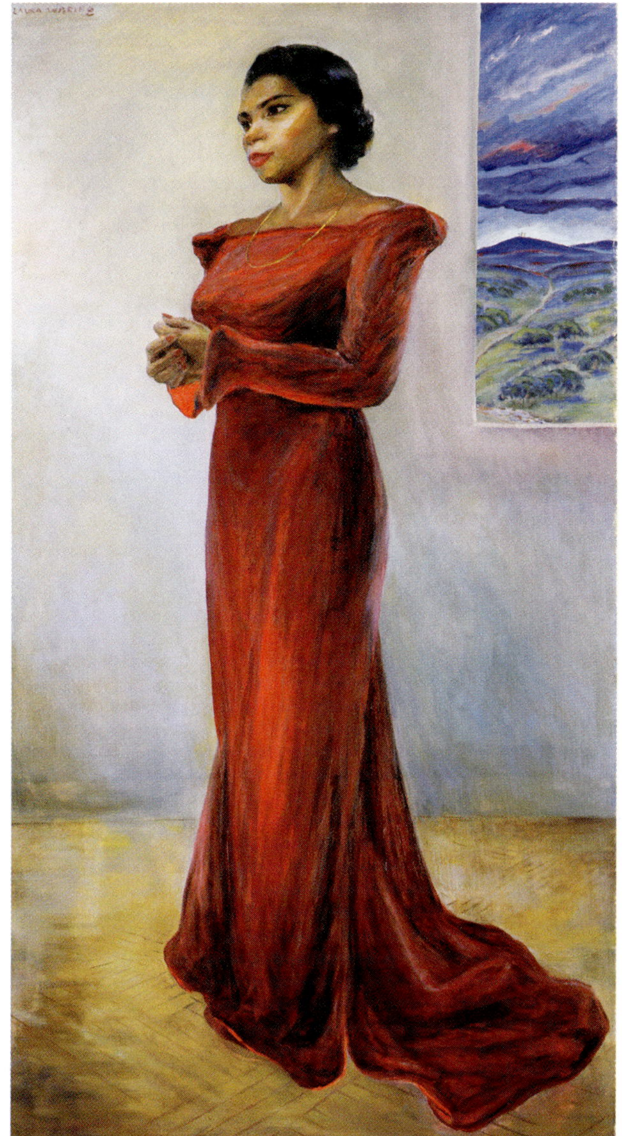

Fig. 3–10 **Even though the subject is turned slightly, notice the proportions of her head, sholders, elbows, and hips.**

Laura Wheeler Waring, *Marian Anderson*, 1944. Oil on canvas, 76 1/8" x 40" (193.3 x 101.6 cm). National Portrait Gallery, Smithsonian Institution, Washington, DC. Gift of the Harmon Foundation. Photo: National Portrait Gallery, Smithsonian Institution/Art Resource, NY.

The Human Figure Notice that the height of most people age twelve and up is about seven or eight times the height of the head. The hips are about halfway between the feet and the top of the head. The elbows and waist are just above the hips. The shoulders are about halfway between the top of the head and the waist. The knees are about halfway between the feet and the hips.

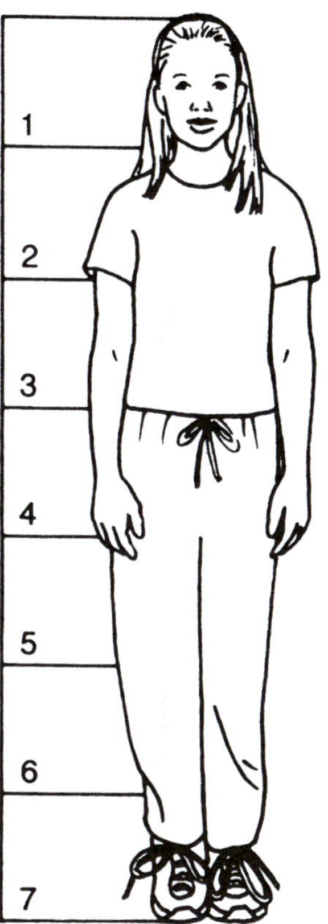

Observe Study the proportions of the human figure on this page. Notice the eight horizontal lines, all the same distance apart. The head fills the top space, and the feet rest on the bottom line.

Tools: Paper, rulers, and pencils.

Practice: Figure Drawing

Practice your understanding of proportions by creating several sketches of the human figure.

- Have a classmate pose for you or work from a photograph.
- First, sketch a standing figure from the front.
- Then, sketch a standing figure from the back and one from the side.
- Next, try sketching a seated figure from the side.

Each time, be careful to use the same proportions. Use a full sheet of paper for each drawing.

The Human Face Notice that the eyes are about halfway between the top of the head and chin. The space between eyes is about one eye width. The bottom of the nose is about halfway between eyes and chin. The mouth is slightly higher than halfway between chin and nose. Its corners are directly below the center of each eye. Ears are about parallel to the eyelids and bottom of the nose.

Observe Study the proportions of the faces on this page. Notice that additional proportions exist. For example, the top of the ear is about halfway between the eye and the back of the head. What other proportions can you find?

Tools: Paper, rulers, and pencils.

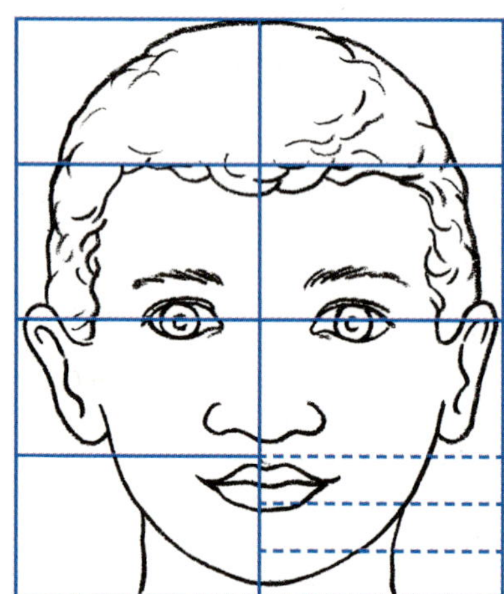

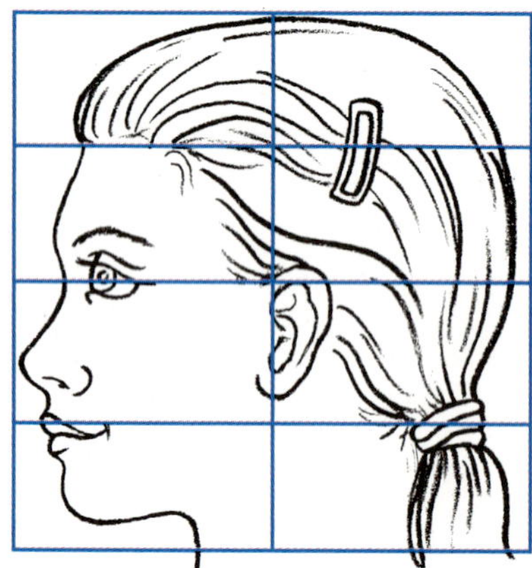

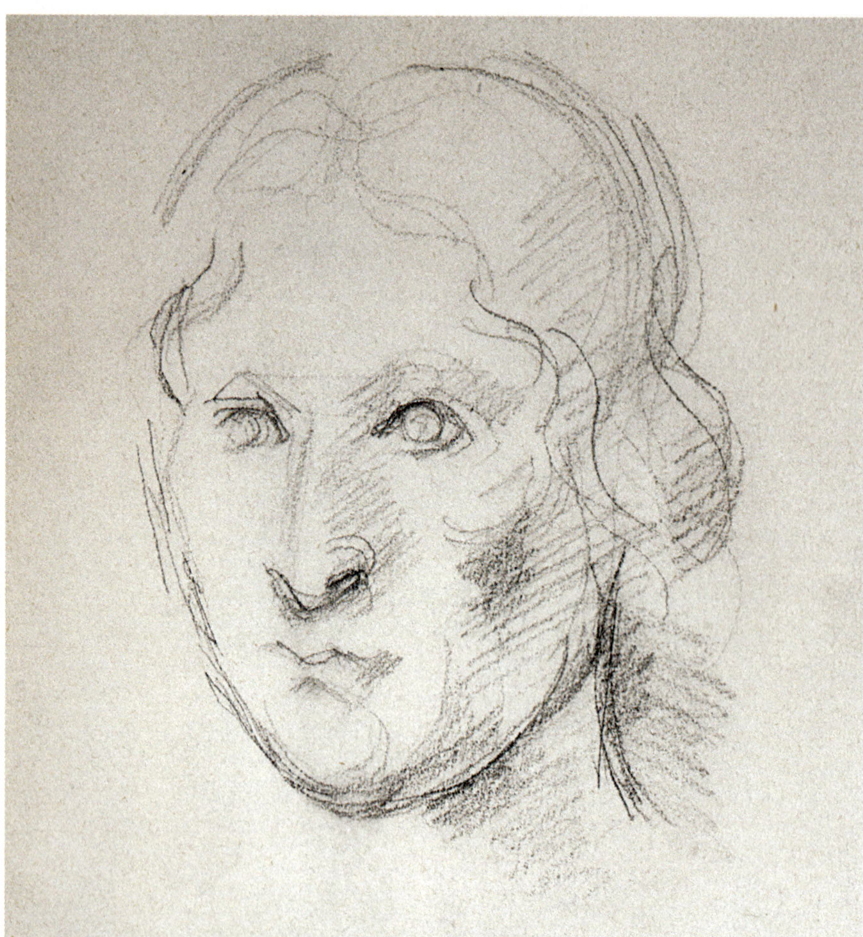

Fig. 3–11 **Look at the features of the face in this image. How can you tell if the face has typical human proportions?**

Paul Cézanne, *Head of a Man*, 1882–90. p.23 (recto) from Sketchbook 1, graphite tintel on wove paper (1882–90). 31 15/16" x 39 7/16" (18.2 x 11.6 cm). Philadelphia Museum of Art, gift of Mr. And Mrs. Walter H. Annenberg, 1987.

Practice: Portraits

Practice your understanding of these proportions by creating sketches of the human face.

- Have a classmate pose for you or work from a photograph.
- First, sketch a face from the front.
- Then, sketch a face in profile. You could also draw yourself while looking into a mirror.

Check Your Understanding

1. Define *proportions* in your own words.
2. In terms of proportions, how do you think drawing a human face is different from drawing a cat's face?
3. Why is it important for artists and designers to have knowledge of human proportions?

Studio Time

A Detailed Portrait

Draw a detailed portrait of yourself or a classmate.

- You might start by drawing an oval shape with light pencil lines for the eyes, nose, lips, and ears (as described in this lesson).
- Then, observe the specific characteristics of your subject. What are the proportions?
- Adjust your marks, if necessary, to show the correct proportions.

Reflect on the realism of the proportions and details in your portrait.

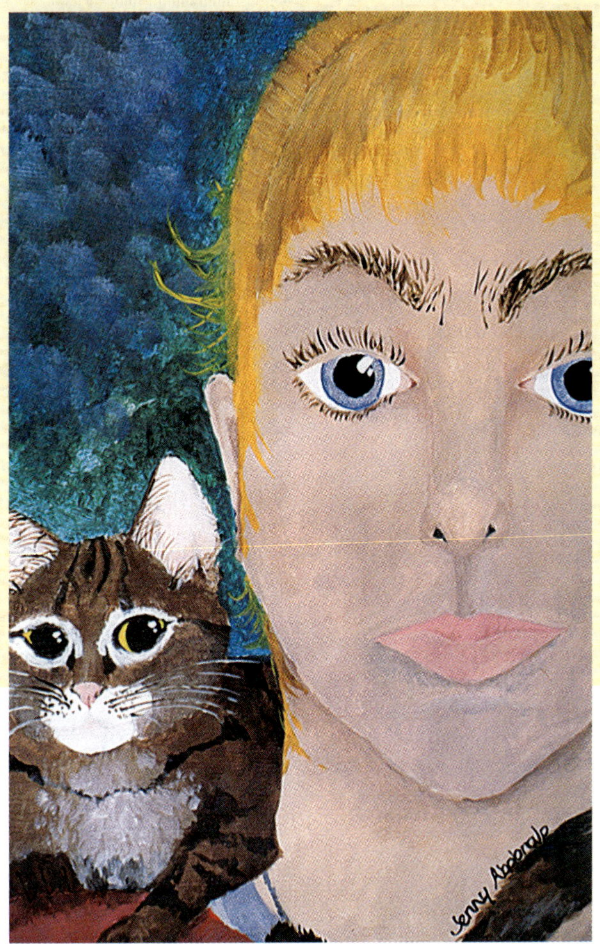

Fig. 3–12 Student artwork

Design an Outfit

Studio Background

Fashion designers such as Issey Miyake create clothing and accessories for a wide variety of people and uses. They experiment with fabrics, colors, and patterns. They also care about how clothing will look and feel to the person who wears it. Fashion designers often look to leaders in their field for inspiration.

In this studio exploration, you will design an outfit or uniform for yourself or someone else. You'll make a cardboard figure on which to attach the outfit. How will your outfit be used? What features does it need? Will you create a design that is entirely from your own imagination? Or will you borrow ideas from leading designers?

You Will Need

- lightweight cardboard
- scissors
- drawing paper
- pencil
- markers, crayons, colored pencils
- white glue or cellophane tape (optional)

Step 1 Plan and Practice

- Brainstorm a list of specific people. Some possibilities are athletes, friends, artists, and teachers.
- Choose one person from your list and think about what kind of outfit the person would need or want.
- Look through magazines or other sources to see examples of similar outfits.
- Make several sketches to help you decide on a design.

Things to Remember:

✓ Draw your figure to reflect typical human proportions.

✓ Pay attention to how the outfit looks and how well it fits the needs of the person who will wear it.

✓ Present your cardboard figure with its outfit in a particular pose.

Inspiration from Our World

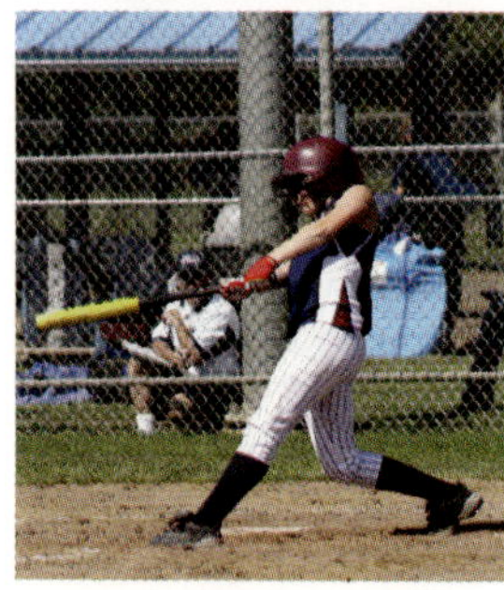

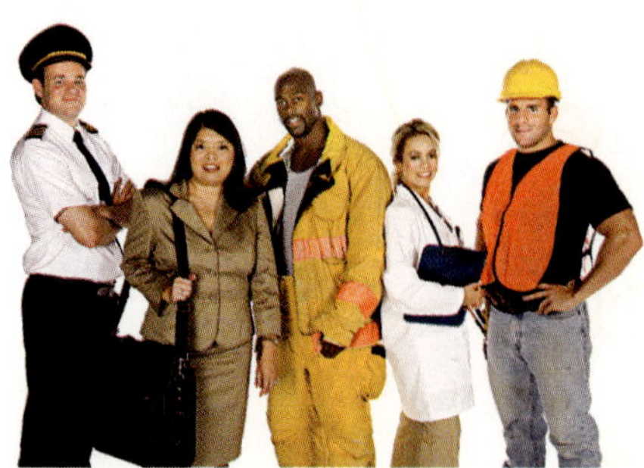

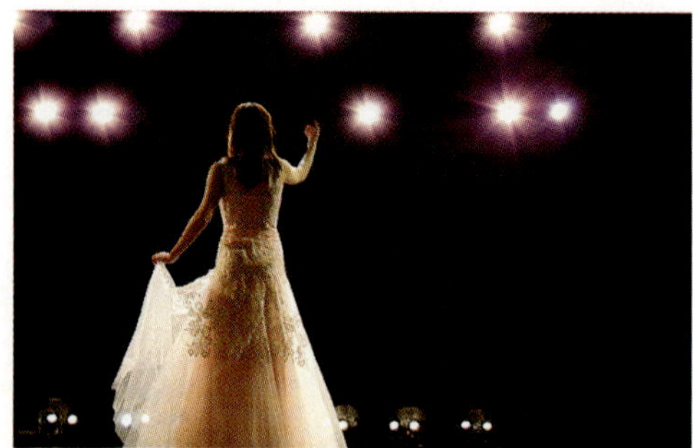

Inspiration from Art

All designers go through a similar series of steps. At each stage of the design process, they ask important questions.

1. **Identify the problem.** What do clients want and need? Which is more important: the product's look or the way it will be used?
2. **Explore the problem.** What designs of the product already exist? Who will use the product?
3. **Brainstorm.** What are possible solutions to the design problem? In this stage, designers make rough sketches or models.
4. **Plan.** Which idea needs more work? How should the idea be changed or improved? Several people usually are involved in choosing and developing one of the sketches.
5. **Produce.** In this stage, a prototype may be created and shown to the client. A prototype is a sample of a product.
6. **Evaluate.** Does the product solve the problem? What parts of the process worked well? How can the product and the process be improved?

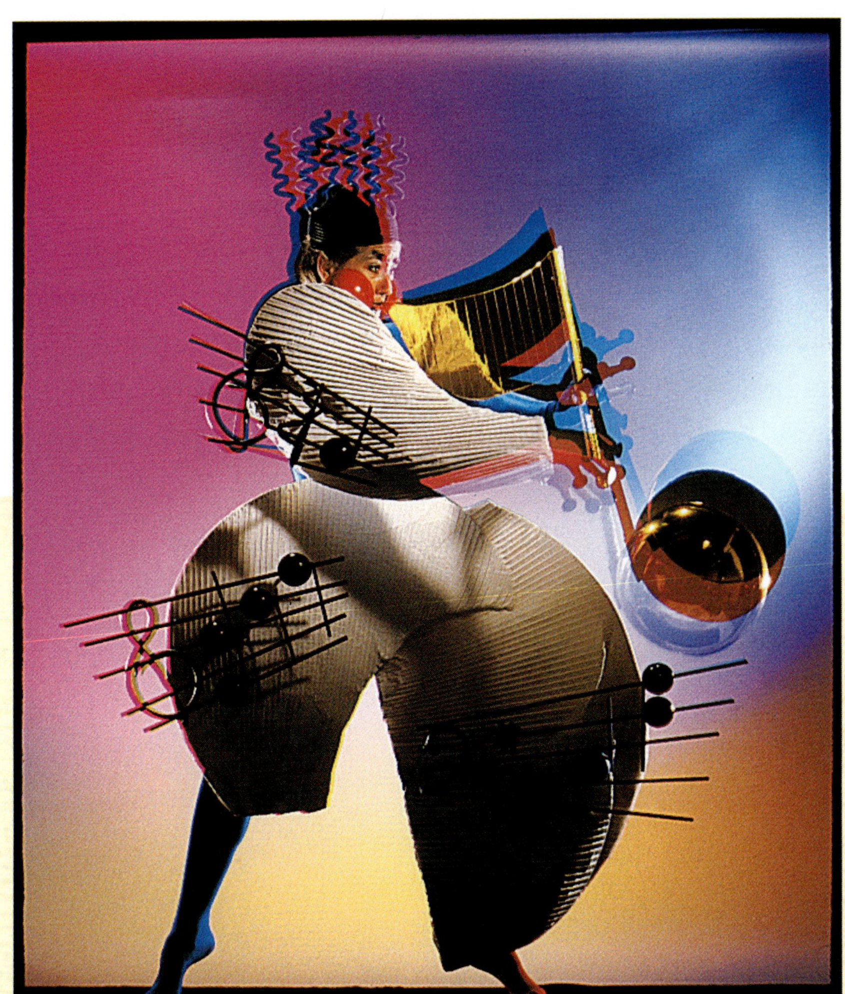

Fig. 3–13 **The artist who made this design for clothing often creates wearable sculpture and performs in what she designs. How is this design unique? Why might someone wear it?**

Pat Oleszko, *Jazzmin*, 1994. Mixed media, for clothing design, 4' x 2' x 7' (122 x 61 x 213 cm). Courtesy of the artist. Photo: Neil Selkirk.

Step 2 **Begin to Create**

- Create a paper figure of the person you chose. **Draw the outline of the person on lightweight cardboard.**

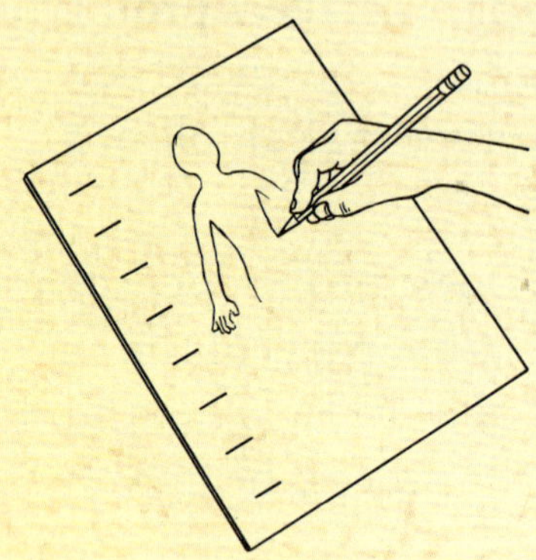

- Think about body proportions. How long should the arms and legs be? How large should the head be? Cut out the figure.
- Lightly trace the figure on drawing paper.
- **Sketch the features of the clothing on the trace.** What features—such as puffy sleeves, a sash, or special hat—do you need? Remember to create a front and back view of your design.

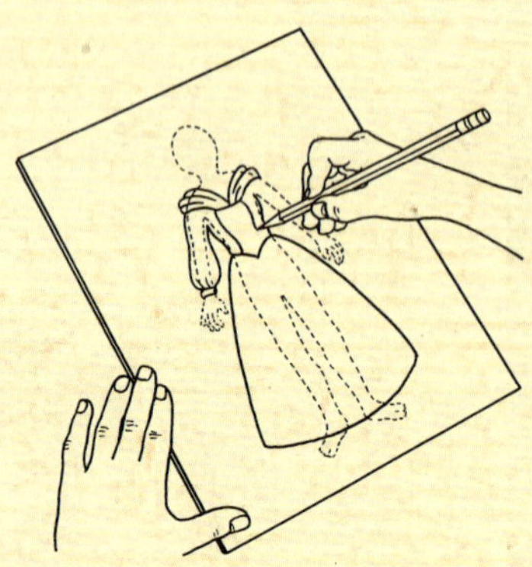

- **Color your design and create patterns.** Will you create an all-over pattern, areas with different patterns, or simply a border design?

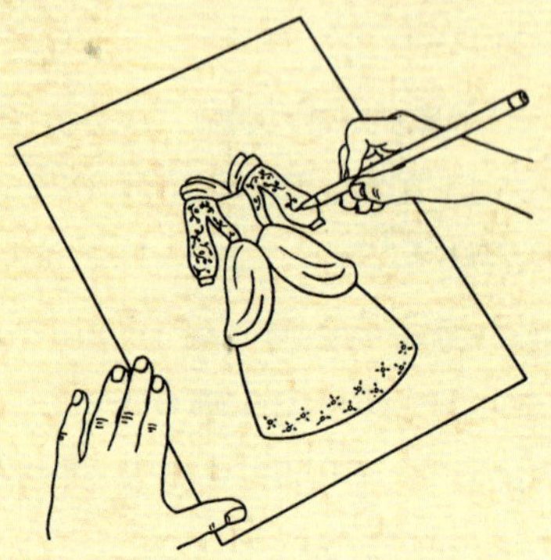

Step 3 **Revise**

Did you remember to:

- ✓ Draw your figure to reflect typical human proportions?
- ✓ Pay attention to how the outfit looks and how well it fits the needs of the person who will wear it?
- ✓ Present your cardboard figure with its outfit in a particular pose?

Adjust your work if necessary. In your sketchbook, make a note of your revisions and why you made them.

Step 4 **Add Finishing Touches**

- Carefully erase any unwanted trace lines. If you want, cut out the clothing and attach it to your figure.

Step 5 **Share and Reflect**

- Write a letter to the person for whom you have designed the outfit.
- Explain why you designed it the way you did.
- Tell the person the steps of the design process you followed as you worked.
- Share your letter with a classmate.
- What different ideas did you have in the beginning? How did you decide which idea, or ideas, to use?
- What do you like about your fashion design? What changes, if any, would you make the next time?

Art Criticism

Describe What kind of outfits did the student artist design? How do you know?

Analyze How has the artist used human proportions in these designs?

Interpret What does this presentation say to you about the design of these outfits?

Evaluate Why do you think these designs might appeal to people?

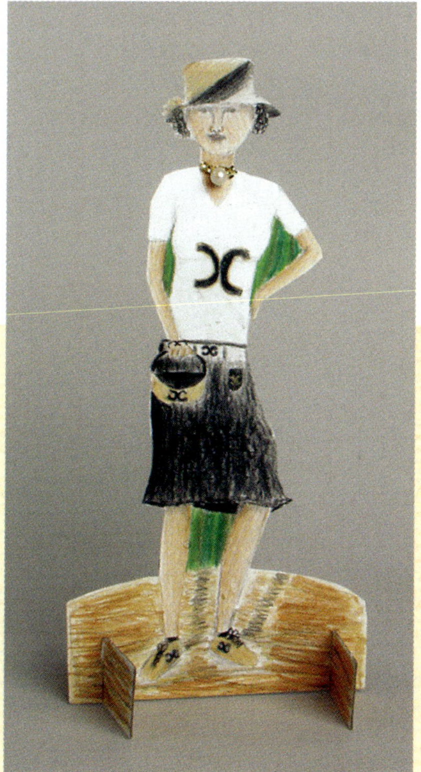

Fig. 3–14
Student artwork

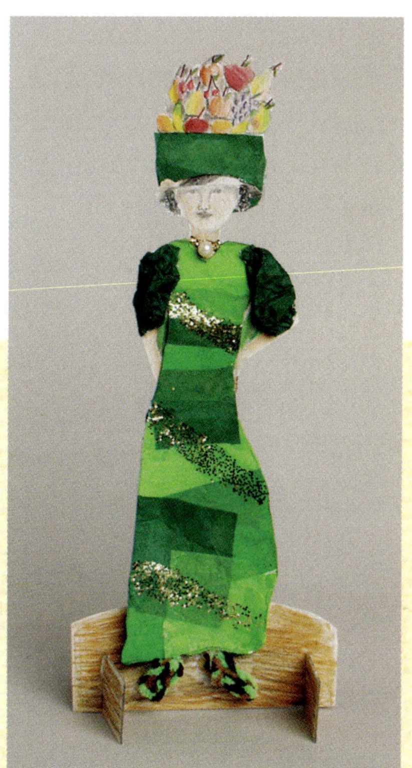

Fig. 3–15
Student artwork

A Tradition of Design for Living

People have always designed functional objects to meet their basic needs. The urns and vases of the ancient Greeks, such as the one shown on this page, are excellent examples of well-designed functional objects. The function, or use, of a vessel determined how it looked. This is also true today.

Movements in Design The world changes rapidly, as does the design of objects. Many things we think of as normal today were beyond people's imagination a hundred years ago. A movement is a trend reflected by the efforts of many artists. Throughout the 1900s, different movements influenced the design of objects.

One movement was begun by a school called the Bauhaus. It was founded in 1919 by a group of artists, architects, and designers in Germany. Bauhaus designers used modern industrial materials without decoration. Fig. 3–17 is an example of Bauhaus design.

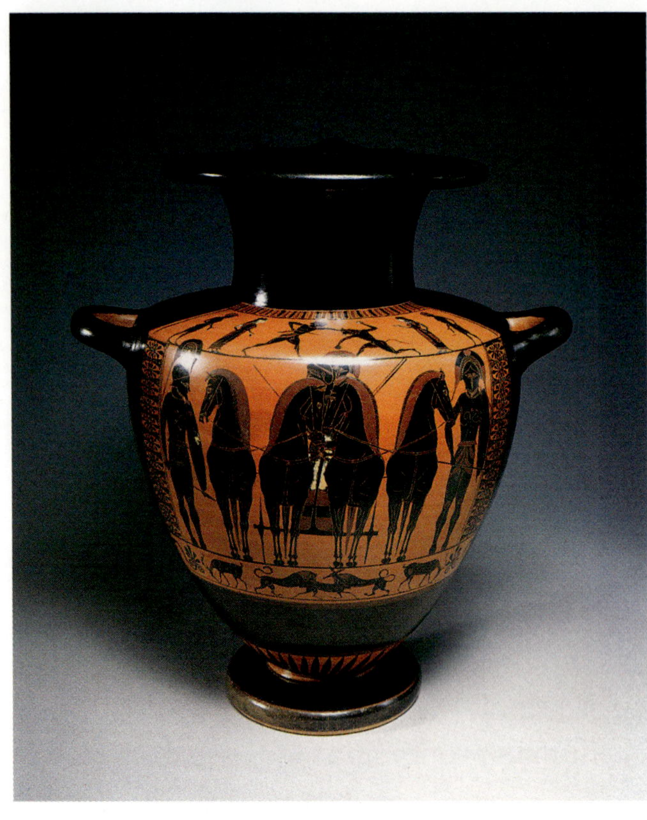

Fig. 3–16 **Study this example of a functional, decorated design. What function might this vase have served?**

Attributed to Antimenes Painter (Greek) *Hydria* c. 520 BC. Black-figure terracotta, h. 42.2 cm. The Cleveland Museum of Art, Purchase from the J. H. Wade Fund, 1975.1.

500s BCE

ca. 530–10 BCE *Hydria*

1800s

1817 First bicycle

1862 Plastics introduced for the first time

1873 First blue jeans

1900s

1914 World War I begins

1919 Bauhaus founded

1932 Breuer, *Side Chair*

1953 First color television

1980 Shire, *Peach Cup*

1985 Graves, *Tea Set*

1986 Graves, *Clock*

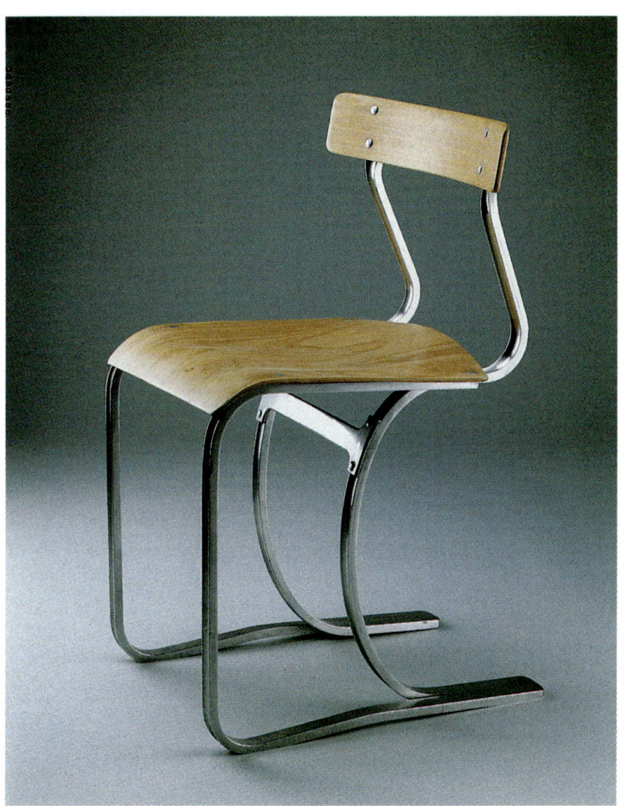

Fig. 3–17 **At first glance, this chair does not look as though it would support a lot of weight. What gives this chair its strength?**

Marcel Breuer, *Side Chair, Wohnbedarf Model 301*, 1932–34. Manufactured by Embru-Werk A.G., Ruti, Switzerland for Wohnbedart, Zurich, Plywood, aluminum 29" x 17" x 18 ½" (73.7 x 43.2 x 47.0 cm) The Wolfsonian-Florida International University, Miami Beach, FL The Mitchell Wolfson, Jr. Collection TD1993.81.2 Photo: Bruce White.

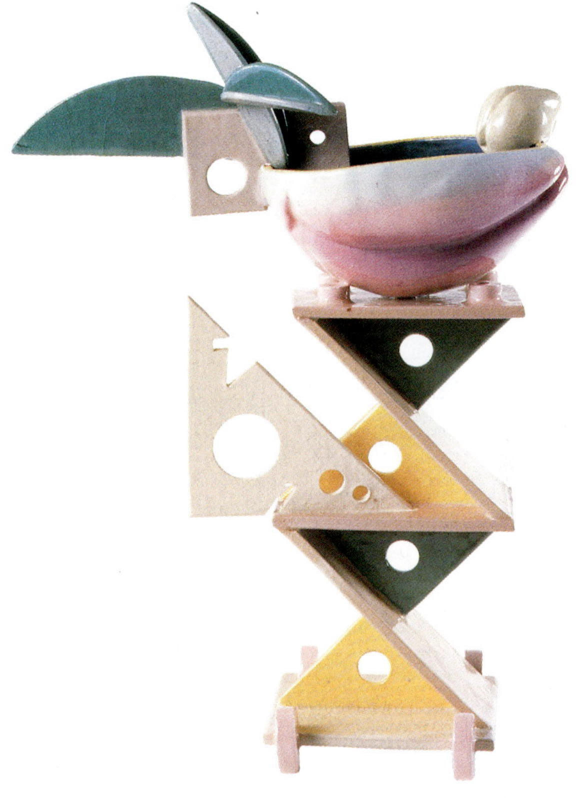

Fig. 3–18 **What shapes are repeated on this cup? Why is this cup a good example of a design by the Memphis Group?**

Peter Shire, *"California Peach" Cup, Memphis*, 1980. Glazed earthenware. Cooper-Hewitt National Design Museum, Smithsonian Institution/Art Resource, NY. Gift of Denis Gallion and Daniel Morris, 1988-60-3.

Design in Your World In 1981, the Memphis Group was founded. Their designs included furniture, fabric, and ceramics, such as the cup on this page. The group used bold colors in new ways. They also borrowed from many sources, including the architectural styles of ancient Greece and Rome.

Since the 1980s many designers have become interested in "people friendly" creations. Their designs are ergonomic. Ergonomic designs are built to help the user be more comfortable, usually at work. Designers use their knowledge of the human body to create objects that people can use easily and safely. Look around your home and school for examples of ergonomic design.

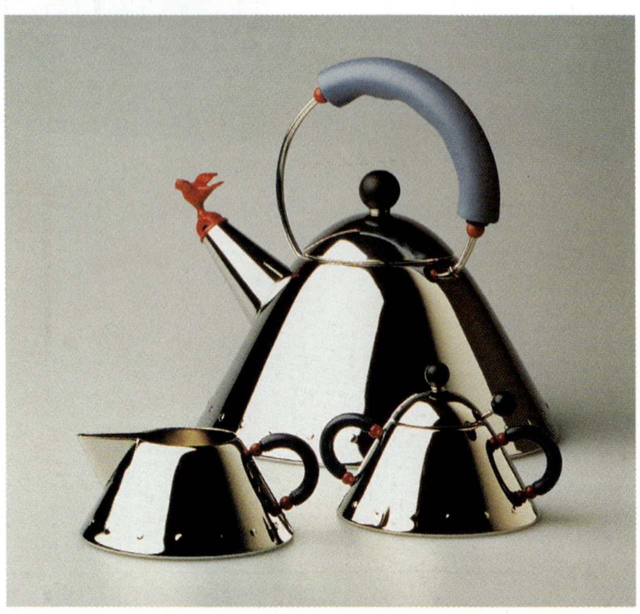

Fig. 3–19 **What visual elements were repeated in this tea set? Why did Graves put a bird on the spout of the kettle?**

Michael Graves, *Whistling Bird Teakettle*, 1985. Stainless steel and plastic, height (teakettle): 9.5" (24 cm). Alessi, S.p.a., Crusinallo, Italy.

Designers today also think about how their objects will fit into modern society. Designer Michael Graves has an educated eye and whimsy, which is a kind of humor. He designs products that are both classic and fun.

The Art of Design Graves, who is also an architect, looks to traditions of architecture when making many of his designs. This clock **(Fig. 3–20)** shows how he mixes classical, simple styles with his imagination. The clock that Graves made looks like a building. Many of his products have symmetry, or similar placement of parts on opposite sides. But Graves always adds something different to create a sense of fun.

Meet Michael Graves

As a child in Indiana, Michael Graves loved to draw. "The more I drew, the better I got," he says. As an architecture student, he experimented with product design. He filled his sketchbooks with designs for furniture and other objects. His sketches were soon made into real products. Graves has created his own special designs for many products. During the 1980s, he designed for the Memphis Group. Today, his products are very popular.

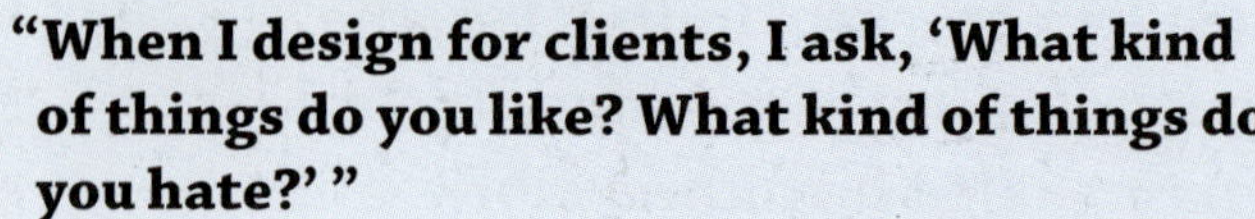

"When I design for clients, I ask, 'What kind of things do you like? What kind of things do you hate?' "

— Michael Graves (born 1934)

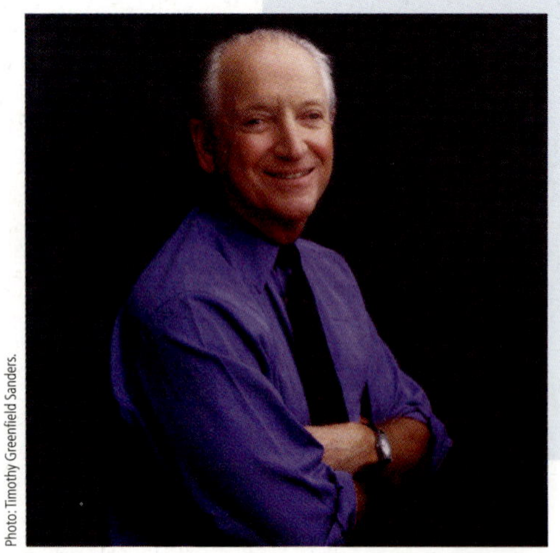

Photo: Timothy Greenfield Sanders.

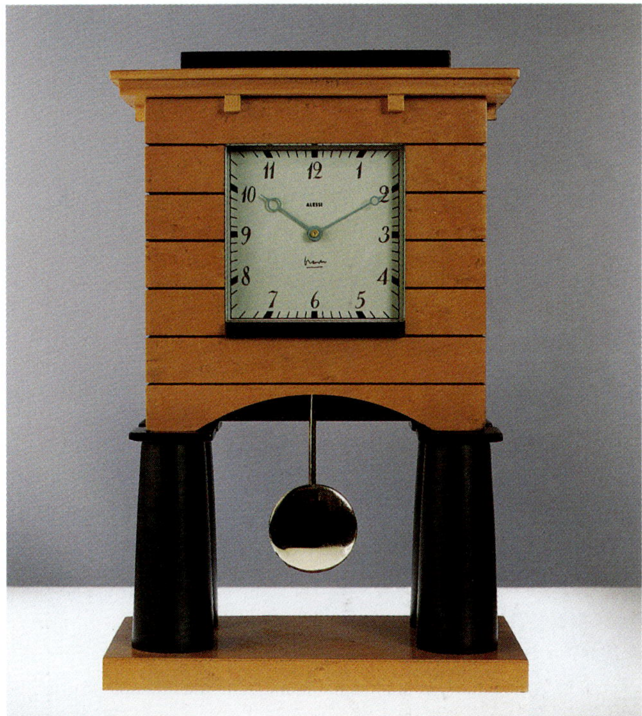

Fig. 3–20 **What parts of classical Greek buildings do you think influenced Graves when he designed this clock?**

Michael Graves, *Mantel Clock for Alessi*, 1986. Ebonized wood, stained birdseye maple, green oxidized metal watch hands, 18k gold dot at center hand pivot, terra cotta numerals, off-white face, 18k gold pendulum with satin fish. Photo by William Taylor. Alessi, S.p.a., Crusinallo, Italy.

Check Your Understanding

1. What qualities does Michael Graves bring together in his designs of products?
2. Compare and contrast Bauhaus and Memphis designs.
3. Look at the chair in Fig. 3–17. How does its function determine its form?

Studio Time

Form and Function

Make a ceramic container, such as a teacup, that has a specific purpose.

- Use slab, coil, and pinch methods, alone or in combination. As you design your container, think about its function and the form you want it to have.
- Will your container be as simple and functional as possible? Any surface patterns should be functional. For example, a pattern of tea leaves would suggest the use of a teacup.
- Or, will your container be functional, but be more playful with its design and surface pattern? For example, you could use the slab method to make your teacup out of a three-dimensional "T."

Reflect on how well form and decoration contribute to the function of your container.

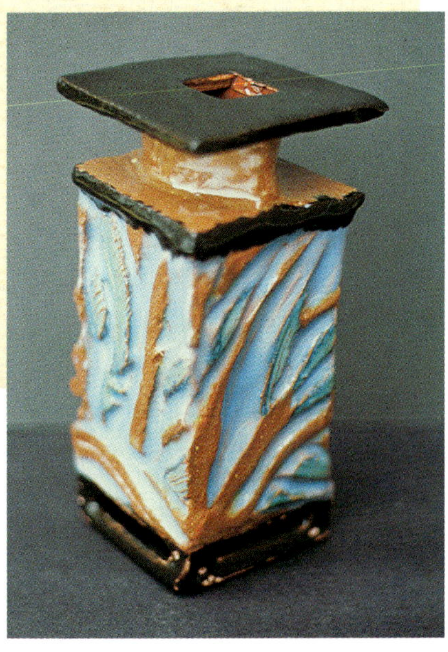

Fig. 3–21
Student artwork

Design in Japan

A Tradition of Product Design The design of functional and beautiful everyday objects has a long history in Japan. Artists created by hand the many objects used in daily life. Many artists followed traditional rules of design. One rule, *wabi*, is the idea of finding beauty in simple, natural things. *Wabi* also means enjoying things that are not perfect or regular. Another rule, *sabi*, refers to timelessness and simplicity.

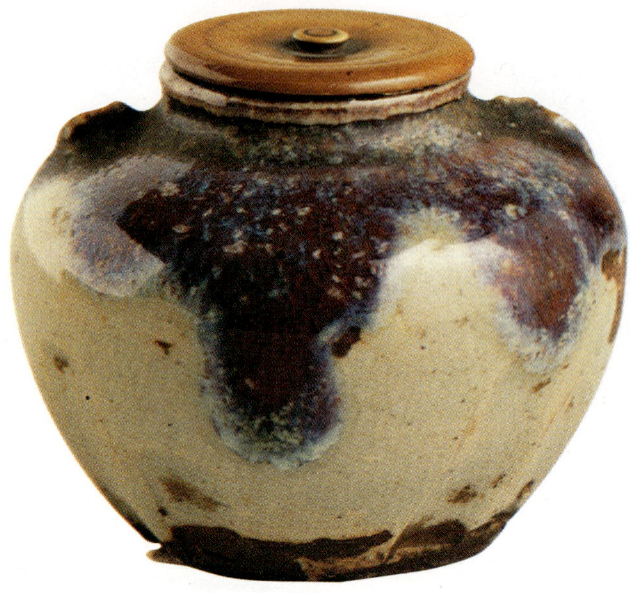

Fig. 3–22 **Look at the design on this tea jar. How does it reflect the tradition of *wabi?***

Japan, Owari province, *Tea Jar*, 19th century. Pottery, height: 1 ¾" (4 cm). Philadelphia Museum of Art: The Louis E. Stern Collection. Photo by Eric Mitchell, 1981.

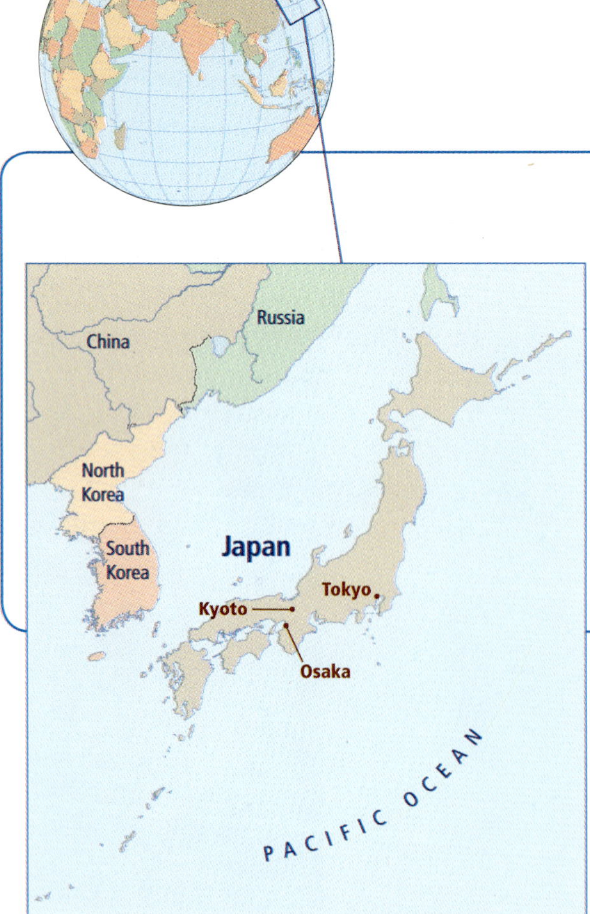

Social Studies Connection

Japan is an island nation in the West Pacific. Its weather and geography make it a great place for growing tea on steep hillsides. Tea has long been an important part of Japanese life. For centuries, preparing tea leaves and serving tea have been performed in a ritual known as the tea ceremony. An important part of the ceremony is the use of beautiful utensils.

Designs Tied to Nature Today, some Japanese designers still create objects for traditional ceremonies, as they have done for centuries. They want their designs to be beautiful and natural looking. These designers make products with simple shapes, small sizes, and fine details, such as the kettle on this page. Many products made in Japan today, such as high-tech electronic products, are not tied to tradition. However, today's designers still create products with natural-looking forms.

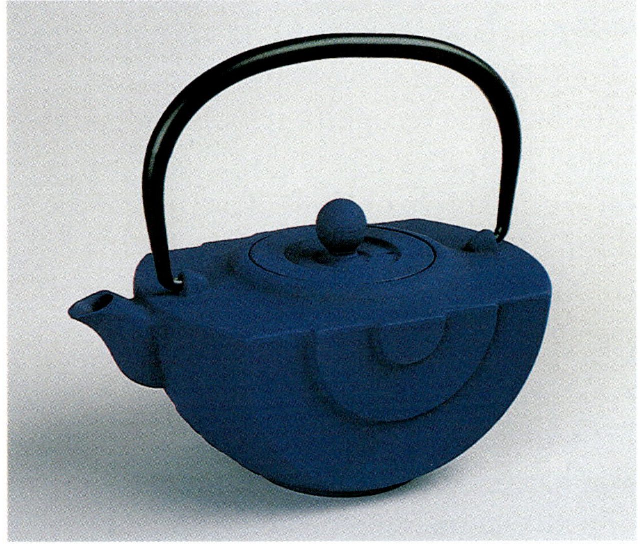

Fig. 3–24 **Compare and contrast this teakettle to those you are familiar with. How are they alike? How are they different?**

Japan, *Nanbu Iron Kettle*, 21st century. Cast iron, height: 5 ½" (14 cm). Photo courtesy of Davis Art Images.

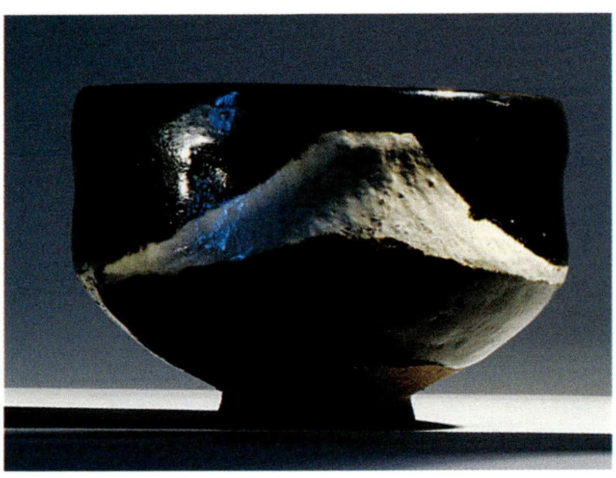

Fig. 3–23 **What was the inspiration for the decoration on this teacup?**

Cup used in the tea ceremony, bearing an image of Mount Fuji. Coll. Philip Goldman, London, Great Britain. Photo Credit: Werner Forman / Art Resource NY.

Visual Culture

In most communities, there are shops and stores that specialize in products for the home such as dishes, glasses, and cooking and eating utensils. Take some time to look at the many different styles and types of utensils that are available in these stores or in catalogues. Why do you think there are so many different varieties of the same thing? What items in particular catch your eye? Why do they appeal to you?

3.5 Continued

Designing for Daily Life Toshiyuki Kita, a well-known Japanese designer, is a careful observer of people's daily lives. Kita uses both Japanese and Western ideas about design in clever ways. He gained international recognition for his adjustable *Wink Chair*, shown below, which builds on the Japanese practice of sitting on the floor. At the same time, it provides the comfort and support of a recliner chair that is popular in Western design.

Designing for the Future Kita designs his products to be comfortable, functional, and natural looking. He considers the effect of new technologies on lifestyles and the environment and explores the relationship between people and materials. When he designs, he tries to hold on to the past while taking a giant step forward. In his designs, such as the tableware shown on the next page, Kita looks to past traditions in Japan while creating products for the future. What is modern about this design?

Meet Toshiyuki Kita

Toshiyuki Kita is a Japanese industrial designer who works in Osaka, Japan. He was born in 1942 and took an early interest in traditional Japanese craftwork. He designs objects that look beautiful and meet human needs. When he designs, he thinks of the tools we use daily.

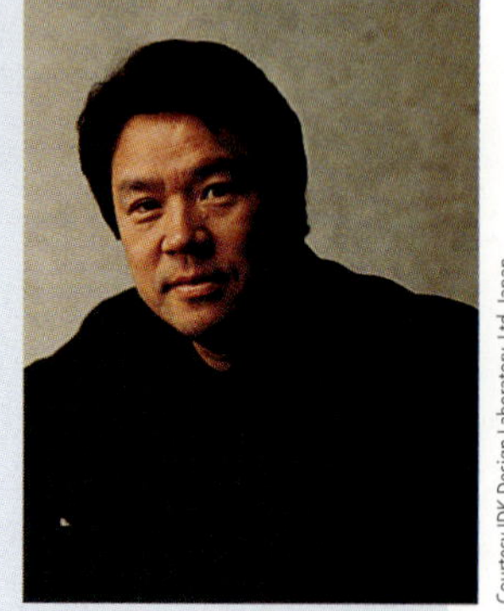

Courtesy IDK Design Laboratory, Ltd. Japan.

Kita's designs show his interest in the harmony of technology and people's lives. He thinks about the look of objects from the past, the needs of the present, and meanings for the future.

"Design has no national border."

— Toshiyuki Kita (born 1942)

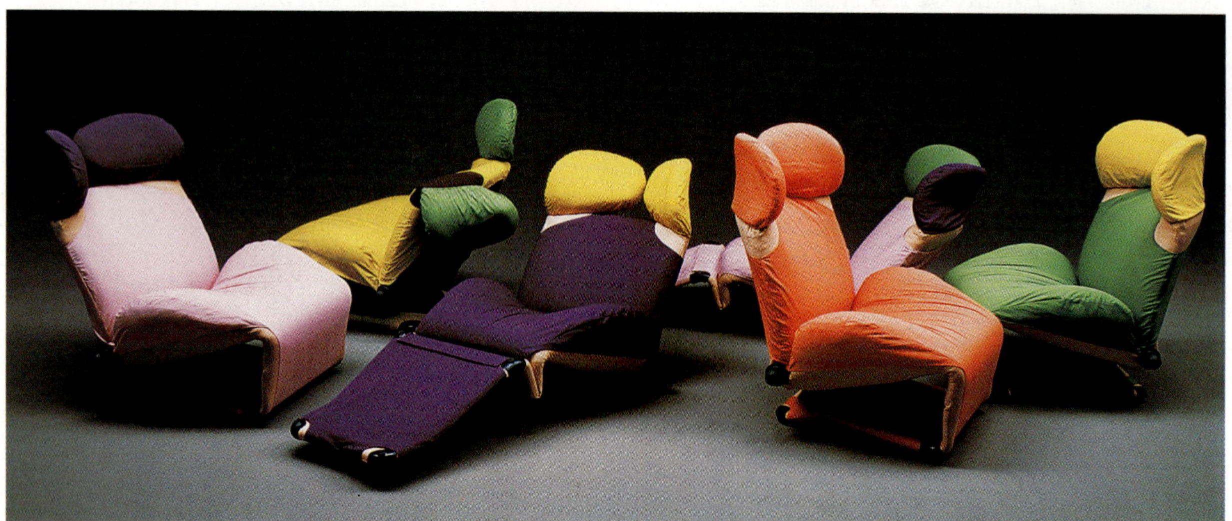

Fig. 3–25 **What design elements make these chairs seem comfortable? Why do you think the designer named them *Wink Chairs*?**

Toshiyuki Kita, *Wink Chairs*, 1980. Steel, foam, polyurethane, dimensions variable, in upright position: 34 ½" x 30 ½" x 37 ½" (90 x 78 x 95 cm). Courtesy IDK Design Laboratory, Ltd., Japan.

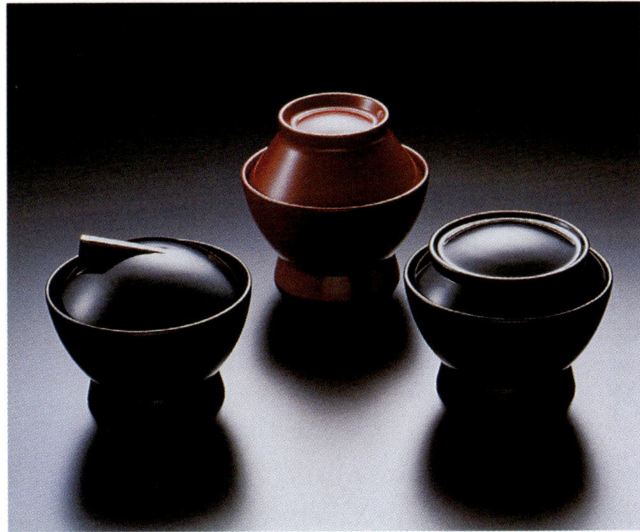

Fig. 3–26 **This tableware is lacquered, which makes it appear highly polished. Using wood for tableware is a strong tradition in Japan. How are these bowls examples of simplicity in design?**

Toshiyuki Kita, *Urushi Tableware*, 1986. Lacquered wood, height: 3 3/16" (8.1 cm), diameter 5 1/8" (13 cm). Omukai Koshudo Company, Wajima, Japan. Courtesy of IDK Design Laboratory, Ltd., Japan.

Check Your Understanding

1. What are two rules of traditional Japanese design, and what do they stand for?
2. What does the design of many Japanese high-tech products have in common with that of traditional everyday objects?
3. Review the products in this lesson that were designed by Toshiyuki Kita. Give an example of how he combines Japanese and Western ideas about design. What three things does Kita try to create in a well-designed product?

Studio Time

A 3-D Prototype

You can develop a 3-D prototype (model) for a new product line of tableware.

- Start by making a series of pencil sketches as a way to explore different possibilities for the design of utensils we use every day for eating—knives, forks, and spoons.
- You might start by drawing a set of tableware from observation. Then think about how you want to change the look of the utensils.
- Consider both decorative and practical features as you design your flatware.
- To make the three-dimensional models, consider using cardboard, wire, aluminum foil, metal tooling foil, or found materials.

Reflect on the decorative and practical features of the forms you create.

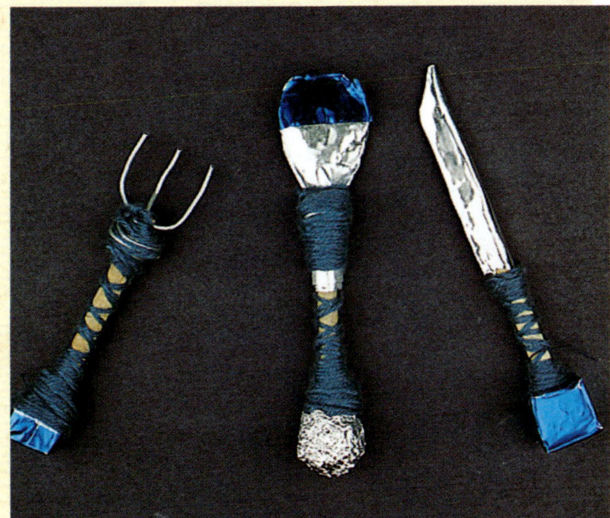

Fig. 3–27 Student artwork

Marketing in Three Dimensions

Studio Background

As you walk down the cereal aisle of your grocery store, which packages catch your eye? Some cereal boxes have bright and exciting designs that seem to say, “If you buy this cereal, you will have fun!” Other designs send messages about how healthy you can be if you eat the cereal inside.

Businesses use graphic designers to help market and sell their products. Graphic designers are artists who create artwork for packages, posters, and other printed material. With so much product competition, package designs need to be visually appealing.

In this studio exploration, you will create a package design for a product or store of your choice. Choose a product or kind of store for which you would like to design a package. For example, you may want to design the packaging for a toy, a shoebox, or a music store shopping bag. Use line, shape, color, and pattern to send a message about your product or store. A pattern is made up of lines, colors, and shapes repeated in a planned way.

You Will Need

- cardboard box or shopping bag
- construction paper
- markers
- scissors
- glue
- collage materials

Inspiration from Our World

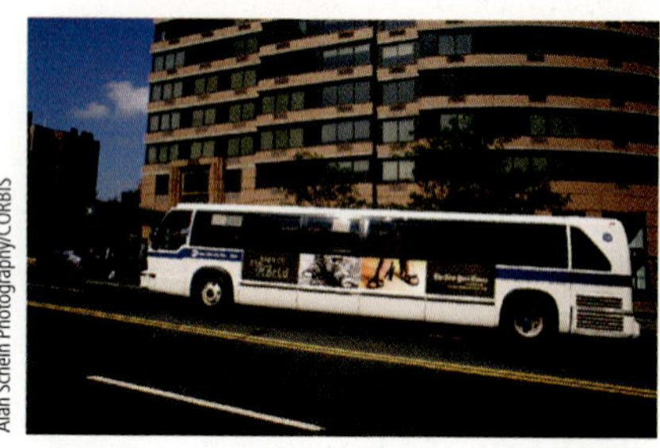

Alan Schein Photography/CORBIS

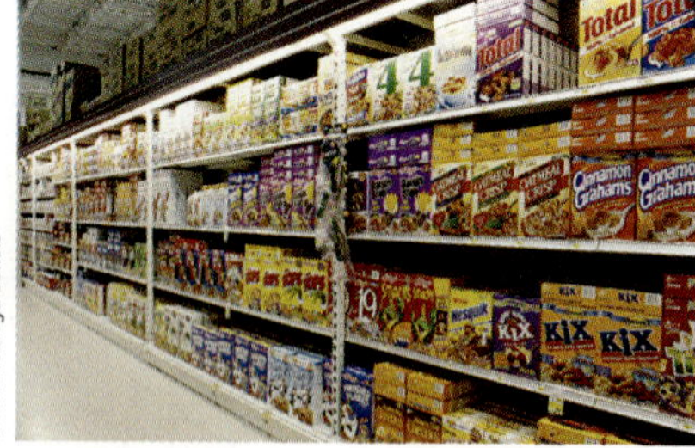

© Chuck Savage/CORBIS

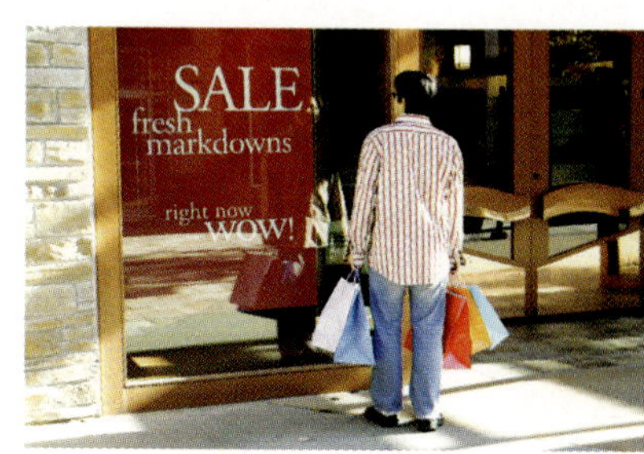

Step 1 **Plan and Practice**

- Choose the product or kind of store for which you will design a package.
- Identify the message you want your packaging to express.
- Decide what size and shape the package should be.
- Draw a rough sketch of your design idea.

Things to Remember:

✓ Choose colors, shapes, materials, words, and images that will make your design exciting.

✓ Use graphics and other elements of design, such as patterns, to help express your message.

✓ Design the package so it will appeal to your target audience (the people who will buy the product).

Inspiration from Art

Today, there are millions of products and hundreds of stores from which to buy them. Graphic designers create packages that will sell a product or promote a store. For example, they might try to make one kind of shampoo or one brand of cold medicine stand apart from the rest. They might also make the corporate image of a store stand apart from other stores. They may create designs to fit a standard container, such as a coffee can, perfume box, or shopping bag. They sometimes design packages that have one-of-a-kind forms.

Graphic designers answer several questions as they create a package design. The ability to answer questions like these is the key to designing successful packaging:

- What size and shape should the package be?
- What materials should be used?
- What message should the design send?
- Who will buy the product?
- What kind of graphics will best send the message?

Fig. 3–28 **How does this package help you recognize the product? Why is this package an example of effective graphic design?**

The Museum of Modern Art.

Step 2 **Begin to Create**

- **Think about the product or store you want to promote on your container.** What images come to mind when you think of your subject? What name, brief saying, or other words can you include to attract the buyers' attention? Look at the questions in the Inspiration from Art section on the previous page for ideas.

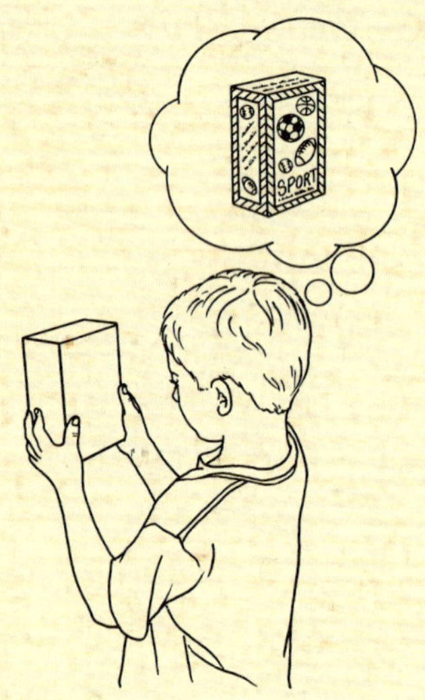

- Design your container. Notice the shapes and sizes of the front, back, and sides of your container. Remember that the design is seen on all sides of the package. How can you use these spaces to create an exciting design? Where can you use a pattern?

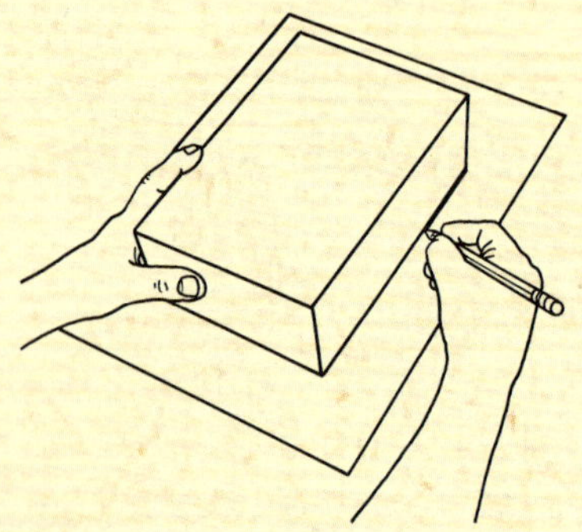

- **Trace the sides of your container onto construction paper** and cut out the panels to create a background.
- Choose one or more paper colors that will best express your message.
- **Use markers and collage materials to create words and images for your package.** Will you create a pattern in the background or in the images and words? Will you create your own images or cut them out of a magazine? Will you draw your words, or will you cut letters out of paper and glue them onto the panels?

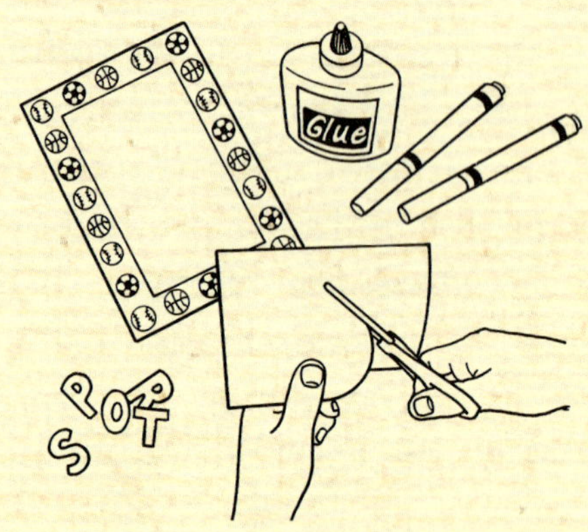

- **Put it together.** Carefully glue the construction-paper panels to the sides of your box or bag.

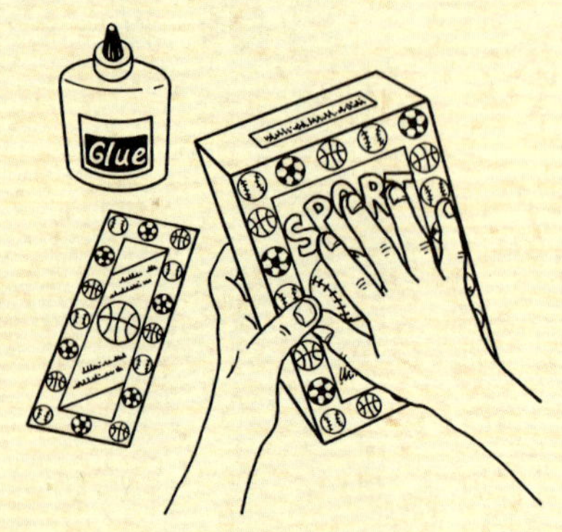

Step 3 **Revise**

Did you remember to:

✓ Choose colors, shapes, materials, words, and images that will make your design exciting?

✓ Use graphics and other elements of design, such as patterns, to help express your message?

✓ Design the package so it appeals to your target audience (the people who will buy the product)?

Adjust your work if necessary. In your sketchbook, make a note of your revisions and why you made them.

Step 4 **Add Finishing Touches**

- Are there any images, shapes, words, or colors that you want to add?
- Can additional patterns make the packaging more interesting or visually appealing?

Step 5 **Share and Reflect**

- When designers complete a project for a client, they present their ideas and explain what they have done and why. Prepare a presentation about your package design.
- Get together with two of your classmates, and take turns playing the roles of presenter and clients.
- Be sure to explain how your design decisions fit the audience and your client's intended message.
- What does your design suggest about your product or store?
- How will this design appeal to your customers?

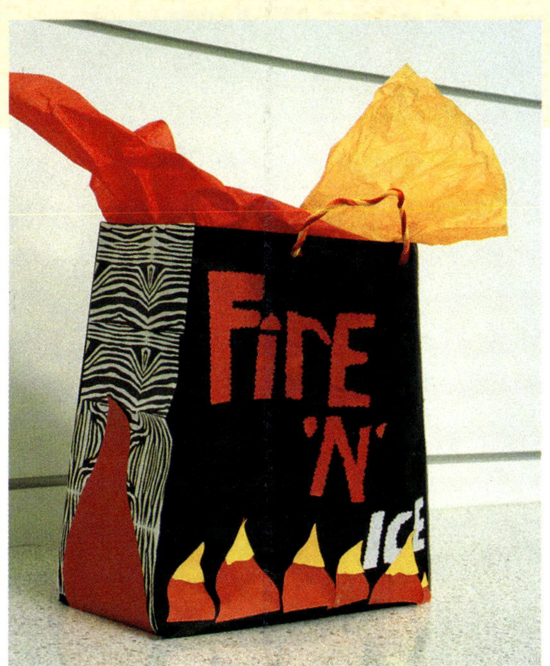

Fig. 3–29 Student artwork

Art Criticism

Describe What colors, words, and images did the artist use for the design of this shopping bag?

Analyze How did the artist use pattern in the design of this package?

Interpret What message is conveyed by the design of this shopping bag?

Evaluate What's especially effective about the design of this shopping bag?

Mathematics

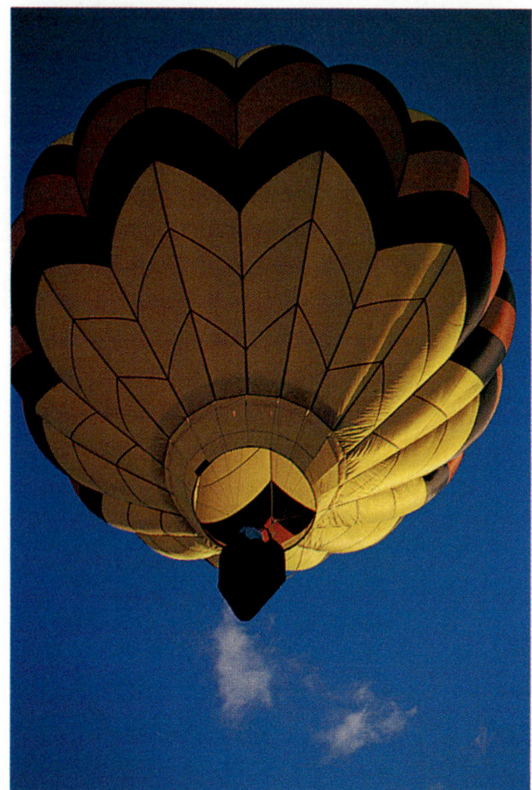

Fig. 3–30 **What other objects can you think of that illustrate the concept of cylindrical symmetry?**

Photo: courtesy of Anette Macintire.

Hot-air balloons, jellyfish, and umbrellas all share a mathematical concept called cylindrical symmetry. The top and bottom of an object with cylindrical symmetry may be different, but all distances are the same from its vertical axis. You may remember a childhood toy that included a set of different-sized rings that you placed over a central rod. The rings were different sizes, but they shared a vertical axis, and thus were cylindrically symmetrical.

Theater

Theater requires the talent of many different special designers. The stage designer creates a set that communicates the mood of the show. Lighting designers decide which parts of the set and which actors to call attention to. The lighting (for example, a spotlight on characters who are saying important things) helps direct the audience's attention. The costume designer uses clothing to help express the personalities of different characters. What other features do you think add to a theater performance?

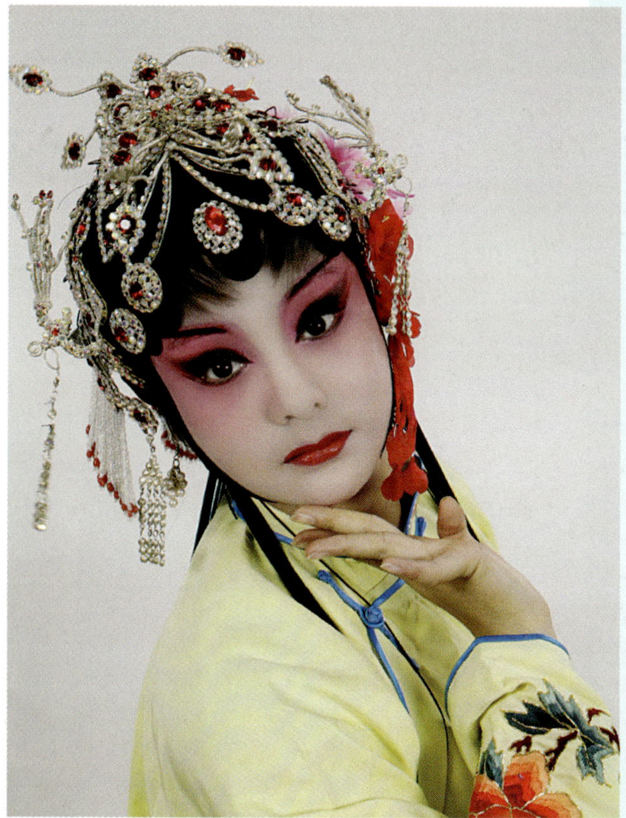

Fig. 3–31

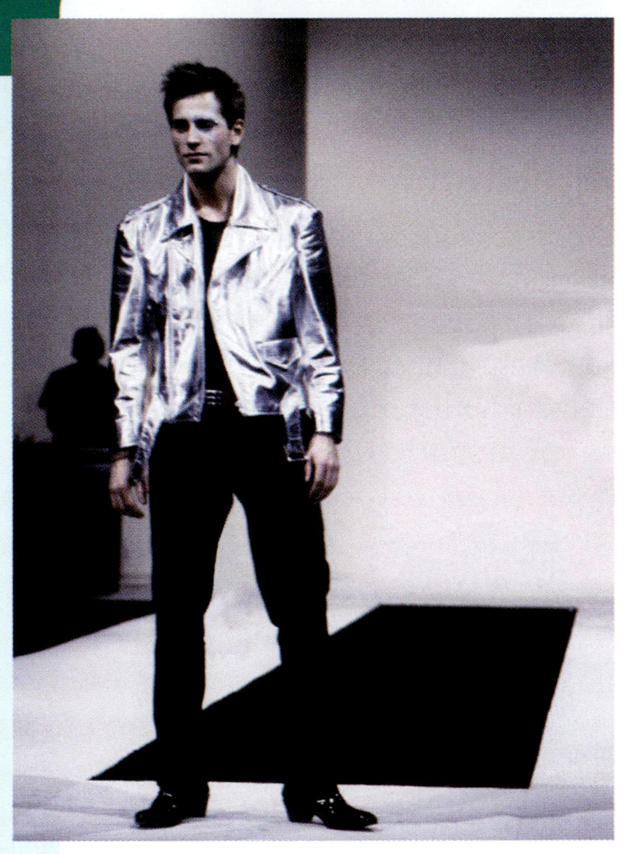

Careers **Fashion**

Fashion designers help create the many clothing articles, shoes, and accessories that people buy each year. Some fashion designers are well-known because of their creations for music and movie stars. Many lesser-known fashion designers sell their work through department stores, specialty stores, and mail order or online catalogues. Students interested in a career in fashion design may earn degrees in fashion merchandising or fashion design through college or university art departments or fashion-design institutes.

Fig. 3–32 **Fashion designers may specialize in women's, men's, or children's clothing. They may design casual, business, or formal clothing. What might this designer's specialty be?**

Photo © Andres Aquino, FashionSyndicatePress.com

Daily Life

You may not pay much attention to many of the designed objects that surround you. The toothbrush you use, the clothes you wear, and the wrapper on your gum are all objects that were designed with a purpose. They are designed to work properly, to attract your attention, to make you comfortable, to fit your body, or to encourage you to buy. Try to notice these objects for one day and see how many you can count.

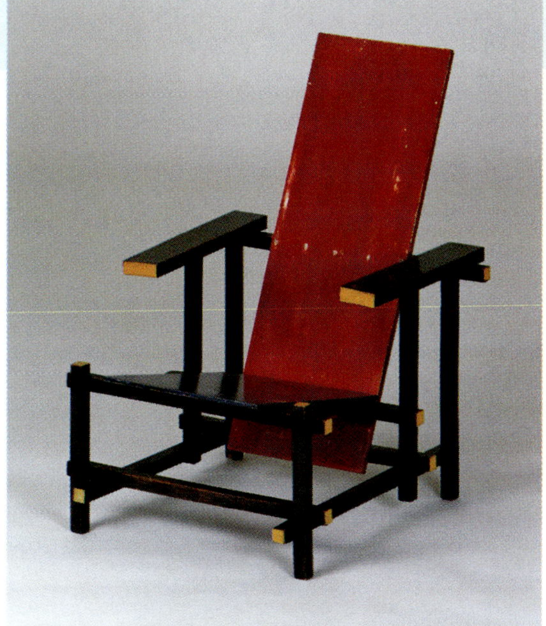

Fig. 3–33 **How would you describe the form of this chair? How does the chair fulfill its function?**

Gerrit T. Rietveld, *Rood Blauwe Stoel (Red Blue Chair)*, 1918. Painted wood, 34 ½" to 26" to 32 ½" (88 x 66x 83 cm). G. van de Groenedkan, NL–Utrecht. Vitra Design Musuem, Weil am Rhein. Artists Rights Society (ARS), NY.

Vocabulary Review

Match each art term below with its definition.

graphic designer
ergonomic
proportions
function
form
pattern

1. how a product looks
2. the size relationship between one part of the body and another
3. how a product works
4. built to help a user be more comfortable, usually at work
5. repetitions of lines, shapes, or colors
6. an artist who creates the artwork for packages, posters, and other printed material

Aesthetic Thinking

Designers consider form and function when creating artworks. When do you think about the form and function of something you create? Your list might include the way you organize your room or take notes.

Write About Art

In this scene from *Major Barbara*, the scenic designer Robert Mark Morgan captures a main character's visions of war. Morgan represents these visions using small- and large-scale models, that when combined create a powerful image. Why might this scene shock its viewers? How is this stage design similar to a painting? How is it different?

Fig. 3–34 Robert Mark Morgan, *Act III Major Barbara Stage Design,* San Jose Repertory Theatre. Photo: Robert Mark Morgan.

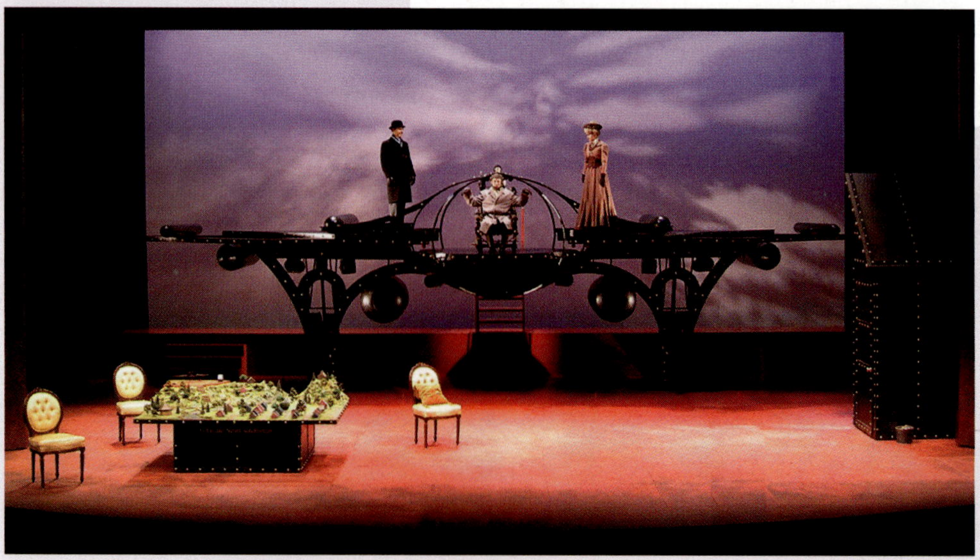

Art Criticism

Describe What do you see in this photograph of a vessel?

Analyze How do the surface designs reflect the shape of this drinking cup?

Interpret What do the two large handles tell us about the function of this vessel?

Evaluate Do you think that the artist thought of this cup primarily as a functional object or as a work of art?

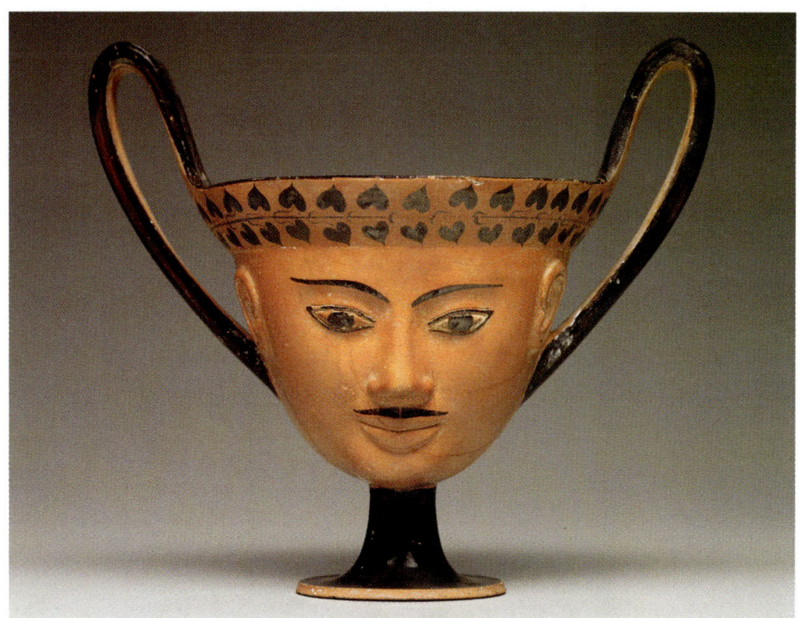

Fig. 3–35 Greek, East Greek, *High-handled drinking cup (kantharos)*, Archaic period, 550–525 BC. Asia Minor (Turkey), Ionia, Miletus Ceramic, Black Figure Height: 6 13/16" (17.3 cm). Museum of Fine Arts, Boston Henry Lillie Pierce Fund, 98.925.

Meet the Artists

Ancient Ceramic artists in ancient Greece worked in one of two main styles: black-figure and red-figure. In the black-figure style, shown in the drinking cup in Fig. 3–35, the artist painted the shapes using black slip—or watered-down clay—against the natural terra-cotta background.

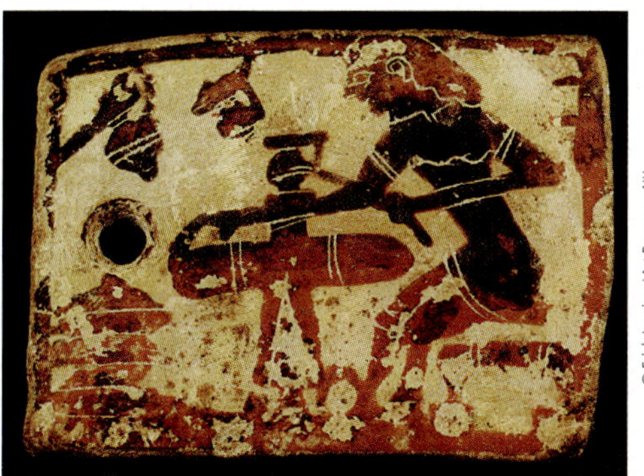

For Your Sketchbook

Use your sketchbook to collect images you see in the world and in print. On a page, paste an envelope or pocket for keeping clippings of designs you like.

For Your Portfolio

Choose one of your artworks from this unit. Identify its form and function. Think about what you like about the artwork and what you would change if you reworked it.

Unit 4

Artists Are Teachers

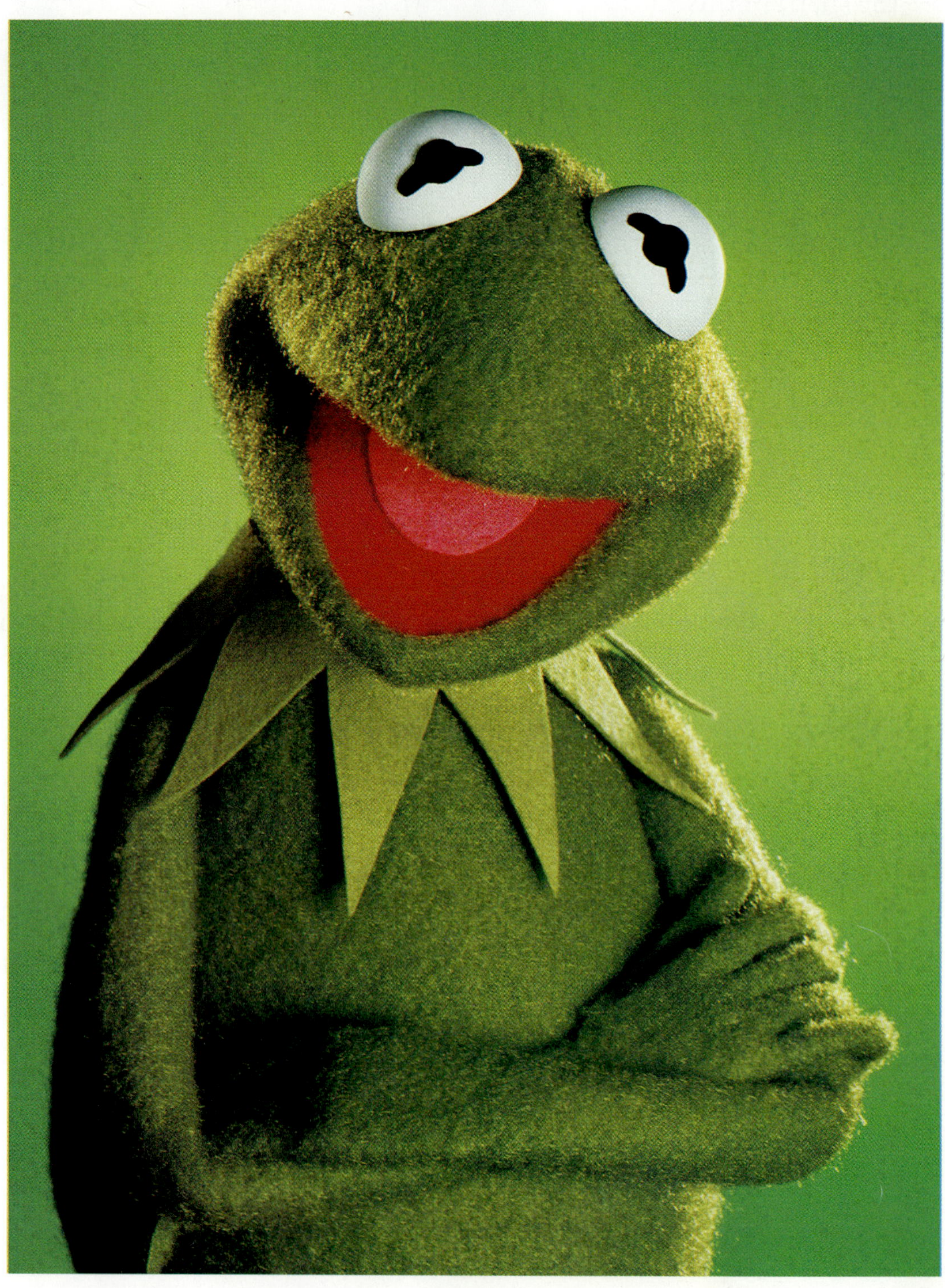

Fig. 4–1 **Kermit has become familiar to children and adults throughout the world. What lessons do you remember learning from puppets or fictional characters such as Kermit?**

Kermit ©The Jim Henson Company.

Parents and siblings teach us how to do many things—tie our shoes, ride a bike, and even to read. We learn from our classmates and teachers too. For example, we learn about important people, events in history, and ideas in science and math.

We also learn from our experiences outside of home and school. Some of the most important things we learn are good habits (such as working hard) and values (such as the importance of caring for the environment). Grandparents, neighbors, and people we see on television are some of the teachers among us.

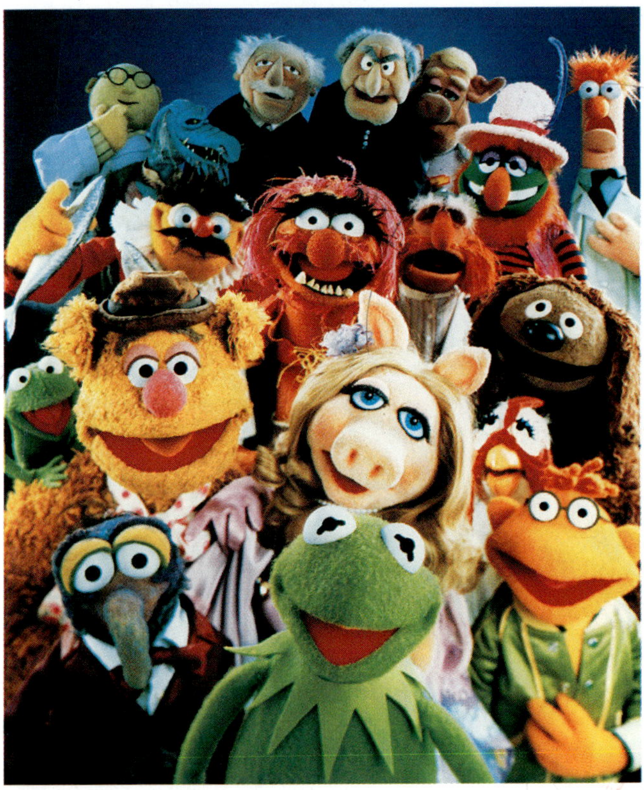

Fig. 4–2 **Muppets are soft and flexible. This allows them to show different facial expressions. Why might this be important for a teaching puppet?**

In this unit, you will learn:

- How artists create artworks that teach values and beliefs.
- How to make sculptures and drawings to teach important lessons.
- How to look at artworks and see meaning through images, objects, and words.

Making a Point

The artist Jim Henson created Kermit the Frog and other Muppets. For over thirty years, his *Sesame Street* characters have taught small children important lessons, such as to count and sound out words, and to be polite and responsible in daily life.

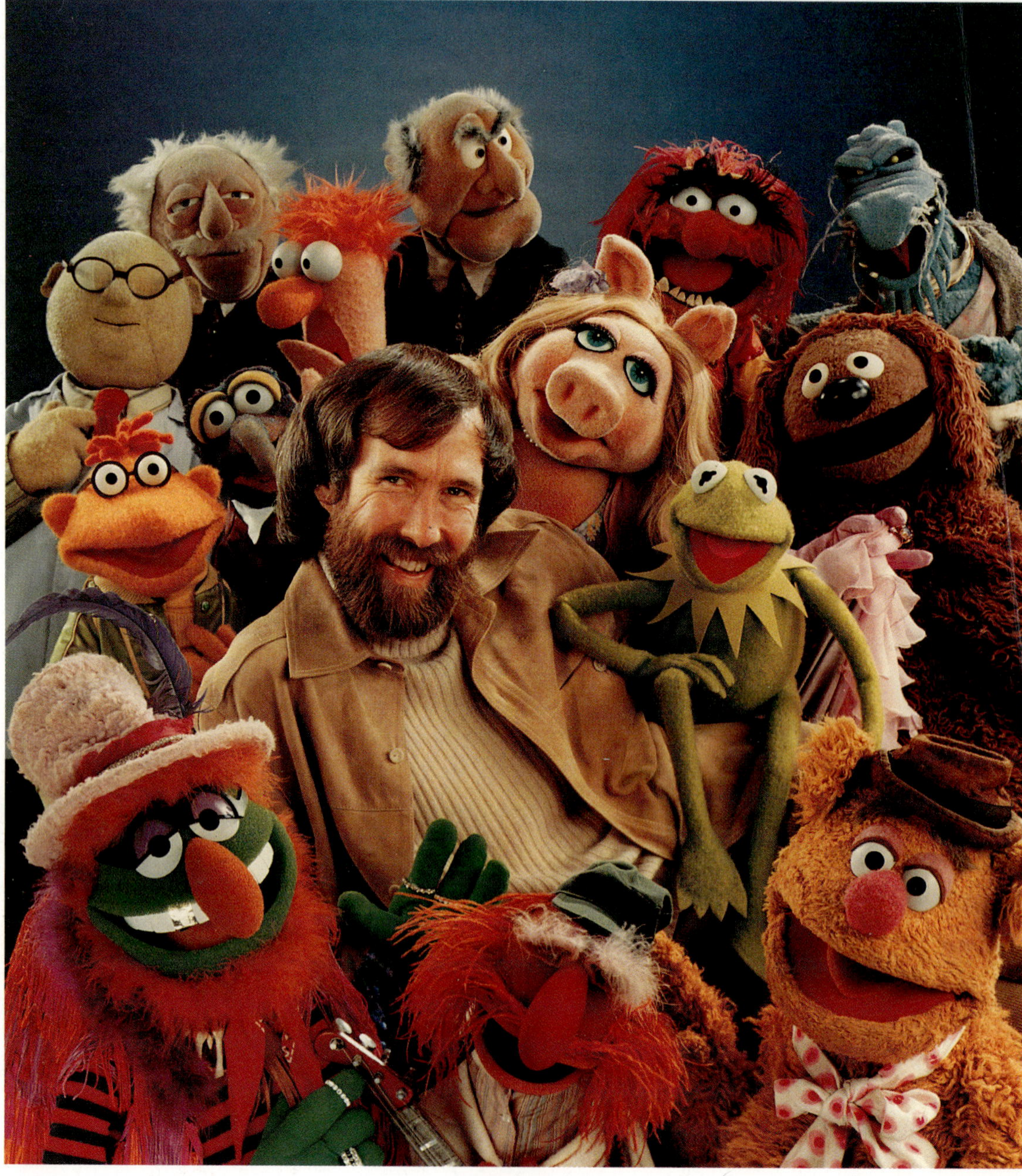

Fig 4–3 **Jim Henson used his sense of humor to create characters that children enjoyed. What is your first impression of the characters in this image?**

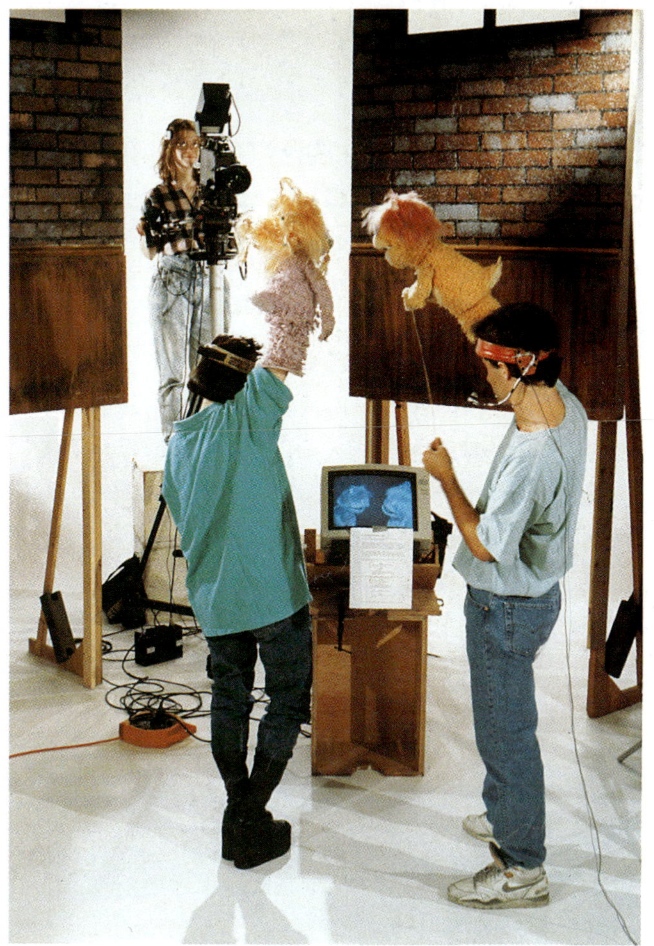

Fig. 4–4 **The arms or hands of Muppets are attached to rods. The rods are controlled from below by puppeteers.**

Puppeteers Handling Muppets. ©The Jim Henson Company. Photo: John E. Barrett.

Working Together From early on, Henson collaborated, or worked with others. He and Jane Nebel, whom he later married, brought in others to work with them. Eventually, Henson created a group of puppets for a new show called *Sesame Street*. His work resulted in the "birth" of the Muppets: Ernie and Bert, Oscar the Grouch, Grover, Cookie Monster, and Big Bird. Collaboration is important because it takes many people to operate the Muppets. The puppeteers all must work together to make a successful show.

Meet Jim Henson

When Jim Henson was a boy, he loved to use different art materials and techniques to make things. Henson's interests in art, theater, and television all came together when he got a job as a puppeteer on a local children's television show. He was only eighteen. One year later, Henson created Kermit, his most famous puppet.

Over the years, Henson and his team created many more Muppets for *Sesame Street* and other television shows and movies. Henson's great sense of humor helped his characters teach important information and good habits in a fun and entertaining way.

"My hope still is to leave the world a little bit better for my having been here."

—Jim Henson (1936–1990)

©The Jim Henson Company.

4.1 Continued

Teaching for a Better World Through artworks, artists can teach people about cultural traditions, community values, and historical facts. Artists must make choices about what lesson to teach and how to help their viewers learn that lesson. To do so, one thing artists think about is scale (the size of the artworks they will create). Small figures and other small-scale objects are very useful for teaching. For example, the Hopi of the American Southwest use kachina figures like those shown here **(Fig. 4–5)** to help teach about important Hopi religious beliefs.

Learning from the Past Throughout history, artists have created artworks for religious or public buildings. These artworks remind people of shared values and beliefs. Artists have also created structures to teach about events and people from the past. In recent times, artists have created artworks to teach us to think differently about issues facing our society. In her installation called *The Dinner Party*, artist Judy Chicago teaches about the historical contributions of women. Each place setting at the table represents an important woman in history.

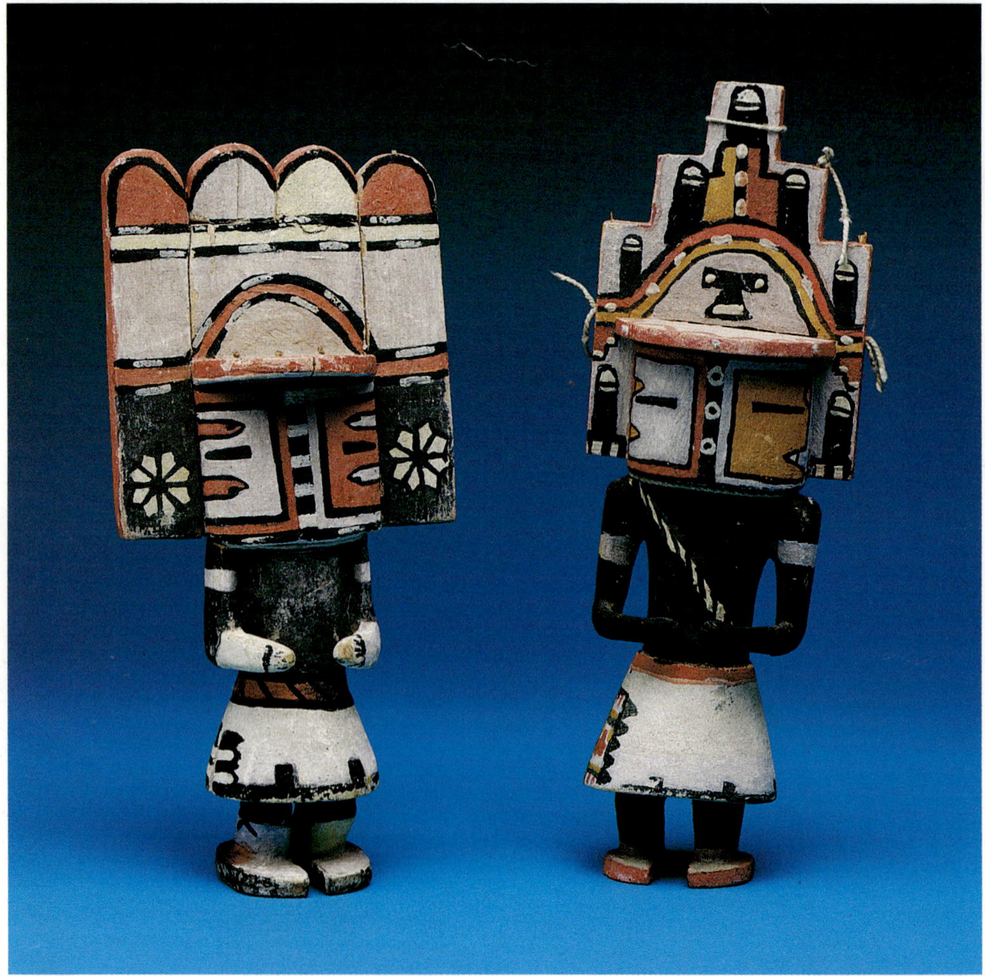

Fig. 4–5 **Hopi children use figures such as these to help them remember each kachina's story and special religious function.**

Native American (Hopi), *Si'ohemiskatsina* (right) and *Nimankatsina* (left), c. 1900. Carved and painted wood. Fred Harvey Collection, Heard Museum, Phoenix, Arizona.

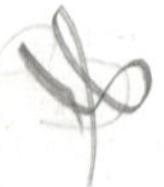

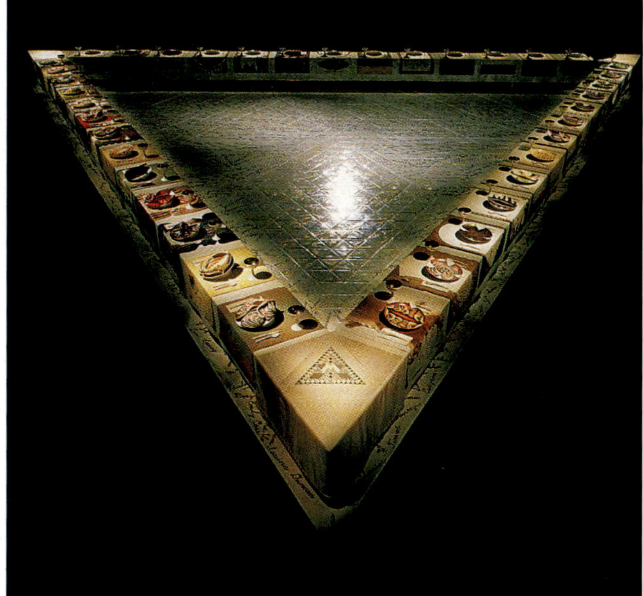

Fig. 4–6 **Judy Chicago gathered many people together to help her create this installation. When assembled, it fills an enormous room.**

Judy Chicago, *The Dinner Party*, 1979. Mixed media. 48' x 42' x 3' (15 x 13 x 1 cm) Collection: The Dinner Party Trust. Photo: Donald Woodman. © 2001 Judy Chicago/ Artists Rights Society (ARS), New York.

Check Your Understanding

1. When artists plan to make artworks for the purpose of teaching, what must they think about?

2. Compare and contrast Jim Henson's Muppets and Hopi kachina figures. In what ways are they the same? How are they different?

3. How do artworks about the past help you learn?

Studio Time

A Current Collage

Create an artwork about a news event that concerns you.

- Use different kinds and colors of paper. Experiment with parts of images from magazines and newspapers.
- Try to use an abstract or nonobjective style to show the emotions surrounding this event and your feelings about it.
- Show your work to a partner. What does he or she think the meaning of your artwork is?
- Have your partner point to specific details in your work to support his or her understanding. Why might people have different reactions to the same work of art?

Reflect on how well your collage communicates your intended message.

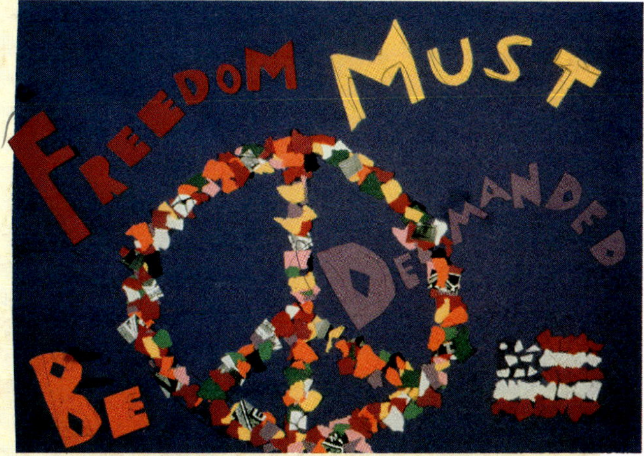

Fig. 4–7 Student artwork

Lettering and Calligraphy

Writing with Calligraphy Calligraphy is a form of beautiful lettering. For years, people have used it to record ideas in books, on scrolls, and in other important documents. During the Middle Ages in Europe, monks and nuns used calligraphy to make copies of religious books.

In Japan, there is a long tradition of practicing calligraphy as a form of self-discipline and meditation. Today, people still use calligraphy to create special handwritten messages.

abcdefghijklm
nopqrstuvwxyz
ABCDEFGHIJKL
MNOPQRSTUVW
XYZ

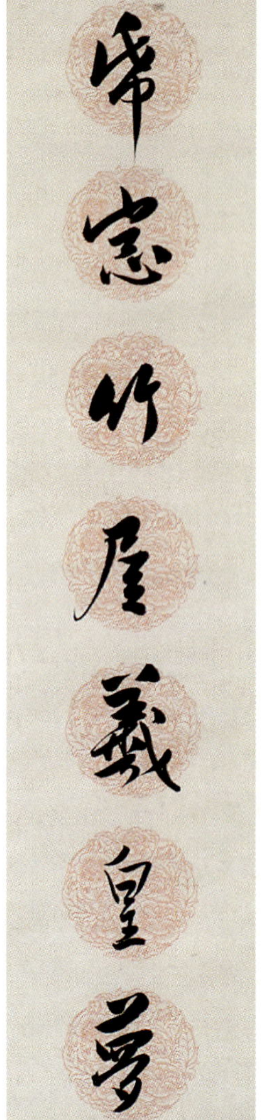

Fig. 4–8 **Notice the intricate designs in this image. Why might people consider this scroll a work of art?**

Pu Ru (Chinese), *Second line of calligraphy couplet*, 20th century. Ink on paper with red woodblock prints. Museum of Fine Arts, Boston. Frederick L. Jack Fund and Marshall H. Gould Fund, 1974.304.2.

Observe Look at the alphabet in the image shown on page 98. Notice that the height of each capital letter is about seven times the width of a pen nib, which is the writing point of a pen. The height of small lowercase letters, such as *a*, should be about five times the width of the nib. Tall lowercase letters, such as *h*, are the same height as capital letters. The width of letters will vary slightly, but as a general rule, each should be similar to the height of a lowercase *a*.

Tools: Calligraphy pen with a medium nib and chisel point, or chisel-point, felt-tip pen, and lined notebook paper.

Practice: Calligraphy Writing

- Practice making rows of diagonal, vertical, horizontal, and curved strokes with a calligraphy pen on lined notebook paper.
- Be sure to hold your pen at a constant angle and pull the nib toward you.
- Now combine strokes to create letters.
- Practice writing each letter.

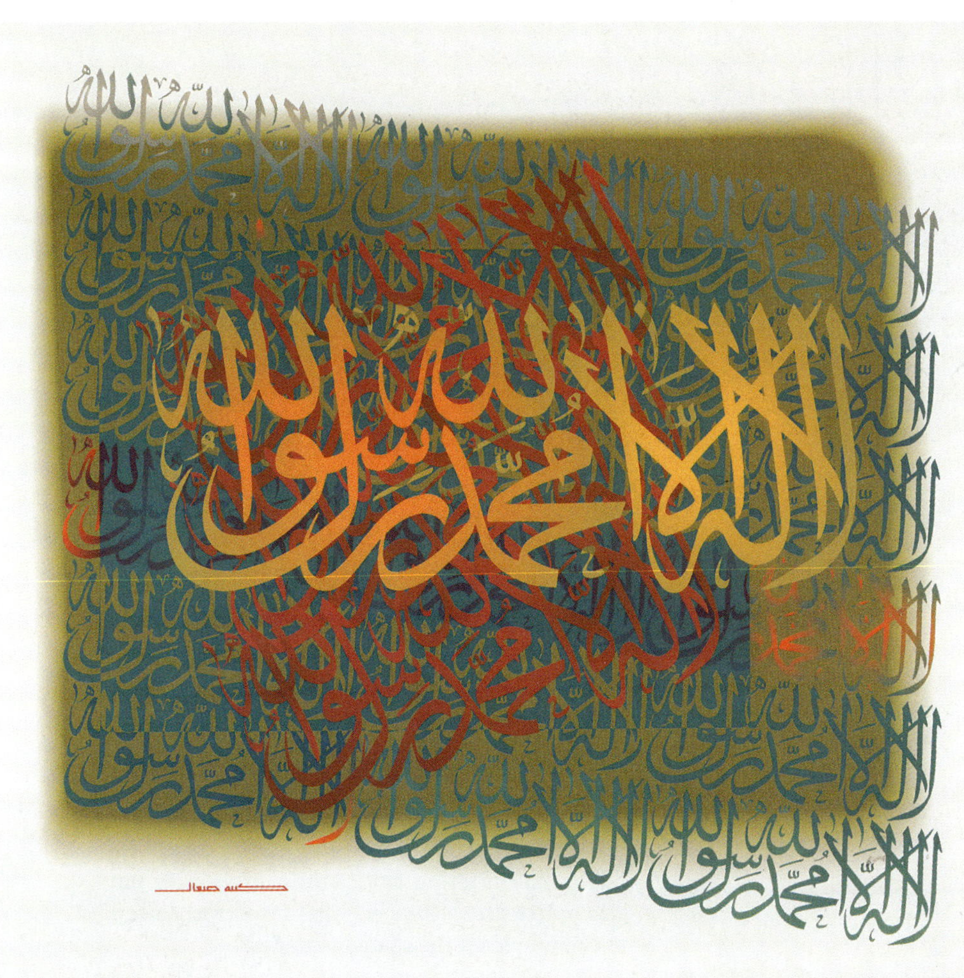

Fig. 4–9 **Compare the content of this image with the letters of our own alphabet. How is it similar? How are they different?**

Mamoun Sakkal, *Shahadah*, 1994. Inkjet print, 19" x 19 ½" (48.3 cm x 49.5 cm). Courtesy of the artist, www.sakkal.com.

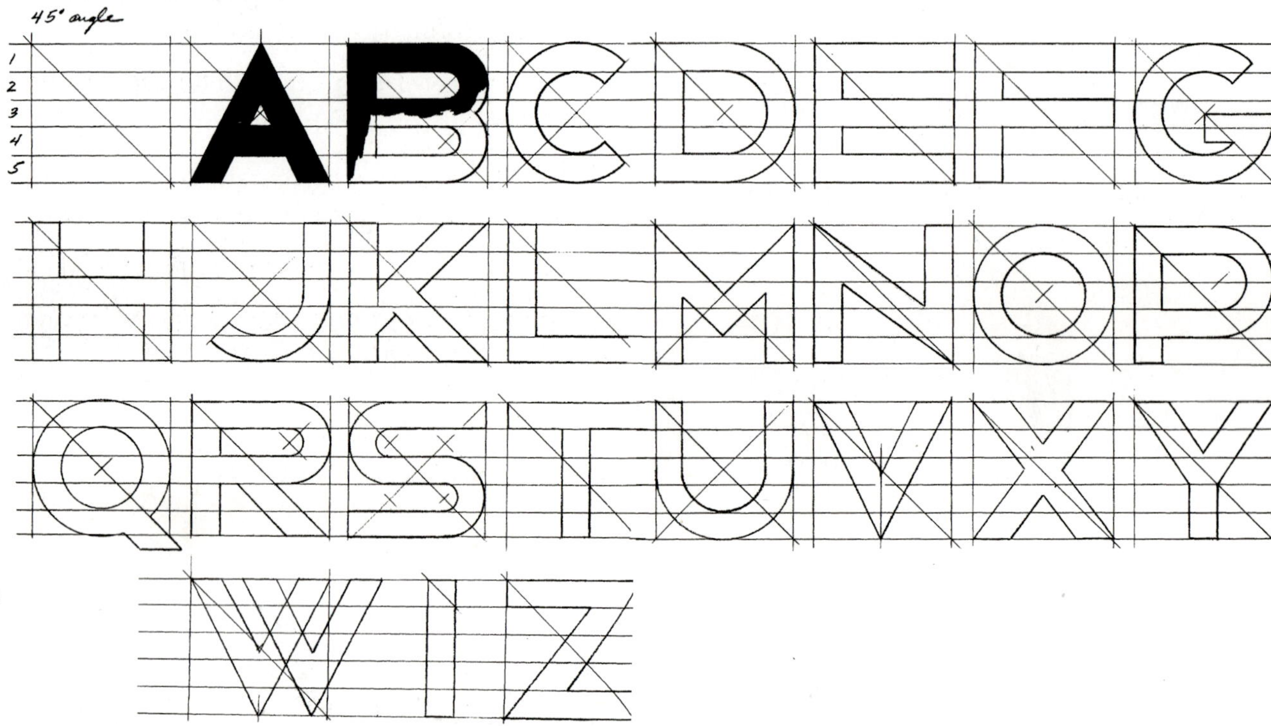

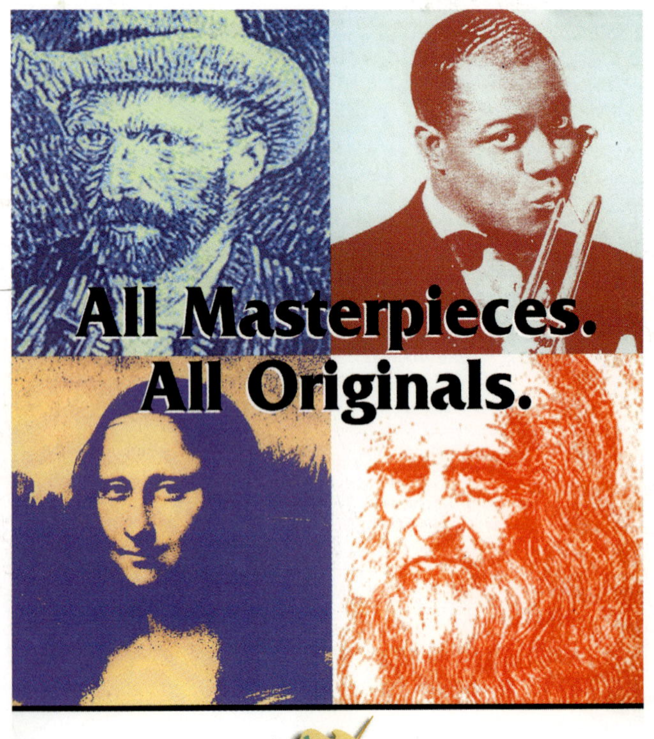

Mechanical Lettering Mechanical lettering is different from calligraphy. Graphic designers often use this type of lettering on posters and billboards.

Observe Look at the letters in the image above. Notice that the letters are all capitals. Also, each letter is a square—five spaces high and five spaces wide. Some of the parts of individual letters are created by drawing a 45-degree angle from one corner of the square to the other.

Tools: Drawing tools such as pens or pencils, lined notebook paper, and a ruler.

Fig. 4–10 **Compare the lettering on this page with calligraphy lettering. Notice their differences, but also notice that letters in either form can be used to communicate the same message.**

Practice: Mechanical Lettering

- Practice writing your name with mechanical lettering. The next time you plan a poster or design a bulletin-board message, try using mechanical lettering. You might paint the letters or draw them on construction paper and cut them out.

Check Your Understanding

1. Use your own words to describe calligraphy.
2. Compare and contrast letters used in mechanical lettering to those used in calligraphy.
3. If you were skilled in both calligraphy and mechanical lettering, which would you use to write a thank-you note to a friend? Why?

Studio Time

Learn from a License Plate

Create a license plate that teaches about you and the state you live in.

- Cut a piece of paper to the size and shape of a license plate. Use colored pencils, markers, or crayons to design your plate.
- Use mechanical lettering to personalize the middle of your license plate with letters, numbers, or a combination of both. The numbers and letters that you choose should have meaning and teach something about you.
- Create a background that represents the state you live in. Across the bottom of the license plate, write words that teach something about your state.

Reflect on the neatness of your lettering.

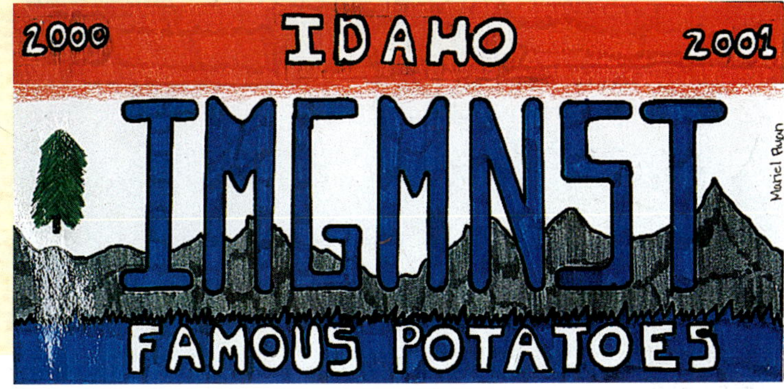

Fig. 4–11 Student artwork

A Poster that Teaches

Studio Background

Do you use posters to decorate the walls of your room? Have you seen large ads for movies or concerts? Have you noticed billboards along the highway? These are all examples of posters. A poster is an artwork that combines one or more pictures with words to send a message or teach a lesson. Posters teach by making us aware of public concerns and events. Sometimes posters are announcements about events, pleas to protect wildlife, or warnings about something that could be dangerous.

In this studio exploration, you will design a poster that will teach a lesson. Choose a topic that is important to you. What ideas come to mind? Think about your audience as you design the poster. Where will your audience see it? How large or small should it be to grab your audience's attention? Will you use calligraphy or mechanical lettering?How can you design the poster to best teach your lesson?

You Will Need

- sketch paper
- pencil and eraser
- ruler
- large drawing paper
- colored pencils, markers, or crayons
- newspapers or magazines (optional)
- scissors (optional)
- glue (optional)

Step 1 Plan and Practice

- Choose a topic for your poster.
- How much of your poster will be pictures and how much will be words?
- Will you use calligraphy, mechanical letters, or cut letters from magazines?
- How large will your words and pictures be in relation to one another?

Things to Remember:

- ✓ Design your poster so the words and images you choose fill the page.
- ✓ Use color and size of both images and words to send your message.
- ✓ Use specific words or images that will make your message stronger.

Inspiration from Our World

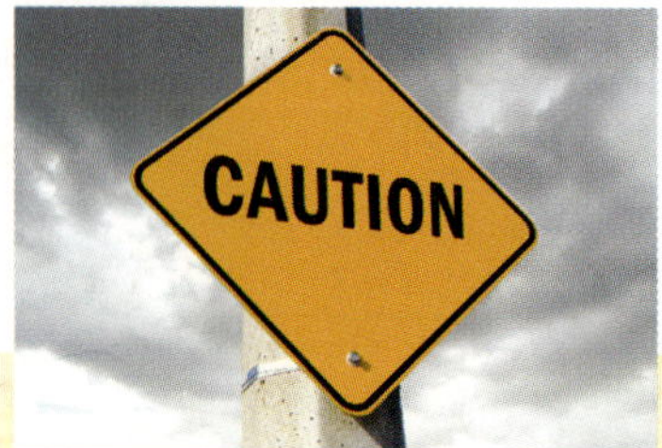

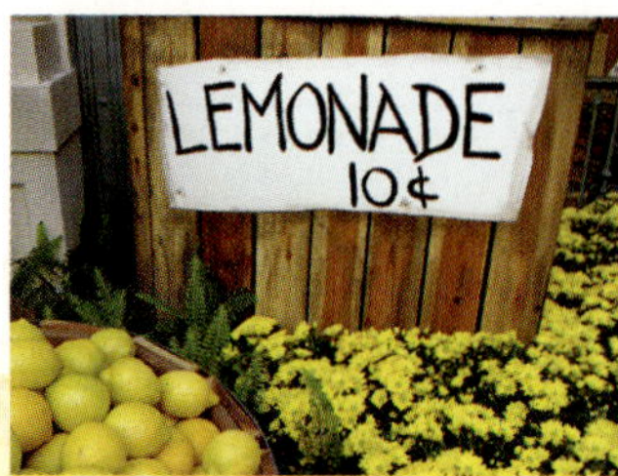

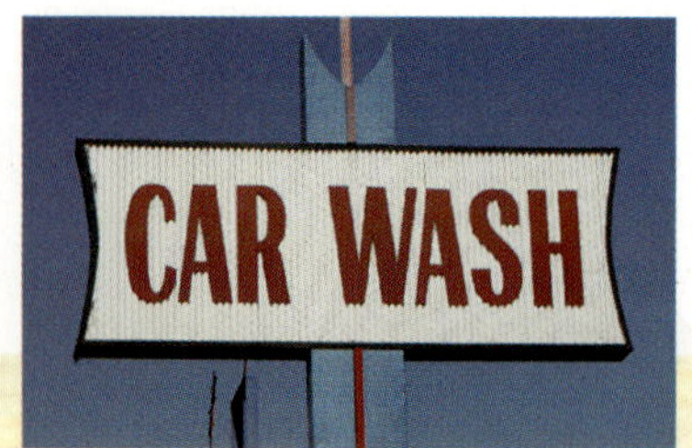

Inspiration from Art

Artists began making posters as a way to communicate to a large audience. The posters you see here were designed for the purpose of teaching. The poster by illustrator Norman Rockwell shown below reminds Americans about the importance of freedom of speech. Ben Shahn, an artist known for his style and interest in lettering, created a poster to teach others about human rights.

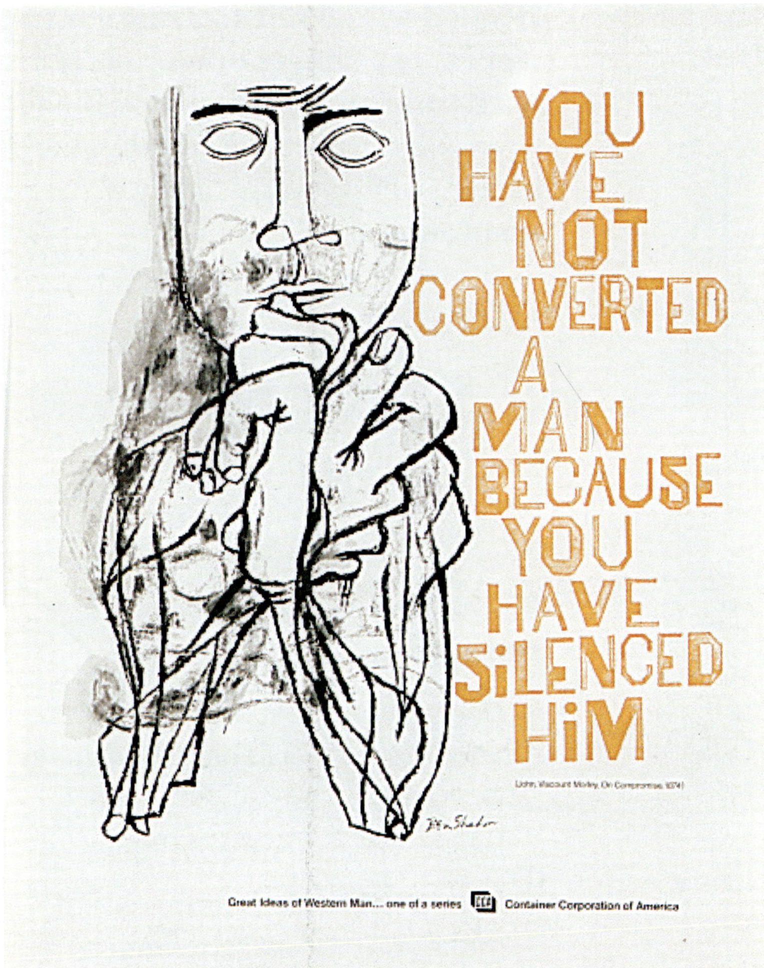

Fig. 4–12 **How did the artist use proportion to strengthen his message?**

Ben Shahn, *You Have Not Converted a Man Because You Have Silenced Him*, 1968. Offset lithograph, 45" x 30" (114 x 76 cm). National Museum of Art, Smithsonian Institution. Gift of the Container Corporation of America. ©Estate of Ben Shahn/Licensed by VAGA, New York, New York.

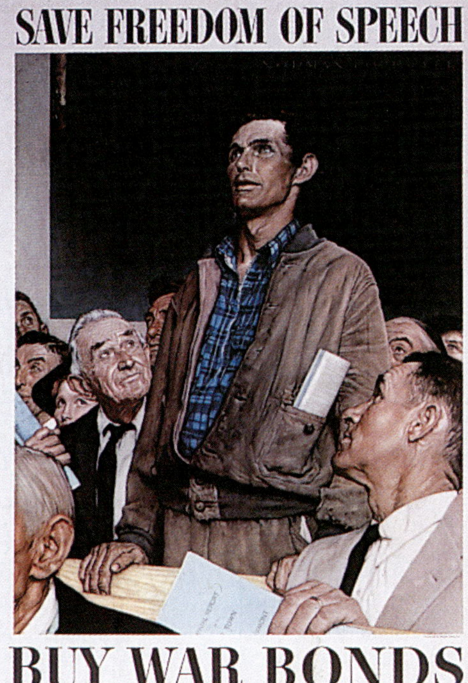

Fig. 4–13 **This poster, from a series of four that Norman Rockwell designed, encouraged Americans to preserve their basic freedoms.**

Norman Rockwell, *Save Freedom of Speech*, 1943. Color lithograph, 40" x 28 ½" (102 x 72 cm). Hoover Institute Archives, Stanford University. Printed by permission of the Norman Rockwell Family Trust. Copyright ©2001 The Norman Rockwell Family Trust.

Step 2 Begin to Create

- **Sketch your plans using different proportions and scale.** One sketch can show larger text with a smaller picture. In another sketch you might make the image larger than the text. Try different placements for the text and image.

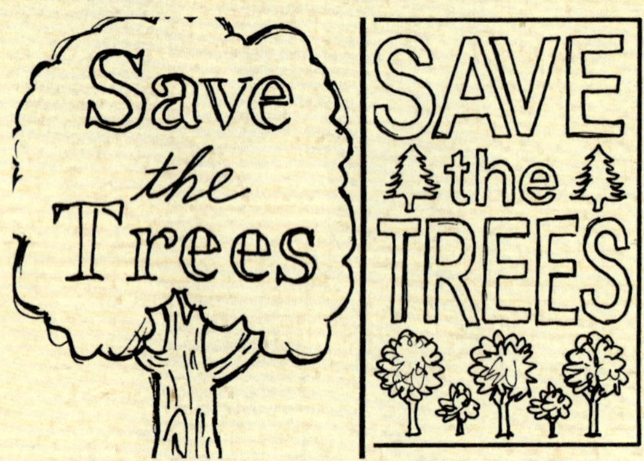

- How large will your words and pictures be? Will letters in all the words be the same size and type? Will the letters print over the picture? How can your design decisions make your teaching stronger?
- Choose the idea that you think works the best. **With a pencil, lightly draw your design on drawing paper.**

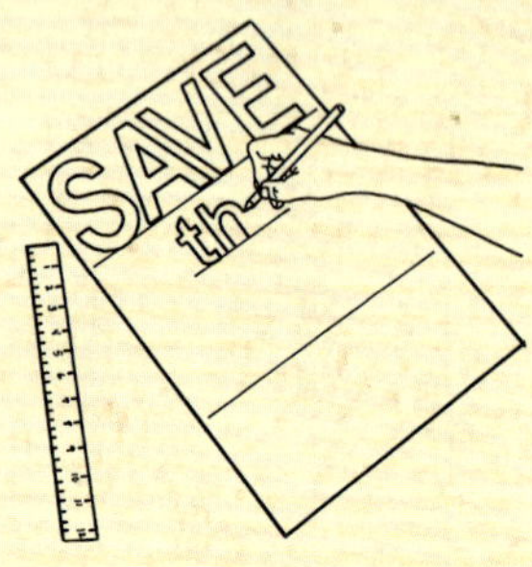

- Fill in areas with color. What colors will enhance your teaching? Think about the mood you want to express and how you can use color to express it.
- **If you decided not to draw your words, cut letters or words from a magazine or newspaper.** Arrange the words on the poster. Carefully glue them in place when you are happy with the arrangement.

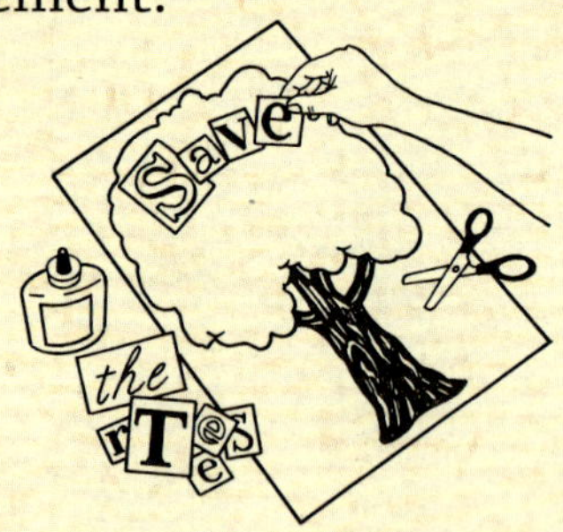

Step 3 Revise

Did you remember to:

- ✓ Design your poster so the words and images you chose fill the page?
- ✓ Use color and size of both images and words to send your message?
- ✓ Use specific words or images to make your message stronger?

Adjust your work if necessary. In your sketchbook, make a note of your revisions and why you made them.

Step 4 **Add Finishing Touches**

- When you are finished with your poster, carefully erase any unwanted lines.
- Add any additional color or images that you think may be needed to pull your poster together.

Step 5 **Share and Reflect**

- Share your poster with a group of your classmates.
- Ask a group member to tell what lesson your poster teaches. Was this what you wanted the poster to teach?
- Have group members talk about what they noticed first in each poster.
- Talk about the size relationships between words and pictures. Which ideas work better? What improvements could be made?
- What changes, if any, would you make if you had the chance to make this poster again?

Art Criticism

Describe What image did the artist show in this poster?

Analyze What did the artist do to call the viewer's attention to the message?

Interpret How did the artist use color to show positive feelings about beaches?

Evaluate What has the artist done especially well?

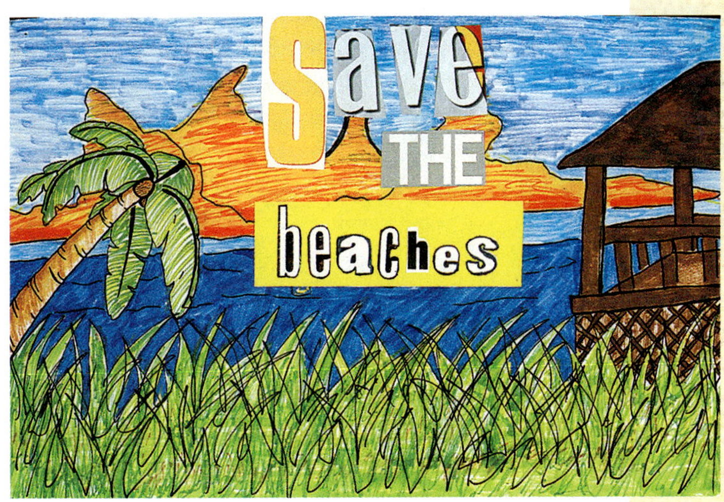

Fig. 4–14 Student artwork

Art and Beliefs

Throughout history, art has been used to teach religious and political beliefs. In the Middle Ages, stained-glass windows and mosaics in churches reminded people of important religious lessons. In the Renaissance, artists used frescoes like *Peaceful City*, and sculptures in government buildings and other public places to teach political beliefs.

Today, murals and billboards can teach about social concerns and cultural identities. What all of these art forms have in common is their size: they are all large in scale.

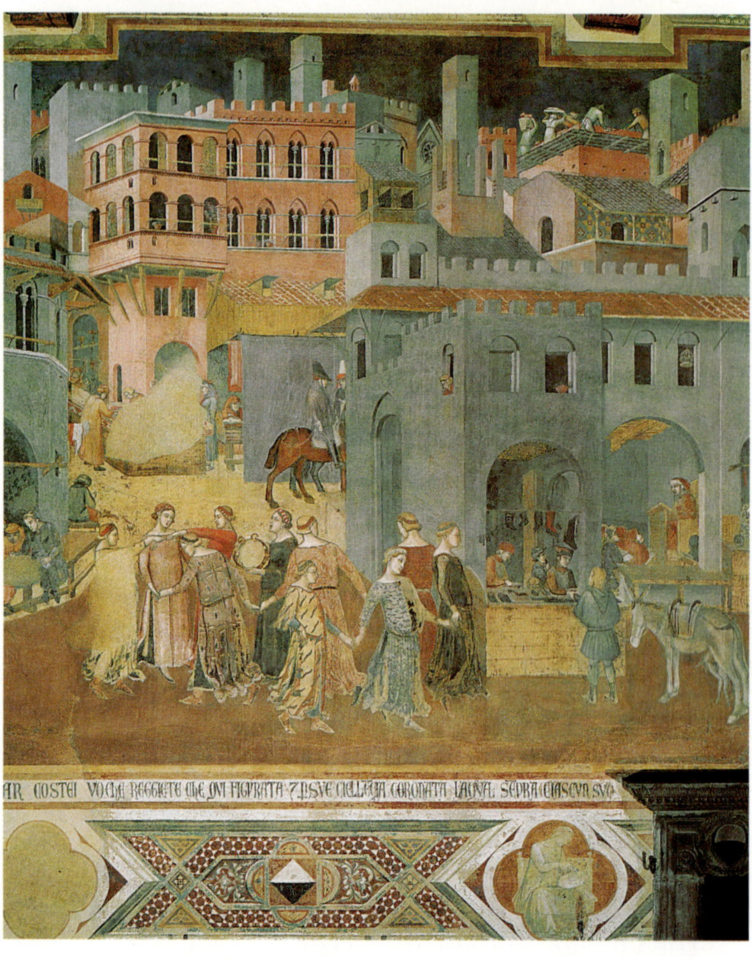

Fig. 4–15 **This is a detail of a fresco that covers the walls of a large room. What lesson do you think this image teaches?**

Lorenzetti Ambrogio, *Effects of Good Government in the City and the Country* (central part), 14th century. Fresco. Palazzo Pubblico, Siena, Italy. Photo credit: Scala/Art Resource, NY.

1300s–1700s

- **1300s** Lorenzetti, *Effects of Good Government*
- **1489** The first math book that uses plus and minus signs is published.
- **1643** Boston Latin School, the oldest U.S. public school, is founded.
- **1776** American Revolution begins

1900s

- **1923** Rivera, *The People Receive Books*
- **1945** World War II ends
- **1967** *Wall of Respect*
- **1969** First episode of *Sesame Street*
- **1990** Kruger, *Think Twice*

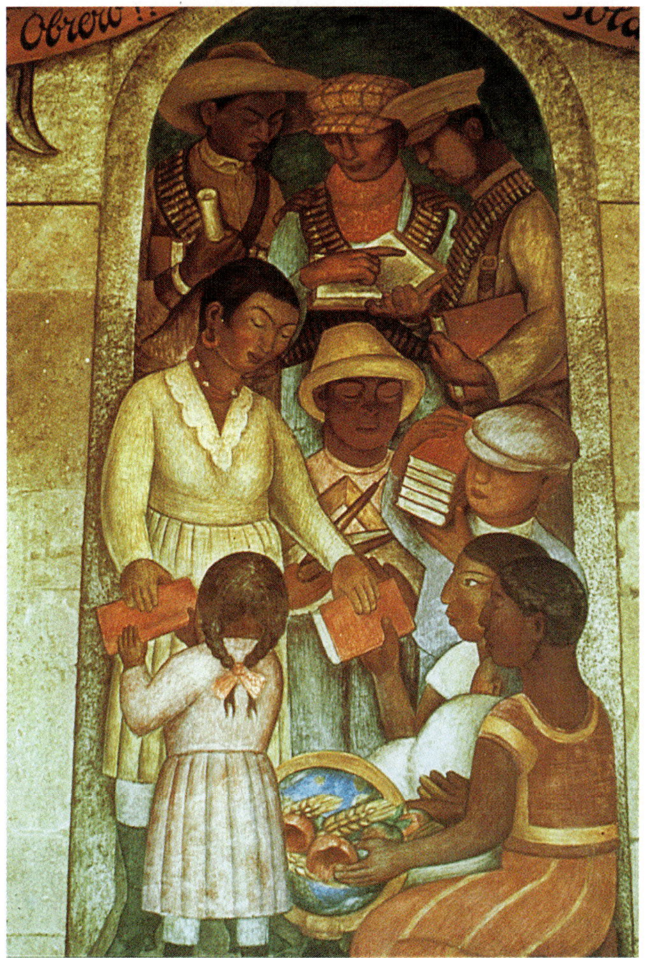

Fig. 4–16 **Diego Rivera's murals remind people of the past and give them hope for the future. How is a mural useful in teaching?**

Diego Rivera, *The People Receive Books*, 1923–28. Fresco. Located in the Education Ministry, Mexico City, Mexico. Photo by Mark Rogovin. Courtesy of Davis Art Images.

Murals that Teach A **mural** is a large artwork that is usually painted on the wall or ceiling of a public building. Murals are one way to remember the people and events that helped shape a nation. Some of the most beautiful murals are those created in the early 1900s in Mexico City. The large-scale murals by Diego Rivera **(Fig. 4–16)** are used to teach the Mexican people about their country's history.

Contemporary Murals *The Original Wall of Respect* in Chicago **(Fig. 4–17)** was an important teaching mural painted in the late 1900s. It showed a number of African-American political, historical, and popular figures. The mural was painted in 1967 on an abandoned building that was destroyed, along with the mural, in 1971. But it inspired hundreds of similar murals in neighborhoods across America. These murals, like so many artworks before them, teach us about the past and what should be remembered in the future.

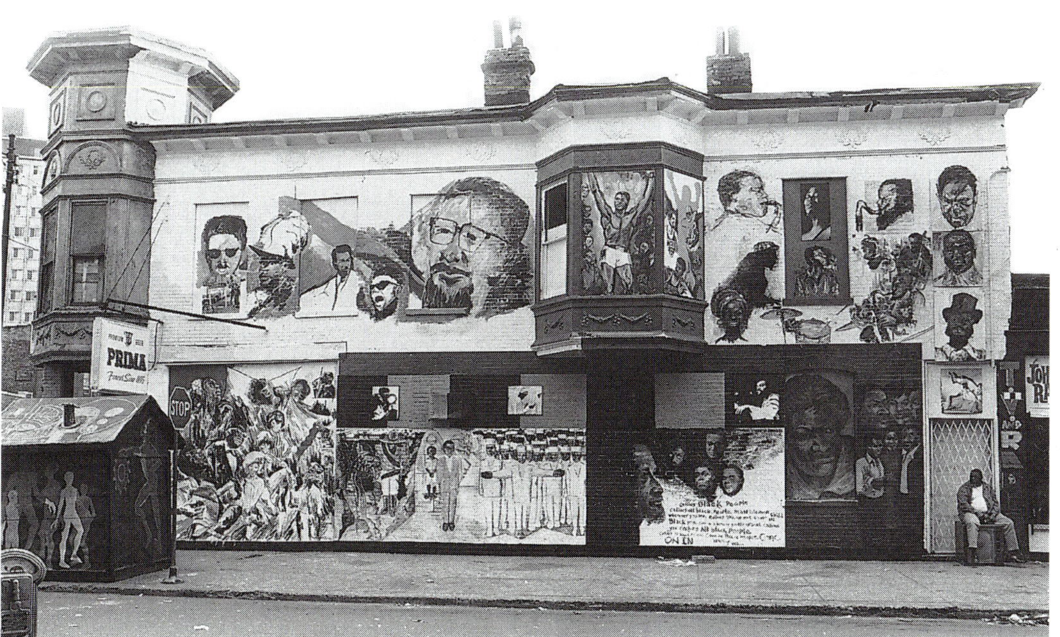

Fig. 4–17 **How can a mural on the side of a building help you feel connected to the place you live?**

The Original Wall of Respect, 1967; destroyed 1971. Originally at 43rd and Langley, Chicago, Illinois. ©1967 Robert A. Sengstacke.

Teaching with Pictures and Words

Barbara Kruger does not say that her artworks teach, but they do challenge you to think about, and even to reject, a message or idea. Her work teaches because she shows stereotypes and overused sayings called *clichés*. The artist seems to be saying "Here's the issue and what it looks like to me; what do you think?"

Kruger creates her art by focusing on one part of an existing photograph, making it larger or smaller, and placing type over the image. The artworks on these pages show some of her works that were used as billboards. Notice how large they are.

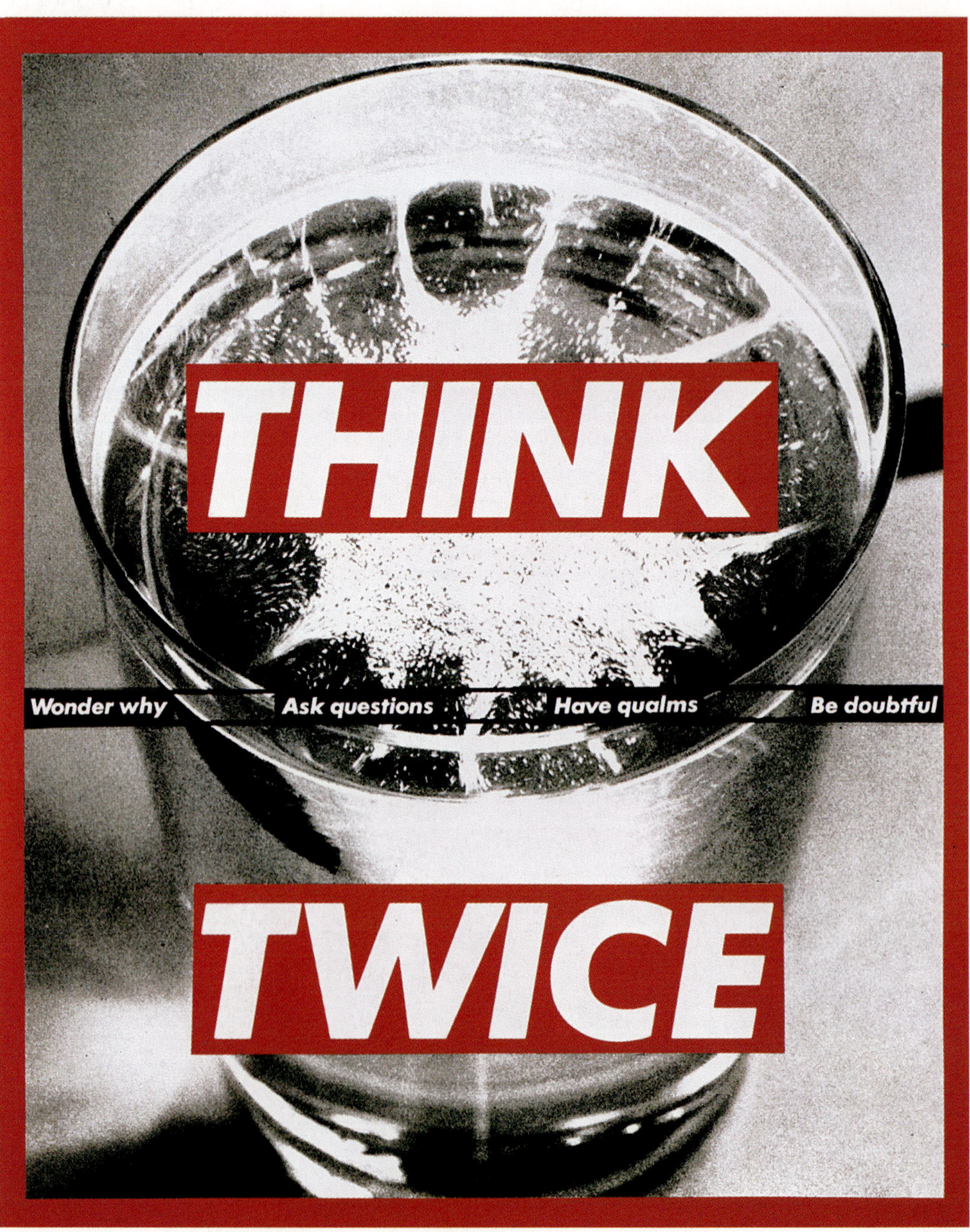

Fig. 4–18 **What issue is the artist raising in this image? How would seeing this image as a billboard differ from seeing it as a small painting on a museum wall?**

Barbara Kruger, *Untitled (Think Twice)*, 1992. Photographic silkscreen on vinyl, 102" by 82 ½" (259 x 209.5 cm). Courtesy of Mary Boone Gallery, New York.

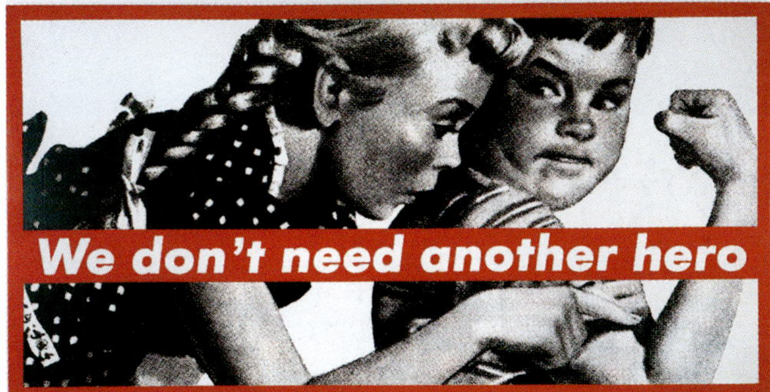

Fig. 4–19 **What do you think Barbara Kruger was trying to say with this billboard?**

Barbara Kruger, *Untitled (We Don't Need Another Hero)*, 1987. Photographic silkscreen on vinyl, 109" x 210" (276.9 x 533.4 cm). Courtesy of Mary Boone Gallery, New York. Emily Fisher Landau Collection, New York.

Meet Barbara Kruger

Growing up in New Jersey, Barbara Kruger took photographs of buildings and neighborhoods. But she lost interest in that when she started working for magazines. As a graphic designer, she learned to look carefully at photographs. This experience gave her confidence to use "found" images to create her own art. Working mainly using black, white, and red, Kruger changes images and attaches powerful words to prompt an emotional response.

"I just say I'm an artist who works with pictures and words."

—Barbara Kruger (born 1945)

Photo: Timothy Greenfield-Sanders.

Check Your Understanding

1. What is a mural?
2. Compare and contrast stained-glass windows, murals, and billboards.
3. How do Barbara Kruger's artworks teach?

Studio Time

Town History Mural

Paint a group mural to teach about your town—its history and goals, what makes it a special place, and so on.

- You can paint the mural on large sheets of paper and display it in the school or community on a temporary basis.
- Or you may wish to create a mural that is more permanent.
- Think about how you can communicate ideas without words.

Reflect on what your mural communicates about your town.

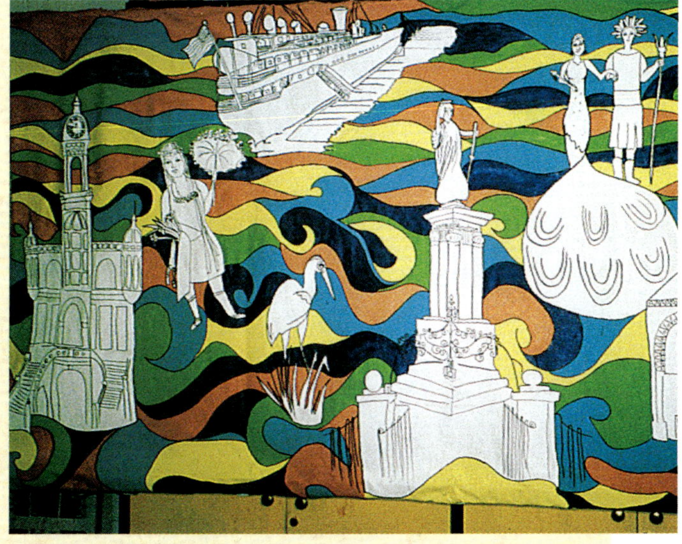

Fig. 4–20 Student artwork

The Islamic Art of North Africa

Calligraphy of Islam Calligraphy, the art of beautiful handwriting, is highly developed in Islamic art. It is one of Islam's important artistic contributions. The teachings of Islam are often written in calligraphic script.

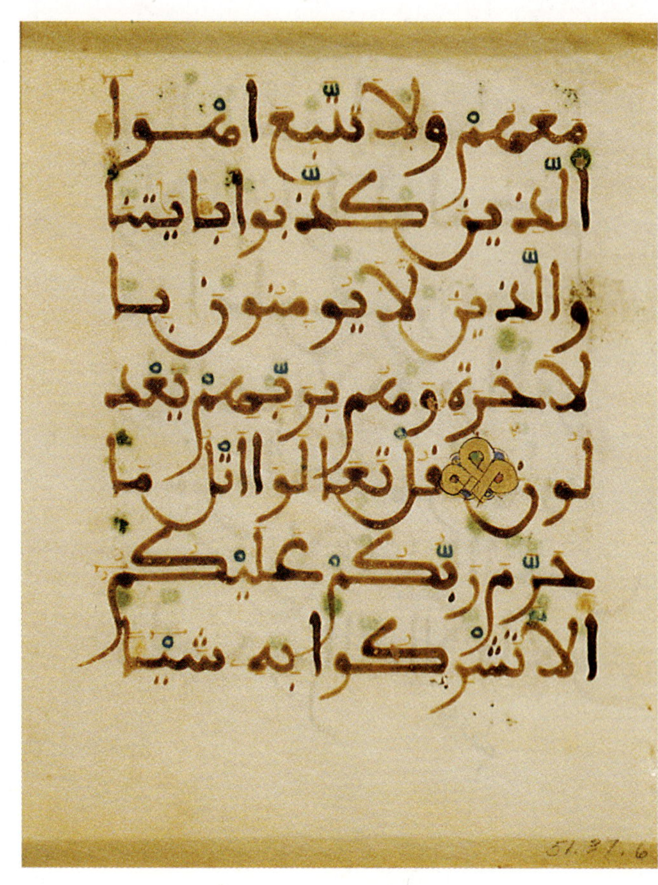

Fig. 4–21 **Look closely at the page from the Koran for any characters that repeat.**

North African (Egypt?), *Two Text Pages from Sura 6 of the Koran*, 12th century. Ink, colors and gold on paper, 5 ¼" x 6 ¼" (13 x 16 cm). Bequest of Mrs. Margaret McMillan Webber in memory of her mother, Katherine Kittredge McMillan. The Minneapolis Institute of Arts.

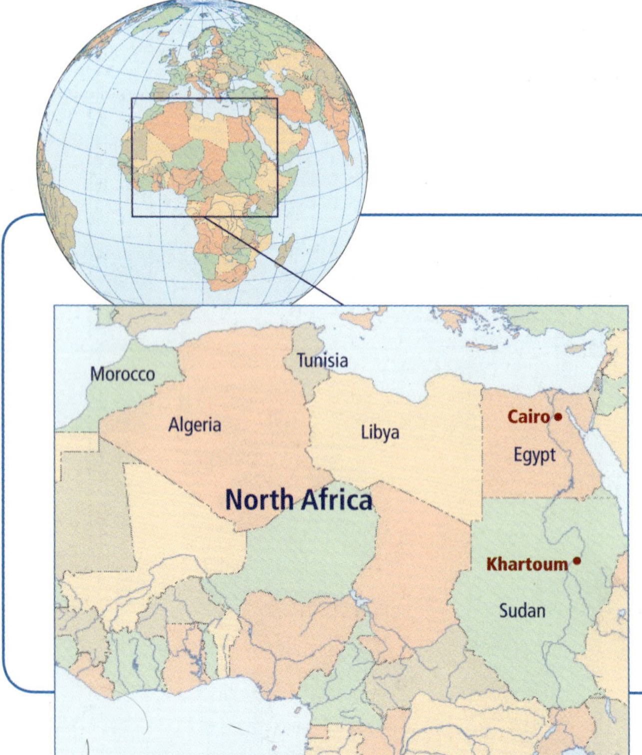

Social Studies Connection

The Islamic religion was started in 622 CE by the Arabian prophet Muhammad. Within the next one hundred years, the religion had spread from Saudi Arabia to **North Africa**. Like all Muslims, North African followers of Islam found their guidance in the text of the Quran (or Koran), a holy book **(Fig. 4–21)**. The Islamic religion brought about an artistic and cultural unity in North Africa.

North African Islamic artists use calligraphy to decorate many kinds of handmade objects, such as the lamp in **Fig. 4–22**. Decorative writing often covers objects made by blacksmiths, leather workers, dyers, jewelers, and metal workers.

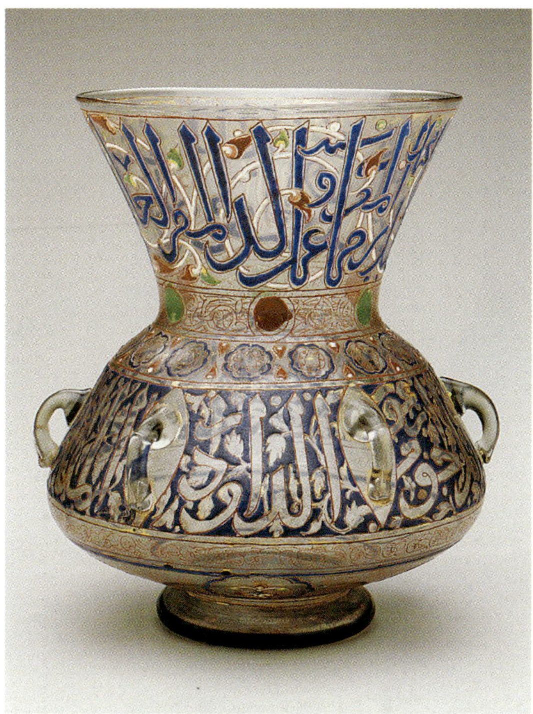

Fig. 4–22 **Why would an artist want to add writing to such an object?**

Islamic, Egypt, *Mosque Lamp*, 1331–35. Blown glass with enamel, gilded; height: 10 13/16" (27.5 cm). The Toledo Museum of Art. Purchased with funds from the Libbey Endowment, Gift of Edward Drummond Libbey, acc. no. 1940.118.

Visual Culture

Look at displays of greeting cards. Pay attention to differences in lettering. Why do you think the lettering on a sympathy card might be different from the lettering on a humorous birthday card? If you wanted to send a card with a serious message, what style of lettering would be most appropriate?

Writing Boards and Arabesques

The writing board **(Fig. 4–23)** is also an important art form associated with Islam in North Africa. Writing boards are made of wood and are used to teach children the sacred writings of Islam. Calligraphers write the lessons in precise, bold, and rounded Arabic script. The Arabic script on writing boards is often richly decorated with geometric designs and calligraphic curves known as arabesques.

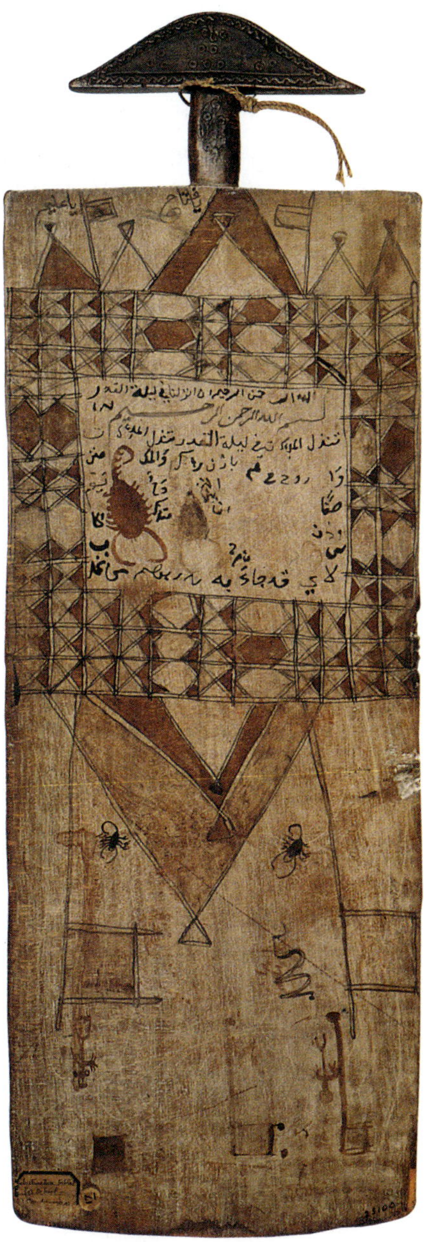

Fig. 4–23 **Compare and contrast this writing board with the boards in your classroom.**

Koranic Board, late 19th or early 20th century. Wood, paint, string, 31 7/8" x 11" (81 x 28 cm). Brooklyn Museum 22.231 Museum Expedition 1922. Robert B. Woodward Memorial.

A Master of Calligraphy Today, many North African artists continue the art of calligraphy. One such artist was Osman Waqialla. In the 1940s, Waqialla studied art in London and then studied in Egypt, at the School of Arabic Calligraphy and College of Applied Arts. Here, he explored Arabic calligraphy and developed his unique style. Waqialla has since mastered the skills of traditional calligraphy. This mastery allows him to be more expressive in his script. As you will notice in the two images on these pages, Waqialla often varies the size and shape of letterforms and even overlaps letters to create decorative effects.

Meet Osman Waqialla

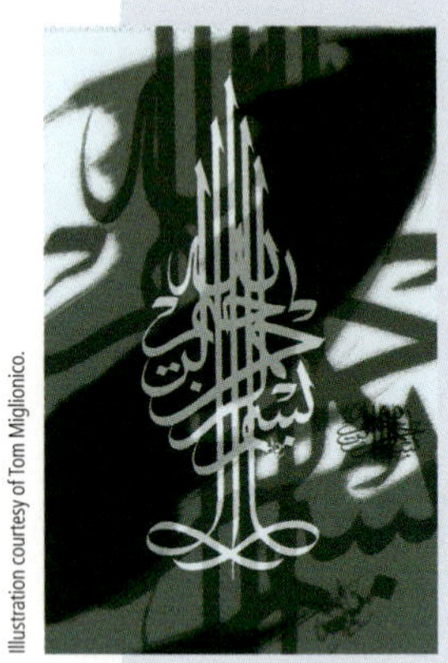

Illustration courtesy of Tom Miglionico.

From Sudan, North Africa, Waqialla is a calligrapher, poet, journalist, and teacher. His art education was based on both European influences and African traditions. In addition to the scripting of religious texts, Waqialla also created non-religious works of modern poetry. His artworks that focus on Arabic and Islamic identity have influenced a movement in calligraphic style known as the Khartoum School. Like those who have followed his lead, Waqialla sees the letters of Arabic script as beautiful forms of artistic expression.

"Visualize letter forms as living elements."

—Osman Waqialla (1905–2007)

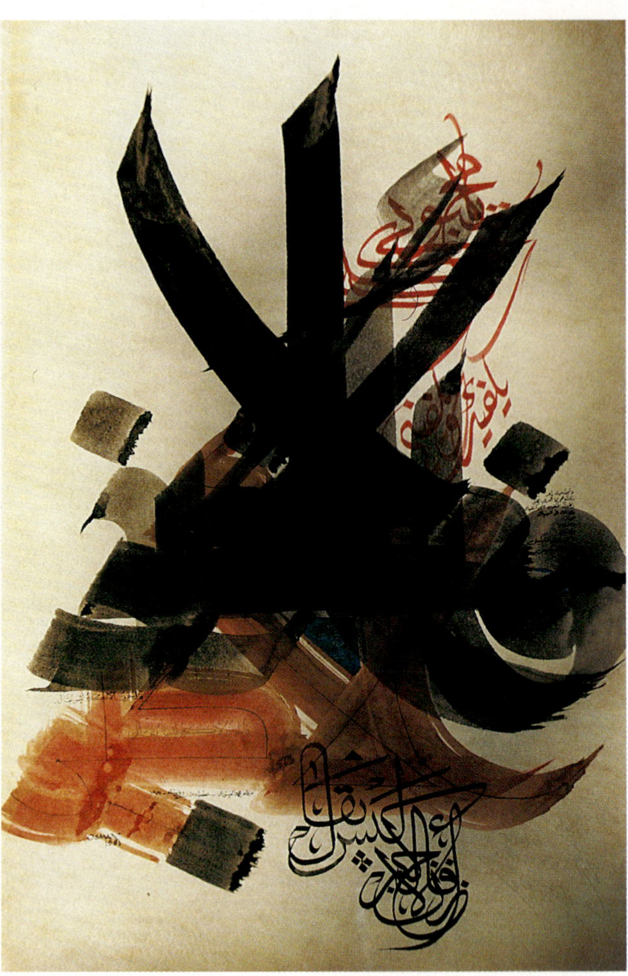

Fig. 4–24 **What reason might the artist have had for making some letterforms much larger than others?**

Osman Waqialla, *Calligraph: "Deep sorrow defies definition"* (Arabic text from poem "The Wandering Dervish" by Mohammed Alfeytoori), n.d. Ink on paper, 16 ½" x 23 ⅜" (42 x 60). Courtesy Osman Waqialla/Napata Graphics.

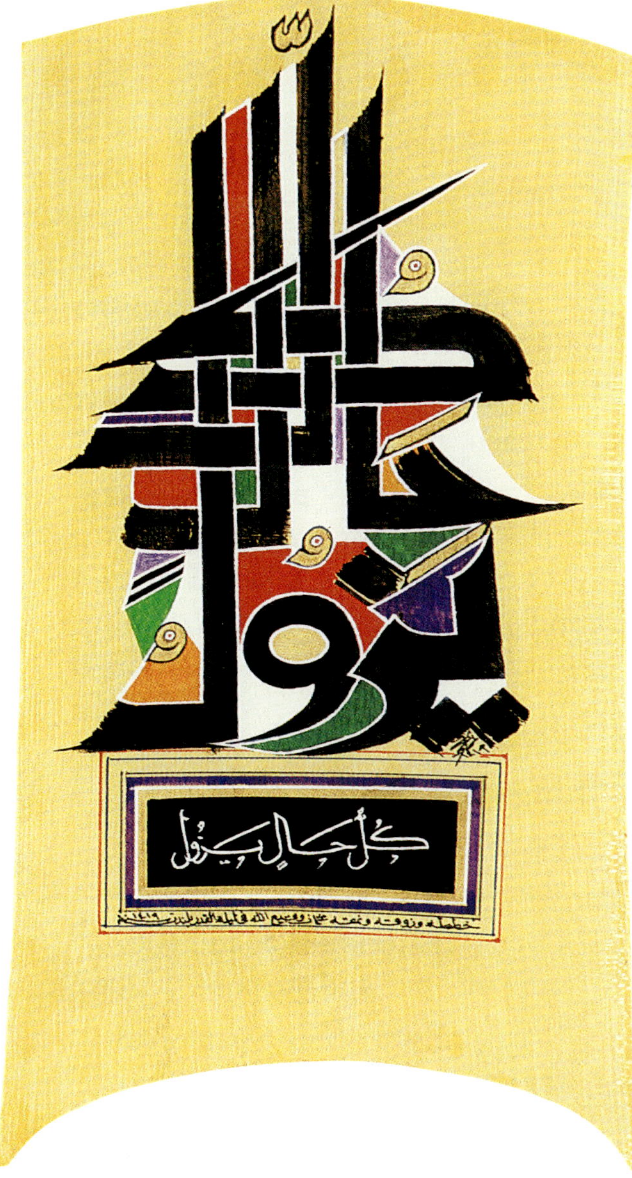

Fig. 4–25 **How did the artist make some shapes stand out?**

Osman Waqialla, *Calligraph* (text from one of the gospels), 2001. Wood writing plaque, 16 ½" x 23 ⅜" (42 x 60 cm). Courtesy of Osman Waqialla/Napata Graphics.

Check Your Understanding

1. How are writing boards used in Islam?
2. Compare and contrast the Islamic calligraphy in North Africa with the calligraphy you learned about in lesson 2 of this unit.
3. What do you think Waqialla meant when he said, "Visualize letter forms as living elements?" Why do you think he would say this?

Studio Time

A Decorative Plaque

Create a decorative board or plaque that teaches something important, such as a proverb, saying, or rule.

- Think of an imaginative shape for the plaque.
- Practice calligraphy and decorative lettering before applying them to the plaque. Add decorative details.
- Your plaque can be of heavy cardboard, foam core, or wood. Because the presentation of your written words is important, consider how the plaque will be displayed.

Reflect on how you have presented your written words and the importance of their message.

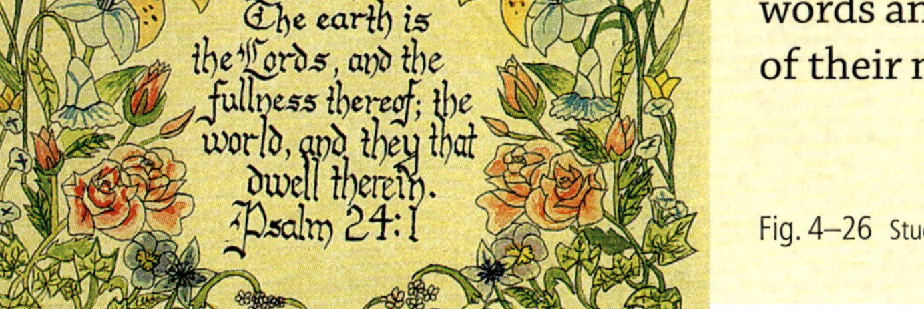

Fig. 4–26 Student artwork

4.6 Studio Exploration — Puppetry

A Teaching Puppet

Studio Background

When artists create artworks for the purpose of teaching, they must think about what they want to teach and how they will teach it. Puppeteers are no different. What questions do you think Jim Henson asked himself when he created his Muppets?

In this studio exploration, you will create a puppet that will help you teach something important. Do you want to teach an event in history, the importance of good habits, or something about caring for the environment?

You Will Need

- puppetmaking materials
- scissors
- white glue
- markers (optional)
- tempera paint and brushes (optional)

Step 1 Plan and Practice

- List some ideas of important things you want to teach.
- Think about the audience to whom you will teach.
- Decide what kind of puppet to make. What kind of puppet character can best help you teach? Will you create a hand puppet, a marionette, or a finger puppet? Will you make an even larger puppet?

Things to Remember:

- ✓ Decide on a size for your puppet that fits your intended audience.
- ✓ Choose materials that suit your puppet's size and purpose.
- ✓ Use details to create a personality for your puppet.

Inspiration from Our World

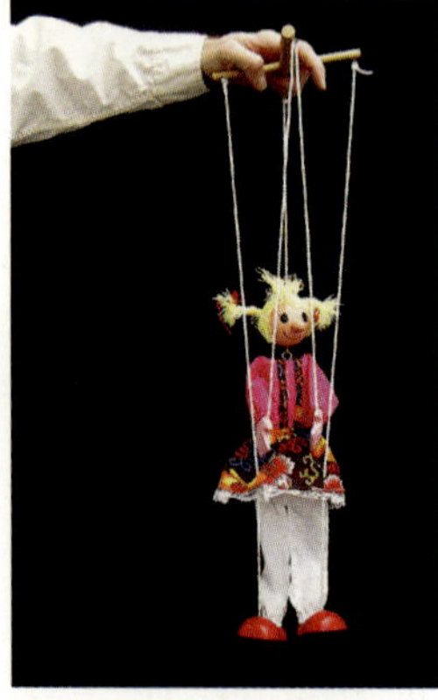

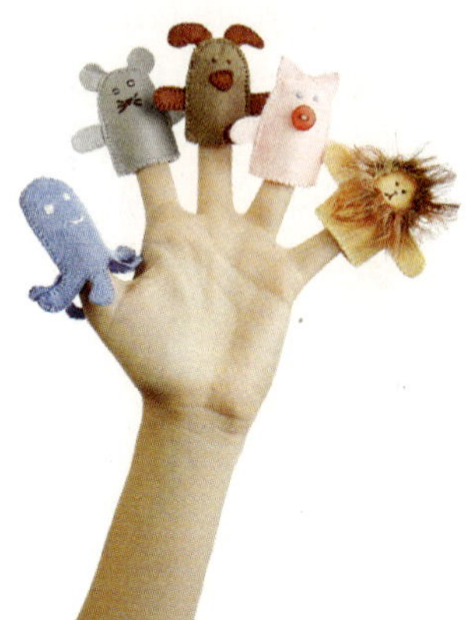

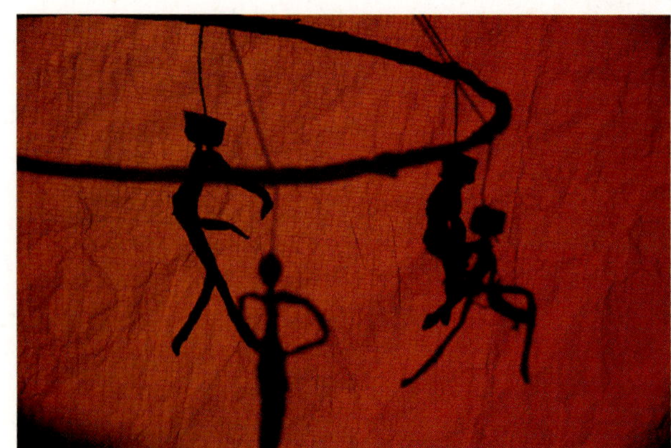

Inspiration from Art

For hundreds of years, people around the world have used puppets to tell stories and teach important lessons. In some cultures, puppet theater is almost as popular as television.

Puppets come in all shapes and sizes. Some of the largest puppets in the world can be found in Japan. *Bunraku* is a traditional form of Japanese puppetry used to tell stories about the past. A Japanese *bunraku* puppet is shown in **Fig. 4–27**. Because the puppets can be almost four feet tall, three people are needed to control each one.

On a smaller scale, hand puppets are another popular form of puppetry. Perhaps the smallest puppets are finger puppets. In ancient China, children played a game in which their fingers were painted. Today, finger and hand puppets are made from many different materials.

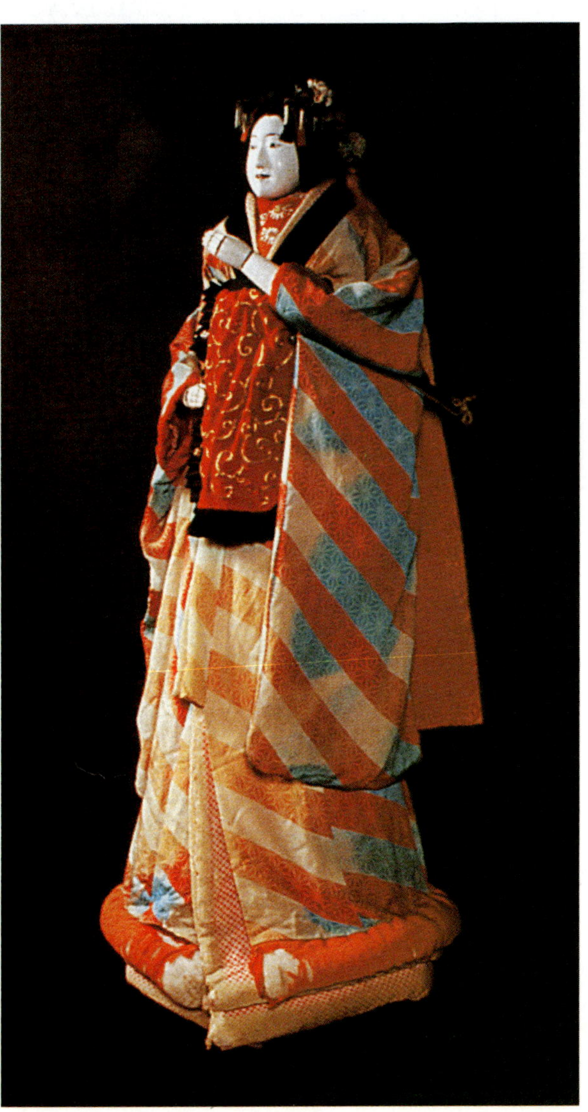

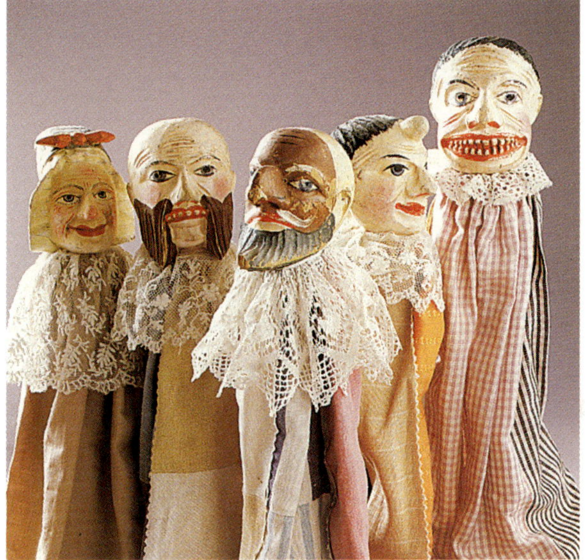

Fig. 4–28 **Hand puppets are often used to tell fables and other stories that teach a lesson.**

Western Europe, *Hand Puppets*, late 19th–early 20th century. Painted wood, average height: 16" (41 cm). Girard Foundaton Collection in the Museum of International Folk Art, a unit of the Museum of New Mexico, Santa Fe. Photo by Michel Monteaux.

Fig. 4–27 **Bunraku puppeteers move the puppet's eyes, eyebrows, and sometimes its mouth, arms, and feet, while other artists play music and tell the story.**

Japan, *Bunraku puppet*, 20th century. Courtesy of the Sheehan Gallery at Whitman College, Walla Walla, Washington.

Step 2 **Begin to Create**

- **Plan and assemble your puppet.** What features will it have? What materials will you use to create the puppet? Choose materials that will suit the size and purpose of your puppet. Think about what you want the puppet to do: If you want it to be flexible and able to move easily, choose soft, pliable materials; if you want it to hold its shape, choose firmer materials.

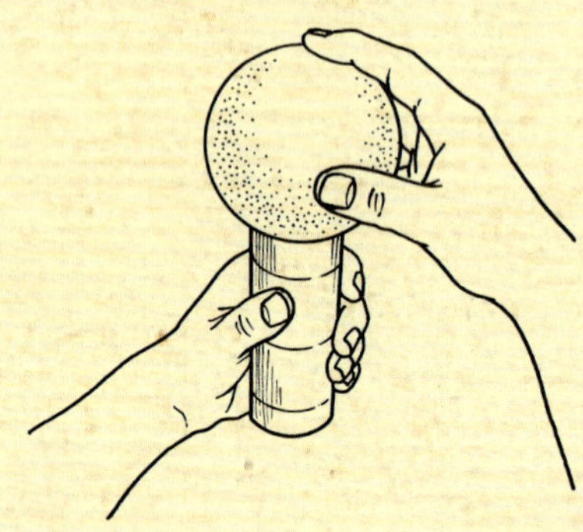

- **When the main forms of your puppet are finished, glue on smaller items.** Use materials such as sequins, yarn, buttons, and the like. How can you use details to create a personality for your puppet? How can that personality help teach your lesson?

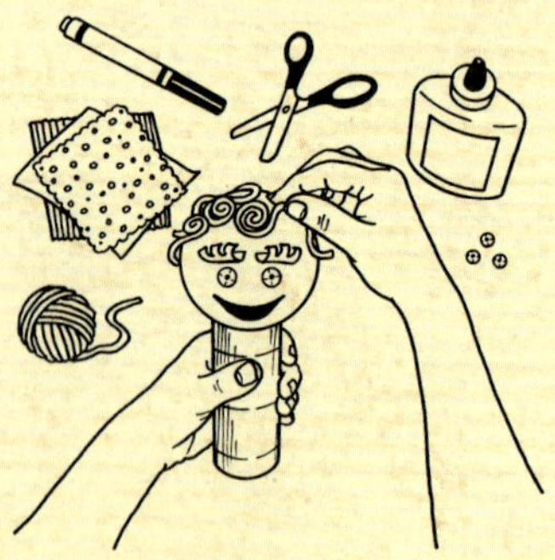

Step 3 **Revise**

Did you remember to:

✓ Select a size for your puppet that fits your audience?

✓ Choose materials that suit your puppet's size and purpose?

✓ Create a personality for your puppet?

Adjust your work if necessary. In your sketchbook, make a note of your revisions and why you made them.

Step 4 **Add Finishing Touches**

- Add other details as needed with paint or marker. If you are making a marionette, you will have to attach the strings.

Step 5 **Share and Reflect**

- With your classmates, talk about why you decided to make your puppet the way you did.
- Explain what lesson you want to teach with your puppet. Who is your audience? How did your chosen lesson and audience affect your decisions?
- How did you use materials and details to create a personality that helped teach your lesson?
- What was the most challenging part about making your puppet? Why?
- What have you learned about puppet-making that will help you make puppets in the future?

Art Criticism

Describe Tell what these puppets look like.

Analyze How have the parts been arranged and assembled?

Interpret What impressions would these puppets make on an audience?

Evaluate What have the student artists done especially well?

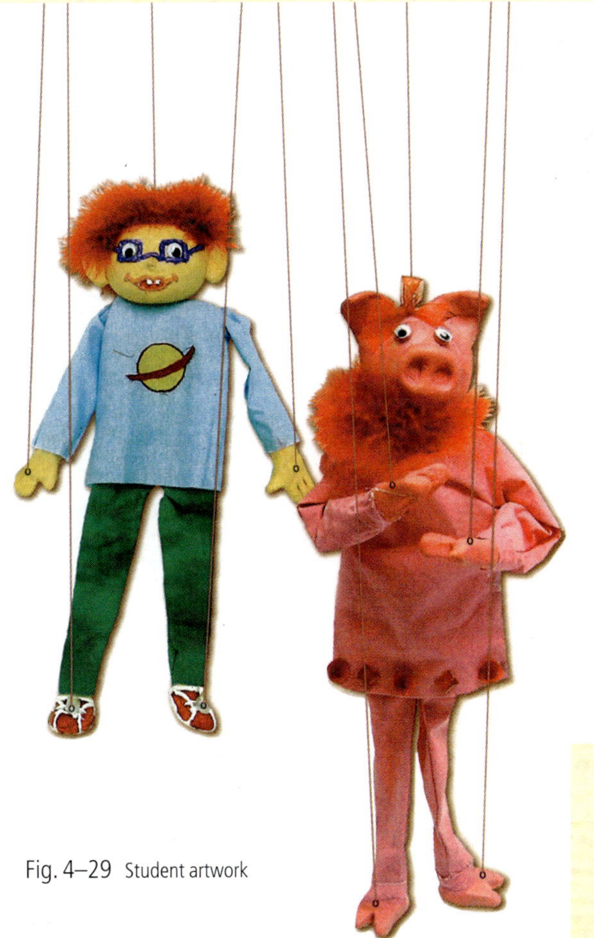

Fig. 4–29 Student artwork

Social Studies

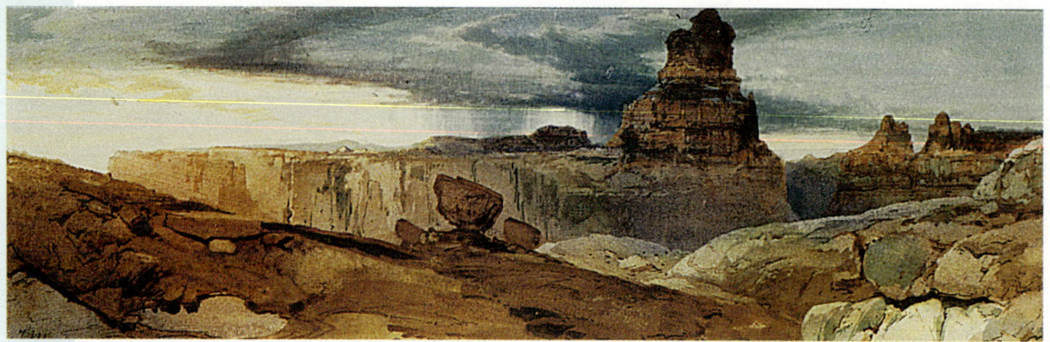

Fig. 4–30 **This painting was used to encourage the establishment of the first national parks, in order to preserve and protect the region's beauty and natural environment.**

Thomas Moran, *Shin-Au-Av-Tu-Weap (God Land), Canyon of the Colorado, Utah*, ca. 1872–73. Watercolor and pencil on paper. 4 13/16" x 14 9/16" (12.2 x 36.9 cm). Photo credit: Smithsonian American Art Museum, Washington, DC. Gift of Dr. William Henry Holmes 1930.12.42. Courtesy Art Resource, NY.

You can learn a great deal from artworks that show the world's natural environments. Have you ever visited or read about the Grand Canyon in Arizona? In the 1800s, many artists and photographers traveled to this area. They captured its natural beauty in hundreds of paintings and photographs. These artworks were often used to teach people in the East about the West. They were also meant to encourage people to move into and settle the region.

Theater

In many cultures, puppets act out stories that are meant to teach. Well-known tales, myths, legends, and reflections of daily living are performed to educate audiences. They learn about history, morals, values, and beliefs. One of the oldest storytelling traditions is the shadow-puppet theater known as *wayang kulit*, from the Indonesian island of Java. The puppetmaster is called *dalang*. The dalang is highly respected by the community for his role as an actor, historian, and teacher.

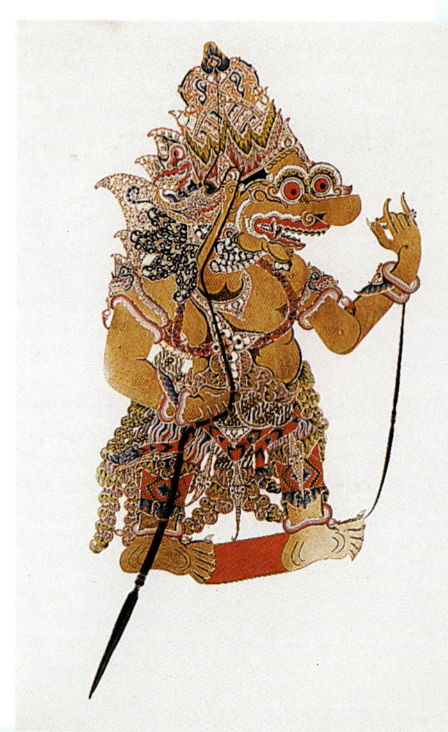

Fig. 4–31 **The flat, cutout puppet is attached to rods that the puppeteer uses to move the puppet in front of a light. The audience, seated in front of a screen, sees only the puppet's shadow.**

Indonesia, Central Java, *Wayang Kulit* (Shadow Puppet), c. 1950. Cut, painted leather, height: 31 ½" (79 cm). Museum of International Folk Art, a unit of the Museum of New Mexico, Santa Fe.

Careers **Documentary Filmmakers**

Documentary filmmakers are artists who make moving pictures about real events. Documentary filmmakers may teach about the past through their work, or they may teach about the present.

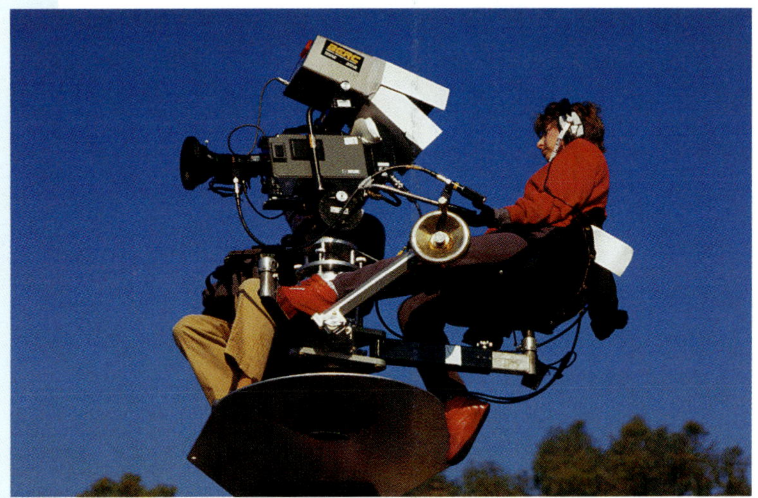

Like other filmmakers, many documentary filmmakers attend film school and have art and design backgrounds. They may work as producers, coordinating the work of all the people working on a film. They may also serve as directors, heading production and shaping the film from the original script, or draft, to the final arrangement of moving images.

Fig. 4–32 ©Joseph Sohm/Visions of America/CORBIS.

Daily Life

There are many people who serve the role of teacher in your life. But do you serve that role for anyone else? The word *teacher* means "one who instructs." No matter how young or how old you are, you can teach by example, by instruction, or by working with others. You may be a teacher to younger brothers and sisters, to children you babysit, to neighbors you help, or to friends at school or in clubs.

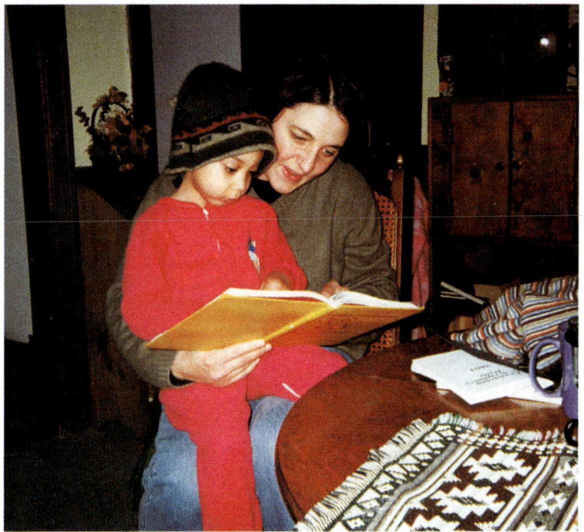

Fig. 4–33 **What situations can you think of in which you act as a teacher?**

Photo courtesy of Gen Gaidis.

Unit 4 Vocabulary and Content Review

Vocabulary Review

Match each art term below with its definition.

calligraphy
arabesques
poster
mural

1. artwork that combines pictures with words to teach a lesson
2. a large artwork painted on the wall or ceiling of a public building
3. a form of beautiful lettering
4. geometric designs and calligraphic curves

Aesthetic Thinking

Have you ever disagreed with the message an artist made with their artwork? Does the artwork still have value? What might you gain from artworks such as this?

For Your Portfolio

Review your artworks from this chapter. Look for a good example of artwork that teaches a visual lesson.

Write About Art

Artist Ben Shahn made this poster in 1968 to illustrate a quotation by John Morley, a British politician. Explain whether you think the quotation is still relevant today. If so, what contemporary image might you use to illustrate it?

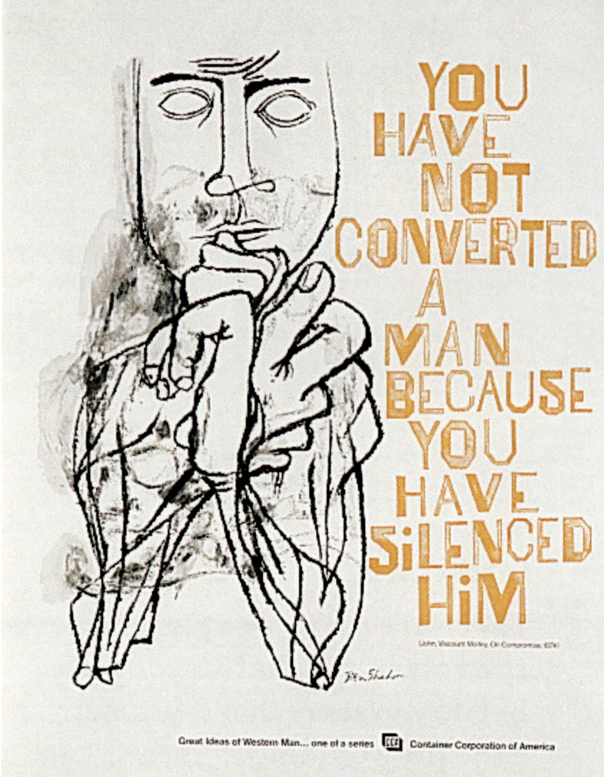

Fig. 4–34 Ben Shahn, *You Have Not Converted a Man Because You Have Silenced Him*, 1968. Offset lithograph, 45" x 30" (114 x 76 cm). National Museum of Art, Smithsonian Institution. Gift of the Container Corporation of America. ©Estate of Ben Shahn/Licensed by VAGA, New York, New York.

Art Criticism

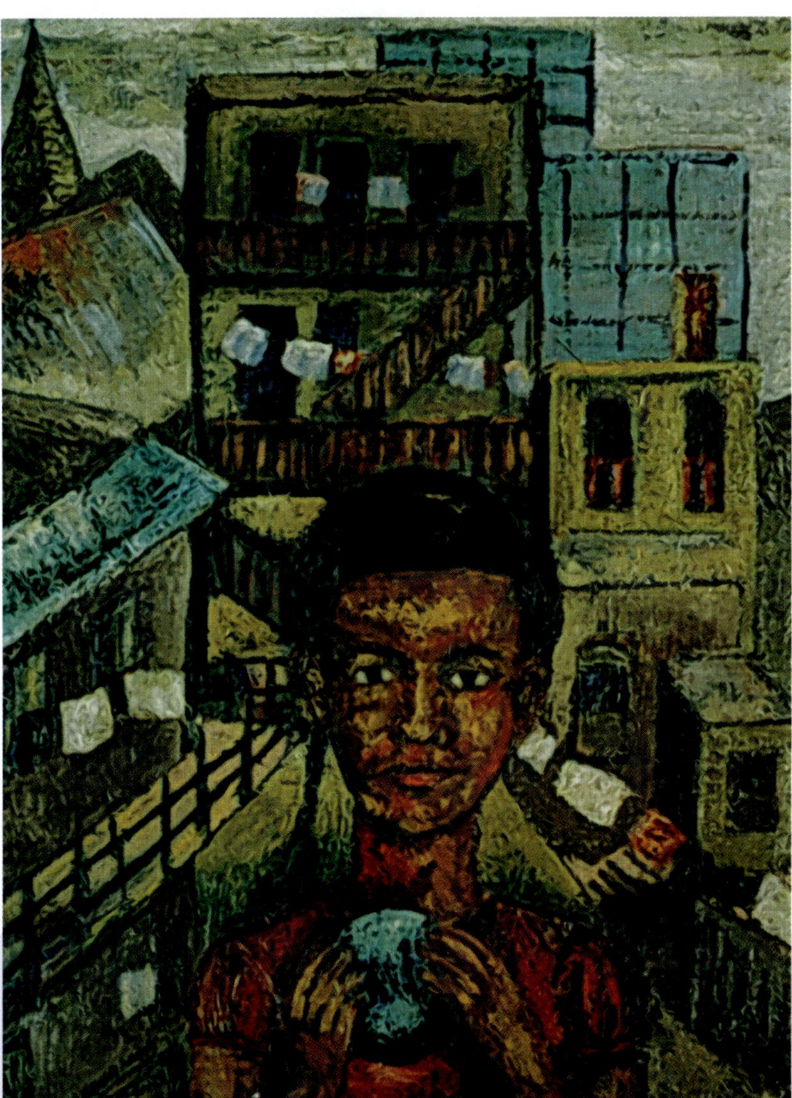

Describe What do you see in this print?

Analyze How did the artist emphasize the main figure?

Interpret How do the colors of the buildings help create a mood? How would you describe the mood?

Evaluate How does the artist teach a lesson with this artwork? What lesson or lessons does it teach?

Fig. 4–35 **What stories does this portrait suggest to you?**

Margaret Taylor Burroughs, *Slum Child*, 1960. Oil on canvas, 37 ½" x 28" (95.3 x 71.1 cm). Courtesy of the Hampton University Museum.

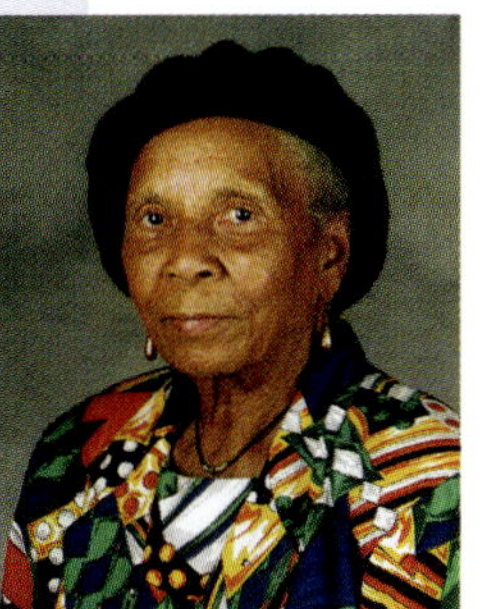

Courtesy of Dr. Margaret Taylor Burroughs.

Meet the Artist

Margaret Taylor Burroughs (born 1917) was born in Louisiana, but lived most of her life in Illinois. She attended art school and taught art for more than twenty years. She also wrote and illustrated many children's books. Burroughs and her husband founded the DuSable Museum of African-American History in Chicago.

For Your Sketchbook

Select a letter of the alphabet. Fill a page with variations (fonts) of the letterform. Match letterforms with a particular audience.

Unit 5

Artists Are Naturalists

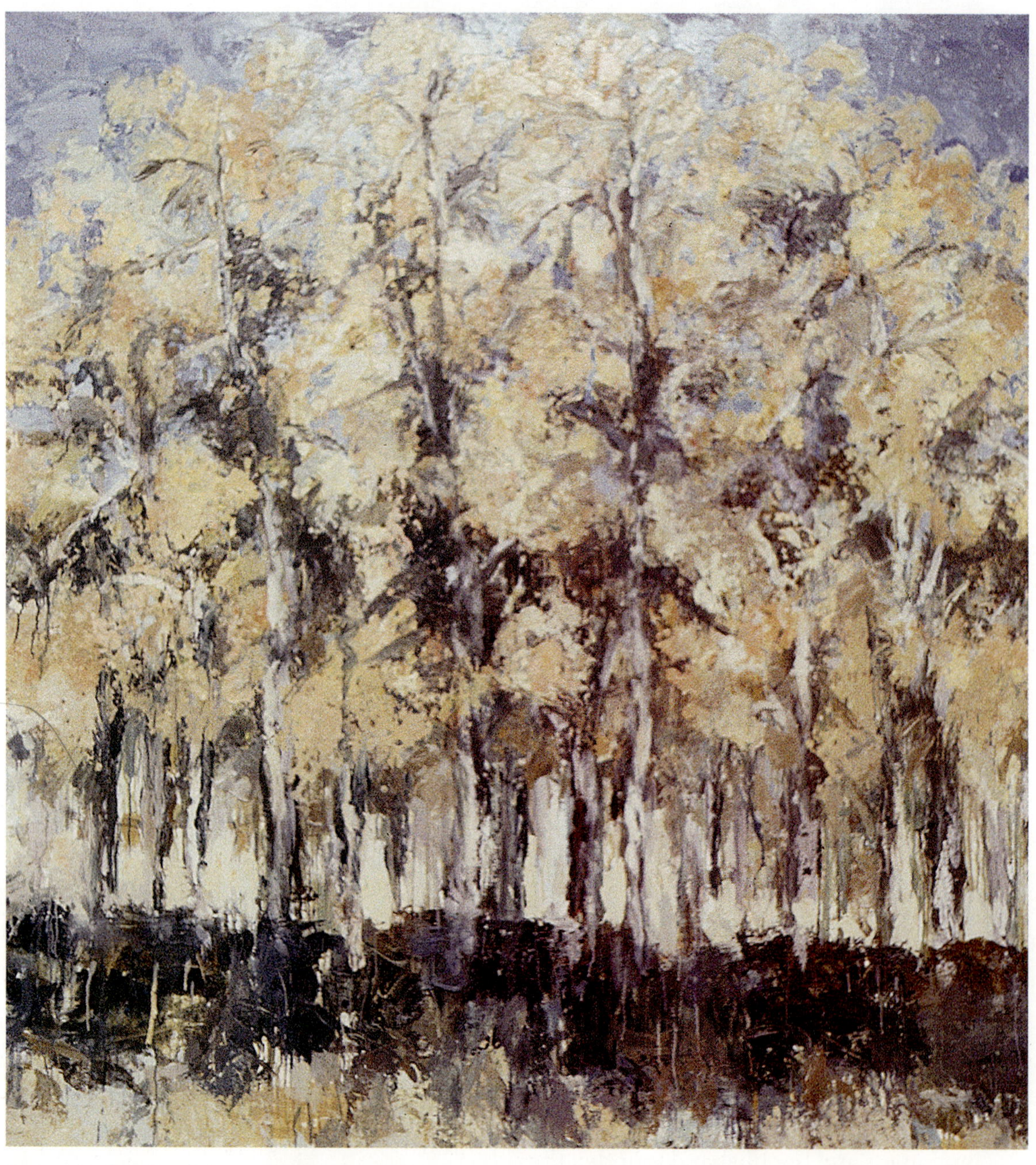

Fig. 5–1 **Artist Theodore Waddell sees all of nature as connected. How did he show this idea in his painting of aspen trees?**

Theodore Waddell, *October Aspen*, 2005 Oil, encaustic on canvas, 84" x 72" (213.4 x 183 cm). Courtesy of the artist.

People react to nature differently. For example, when you come across a spider web, what is your reaction? Do you see it as a nuisance to get rid of immediately, or as a sign that there is an interesting insect nearby? Maybe you see it as a beautiful pattern of lines. One person might think that the web is creepy. Another might show it to friends and talk about its delicate design. The way we react to nature depends on how we think about and interpret, or explain, it.

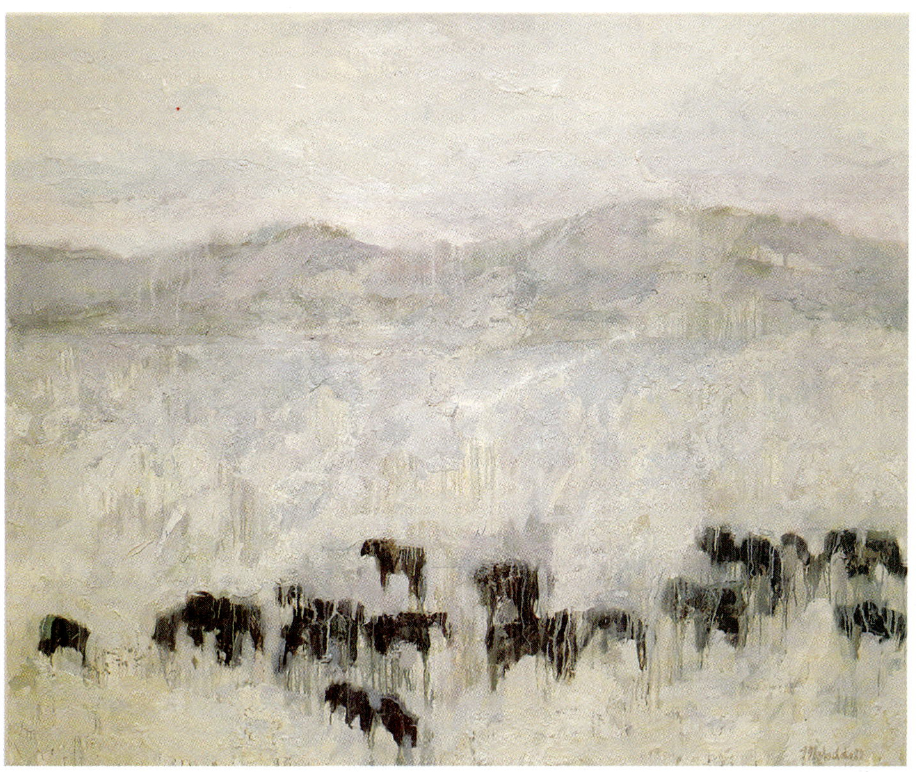

Fig. 5–2 **Waddell notices how the grazing animals in Montana seem to blend into the landscape. How did he use paint to show this?**

Theodore Waddell, *Monida Angus #7*, 2000. Oil, encaustic on canvas, 60" x 72" (152 x 183 cm). Courtesy of the artist.

In this unit, you will learn:

- How artists express ideas about nature using different materials.
- How to paint and sculpt animals in ways that help express your own ideas about them.
- How to view artworks as thoughtful expressions of feelings and ideas about the natural world.

Observing Your Environment

Artists such as Theodore Waddell give us new ways of thinking about what nature provides. He often looks at animals in the environment. Waddell notes how colors in nature change with the seasons and with the time of day. He shows how animals seem to merge with their surroundings, showing the two as if they are one.

Observing Nature Waddell begins by carefully observing his surroundings. He notices that things look different as the seasons change. For example, summer light brings out colors not seen in winter. Horses in the spring reflect the colors of the sky, the grass, and the sunlight. In winter, the horses' forms emerge through snow that Waddell paints in purples, pinks—even black!

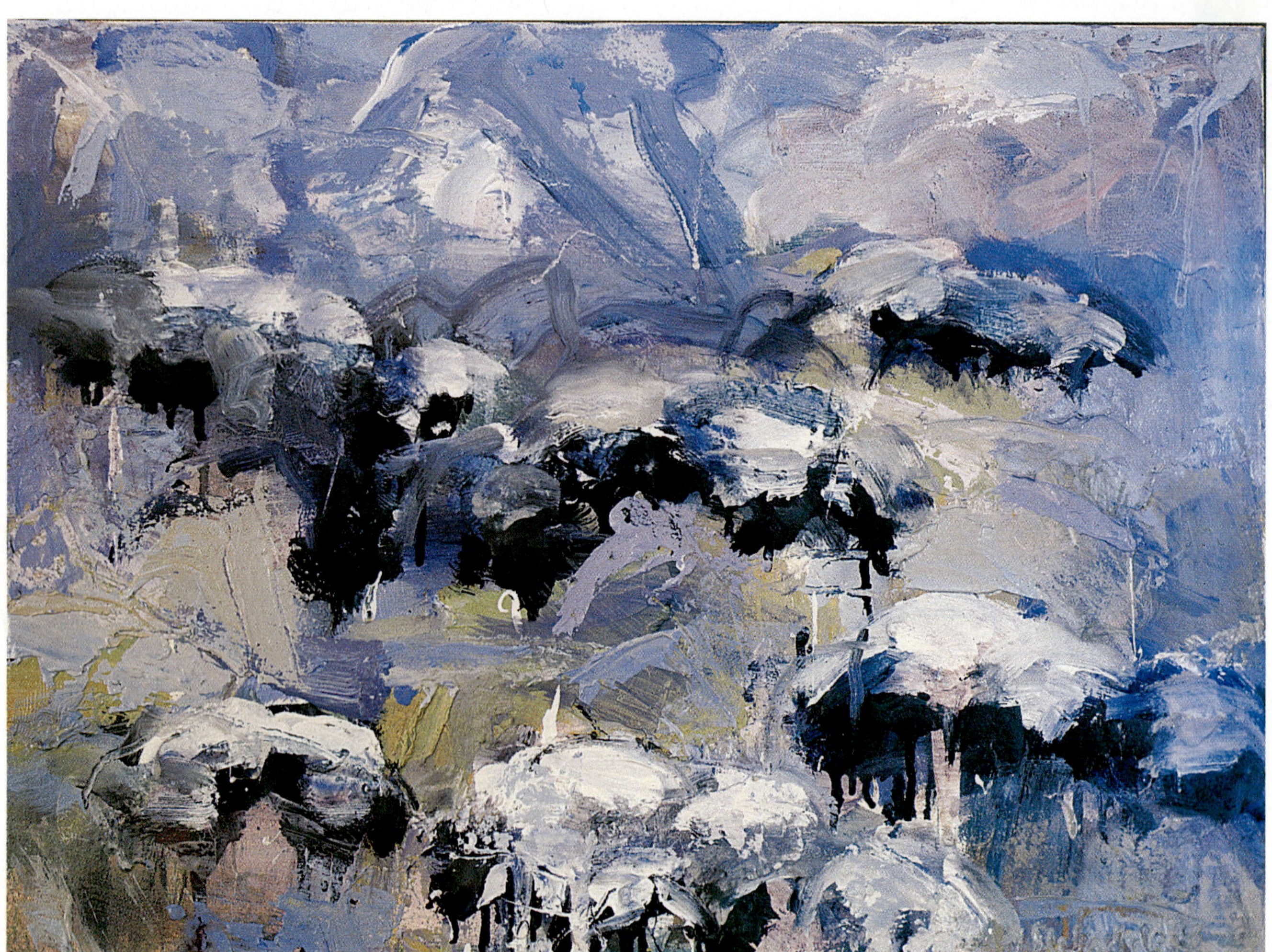

Fig. 5–3 **The painting's title refers to the Impressionist painter Monet, who painted the effects of sunlight. What painting techniques did Waddell use when creating this artwork?**

Theodore Waddell, *Monet's Sheep #3*, 1993. Oil, encaustic on canvas, 18" x 24" (46 x 61 cm). Courtesy of the artist.

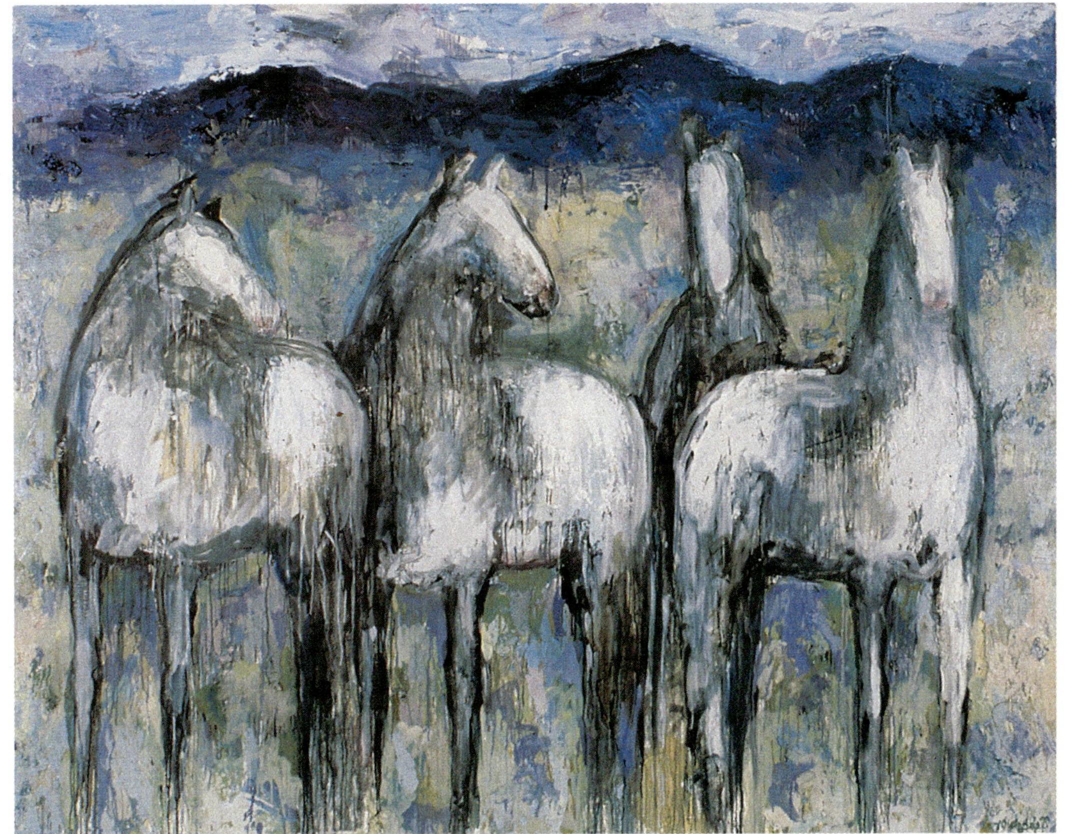

Fig. 5–4 **Waddell paints horses, sheep, and cattle in different ways. How does this painting differ from his paintings shown in Figs. 5–1 and 5–2?**

Theodore Waddell, *Ennis Horses #5*, 1998. Oil, encaustic, graphite, on paper. Courtesy of the artist.

Study the paintings on these two pages. Notice how Waddell experiments with ways to use paint. In his early paintings, he applied paint thickly. To create interesting effects and textures, he applied paint with a brush, a rag, and the heel of his hand. In more recent paintings, he uses thinned paint, quick brushstrokes, and allows the paint to drip.

Meet Theodore Waddell

Theodore Waddell is an artist and a rancher who grew up and still lives in Montana. He left home to study art in college and graduate school, where he was especially interested in making sculpture. When Waddell returned to Montana and took up ranching, he turned to painting because he thought that would be the best medium to show the wide-open spaces of the landscape he loved. Waddell's painted interpretations reveal his thinking about how, in nature, everything is connected.

"I spend a lot of time observing before I begin painting. How animals move on a plain...constantly changing and yet remaining the same."

— Theodore Waddell (born 1941)

Photo by Lynn M. Campion, ©1997.

Communicating Ideas About Nature

Artists from cultures around the globe have found beauty in the natural world. Some artworks show nature as magnificent or grand, while others show it as peaceful or calm. One artist may interpret nature as friendly, but another may find it threatening.

Artists bring their own ideas about nature to their work. Each artist thinks about and interprets nature uniquely. When artists observe nature, they look for and see different features. Some artists are very careful and show every detail of a plant or animal. Other artists want to express a general idea about nature.

You can find interpretations of the natural world in paintings, sculptures, and other types of artworks. Many objects you encounter every day are decorated with artists' images of nature. For example, notice birds and trees on greeting cards. Whenever you see images of nature, try to determine how the artist showed it. Is nature presented as serious or silly? Delicate or bold? Pay attention to the use of color and other art elements to express different moods, feelings, and ideas.

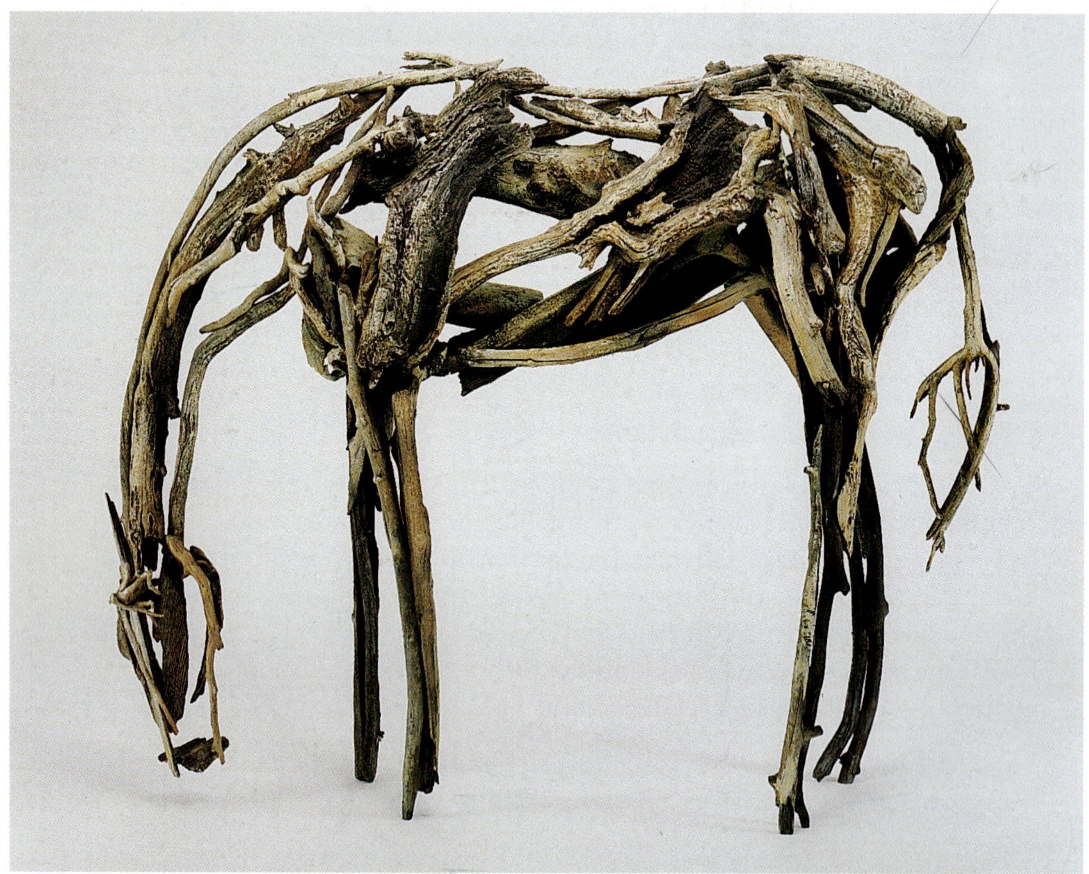

Fig. 5–5 **Deborah Butterfield uses wood, metal, and straw to create large-scale sculptures. This horse sculpture appears to be made of wood, but it is actually sculpted in bronze. How would you describe Butterfield's interpretation of nature?**

Deborah Butterfield, *Cottonwood Creek*, 1995–96. Cast bronze, 81"x 96"x 26" (206 x 244 x 66 cm). Courtesy Buck-Butterfield, Inc. Collection of Art & Sherry Zimand, Orlando, Florida. ©Deborah Butterfield.

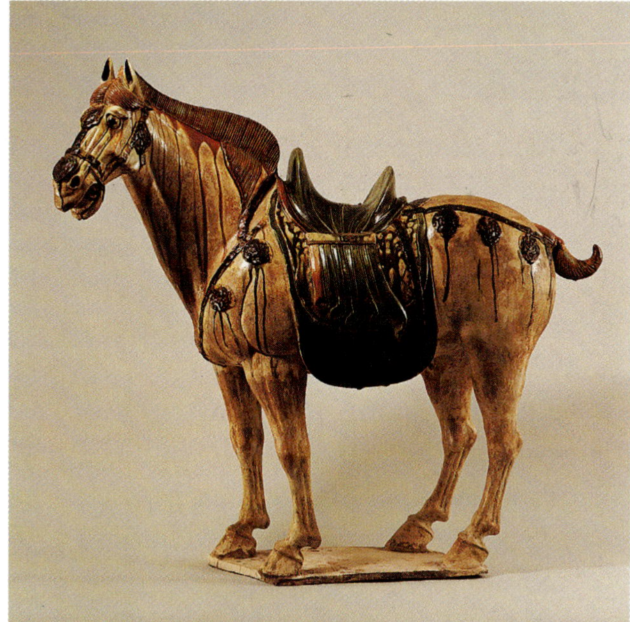

Fig. 5–6 **In China, the horse has always been a revered animal. How does this sculpture show the artist's respect for the importance of the horse?**

China, Tang dynasty, *Horse*, early 8th century. Glazed earthenware, length: 31 ½" (80.5 cm). Soloman Gift Inv.: C50-1964. Photo credit: Victoria and Albert Museum, London/Art Resource, NY.

Check Your Understanding

1. Why might two paintings of the same scene painted by two separate artists look very different?

2. Compare and contrast the artists' interpretations of nature in **Fig. 5–5**, *Cottonwood Creek*, and **Fig. 5–6**, *Tomb Figure of a Saddle Horse*.

3. Why would an artist want to experiment with color when painting an interpretation of nature?

Studio Time

Expression in Wire

Work with wire to create a sculpture of an animal.

- Look at pictures of animals for ideas. Observe basic forms and details.
- Make several contour sketches of animals using a continuous line without lifting your pencil from the paper.
- Use long pieces of flexible aluminum wire to create the three-dimensional form for your animal. Think of the wire as the lines in your contour drawing.
- Try bending, looping, twisting, and joining pieces of wire together to add features and details to your animal.
- With staples or tacks, attach your sculpture to a wood base.

Reflect on the realistic and imaginative aspects of your animal form.

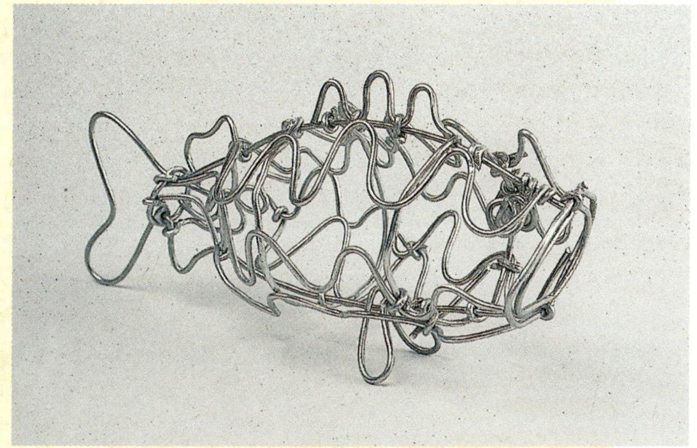

Fig. 5–7 Student artwork

Color Mixing

Knowing Your Color Vocabulary The three primary colors, red, yellow, and blue, are the colors from which all other colors are made. But, do you know how all the other colors are made from these three hues, or colors? Different combinations of the primary colors produce new colors.

Observe Look at the example of mixing primaries. Notice the various colors that are created by mixing combinations of the primary colors.

Tools: Red, yellow, and blue tempera paint, paintbrush, either a paper plate, piece of cardboard, or a disposable palette, and a large sheet of manila paper.

Practice: Mixing Primary Colors

- Begin by painting a small circle of each of the primary colors on the manila paper. Remember to wash, wipe, and blot your brush between colors.
- Then, on a paper plate, piece of cardboard, or disposable palette, mix one primary color with one other primary color.
- Paint another circle with this color, and label it with the names of the colors you mixed.
- Continue practicing until you have mixed a variety of combinations, including a mixture of all three colors.

Mixing Primaries

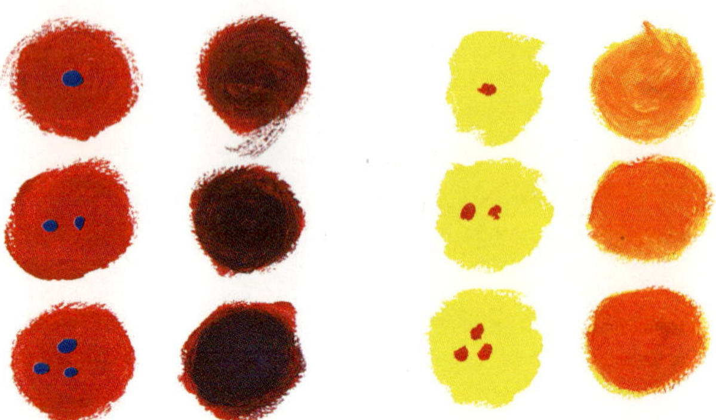

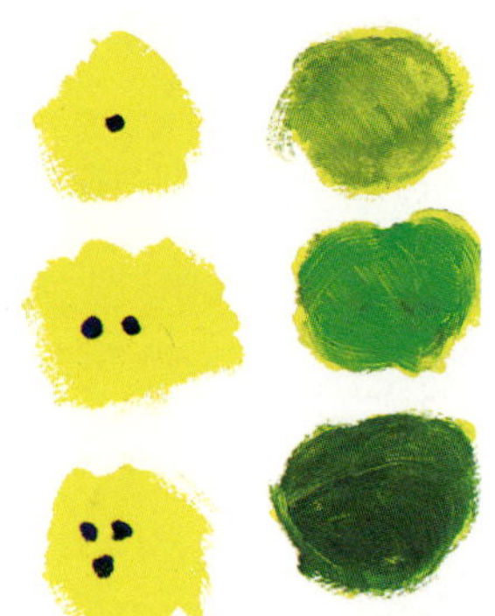

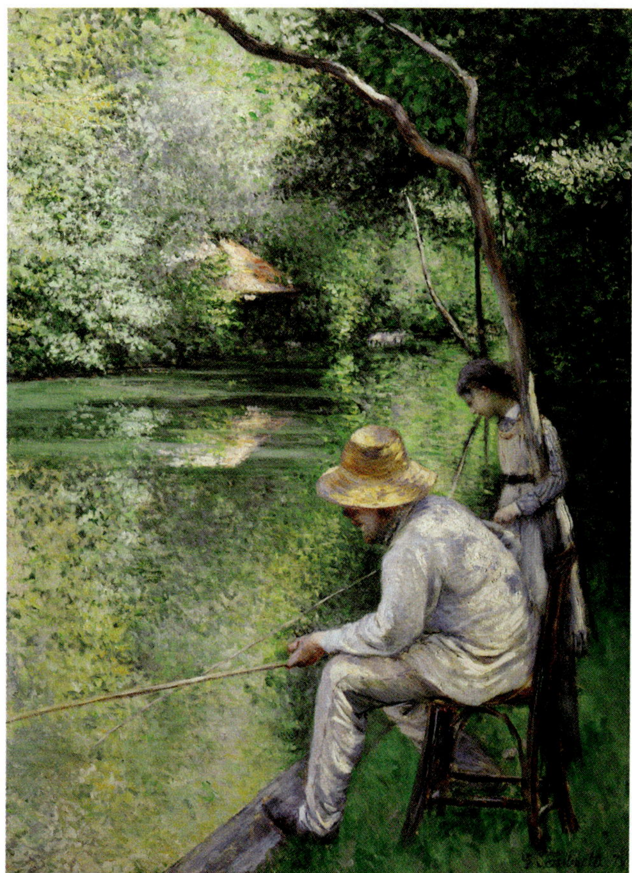

Fig. 5–8 **How did the artist use tints and shades to create this painting?**

Gustave Caillebotte, *Pêche a la ligne—Fishing*, 1878. Location: Private Collection, France. Photo: Erich Lessing / Art Resource, NY.

Mixing Tints

Mixing Shades

Creating Tints and Shades Mixing colors with white makes them lighter. A lighter value of a color is called a tint. Adding black makes a color darker. A darker value of a color is called a shade.

Observe Notice how tints and shades are mixed below. What happens when small amounts of red are mixed into a patch of white? When black is added to a patch of red?

Tools: Red, yellow, or blue tempera paint, white and black tempera paint, paintbrush, and manila paper.

Practice: Tints and Shades

- On manila paper, begin with three small circles of white paint.
- Add a drop of either red, yellow, or blue paint to one circle, and mix.
- Add two drops of the same color to the second circle, and mix.
- Add three drops of the same color to the third circle, and mix.
- Label each circle with the names and amounts of colors you mixed.
- Repeat the process, this time starting with three circles of either red, yellow, or blue paint, and adding first one, then two, and finally three drops of black to each.

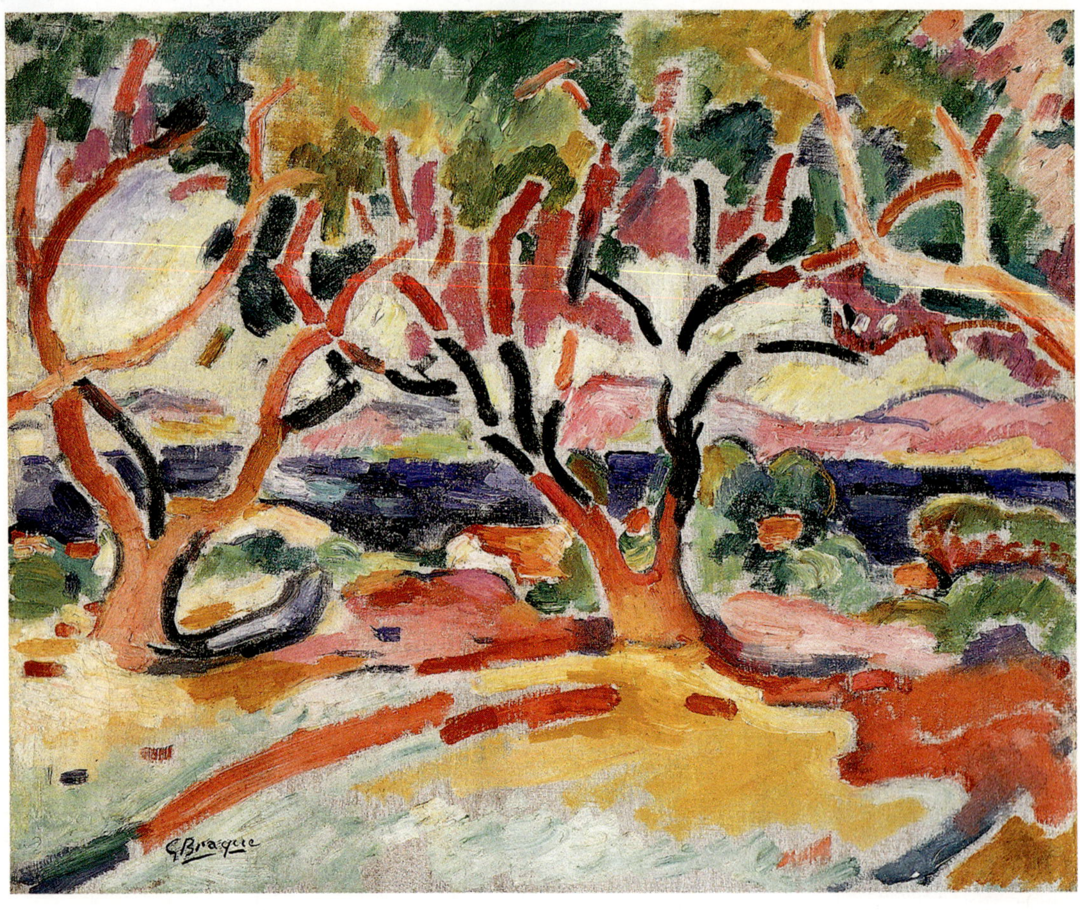

Fig. 5–9 **What colors appear in different intensities? What do you think the artist's interpretation of this nature scene is?**

Georges Braque, *Olive Trees*, 1907. Oil on canvas, 14 15/16" x 18 ¼" (38 x 46.3 cm). Worcester Art Museum, Worcester, Massachusetts, 1970.122 Gift from the estate of Mrs. Aldus Chapin Higgins. ©Artists Rights Society (ARS), New York/ ADAGP, Paris.

Changing Intensities In art, the word **intensity** refers to how bright or dull a color is. To make a color duller, you can add a small amount of its complement. A **complement** is the color opposite a color on the color wheel. For example, green is the complement of red. Adding a very small amount of green to red will make the red duller.

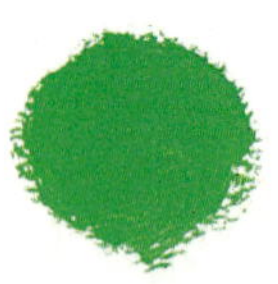
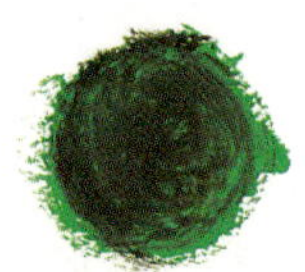
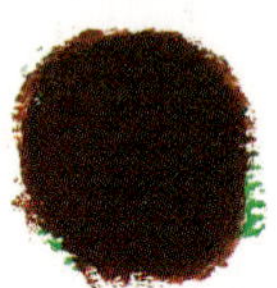
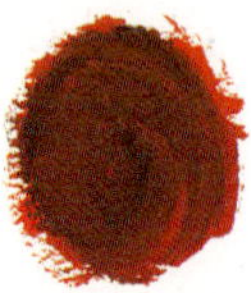
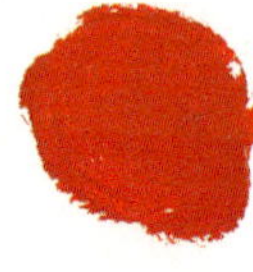

Intensity Scale

Observe Look at the intensity scale example on this page. How do the five circles differ in intensity?

Tools: Yellow, violet, red, green, orange, and blue tempera paint, paintbrush, and manila paper.

Practice: Intensities

- Practice changing the intensity of a color. First, paint three circles of yellow on manila paper.
- Leave the first circle alone. Add a drop of violet to the second circle, and mix.
- Add two drops of violet to the third circle, and mix.
- Label each circle with colors and amount of paint mixed.
- Try the same experiment with red and green, and orange and blue.

Check Your Understanding

1. How are all non-primary colors made?
2. Compare and contrast how the process of changing the intensity of a color is different from and similar to the process of changing the value of a color.
3. Why would you want to mix colors when you paint?

Studio Time

Color in Nature

Choose a subject from nature for a small tempera painting on paper.

- You might decide to create a landscape, or you might focus on certain animals, trees, or plants.
- Think about the natural colors of your subject. Mix your own colors and change the intensity to make the colors appear more realistic.
- Be sure to include at least one primary color, one tint, and one shade.

Reflect on the variety of colors, values, and intensities in your artwork.

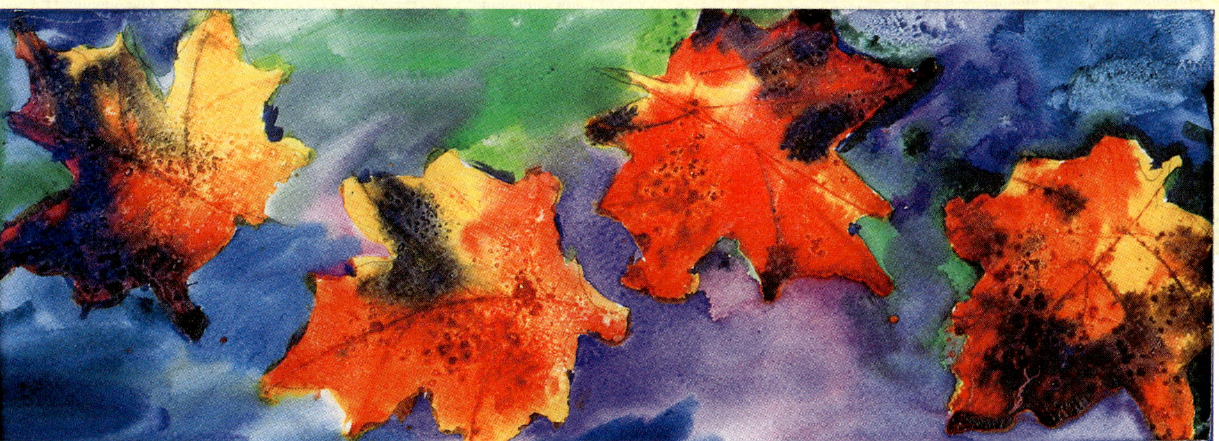

Fig. 5–10 Student artwork

Painting Nature's Creatures

Studio Background

Before interpreting nature in an artwork, an artist first looks carefully at the natural world. The artist probably has some ideas about nature, such as whether it should be controlled or left alone. As a painter, the artist must decide which techniques and colors will best express those ideas. How would you express your interpretation of your natural environment?

In this studio exploration, you will create a painting of an animal in natural surroundings. Through your artwork, you will express feelings and ideas. As you work, remember that your painting will be viewed as your interpretation of the animal.

You Will Need

- heavy drawing paper
- pencil and eraser
- white construction paper, 2 sheets
- tempera paint
- variety of paintbrushes
- water
- palette or disposable plate

Step 1 Plan and Practice

- Choose an animal that interests you. What is its environment?
- Think about the ideas you have about the animal and its environment. How do you want to express these ideas?
- Think of ways to show the animal. Do you want it to look powerful and strong or in need of protection?

Things to Remember:

✓ Include background scenery.

✓ Add details that help express feelings and ideas about the animal.

✓ Mix colors to create various tints, shades, and intensities.

Inspiration from Our World

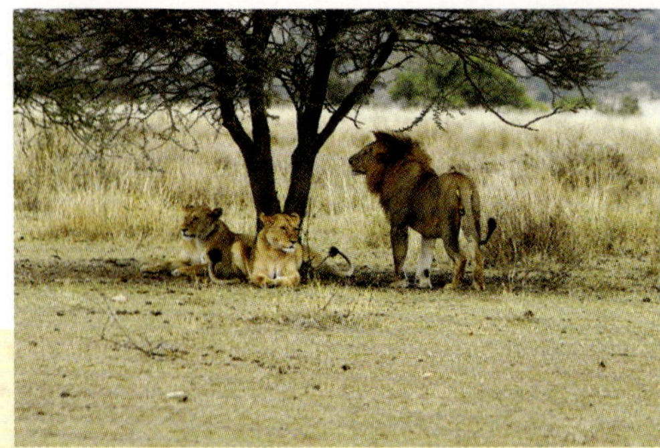

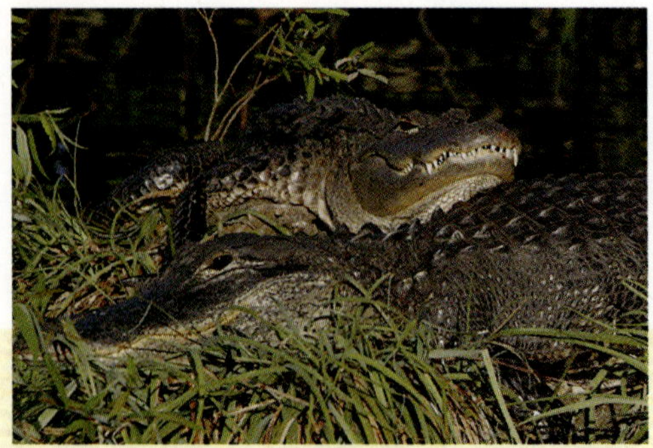

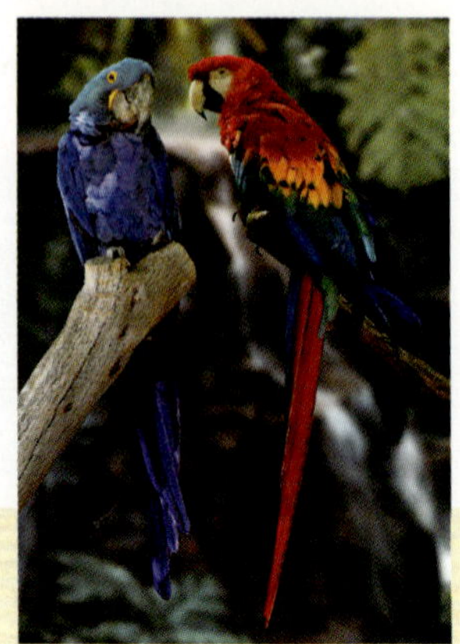

Inspiration from Art

Elements of art, such as line, color, value, and texture, help artists show their ideas more clearly. When artists interpret the natural world in a painting, they decide how they will use these elements to express their ideas and feelings.

Painters may use lines that are sharp and clear, or soft and blurred. They may decide to use many colors or just a few, and may have them range from light to very dark values. To create a mood, painters may create a work with dramatic lighting and shadows—or one with very little contrast. Painters may also use texture to create what looks like a rough or smooth surface, or one of many different textures. Look at the painting on this page. Which elements of art did Franz Marc use and how did he use them?

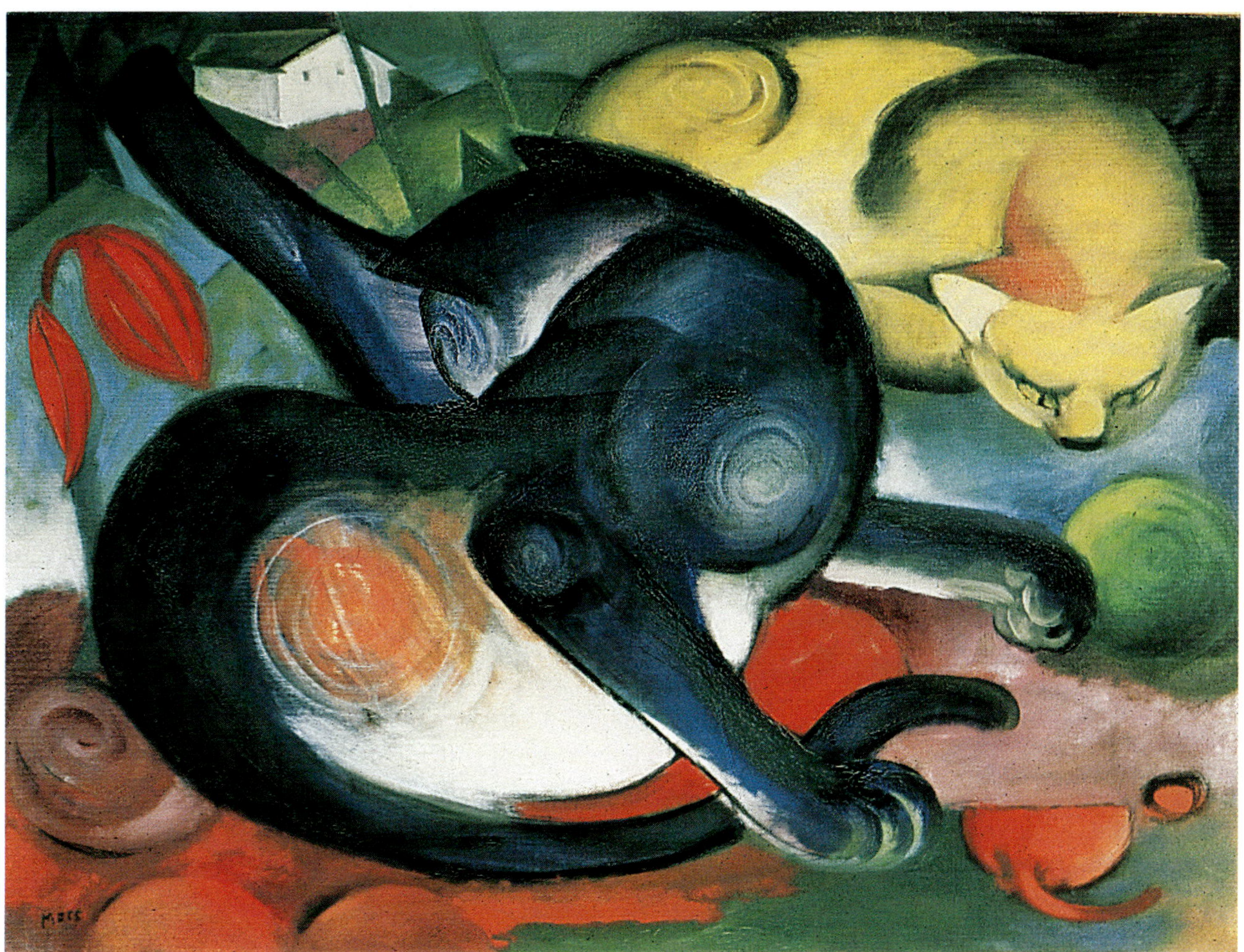

Fig. 5–11 **When painting a scene or object from nature, artists sometimes use expressive colors. What feelings or ideas did Franz Marc express in this painting?**

Franz Marc, *Two Cats, Blue and Yellow,* 1912. Oil on canvas, 74" x 98" (188 x 249 cm). Oeffentliche Kunstsammlung, Basel, Switzerland. Photo credit: Art Resource, NY.

Step 2 Begin to Create

- On drawing paper, create a sketch of your animal and its surroundings. Sketch the largest shapes first.
- **As you sketch, think about where you will place the animal on the page and from what angle you will show it.** Will it be doing something? What kind of background scenery will you include?

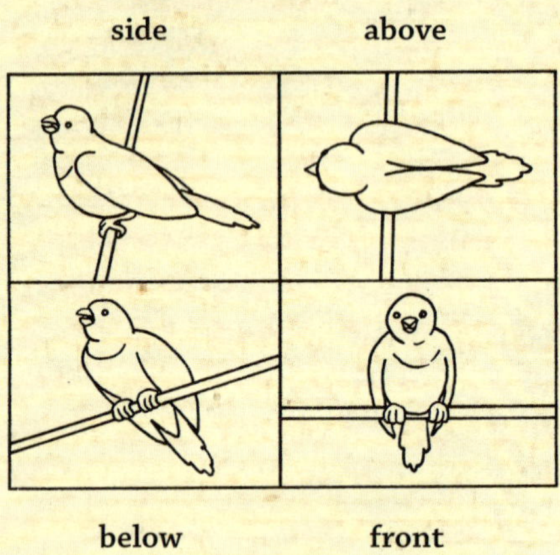

- Experiment with mixing colors of paint on a plate.
- On a sheet of white construction paper, test the colors you mix.
- Decide which colors will best express your interpretation of the animal. Will you use expressive color—color that expresses feelings or ideas of the subject? Or will you use local color—color that you see in the natural world?
- On another sheet of construction paper, **experiment making brushstrokes using a variety of paintbrushes.** What textures and effects can you make? How can you use them to create the forms and details of your scene?

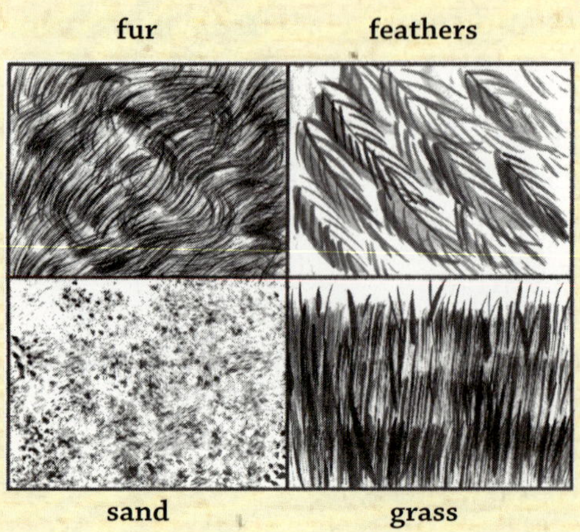

- **Begin adding color to your sketch.** Paint large areas of color first.

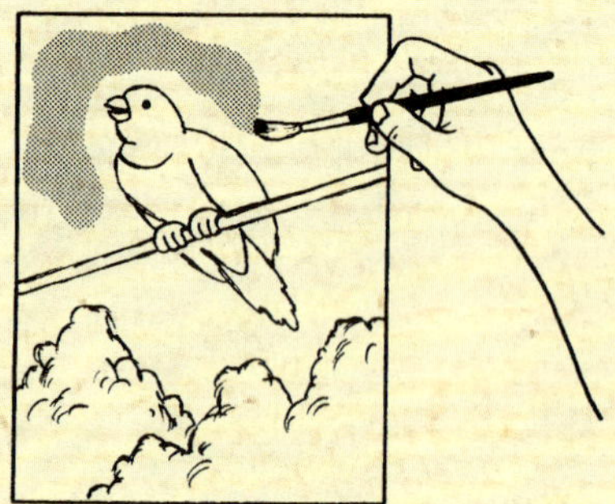

Step 3 Revise

Did you remember to:

✓ Include background scenery?
✓ Add details that help express feelings and ideas about the animal?
✓ Mix colors to create various tints, shades, and intensities?

Adjust your work if necessary. In your sketchbook, make a note of your revisions and why you made them.

Step 4 **Add Finishing Touches**

- When the paint is dry, add final details to your painting.

Step 5 **Share and Reflect**

- Share your finished painting with a group of classmates.
- Discuss the overall process of creating your artwork. How did you use paint to create an animal in natural surroundings? What kinds of brushstrokes did you experiment with and use?
- What ideas and feelings did you try to express with your painting? How did you use color, line, shape, and texture to convey these feelings?

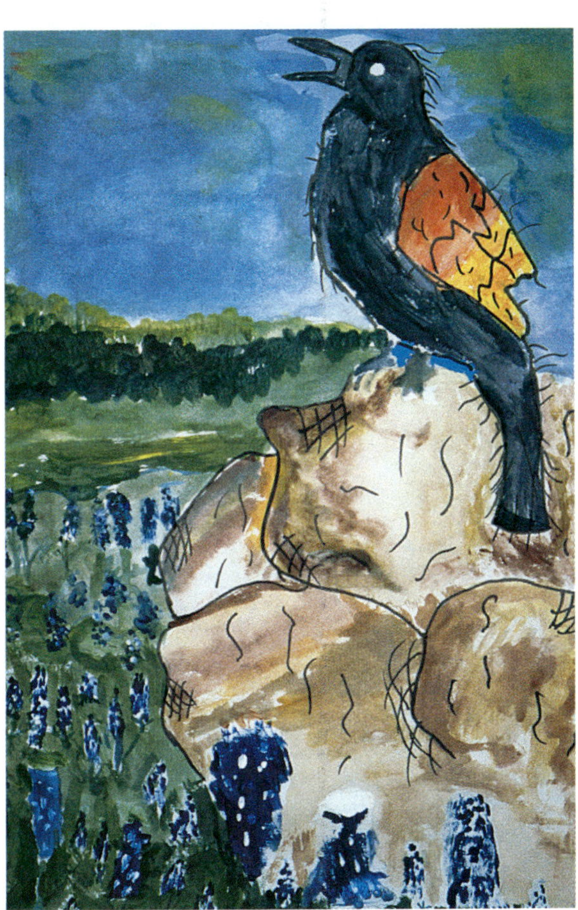

Art Criticism

Describe What does the artist show in this painting?

Analyze How has the artist used color and balance to organize this artwork?

Interpret What ideas and feelings about nature seem to be expressed in this artwork?

Evaluate What has the artist done especially well in this painting?

Fig. 5–12 Student artwork

A Tradition of Landscape

Throughout history, artists have interpreted the land in many different ways. Some have shown the land as a decorative pattern, while others have shown it as a dreamlike vision. Dutch painters of the 1600s, such as Jacob van Ruisdael **(Fig. 5–13)**, were interested in the quality of light and open space. By studying every color and detail, these painters were able to capture the shifting shapes formed by clouds and the changing effects of sunlight on water. Their interpretations of the landscape were both dramatic and natural.

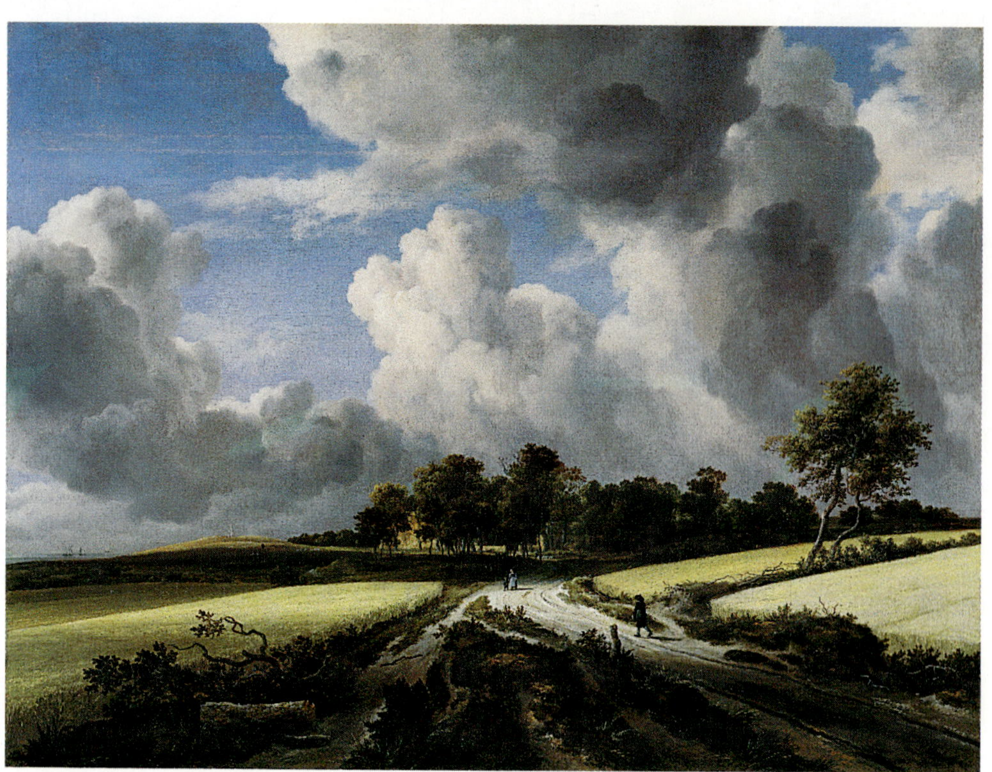

Fig. 5–13 **Note the band of sunlight through the lower third of the painting. What happens to the colors of a landscape when clouds block the sun?**

Jacob van Ruisdael, *Wheatfields*, 1670. Oil on canvas, 39 ⅜" x 51 ¼" (100 x 130 cm). Metropolitan Museum of Art, Bequest of Benjamin Altman, 1913 (14.40.623). Photograph ©1994 The Metropolitan Museum of Art.

1600s

1617 The Pilgrims leave Holland to start their voyage to America.

1670 van Ruisdael, *Wheatfields*

1800s

1825 The Erie Canal is completed, connecting Lake Erie and the Hudson River.

1835 Turner, *The Burning of the Houses of Lords and Commons*

1859 Charles Darwin's *The Origin of Species* is published.

1863 Heade, *Sunset Over the Marshes*

1900s

1983 Gornik, *Divided Sky*

1991 Gornik, *Light at the Equator*

1997 The Kyoto Protocol, a program aimed to curb global warming, is established.

Interpreting Land, Sea, and Sky Many European and North American artists of the 1800s continued to interpret the character of the landscape. One of these artists was J.M.W. Turner **(Fig. 5–14)**, a Romantic artist. Romantic artists focused on dramatic, emotional interpretations of nature's power and beauty. Realist artists, on the other hand, concentrated on the realistic appearance of the land, sea, and sky.

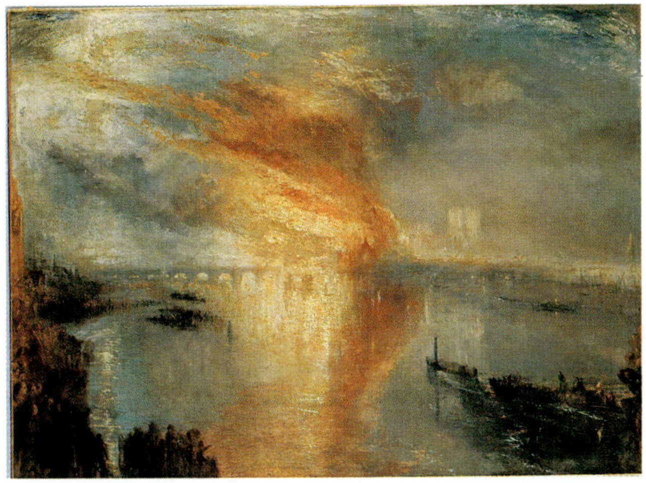

Fig. 5–14 **Why is Turner called a Romantic painter? How did he use colors to show the elements of fire, water, and air?**

J. M. W. Turner, *The Burning of the Houses of Lords and Commons, October 16, 1834*, 1835. Oil on fabric, 36 ½" x 48 ½" (93 x 123 cm). © The Cleveland Museum of Art, Bequest of John L. Severance, 1942.647.

Luminous Landscapes The study of light on the landscape was very important for a group of American artists in the mid-1800s. Art historians now refer to this interest in natural light as Luminism. The American Luminist painters were concerned mostly with showing water and sky. Their works were realistic and had no sign of brushwork. The artists were precise in showing different textures and the colors created by reflected and direct light. The image in **Fig. 5–15** shows one artist's interpretation of the effects of light at sunset.

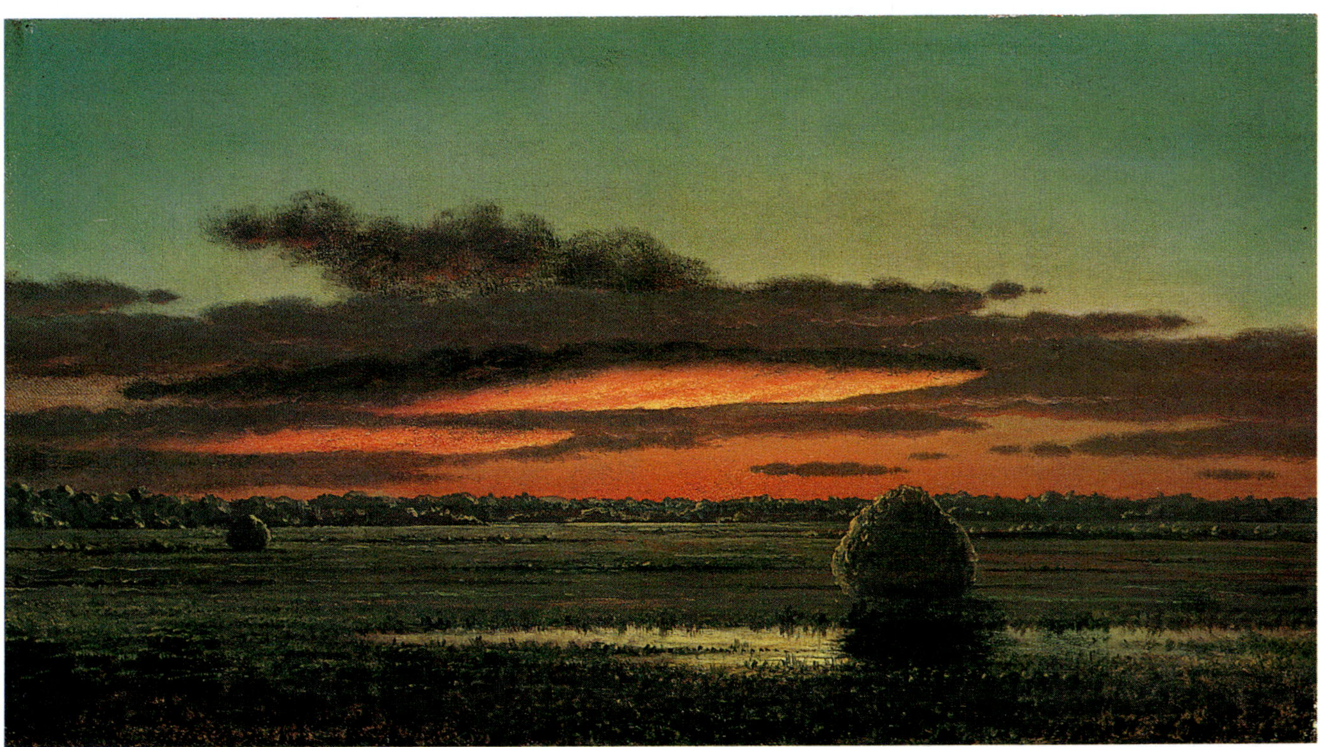

Fig. 5–15 **How did the artist use variations in color to create a feeling of deep space?**

Martin J. Heade, *Sunset over the Marshes*, about 1890–1904. Oil on canvas 10 ¼" x 18 ¼" (26.03 x 46.35 cm) Museum of Fine Arts, Boston. Gift of Maxim Karolik for the M. and M. Karolik Collection of American Paintings, 1815–1865.

Contemporary Landscape Art The challenge facing today's landscape artists is that they want to do more than paint what they see. They also want to communicate feelings and ideas about the natural forms of the landscape. American artist April Gornik achieves that balance by observing and interpreting nature.

Look closely at Gornik's paintings *Divided Sky* and *Light at the Equator* **(Figs. 5–16, 5–17)**. Notice how she focuses on the pureness of light, color, and the natural landscape. Her large drawings and paintings can be described as luminous because light seems to shine through her colors. Although her work is often compared to the American Luminist painters of the 1800s, Gornik does not try to capture a specific place, time, or climate. Instead, she sets out to make something extraordinary—a beautiful artwork.

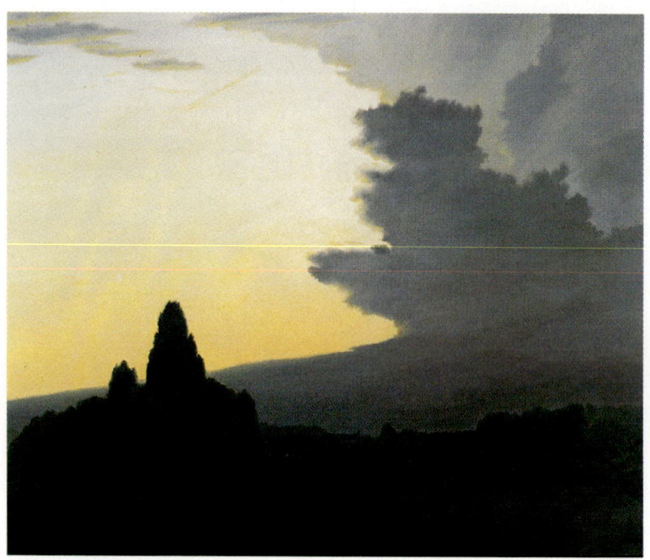

Fig. 5–16 **What do the clouds in this painting suggest to you?**

April Gornik, *Divided Sky*, 1983. Oil on canvas, 72" x 85" (183 x 216 cm). Jack S. Blanton Museum of Art. The University of Texas at Austin. Gift of Mr. and Mrs. Jack Herring, 1984.

Fig. 5–17 **The artist probably started this work with a series of small sketches. She then worked on one image and enlarged it, with pencil, on a canvas.**

April Gornik, *Light at the Equator*, 1991. Oil on linen, 74" x 131" (188 x 333 cm). Courtesy of the artist.

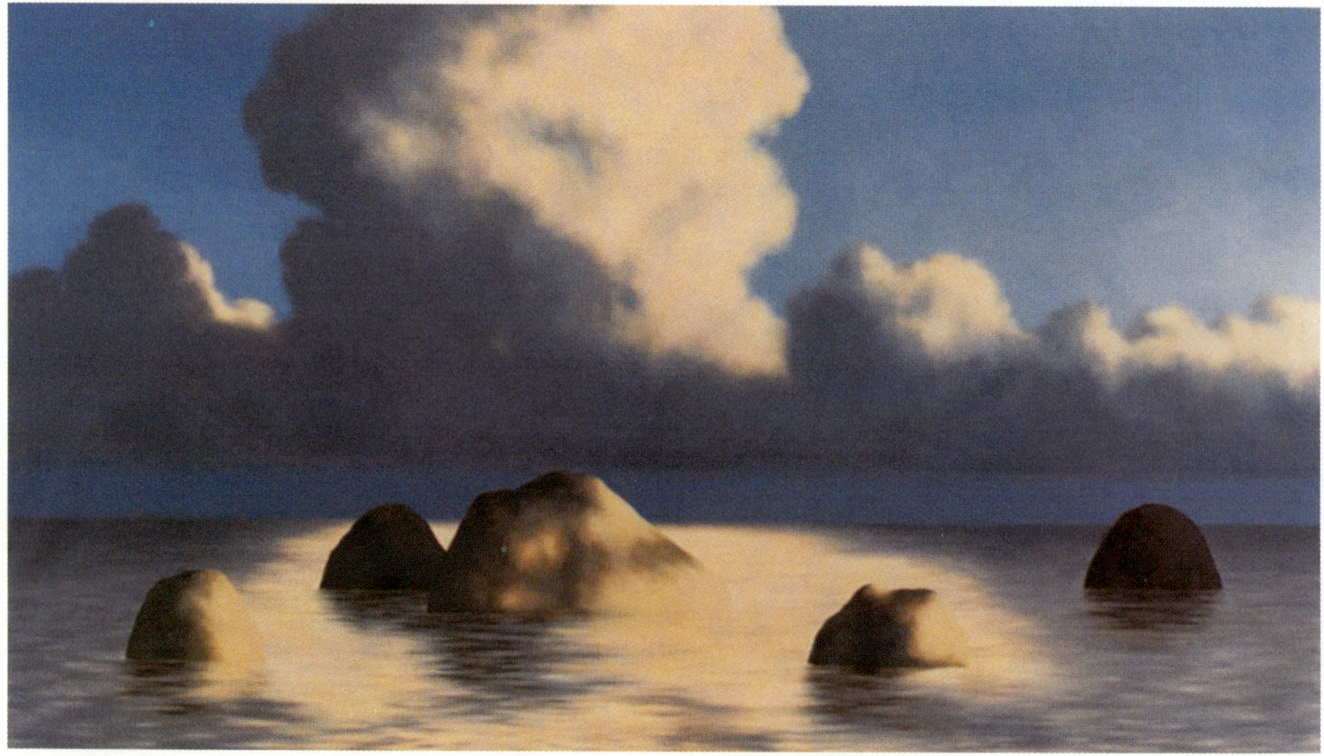

Meet April Gornik

Artist April Gornik remembers that as a child in Ohio, she would go outside and look for storms. She saw the sky as a way to reach beyond the limits of her world. Once she finished school, Gornik got the chance to travel to Europe. Here, in a small Dutch museum, she saw Jan Vermeer's *View of Delft*, a landscape painting from the 1600s. She did not know it at the time, but this visit influenced her own future creations.

When Gornik returned to the United States, she started painting landscapes. Years later, when she again viewed Vermeer's work, she realized that elements in *View of Delft* were what she was creating in her own landscapes.

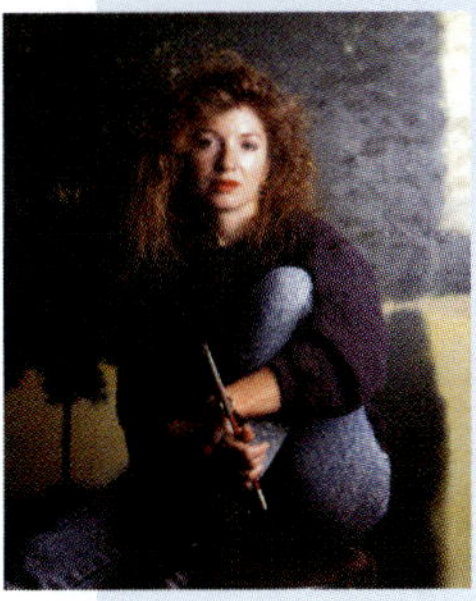

Photo: Timothy Greenfield-Sanders

As an artist, April Gornik wants her landscapes to have a fictional, "other world" quality. She wants viewers to put themselves into her landscapes and experience the space.

"I really do love beauty."

— April Gornik (born 1953)

Check Your Understanding

1. What is *Luminism*?
2. What are some similarities and differences between the work of April Gornik and the work of other artists in this lesson?
3. Why are the qualities of light and color important to landscape painters?

Studio Time

A Colorful Outdoor Scene

Using pastels on colored paper, interpret and draw an outdoor scene.

- Think about what you will draw. How much of your paper will you use for the sky? What colors will you use?
- Choose if you will show things up close or far away. Will you focus on a specific part of the outdoor scene?
- Think about how you will show light and dark areas. How can you show the brightness or gloominess of the sky? How can you show where the light comes from?

Reflect on how well your drawing captures the effects of light on the landscape.

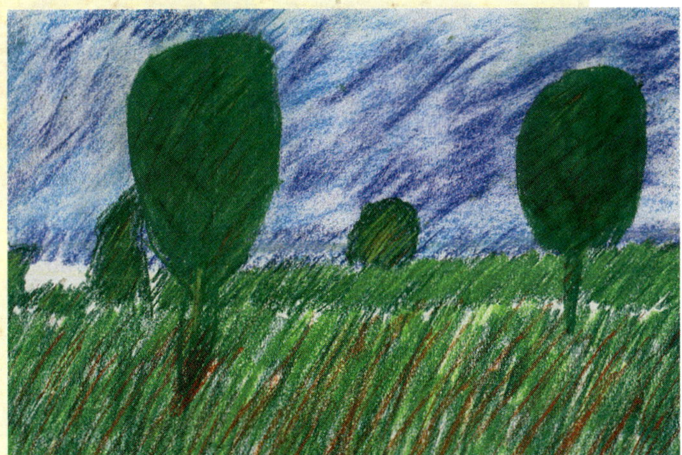

Fig. 5–18 Student artwork

Chinese Nature Paintings

Nature Scenes on Crafted Objects At the beginning of Chinese culture, artists looked to nature for ideas. They decorated vessels with images of plants and animals. Artists studied the natural world to get ideas for decorating precious objects. They often covered objects, such as the pieces shown in **Figs. 5–19** and **5–20**, with images from nature.

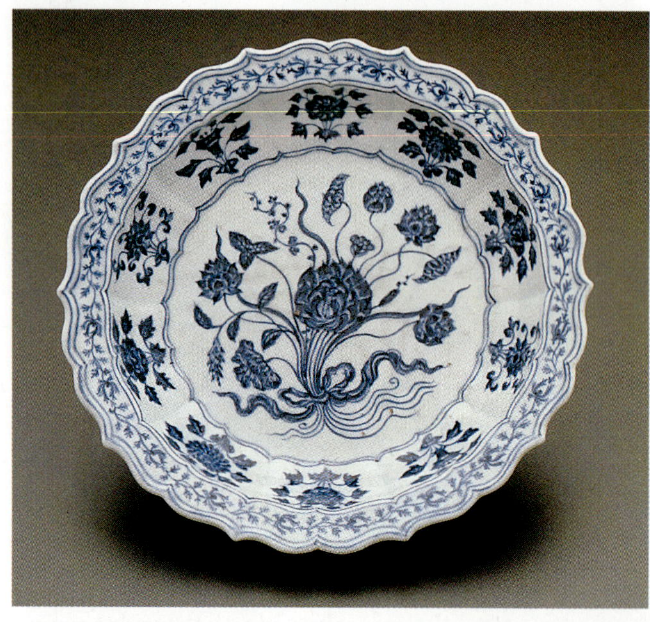

Fig. 5–19 **What ideas about nature do you see here?**

China, Ming dynasty, Xuande period, *Dish*, 1426–35. Porcelain with underglaze blue decoration, height: 2" (5.1 cm). Gift of Russell Tyson, 1955.1204. Photograph: Christopher Gallagher. The Art Institute of Chicago, Chicago, Illinois.

Learning to Paint Nature Painters during the Ming dynasty and other dynasties were well-educated. An important part of this education was nature painting. Artists interpreted the beauty of nature in their artworks, which helped the emperors stress the importance of harmony between humans and nature.

Learning from Past Artists The Ming dynasty artistic rules were based on ideas and methods from earlier times. Artists were educated to paint the natural world in the styles of the well-known artists of the past. Thus, an artist such as Wen Boren **(Fig. 5–21)** could paint in at least six different styles and produce landscapes ranging from dramatic to peaceful.

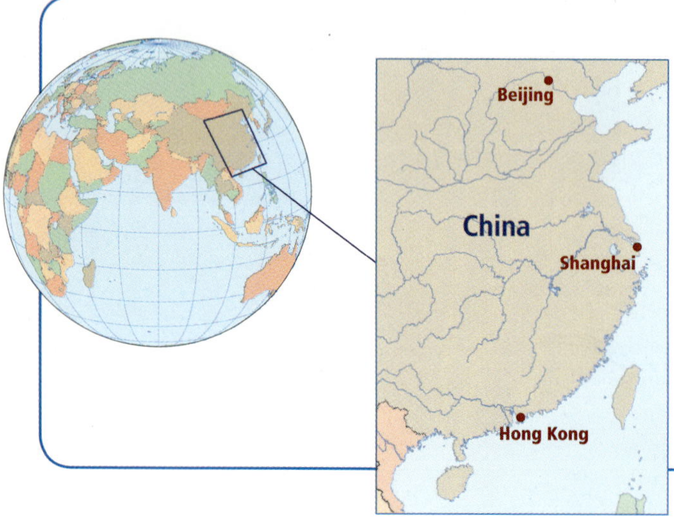

Social Studies Connection

For thousands of years, **China** was governed by many dynasties. Dynasties are powerful family groups who rule through many generations. Under the emperors who controlled these dynasties, the arts in China grew. The change of powerful emperors from one dynasty to another often resulted in a change in the look of China's art. This was especially so during the Ming dynasty (1368–1644).

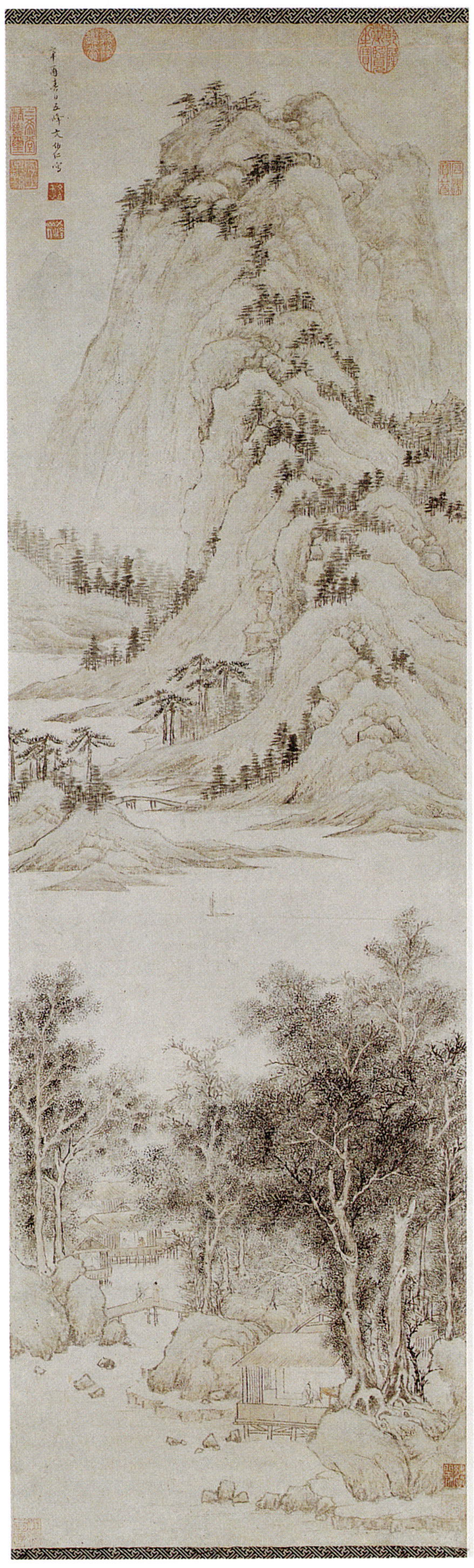

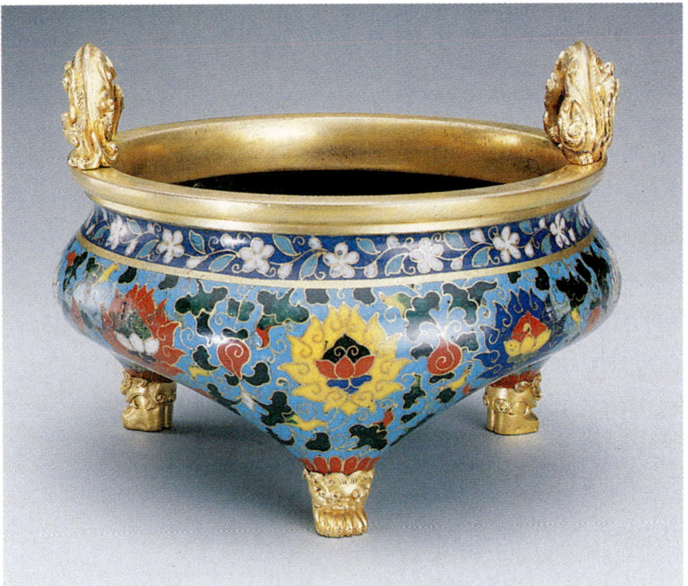

Fig. 5–21 **What elements of nature are included on this burner? Why do you think the artist used such bright colors?**

China, Ming dynasty, *Incense Burner*, 16th century. Cloisonné enamel. Freer Gallery of Art, Smithsonian Institution, Washington, DC. F1961.12.

Visual Culture

Like traditional Chinese artists, many designers and decorators today are influenced and inspired by nature. Look around your home and community. What objects in your home have designs that have been inspired by nature? What products that you see in stores and markets come in packages decorated with a nature theme?

Fig. 5–20 **What words would you use to describe this artist's interpretation of nature?**

Wen Boren, *River Landscape with Towering Mountains*, 1561. Hanging scroll, ink and color on paper. Eugene Fuller Memorial collection, Seattle Art Museum.

Understanding the Artist's Process

Like past artists, contemporary artists in China study the masterworks of Chinese art. Chao Shao-an's paintings show his strong attachment to nature. Before beginning to paint, he carefully studied subjects in nature. He interpreted his subjects according to his own mood or feeling. He also based his interpretations on his own ideas about color, light and shade, and perspective. Although most of his compositions appear to be very simple, Chao planned them carefully.

Combining the Past with the Present

In paintings such the ones shown on this page, Chao Shao-an used modern techniques to show traditional subjects. Art critics call attention to the modern look of his brushwork. Chao used dry and loose brushstrokes to create textures and to catch his subjects' natural beauty. He skillfully built up layers of ink and color washes, where strong colors gradually fade into soft tones.

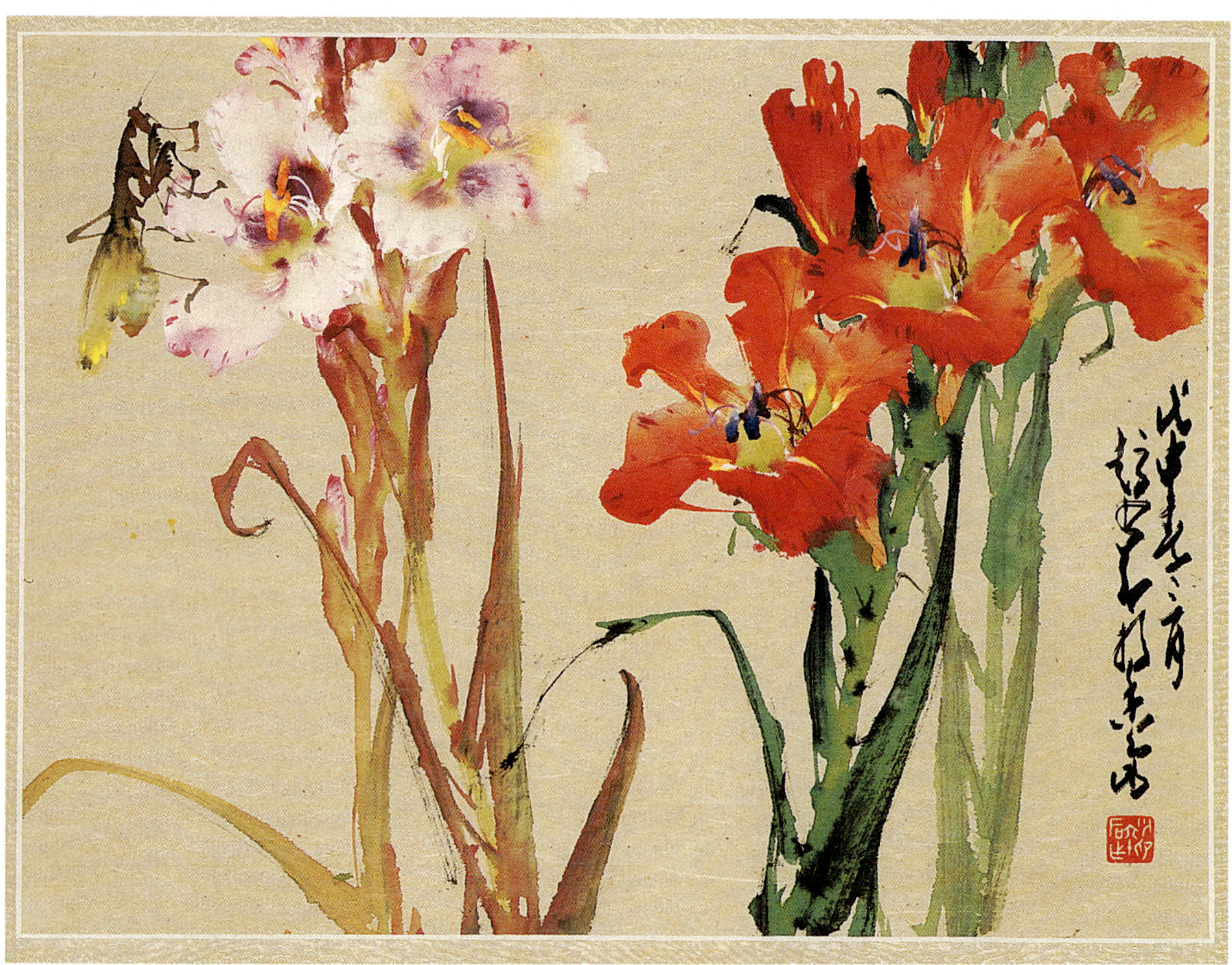

Fig. 5–22 **How did the artist use colors in his interpretation of these flowers?**

Chao Shao-an (China), *Gladioli*, 1968. Ink and colors on paper. Collection of Master Chao Shao-an, 1992.248. Image ©Asian Art Museum of San Francisco. Used by permission.

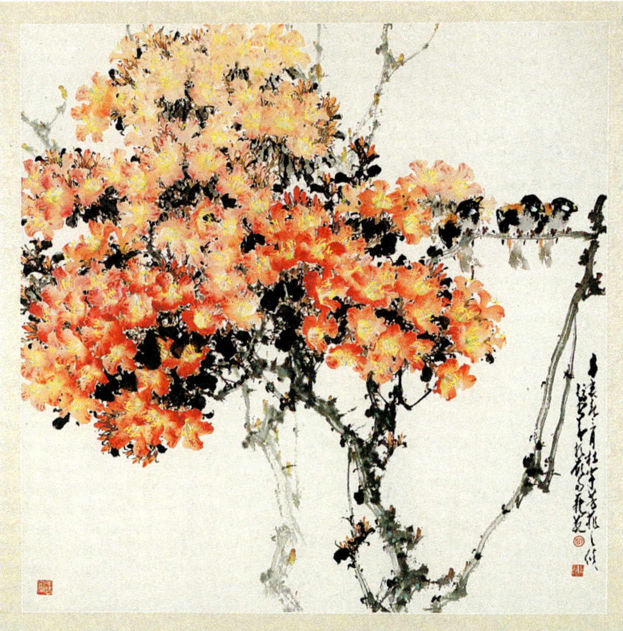

Fig. 5–23 **How did the artist reflect the warmth of azaleas in springtime?**

Chao Shao-an (China), *Azaleas*, 1971. Ink and colors on paper. Collection of Master Chao Shao-an, 1992.239. Image ©Asian Art Museum of San Francisco. Used by permission.

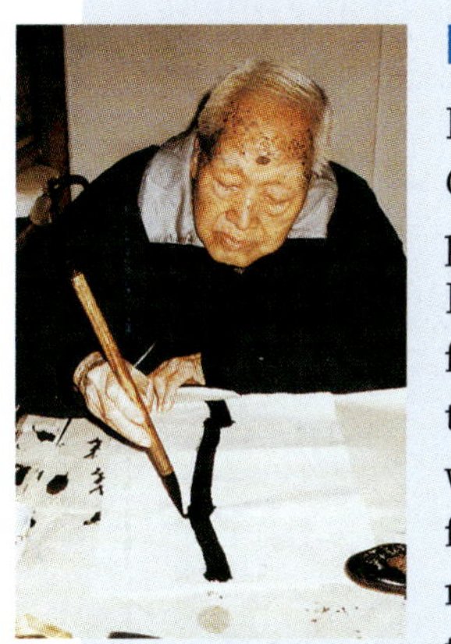

Asian Art Museum of San Francisco.

Meet Chao Shao-an

Like many young Chinese, Chao Shao-an drew from pictures and old paintings. He was interested in art from an early age and taught himself to paint in watercolors. When he was fifteen, he studied with a master painter and continued to polish the techniques used by the old masters. He also learned new methods of drawing from life. He soon became known as a creative painter of birds, animals, and flowers.

"I recall fondly a life devoted to books."

—Chao Shao-an (1905–1998)

Check Your Understanding

1. When and why did the style of art change in China?
2. Compare and contrast Chao Shao-an's art with that of Wen Boren. How are they similar? How are they different?
3. How does artwork from the past influence your style? Explain.

Studio Time

Watercolor Flowers

Use the qualities and techniques of watercolor in your interpretation of flowers, leaves, and branches in a vase.

- Think about how you will arrange your composition to make a colorful interpretation of floral forms. Will your paper be vertical or horizontal?
- Make a light pencil sketch showing shapes and details.
- Experiment with watercolor washes and thick and thin brushstrokes.

Reflect on the variety of brushstrokes you have used.

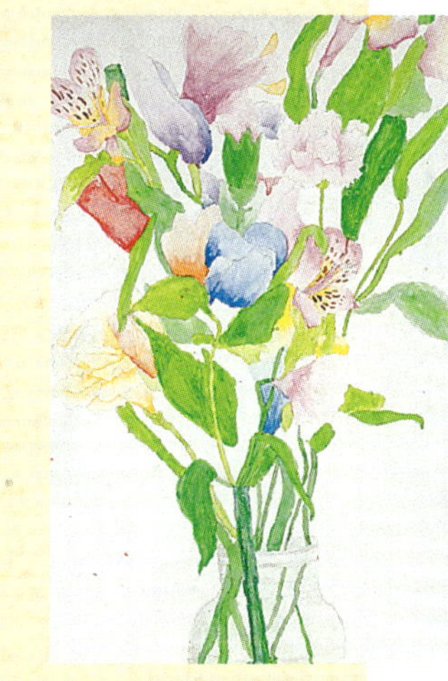

Fig. 5–24
Student artwork

From Branches to Animals

Studio Background

Have you ever seen a cloud shaped like a walrus? How about tree branches in the shape of a horse? Shapes and forms we see in nature can excite our imagination, and can inspire artists to make fantastic creations. Artists often respond to qualities, such as shape, form, and color, that art materials offer.

In this studio exploration, you will build a sculptural animal out of wood scraps and branches. Look carefully at collected scraps of wood. Find interesting wood forms or branches or twigs that have fallen from trees. Turn the wood pieces and look at all the sides and angles. Do any pieces look like animal shapes? Let the shapes and forms of the wood inspire you.

You Will Need

- wood scraps
- small tree branches, twigs, or sticks
- rasps, files, coping saw, sandpaper
- wood glue
- tempera or acrylic paint
- paintbrushes

Step 1 Plan and Practice

- Decide whether you will use wood scraps or branches to create your animal. You may use both.
- Spend some time looking at the wood to get your ideas.
- Decide what animal you will sculpt.
- Select your materials. Choose one or two pieces from which to create the main form of the animal. What small pieces can you add to create ears, legs, a tail, or other features?

Things to Remember:

- ✓ Choose wood scraps or branches that help show your animal's form and characteristics.
- ✓ Arrange and shape parts of your sculpture to suggest movement or a pose.
- ✓ If you use paint, choose paint colors that express a specific mood.

Inspiration from Our World

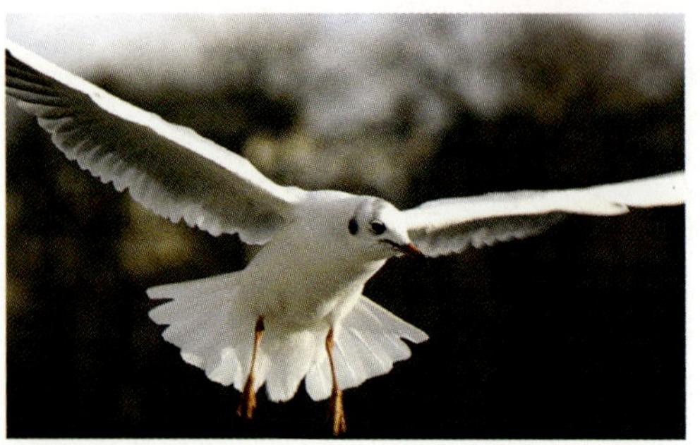

Inspiration from Art

Woodcarving from twisted tree branches is a popular art form among the Zapotec of southern Mexico's Oaxaca Valley. Artists carve animal sculptures, usually ones that show movement and expressive poses. The shapes of the branches help the artists decide what animals to make.

Oaxacans have carved toys and masks for hundreds of years. Today, over 200 Oaxacan families of woodcarvers produce sculptures. Some family members carve the sculptures, and others paint them. Although the carvers sign the sculptures, the entire family plays a part in their production.

The decorating of the sculptures is as important as the carving. Instead of turning to nature for decoration ideas, the artists use colors and patterns that are brighter, bolder, and fancier than those in nature. Imagine seeing a bright-blue lizard with lavender and red flames, or a green-and-orange-spotted antelope with pink hooves!

Fig. 5–25 **Look at the shape of this sculpture. How did the artist show movement in it?**

Fuentes family, *Untitled (Fish)*, 2000. Carved copal wood, 10" x 3" x 5" (25 x 8 x 13 cm). Photo courtesy of Eldon Katter.

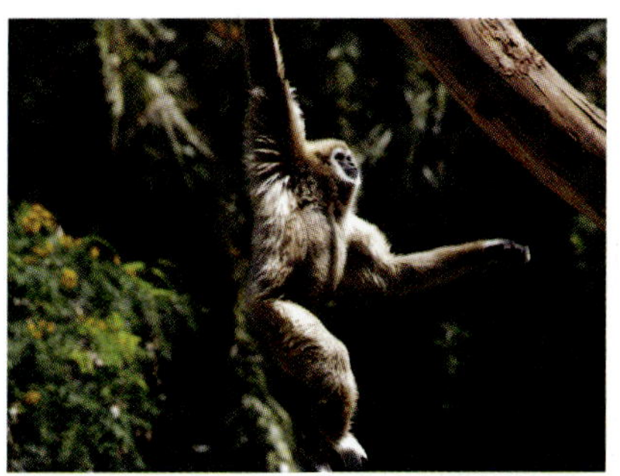

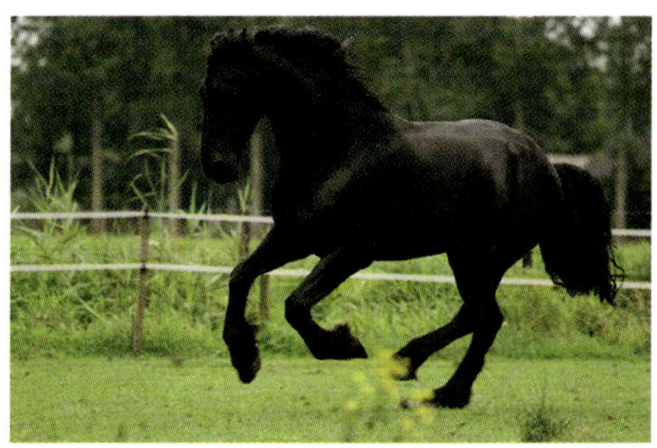

Step 2 Begin to Create

- **Arrange and shape the pieces to suggest movement or an expressive pose.**

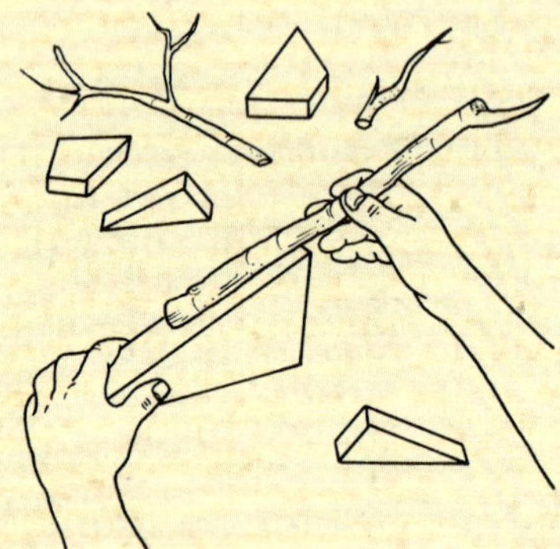

- **Carefully shape the main form with a saw or other tools.** If you use more than one piece of wood, glue the main forms together. Then add the smaller features.

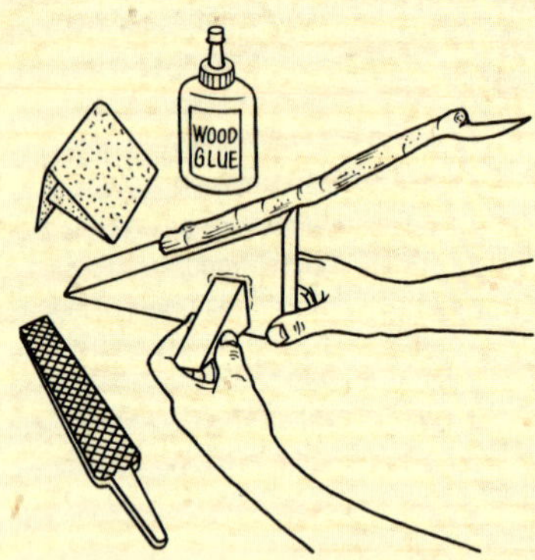

- After you have assembled your animal, decide whether you will decorate it. Will you leave your sculpture natural, with or without the tree bark? Or will you paint it?

- **If you decide to paint your sculpture, think about color and pattern.** Be as creative as you can! What mood do you want your colors to suggest? What colors can create a happy, scary, dangerous, gentle, or peaceful animal?

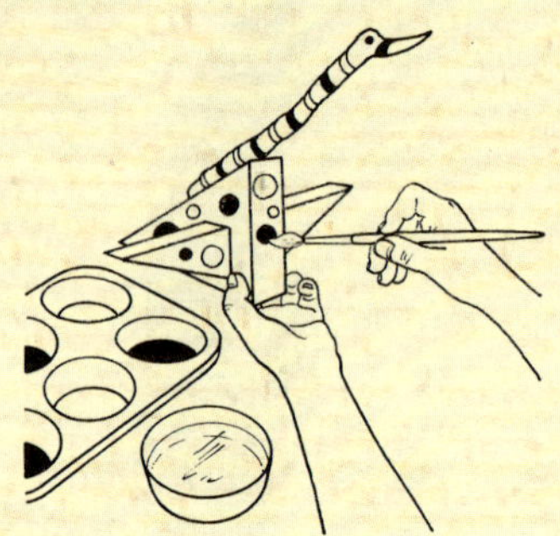

Step 3 Revise

Did you remember to:

✓ Choose wood scraps or branches that help show your animal's form and characteristics?

✓ Arrange and shape parts of your sculpture to create movement or a pose?

✓ Choose paint colors that express a specific mood?

Adjust your work if necessary. In your sketchbook, make a note of your revisions and why you made them.

Step 4 Add Finishing Touches

- Examine your sculpture and add any desired details.

Step 5 **Share and Reflect**

- Share your sculpture with your classmates.
- Discuss how you came up with the idea for your animal sculpture.
- How did the shape of the wood add to the shape and pose of your animal?
- How did details, or lack of details, help to create a mood?

Art Criticism

Describe Tell what you see in these sculptures.

Analyze How have the artists utilized the natural form of the wood to create their creatures?

Interpret What moods and feelings do these sculptures suggest?

Evaluate Why might people find these sculptures appealing?

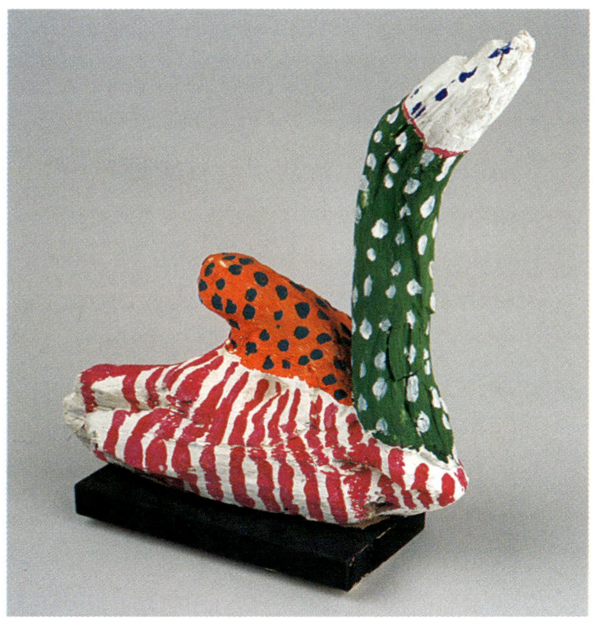

Fig. 5–26 Student artwork

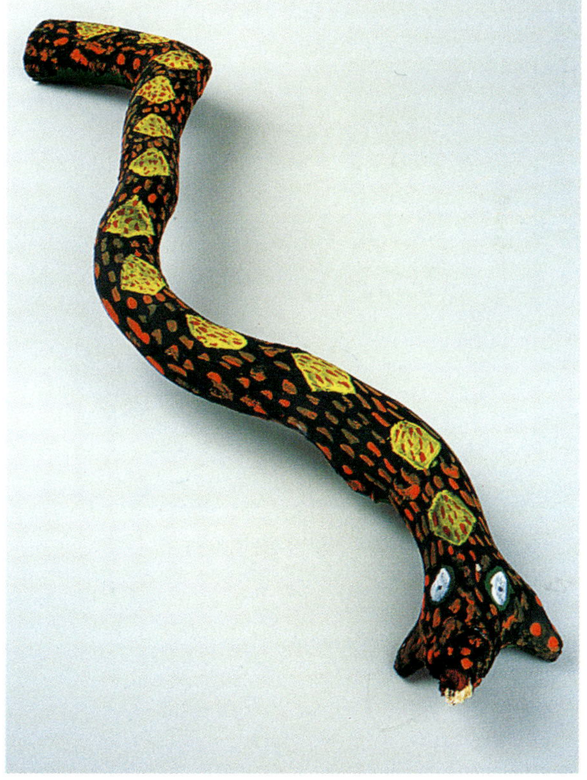

Fig. 5–27 Student artwork

Language Arts

One longtime challenge for researchers was the interpretation of ancient Egyptian hieroglyphs. Hieroglyphs are a writing system that uses symbols or pictures instead of words. In 1799, the discovery of the Rosetta Stone presented scholars with a chance to break the code. A passage written in three languages was carved into the stone. These languages were hieroglyphic, demotic (a shorthand form of hieroglyphs), and Greek. Scholars used their understanding of Greek to make sense of the words in the two other languages.

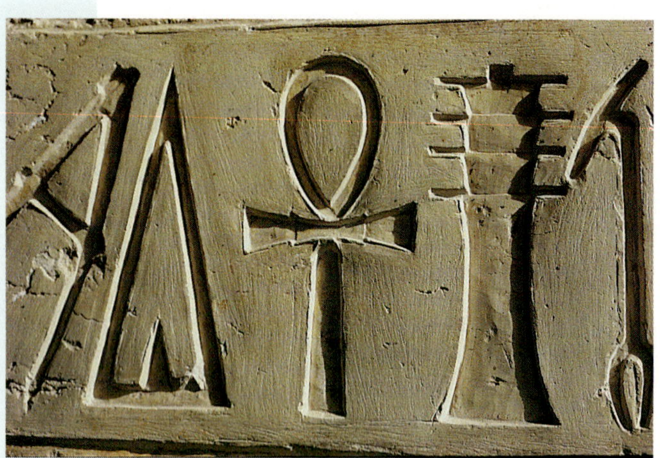

Fig. 5–28 **If you were creating your own hieroglyphic language, what kinds of pictures or symbols would you use?**

Photo courtesy of Helen Ronan.

Music

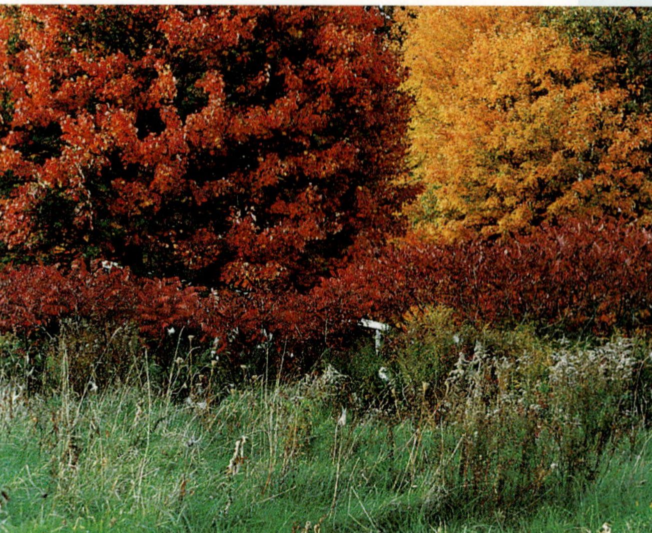

Fig. 5–29 **Some composers have created music based upon the seasons. Can you imagine music inspired by this scene? How would it sound?**

Photo courtesy of Anette Macintire.

Musicians interpret nature in many different ways. Sometimes, nature itself has been used as part of the performance. In 1952, composer John Cage shocked his audience. Rather than playing the piano, Cage sat completely still during the performance. He allowed the silence to be filled with the "music" of the everyday world. Because the performance hall was open in back, nature's noises, along with rustling programs and audience coughs, became the music. Explain whether or not you think this performance would be as shocking today?

Careers **Art Critics**

Art critics are art experts who write reviews about contemporary art. They usually write about artworks that they enjoy and want others to appreciate. Although art critics sometimes make judgments about artworks, they more often write to address the question, "What is this artwork *about?*" To answer this question, the art critic must observe and describe the artwork carefully while offering an interpretation. What do you think an art critic needs to know? Most art critics are skilled in persuasive writing.

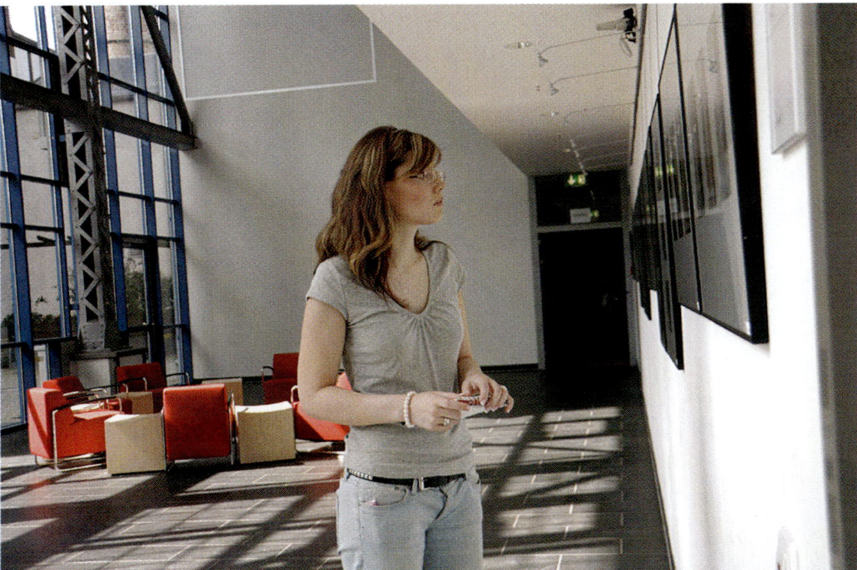

Fig. 5–30

Daily Life

Popular culture is made up of the ideas, people, and things that society likes during that time period. This may include current television shows, songs on the radio, or clothing trends. Popular culture may be interpreted differently by you than by your family members. How do their tastes about movies, music, and clothing differ from yours? How do you think today's popular culture is different from that of thirty or forty years ago?

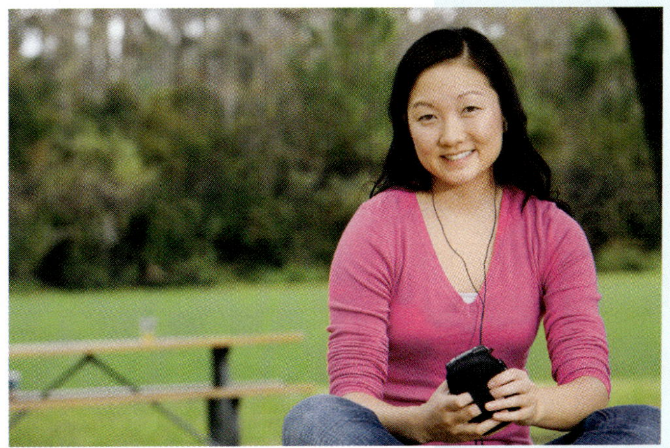

Fig. 5–31

Unit 5 Vocabulary and Content Review

Vocabulary Review

Match each art term below with its definition.

complement
intensity
primary colors
tint
shade

1. the brightness or dullness of a color
2. a darker value of a color
3. the colors you can mix to make other colors
4. a color mixed with white
5. the color directly opposite another color on the color wheel

Aesthetic Thinking

Do artists need to find new ways of depicting the environment in landscape paintings? Why or why not?

For Your Sketchbook

Use a nature motif to design a border on a sketchbook page. On the same page, write about how you view nature, and list ways you might show your views in future artwork.

Write About Art

Imagine yourself as the man in this painting and write a description of your experience on the beach. Tap into all your senses: what do you see, smell, hear, and feel?

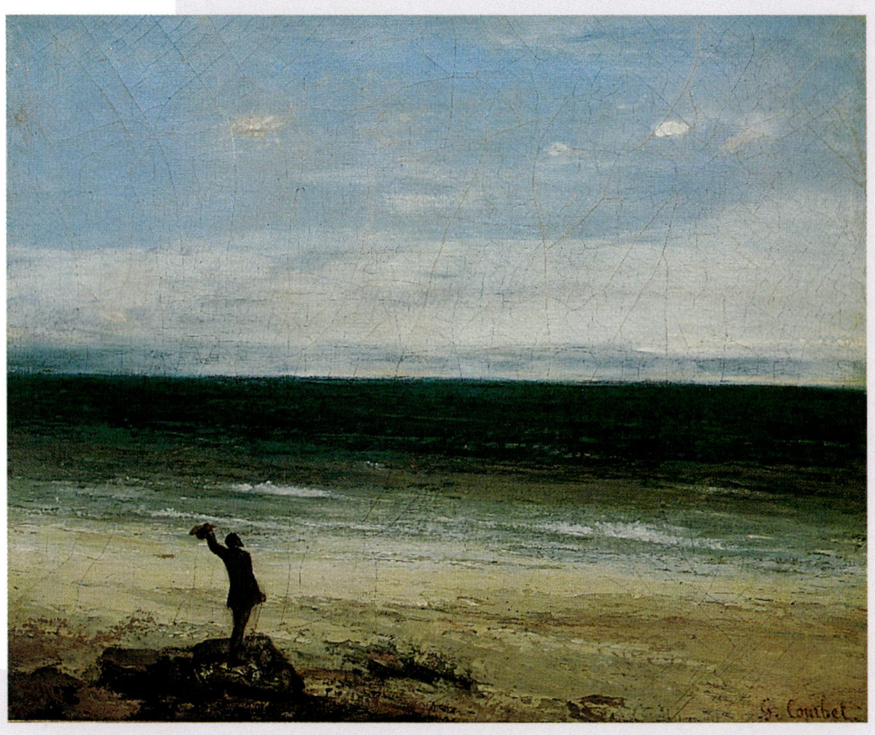

Fig. 5–32 Gustave Courbet, *Seaside at Palavas*, 1854. Oil on canvas, 10 5/8" x 18 1/8" (27 x 46 cm). Musée Fabre, Montpellier, France, Erich Lessing/Art Resource, New York.

Art Criticism

Describe What do you see in this sculpture? Describe both the shape and the decoration.

Analyze How did the artists create a sense of movement in this sculpture?

Interpret In what ways does this sculpture remind you of a real lizard? In what ways is it different?

Evaluate One artist carved this sculpture and another artist painted it. Do you think their interpretations work well together?

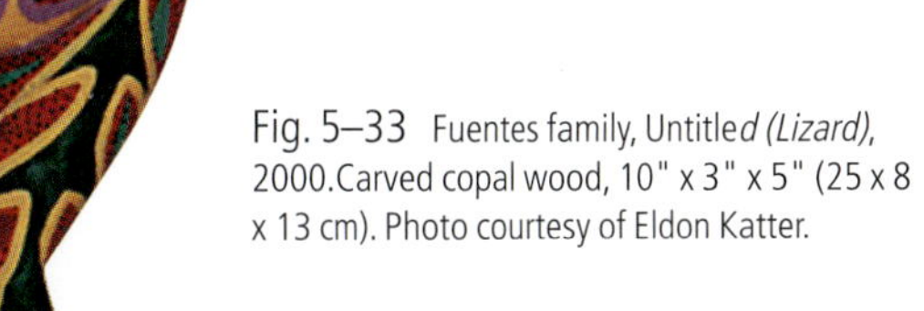

Fig. 5–33 Fuentes family, Untitled *(Lizard)*, 2000. Carved copal wood, 10" x 3" x 5" (25 x 8 x 13 cm). Photo courtesy of Eldon Katter.

Meet the Artist

Zeny Fuentes (born 1975) is a Zapoteca Indian who was born in Oaxaca, Mexico. He and his brothers Efrain and Ivan were taught to carve by their father, Epifanio Fuentes. Zeny began carving animal figures when he was seven years old.

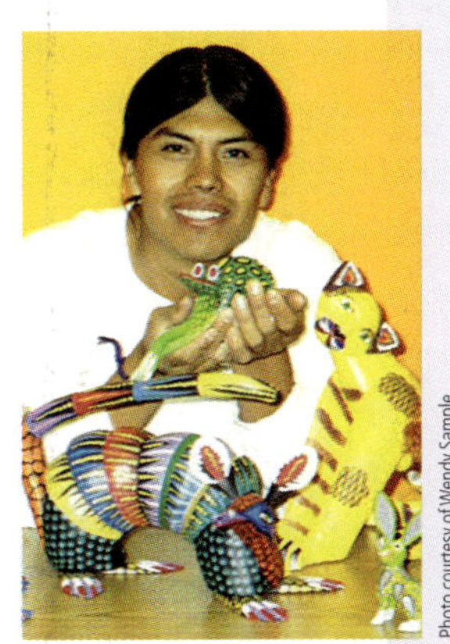

Photo courtesy of Wendy Sample.

For Your Portfolio

Create two artworks that each show a different interpretation of nature; for example, humorous and scientific, or realistic and fanciful. Title your artworks, add your name and date, and put them into your portfolio.

Unit 6

Artists Are Messengers

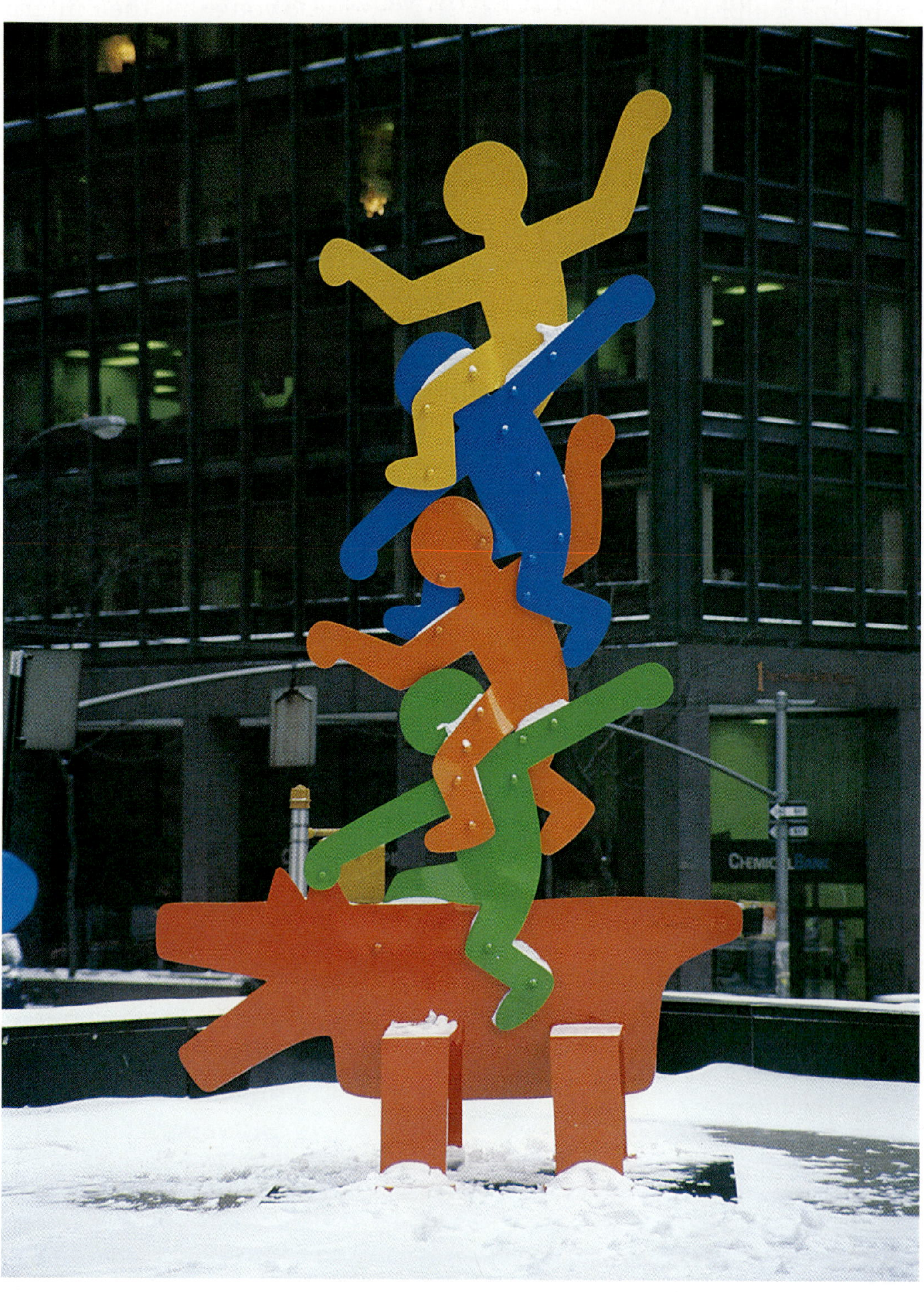

Fig. 6–1 **How did this artist create a sense of energy and playfulness in this sculpture?**

Keith Haring, *Untitled*, 1985. Polyurethane paint on aluminum. ©The Estate of Keith Haring. Photo: Ivan Dalla Tana.

Have you ever had a sore throat that made it impossible for you to talk? How did you communicate with family members? Did you write messages on a notepad, draw pictures, or make hand gestures? We rely so much on speaking and writing that we sometimes forget other ways of communicating. Sometimes a look will "speak" a hundred words.

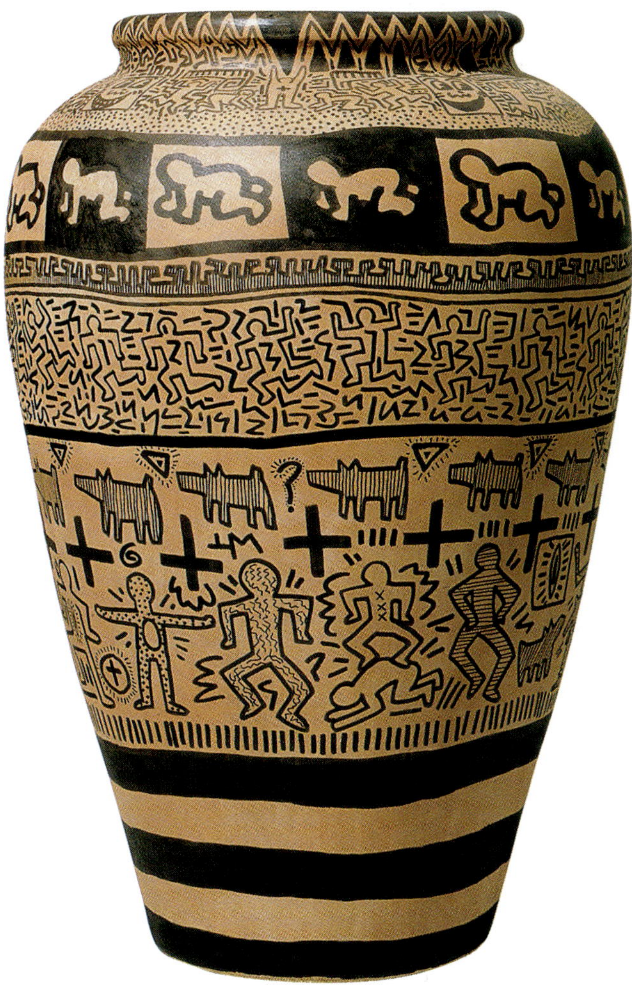

Fig. 6–2 **Haring studied artworks by the Egyptians, Greeks, and other cultures. What evidence of this do you see?**

Keith Haring, *Untitled*, 1981. Felt-tip pen on fiberglass vase. ©The Estate of Keith Haring.

Artists communicate using images. They use images to tell stories, to persuade others, and to tell about beauty. Like poets or writers, who use combinations of words, artists create combinations of visual imagery to send messages to their audience.

In this unit, you will learn:

- How artists use symbols to communicate a message.
- How to create monoprints and linoleum block prints.
- How to look at artwork to find meaning in visual messages.

Recognizing Messages

Artist Keith Haring made playful artworks with serious messages. He used visual symbols to comment on life in the 1980s. **Symbols** are images that "stand for" and communicate certain ideas. Like many people, Haring was worried about problems he saw. Haring's messages were concerned with the environment, human cruelty, and the negative effects technology might have on us. He did not want us to forget about the really important things in life—family and other people we love.

People quickly learn to "read" pictures. Think about how young children name objects in picture books. As we develop, we are able to understand the meanings of images. We know that a certain shape is a symbol for a ball or a cat. In Haring's work one symbol, a glowing or "radiant" baby, represents innocence and joy. Another of Haring's symbols, a barking dog, represents the family dog, always there to watch what's going on and to protect us.

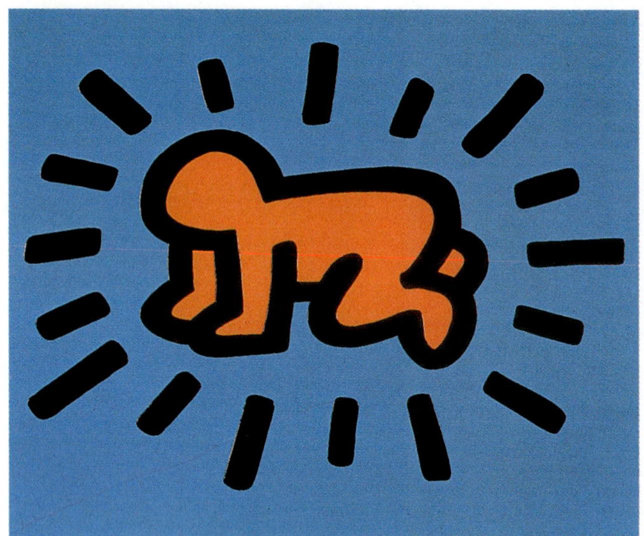

Fig. 6–3 **Haring sometimes surrounded his images with lines. What effect is created by the lines surrounding this figure?**

Keith Haring, *Icons* (Radiant Baby), 1990. Silkscreen with embossing. 21" x 25" (53 x 63.5 cm). ©The Estate of Keith Haring.

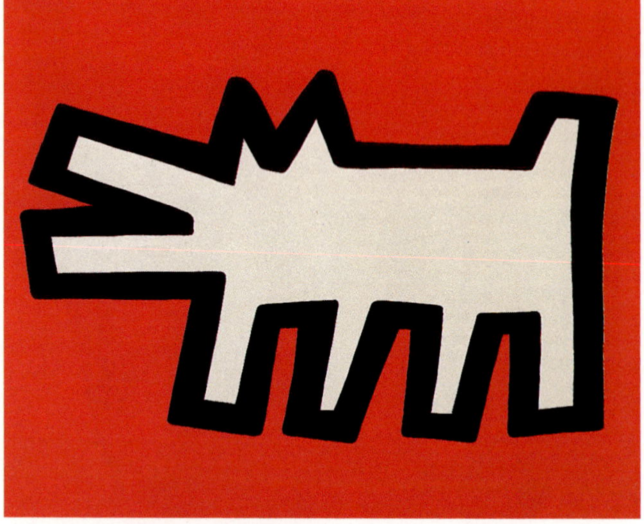

Fig. 6–4 **How would combining the two symbols of a baby and a dog affect their meaning?**

Keith Haring, *Icons* (Barking Dog), 1990. Silkscreen with embossing. 21" x 25" (53 x 63.5 cm). ©The Estate of Keith Haring.

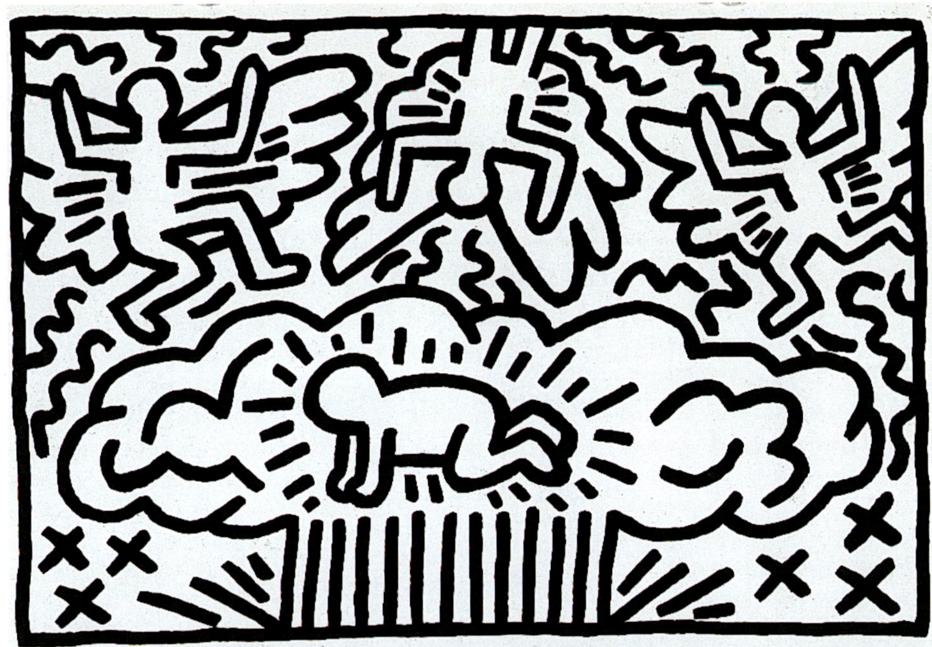

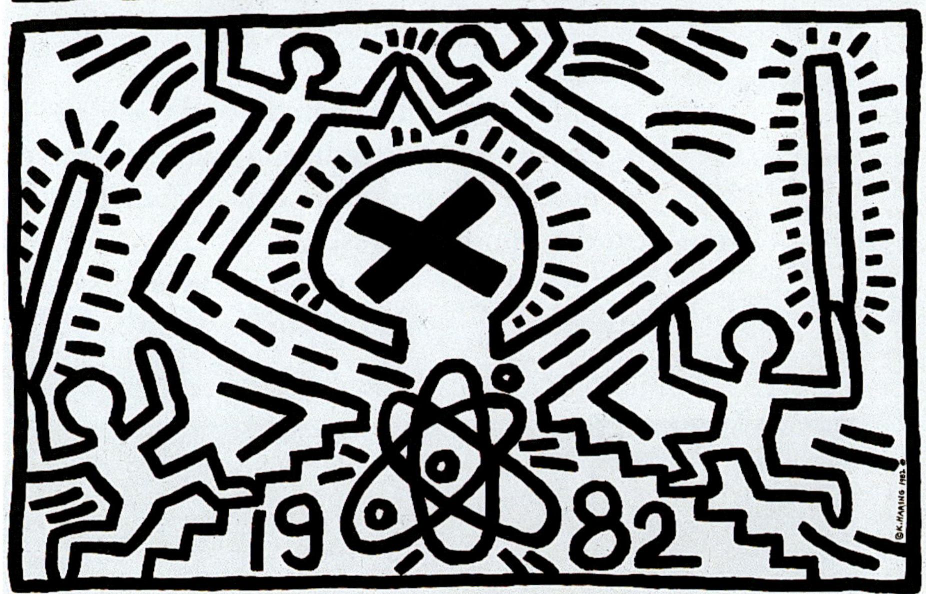

Fig. 6–5 **What makes this a powerful message? What symbols do you see? What do you think they mean?**

Keith Haring, *Untitled* (Poster for antinuclear rally, New York), 1982. ©The Estate of Keith Haring.

Meet Keith Haring

As a child, Keith Haring liked to draw with his father and his youngest sister. He also enjoyed looking at cartoons and illustrations. These inspired the simple cartoonlike forms in the drawings, paintings, murals, and sculptures that he made as an adult. Throughout his life, Haring continued to draw. He often drew the same forms over and over. Haring often drew Disney characters, but also included computers, spaceships, dolphins, and people at work and play.

"I am intrigued with the shapes people choose as symbols to create a language."

— Keith Haring (1958–1990)

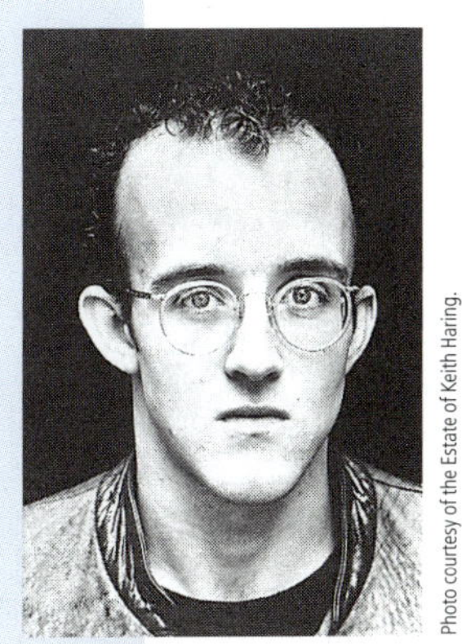

Photo courtesy of the Estate of Keith Haring.

Messages with Symbols

People have long used pictures to communicate. The earliest forms of writing were called pictograms. Pictograms are simple pictures that represent objects. Pictograms were easily understood and "read" by community members. Many artists throughout history have developed their own sets of symbols.

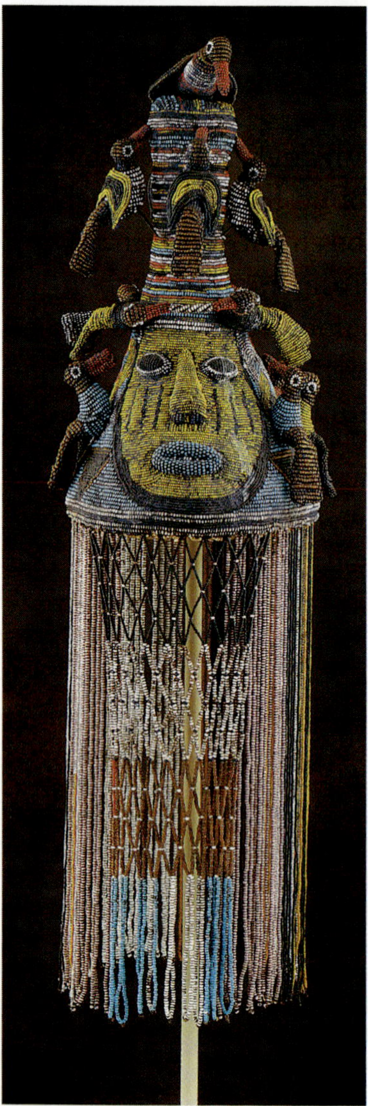

Fig. 6–6 **In Yoruban culture in the 1800s, only the most important people were allowed to use or wear beaded objects.**

African, Nigeria (Yoruba), *King's Crown*, 19th century. Beads, leather, canvas, and wicker, height: 30" (76 cm). The Minneapolis Institute of Arts (The Ethel Morrison Van Derlip Fund 76.29).

Understanding Symbols When we study artworks from the past or from different cultures, we do not always understand the artists' symbolism. You may understand the message of **Fig. 6–7** to be "Look at these beautiful things." However, if you had lived in the Netherlands during the 1620s, you would have known that the artist was saying, "Time passes quickly and life is short."

In the 1800s, an artist in the African kingdom of Yoruba covered a king's crown with symbols to show the power of the king **(Fig. 6–6)**. The lines on the face stand for the ruler's family, and the birds represent his skill in dealing with the forces of evil. When people saw the crown, they understood its messages. Whenever artists communicate, they must use symbols or images that others will understand.

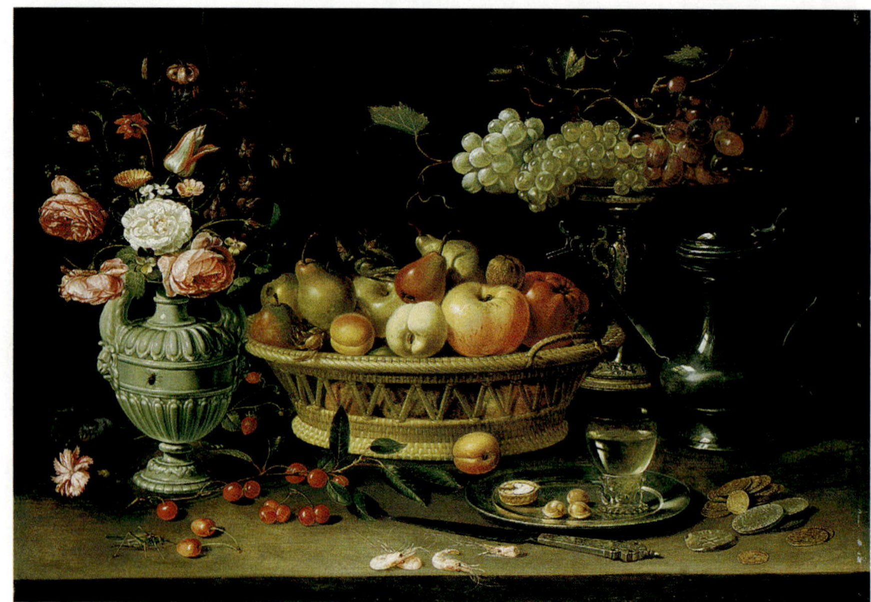

Fig. 6–7 **This painting is an example of a *vanitas* painting, a kind of still-life painting. The message of such paintings is that, like flowers and fruit, people don't live forever.**

Clara Peeters, *Still Life of Fruit and Flowers*, after 1620. Oil on copper, signed on knife handle, 25" x 35" (64 x 89 cm). Ashmolean Museum, Oxford. Bequeathed by Daisy Linda Ward, 1939. ©Ashmolean Museum, Oxford.

Studio Time

Thinking Visually

When someone says to you, "close your eyes and try not to think of about the elephant in this room," the chances are that you will have a visual image of an elephant. You will not see the word elephant, just a picture of one. This is visual thinking.

In this studio experience, you can make a drawing to illustrate what it means to think with pictures, or to "think visually."

- Without using words in your picture, create a drawing that shows what someone is thinking about.
- Sketch some ideas first. Then use pencil to plan your final drawing on larger paper.
- Remember to include a background to show where the person is and what she or he is doing.
- Use colored pencils to complete your drawing.

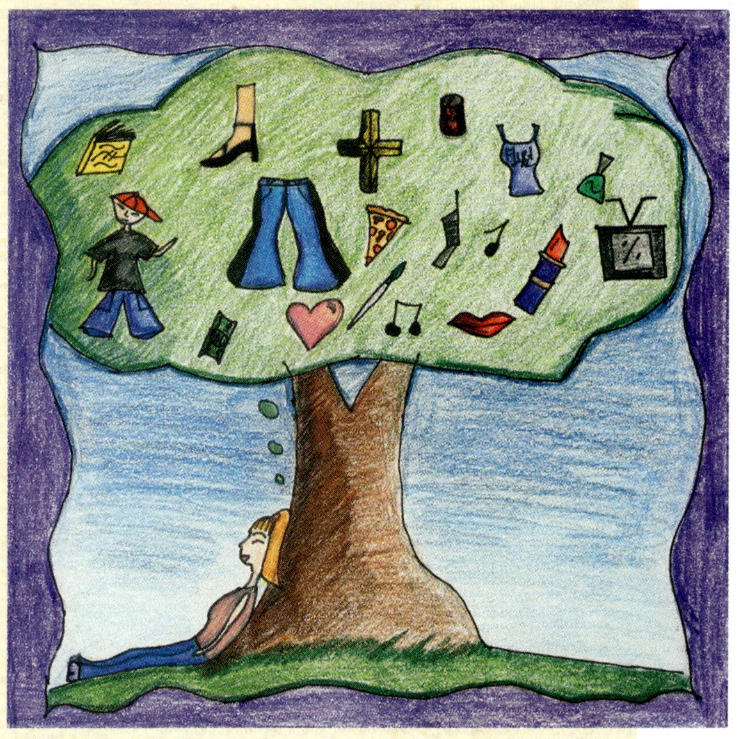

Fig. 6–8 Student artwork

Reflect on how well your drawing sends a visual message. Think about the similarities between your drawing and the "picture writing" that people used long, long ago before there were alphabets.

Check Your Understanding

1. What is a symbol?
2. Compare and contrast Keith Haring's *Radiant Baby* and the Yoruban *King's Crown*.
3. Why is it sometimes difficult to interpret symbols from other times and places?

One-of-a-Kind Prints

The prefix *mono-* means "one." In printmaking there are two ways to create one-of-a-kind prints. One is called a monotype, and the other is called a monoprint. A **monotype** is a print made by drawing in ink or paint that has been spread over a smooth surface. The plate used to make a monotype has no permanent marks on its surface. A **monoprint** is made by carving into the surface of a plate and adding or changing the printing ink each time the print is made.

In other methods of printmaking, you can make many prints from the same plate. When you make a monotype or monoprint, you can prepare the plate in several ways, but the preparations on the plate usually do not survive after the first print.

Monotypes and monoprints allow an artist to experiment and create works that are loose and free. They are also a good way to explore the use of various materials and contrasts, such as the relationship between thick and thin lines or between areas of dark and light.

Methods of Making a Monotype

To create a monotype, you can prepare the plate in several ways. Each method requires a smooth, nonabsorbent surface. You might use a piece of rigid plastic or Formica or even a cookie sheet. And remember: your print will be the reverse of the drawing or painting you create on the plate.

Method 1 This method for creating a monotype works well for still lifes or abstract designs.

Observe The monotype (Fig. 6–9) on the next page was made using the method detailed below. What different textures do you see?

Tools: Tempera paint and a surface to paint on.

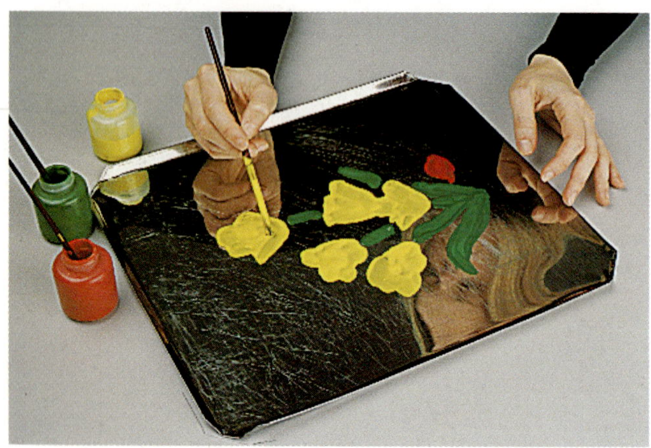

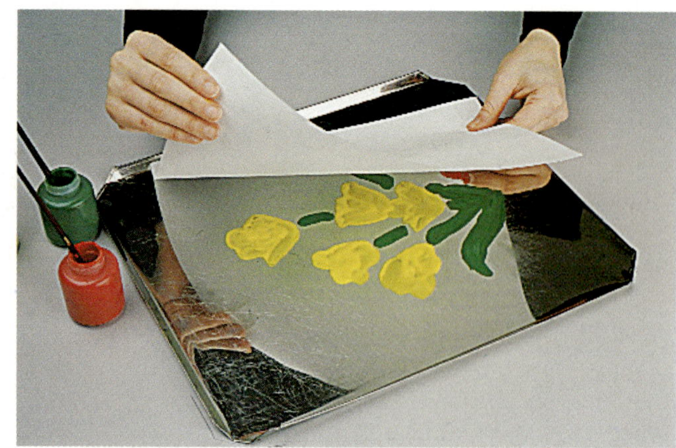

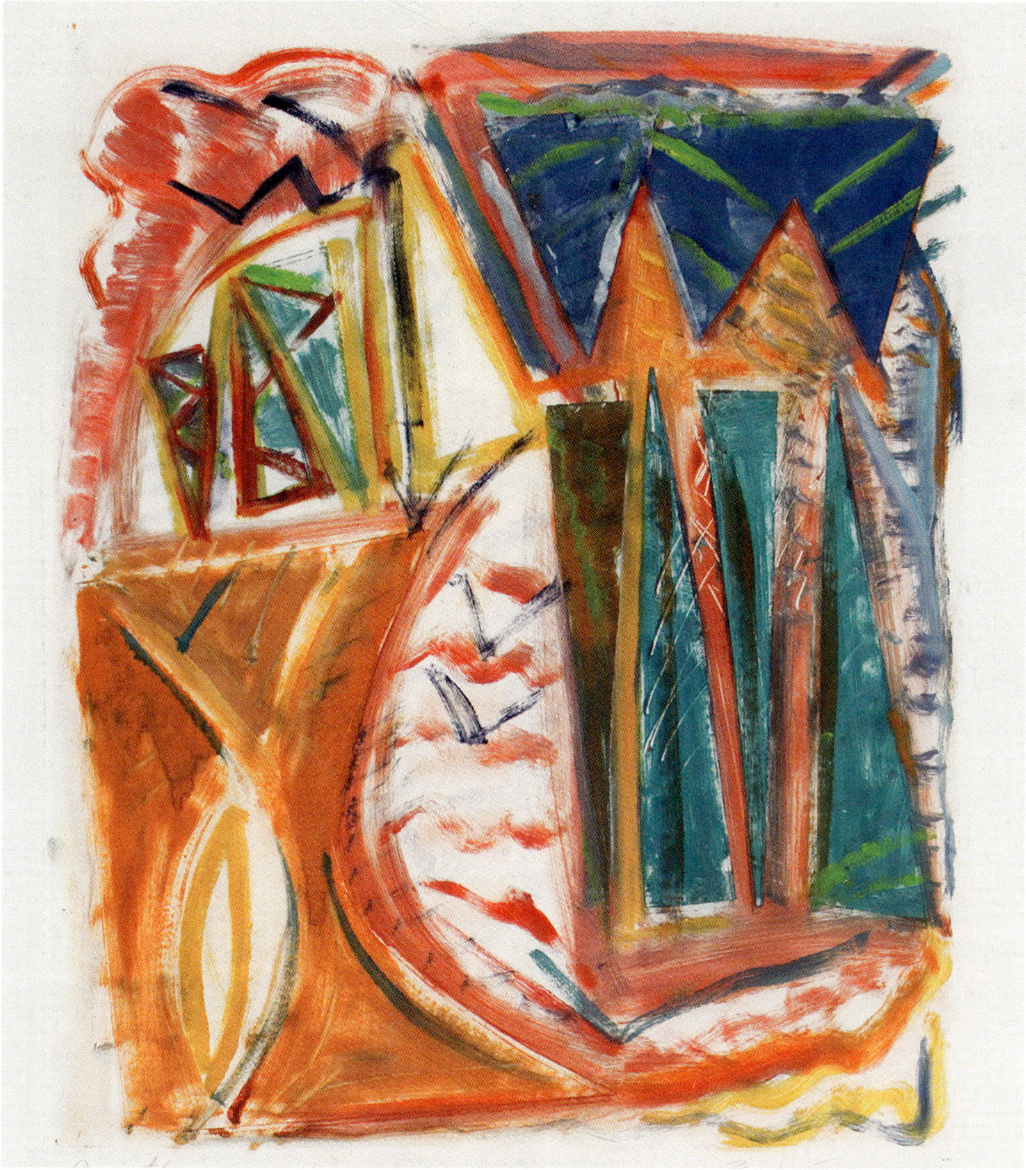

Fig. 6–9 **What does this printing method allow the artist to do?**

Phyllis Ewen, *Quiver #6* from the *Artist's Proof Studio Archival Portfolio II, 2000*, 1983. Oil monotype, 19 ½" x 16 ½" (49.5 x 39.4 cm). Museum of Fine Arts, Boston Gift of Artist's Proof Studio 2002.633.5.

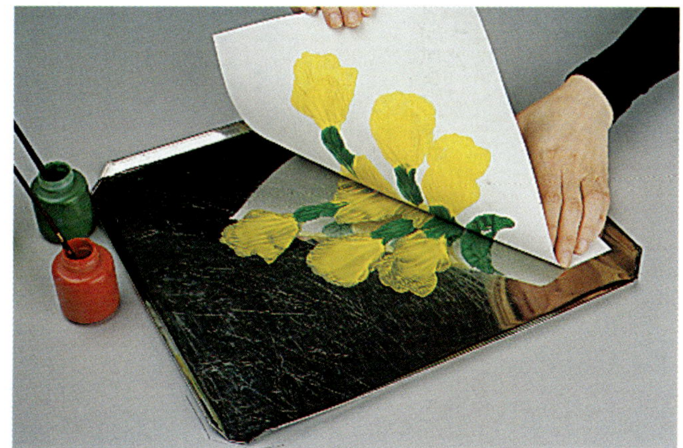

Practice: Method 1

- Paint an image with tempera paint on a smooth, nonabsorbent surface. Work quickly so that the paint stays wet.
- Place a sheet of paper over the painted image.
- Rub it evenly but lightly with your hand.
- Then pull the print by lifting the paper away from the surface.

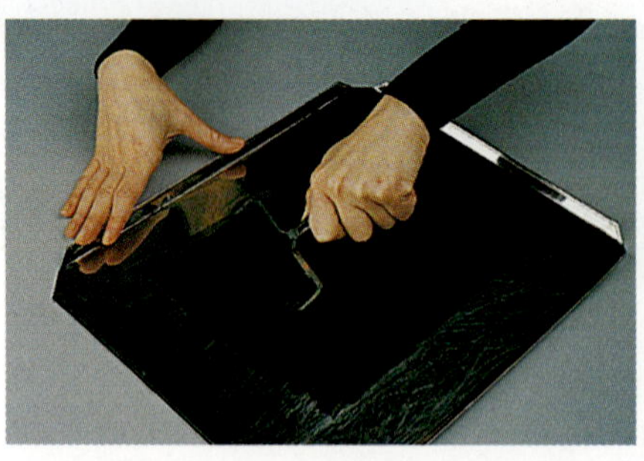

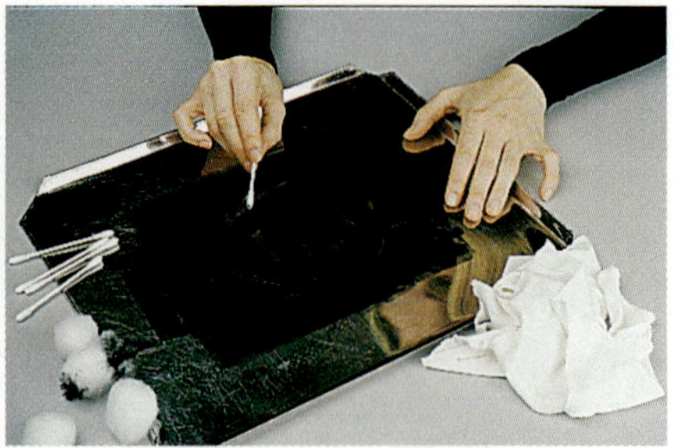

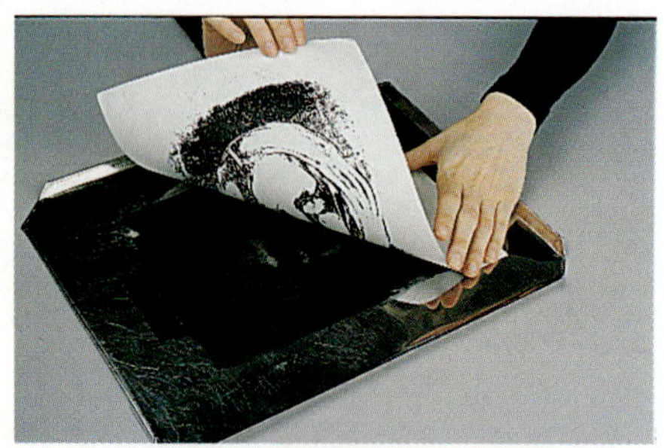

Method 2 This monotype method is good for creating portraits.

Observe Notice how the painting in **Fig. 6–10** contrasts areas of light and dark to create an eerie composition.

Tools: Ink, a surface to spread ink on, and a drawing tool.

Practice: Method 2

- Roll out a thin layer of ink on a smooth, nonabsorbent surface.
- Draw directly into the ink with a tool such as a toothpick, pencil eraser, cotton swab, facial tissue, or old comb.
- Place a sheet of paper over the design.
- Rub it evenly but lightly with your hand.
- Then pull the print by lifting the paper away from the surface.

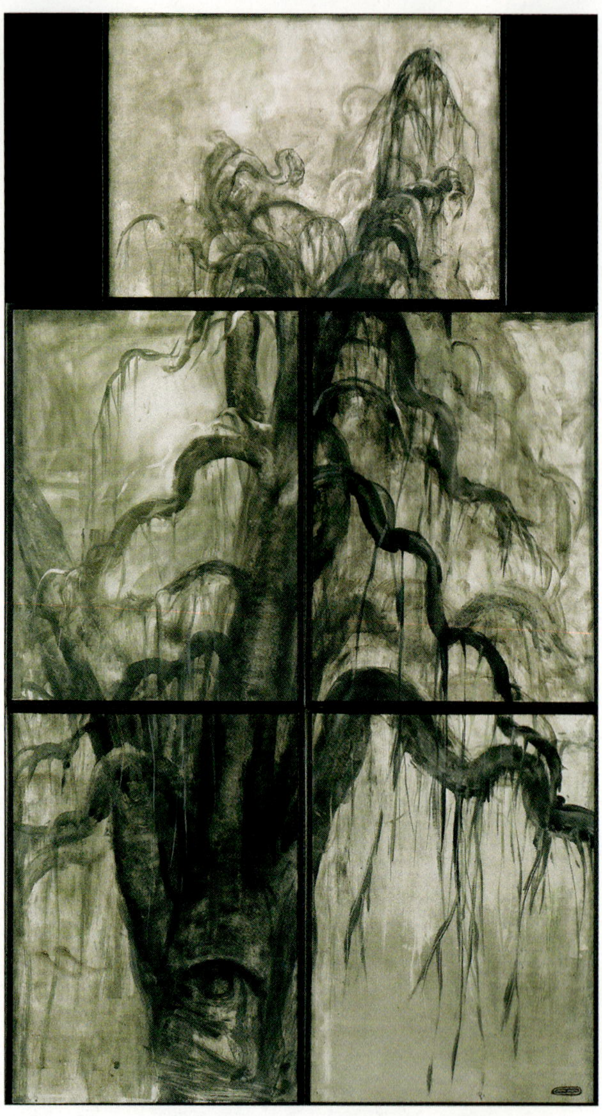

Fig. 6–10 **How did the artist use thick and thin lines?**

Michael Mazur, *Weeping Beech*, 1988. Monotype on silk charmeuse, 31" x 12" (78.7 x 58.5 cm). Museum of Fine Arts, Boston. Gift of the artist, 1990.305a-e.

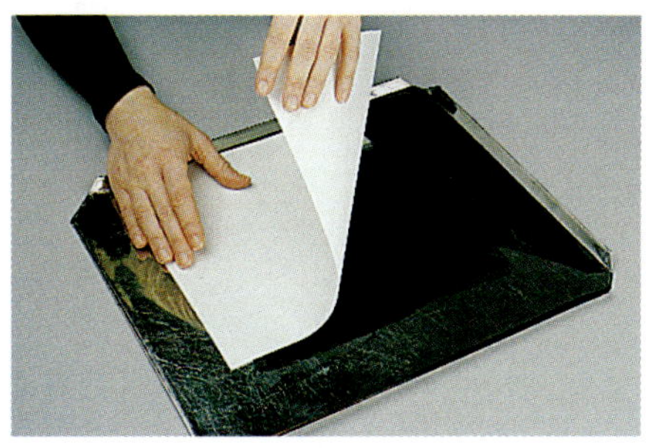

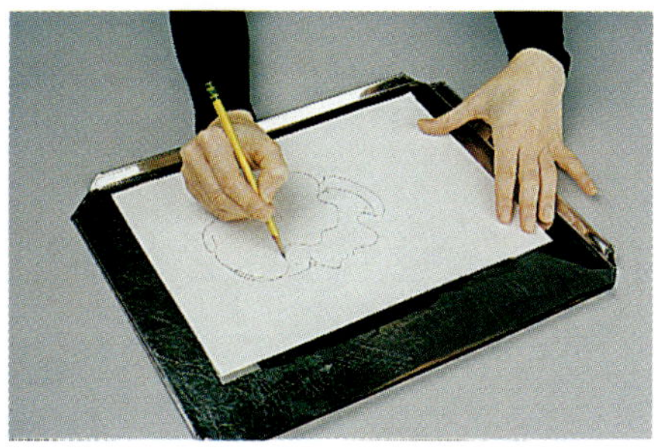

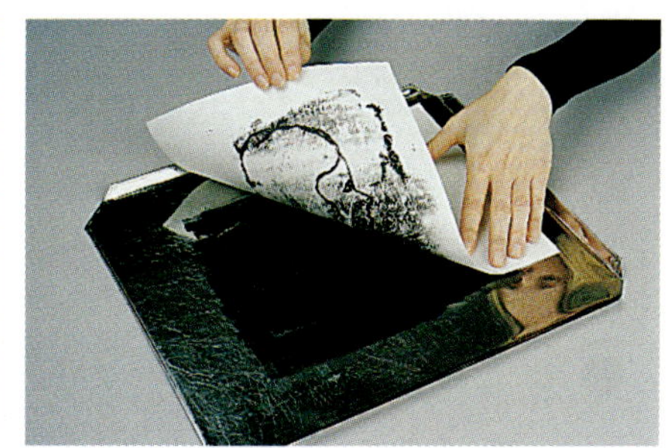

Method 3 When you try this method for the first time use only one color.

Observe Look at Fig. 6–10. Notice how the artist created interesting textures using only one color.

Tools: A surface for spreading ink, a pencil, and ink.

Practice: Method 3

- Roll out a thin, even layer of ink on a smooth, nonabsorbent surface.
- Place a sheet of paper over the inked surface, but do not rub it.
- Using a pencil, draw an image on the paper.
- Then pull the print by lifting the paper away from the surface.

Check Your Understanding

1. How is making monotypes and monoprints different from making other types of prints?
2. Compare and contrast the different results that you get with each method of monotype printing.
3. The act of pulling a print from its surface will create interesting textures in the image. What other ways might you create textures when making a monotype?

Studio Time

Make a Monotype

Create a monotype by using one of the methods discussed in this lesson.

- Choose a method that works well with your subject. For example, method 1 works well for still lifes or abstract designs. Method 2 works well for portraits.
- Use copy paper or drawing paper to pull the print.

Reflect on your work and discuss the methods you used to create your monotype.

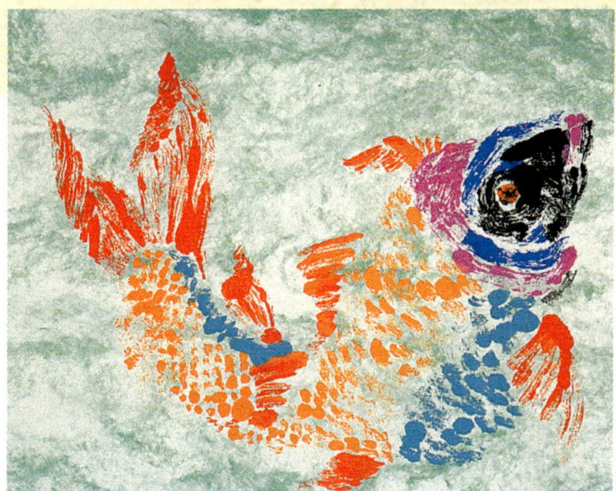

Fig. 6–11 Student artwork

Printing Symbols

Studio Background

Do you ever fill notebook pages with playful scribbles or drawings? The shapes and patterns that come into your mind as you doodle can become part of your own set of symbols. Like Keith Haring, you can combine your symbols to send messages.

In this studio exploration, you will make a set of symbol stamps and use them to create a print. Without using words in your print, express a message about a social issue. What issues concern you? Abandoned pets? Global warming? Water pollution? Hunger? Develop at least six different symbols that you can use to express your concern about one issue. Create a stamp for each symbol.

You Will Need

- sketch paper
- pencil and eraser
- black marker (optional)
- stiff cardboard
- string, lightweight cardboard, sponges
- scissors
- glue
- newsprint paper
- drawing paper
- stamp pad
- tempera paint
- damp paper towels

Step 1 Plan and Practice

- Think about the social issues that are important to you. Make a list of those issues on a piece of paper.
- Imagine how you might use symbols to represent each issue.
- Choose one issue that you can visualize well.

Things to Remember:

✓ Create symbols that are all related to a single social issue.

✓ Use lines to make your symbols more effective.

✓ Use size, shape, and color to create emphasis in your print

Inspiration from Our World

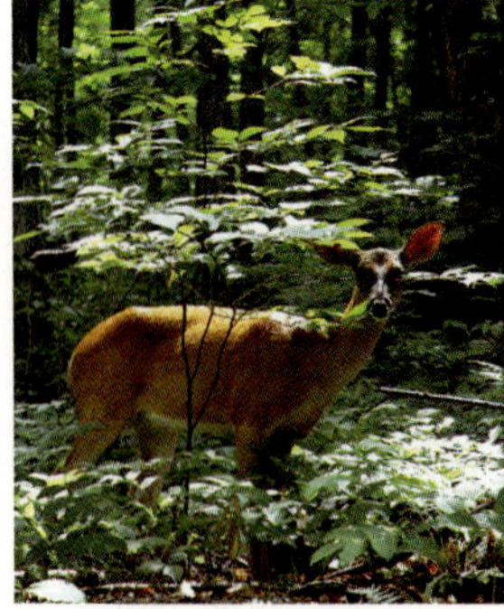

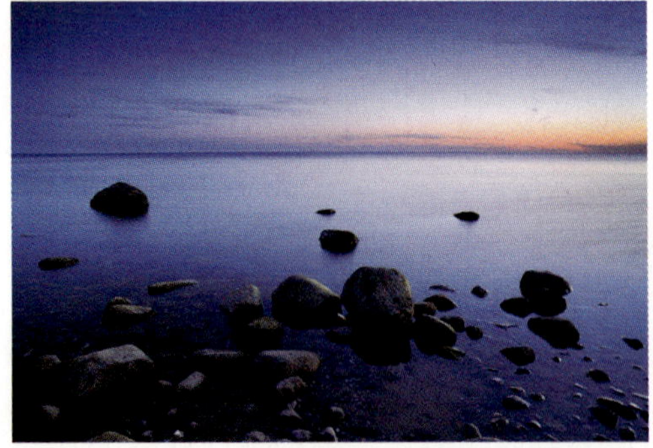

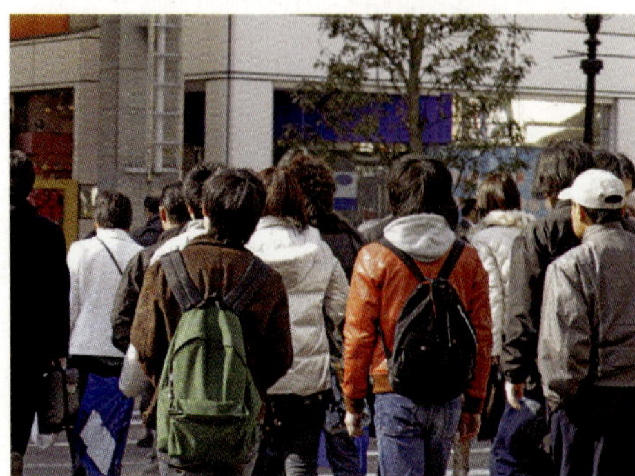

Inspiration from Art

Every day, we come upon hundreds, perhaps thousands, of symbols: the 26 letters of the alphabet, which are symbols for sounds; mathematics symbols at the grocery store or bank; and traffic lights and other signs for drivers. But what do all symbols have in common? They send messages. Anyone can create a symbol for any reason. For the poster *Running Water* **(Fig. 6–12)**, Lester Beall used a few simple shapes to tell how electricity would improve people's lives.

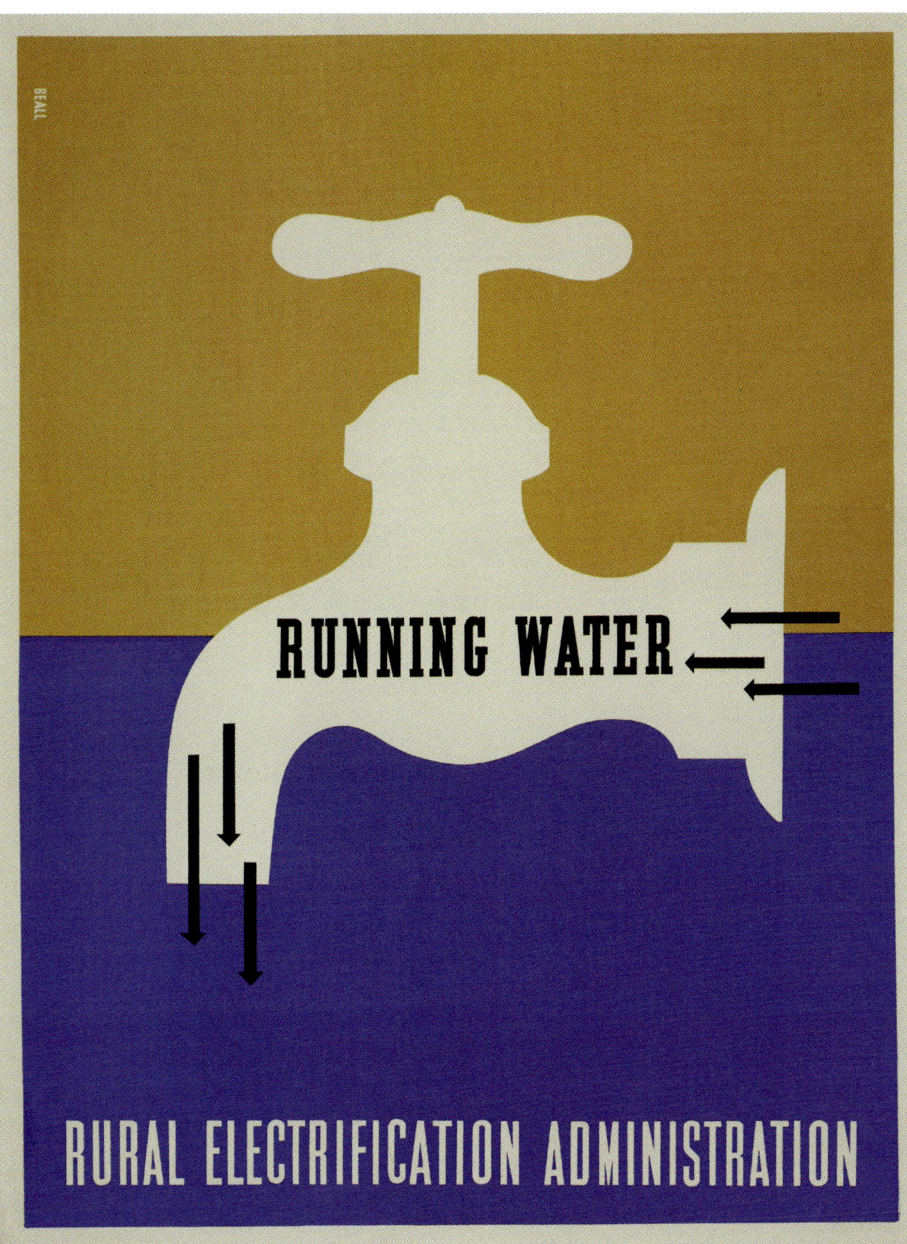

Fig. 6–12 **What two symbols has the artist used in this poster?**

Lester Beall, *Running Water—Rural Electrification Administration*, 1937. Silkscreen, 40" x 30" (101.6 x 76.2 cm). Gift of the designer. (223.1937). The Museum of Modern Art, New York, NY. Digital Image ©The Museum of Modern Art/Licensed by SCALA/Art Resource, NY. ©VAGA, NY.

Step 2 Begin to Create

- Begin by filling a page with doodles. Focus your ideas on your chosen social issue.
- **Choose six doodles that you will improve for your symbols.**

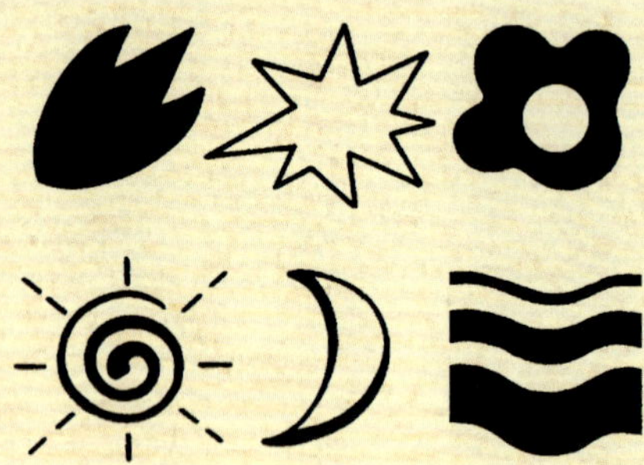

- What kinds of lines will make the symbols more effective? What positive and negative shapes can you create?
- **Decide which materials you will use.** Will you glue string, cardboard pieces, or sponge onto the cardboard? What sizes will your stamps be?

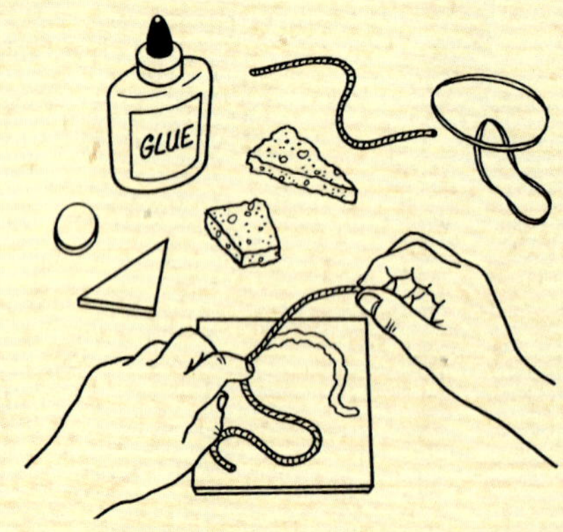

- Place about a teaspoon of paint on a stamp pad. **Practice stamping on newsprint.** Carefully wipe off the stamps between colors.

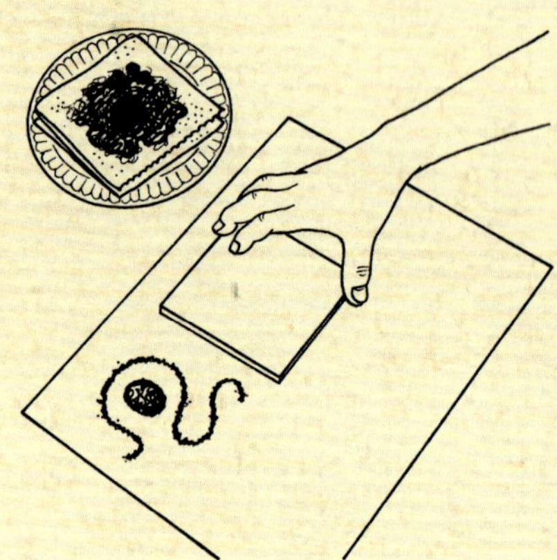

- Create your print on drawing paper. How will you use the size, shape, color, and arrangement of your stamps to create emphasis? How will you use the stamps to best express your message?

Step 3 Revise

Did you remember to:

✓ Create symbols that are all related to a single issue?

✓ Use lines to make your symbols more effective?

✓ Use size, shape, and color to create emphasis in your print?

Adjust your work if necessary. In your sketchbook, make a note of your revisions and why you made them.

Step 4 **Add Finishing Touches**

- Review your stamps and symbols to make sure they effectively represent your social issue. You can add lines or colors to emphasize certain symbols.

Step 5 **Share and Reflect**

- Share your finished print, your stamps, and your doodles with a group of your classmates.
- Discuss your doodles. How do your original symbols compare with the final print?
- Discuss your method of creating your stamps. What kinds of material did you use? How did you choose the size of your stamp?
- Talk about your final print with your classmates. Why did you choose your symbols? What social issue did you focus on? How did you choose the arrangement of your symbols in the final composition of your print?

Art Criticism

Describe What things do you recognize in this artwork?

Analyze How did this artist use shape and line to send her message?

Interpret What do you think is the message of this artwork?

Evaluate Why do you think this artwork is effective?

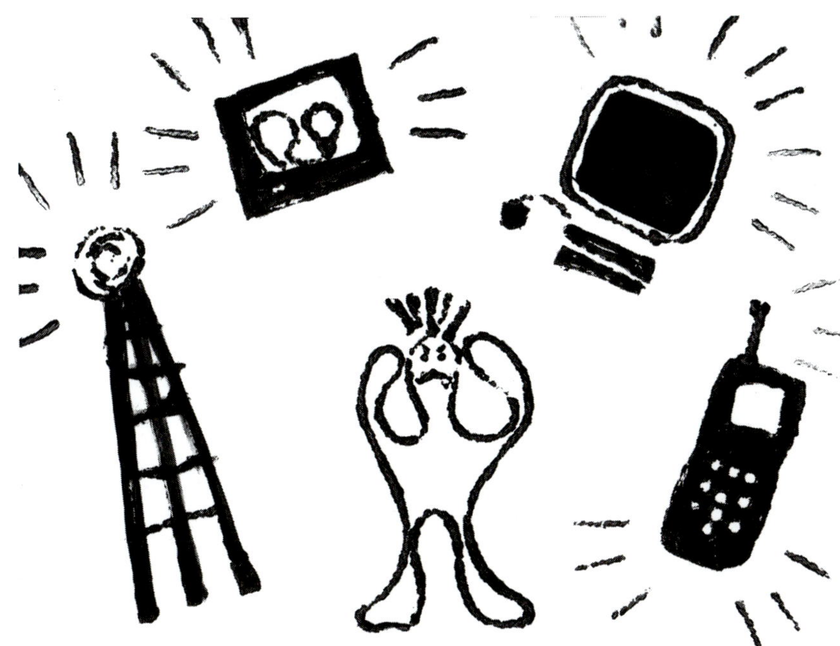

Fig. 6–13 Student artwork

Symbolism in Portraits

An artist's likeness of a person is called a portrait. From ancient Egypt to today, portrait artists have represented the special qualities of a person in different ways. Portrait artists from the 1400s through the 1800s used objects as symbols to tell about a person. The Renaissance portrait *The Ambassadors* **(Fig. 6–16)**

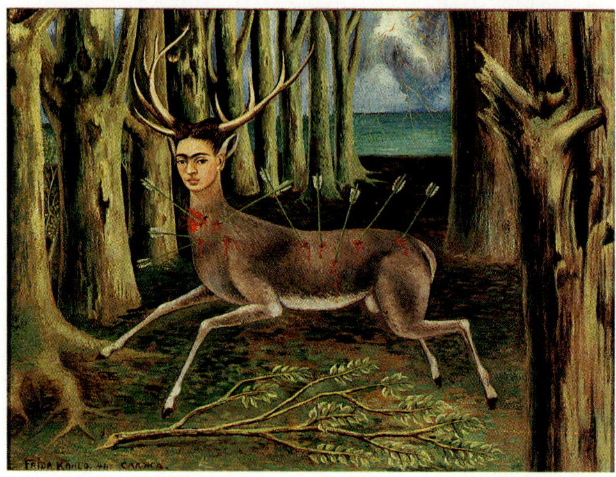

Fig. 6–14 **How does this artwork communicate the idea of pain and suffering? What makes this such a powerful message?**

Frida Kahlo, *The Little Deer*, 1946. Oil on canvas, 8 ¾" x 11 ¾" (22.5 x 29.9 cm). Private Collection. Photo: Hayden Herrera. Courtesy of Mary-Anne Martin/Fine Art. ©2001 Banco de México, Diego Rivera & Frida Kahlo Museums Trust, A. Cinco de Mayo No. 2, Col. Centro, De.Cuauhtémoc 06059, México. D. F.

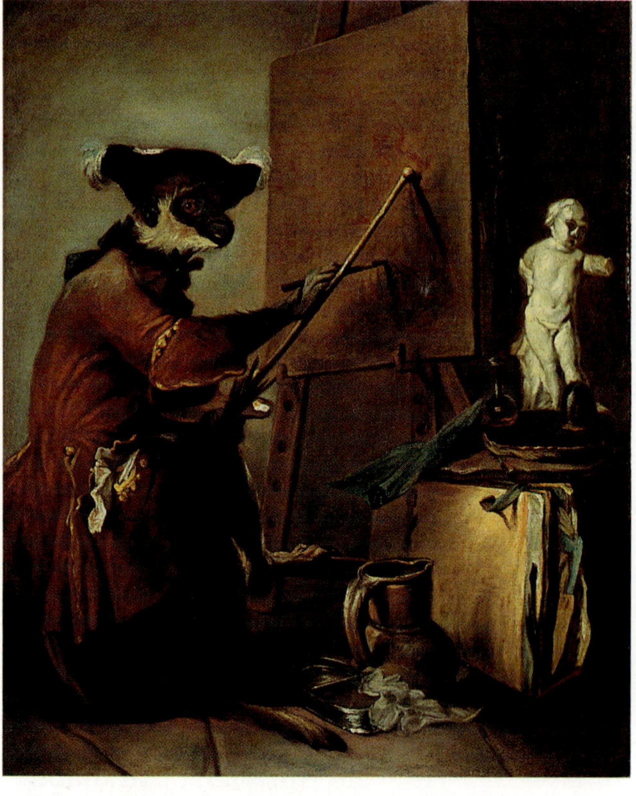

Fig. 6–15 **Chardin was a still-life painter. What clues can you find to tell you that this could be the artist's self-portrait?**

Jean-Baptiste-Siméon Chardin, *The Monkey as Painter*, 1740. Oil on canvas, 28 ¾" x 23 ½" (73 x 59.5 cm). Louvre, Paris, France. Photo credit: Erich Lessing/Art Resource, New York.

1500s–1700s

1517
Martin Luther posts his 95 theses on a church door, beginning the Protestant Reformation.

1533
Holbein, *The Ambassadors*

1740
Chardin, *The Monkey-Painter*

1800s–1900s

1874
Treaty of Berne, which is signed by 22 countries, establishes a universal postal code.

1891
The first underwater long-distance telephone cable linked France and England.

1946
Kahlo, *The Little Deer*

1961
The Berlin Wall is built, dividing Germany into two separate countries.

1981
Fonseca, *Rose and the Reservation Sisters*

Fonseca, *Coyote Leaves the Reservation*

shows how individuals were placed in settings with objects that represented their interests, greatness, or character. In the 1900s, artists continued to use symbols to portray themselves and others, as well as their culture and their life.

Portraits as Messages What can a portrait communicate? Happiness? Shyness? Regardless of the art form, portraits send messages. Artists use portraits to show more about a person than their appearance. They create symbols to send messages about the subjects—what they enjoy, what they do for a living, or what they think.

The Messages of Symbols In the 1700s, the French artist Jean-Baptiste-Siméon Chardin painted an unusual self-portrait **(Fig. 6–15)**. A self-portrait is a picture an artist makes of him or herself. He used a monkey to symbolize someone trained to act in a certain way and to repeat the same actions. What message might Chardin have been trying to send?

The Mexican artist Frida Kahlo used plant and animal symbols to tell about her personal life. In her self-portraits and portraits, Kahlo used symbolism to express feelings and emotions. The artist painted her own face on the body of a deer in *The Little Deer* **(Fig. 6–14)**, a self-portrait from 1946. What message was Kahlo trying to give to viewers?

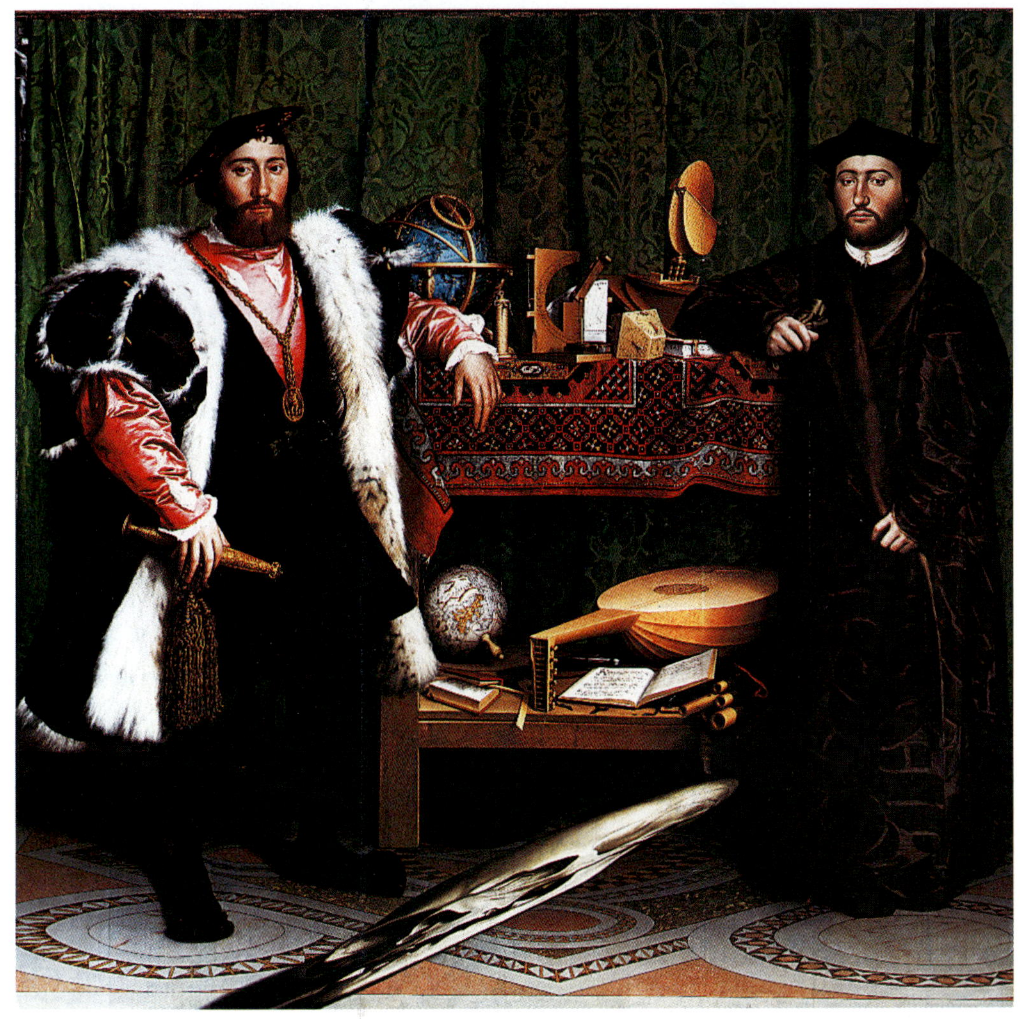

Fig. 6–16 **This painting shows two wealthy French ambassadors in England during the 1500s. Why do you think the artist showed them surrounded by books, a globe, and other instruments?**

Hans Holbein the Younger, *The Ambassadors*, 1533. Oil on wood, 81 ½" x 82 ¼" (207 x 209.5 cm). Courtesy of The National Gallery, London, England. ©The National Gallery, London.

Cultural Symbols You have seen how artists of the past used symbols to comment on their personal experiences and society. Contemporary artist Harry Fonseca uses traditional symbols to tell about modern-day Native Americans.

One of Fonseca's favorite symbols is Coyote, a character who plays tricks in many Native American cultures. Some tribes, like the Nisenan Maidu of northern California, use Coyote's tricks to teach lessons about being safe and responsible. Fonseca uses Coyote's image to show a survivor who knows how to fit in, understand, and even outsmart the non-Native cultures in America. In the paintings shown in **Figs. 6–17** and **6–18**, Fonseca uses Coyote to question and poke fun at cultural stereotypes, or overused images.

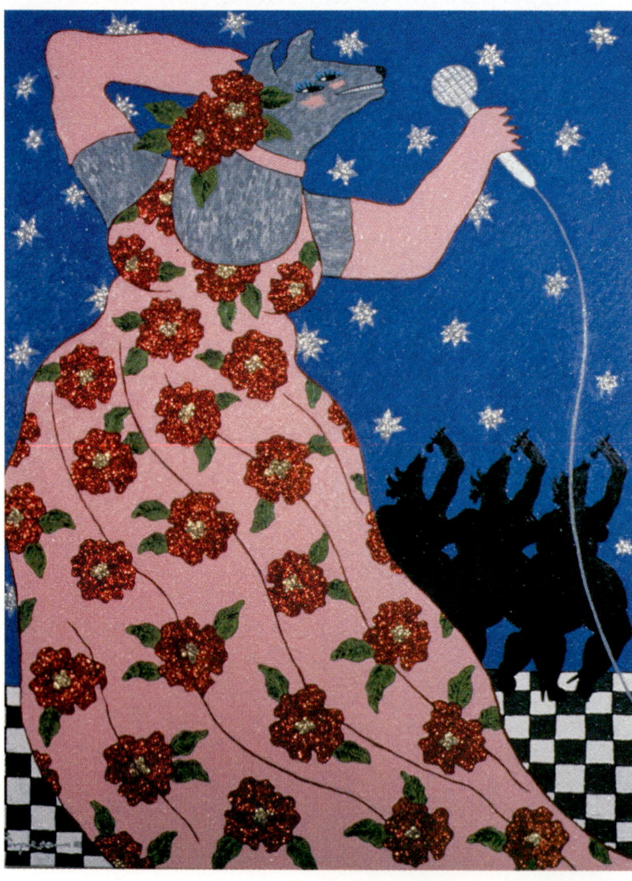

Fig. 6–17 **Here, Coyote is dressed as a singer. Why might artists use humor to send messages about important issues?**

Harry Fonseca, *Rose and the Reservation Sisters*, 1981. Oil and glitter on canvas, 30" x 40" (76 x 102 cm). Courtesy of the artist.

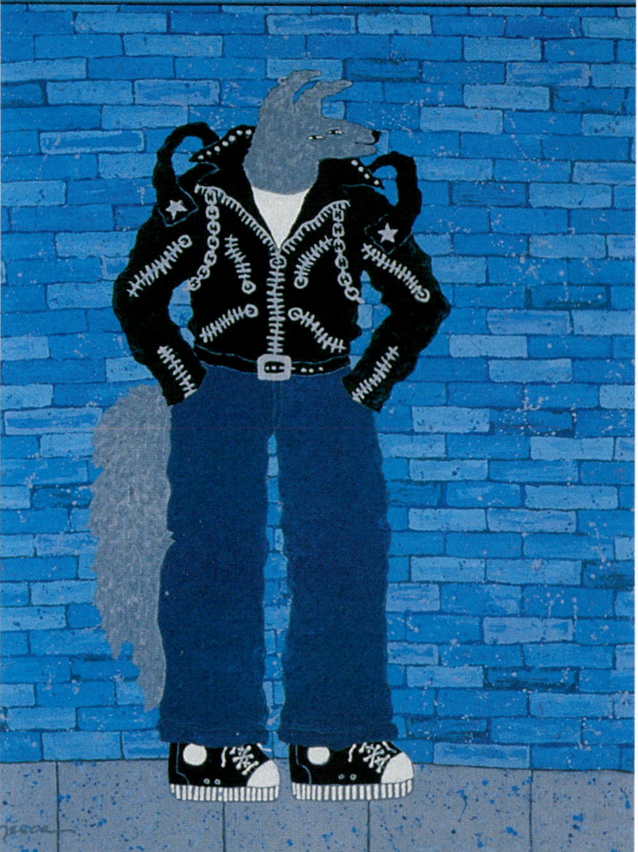

Fig. 6–18 **What messages can you "read" in this Coyote painting?**

Harry Fonseca, *Coyote Leaves the Reservation*, 1981. Oil on canvas, 72" x 60" (183 x 152 cm). Courtesy of the artist.

Meet Harry Fonseca

Harry Fonseca always loved to draw and paint. In high school, his art teacher introduced him to the masterpieces of art history. Fonseca studied fine arts in college, but he always held on to some of the self-taught techniques he developed when he was young. He also researched his Native American background. Fonseca is of Portuguese, Hawaiian, and Nisenan Maidu descent. His mixed cultural background enriches the symbolism in his work. His personal interests and professional training influence the many messages he sends about himself and about Native Americans in society.

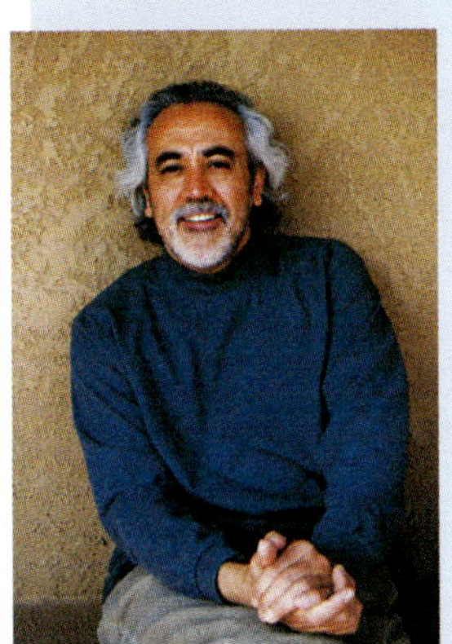

Photo courtesy of the artist.

"My work is of the old, transformed into a contemporary vision."

— Harry Fonseca (1946-2006)

Check Your Understanding

1. What kinds of messages can portraits send?
2. What are the differences between the ways Chardin and Kahlo use animals to symbolize themselves?
3. What animal would you choose to symbolize yourself in a painting? What would surround the animal?

Studio Time

Animals as Symbols

Create a character that symbolizes you.

- Use colored pencils to create your character, possibly an animal, that sends a message about you, your culture, and what you care about.
- Include other symbols, such as objects that reflect your interests, feelings, and experiences.
- To create emphasis, experiment with different types and directions of lines.

Reflect on how well your symbolic portrait reflects your true nature.

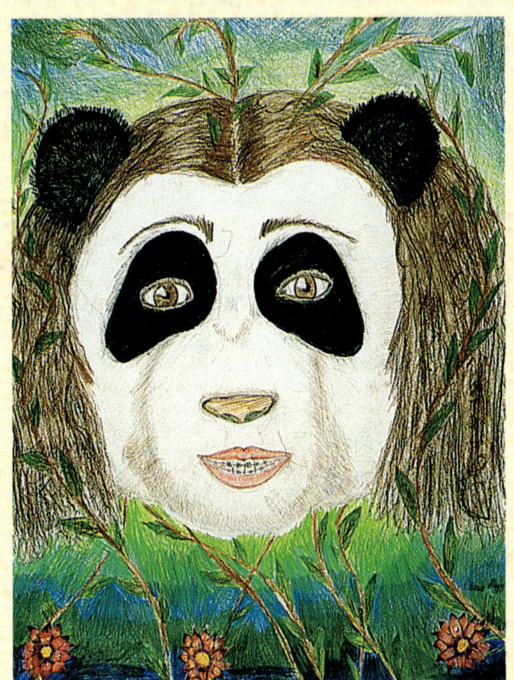

Fig. 6–19 Student artwork

Australian Aboriginal Symbols

Statements of Power Knowledge is important in Australian Aboriginal culture. In this culture, knowledge determines a person's importance and influence in the community. Aboriginal art is an expression of knowledge, making it a statement of authority.

Aboriginal artists use symbols and designs inherited from their ancestors. Most families have their own sets of symbols and designs. For example, patterns of crosshatched lines **(Figs. 6–20 and 6–21)** identify a family and their ancestors.

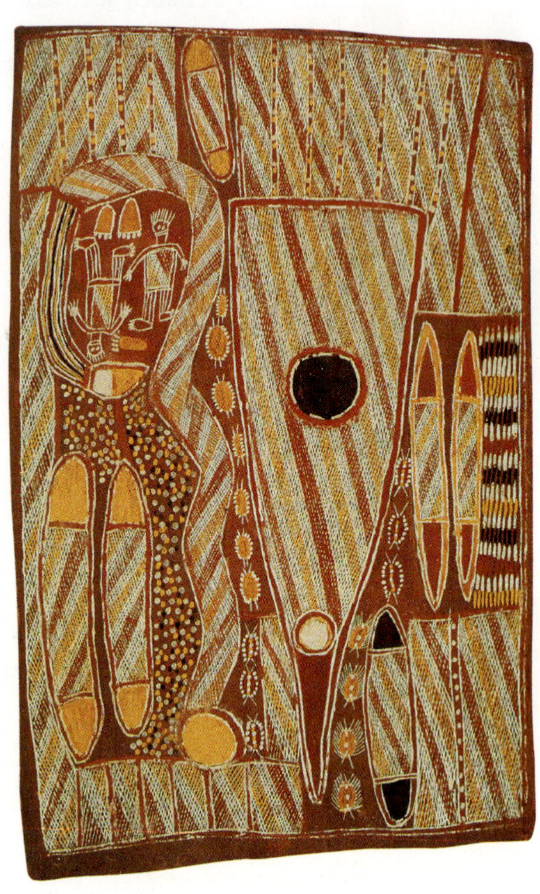

Fig. 6–20 **Note the pattern of crosshatched lines, which symbolizes an ancestor of the artist. What different crosshatched patterns could you make to represent some of your ancestors?**

Australian Aboriginal, *Painted Tree Bark with Crosshatching Pattern*, 20th century. Courtesy the Archivo Fotografico del Museo Preistorico de Etnografico L. Pigorini, Roma.

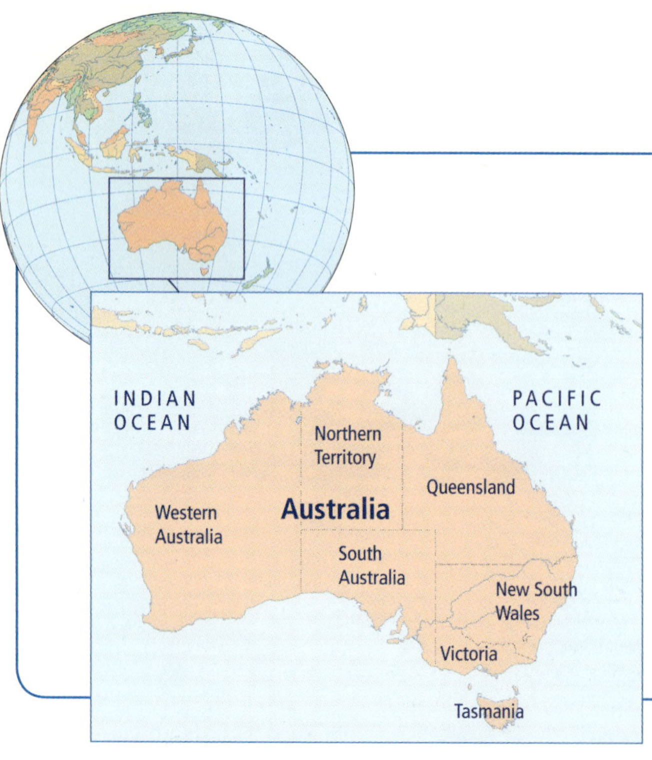

Social Studies Connection

The first inhabitants of **Australia**, called Aborigines, probably arrived on the continent thousands of years ago. They settled in many different areas. Some formed communities in the northern tropical regions or the mild climates of the south. Others settled in the fertile river lands or the harsh deserts. Each group developed a distinct language and artistic style because they were separated by large distances. However, in all Aboriginal groups, art is very important.

They also use the symbols to look at the relationships between individuals and groups, people and the land, and people and their ancestors.

Messages About the Land In Australia, symbols and designs are different depending on where an artist lives. Artists of the Northern Territory use dot-and-line designs **(Fig. 6–22)**. Some of their symbols include dots, which stand for clouds, rain, or fire; curving lines, which may indicate a river or animal tracks; or zigzag lines, which symbolize lightning. Artists often combine designs to communicate a message known only to their Aboriginal group.

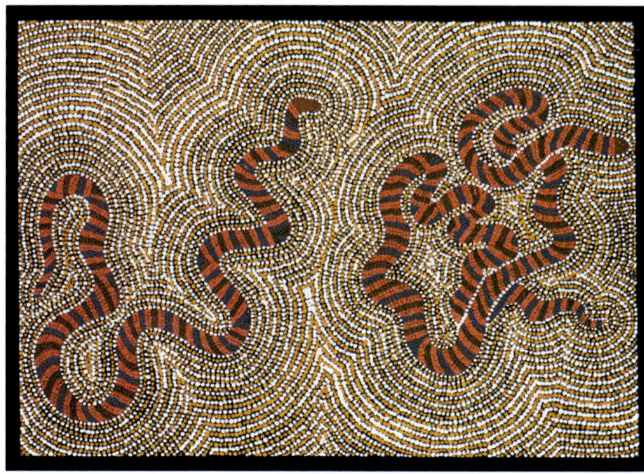

Fig. 6–22 **Do you see dots or lines? Dotted lines often symbolize certain landforms, paths, or trails. The lines may also be decorative.**

Rene Ronibson, *Snake Dreaming,* 20th century. Acrylic on canvas. Aboriginal Artists Agency Ltd. Photo credit: Jennifer Steele/Art Resource, New York.

Visual Culture

Look in magazines, newspapers, books, and use the Internet to find symbols that are widely known or commonly used for ideas such as peace, love, friendship, war, death, danger, and so forth. Draw or make copies of these symbols and share with your classmates. What new ideas for symbols can you design?

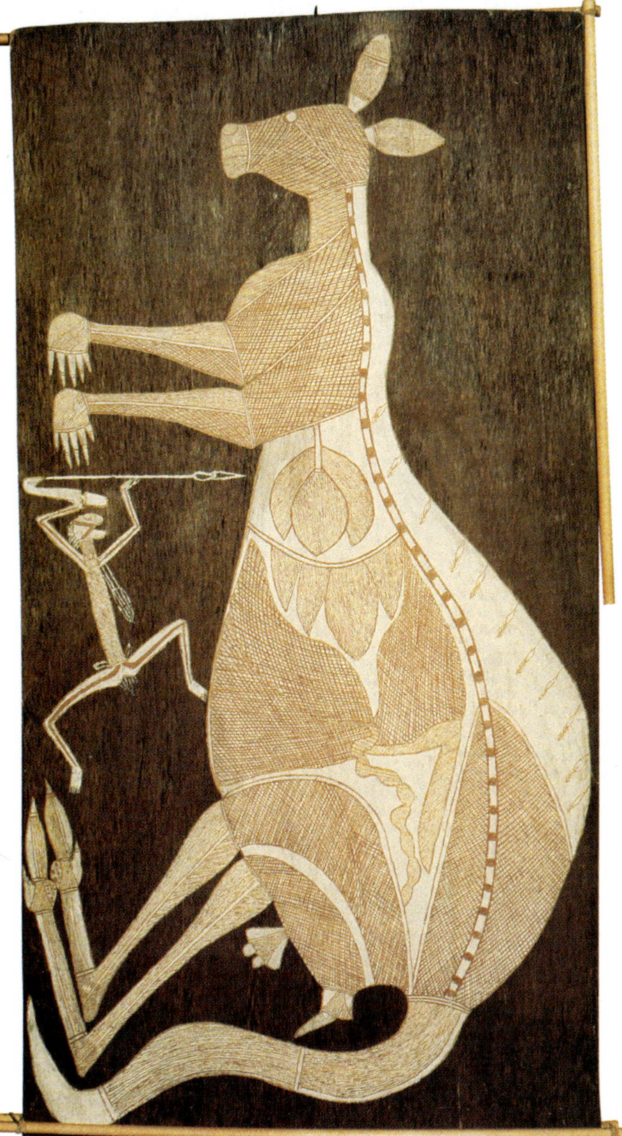

Fig. 6–21 **Why might outsiders refer to this way of painting as "X-ray" style? Why would the artists want to show the internal organs of the animals in their region?**

Australian Aboriginal, Western Arnhem Land, *Kangaroo and Hunter,* 20th century. X-ray style painting on bark. Private Collection, Prague, Czech Republic. Werner Forman/Art Resource, New York.

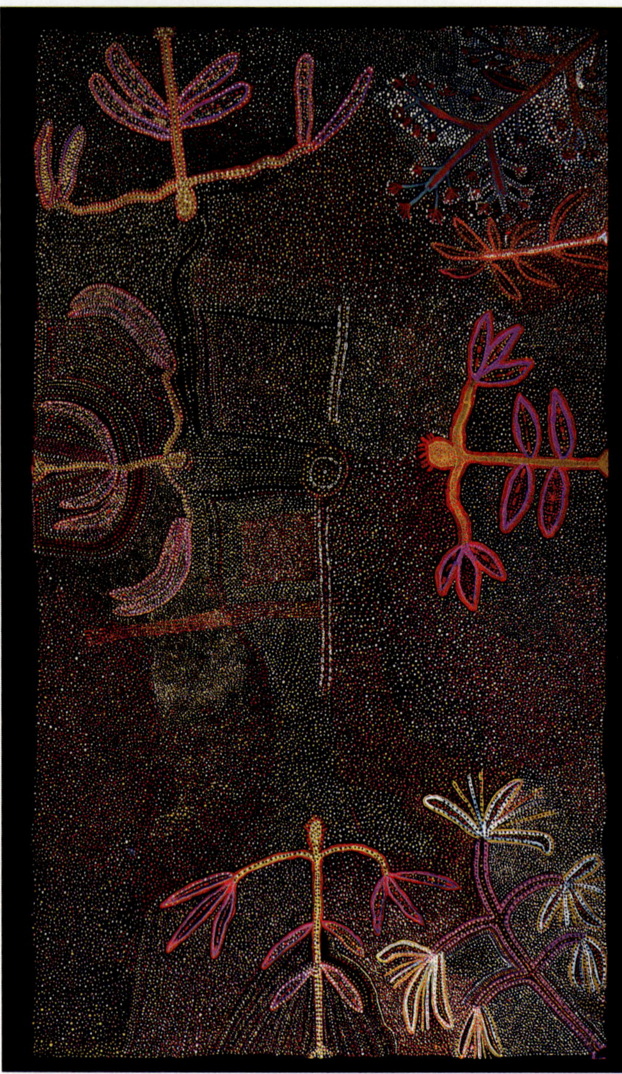

Fig. 6–23 **Every mark in this painting is a symbol. What symbols do you think you recognize?**

Ada Bird Petyarre, *Sacred Grasses*, 1989. Synthetic polymer paint on canvas, 51" by 90 ½" (130 x 230 cm). Collection: National Gallery or Australia, Canberra.

The Meaning of Patterns Ada Bird Petyarre has worked in batik, watercolor, woodblock prints, and sculpture. Her most recent works are acrylic paintings on canvas. Each canvas is a pattern of repeated elements such as dots, lines, and circles. The patterns often have important meaning for her family group. Petyarre also uses symbols that look like plants. They represent sacred desert plants and grasses or the large number of wildflowers that sprout after a good rain. The painted patterns are her personal statements about her world. In *Sacred Grasses* **(Fig. 6–23)**, the symbols are easy to recognize as plant forms. For her work *Mountain Devil Lizard* **(Fig. 6–24)**, she repeated lines to create patterns. These patterns represent designs that are painted on the bodies of dancers in special ceremonies.

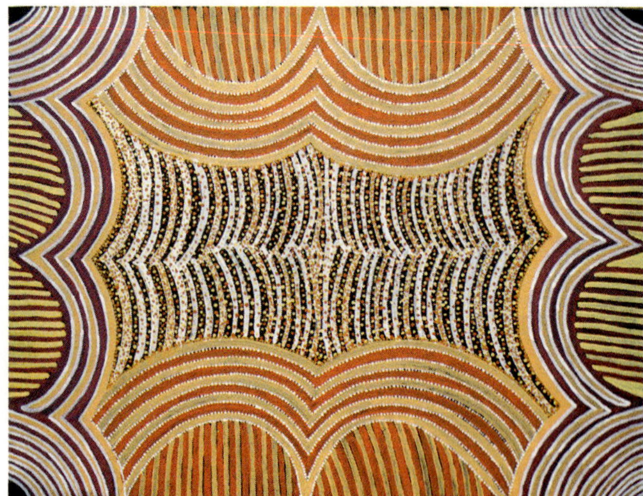

Fig. 6–24 **How would you describe the lines in this painting?**

Ada Bird Petyarre, *Mountain Devil Lizard,* 1992. Acrylic on canvas. Courtesy of the artist and Jinta Desert Art, Sydney, Australia.

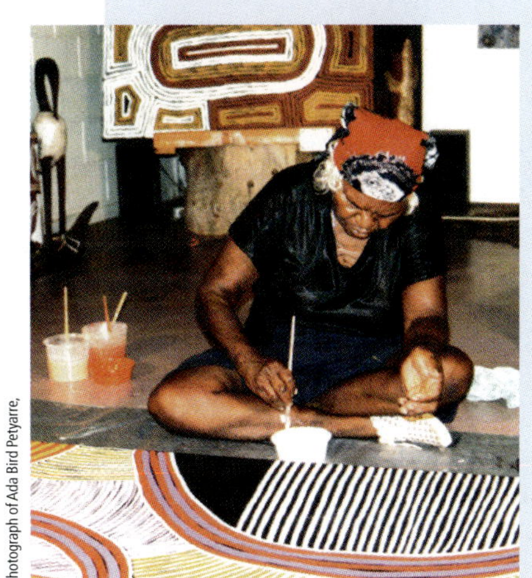

Photograph of Ada Bird Petyarre,

Meet Ada Bird Petyarre

Artist Ada Bird Petyarre is a spokesperson for her native Aboriginal group. She was born in the desert part of Australia's Northern Territory, a land well represented in her artworks. Petyarre is the oldest of five sisters, who are each well-known artists too. Petyarre and her sisters have a common knowledge of stories, dances, songs, and ceremonies. They also share the responsibility of preserving and passing on the symbols of their ancestors.

"I draw from designs that I understand from my own background."

— Ada Bird Peyarre (born 1930)

Studio Time

A Stencil Pattern

Make and use stencils to create repeated shapes on one piece of paper.

- Use the stencils to create a pattern that sends a personal message.
- Before you create your stencil pattern, practice with a sponge or stiff bristle brush to stipple paint around or through the openings in the stencil shape itself.
- Consider overlapping the stencils and using different colors for emphasis.

Reflect on how you created a variety of patterns.

Check Your Understanding

1. What are some symbols used in Aboriginal art?
2. Compare and contrast the meaning of symbols and patterns from one part of Australia to another.
3. What patterns and symbols would you use to symbolize your town or city?

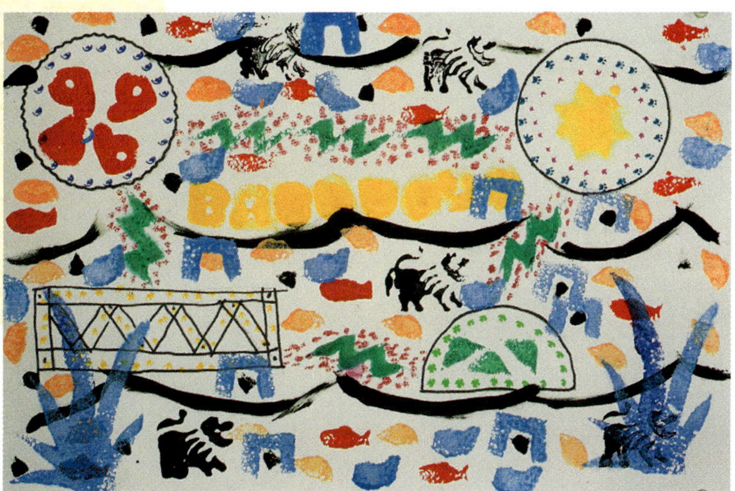

Fig. 6–25 Student artwork

Send a Message without Words

Studio Background

Messages can come in many forms. They can be written, spoken, signaled, or communicated by codes and symbols. For example, think about the last television commercial that caught your eye. How did it make you feel? What do you think it means? Your answers probably tell you the message that the commercial was trying to send. But commercials are not the only medium that sends messages; artworks can send messages as well.

In this studio exploration, you will create a linoleum print that sends an important message. First, choose a topic for your message, such as littering, animal rights, or school dress codes. What kind of image will best express the seriousness, humor, or concern you feel about your topic? How will you get people to notice and understand your message? How will you use lines and shapes to create emphasis? Will you outline the positive and negative shapes? Will you use lines to create patterns and visual texture?

You Will Need

- sketch paper
- pencil
- linoleum block
- carving tools
- bench hook
- ink
- brayer
- construction paper

Step 1 Plan and Practice

- Choose a topic for your message.
- Think of an image that will best show the viewer how you feel about your topic.
- How will you use lines, shapes, and textures to support your message?

Things to Remember:

- ✓ Communicate a message about a topic or issue.
- ✓ Create emphasis with lines, shapes, and textures.
- ✓ Use care while inking the surface and pulling the print.

Inspiration from Our World

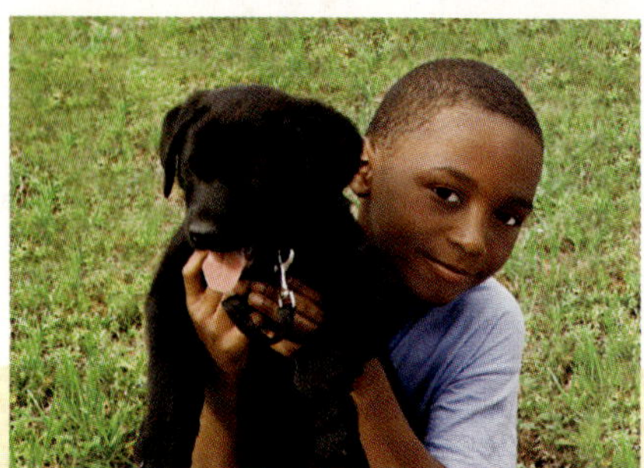

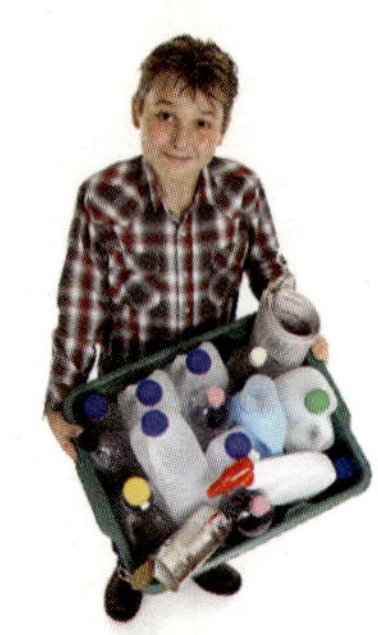

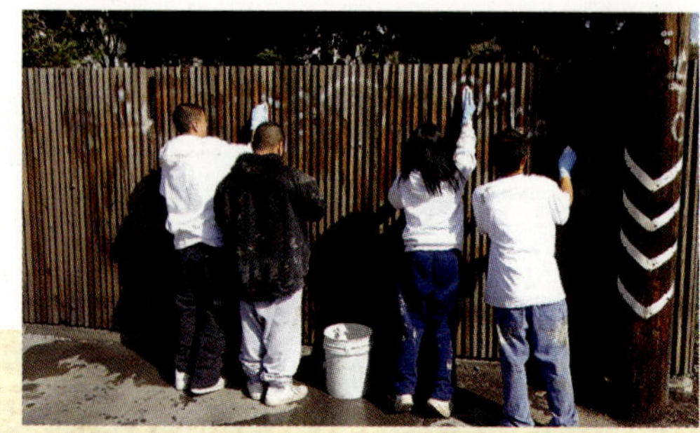

Inspiration from Art

Some artists make prints so that many people will see their messages. Printmaking allows artists to create more than one copy of their artwork. Relief printmaking is one of several basic printmaking methods. A **relief print** is made from a design that is raised from a flat background. Two traditional relief-printmaking processes are woodcuts and linoleum, or lino, cuts. Both involve carving the surface of a block to create an image. The raised areas will create lines and positive shapes in the print. The areas that are cut away will create negative shapes.

On the carved block, the artist coats the raised areas with ink and then places a sheet of paper on the inked surface. When he or she presses down on the paper, the inked image is transferred to it. The artist then "pulls the print" by carefully peeling the paper away from the block.

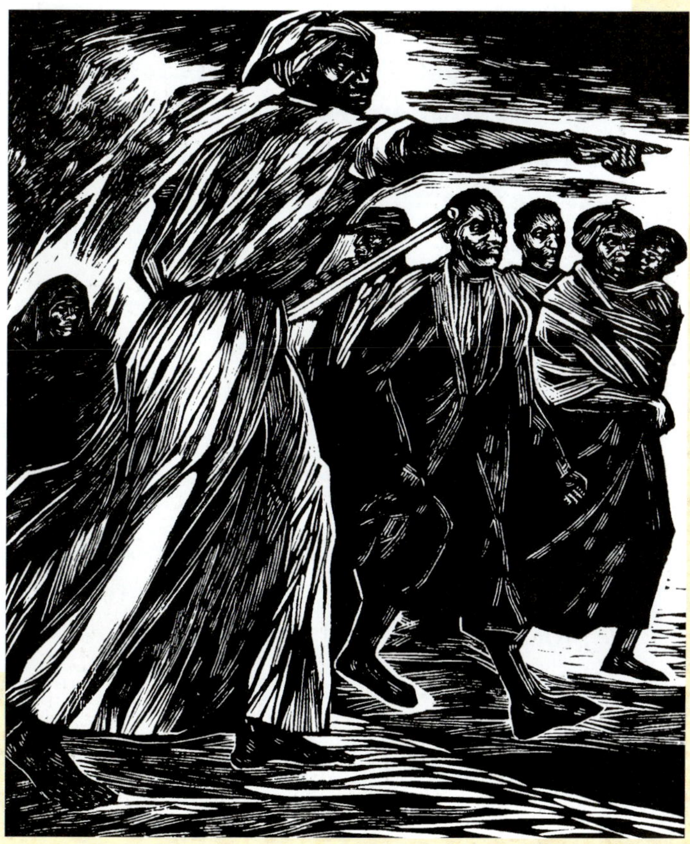

Fig. 6–26 **How did the artist show the heroism and strength of Harriet Tubman? How did she use contrast to emphasize her message?**

Elizabeth Catlett, *Harriet*, 1975. Linocut, 12 ½" x 10 ⅛" (32 x 26 cm). Courtesy Sragow Gallery, New York. © Elizabeth Catlett/Licensed by VAGA, New York, NY.

Step 2 Begin to Create

- Trace the edges of your block on sketch paper. Draw your design inside the lines of the trace with a soft-leaded (#2) pencil.
- Think about which areas will print and which will be the color of the paper. With your pencil, fill in the areas that will print.
- **Carefully lay your design facedown on the linoleum side of the block. Make sure that the edges of the trace line up with the edges of the block.**

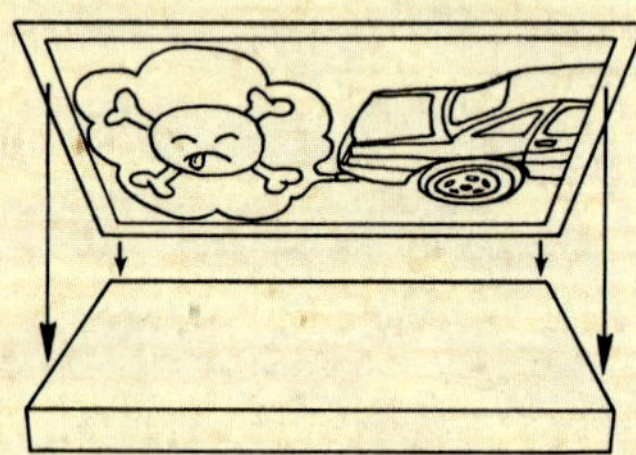

- With your hand, rub the back of the paper to transfer your design onto the block.
- Check the darkness of the image that is now on the block. Darken any lines that you think are too light.
- Place the block on a bench hook. **Carefully carve away the areas of your design that will not print.**

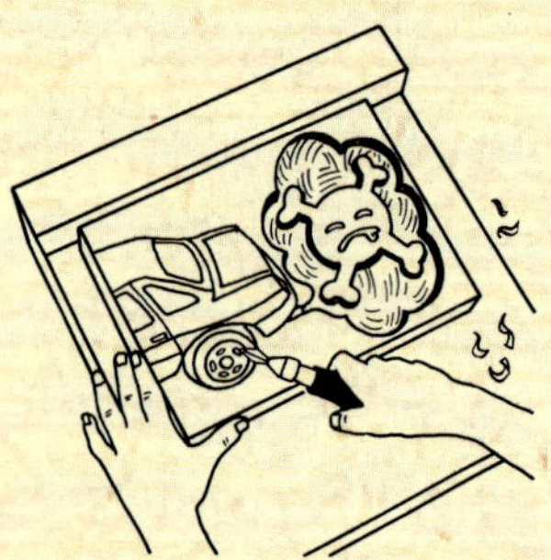

- **Use a brayer to roll a thin, even layer of ink onto the raised surfaces of your block.**

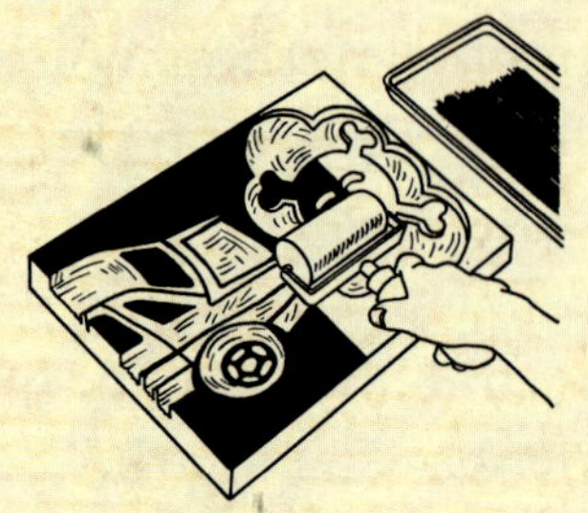

- Carefully place your printing paper over the block. Gently rub the back of the paper. **When you see the faint impression of your design on the back of the sheet, slowly pull the print away from the block.**

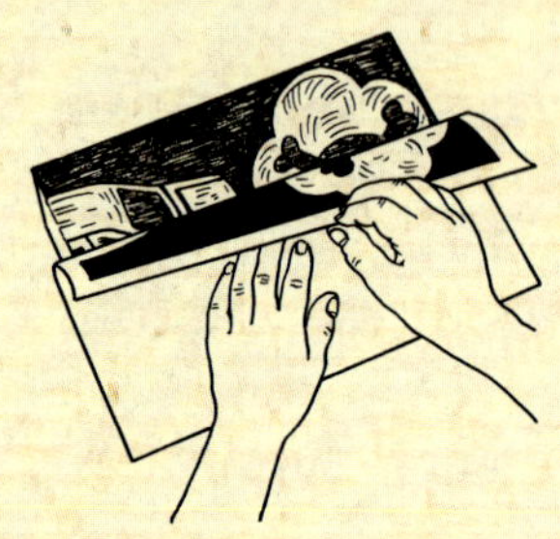

Step 3 Revise

Did you remember to:

- ✓ Communicate a message about a topic or issue?
- ✓ Create emphasis with lines, shapes, and textures?
- ✓ Use care while inking the surface and pulling the print?

Adjust your work if necessary. In your sketchbook, make a note of your revisions and why you made them.

Step 4 **Add Finishing Touches**

- Give your print a title.
- When it is dry, sign and date your print.

Step 5 **Share and Reflect**

- Display your artwork. Ask your classmates if they can "read" the message of your artwork. What issue did you focus on?
- Discuss the ways you used lines, textures, and shapes to emphasize your message.
- Point out where you can see positive and negative shapes in your own work and the work of your classmates.
- What did you find challenging about this project?

Art Criticism

Describe What do you see in this artwork?

Analyze How has the artist arranged the parts in this print?

Interpret What message do you think the artist was trying to send?

Evaluate What makes this a powerful image?

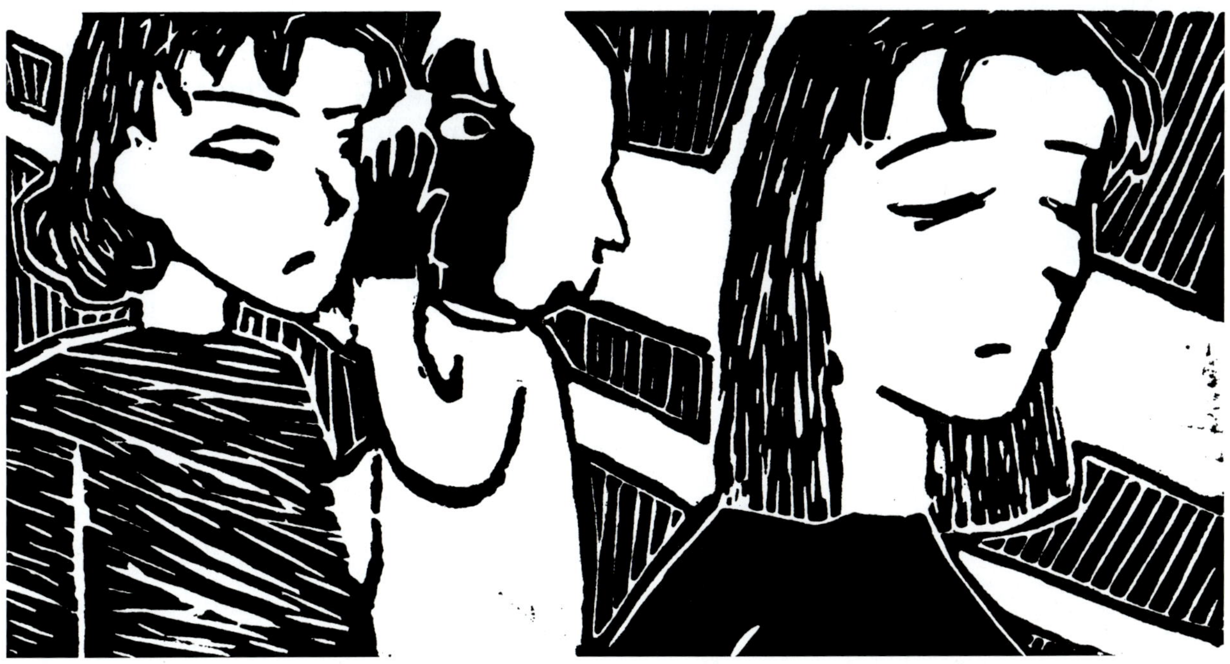

Fig. 6–27 Student artwork

Social Studies

Since the beginning of history, people have used banners and flags. They have used them to identify friends and enemies, to show allegiance, or to promote pride. The designs on the flag or banner often send a message. George Washington explained the message of the first American flag in these words: "We take the stars from heaven, the red from our mother country, separating it by white stripes, thus showing that we have separated from her, and the white stripes shall go down to posterity representing liberty."

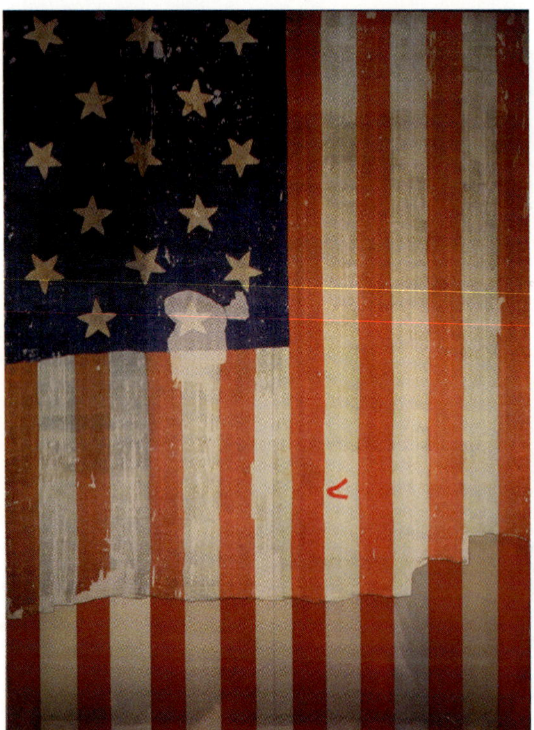

Fig. 6–28 **Compare this American flag to the flag you can see today. What message does the flag send to you?**

Mrs. Mary Pickersgill, Baltimore, *Star-Spangled Banner*, 1813. Cotton, wool bunting, Irish linen, 30' x 34' (originally 30' x 42'). Courtesy of Smithsonian Institution.

Theater

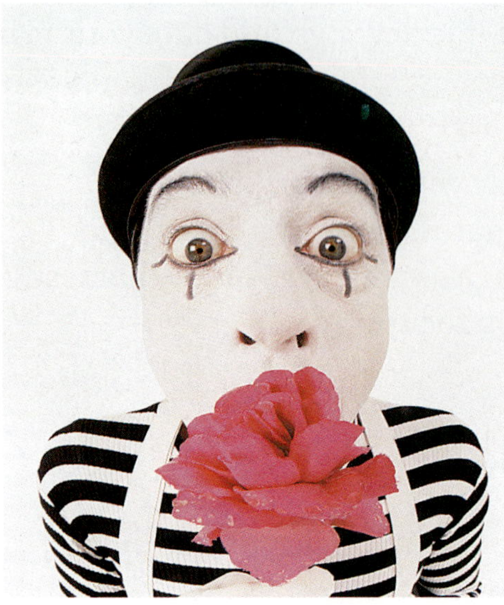

Fig. 6–29 **Clowns first appeared in early European pantomime plays that mixed music, song, dance, and acrobatic tricks. Why can people of different cultures and languages understand pantomime?**

Courtesy of SuperStock.

Mimes are performers who communicate without words. They use movements and facial expressions to act out scenes. They do not speak while they are acting. This art form began in ancient Rome. It is called pantomime. In Roman plays, a chorus told the story and a single dancer pantomimed the actions of the characters. Today, pantomime is part of many circus clown acts. Think about times when you have communicated something without using words. How can you communicate with your eyes, your hands, your shoulders, your head?

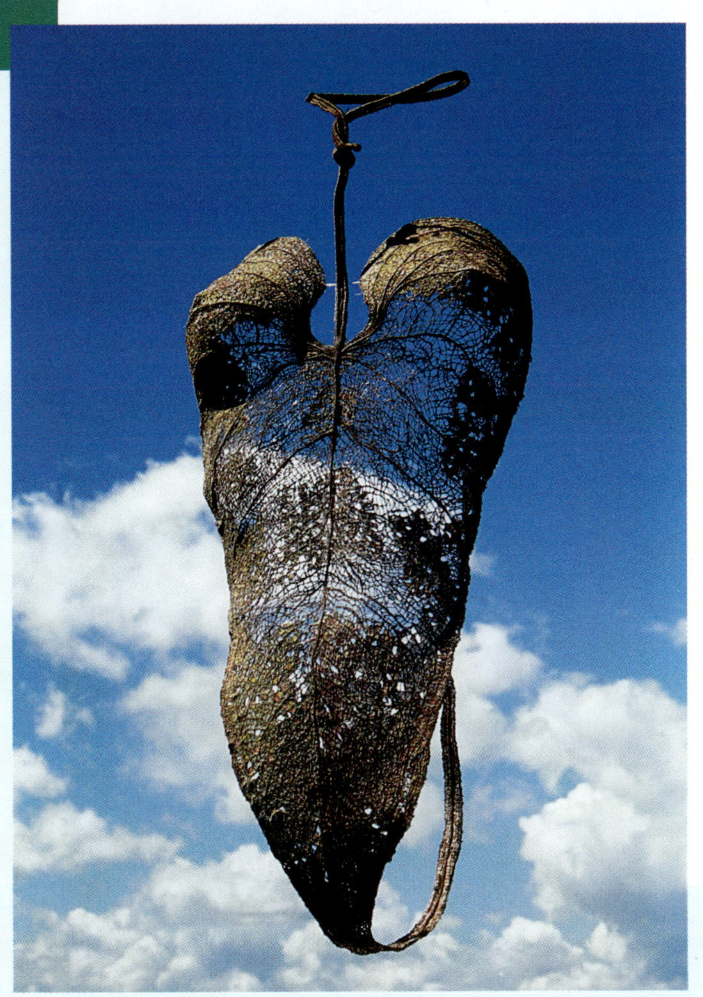

Careers **Aestheticians**

Aestheticians are people who think about art and how people respond to it. Have you ever seen an artwork that you didn't understand? Did you wonder why some people called it a great work of art? Aestheticians have many questions concerning the way people think about art. They wonder what makes something an artwork. Most aestheticians earn degrees in philosophy from a college or university.

Fig. 6–30 **Thinking like an aesthetician, what questions would you ask about this artwork?**

Anda Klancic, *Embraced by Nature*, 1998. Flax, cotton, polyester, metal filament, PVA fabric, 27 ½" x 10 ½" x 9 ½" (69.8 x 26.7 x 24.1 cm). Courtesy of Browngrotta Art.

Daily Life

Before the 1980s, people your age communicated with their friends and family using telephones or sending letters by mail. With today's technology, we can communicate using computers, cellphones, and text messaging. Now instead of sending a letter by mail, you probably send an e-mail. What new inventions can you imagine that might make communication around the world even easier and faster?

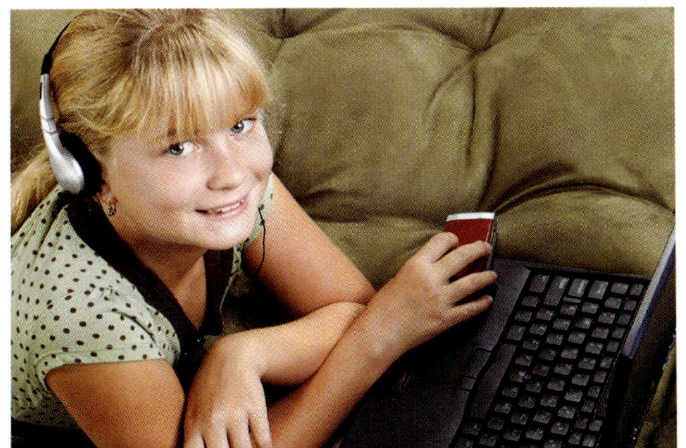

Fig. 6–31

Unit 6 Vocabulary and Content Review

Vocabulary Review

Match each art term below with its definition.

symbols
pictograms
monotype
relief print
monoprint

1. a print made by drawing in ink
2. a print made from a design that is raised from a flat background
3. images that stand for and communicate certain ideas
4. a print made by carving into a surface and adding or changing ink with each print
5. an early form of writing

Aesthetic Thinking

Does an artwork have to be a self-portrait to be about the artist? Do all artworks tell us something about the artists who made them? Is it possible for artists to ever completely remove themselves from the work they make? Why or why not?

For Your Portfolio

Review your artwork from this unit and choose the work you think sends the most effective message. Write a brief artist's statement explaining what the message is and why you think it is effective.

Write About Art

Art historians have described Bill Traylor's paintings as displaying both fear and joy. Do you see fear, joy, or both in this painting? Write an explanation of your answer.

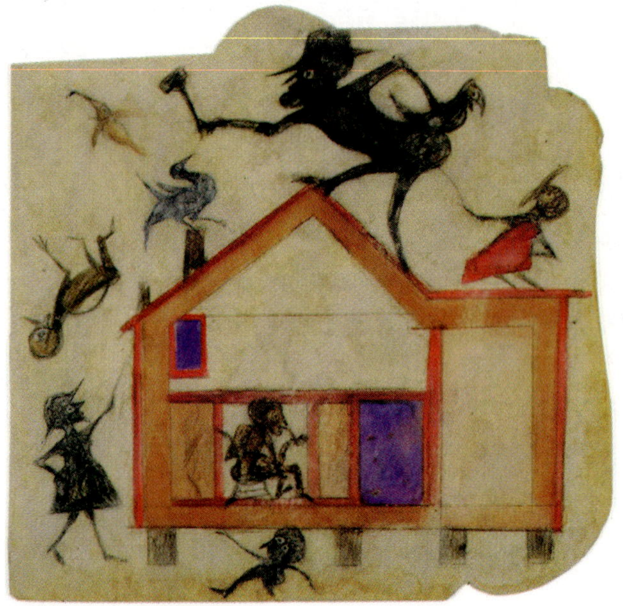

Fig. 6–32 **How does the artist use color to send a message in this artwork?**

Bill Traylor, *Untitled (Exciting Event: House with Figures)*, c. 1939–47. Poster paint and pencil on cardboard. High Museum of Art, Atlanta. T. Marshall Hahn Collection, 1997.114.

Art Criticism

Describe What do you see in this print?

Analyze How does the artist use line in this print?

Interpret The artist has made the heads of the flowers very detailed while leaving the stems and flowers sketchy. What is the effect of this decision?

Evaluate Why do you think the artist included the sunflower's "ghost"?

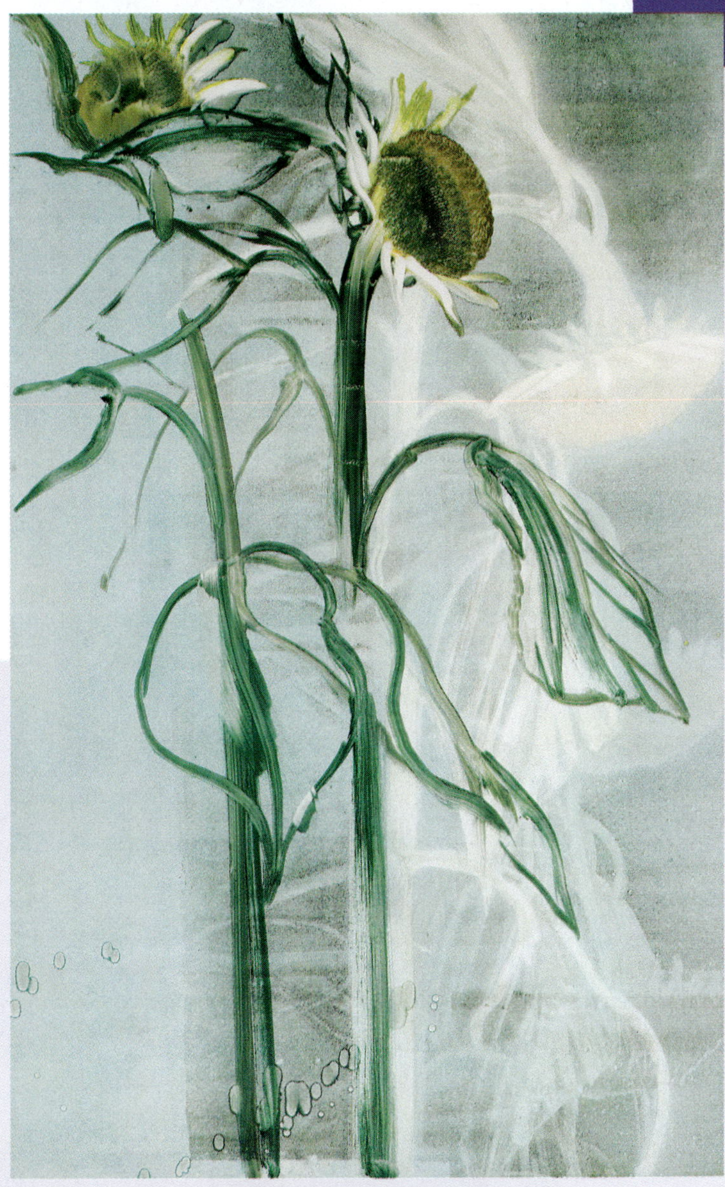

Fig. 6–33 Michael Mazur, *Night Sunflowers (Cognate II)*, 1982. Color monotype, 47 ¼" x 29 ⅜" (120 x 74.6). Museum of Fine Arts, Boston. Fund in memory of Horatio Greenough Curtis, 1983.228.

Meet the Artist

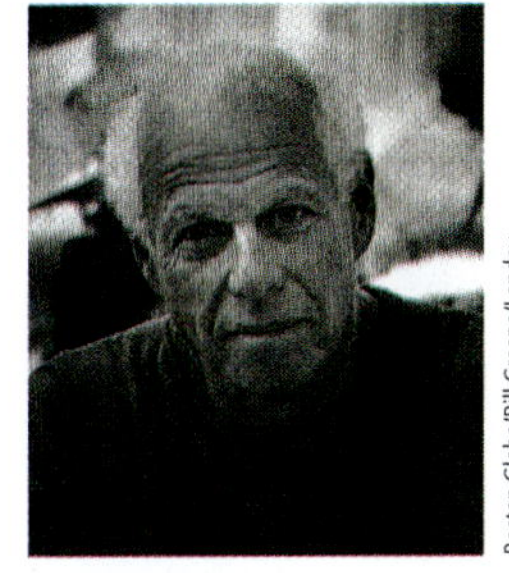

Boston Globe/Bill Greene/Landov.

Michael Mazur was born in New York and now lives in Massachusetts. Throughout his career, he has experimented with many different ways of making prints. Mazur's work focuses on the natural world. Some of his work shows flowers or landscapes; other prints are more abstract but still suggest nature.

"Whenever you work with materials... you have to listen in a certain way. They may not be doing exactly what you wanted them to do. But they may be telling you something about what they can do."

— Michael Mazur (born 1935)

For Your Sketchbook

Fill a sketchbook page with different kinds of lines. Identify those lines that might be used to symbolize or express different moods and feelings, such as energy, calm, or joy.

Unit 7

Artists Are Inventors

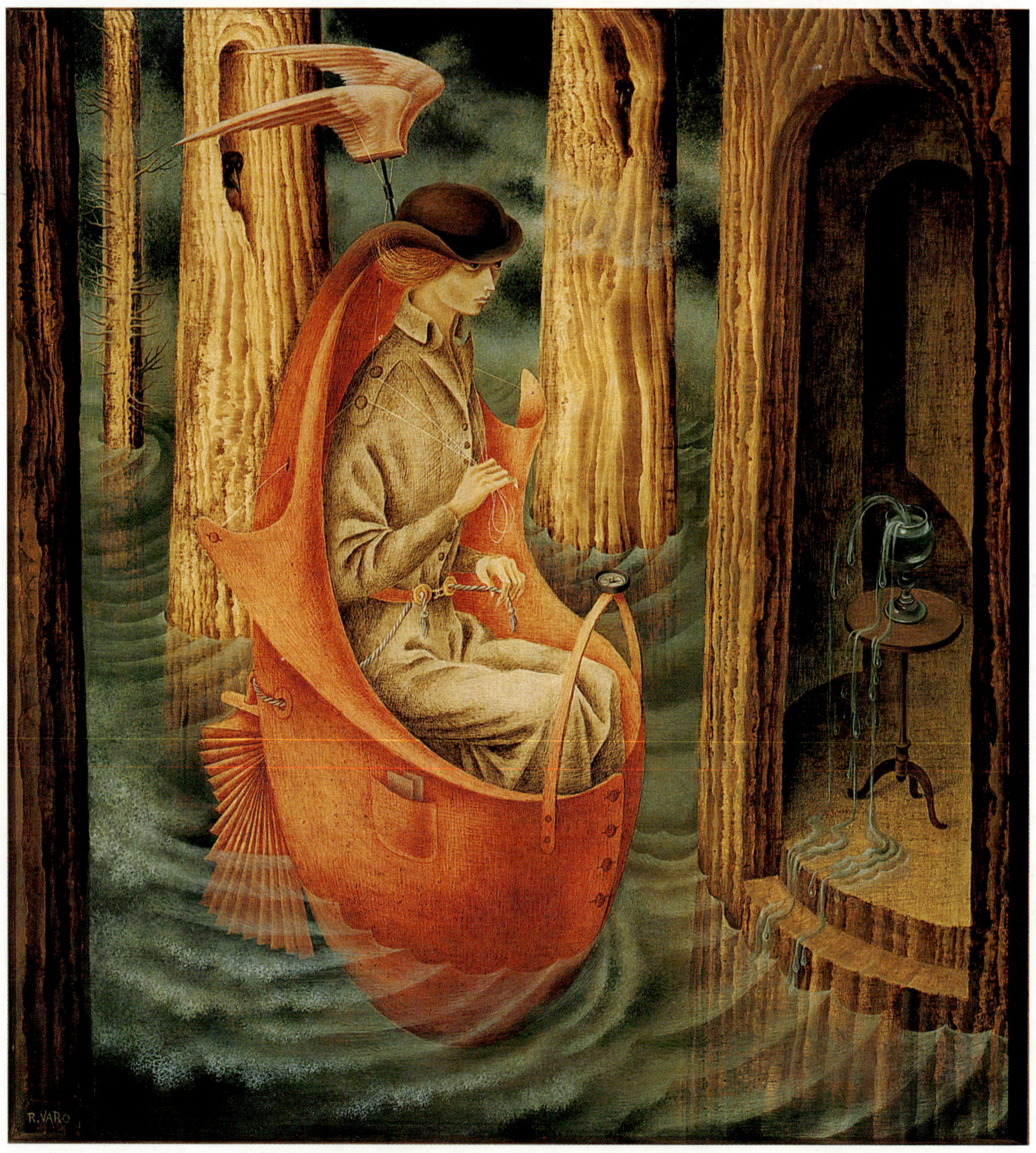

Fig. 7–1 **Remedios Varo often showed imaginary journeys in her paintings. What ordinary item of clothing did she transform into a boat?**

Remedios Varo, *Exploration of the Sources of the Orinoco River*, 1959. Oil on canvas, 17 ½" x 15 ½" (44 x 39.5 cm). Private collection. Courtesy of Anna Alexandra and Walter Gruen.

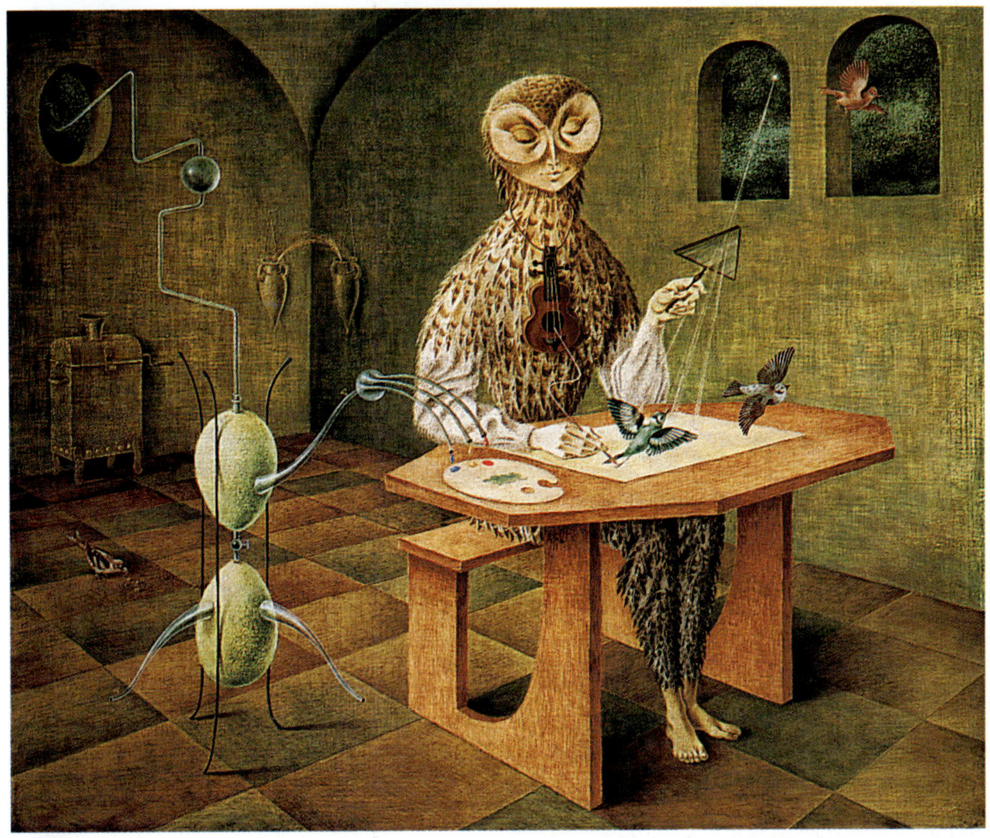

Fig. 7–2 **What question do you think Remedios Varo was trying to answer with this painting?**

Remedios Varo, *Creation of the Birds*, 1957. Oil on masonite, 21 ¼" x 25 ¼" (54 x 64 cm). Courtesy of Anna Alexandra and Walter Gruen.

Have you ever imagined a world where things happened in strange or unusual ways? Perhaps you dreamed of a place where weird creatures roamed the land. Or maybe you pretended to live on a faraway planet, where everything is upside-down or topsy-turvy.

Mysterious worlds are often subjects of artworks. Artists, like most of us, are interested in what appears not to be of this world. By focusing on dreams and fantasies, artists invent imaginative worlds for us to consider. They are worlds where objects come alive, people become plants, and nothing is as we expect it to be.

In this unit, you will learn:

- How artists create the worlds they dream and imagine.
- How to use perspective and other techniques to create the illusion of depth.
- How to recognize the many ways artists use invention and fantasy.

Asking "What If...?"

Artist Remedios Varo was fascinated with the way things worked. Like a scientist, she focused on mechanical objects and things in nature. To create the invented worlds of her paintings, Varo asked questions and then explored possible answers. She would ask, for example, what the moon would look like if someone could capture it and put it into a cage. With her "What if?" questions, she allowed herself to ignore science's explanations of our world.

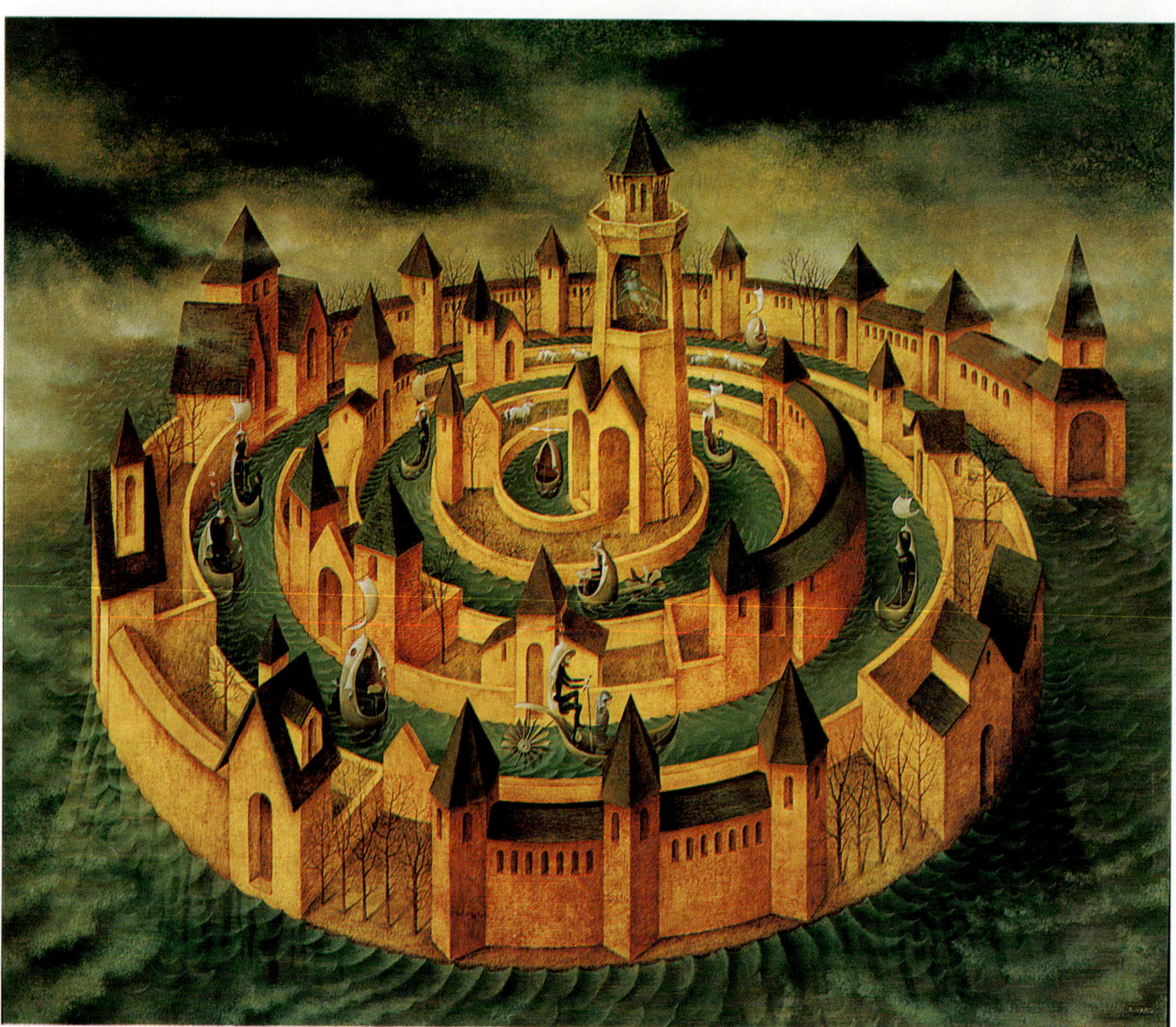

Fig. 7–3 **In this artwork, travelers in tiny vehicles make their way through winding waterways. What parts of the scene look invented?**

Remedios Varo, *Spiral Transit*, 1962. Oil on masonite, 39 ⅜" x 45 ¼" (100 x 115 cm). Private collection. Courtesy of Anna Alexandra and Walter Gruen. Photo by Javier Hinojosa.

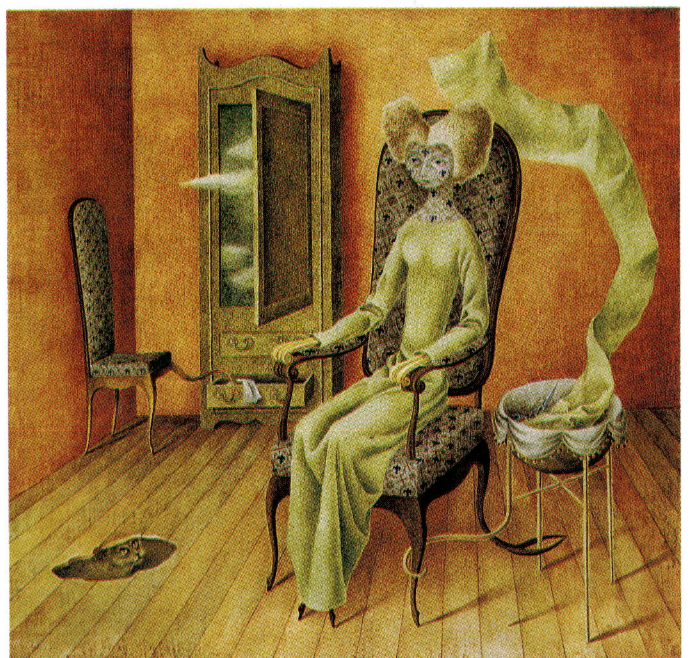

Fig. 7–4 **Here, the artist twisted reality around. Chairs and other ordinary objects seem to come to life.**

Remedios Varo, *Mimesis*, 1960. Oil on masonite, 19" x 19" (48 x 50 cm). Courtesy of Anna Alexandra and Walter Gruen.

Art from the Imagination Varo was not the first to explore "What if?" questions. Centuries before science would explain much of our universe, people used their imagination to explain what they could not understand. They wondered about the origin of fire or how the sun "moved" across the sky. They asked questions to help them find solutions to the puzzles. They asked, "What if all the fire in the world came from a fire-breathing dragon?" or "What if a chariot pulled by a team of horses moved the sun across the sky?" Their artworks showed what they imagined when they asked these questions.

Meet Remedios Varo

As a child in her native Spain, Remedios Varo often copied her engineer father's detailed mechanical drawings and plans. She also loved fairy tales and magic stories, which inspired her to add fantasy-like elements to her drawings.

Varo studied at an art academy for seven years, developing her drawing talent and studying art history. She later journeyed to Paris, where she became familiar with the Surrealists. The Surrealists were artists who were interested in dreams and the workings of the subconscious. (See more Surrealist art on pages 193 and 196–199.) In the 1940s, Varo fled Paris because of World War II. She moved to Mexico, where she developed her personal artistic style and pursued her interests in magic, fantasy, and science.

"I took advantage of all that I learned, in painting the things that interested me...which could be called, together with technique, the beginning of my personality."

— Remedios Varo (1908–1963)

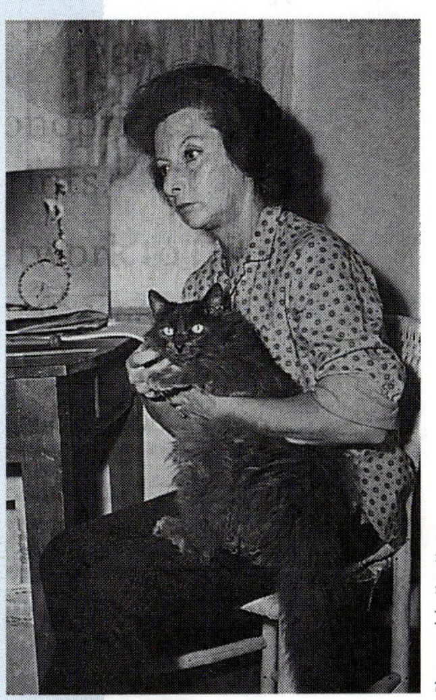

Photograph by Katy Horna.

Artistic Tricks Some artists seem to love to fool us with optical tricks. In the mid-1500s, artist Giuseppe Arcimboldo invented a unique approach to fool the eye. The painting *Vertumnus* (Fig. 7–5) shows the technique he developed. Arcimboldo created fantasy portraits by combining images of different fruits, vegetables, and other natural objects.

Artists also may use mathematical and scientific approaches to make their unreal worlds appear real. They create optical tricks through the use of perspective. Perspective is a technique for creating the illusion of depth on a two-dimensional surface. Artist M. C. Escher, for example, distorted perspective and worked with several vanishing points in order to make impossible scenes look real. In his artwork *Another World II* (Fig. 7–6) how many different ways to look into space did the artist create?

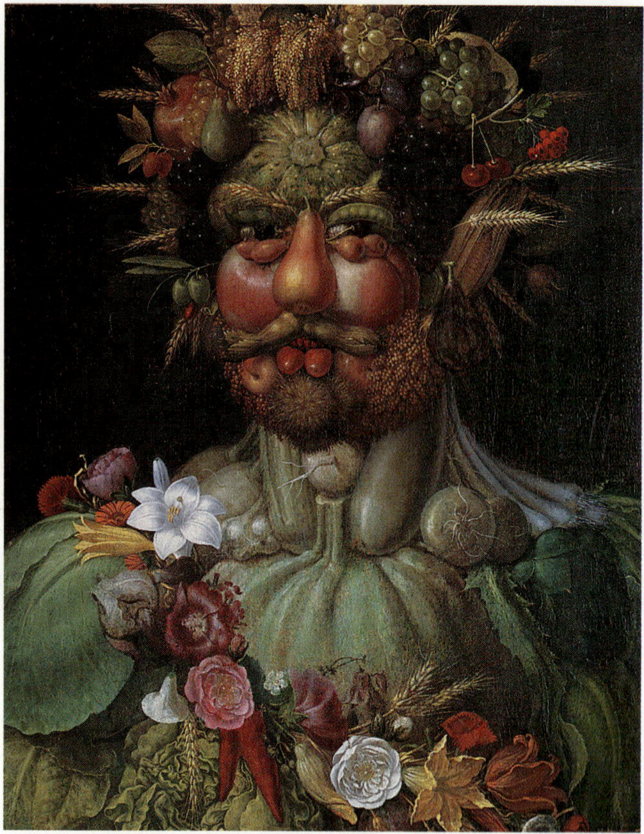

Fig. 7–5 **What things from nature can you find in this fool-the-eye painting?**

Giuseppe Arcimboldo, *Vertumnus*, (Emperor Rudolf II), 1590. Oil on wood. 27 ¾" x 22 ½" (70.5 x 57.5 cm). Slott, Skokloster, Sweden. Photo credit: Erich Lessing/Art Resource, NY.

Check Your Understanding

1. What is perspective?
2. How is art from the imagination different from other forms of art?
3. Why are dreams a good source of imaginative art?

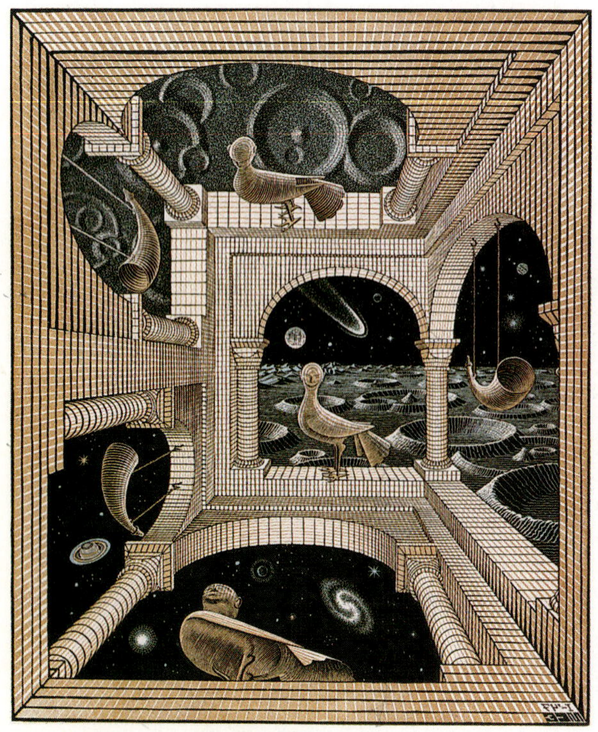

Fig. 7–6 **How did this artist use perspective to create an optical illusion?**

M.C. Escher, *Another World II*, 1947. Wood engraving printed from three blocks, 12 ½" x 10 ¼" (31.5 x 26 cm)

Studio Time

It's An Illusion

You can use a unique "checkerboard" grid to create an optical illusion. As you work, remember the "four peas in a pod" requirement: Practice, Planning, Precision, and Patience.

- One way to begin is to use a light pencil line to draw a small circle near the center of the paper. Continue to draw concentric circles to the edges of the paper. Complete your "fool the eye" drawing by adding wavy lines across the paper.
- You can also start with a small square in the very center of the paper and continue to draw larger and larger squares toward the edges. Then draw radiating lines from the center of the paper to the corners and edges.
- With both techniques, apply color in the alternate spaces. Start at the top corner of the paper and place a light pencil mark in every other space. Continue in rows across and down the paper.
- Precision and practice are required when adding color to the marked spaces. Work slowly and carefully. Concentrate and stay focused on the task.

Reflect on the visual effects your optical illusion creates.

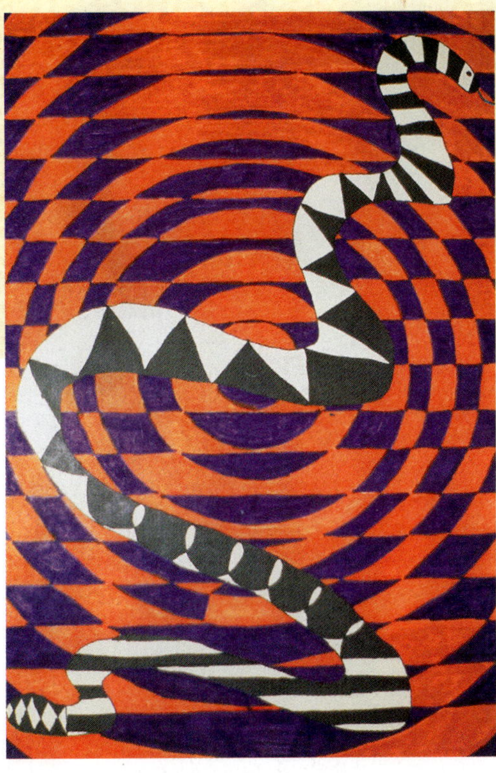

Fig. 7–7 Student artwork

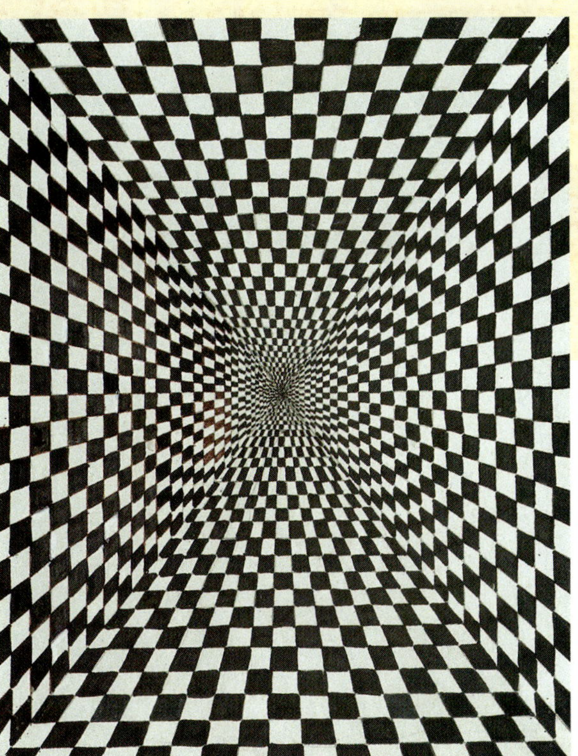

Fig. 7–8 Student artwork

Perspective

Linear perspective is a system of using lines to create the illusion of three-dimensional space. Artists use this system to create a sense of depth in a painting or drawing. Other ways to create the illusion of three-dimensional space include: overlapping, shading and shadow, placement, size, color and value, and focus. Artists have found inventive ways to combine these methods with one- and two-point perspective.

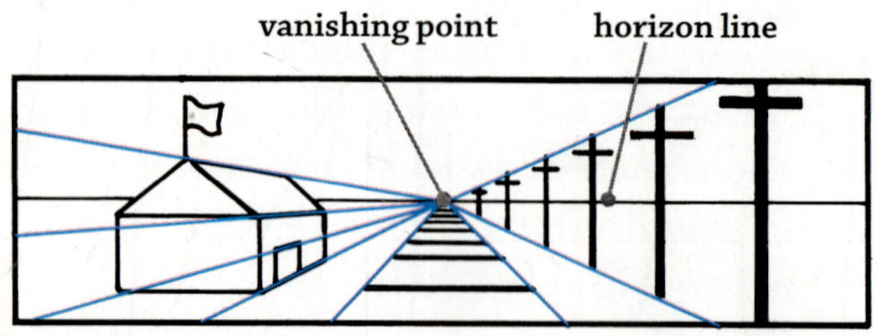

One-Point Perspective Artworks that show landscape usually show it from the eye level of an imagined viewer. Artists create a horizon line to help make the image more like scenes we are used to seeing.

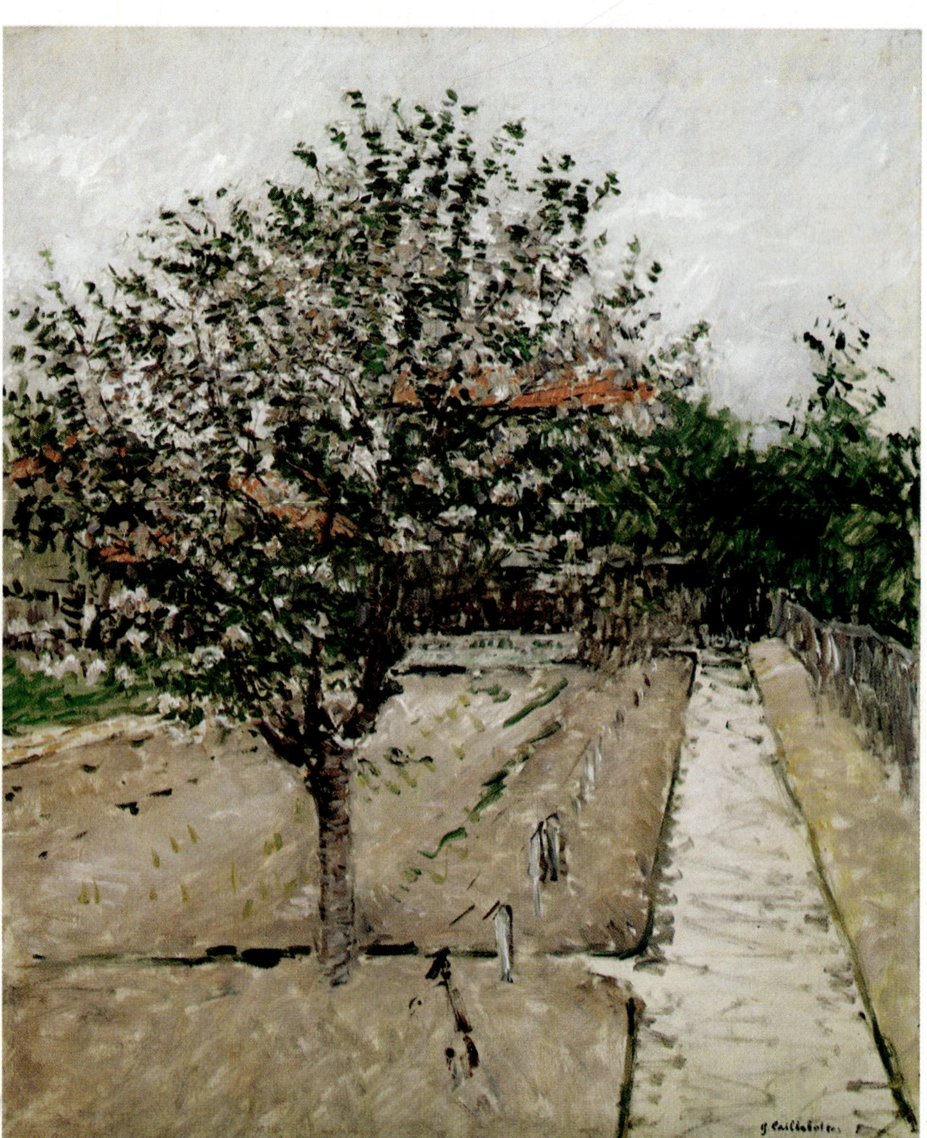

Fig. 7–9 **This artist has used linear perspective to create the illusion of three dimensions. Which images in this work form the horizon line?**

Gustave Caillebotte, *Pommier en fleurs (Apple Tree in Bloom)*, c. 1885. Oil on canvas, 28 7/8" x 23 5/8" (73.3 x 60 cm). Brooklyn Museum 1992.107.2 Bequest of William K. Jacobs, Jr.

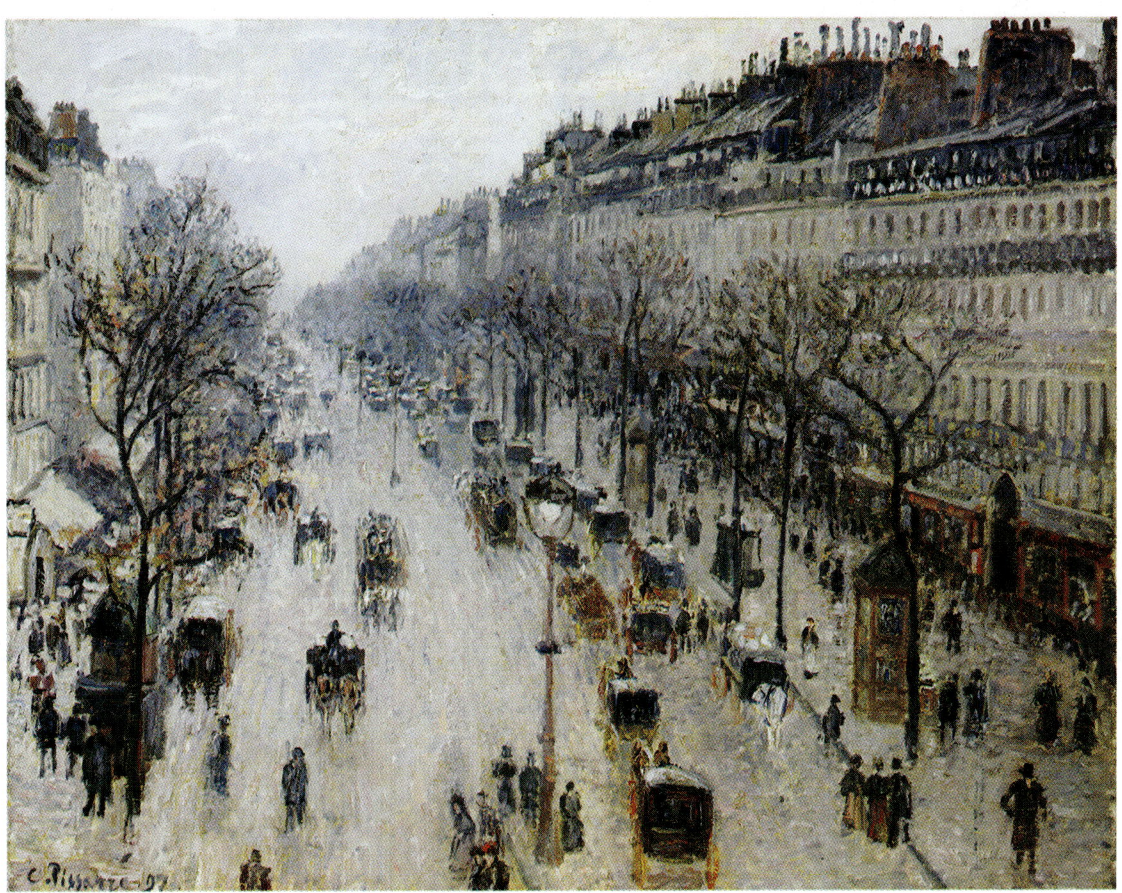

Fig. 7–10 **How is the vanishing point created in Pisarro's picture?**

Camille Pissarro, *The Boulevard Montmartre on a Winter Morning,* 1897. Oil on canvas, 25 ½" x 32" (64.8 x 81.3 cm). The Metropolitan Museum of Art, Gift of Katrin S. Vietor, in loving memory of Ernest G. Vietor, 1960 (60.174), Image ©The Metropolitan Museum of Art.

The horizon line is the area in an artwork where the earth appears to meet the sky. The vanishing point is the place where parallel lines seem to meet in the distance.

Observe Look at the one-point perspective diagram on page 188. Notice that the vanishing point is located on the horizon line.

Tools: A yardstick and fine-tipped drawing tools, such as pencils, markers, or pens.

Practice: One-Point Perspective

Refer to the one-point perspective diagram for help in setting up your drawing.

- Use a yardstick to draw a straight line lightly across a sheet of paper. This represents the horizon line.
- Add a vanishing point at or near the center of the horizon line.
- Next, draw a row of buildings, houses, or other boxlike objects that seem to recede—go back into space and get smaller—as they approach the vanishing point.
- Be sure that all vertical lines remain parallel to the side of the paper. All horizontal lines should remain parallel to the top and bottom of the paper.
- You may wish to add diagonal guides for lines that recede to the vanishing point.

Two-Point Perspective Artists use this system of linear perspective when they view an object or building from an angle or corner.

Observe Look at the two-point perspective diagram. Notice that in two-point perspective there are two vanishing points on the horizon line.

Tools: A yardstick and fine-tipped drawing tools, such as pencils, markers, or pens.

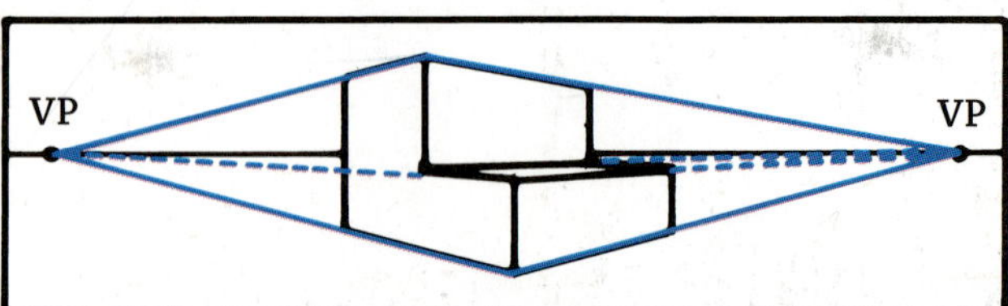

Check Your Understanding

1. How do the horizon line and the vanishing point create perspective?
2. In your own words, explain how an image created using one-point perspective looks different from an image created using two-point perspective.
3. Why is a yardstick—rather than a ruler—helpful in making a perspective drawing?

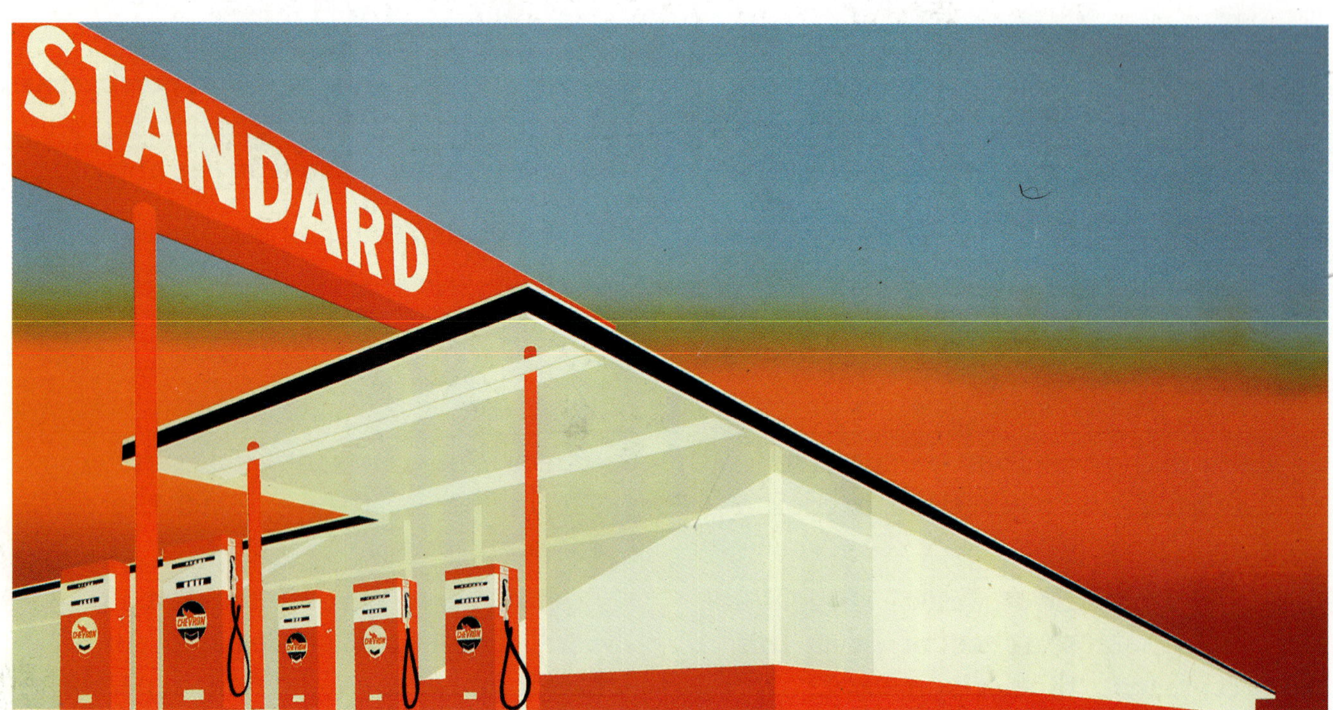

Fig. 7–11 **Ruscha used two-point perspective to create this picture. Locate the two vanishing points.**

Ed Ruscha, *Standard Station*, 1966. Screenprint, printed in color, composition: 19 5/8" x 36 15/16" (49.6 x 93.8 cm). John B. Turner Fund. (1386.1968) The Museum of Modern Art, New York, NY. Digital Image ©The Museum of Modern Art/Licensed by SCALA / Art Resource, NY.

Practice: Two-Point Perspective

Study the two-point perspective diagram for help in setting up your drawing.

- Use a yardstick to draw a horizon line lightly across a sheet of paper.
- Add two vanishing points to the horizon line. These should each be about the same distance from the left and right edges of the paper.
- If the vanishing points have to be placed off the edges of the paper, you can tape your drawing onto a larger sheet. Then extend the horizon line onto the larger sheet and locate the vanishing points.
- Next, draw a single building, house, or other boxlike object at the center of the paper.
- As in one-point perspective, lines above the horizon line slant downward, and lines below the horizon line slant upward. Your subject should be turned so that one corner is closer to the viewer.

Studio Time

The Illusion of Depth

Use a yardstick to create a perspective drawing, such as a street scene, a cityscape, or a still life that includes boxlike forms (such as milk cartons, blocks, wrapped gifts, or books).

- You also could choose to draw an imaginary collection of boxes of different sizes as though they were flying above the horizon line.
- Use one-point or two-point perspective as necessary to create the illusion of depth in your drawing.
- Include other ways of creating the illusion of three-dimensional space where needed.

Reflect on the three-dimensional illusion in your drawing.

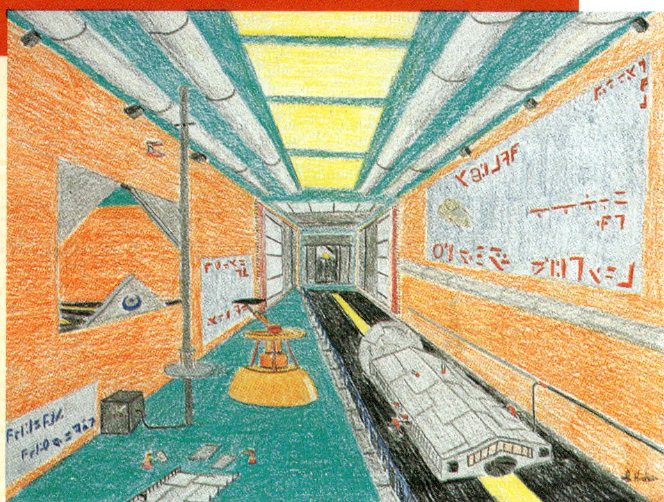

Fig. 7–12 Student artwork

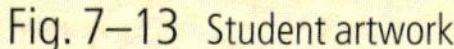

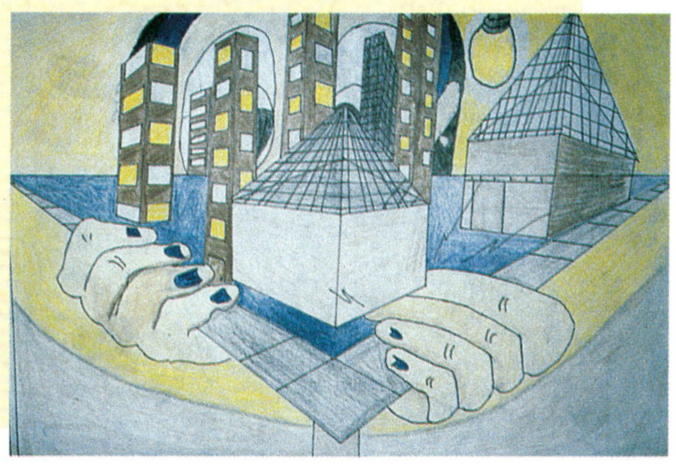

Fig. 7–13 Student artwork

7.3 Studio Exploration — Drawing

Creating a Fantasy World

Studio Background

What strange and wonderful places do you see in your daydreams or your sleep? You have seen how Remedios Varo and other artists use their imagination to create invented worlds. Now it's your turn to create a fantasy world where unexpected things occur.

In this studio exploration, you will use colored pencils to create an invented scene from a world where fantasy is combined with reality. As you make your detailed drawing, ask some "What if?" questions: What if people looked like plants? What if birds grew from seeds? Think of ways to draw and arrange lines and shapes to create rhythm and movement. Consider how you could use perspective to create the illusion of both deep and crowded spaces in your scene.

You Will Need

- drawing paper
- pencil
- eraser
- ruler or yardstick
- colored pencils or markers

Step 1 Plan and Practice

- Decide how you will create the illusion of deep space in your scene. Will you use linear perspective, placement, overlap, size, and/or color?
- Decide how you will combine methods of perspective to get the look of space you want.

Things to Remember:

✓ Combine images from the real world with images from a fantasy world.

✓ Use linear perspective and other techniques, such as overlapping and size, to create the illusion of depth.

✓ Draw and arrange lines and shapes in a manner that adds rhythm and movement to your invented world.

Inspiration from Our World

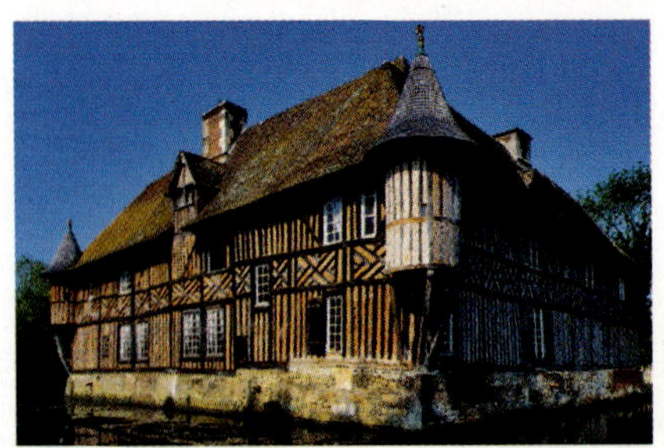

© Hemis/Corbis

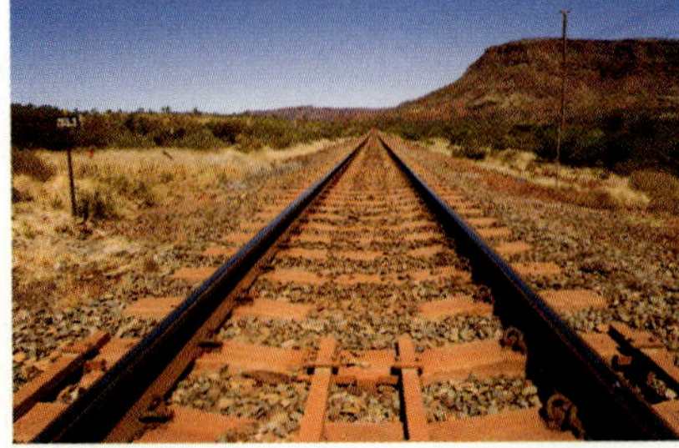

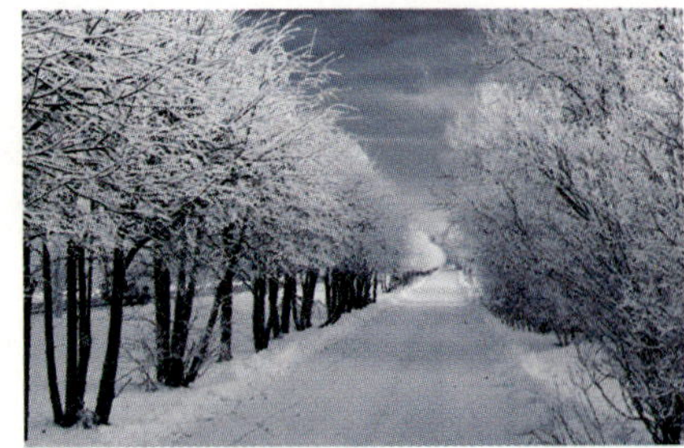

Inspiration from Art

Renaissance artists discovered that parallel lines seem to recede, or move back in space, to a vanishing point. An artist's use of lines to create depth is called linear perspective.

Artists may use techniques other than perspective to create the illusion of depth. They may place shapes high on a paper or canvas so that they appear to be far away. Artists may also overlap shapes. By doing so, the topmost shape will appear to be in front of other shapes. The drawing of similar shapes in different sizes is another way that artists create depth. The smaller shapes will seem farther away than the larger ones. Artists also use color and value to give the illusion of depth. Bright colors appear to move forward, and light shades and dull colors appear to recede.

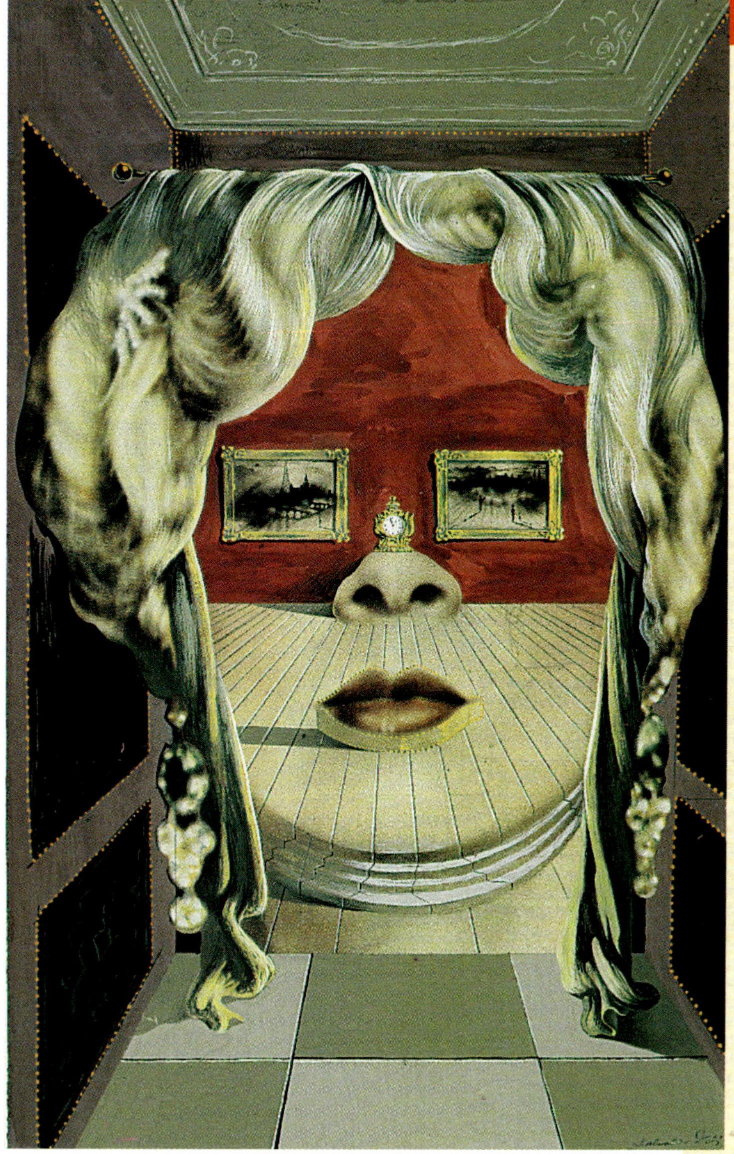

Fig. 7–14 **Salvador Dalí was a Surrealist. How did he use perspective to create the illusion of depth?**

Salvador Dalí, *Mae West*, c. 1934. Gouache, with graphite on commercially printed magazine page, 11" x 7" (28.3 x 17.8 cm). Gift of Mrs. Gilbert W. Chapman, 1949.517. Photograph ©2001, The Art Institute of Chicago, All Rights Reserved. ©2001 Kingdom of Spain, Gala-Salvador Dalí Foundation/Artists Rights Society (ARS), New York.

Step 2 Begin to Create

- If you have decided to use linear perspective, lightly draw your guides with a pencil and ruler or yardstick. **Position your vanishing point.**

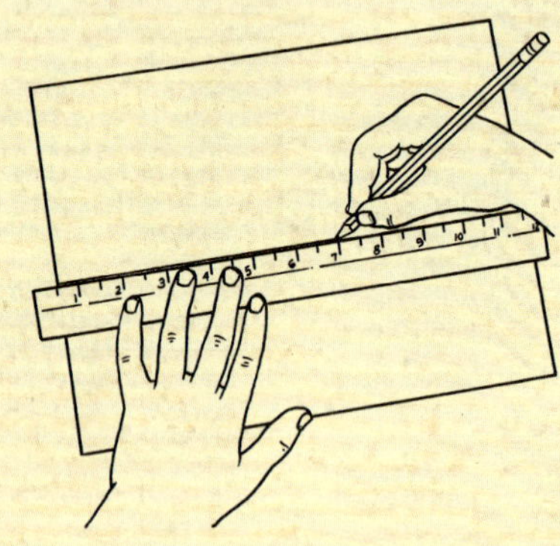

- **Sketch the main features of your scene.** What buildings, objects, and life forms will you include? Which elements will be from the real world? Which will be from a dreamlike world?

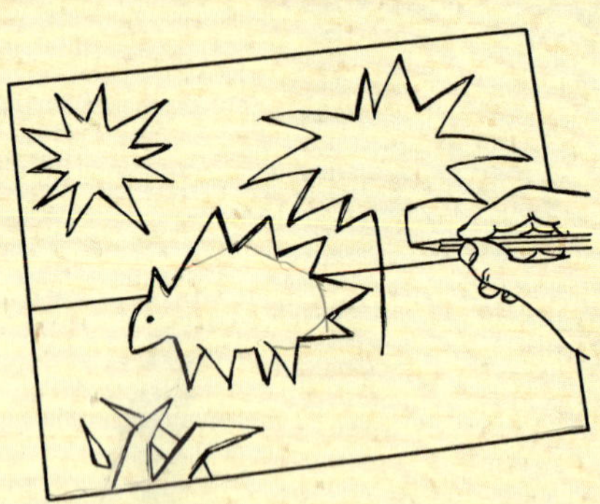

- **Think of ways to draw and arrange lines and shapes to create rhythm and movement.** Will your shapes swirl or float in rhythmic patterns? Will they collide and create jerky or jagged patterns?

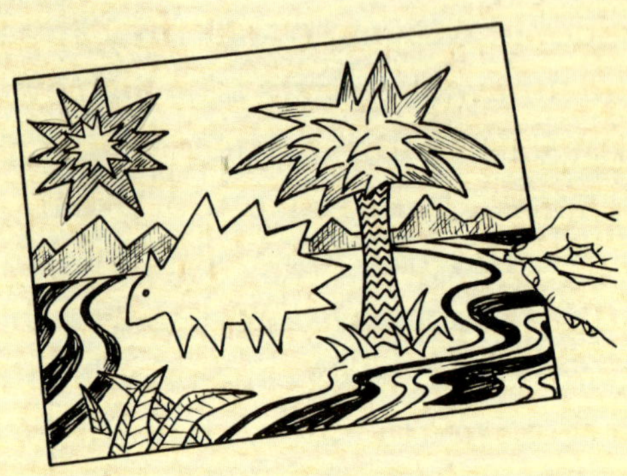

Step 3 Revise

Did you remember to:

✓ Combine images from the real world with images from a fantasy world?

✓ Use linear perspective and other techniques such as overlapping and size, to create the illusion of depth?

✓ Draw and arrange lines and shapes in a manner that adds rhythm and movement to your invented world?

Adjust your work if necessary. In your sketchbook, make a note of your revisions and why you made them.

Step 4 **Add Finishing Touches**

- Fill in color and add details with colored pencil. Remember that shapes in the distance have less detail than those close up. How could you use value, or light and dark colors, to add to the illusion of depth?

Step 5 **Share and Reflect**

- Pair up with a classmate to talk about your completed drawings.
- Which "What if?" question did each of you explore?
- What parts of your drawing show things from the real world? What parts are from a fantasy world?
- How did you create the illusion of space?
- Where did you create rhythm and movement?

Art Criticism

Describe What does the artist show in this artwork?

Analyze How did the artist show space and illusion of depth in this drawing?

Interpret What do you think this drawing is about?

Evaluate What makes this a successful drawing?

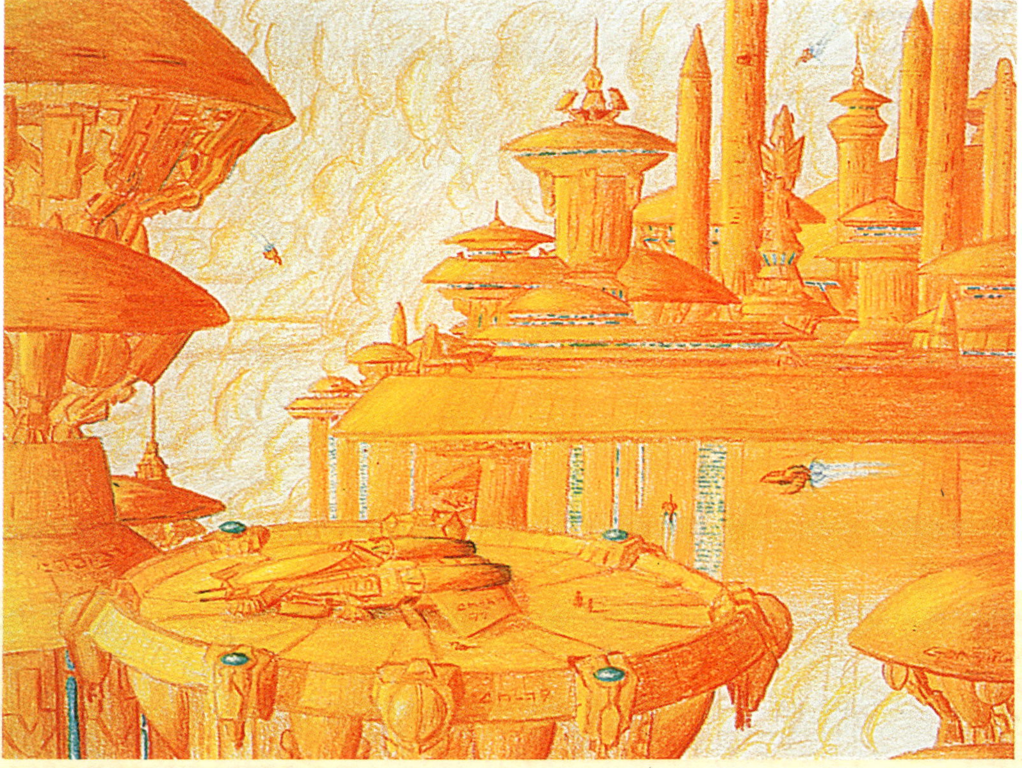

Fig. 7–15
Student artwork

Fantasy in Art

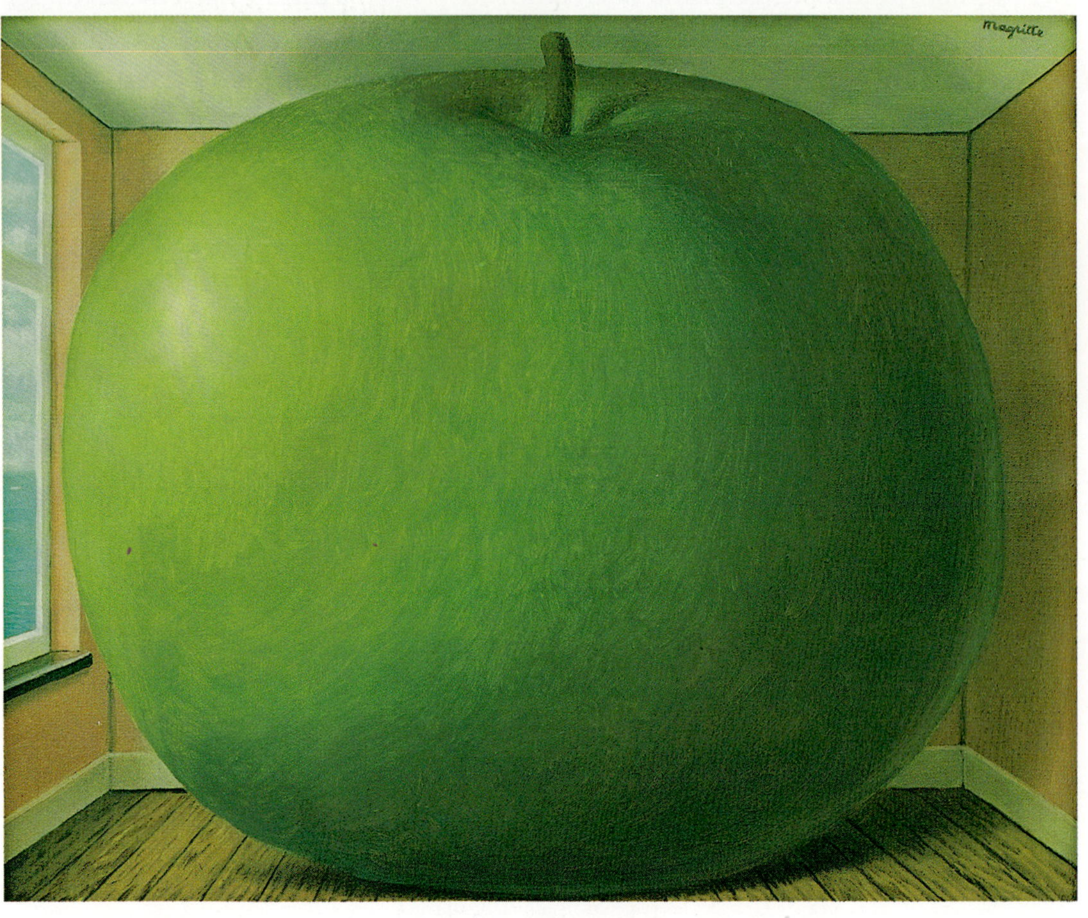

Fig. 7–16 **By changing the usual scale of the object in relation to its setting, the artist invented a dreamlike space. Do you get the feeling that something is about to happen?**

René Magritte, *The Listening Room*, c. 1958. Oil on canvas 15" x 18" (38 x 46 cm). Kunsthaus, Zurich, donated by Walter Haefner. Photo AKG London. ©2001 C. Herscovici, Brussels/ Artists Rights Society (ARS), New York.

The invention of stories and special creatures has always been important to people. These inventions often help people to "explain the unexplained." Throughout history, artists have depicted fantasy scenes in different ways. In the Middle Ages, for instance, European artists carved grotesque creatures in stone and painted pictures of dragons, even though these creatures did not exist. In the 1900s, artists made things seem unreal by putting real things in invented, dreamlike settings.

More Real than Life Surrealist artworks are based on the idea that dreams and fantasies often seem "more real" than real life. Surrealist artists in the first half of the 1900s were interested in shocking their viewers. The Surrealists would mix up everyday objects with dreamlike settings. Some artists carefully arranged their odd combinations. Others allowed chance or coincidence to create surprises.

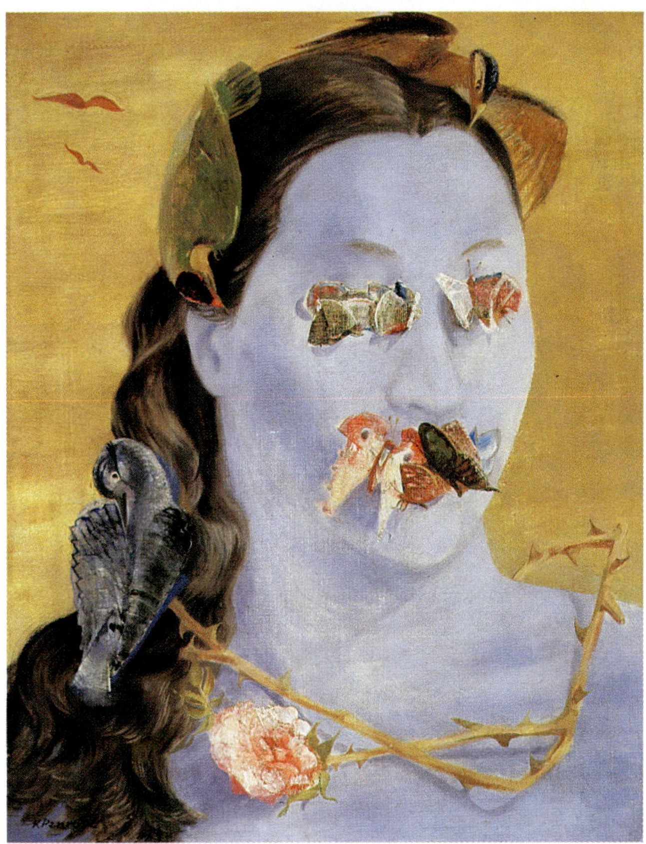

Fig. 7–17 **The title of this portrait is *Winged Domino.* A domino is a type of mask. Do you see a mask in this work?**

Roland Penrose, *Winged Domino—A Portrait of Valentine*, 1938. Oil on canvas. ©Estate of the artist.

Visual Tricks The paintings of René Magritte are like dreams. In such artworks as *The Listening Room*, he made familiar objects seem strange. The objects look real, but what the viewer sees could not possibly be. To play his visual tricks on viewers, Magritte placed objects in invented places or showed objects in unreal sizes.

Surrealist Roland Penrose also seemed to play tricks on viewers. In a portrait of his wife, *Winged Domino,* he showed her covered with butterflies and birds. He covered normally recognizable features—eyes and lips—with winged creatures.

1900s

1934
Dalí,
Mae West

1938
Penrose,
Winged Domino

1945
The first atomic bomb test occurs in New Mexico.

1958
Magritte,
Listening Room

1961
Yuri Gagarin, a Russian astronaut, performs the first single-orbit space flight.

1968
Ralph Baer invents the first video game console, called the "Brown Box."

1970
Lanyon,
Chemistry Versus Magic

1975
Lanyon,
The Disguise

1989
The World Wide Web is created by Tim Berners-Lee, a British scientist.

7.4 Continued

Fantasy Inventions Ellen Lanyon is an artist who is always on the lookout for postcards and souvenirs. She often copies parts of postcard scenes and puts them into her own paintings. She also draws from a huge collection of found objects, carefully observing their details.

Lanyon's drawings and paintings are realistic, but she often puts images of animals, plants, and found objects together to form fantasy settings. Many of her artworks show human-made objects in settings with animals or plants. In such paintings as *Dragons and Dominoes* and *Chemistry Versus Magic*, Lanyon seems to want us to think about our relationship to the natural world.

Lanyon also likes to show transformations in her artworks. By transforming, or changing, things, she creates an illusion—things look real, yet they are not real.

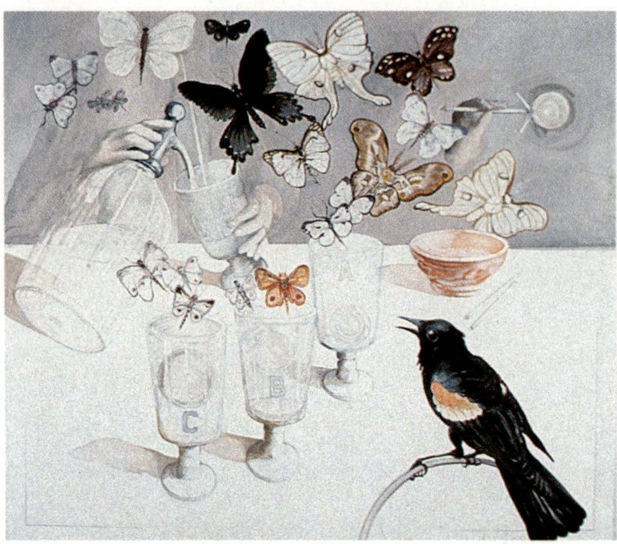

Fig. 7–19 **Compare this work to *Creation of the Birds* (Fig. 7–2) by Remedios Varo. How are the two works alike? How are they different?**

Ellen Lanyon, *Chemistry Versus Magic*, 1970. Acrylic on canvas, 60" x 60" (152 x 152 cm). The Letitia and Richard Kruger Collection. Courtesy of the artist.

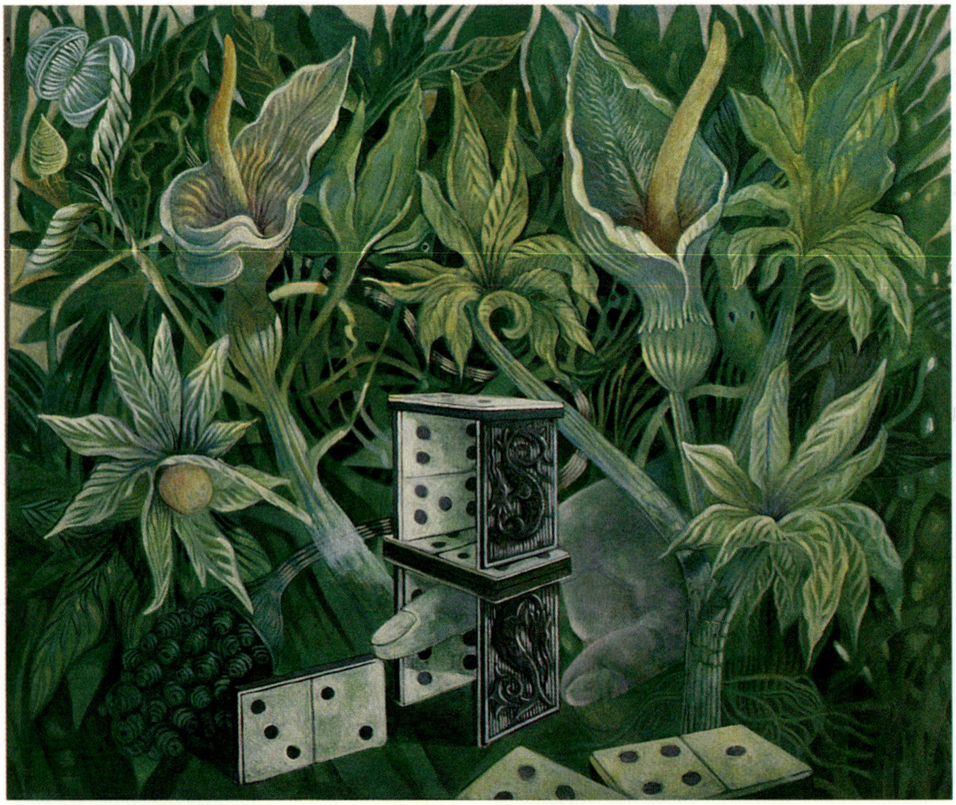

Fig. 7–18 **What did the artist do to make the space seem crowded?**

Ellen Lanyon, *Dragons and Dominoes*, 1999. Acrylic on canvas, 45" x 52" (114 x 132 cm). Courtesy of the artist and Jean Albano Gallery, Chicago, Illinois.

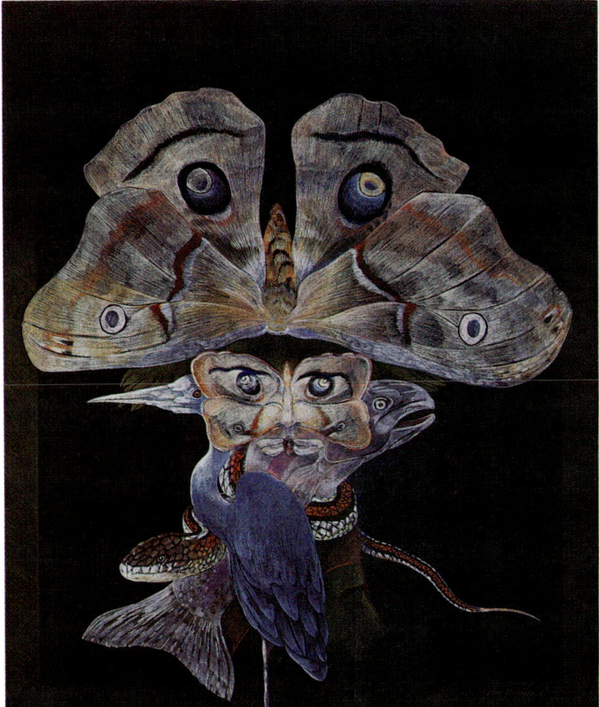

Fig. 7–20 **How would the effect of this picture be different had the artist not overlapped the shapes, but had left more open space between them?**

Ellen Lanyon, *The Disguise*, 1975. Private Collection. Courtesy of the artist.

Studio Time

Fantasy Collage

Use collage materials to invent a fantasy environment filled with ordinary objects.

- Cut materials that are different sizes, shapes, textures, and colors.
- Give your collage meaning by combining things that might not always seem to belong together.

Reflect on how playful you were in arranging your objects.

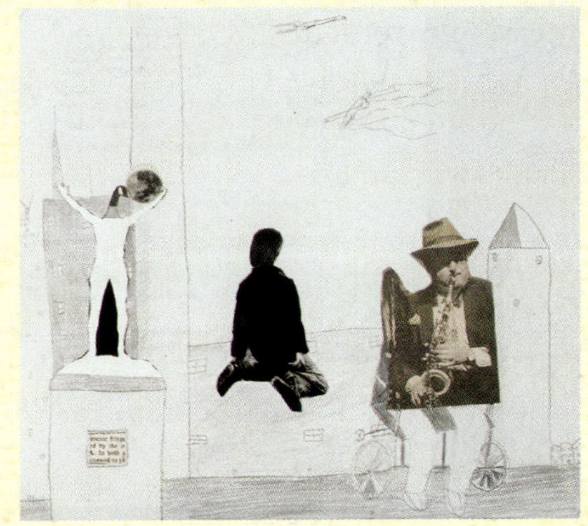

Fig. 7–21 Student artwork

Meet Ellen Lanyon

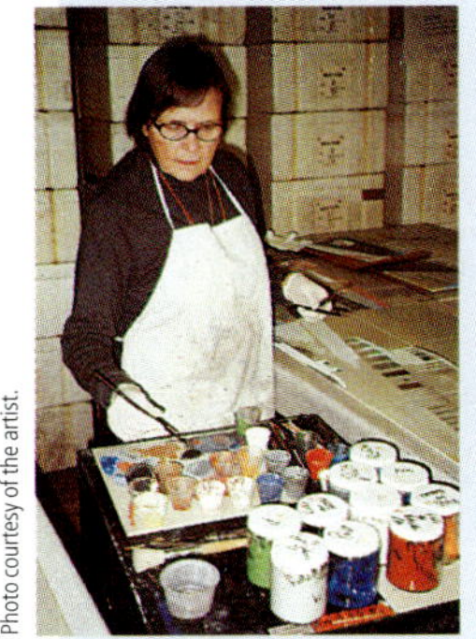

Photo courtesy of the artist.

When she was eight, Ellen Lanyon went to the 1934 Chicago World's Fair, where she played in a miniature village that her grandfather had built. She remembers the village as a storybook setting—very real, yet very magical. Her memories of that childhood experience influence her work today.

Lanyon taught herself to draw by working from photographs. As a teen, she worked part time in a company's drafting department, enlarging designs for machine parts. These early experiences helped her to be inventive.

"I wanted to make magic on a two-dimensional surface."

— Ellen Lanyon (born 1926)

Check Your Understanding

1. Describe three ways artists can act like inventors through their artwork.
2. Compare and contrast the realistic and unrealistic qualities of Ellen Lanyon's depictions.
3. What are some things you could do as an artist to create a fantasy environment?

Puerto Rican Fantasy

Fantasy in Art Since the 1600s, Puerto Ricans have used colorful masks and costumes in their celebrations. Both help create a feeling of an unreal, dreamlike world. In the town of Ponce, the masks typically have long, pointed teeth and tall horns **(Fig. 7–22)**. The masks made in Loiza, however, usually have square mouths, triangular noses, and round eyes. Masks from both areas are colorful and have repeated elements that create visual rhythm and movement.

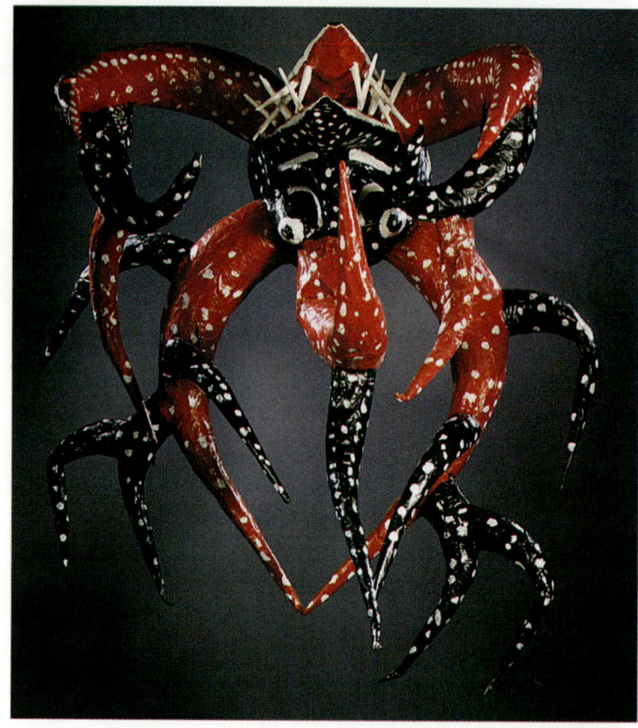

Fig. 7–22 **This mask is made from the traditional material of papier-mâché. It is decorated with the bright colors and patterns that are typical of masks from the town of Ponce.**

Puerto Rico, *Ponce Mask*, 21st century. Courtesy the Smithsonian Institution, National Museum of American History, Teodoro Vidal Collection.

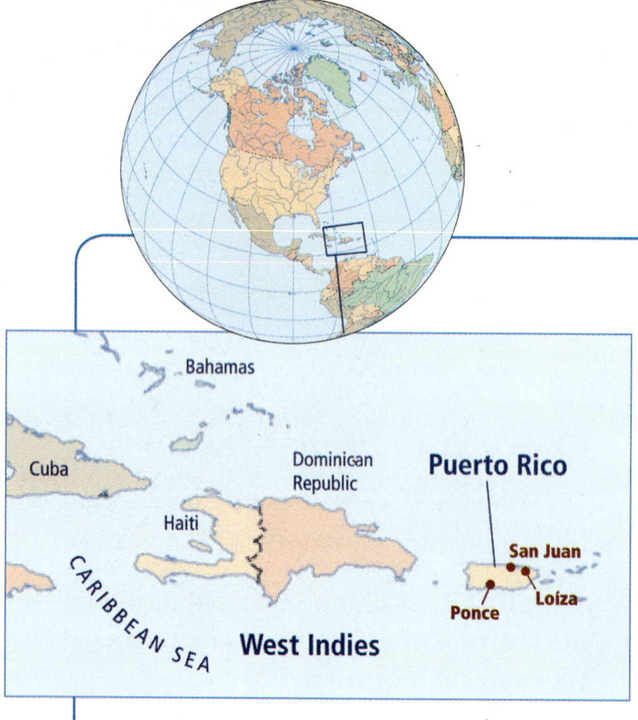

Social Studies Connection

Puerto Rico—a beautiful, fertile island about a thousand miles southeast of Florida—has a diverse history. Its first inhabitants were the South American Arawak Indians. In the 1500s, Spanish colonists established large plantations. They brought Africans to the island to work in the fields and gold mines. In 1898, Puerto Rico became a commonwealth of the United States. Because of their rich heritage, Puerto Ricans celebrate many holidays and festive occasions.

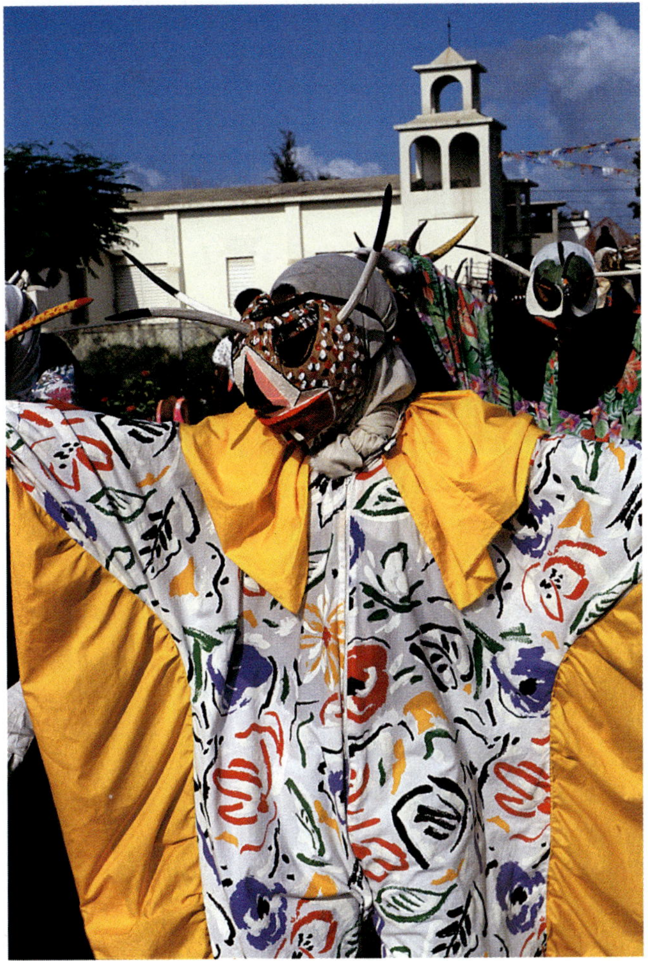

Fig. 7–23 **Why do people wear costumes during celebrations?**

Puerto Rico, *Vejigante Celebrant in Loíza-style Costume and Mask*, 21st century. Photo ©2001 Mark Bacon.

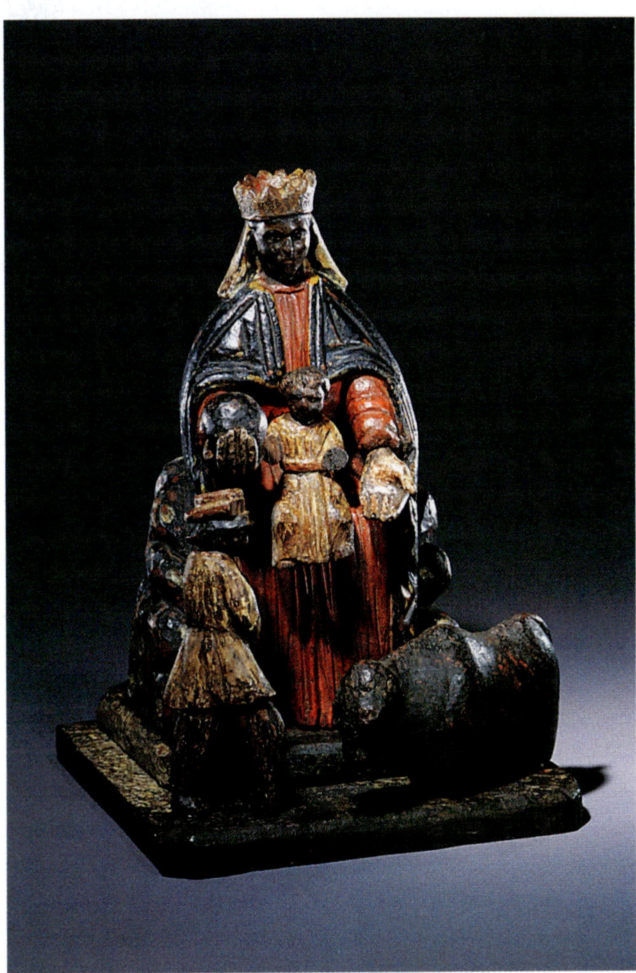

Fig. 7–24 **Carved wooden images such as this are often placed in boxes called niches.**

Puerto Rico, *Santos Figure: Virgen de Hormigueros*, c. 19th century. Carved wood. Smithsonian Institution, National Museum of American History, Teodoro Vidal Collection.

Creative Traditions In addition to these artistic expressions, many artists produce spiritual artworks. Since the 1500s, artists have carved religious figures called santos (Fig. 7–24). Because they do not usually have pictures of the saints from long ago, the *santeros*, or artists who make santos, have invented ways to represent them. They often use symbols to stand for saints and other holy figures from the Catholic religion.

Visual Culture

Masks have many different functions in many different cultures. Look through books, magazines, newspapers, and search the Internet for examples of masks from around the world and that serve different purposes. Find examples of masks that are used for protection in the workplace. What sports use masks for protection? In what kinds of situations might people wear masks for disguise? For entertainment?

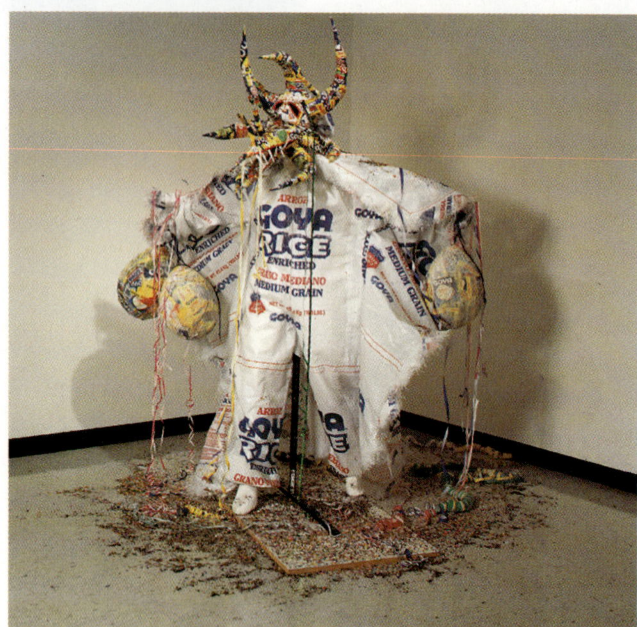

Fig. 7–25 **This sculpture is part of a larger installation. The installation included masks and carnival costumes, as well as drawings and paintings on the theme of carnival.**

Lillian Méndez, *Vejigante Made from Goya Rice Bags*, 1999–2000. Mixed media, 84" x 48" x 24" (213 x 122 x 61 cm). Courtesy of the artist.

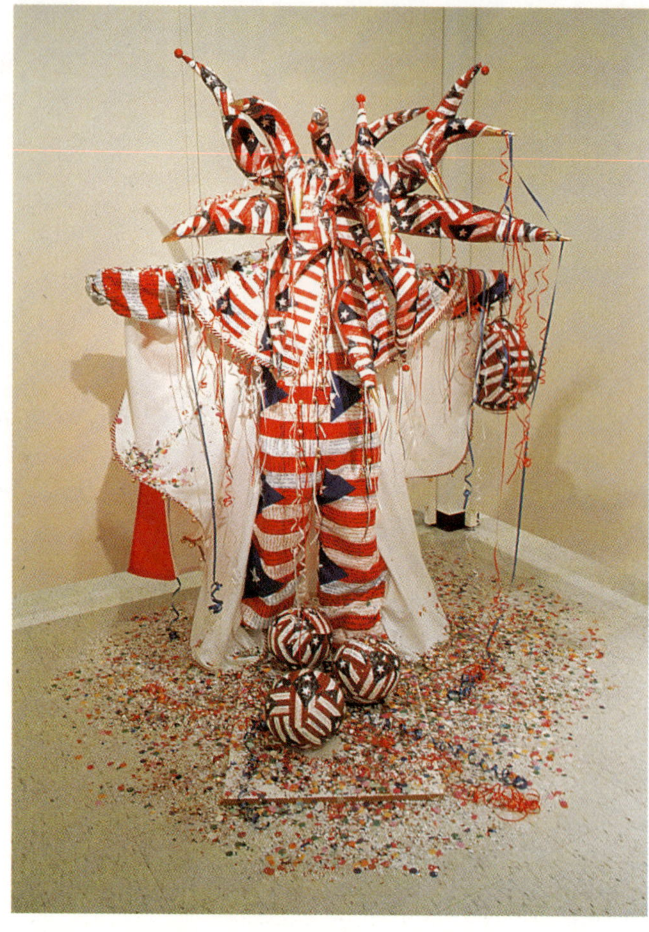

Fig. 7–26 **A *vejigante* is a traditional clown-like character seen often in Puerto Rican festivals. How is this sculpture like a clown?**

Lillian Méndez, *Vejigante Made from Puerto Rican Flags*, 1999–2000. Mixed media, 84" x 48" x 24" (213 x 122 x 61 cm). Courtesy of the artist.

Today, many artists in Puerto Rico continue to use folk-art traditions as inspiration for their artworks. Such artists as Lillian Méndez often balance these traditions with present-day cultural influences.

Méndez sees herself as three different artists: she is a maker of objects, an inventor, and a storyteller. The biographical stories of her art describe her personal journey as a Latina raised in Puerto Rico and now living in the United States. Her childhood experiences add colorful and inventive qualities to the objects she makes. She uses the folk-art tradition of papier-mâché to give her artworks their complicated forms.

Check Your Understanding

1. What are santos, and what role do they play in the lives of the Puerto Rican people?

2. Compare and contrast the costumes shown in this lesson. How are they similar? How are they different?

3. In what way is Lillian Méndez both a storyteller and an inventor?

Meet Lillian Méndez

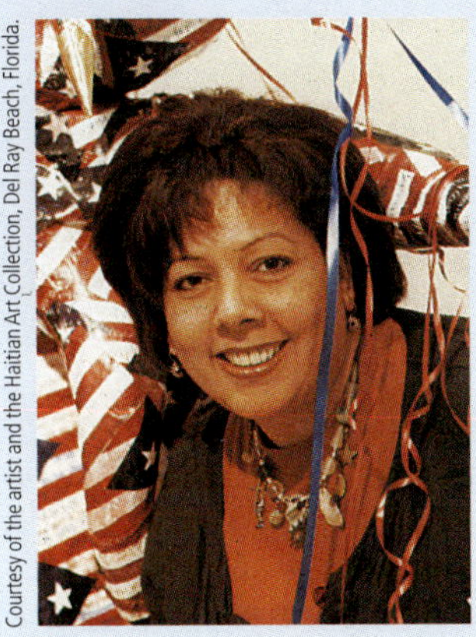
Courtesy of the artist and the Haitian Art Collection, Del Ray Beach, Florida.

In her childhood, Méndez lived by the ocean in southeastern Puerto Rico. She was an inventor at an early age, catching crabs with traps that she designed. As an adult artist, Méndez is still inventing. She makes inventive use of materials, such as the decoration of her costumed figures with Puerto Rican flags. Through her art, Lillian Méndez shares her Puerto Rican heritage with others, developing awareness of the Hispanic/Latino art and culture.

"It's important to educate yourself about your culture. The path that your ancestors have traveled is fertile ground for your own imagination to develop and prosper."

— Lillian Méndez (born 1957)

Studio Time

Cut-Paper Mask

You can create a two dimensional design for a colorful mask.

- Make a detailed paper mask that is decorative and festive.
- Use construction paper, and explore a variety of paper cutting techniques.
- Choose colors that are bright and show contrast.
- Be inventive in creating facial features with cut-paper shapes.
- Use glue to assemble the parts of your mask.

Reflect on the festive and fantasy qualities of your mask.

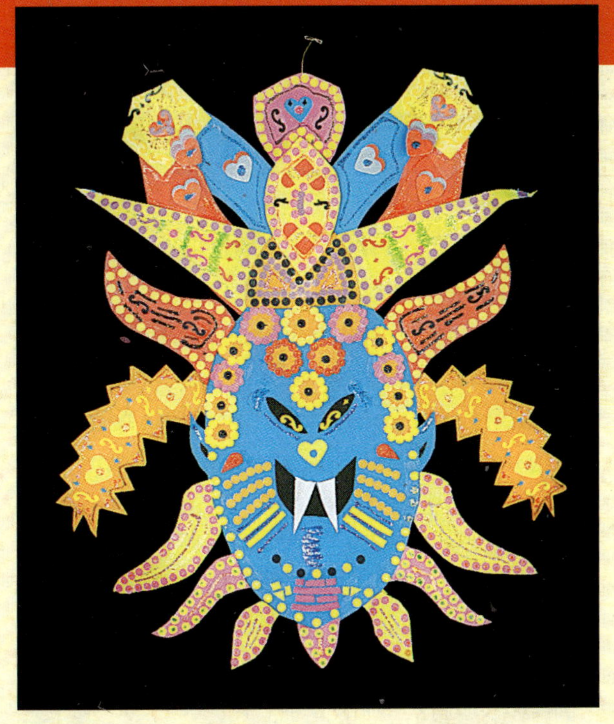

Fig. 7–27 Student artwork

Creating a Fantasy Disguise

Studio Background

In Western culture, people wear masks for fun at Halloween or for other festive occasions such as Mardi Gras. However, in many cultures, masks are an important form of art. They are not just a disguise nor are they always just for fun. Instead, they are used in rituals and ceremonies. In some cultures, artists create masks for traditional plays, dances, and festivals. The masks often portray characters in myths and legends.

In this studio exploration, you will create a fantasy mask that can be used as a disguise or be displayed as a decorative sculpture. As you sketch ideas for your mask, consider the many different ways you can bend and fold a flat, flexible material to create three-dimensional forms. Think about how you want your mask to function. Is it to be worn over the head, or will it hang on a wall? Also think about the mood or feeling you want your mask to convey. Do you want it to scare people or to amuse them?

You Will Need

- brown paper for sketching and practicing (use grocery bags)
- pencil
- scissors
- thick foam rubber (from upholstery shops)
- clear glue
- stapler and staples
- binder clips
- acrylic paint
- markers

Step 1 Plan and Practice

- Work with your classmates in groups. Experiment with different ways to cut and fold brown grocery bag paper to create forms.
- Share ideas and demonstrate discoveries with classmates.
- Discuss ways parts can be combined to create a fantasy mask.
- Think about how the brown grocery bag paper can be used as a pattern for cutting pieces of foam rubber.

Inspiration from Our World

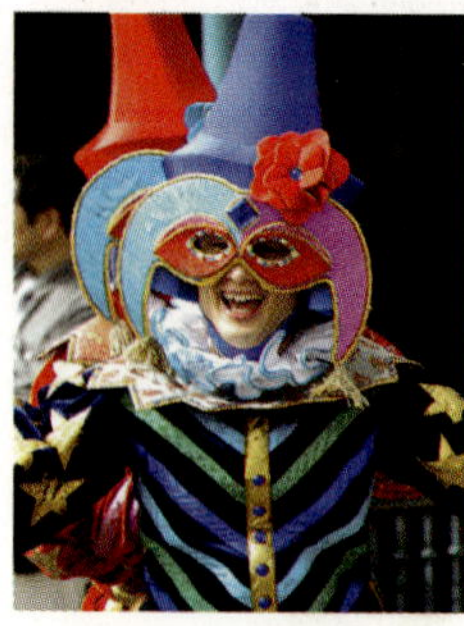

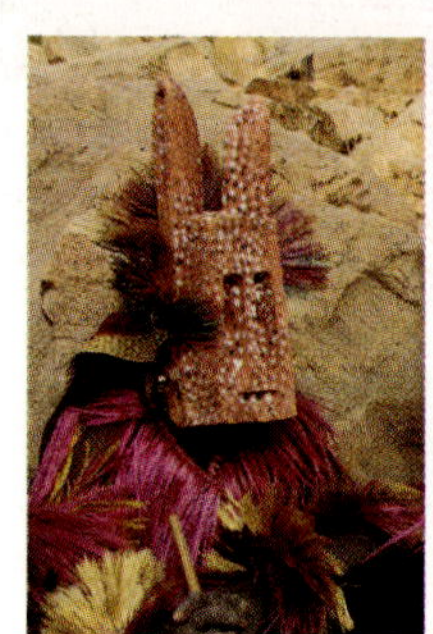

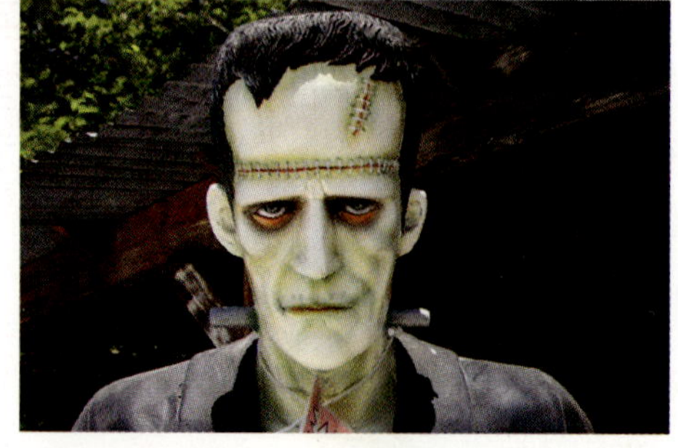

Things to Remember:

- ✓ Create a fantasy creature.
- ✓ Include some features that are decorative and some that function for disguise.
- ✓ Repeat shapes or forms for balance and rhythm.

Inspiration from Art

George Wolfe is a teacher, writer, and artist who is known for finding innovative ways to teach sculpture in his classroom. Wolfe believes that art class is not only a place to make things, but a workshop for challenging ideas where imagination and experimentation are more important than knowledge.

Wolfe often uses materials that can be easily found and manipulated, such as urethane foam. The foam is not as durable as papier-mâché, but it is easier to control. To create imaginative masks, Wolfe manipulates the foam into shapes, and adds and subtracts parts until his mask is complete.

Wolfe once said, "[Creature] masks can be as wild as your imagination."

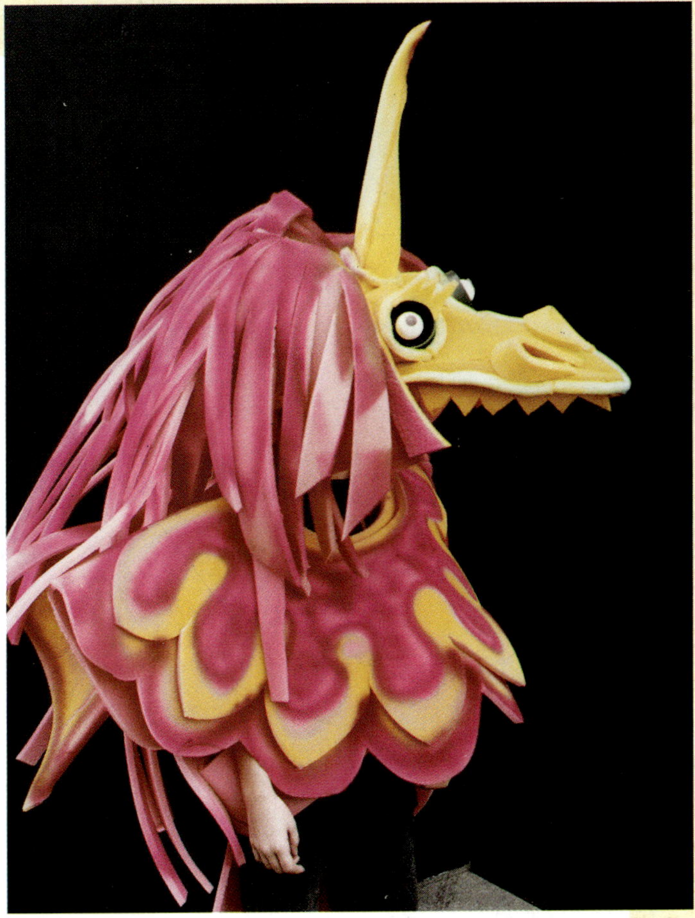

Fig 7–28 **What mood or feeling does this mask convey? What parts of the mask convey this feeling or mood?**

George Wolfe, *The Mask*. From *3-D Wizardry*, ©1995 Davis Publications, Inc. Courtesy of Davis Publications, Inc.

Step 2 Begin to Create

- **Make a paper pattern for your basic mask form.**

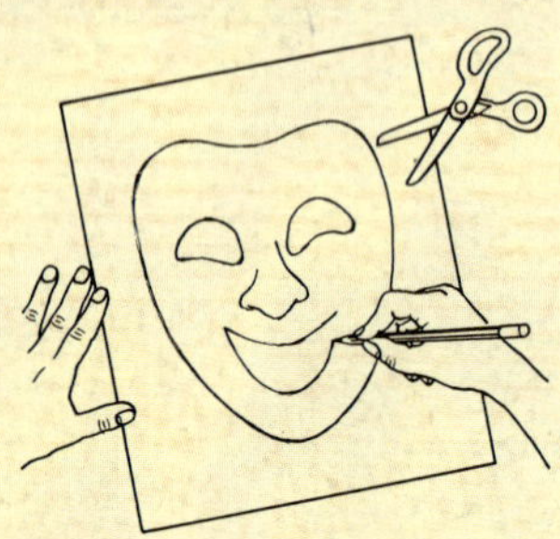

- **Trace around the pattern on your sheet of foam rubber.**

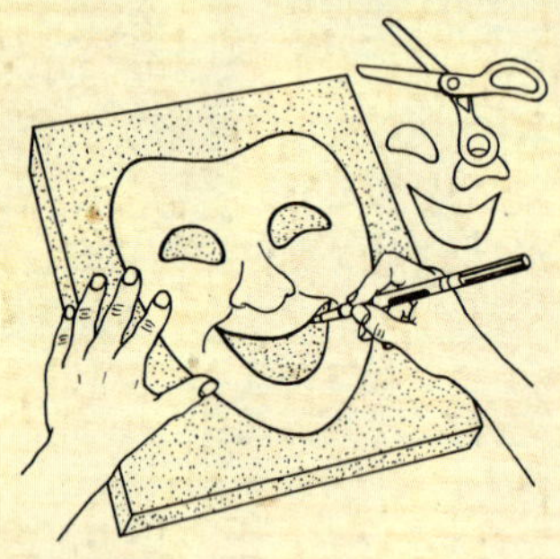

- Use large scissors to cut the foam rubber into the basic shape.
- Cut other parts you will need.
- Make slits so you can twist or bend the foam to create a three-dimensional form.
- Begin to staple or glue the parts of your mask.

Step 3 Revise

Did you remember to:

✓ Create a fantasy creature?

✓ Include parts for the decorative and disguise functions of masks?

✓ Repeat shapes or forms for balance and rhythm?

Adjust your work if necessary. In your sketchbook, make a note of your revisions and why you made them.

Step 4 Add Finishing Touches

- **Add details and color with acrylic paints and markers.**

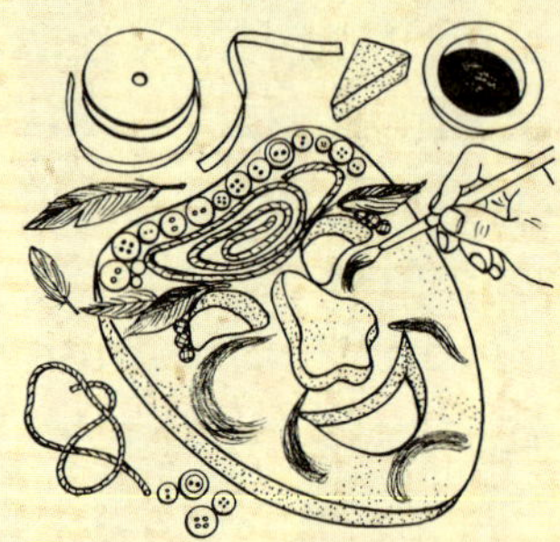

- Do you want to add other objects or sew on buttons, feathers, or ribbons of cloth?
- Have you thought about using repeated elements in your mask?

Step 5 **Share and Reflect**

- Pair up with a classmate to talk about your masks.
- What construction techniques did each of you explore?
- What parts of your masks are fanciful? What parts are based on reality? What parts are for decorative purposes only?
- Where did you repeat shapes or forms?

Art Criticism

Describe What kind of mask did this artist create?

Analyze How did the artist use the materials and arrange the parts to suggest fantasy?

Interpret What do you think about when you look at this mask?

Evaluate What did the artist do especially well?

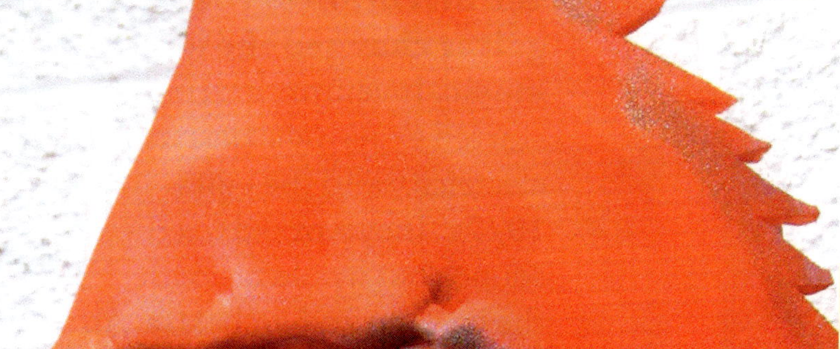

Fig. 7–29 Student artwork

Mathematics

Artists use geometric concepts to create the appearance of depth or distance on a flat surface. Linear perspective is a technique that uses parallel lines to create the appearance of three-dimensional space. Imagine train tracks going away from you, toward a point in the distance. The parallel tracks appear to get closer together as they get farther away from you. This creates a sense of distance. What other connections do you see between math and art?

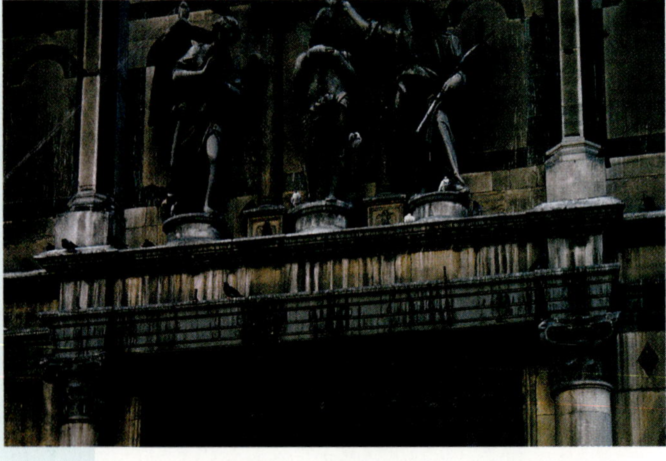

Fig. 7–30 **In the early 1400s, Renaissance artists invented a system of drawing called linear perspective. How does this bronze relief show linear perspective?**

Lorenzo Ghiberti, *Gates of Paradise* (detail), 1425–52. Gilt bronze, approx. 31 ½" x 31 ½" (80 x 80 cm). Courtesy of Davis Art Images.

Music

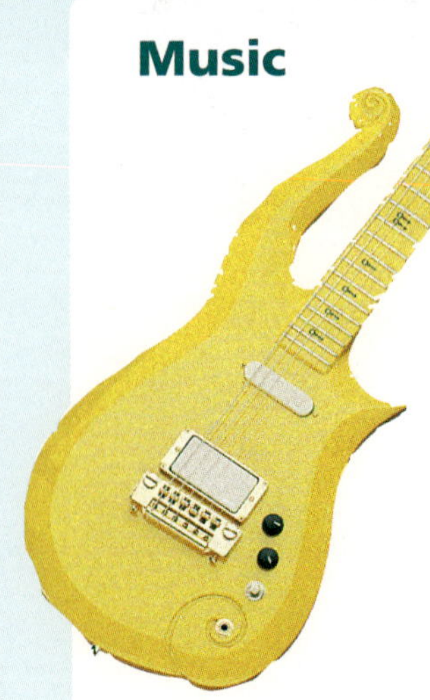

Fig. 7–31 **Musicians have used the electric guitar in new and inventive ways. They have created fresh sounds in jazz, rock, and other forms of contemporary music.**

United States, *Electric Guitar (Flying V model)*. 1967. Mahogany, rosewood, plastic. Manufactured by Gibson, Inc. Smithsonian Institution, National Museum of American History, Division of Cultural History.

The invention of the electric guitar changed the world of music. Inventors and musicians started experimenting with electricity and the guitar in the 1920s. They worked to create a sound that would be louder than the background orchestra. An electric guitar has magnetic devices called "pick-ups." Pick-ups turn the vibrations of the strings into electric signals. These signals then pass through a device called an amplifier. This device increases the sounds of the strings. Which musicians that you listen to today experiment with new sounds?

Careers **Jewelry Maker**

Jewelry has always been an important part of many cultures. Jewelry has been worn for decoration or to indicate wealth. Making and designing jewelry requires great skill and imagination. These artists learn their craft by attending trade schools or through apprenticeships with other jewelry makers and designers. Others may earn a fine-arts degree or teach themselves. Why might jewelry makers and designers be considered inventors?

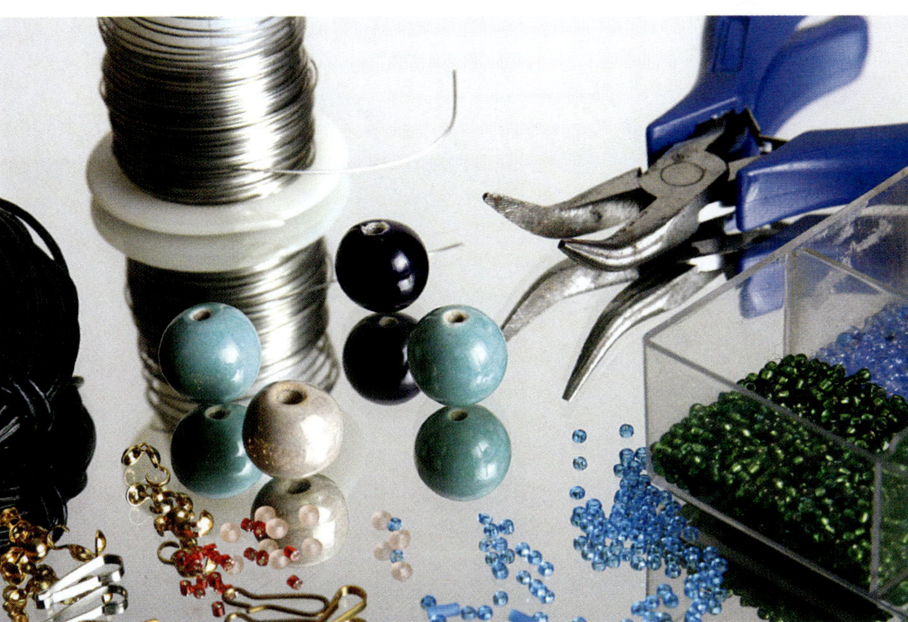

Fig. 7–32

Daily Life

Society benefits from inventions in technology. In your life, you have seen technological advances in devices such as cell phones and the Internet. A person who was born in 1870 may have lived long enough to witness the invention of electric lighting, the automobile, and the airplane. Can you imagine life without any of those things? What other kinds of technological advances do you think you may see in your lifetime?

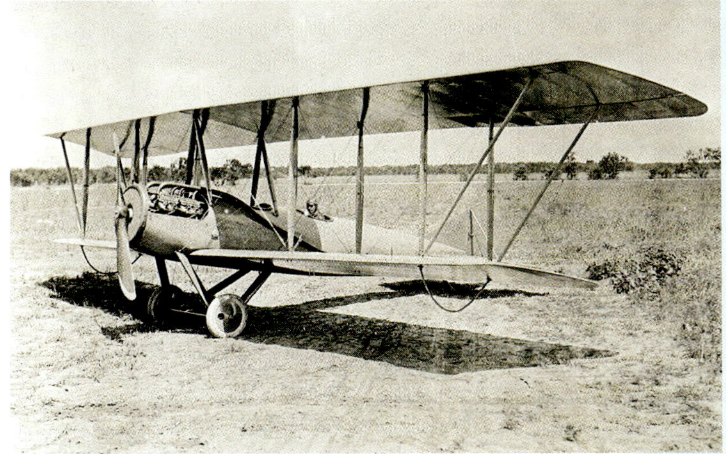

Fig. 7–33

Unit 7 Vocabulary and Content Review

Vocabulary Review

Match each art term below with its definition.

perspective
santos
vanishing point
horizon line

1. the place where parallel lines seem to meet in the distance
2. a technique for creating the illusion of depth on a two-dimensional surface
3. carved figures that represent saints and other holy figures in the Catholic religion
4. represents the eye level of a viewer and is located where the earth appears to meet the sky

Aesthetic Thinking

What do the phrases, "The sky is the limit" and "Think outside the box" mean to you? Artists often invent by making connections or combinations where there formerly were not any. Are there limits for artists? If so, what are they? If not, should there be limits?

Write About Art

Imagine that you are a video game designer asked to transform this painting into an interactive game. Describe how to play the game, earn points, and win. What other creatures might appear?

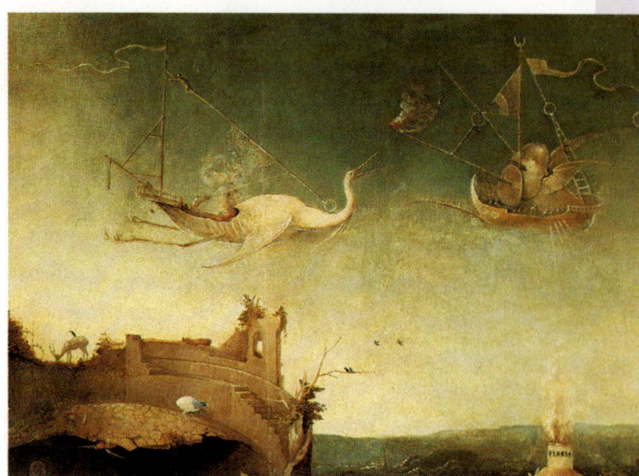

Fig. 7–34 **Look closely at ths image, a detail of a much larger painting. Note how the artist invented travel machines that could exist only in dreams or nightmares. How are these fantasy vehicles like those invented by Remedios Varo?**

Hieronymus Bosch, *The Temptation of St. Anthony* (detail), ca. 1500. Oil on panel, central panel: 51 ¾" × 47" (131.5 × 119 cm). Museu Nacional de Arte Antiga, Lisbon, Portugal. Nicolas Sapieha/Art Resource, New York.

Art Criticism

Describe What do you see in this mixed-media artwork?

Analyze How does the artist use color in this work?

Interpret Do you see any recognizable images or is everything imaginary?

Evaluate The artist believes that pink has "contradictory meanings," noting that it has associations with skin, muscle, and innocence. What meaning do you think the color pink has here?

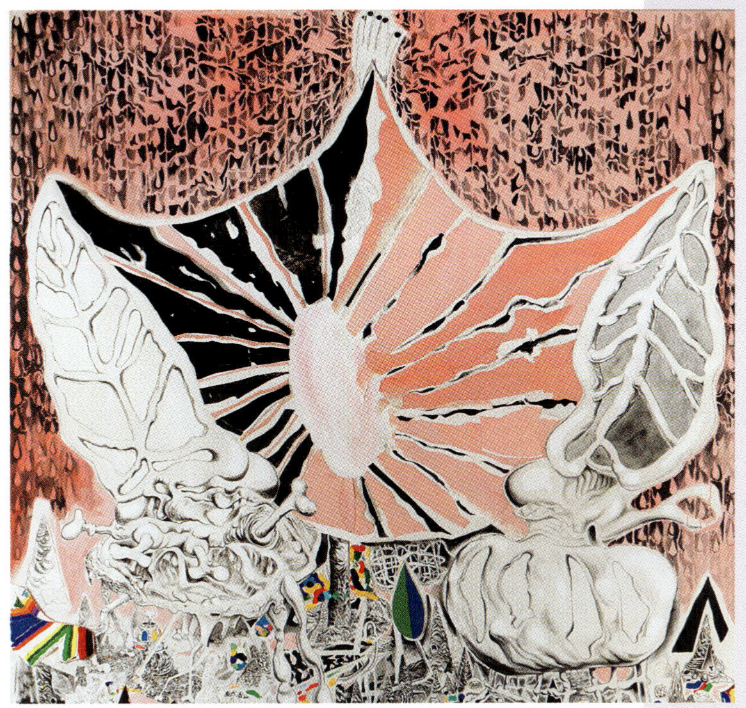

Fig. 7–35 Trenton Doyle Hancock, *Miracle Machine #20 or The Hand of Glory*, 2006, 60" x 60" (152 x 152 cm). Courtesy of the artist , the Museum of Modern and Contemporary Art of Trento and Rovereto, and Dunn and Brown Contemporary.

Meet the Artist

Trenton Doyle Hancock was born in Oklahoma and now lives in Texas. His work tells the story of the "Mounds," imaginary half-animal, half-plant characters. The "Mounds" series includes paintings, drawings, prints, and collages.

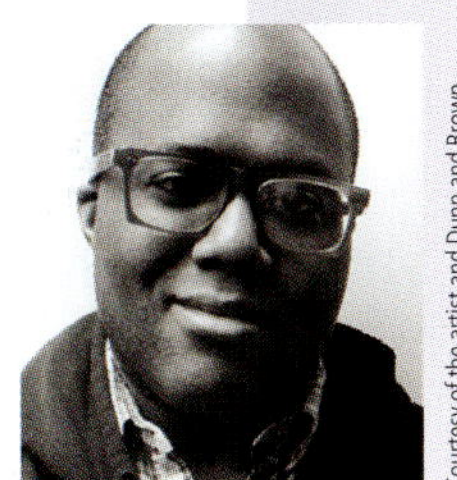

Courtesy of the artist and Dunn and Brown Contemporary.

"I see each character as a separate part of me...And it's kind of like all of these things are inside me at once, battling each other."

— Trenton Doyle Hancock (born 1974)

Trenton Doyle Hancock is one of many contemporary artists featured on the excellent companion website to the Public Television series Art: 21. Visit **www.pbs.org/art21**.

For Your Sketchbook

Use a page of your sketchbook to transform one object into another in a sequence of six sketches. For example, you might change a flower into a butterfly.

For Your Portfolio

Look through this unit and select one artwork that especially appeals to you. How would you describe it? Explain how this artwork suggests a world of fantasy.

Unit 8

Artists Are Planners

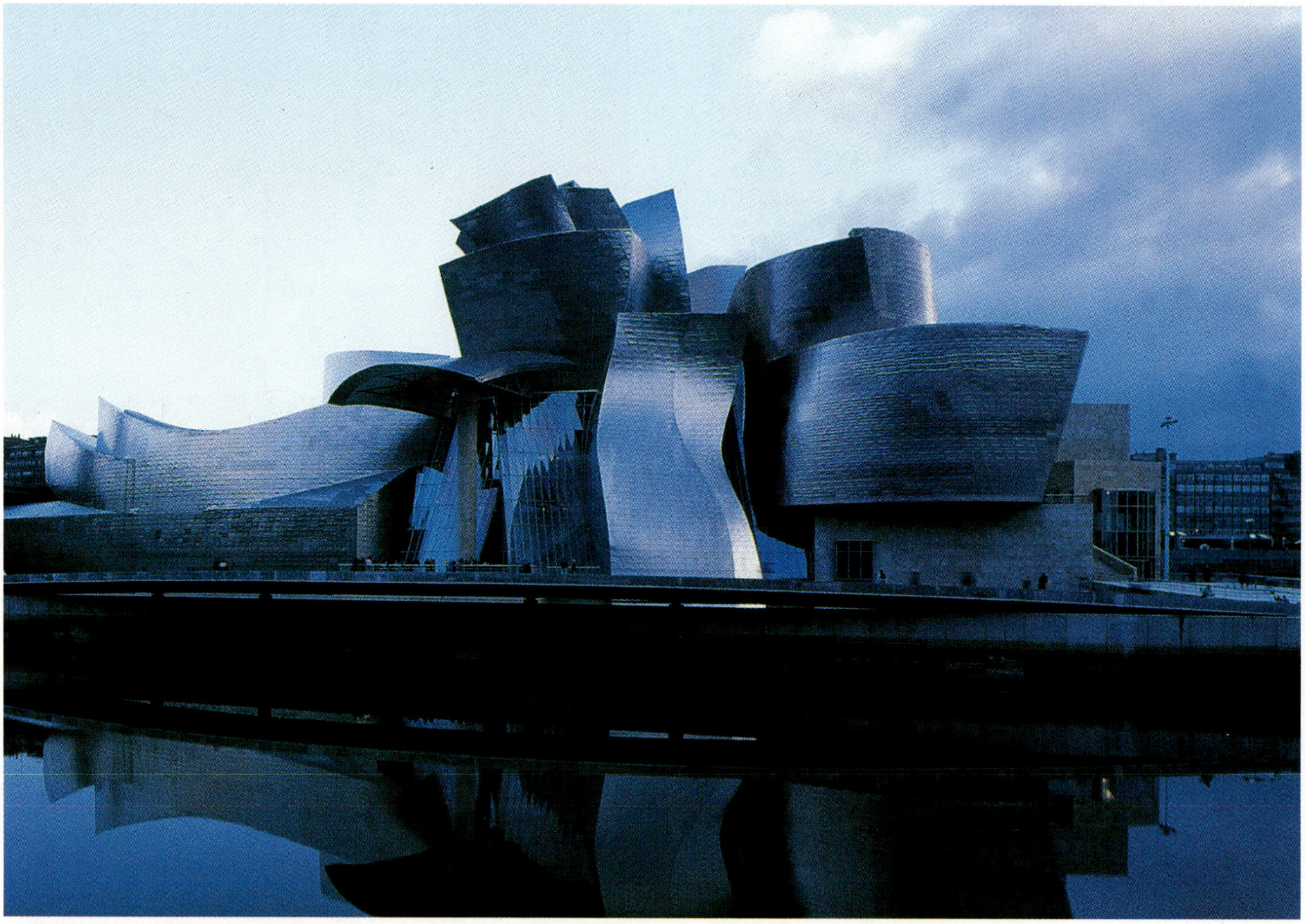

Fig. 8–1 **Gehry is known for creating dramatic forms and using materials in new and unusual ways. How does this museum's design compare with that of other museums you have seen?**

Frank Gehry, *Guggenheim Museum, Bilbao*, 1997/ Bilbao, Spain. Photo ©Ralph Richter/Esto/architekturphoto.

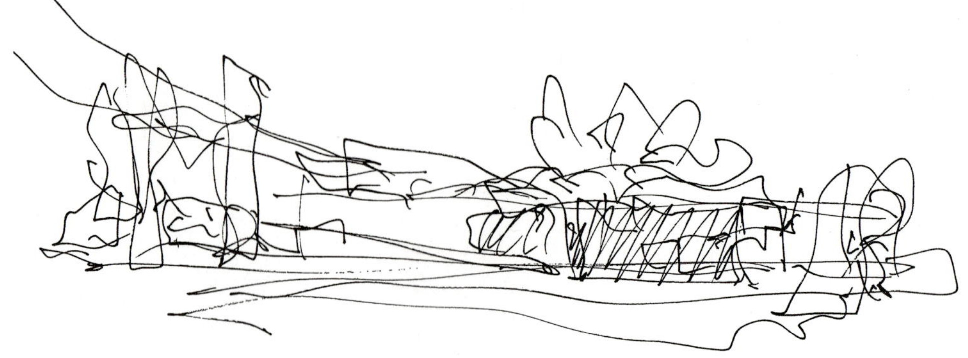

Fig. 8–2 **Many of Gehry's buildings begin as gesture drawings, such as the one shown here. How is drawing helpful in working out ideas?**

Frank Gehry, *Guggenheim Museum, Bilbao, Design Sketch*. Courtesy Frank O. Gehry and Associates, Santa Monica, California.

What is your school building like?

Are the hallways wide and open? Are there many windows? How are the spaces organized? People have always planned the spaces around them. They plan ways to organize inside and outside with places for cooking, washing, sleeping, working, and relaxing. They also plan ways to organize appliances, furniture, and other belongings.

In this unit, you will learn:

- How artists plan buildings and spaces in which people live and work.
- How to plan and build architectural and three-dimensional models.
- How to view buildings and spaces as works of art.

Architecture is the art of planning buildings and spaces. A group of experts work together to create the architecture of a street or neighborhood. These experts include city planners, engineers, builders, and architects. Architects are artists who design buildings. Because people must have places to shop, work, and relax, planners must think about the best use of available spaces for businesses, parks, and roads.

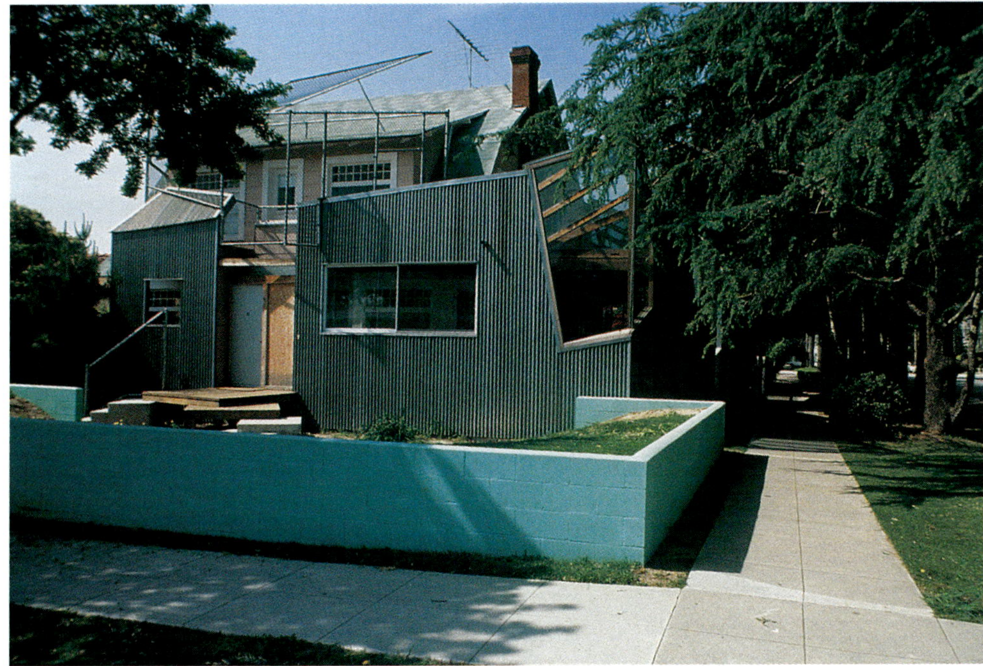

Fig. 8–3 **Gehry's use of inexpensive materials has influenced the plans of many other architects today. What materials can you identify in this image?**

Frank Gehry, *Gehry Residence*, 1978. Santa Monica, California. Photo ©Tim Street-Porter/Esto. All rights reserved.

The Planning Process

Architect Frank Gehry is noted for his experiments with forms, materials, and construction techniques. He first received attention for the unusual design of his own home in California **(Fig. 8–3)**. It was an ordinary pink, two-story house when he began to work on it. Gehry used inexpensive materials, such as plywood, tar paper, chain-link fence, concrete blocks, and corrugated metal. Planning from inside to outside, he expanded the house upward and sideways. He even wrapped parts with metal and wood.

For Gehry, the planning process is very important. He begins with gesture drawings **(Fig. 8–2)**, and then creates three-dimensional models. As he builds his models, he thinks about them as both sculpture and as a place for people to live or work. Gehry and a team of more than 120 people work to plan and create imaginative spaces for clients.

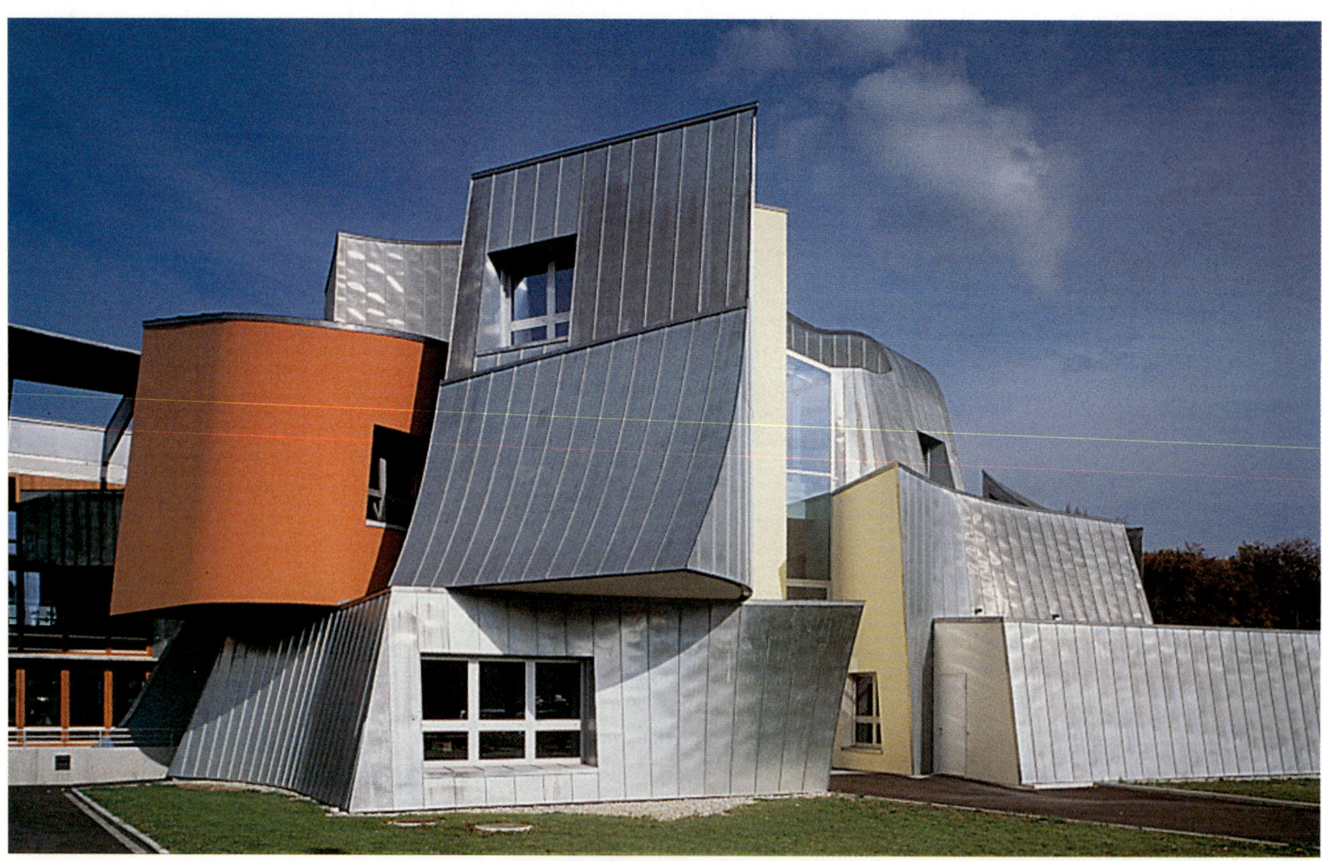

Fig. 8–4 **This building is like a three-dimensional collage. What different forms and materials can you identify?**

Frank Gehry, *Vitra Headquarters*, 1994. Birsfelden, Switzerland. Photo: Tim Griffith/Esto.

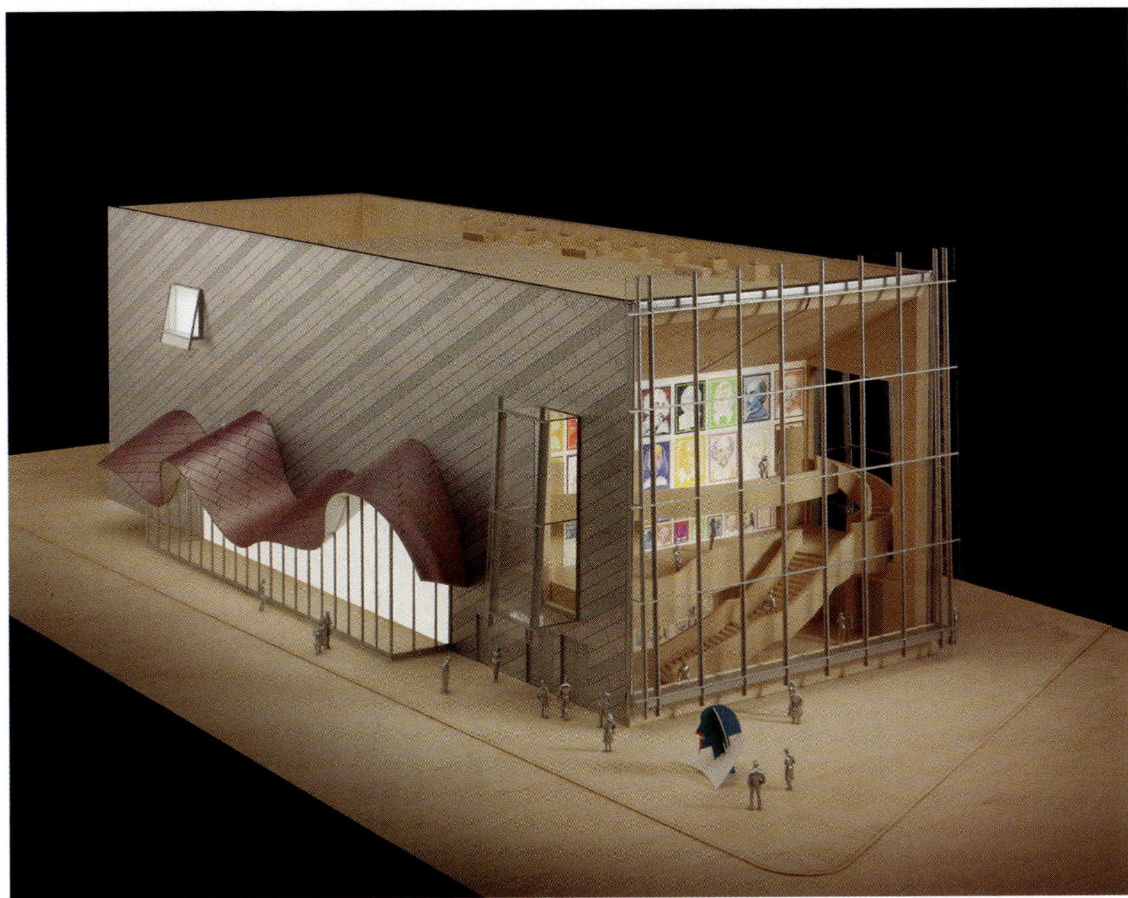

Fig. 8–5 **This type of three-dimensional model helps architects visualize their buildings. What does this model show that a gesture drawing could not?**

H3 Hardy Collaboration, Frank Gehry, *Theatre for a New Audience Model*, Photograph ©Jock Potle/Esto. All rights reserved.

Like many architects working today, Gehry uses the computer to help with design. He works with a computer program that allows him to create surprising-looking buildings whose surfaces bend and ripple. Some have suggested that his space-age buildings seem alive, constantly moving and changing.

Meet Frank Gehry

Frank Gehry grew up in Toronto, Canada. He remembers when, as a child, he made "little cities" out of wood scraps with his grandmother. At 18, he and his family moved to California, where he still lives and works. As an architect, Gehry has produced shopping malls, houses, parks, museums, banks, restaurants—even furniture! Gehry wants people to be comfortable in the buildings and spaces he plans. He thinks about how his buildings will be used daily, by ordinary people. He also pays attention to the community in which his buildings will be built.

Photo by Thomas Mayer.

"I approach each building as...a spatial container, a space with light and air."

— Frank Gehry (born 1929)

Planning Forms for the Future Imagine that you are asked to plan a new city. What kinds of spaces would people need? Where would they live, work, and play?

The idea of planning a new place has always been important. Artists such as Remedios Varo (Fig. 7–3) have created images of fantasy worlds or cities of the future. Architects and other artists think of ways for technology to meet people's needs in years to come. Some planners create new places while also saving the earth's resources. Architect Paolo Soleri has designed a city plan called *Arcosanti* (Fig. 8–7) in which the automobile is not necessary. Renewable resources, such as the sun and wind, provide the city's energy supply.

Planning Decisions Most professional planners, however, must plan buildings, parks, and other spaces within neighborhoods that already exist. When architects plan, they consider how the new site will fit what is already there. A new structure may look similar to the other structures, wildly different, or somewhere in between. Whether designing whole neighborhoods or just one building, planners must consider future needs.

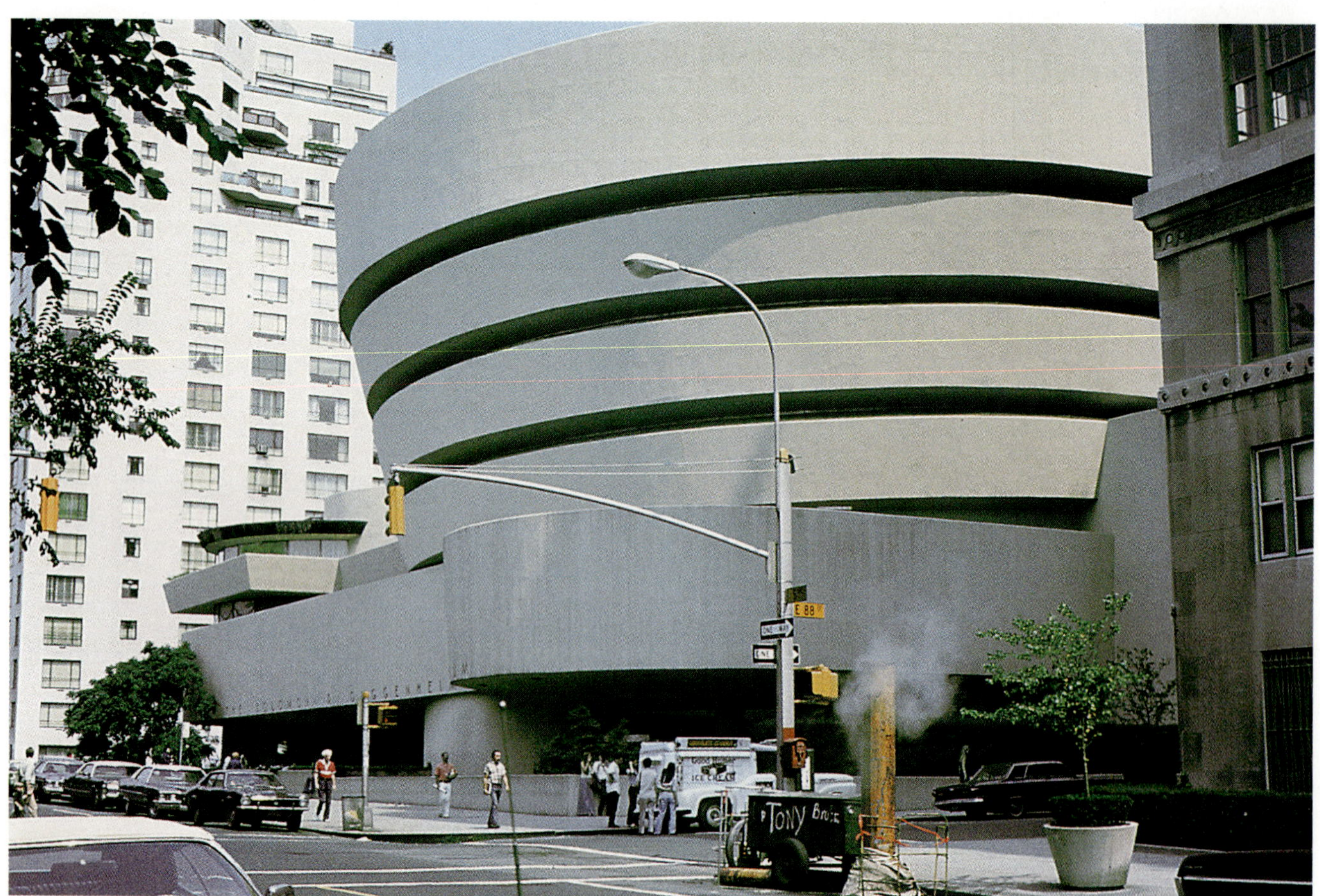

Fig. 8–6 **Architect Frank Lloyd Wright designed a museum with a unique shape. What does its shape resemble? How does it differ from the other buildings shown?**

Frank Lloyd Wright, *Solomon R. Guggenheim Museum*, 1956–59. New York, New York. Courtesy of Davis Art Images.

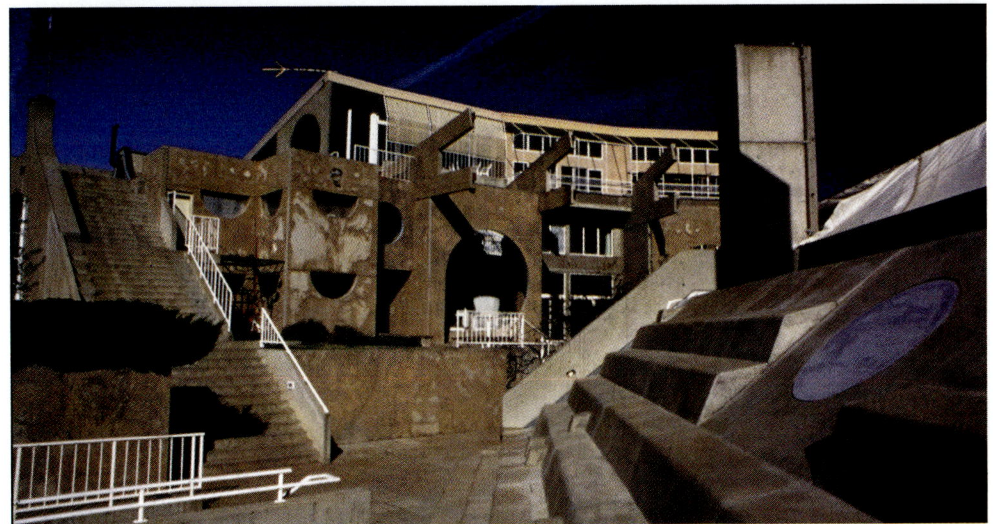

Fig. 8–7 **Architect Paolo Soleri's plan for this city blends architecture with ecology, a combination he calls "arcology." An arcology complex contains apartments, businesses, entertainment, and open spaces.**

Paolo Soleri, *Arcosanti*, 2001. Under construction in central Arizona. Photo courtesy of the Soleri Archives.

Studio Time

Planning a City Block

Plan and draw buildings in a city block.

- Use one-point or two-point perspective to create the illusion of depth in your drawing.
- Think about how the buildings will look side by side. Remember that your buildings will have different functions. For example, you might include a car wash, a movie theater, or a department store.
- Add details to show the functions and placements of your buildings.

Reflect on how well your drawing shows your understanding of perspective.

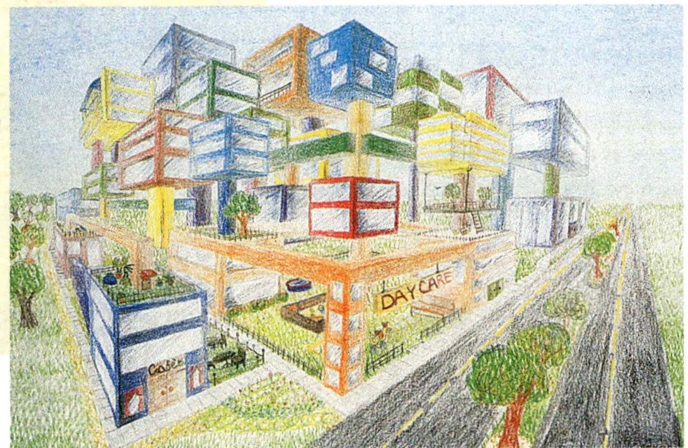

Fig. 8–8 Student artwork

Check Your Understanding

1. What types of questions do architects and planners ask themselves when creating new buildings and spaces?
2. How do Frank Gehry's architectural designs differ from Paolo Soleri's?
3. When planning a building, do you think it is more important for the architect to consider the way the building will function or the way it will look? Why?

Making Three-Dimensional Models

Architects work with many other professionals to plan a building, but they are responsible for deciding how the final building will look. They sometimes plan a building using only a few basic geometric forms, such as a cube for the central space, cylinders for columns, and a pyramid for the roof. In other cases, an architect might decide to combine a great number of forms and shapes, including towers, domes, arches, spheres, barrel vaults, or cones. Look at the drawing of the building on this page. It offers one example of how basic geometric forms can be combined.

During the process of designing a building, architects often create an architectural model. An architectural model is a small, three-dimensional representation of a building. They build the model from paper, cardboard, wood, or other materials. Some of the techniques they use are similar to the ones illustrated on these pages.

When you make a three-dimensional model, you may decide to use some ready-made boxes, tubes, or spheres, if necessary.

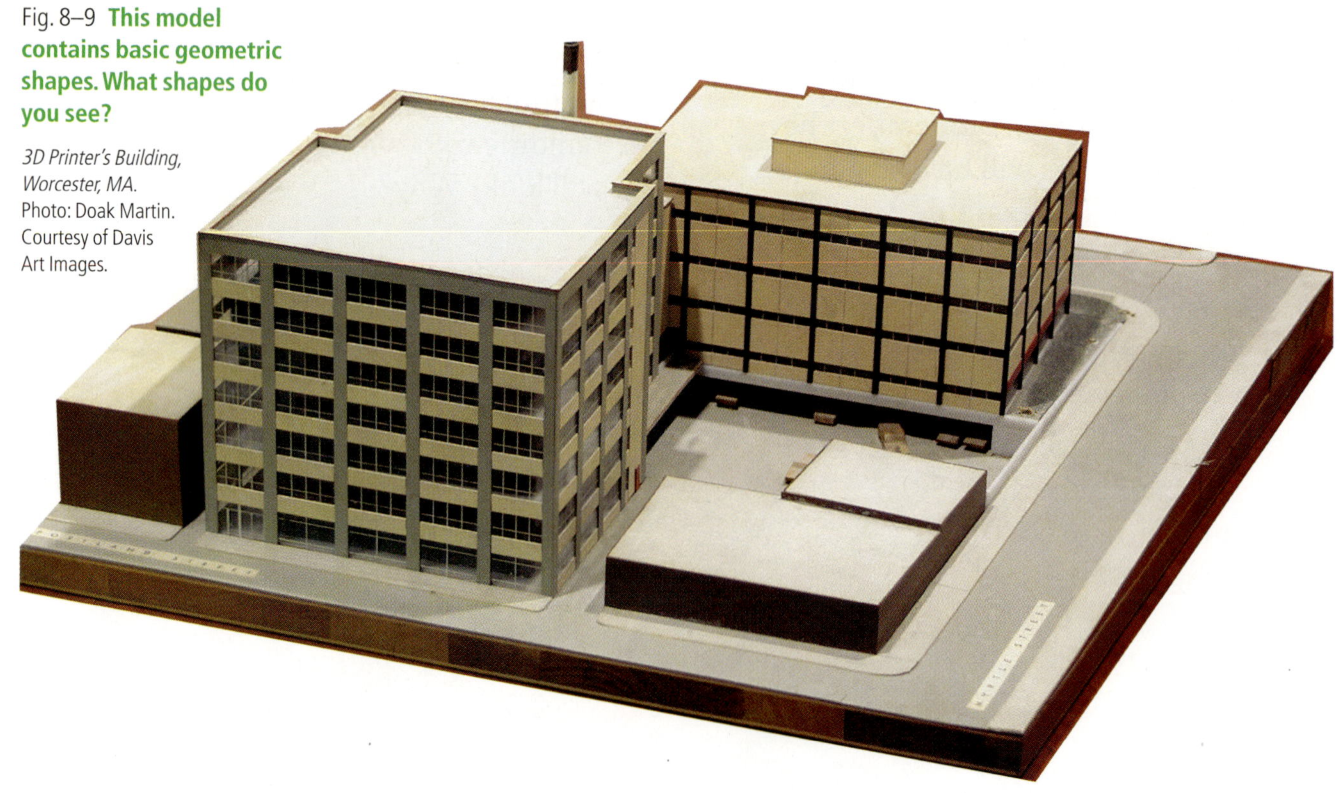

Fig. 8–9 **This model contains basic geometric shapes. What shapes do you see?**

3D Printer's Building, Worcester, MA. Photo: Doak Martin. Courtesy of Davis Art Images.

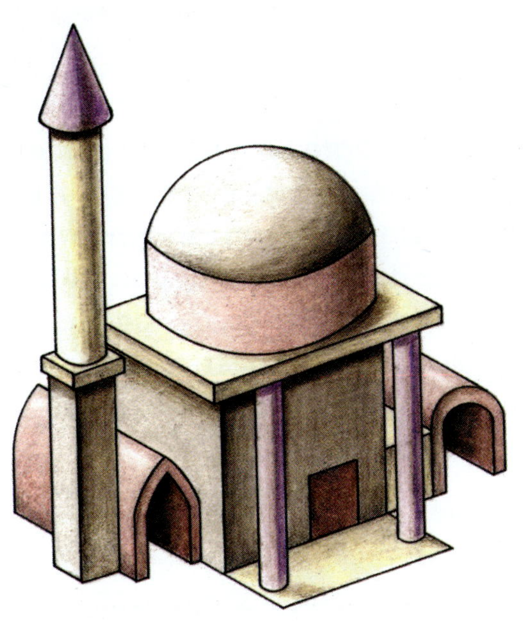

Pyramid, Cone, and Cube Use construction paper, scissors, and glue to make a series of three-dimensional forms: a cube, a cylinder, a cone, a pyramid, and an arch. For additional guidance, study the diagrams provided on these pages.

Observe Look at the model of the buildings on this page. Note that the buildings are made up of basic geometric shapes.

Tools: Construction paper, scissors, glue, ruler, and compass.

Practice: Creating Pyramids, Cubes, and Cones

- Measure carefully before you cut. Make crisp folds and use glue neatly. Use the diagrams on this page to help guide your folding and cutting. Note that in the diagram with a pyramid, cone, and cube, dotted lines are lines to be folded, not cut.

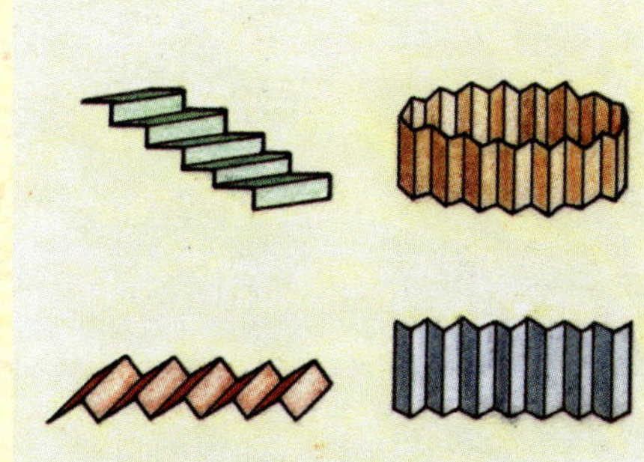

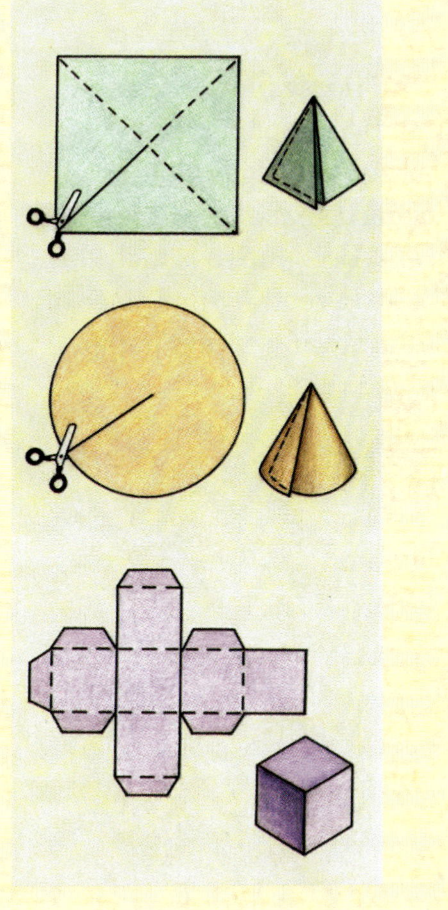

Barrel Vault A barrel vault is an architectural form that is made up of a series of connected arches.

Observe Look at the diagram of the barrel vault below. Notice how a barrel vault has been used in the student model on the following page. What does it add to the design?

Tools: Construction paper, scissors, and glue.

Practice: Creating a Barrel Vault

- Cut out two "horseshoe" shapes from construction paper. Cut small triangular wedges along the outside of each shape, as shown in the diagram. Use glue to attach the two shapes to a rectangular piece of paper. Cut away any excess paper.

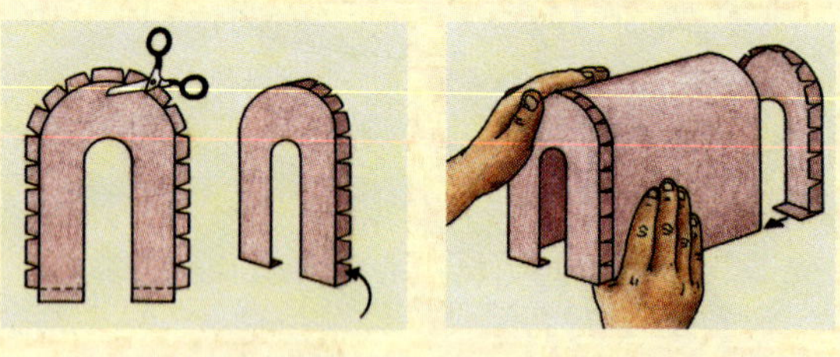

Geodesic Dome Spheres and domes are not easy to make with construction paper and glue. However, you can construct a geodesic dome by folding and gluing together several circles. A geodesic dome is a structure that is nearly spherical and is made up of a network of great circles, also known as geodesics.

Observe Look for an example of a geodesic dome in the student image on page 221. What do you notice about the arrangement of triangles?

Tools: Construction paper, scissors, glue, and a compass.

Practice: Creating a Geodesic Dome

- To make the dome, cut out a circle and fold it on three sides to make a triangle with three flaps. Join many of these forms to make a dome. Look at the diagrams below to guide your construction of your geodesic dome.

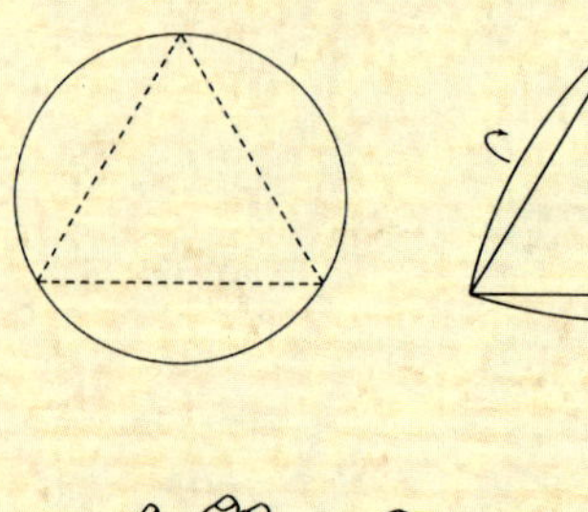

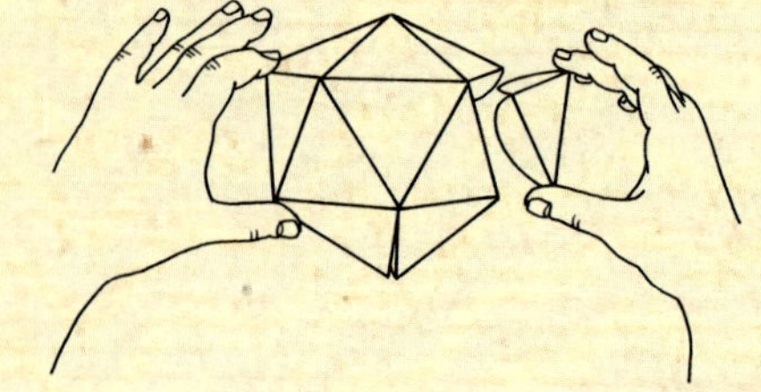

Studio Time

Buildings in Paper

Work with a small group of classmates to construct a three-dimensional model of a building or even a model of a group of buildings.

- First, look at pictures of various buildings. Which basic forms did the architect combine in each one?
- Then, discuss what you might create. Make some sketches to show how your building(s) can be created from basic forms.
- Use construction paper to create a three-dimensional model of your plan.

Reflect on how well the variety of forms create a unified whole.

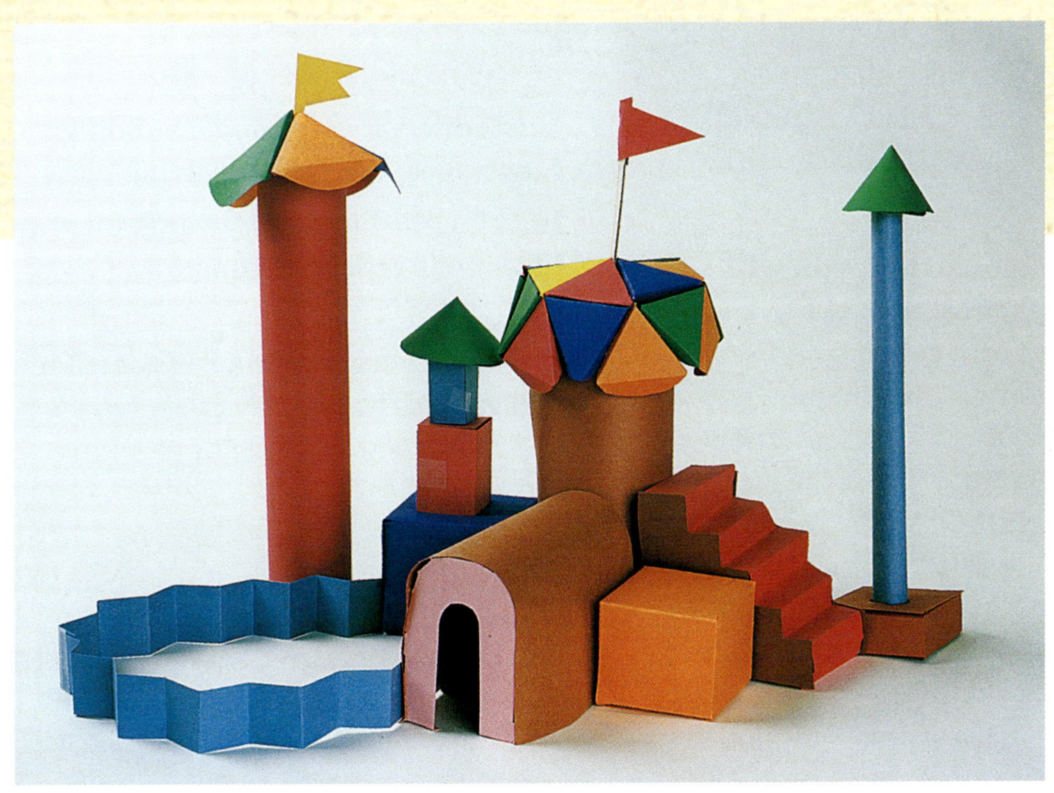

Fig. 8–10
Student artwork

Check Your Understanding

1. What is an architectural model?
2. How does a geodesic dome differ from the dome shown in the diagram on page 219?
3. Why do you think architects usually make three-dimensional models when they design a building?

Building a Model

Studio Background

Before architects like Frank Gehry plan a building, sketch ideas, and make models, they think about the building's use. They ask what activities will take place in it and what needs it must meet. They think about how the building will look on the inside and outside. They ask how the building's appearance will reflect its function. For example, a courthouse could have architectural features that reflect seriousness and justice, such as a broad stairway leading to a large hallway with high ceilings.

In this studio exploration, you will build an architectural model for a certain function and setting. When you look at a building, think about what function it serves. Think also about how its setting, or place, may affect the way it looks. What is the building's overall form? What architectural features does the building have? Imagine what an architectural model of the building would look like.

You Will Need

- construction materials, such as Styrofoam™, foam core board, cardboard, and wood scraps
- scissors
- white glue
- tempera paint (optional)
- brushes (optional)
- water (optional)

Step 1 Plan and Practice

- Think of what your model building's function is. What is its setting?
- Imagine the building's overall form and how it will reflect its function.
- What materials will you need to construct your building? What colors will you use?

Inspiration from Our World

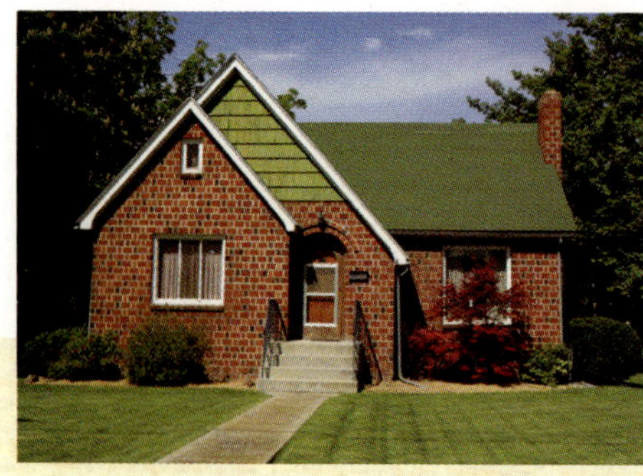

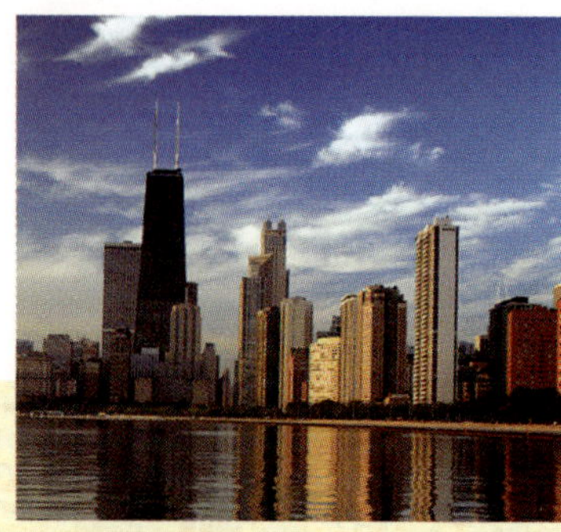

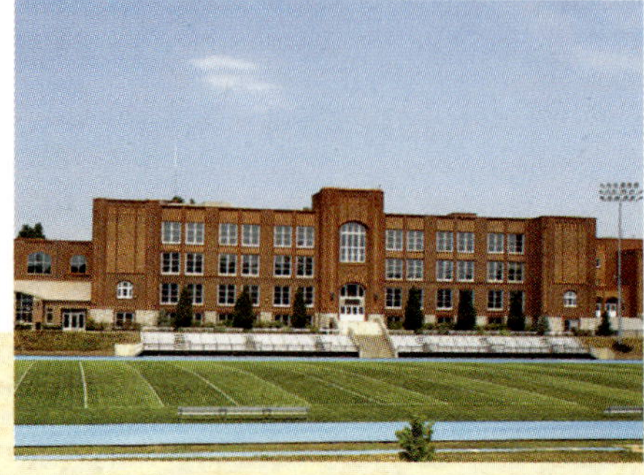

Things to Remember:

- ✓ Assemble the building's forms, such as cylinders, cubes, cones, or pyramids, to create a sense of balance.
- ✓ Create a building that fits well into the setting you have chosen.
- ✓ Create forms for your building that help reveal its function.

Inspiration from Art

For centuries, city and building planners in the Western world have been influenced by ancient Greek and Roman ideas. The Greeks developed innovative ways to build temples and outdoor theaters. The Romans invented concrete and combined it with stone to build huge domed meeting halls and stadiums. Their city plans included the construction of roads, bridges, and aqueducts (channels that transport water) throughout their vast empire.

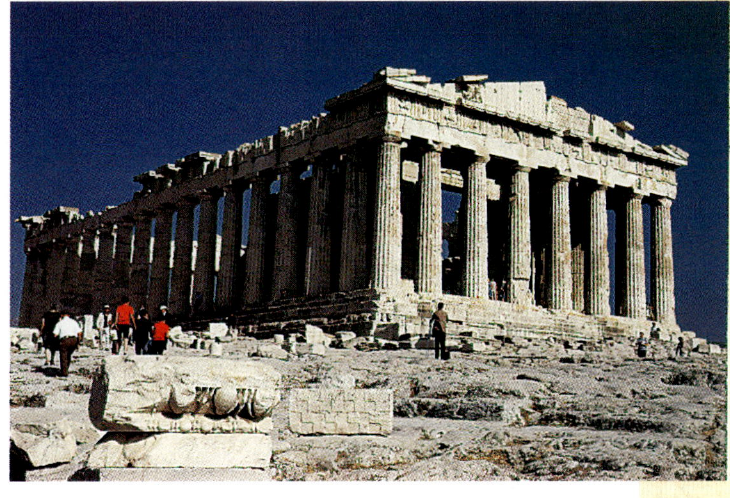

Fig. 8–11 **The ancient Greeks planned their buildings to have parts that are proportional to other parts. What buildings in your town have parts that are proportional?**

Iktinos and Kallikrates, *Parthenon Eastern Façade,* 448–432 BC. The Acropolis, Athens, Greece. Photo credit: Werner Forman/ Art Resource, NY.

Step 2 Begin to Create

- Decide what kind of building model you will create. Will you build a model for a skyscraper, a library, or other type of community building?
- For what setting—city, village, forest, ocean, or outer space—will you create your model?
- How will you use architectural features to express your ideas?
- **Sketch your plan.**

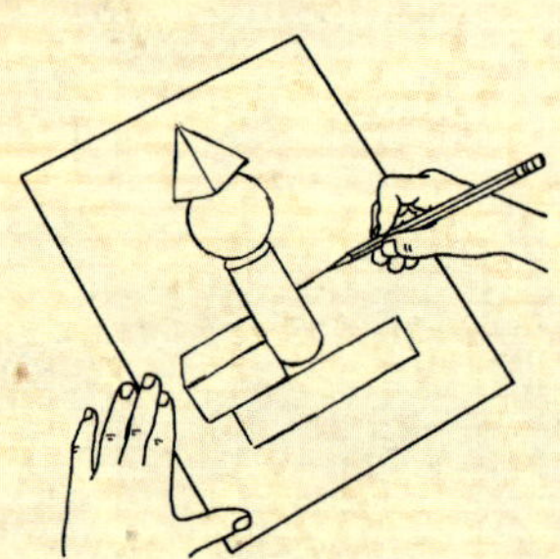

- Choose the forms you need to construct your model. Will you cut or bend any materials to create them?
- **Experiment with the arrangement of the forms.** How will you create balance in your arrangement?

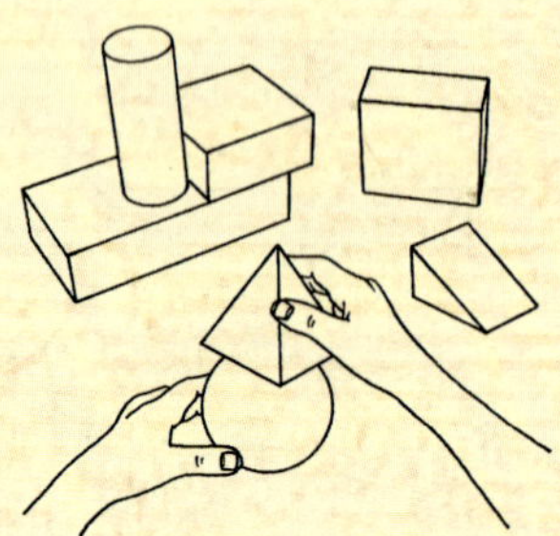

- **When you are satisfied with your arrangement, carefully glue the forms together.** Will you paint your finished model? Or will an unpainted model better express your ideas?

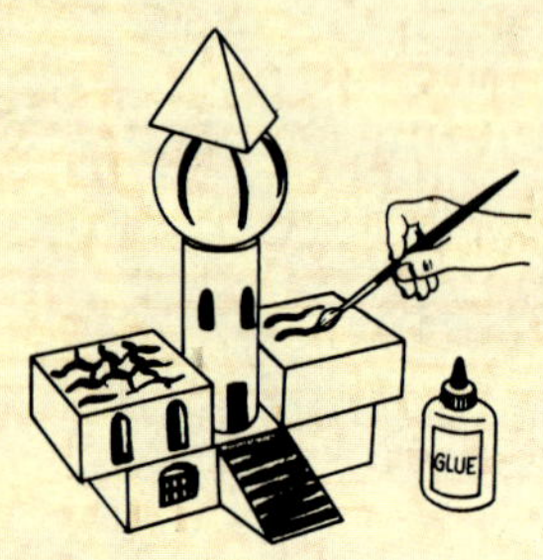

Step 3 Revise

Did you remember to:

- ✓ Assemble the building's forms, such as cylinders, cubes, cones, or pyramids, to create a sense of balance?
- ✓ Create a building that fits well into the setting you have chosen?
- ✓ Create forms for your building that help reveal its function?

Adjust your work if necessary. In your sketchbook, make a note of your revisions and why you made them.

Step 4 Add Finishing Touches

- Add any last features that will complete your model, and place your signature on it.

Step 5 **Share and Reflect**

- Display your architectural model with your classmates' models.
- Talk about the function and setting of each model.
- How does each model's overall form reflect its function?
- Discuss the way that each model would fit in with other buildings that could be planned for the same setting. Does your model fit in with any of your classmates'? How?

Art Criticism

Describe What forms did the artists use to create these models?

Analyze Compare and contrast the design of these two models.

Interpret How do the forms of these buildings suggest their use?

Evaluate What has each artist done especially well in these architectural models?

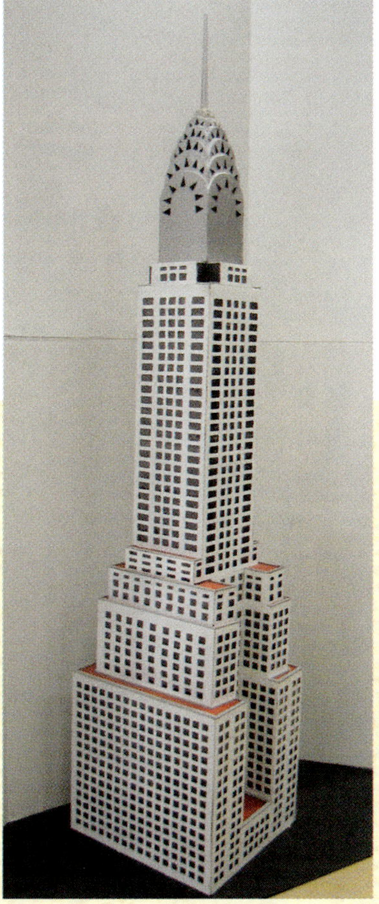

Fig. 8–12
Student artwork

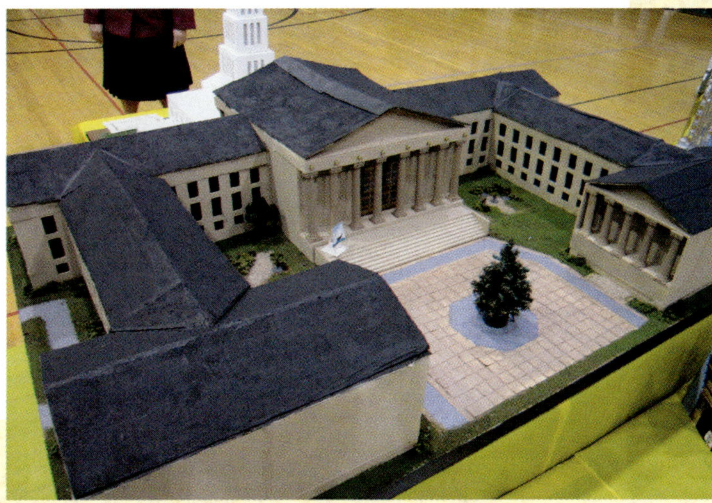

Fig. 8–13 Student artwork

Architecture for Living

There are many kinds of buildings, but the house is probably the most interesting building of all. The first houses were simple wooden shelters built by Paleolithic hunter-gatherers 750,000 years ago. Over time, people discovered new building materials and techniques, and dwelling design changed.

Planning Houses British architect Philip Webb created plans for private homes in the 1800s. One of his best known is *The Red House* **(Fig. 8–14)**, built for William Morris, also a designer. Their goal was to create a contemporary look but also to use architectural features from older styles of buildings.

Creating Form Architects have always created balanced forms. However, in the early 1900s, architects used materials such as steel and iron to create new kinds of balanced forms.

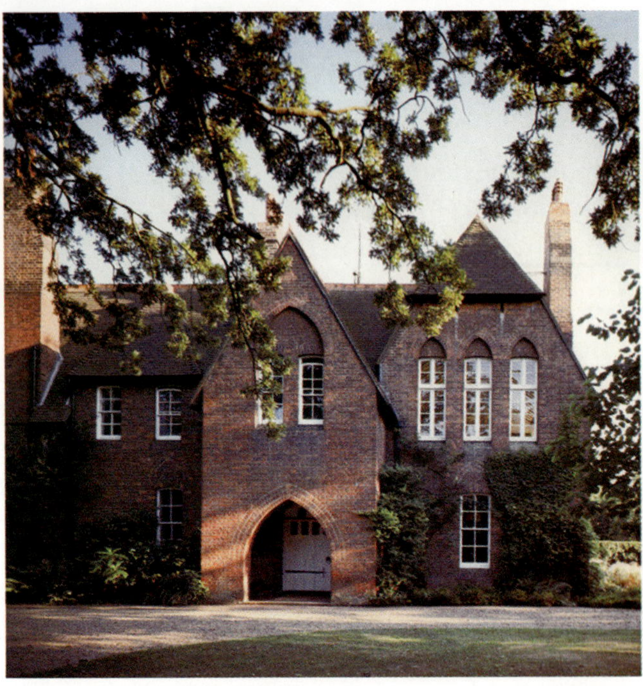

Fig. 8–14 **In what ways does this home remind you of castles from the Middle Ages?**

Philip Webb, *The Red House*, 1859. Bexley Heath, in Kent, England. Niall Clutton/Arcaid.

1700s

1793
With designs from Pierre-Charles L'Enfant, a French engineer, construction begins on Washington, DC.

1800s

1859
Webb, *The Red House*

1864
In the American Civil War, Union troops burn factories and stores in Atlanta, GA.

1889
Eiffel Tower completed in Paris, France.

1900s

1935
Hoover Dam completed.

1936–39
Wright, *Fallingwater*

1937
Golden Gate Bridge opens in San Francisco, CA.

1962
Venturi, *Vanna Venturi House*

1992
Gray, *Gluelam House*

1996
Gray, *The 13° House*

In 1939, Frank Lloyd Wright designed the home *Fallingwater* **(Fig. 8–15)** with a modern look. He used steel to build cantilevered terraces to connect the home with its natural setting. (A **cantilever** is a beam supported at one end and freestanding at the other end.) The cantilevers allow parts of the building to stick out over the water and rocks. Wright's use of cantilevers is an example of asymmetrical balance. **Asymmetrical balance** occurs when objects on each side of a composition are different, but equal in weight or visual interest.

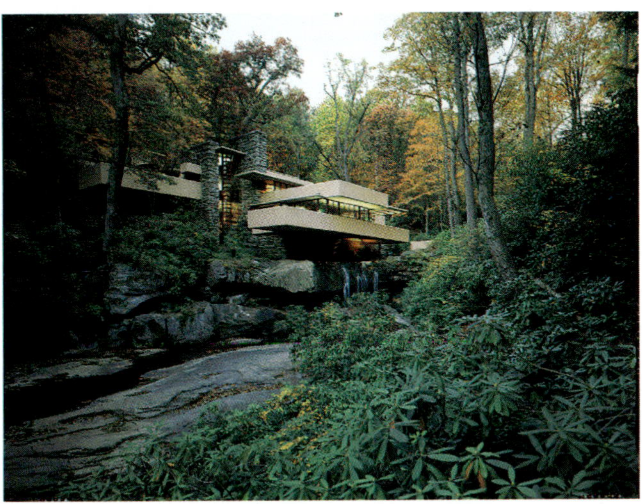

Fig. 8–15 **The hearth, or fireplace, was the central focus of Wright's homes. In making the fireplace the central focus, what image of family life do you think Wright had in mind?**

Frank Lloyd Wright, *The Kaufmann House: Fallingwater*, 1936–39. Bear Run, Pennsylvania. Photo ©Thomas A. Heinz, AIA, Heinz & Co. Artists Rights Society (ARS), NY.

In the mid-1900s, some architects began to plan structures that combined new ideas with traditional architecture. Architect Robert Venturi and others wanted to mix familiar shapes and details in unexpected ways in the façades of their buildings. A **façade** is the front of a house or building. This new trend was called **Post-Modernism**, which literally means "after Modernism," because it broke away from the modern tradition of little or no decoration. Modernism featured sleek, functional buildings with few surprises and little humor. In the *Vanna Venturi House* **(Fig. 8–16)**, Venturi's designs create a playful mix of symmetry and asymmetry.

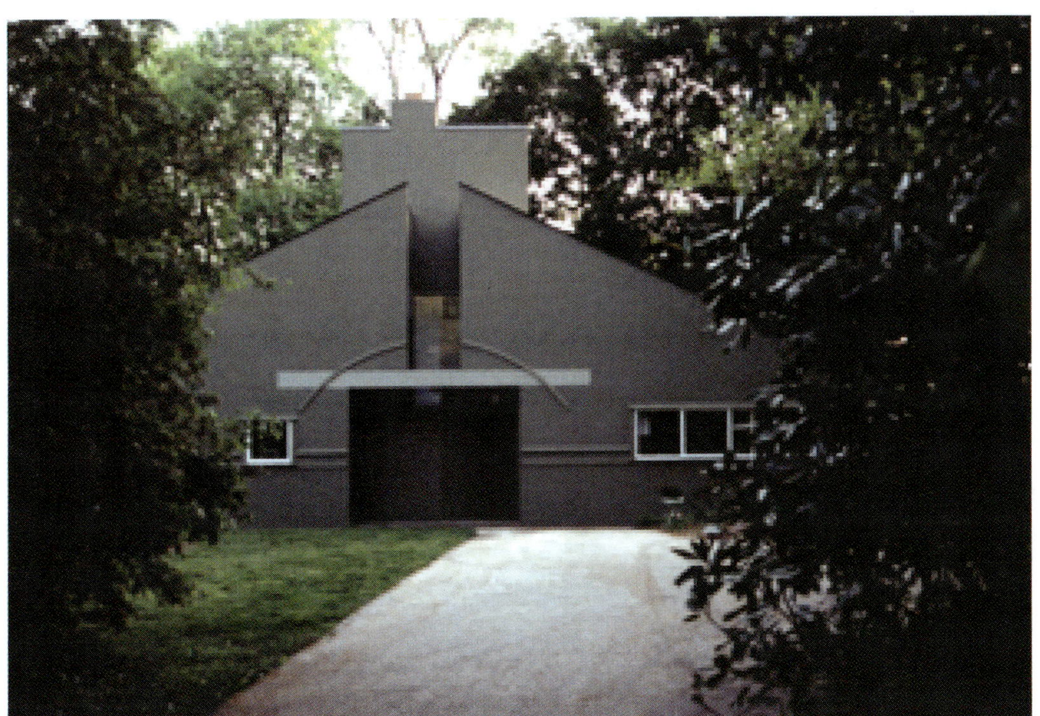

Fig. 8–16 **In what way is the façade of this house symmetrical? What features are asymmetrical, or not equally balanced?**

Venturi, Scott Brown and Associates, *Vanna Venturi House*, 1962. Chestnut Hill, Pennsylvania. Kevin Matthews, ©Artifice Images.

The Order of Architecture

Like many of today's architects, Melinda Gray continues the tradition of creating new spaces for homes. She likes to experiment with materials, and she mixes them in fun, unexpected ways. For example, she will contrast the warmth of natural wood with the coolness of steel or glass. Gray also designs courtyards, gardens, balconies, and other outdoor spaces. These spaces visually extend the house and help people move around easily.

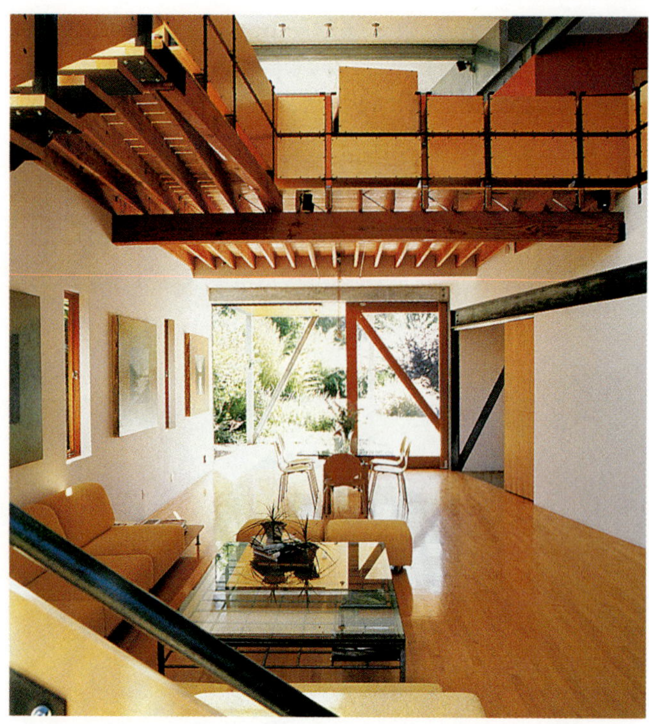

Fig. 8–18 **Gray creates light-filled interior spaces. What makes the interior of this home appealing?**

Melinda Gray, *The Glulam House* (interior), 1992. Santa Monica Canyon, California. Photo by Richard Cheatte. Courtesy of Gray Matter Architecture.

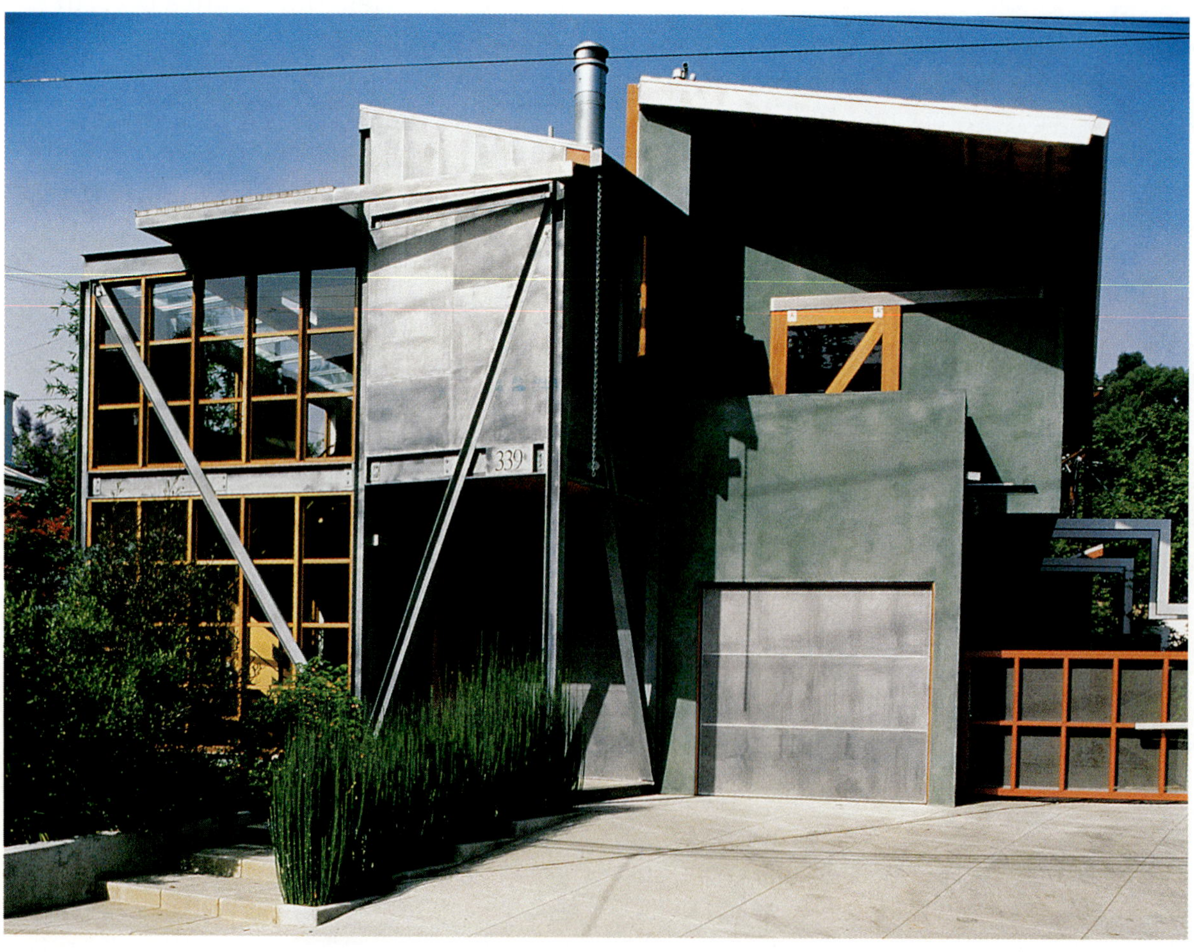

Fig. 8–17 **Melinda Gray plans houses that are full of contrasts, such as curved and straight lines, open and closed spaces, and formal and informal balance.**

Melinda Gray, *The 13° House* (exterior), 1996. Santa Monica Canyon, California. Photo by Grey Crawford. Courtesy of Gray Matter Architecture.

To unify her designs, Gray uses grid patterns. For the exterior of homes such as the *13° House* (Fig. 8–17), she repeats patterns of squares and grouped square windows. She contrasts the strong vertical and horizontal lines with a curved roof. The interiors of the homes are based on cubes and other forms that intersect to create wide, open spaces.

Meet Melinda Gray

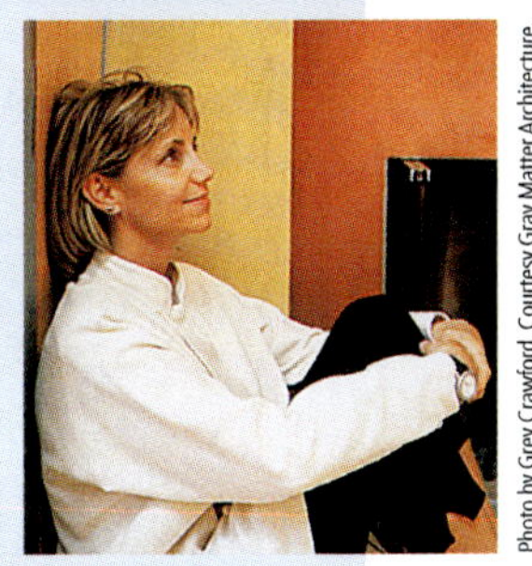
Photo by Grey Crawford. Courtesy Gray Matter Architecture.

Melinda Gray was born in Chicago, Illinois. After college, she studied architecture at the University of California in Los Angeles and apprenticed with a designer of commercial structures. Gray's style is a mix of craftsmanship, careful planning, and experimentation. Her interest in architecture grew out of a love of geometry, and she bases many of her plans on ideas from geometry. She plans her buildings by using shapes and forms that come together in dynamic ways.

"I'm really into order. It affects people even if they don't perceive it."

— Melinda Gray (born 1952)

Check Your Understanding

1. What is Post-Modernism?
2. How does Frank Lloyd Wright's house *Fallingwater* differ from Post-Modern architecture?
3. Describe Melinda Gray's approach to architecture.

Studio Time

Dream House Drawing

Draw an elevation plan or a façade of your dream house.

- Decide whether the front of your dream house will have formal, symmetrical balanced or a more informal, asymmetrical look.
- Choose tools that will help you make even lines and shapes, such as a ruler and compass.
- Make sketches with pencil before creating the final drawing with a fine-tip marker.

Reflect on how well the parts of your house relate to each other.

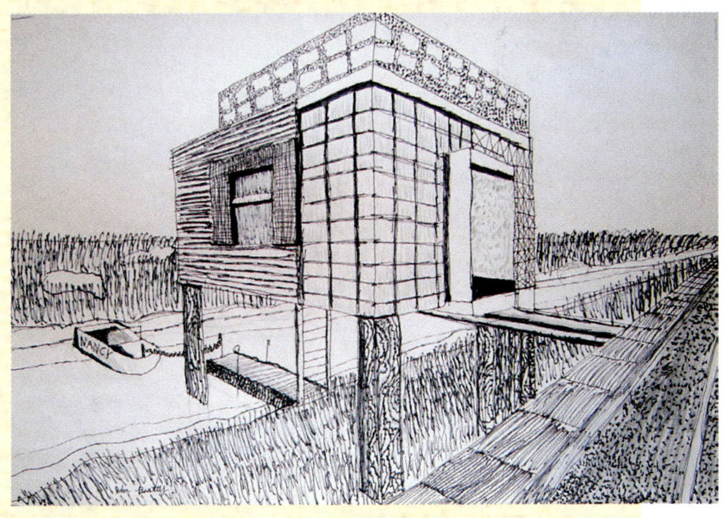

Fig. 8–19 Student artwork

Mexican Architecture

Urban Architecture Before the arrival of Spanish settlers, urban architecture in Mesoamerica began with the creation of ceremonial centers. In these urban centers, large groups of people could watch and take part in rituals and other public events. Early Mexican planners developed architecture with gently sloping walls, as well as plazas, platforms, ramps, and stairs **(Fig. 8–20)**.

These early structures often have inspired today's architects, including Pedro Ramírez Vázquez. For *The National Museum of Anthropology* **(Fig. 8–21)**, Vázquez wanted a place where Mexican people could honor their heritage. He designed the museum around a large central plaza that was protected, yet open, and where people could come and go as they pleased.

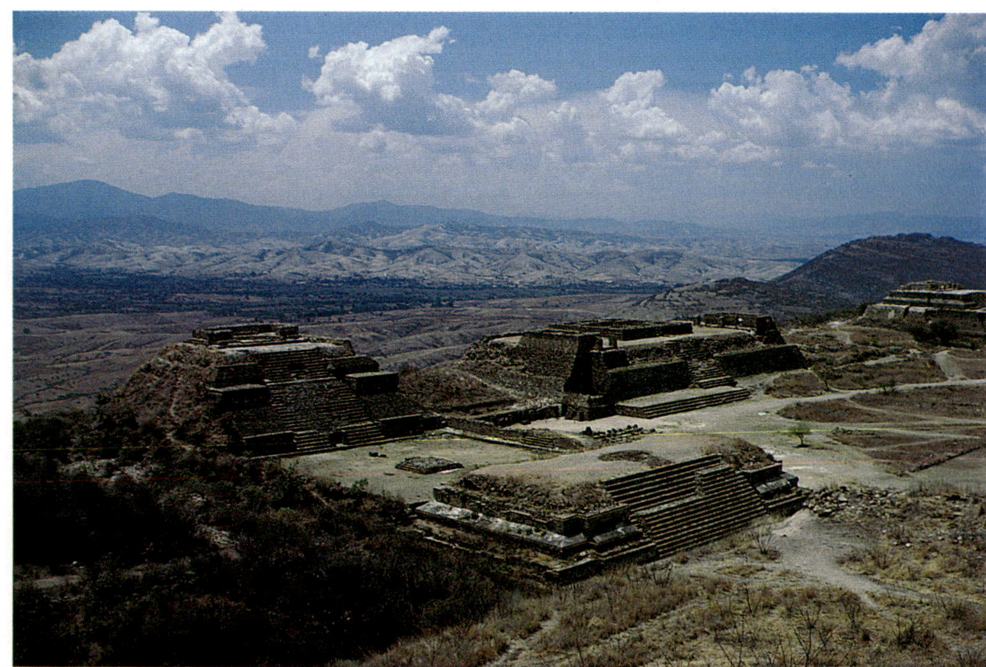

Fig. 8–20 **What is the overall plan of the placement of these structures? What evidence do you see that shows that the planners were thinking about having large groups of people moving about?**

Mexico, *Teotihuacán*, 1st century AD. Photo courtesy of Karen Durlach.

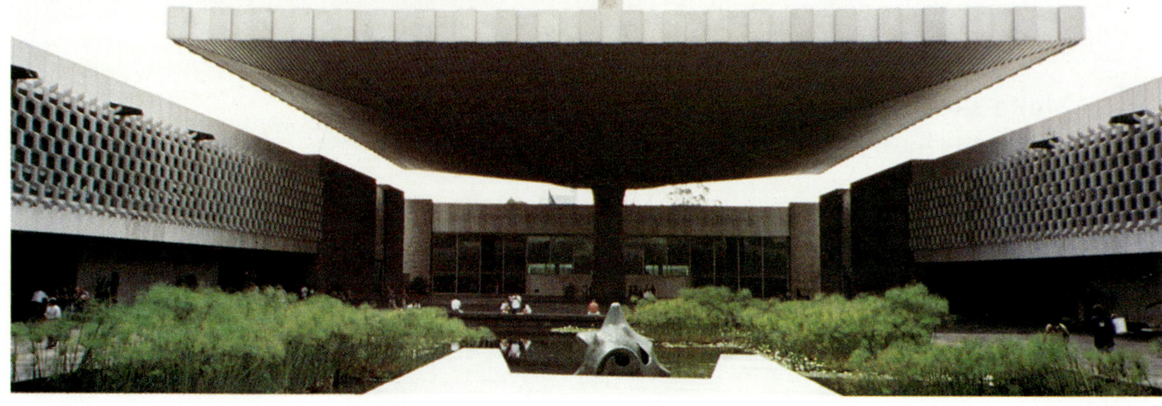

Fig. 8–21 **Why does the overall plan of this space seem balanced?**

Pedro Ramírez Vázquez, *The National Museum of Anthropology*, 1964. Mexico City, Mexico. Photo courtesy of Eldon Katter.

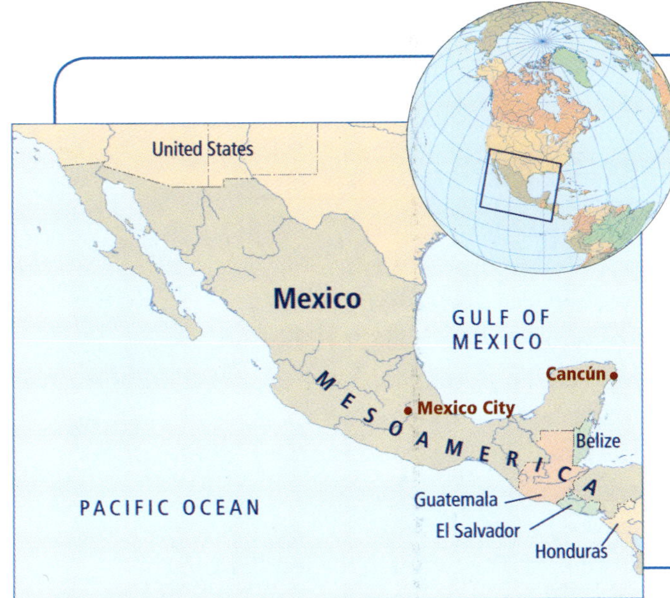

Social Studies Connection

Most of **Mexico** is composed of hills or mountain ranges broken by plateaus. Deep valleys and canyons contrast the mountains. The features of the country's landscape can also be found in its buildings. Structures range from simple adobe homes to complex stone temples. The ruins of pyramids and temples are evidence of the architectural achievements of early civilizations like the Olmec, Maya, Toltec, and Aztec cultures.

Rural Architecture In the 1500s, Spanish settlers in Mexico began to build haciendas. Haciendas are large agricultural estates that house hundreds of workers on a plantation. Today, the hacienda is still a popular style for homes in Mexico. Architect Luis Barragán planned buildings (Fig. 8–22) in a style that is similar to the hacienda's simple, boxlike exteriors.

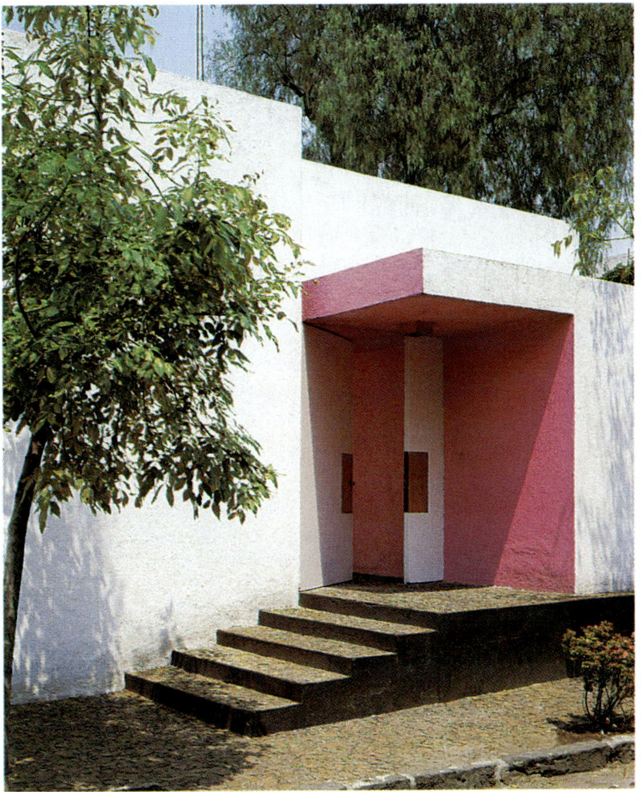

Fig. 8–22 **Barragán was known for the simple style of his buildings. Notice his use of color and asymmetrical balance.**

Luis Barragán, *Casa Antonio Galvez*, 1954. San Angel, Mexico. Courtesy of Elizabeth Whiting & Associates, London.

Visual Culture

Architectural styles differ from one part of the world to another. They also differ from one community to another. Sometimes these differences are due to geography and climate and available materials. Sometimes the differences reflect cultural traditions. Social status and economics are also factors in building designs. Work with your classmates to document differences in architectural styles in your community, state, or region.

Ricardo Legorreta doesn't remember when or how he decided to be an architect. He says that it just happened. His interest in architecture came about in a natural way, from his visits to towns, haciendas, convents, churches, and the Mesoamerican pyramids.

Designing for the Place Ricardo Legorreta's many hotels, like the one in Fig. 8–23, are planned to take advantage of the view and terrain. As in ancient Mexican ceremonial centers, they have open, public spaces. But Legorreta also plans for enclosed and private spaces, following the tradition of convents, haciendas, and smaller Mexican houses. He plans other kinds of buildings, such as the business center in Fig. 8–24, with walls of different size and scale. All of Legorreta's buildings use simple forms, open spaces, sunlight, and carefully planned colors. His architecture is both simple and grand.

Meet Ricardo Legorreta

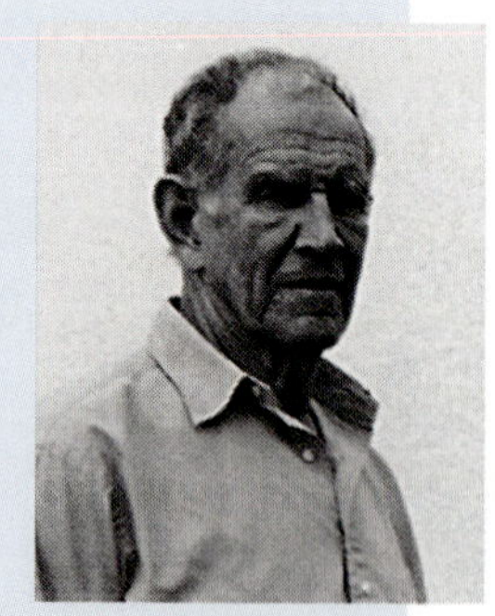

Graciela Iturbide

Ricardo Legorreta was born in Mexico City. He worked as a draftsman while studying architecture at the University of Mexico. Early in his career, he looked to the traditional architectural styles of Mexico. Legorreta worked with elements from both the Spanish haciendas and the pre-Hispanic ceremonial centers. He did not want his buildings to have the chain-restaurant and Hollywood set-design looks of other Mexican buildings. His buildings have the appearance of historical Mexico and the feel of the modern age.

"[The designer must] go to the roots, to the culture, and design for a place. The challenge is to create architecture that everyone feels good in."

— Ricardo Legorreta (born 1931)

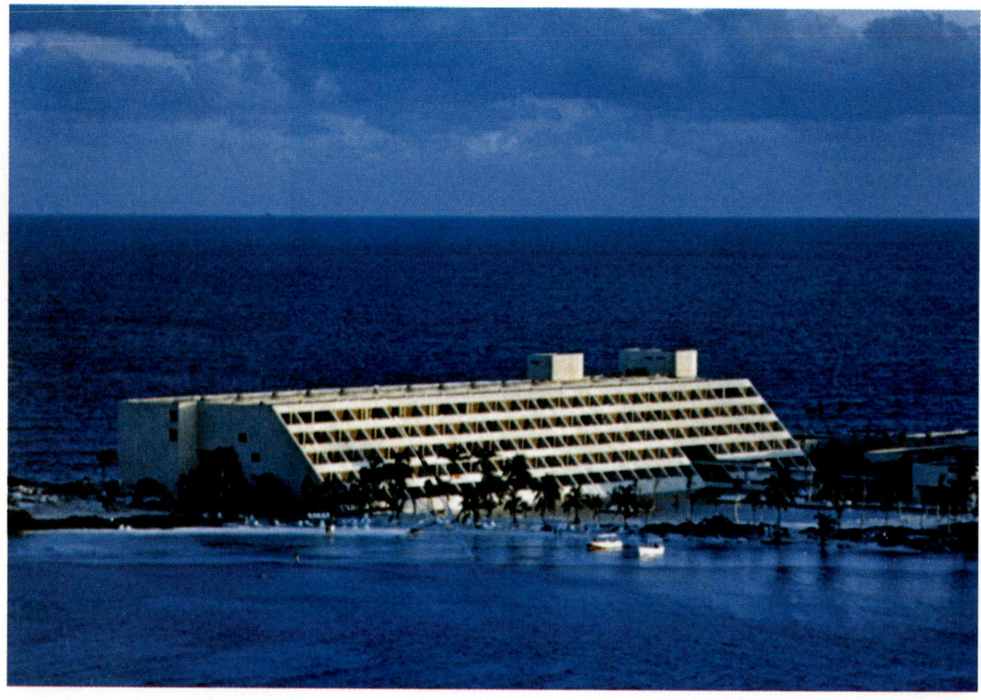

Fig. 8–23 **What features of this structure remind you of the pyramids at Teotihuacán, pictured in Fig. 8–20?**

Ricardo Legorreta, *Camino Real Hotel*, 1981. Cancún, Mexico. Photo courtesy of Legorreta Arquitectos.

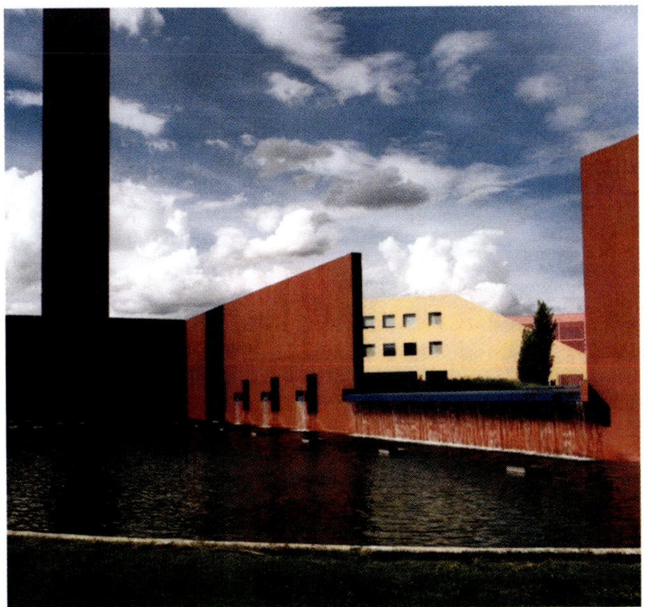

Fig. 8–24 **How did the architect achieve informal balance in the plan for this site?**

Ricardo Legorreta, *Solana Complex*, 1992. Solana, Texas. Photo by Lourdes Legorreta.

Check Your Understanding

1. What kinds of structures were built by the early civilizations in Mexico?
2. Compare features that are similar in many of Legorreta's buildings.
3. If you were to plan a building that shows features from both traditional and contemporary Mexican architecture, what are some things you might include?

Studio Time

Planning a Public Space

Draw a plan or aerial view for a public gathering place, such as a shopping mall or town center.

- Consider how people and traffic will move through this space.
- Think about how you will show details. Will there be places for people to sit? Will there be different levels?
- You may wish to make a three-dimensional model of your public space.

Reflect on how well your drawing shows a plan for an open, public space.

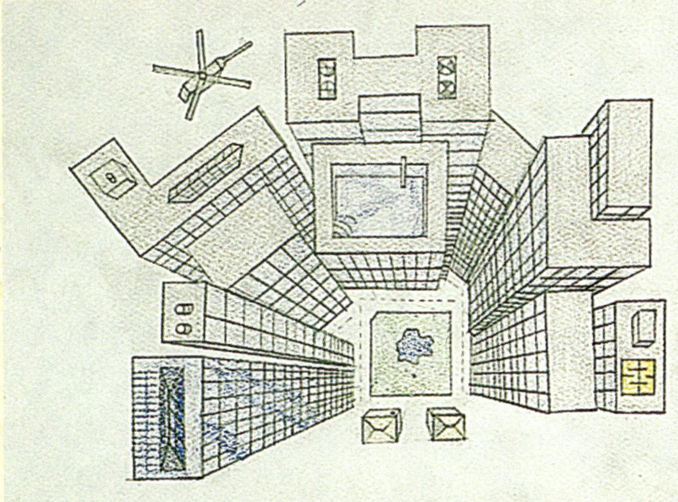

Fig. 8–25 Student artwork

Thrilling Architecture

Studio Background

Do you think of roller coasters as one of life's greatest thrills? Many people do. While riding on a roller coaster, you cannot admire its complex details. But if you look at this ride from the ground, you can see its graceful form and delicate balance.

In this studio exploration, you will plan and construct a track for marbles. How can you build a structure that will direct rolling marbles on a thrilling ride? How will you use form and balance to create a graceful ride for the marbles? Think about curves, gentle and steep rises, and spirals. Think about the kind of motion and speed that these features create.

You Will Need

- sketch paper
- pencil
- corrugated paper or other flexible, sturdy paper
- scissors
- glue

Step 1 **Plan and Practice**

- Think about roller coasters you have seen or ridden. What is their overall shape? What holds the cars up off the ground? How high are they? How steep are the drops?
- Make some sketches of what you remember.

Things to Remember:

✓ Give your form balance. Will it be radial, symmetrical, or asymmetrical?

✓ Create an obvious starting point for your marble.

✓ Make sure your marbles can travel easily through your ride.

Inspiration from Our World

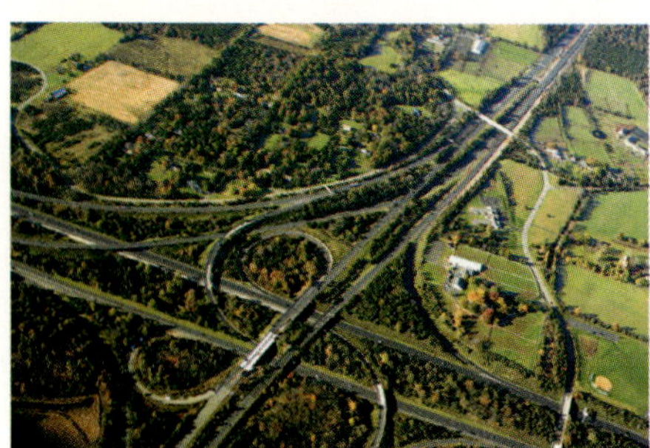

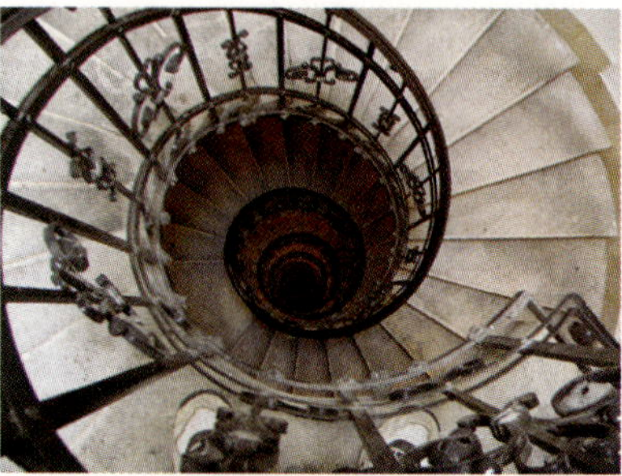

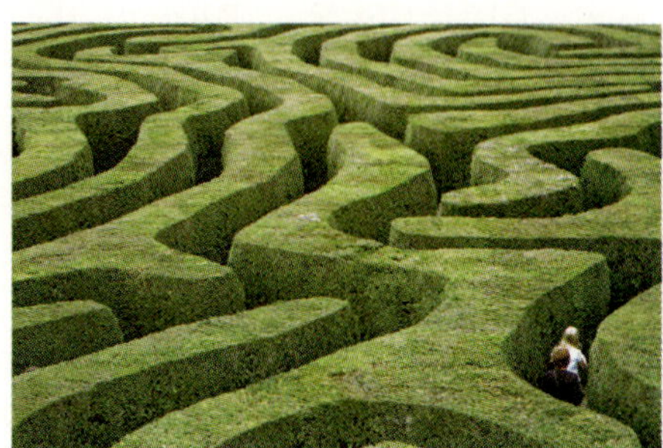

Inspiration from Art

Construction on the Eiffel Tower began in 1887. Because of its size, it was designed to ensure wind resistance. The tower is made of beams, straight pieces of metal. The 18,000 beams are held together by riveting, a tried and tested construction method at the time. The tower needed 2,500,000 rivets. About 300 people were needed to build the tower. It took 22 months to build the structure, which rises 81 stories.

Elevators move up the curving legs from ground level. They lean slightly as the elevator rises, to keep the floor level for passengers. During the Nazi occupation of Paris, the French cut the elevator cables so that Hitler would have to walk all the way up.

More than 200 million people have visited the Eiffel Tower since it opened in 1889.

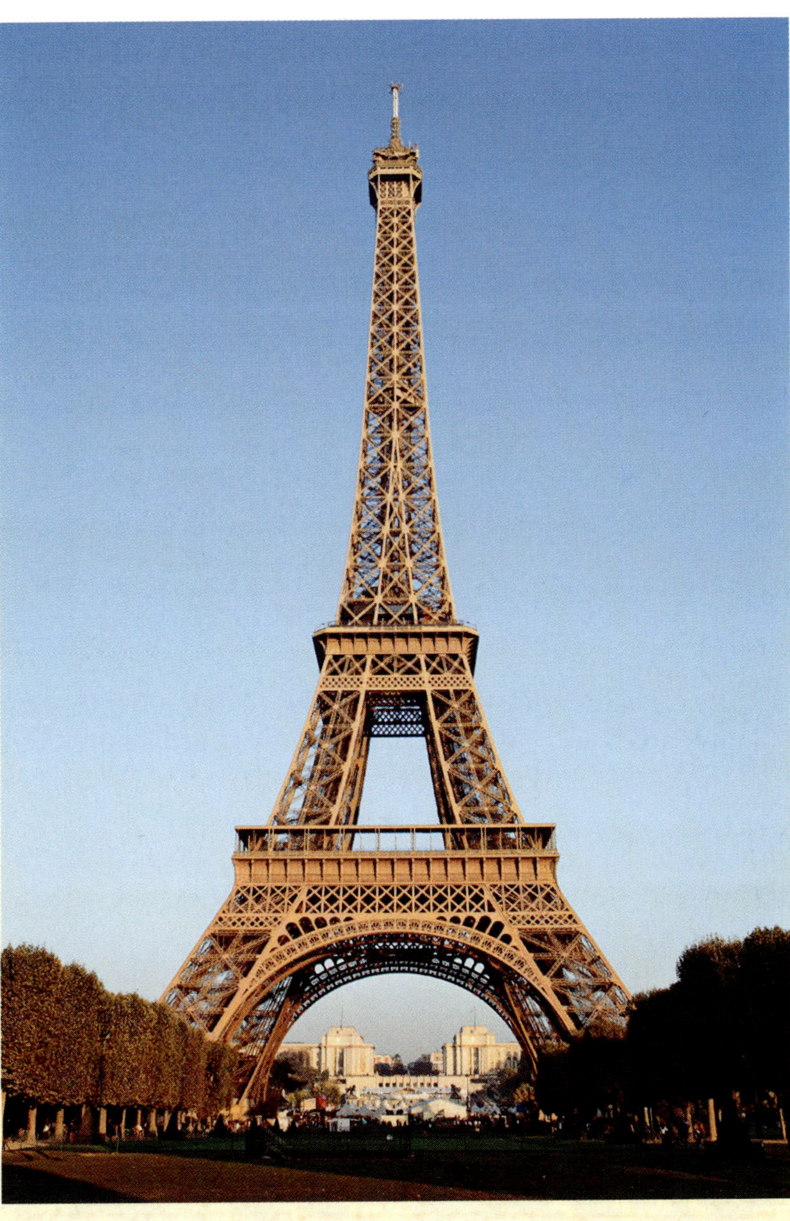

Fig. 8–26 **Eiffel Tower**

Step 2 **Begin to Create**

- Come up with a final plan for your marble roller coaster, and make a more detailed drawing. Will you create a tall spiral or a spiral design that sits flat on a surface? Will it be a maze that the marble will move through? Or will your design use several of these features? What kinds of runways will you design?
- Think about how the parts of your roller coaster will fit together.
- **Construct runways: Glue strips of corrugated paper together.** Remember to consider the size of your marbles when planning the width of runways. Make walls on both sides so that marbles will not fall off.

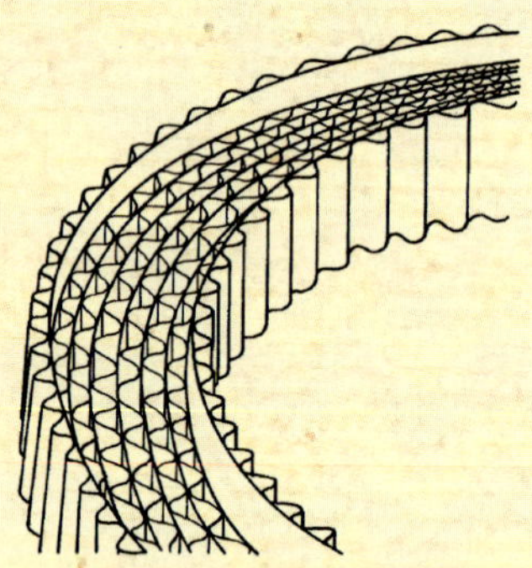

- **If flat, tightly coil a long strip of corrugated paper into a large spiral disk.**

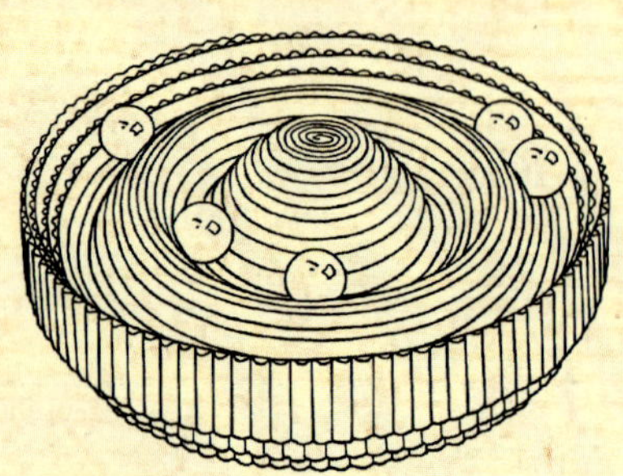

- **If a tall spiral, create a sturdy cardboard cylinder, and wrap a curving runway in corkscrew fashion along its length.**

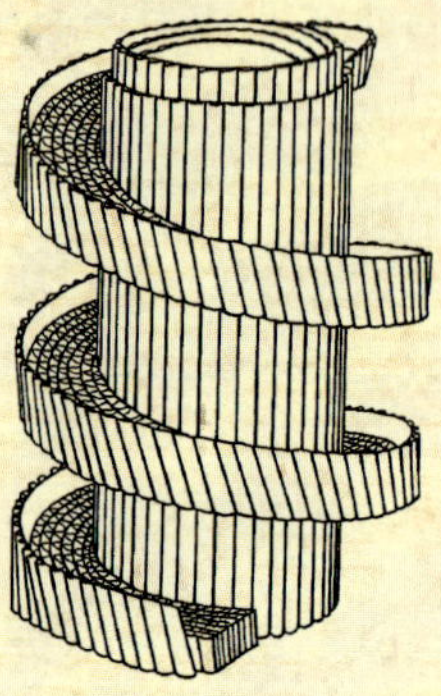

- Construct mazes: Use a sheet of corrugated paper as the "floor." **Create walls by gluing strips to the floor.**

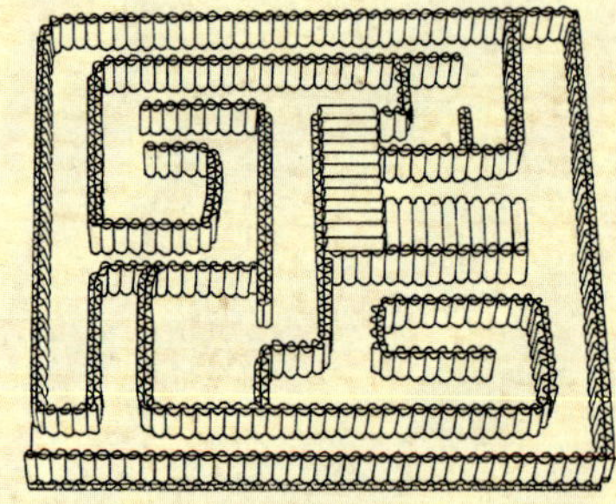

- After you put your roller coaster together, send some marbles on a test run!

Step 3 **Revise**

Did you remember to:

- ✓ Give your form balance?
- ✓ Create an obvious starting point for your marble?
- ✓ Make sure your marbles can travel easily through your ride?

Adjust your work if necessary. In your sketchbook, make a note of your revisions and why you made them.

Step 4 **Add Finishing Touches**

- Will you paint your roller coaster? Will you add details with paint or a marker to make it look like a real one?

Step 5 **Share and Reflect**

- Demonstrate how your ride works.
- Explain how you came up with your ideas. What kinds of forms did you include? How did you create balance?
- What would change if you made another marble track?

Art Criticism

Describe What structural elements do you see in this construction?

Analyze How did the artist arrange the parts of this construction?

Interpret How does the design of this marble run suggest a thrilling ride?

Evaluate What about this marble run appeals to you?

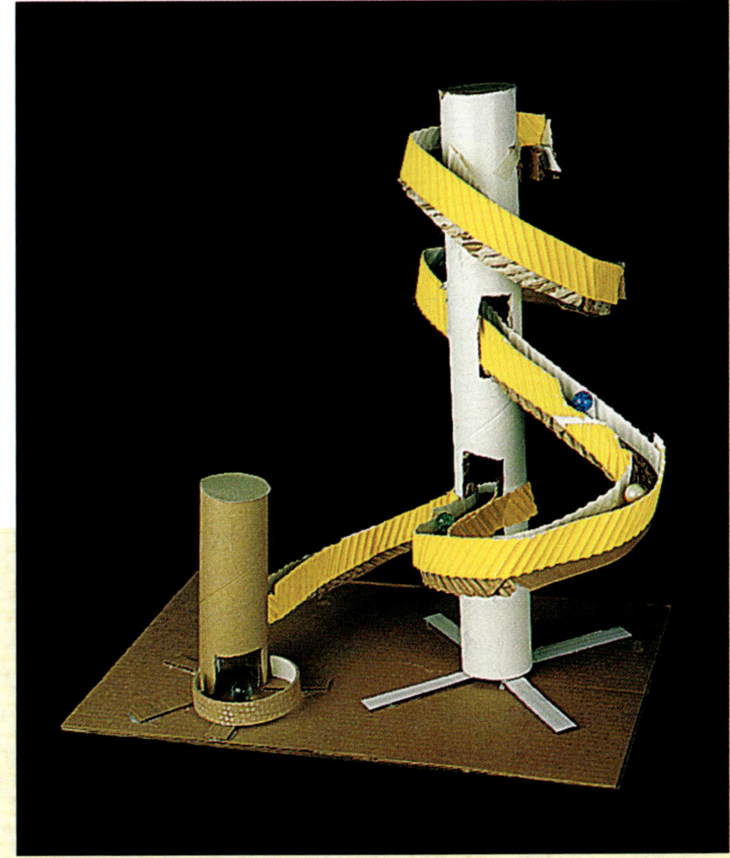

Fig. 8–27 Student artwork

Social Studies

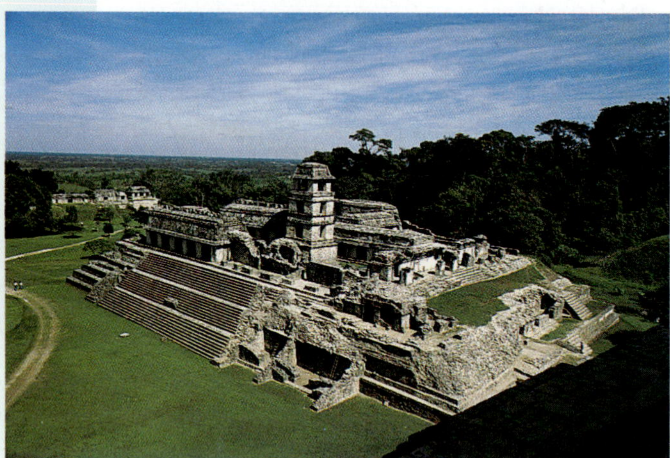

Fig. 8–28 **Archaeology has uncovered and preserved many sites of the ancient Mesoamerican and South American cultures.**

PreColumbian Mexico, Palenque (Maya), *Palace* (general view), c. 720–783 AD. Photo courtesy of Karen Durlach.

How do people find out about the past? Archaeologists are scientists who study past human life by digging for objects and remains. This requires careful planning. First, they must choose and locate a place to dig. They must also learn about the location through research. Then, they use special methods to uncover and identify objects. They preserve what they find by keeping records and carefully packing what they find. What makes each of these steps important?

Dance

Dancers plan their movements using the space around them. The person who plans and arranges the different steps and movements of a dance is called a choreographer. Choreographers may be inspired by a piece of music. Or they may be inspired to create a dance that tells a story. Choreographers work with and without music. When have you seen a dance that may have been arranged by a choreographer?

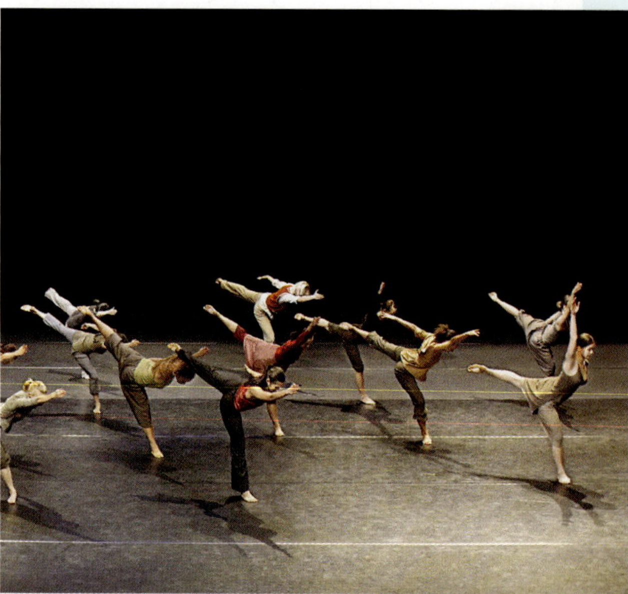

Fig. 8–29

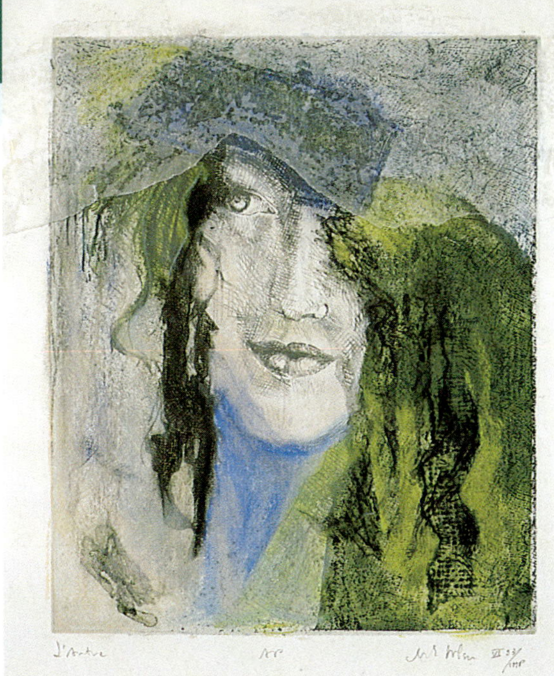

Fig. 8–30 **Printmakers plan their work carefully, deciding where and how to use lines, shapes, colors, and textures.**

Mary Ellen Wilson, *L'Autre*, 1996. Ink and pastel on paper, 8" x 10" (20.3 x 25.4 cm). Courtesy of the artist.

Careers **Printmaker**

Have you ever watched a printmaker transfer an image onto a shirt? This process is similar to what a fine-art printmaker does. Printmakers are artists who use different techniques to produce prints that are original. These prints are usually limited in number and printed by hand. They may use age-old techniques such as etching. Or they may use newer processes like screen or stencil printing. Many universities offer a fine-arts degree in printmaking. Graduates of these programs may teach in a college or university.

Daily Life

Imagine that you were planning a trip to another country so you could look at the artwork. What would you need to do to plan the trip? You might start by doing research about the country and its museums. You may need to get a guidebook or maps. You might need a phrasebook if you do not know the language of that country. You would have to get a passport and make airplane reservations. What are the advantages of careful planning?

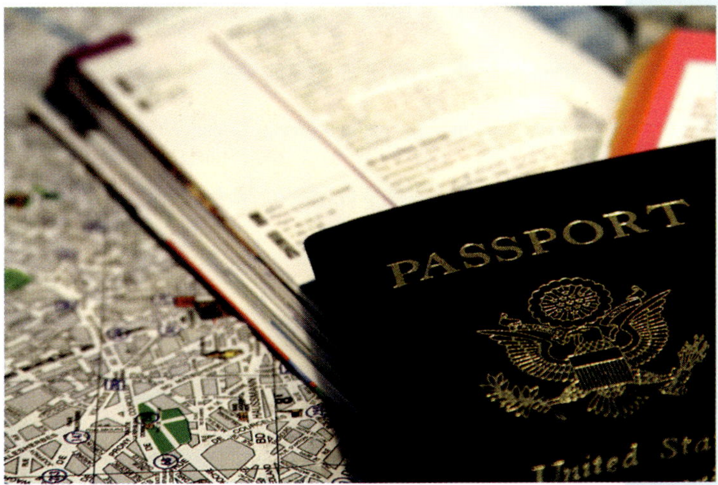

Fig. 8–31

Unit 8 Vocabulary and Content Review

Vocabulary Review

Match each art term below with its definition.

architectural model
hacienda
Post-Modernism
cantilever

1. a large, agricultural estate
2. a small, three-dimensional presentation of a building
3. a trend in architecture which mixes familiar shapes and details in unexpected ways
4. a beam with a supported end and a freestanding end

Aesthetic Thinking

Should architects consult members of the communities for which they design buildings? Why or why not? What should they consider as they go about their work in terms of social responsibility?

Write About Art

Frank Gehry has said: "I approach each building as a sculptural object." Using this building as an example, explain this statement.

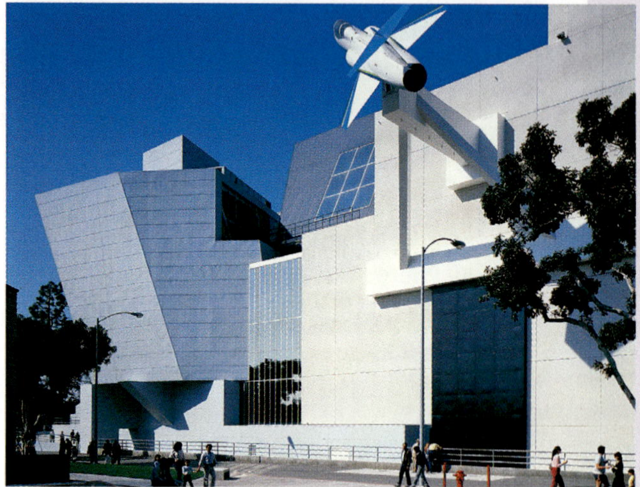

Fig. 8–32 **How does this museum design include humor?**

Frank Gehry, *Aerospace Museum*, 1984. Los Angeles, California. Photo ©Michael Moran.

For Your Sketchbook

Fill a sketchbook page with building designs that show qualities like security or wisdom. For example, you could represent security with a building that has features of a combination lock.

Art Criticism

Describe What do you see in this artwork?

Analyze How does the artist use line?

Interpret Why do you think she created a series of lines over the drawing of the house?

Evaluate Do you think you'd like to live in this house? Why or why not?

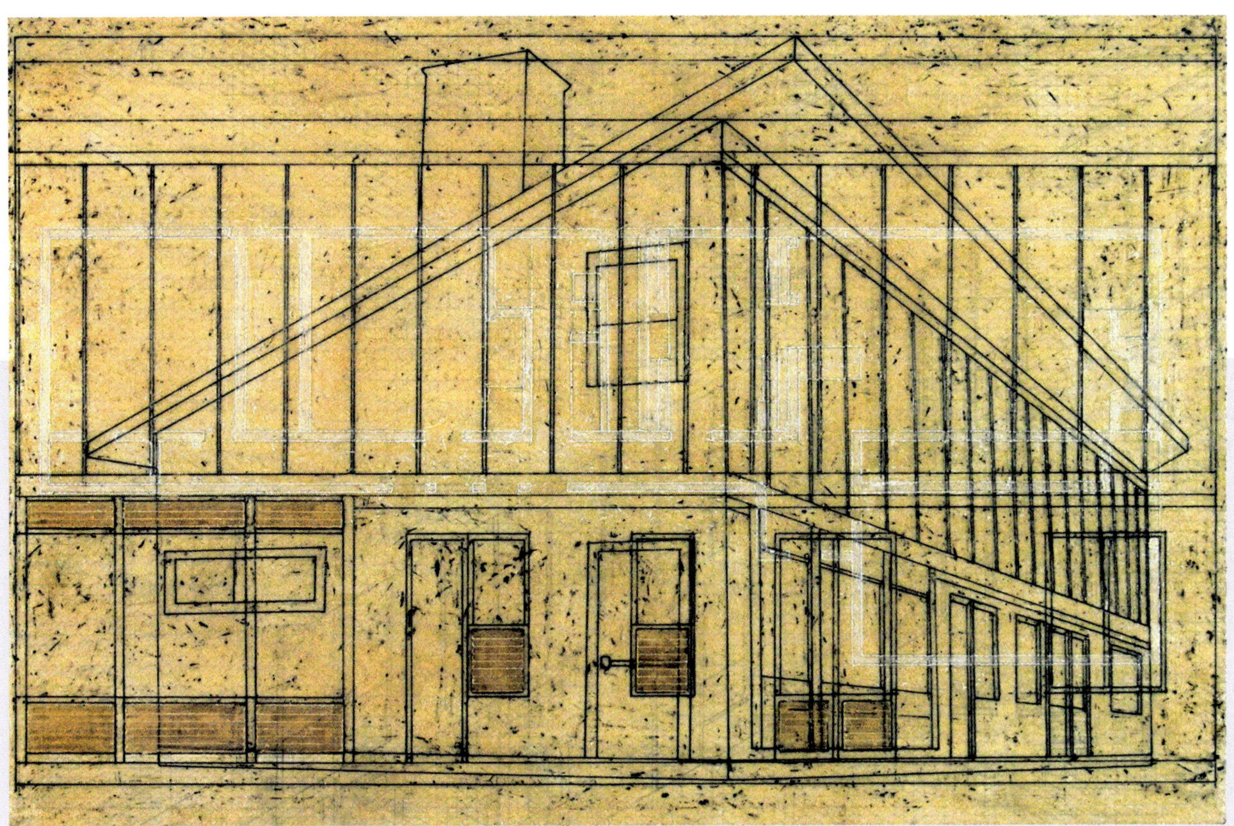

Fig. 8–33 Based on Eleanor Raymond's design. Cheryl Goldsleger, *Solar House*. Photo: Cheryl Goldsleger. Courtesy of Kidder Smith Gallery, Boston.

For Your Portfolio

Keep your portfolio organized. Always date and clearly identify each item in your portfolio, and place a sheet of tissue paper or newsprint between each piece.

Meet the Artist

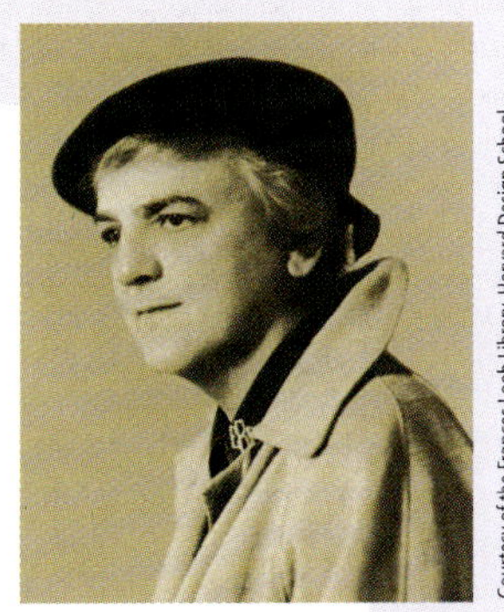

Courtesy of the Frances Loeb Library, Harvard Design School.

Eleanor Raymond (1888–1989) was born in Cambridge, Massachusetts. Educated at The Cambridge School of Architecture and Landscape Architecture, she opened her own architecture office in 1928 and designed homes based on early American architecture.

Unit 9

Artists Are Pioneers

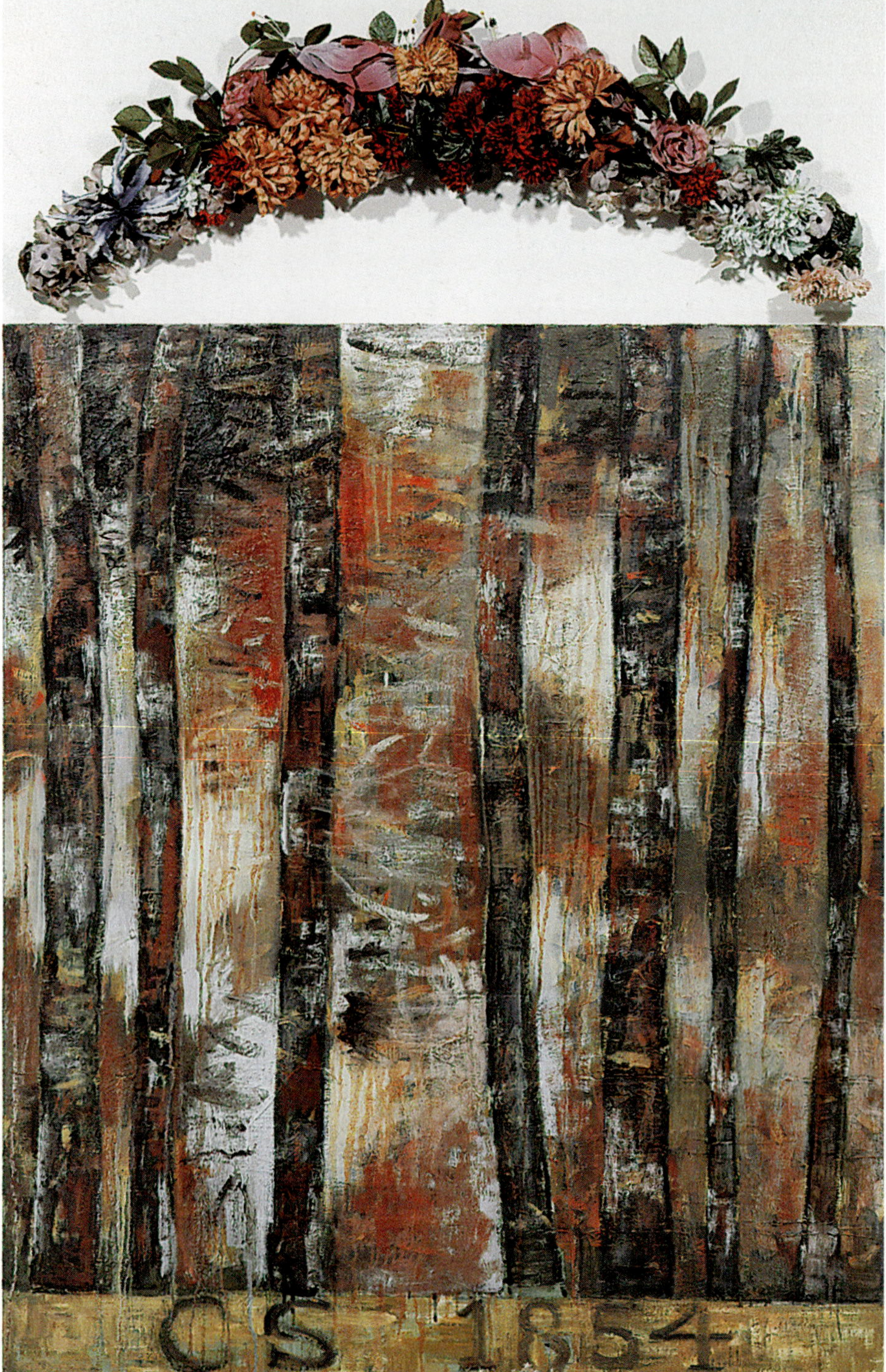

Fig. 9–1 **Smith placed a funeral spray of flowers above her painting. How does this highlight the slow death of our environment?**

Jaune Quick-to-See Smith, *Requiem*, 1990. Oil and beeswax on canvas, silk flower wreath, 48" x 72" (122 x 183 cm).

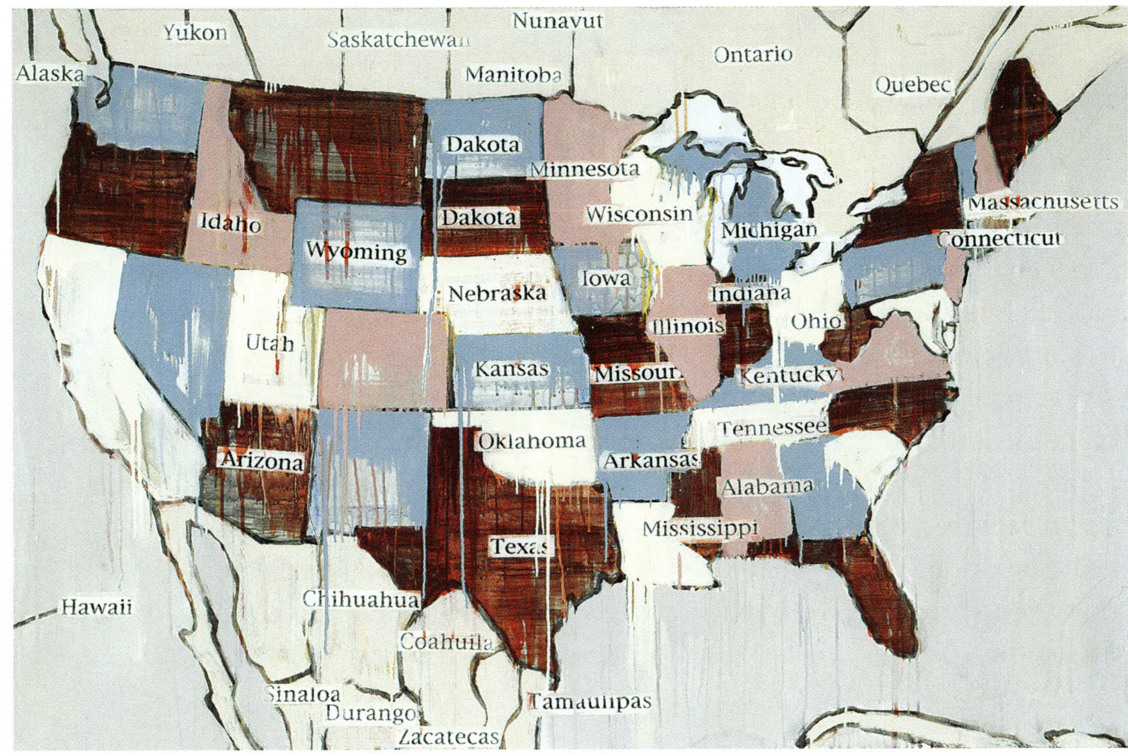

Fig. 9–2 **This artist labeled all of the states that have Native American names. What is your first reaction to this artwork?**

Jaune Quick-to-See Smith *State Names #2*, 2000. Oil and collage on canvas, 48" x 72" (122 x 183 cm).

Imagine traveling to a new "territory," perhaps as far away and as fictional as a new galaxy—or as close and as real as a problem in math class today. Many scientists are pioneers. They can never be sure where their explorations may lead. They think about what they know and then experiment in new directions.

Many artists have also been pioneers. As each age sees developments in technology, artists explore new materials and techniques for making art. Pioneering artists explore new ideas and present them as messages in their artworks, encouraging us to think about, see, and experience the world in new ways.

In this unit, you will learn:

- How artists pioneer new ideas, techniques, and approaches to materials in their artworks.
- How to cast a unique relief sculpture.
- How to notice and interpret new approaches used in artwork.

Breaking New Ground

Artist Jaune Quick-to-See Smith believes that most children learn about Native Americans as if they lived only in the past. As a pioneer of new ways to think about her people, Smith says, "We are very much alive." She challenges over-simplified beliefs called stereotypes, such as those that all Native Americans live in tepees, wear feathered headdresses, or travel in canoes. Some of her artworks point out how Hollywood movies, television, textbooks, and tourist shops do not show Native Americans as they really lived in the past and are living today.

Smith's paintings often send a message that all things, including humans, belong to the earth. Many of her paintings, such as *House* **(Fig. 9–4)**, include pictograms—symbols of plants, animals, humans, and objects. These simple line drawings look like petroglyphs. **Petroglyphs** are rock carvings created by Native Americans hundreds of years ago. Smith layers paint with pictures and words from magazines and newspapers. She says that using familiar images and words creates a way for viewers to see what they already know—but in different ways.

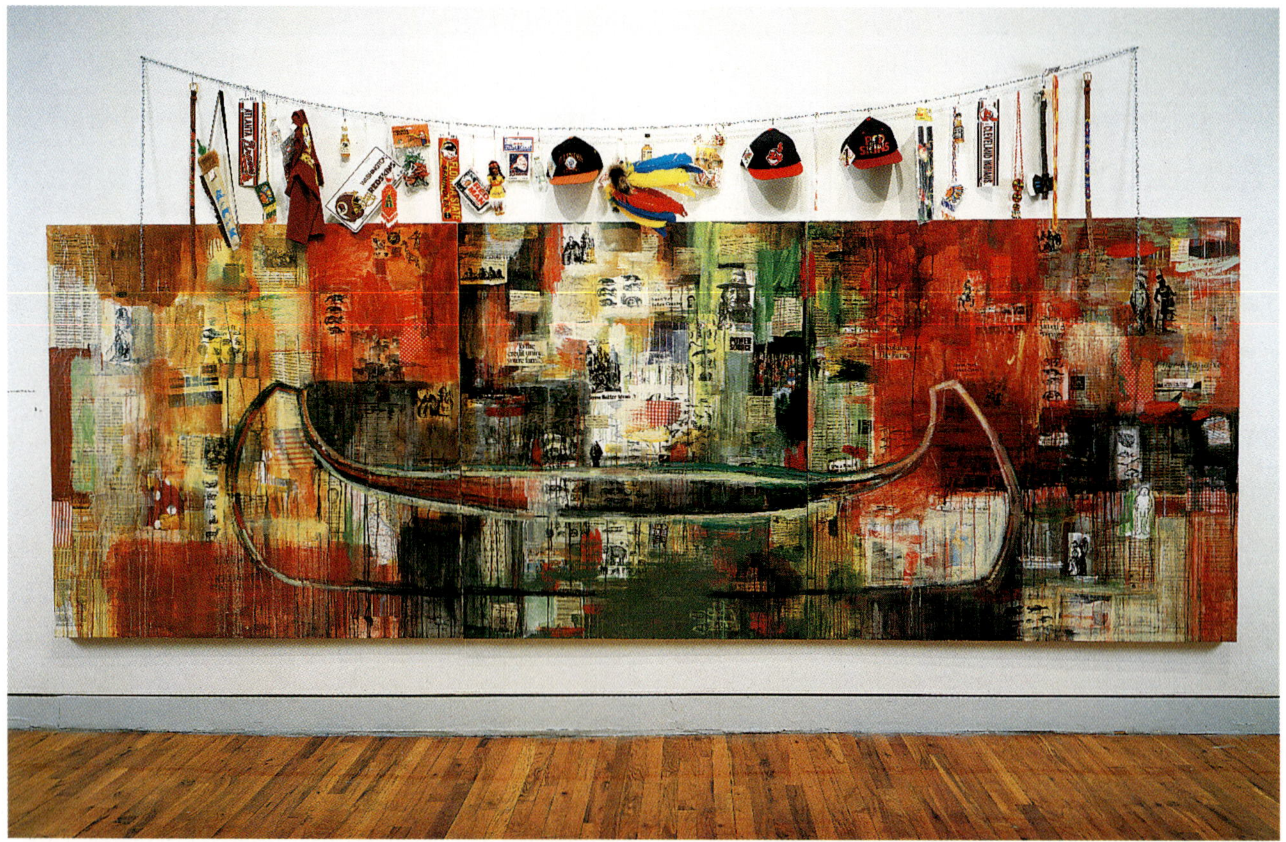

Fig. 9–3 **Smith often points to the ways that Native Americans have been shown. What stereotypes did she explore here?**

Jaune Quick-to-See Smith, *Trade (Gifts for Trading Land with White People)*, 1992. Oil, collage, mixed media on canvas with objects, triptych: 60" x 70" (152 x 178 cm).

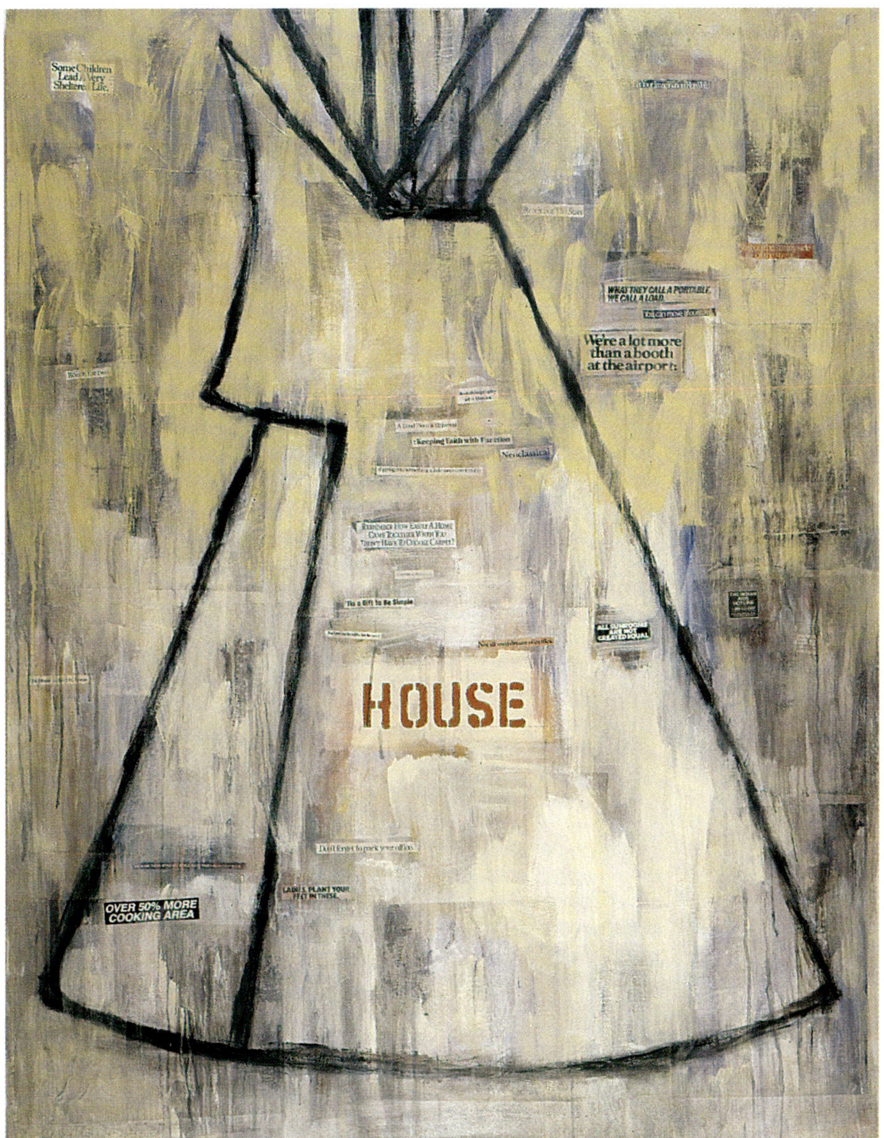

Fig. 9–4 **In this painting, Smith used a pictogram of a tepee and labeled it "HOUSE." What message does this artwork send?**

Jaune Quick-to-See Smith, *House*, 1995. Acrylic, mixed media on canvas, diptych: 80" x 60" (203 x 152 cm).

Meet Jaune Quick-to-See Smith

Born in Montana, Jaune Quick-to-See Smith spent much of her youth traveling. She lived with her father, a rodeo rider and trader. She often worked as a farmhand and used her money from work to take a correspondence art course.

Smith earned a college degree, something few Native Americans of her generation had done. Her artworks today show the influence of artists from the mid-1900s. In addition to making and showing her own artworks, Smith has organized exhibitions for other Native American artists. Her pioneering spirit has helped her create ways for us to see and appreciate their artworks.

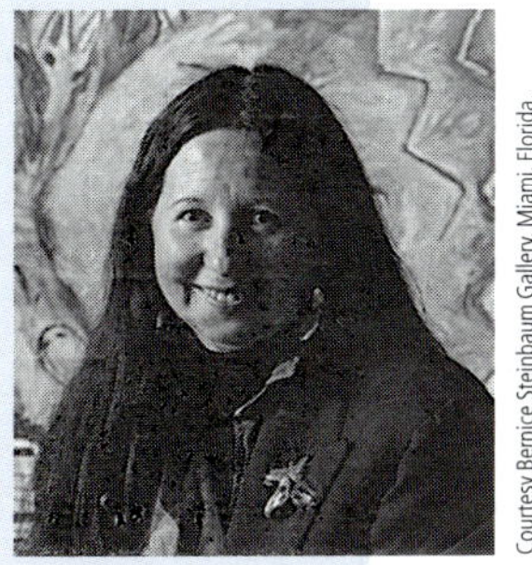

Courtesy Bernice Steinbaum Gallery, Miami, Florida.

"I go from one community with messages to the other and I try to teach and enlighten people."

— Jaune Quick-to-See-Smith (born 1940)

Changing the Way We Think Jaune Quick-to-See Smith thought about what she saw and experimented with new ways to think, work, and act. Other artists have also been pioneers. Marcel Duchamp was among many artists from the 1900s who wanted to make people see art in a different way. In artworks such as *Bicycle Wheel* **(Fig. 9–6)**, Duchamp took ordinary objects and presented them as art. At first, people were shocked by art made from everyday things, but Duchamp's ideas changed what people thought about art. Today, many artworks combine found materials. An assemblage is a sculpture of combined objects, such as boxes, pieces of wood, and parts of old machines.

Romare Bearden was another artist of the 1900s who made artworks by combining found materials. He combined cut and torn images to create his collage paintings. In *Jazz Village* **(Fig. 9–5)**, for example, he combined images from magazines and other sources. An African American, Bearden pioneered powerful messages about his people. He often showed what life was like—both good and bad—for African Americans living in the city.

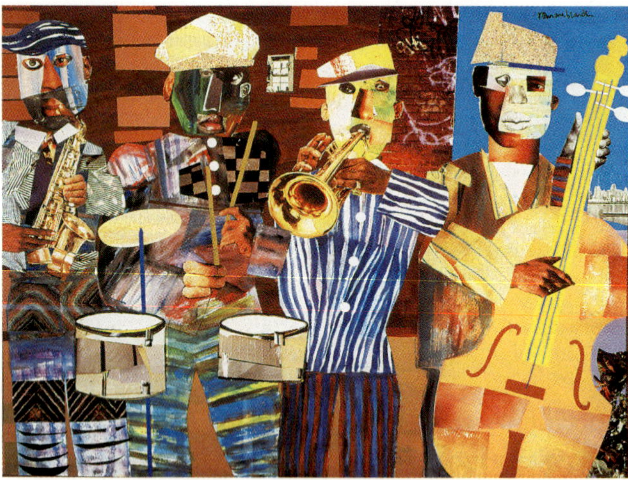

Fig. 9–5 **Romare Bearden often celebrated the importance of music, especially jazz, in African American culture. How do the shapes, colors, and textures connect with the musical form of jazz?**

Romare Bearden, *Jazz Village*, 1967. Mixed media and collage, 30" x 40" (76 x 101.6 cm). ©Romare Bearden Foundation/Licensed by VAGA, New York, New York.

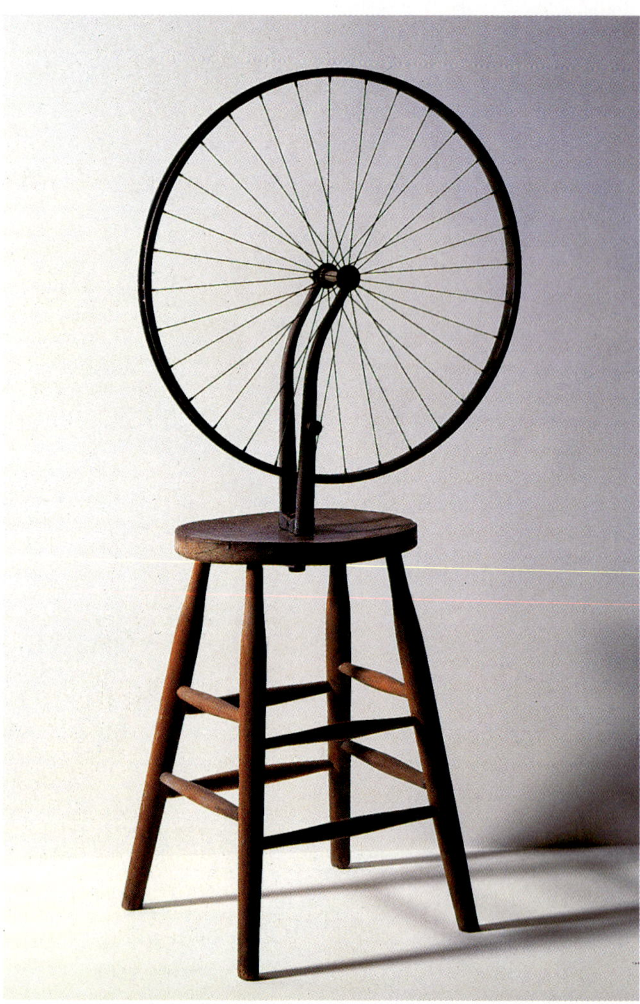

Fig. 9–6 **Why might some people have referred to Duchamp's work as junk sculpture?**

Marcel Duchamp, *Bicycle Wheel*, 1963. Readymade: metal wheel mounted on painted wood stool, height 49 ¼" (125 cm). Collection of Richard Hamilton, Henley-on-Thames, Great Britain. Cameraphoto/Art Resource, New York. ©2001 Artists Rights Society (ARS), New York/ADAGP/Estate of Marcel Duchamp.

Studio Time

Changing Old Habits

Breaking new ground sometimes begins with looking to the past and thinking about how changing things can make a difference. There are risks involved in making changes and breaking new ground.

In this studio experience you can use art that you have made in the past to explore new possibilities for presenting it.

- You can use the actual artwork, or you can make a color copy of it and use the copy.
- Study the artwork carefully and think about how and where to cut it apart. Consider making all horizontal, all vertical, or all diagonal cuts. Will your sections be all the same width or will you vary the size?
- Once you have your work cut apart, play around with different ways to position the strips. Notice how even very small shifts in position can make a big difference in the way things look.
- When you are satisfied with the new look, carefully glue the pieces to a background paper.

Reflect on how you felt about "destroying" an old artwork, and whether you think you improved the artwork by changing it.

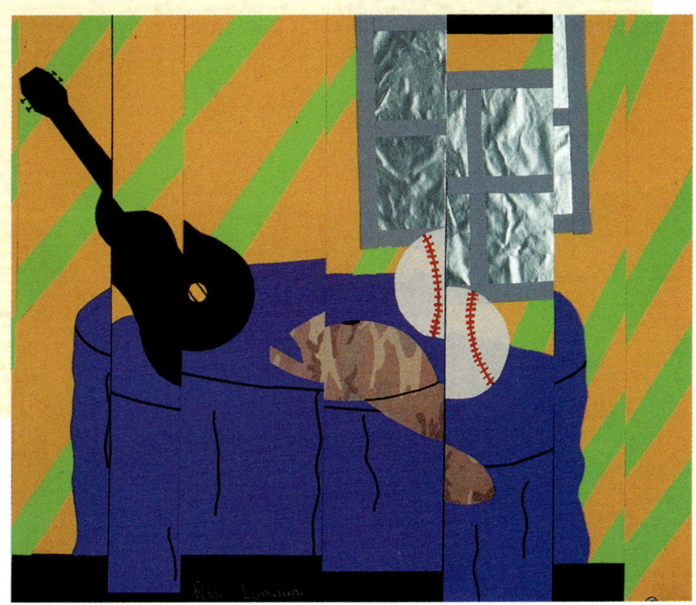

Fig. 9–7 Student artwork

Check Your Understanding

1. What items might be used to create an assemblage?
2. Compare and contrast Jaune Quick-to-See Smith's paintings from this lesson. How are they similar? How are they different?
3. Identify an artist pioneer other than Smith, and explain how one of his or her works showed a pioneering spirit.

Relief Sculpture

If you've ever been in a cemetery, you've probably seen relief sculpture. Relief sculpture is sculpture that projects from a background surface instead of standing on its own. Relief sculptures are made to be seen from one side only, as a wall plaque is. There are two kinds of relief sculpture: high relief and low relief.

High relief sculpture stands sharply off its background, creating deep shadows. Fig. 9–8 is an example of high relief sculpture. Notice the shadowy spaces formed by using thick pieces of wood. Low relief sculpture stands out only slightly from its background, so it produces few shadows. Coins are good examples of low relief sculpture. Some artworks include examples of both high and low relief.

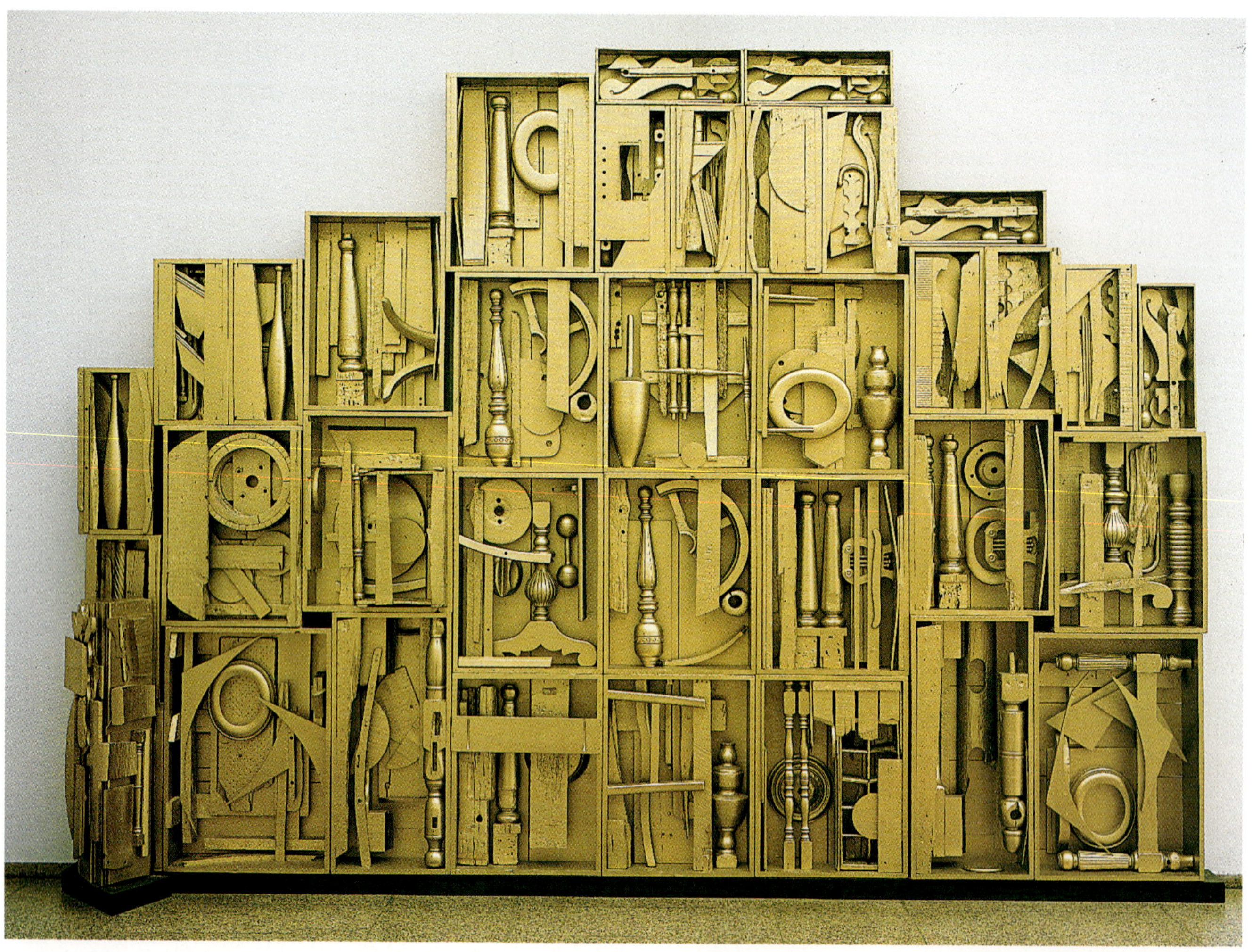

Fig. 9–8 **The artist often assembled found wooden objects and painted them all one color—black, white, or gold.**

Louise Nevelson, *Royal Tide IV*, 1960. Wood painted gold, 132" x 168" x 10" (335 x 427 x 24.4 cm). Stadt Köln, Rheinsches Bidarchiv. ©2001 Estate of Louise Nevelson/ Artists Rights Society (ARS), New York.

Expression in Relief Sculpture Relief sculpture can reflect emotion and ideas, send messages, and make you think, just as any artwork can. Look at Fig. 9–9. What has the artist shown in this low relief sculpture? How is it expressive? Notice the carved muscles on the lioness's front and rear legs, and the way the front of her body reaches upward while she drags her hindquarters.

Low Relief Sculpture You can make low relief sculpture from clay or other modeling materials, soft wood or metal, or from cardboard shapes cut into progressively smaller versions and then glued together. Your sculpture can also be carved or incised. Incise means to cut a shallow line in a material, such as wood.

Fig. 9–9 **The artist created this low relief sculpture to depict a lioness that has been pierced with arrows. How does this sculpture reflect emotion?**

Dying Lioness, Nineveh (Assyria), c. 650 BC. Limestone, height of lion 13 ¾" (35 cm). The British Museum, London.

Observe Look at Fig. 9–9. Where can you see shadows? Are they dark and intense, or delicate? Are they difficult to see? Where does light strike the relief?

Tools: Cardboard, X-Acto™ knife, and glue.

Practice: Cardboard Low Relief Sculpture

- Draw a simple shape on cardboard. Cut it out.
- Trace the cutout shape onto another piece of cardboard. Cut it out, but cut it at a smaller size than the first. Repeat, but cut the third shape smaller than the first two.
- Glue the shapes together, putting the largest shape on the bottom, the next largest on top of it, and so on.
- How have you created relief?

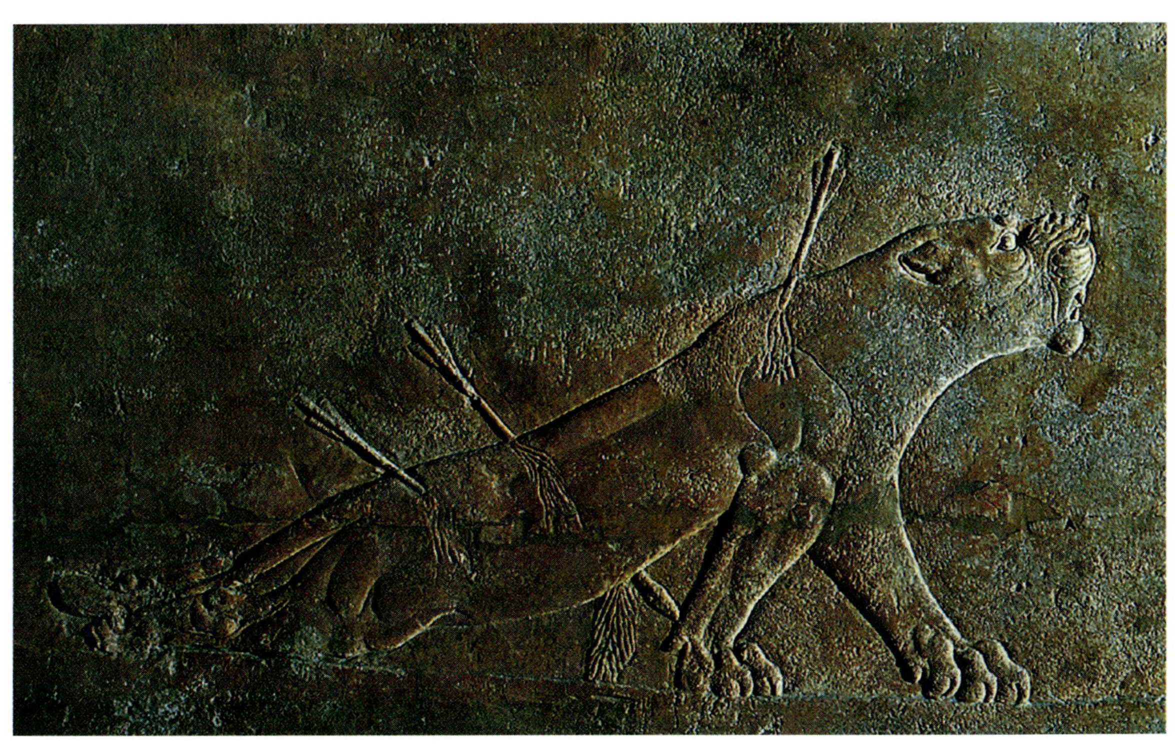

High Relief Sculpture

Artists make high relief sculptures from a number of materials, including found objects, wood, stone, bronze, and plaster. The objects in some high relief sculptures are so close to being three-dimensional that it looks as if you could almost get your hand all the way around them.

Observe Look at Fig. 9–8, which is made of real objects the artist found. Where are the deepest shadows? How deep is the sculpture? Note the deep shadows in Fig. 9–10. How has the artist made the face expressive?

Tools: Modeling clay and clay carving tools.

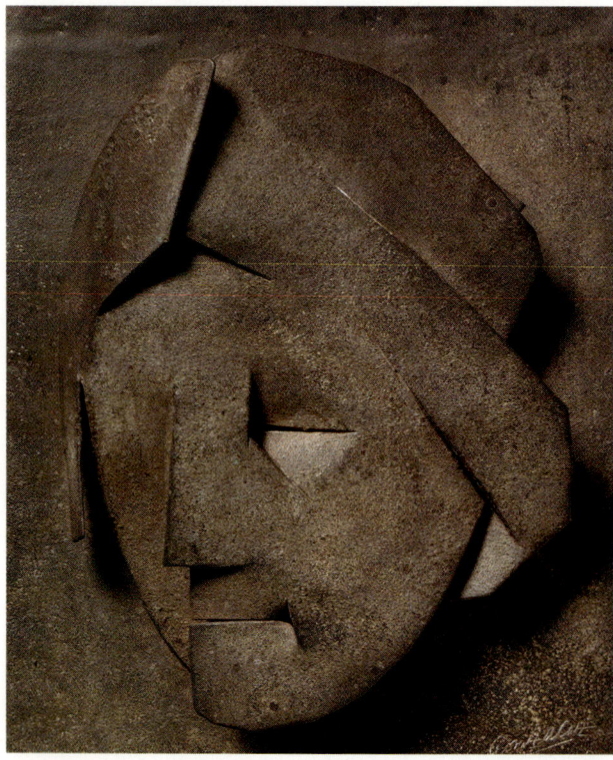

Fig. 9–10 **This is an example of a high relief sculpture. What emotion do you think the artist is trying to express?**

Julio Gonzalez, *Pensive Face*, 1929. Iron mounted on painted wood, 9 5/8" x 7 3/4" (24.5 x 19.7 cm). The Cleveland Museum of Art, Gift of Ralph King, by exchange, 1980.32. Artists Rights Society (ARS), NY.

Practice: Clay Relief

- Draw a simple relief design.
- Work with a square or rectangular slab of modeling clay at least 1" deep.
- Carve, pull, or use small objects to press your design into the clay, making some areas deep. Shine a bright light on the relief. Where are the darkest areas? Where are the highlight areas?

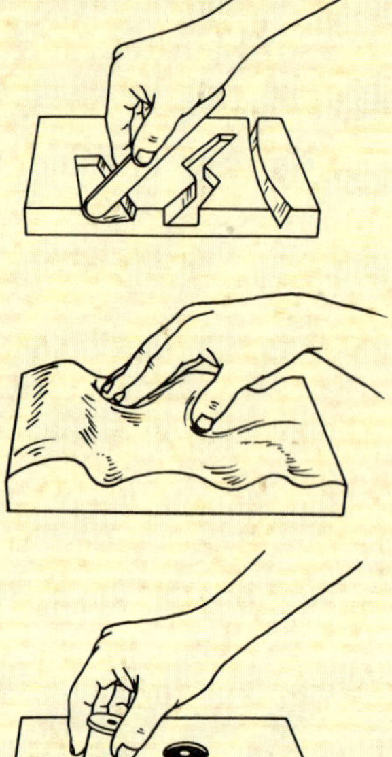

- You can also add small balls and coils of clay to the surface of your slab to create relief.

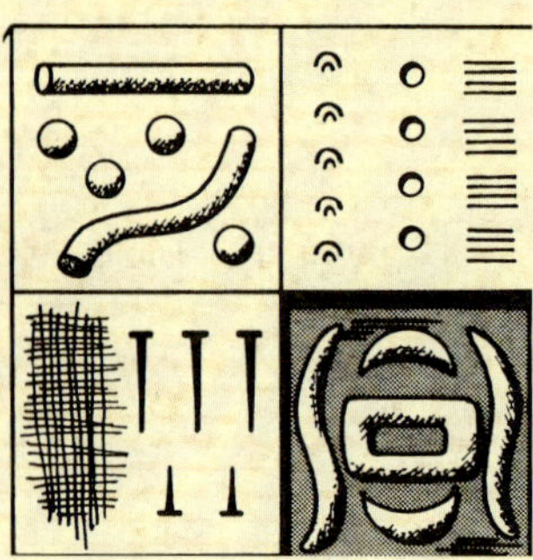

Studio Time

An Expressive Relief

You can create a low-relief sculpture using cardboard and metal foil.

- Begin your relief sculpture as though you were making a collage.
- Collect nearly flat materials such as cardboard, textured paper, fabric, buttons, toothpicks, leaves, weeds, or shells.
- Glue these to cardboard and allow to dry thoroughly.
- Apply thinned white glue to the whole design and place a sheet of metal foil on top of the design.
- Work from the center to the edges, gently pressing the foil down. Fold back the extra foil.
- With a blunt pencil, outline the edges of the shapes you have glued. Add other lines, textures, or patterns to flat areas of the foil.
- To finish your sculpture, brush waterproof ink over the foil. When it is dry, wipe it off with a dry paper towel.

Reflect on the three-dimensional qualities of your relief.

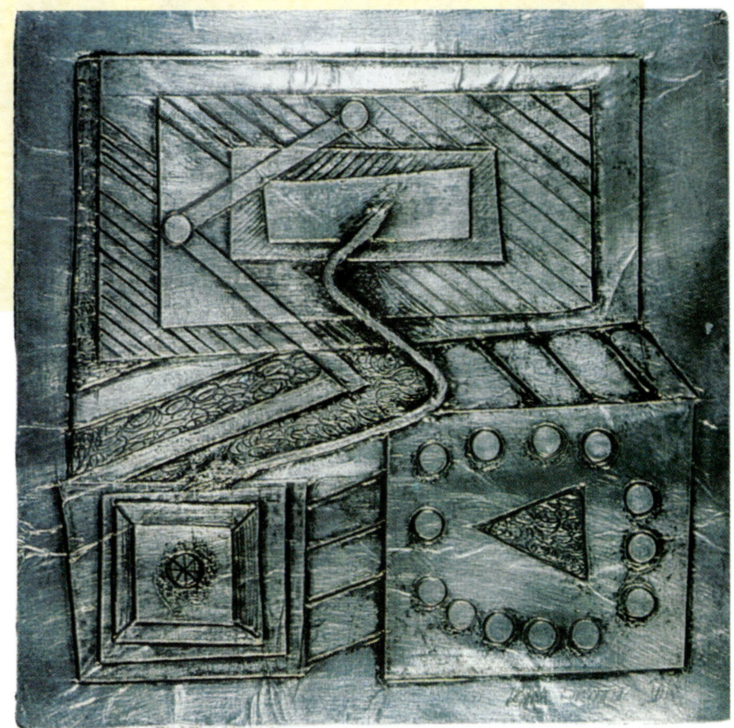

Fig. 9–11 Student artwork

Check Your Understanding

1. What is relief sculpture?
2. Compare and contrast high relief and low relief sculptures.
3. Why might someone want to pay attention to light and shadows when looking at a relief sculpture?

Casting a Relief Sculpture

Studio Background

Many of the sculptures that you see in parks, museums, and galleries are probably made by a process called casting. Casting is a multistep process for creating sculptures in bronze or other materials, such as concrete, plaster, or plastic. Some casting techniques allow an artist to create several identical sculptures from a single mold.

In this studio exploration, you will cast a relief sculpture. You can use wet sand or oil-based clay for the mold. Your final sculpture will be plaster. Think about objects you can press into the sand or clay. What objects would make unusual impressions? How might you combine several objects to make a thought-provoking composition?

You Will Need

- a milk carton or other small box
- scissors
- masking tape
- fine, damp sand or oil-based clay
- one or more textured objects
- plaster

Step 1 **Plan and Practice**

- Choose textured objects for your plaster cast. Look for objects with unusual lines, indentations, and shapes. Will you choose only natural objects, human-made objects, or a combination?
- Will you overlap the objects, or have each appear on its own? Think about size relationships between the objects.
- Remember that all objects will appear plaster-colored when the casting is complete.

Things to Remember:

- ✓ Use a variety of textured objects.
- ✓ Arrange the objects' impressions carefully.
- ✓ Press the objects straight into the sand or clay and lift them straight out again.

Inspiration from Our World

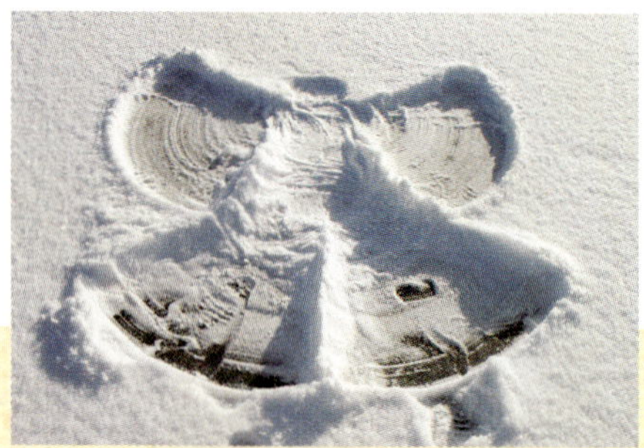

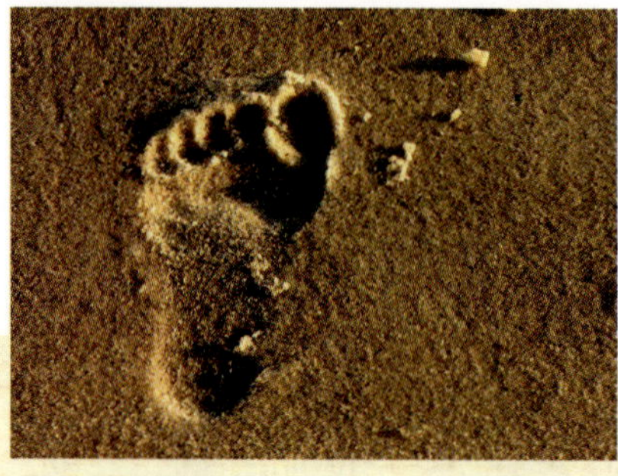

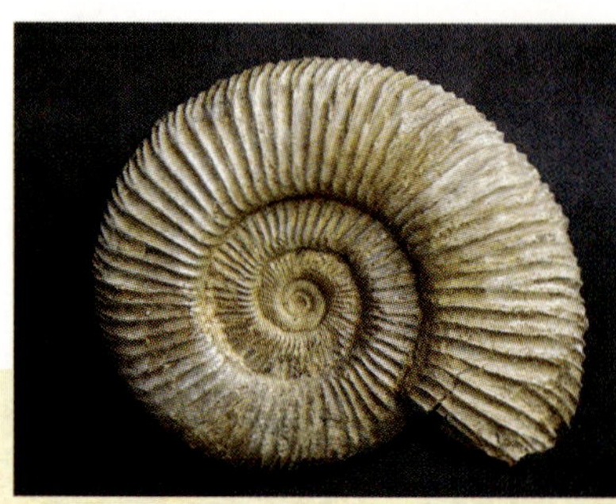

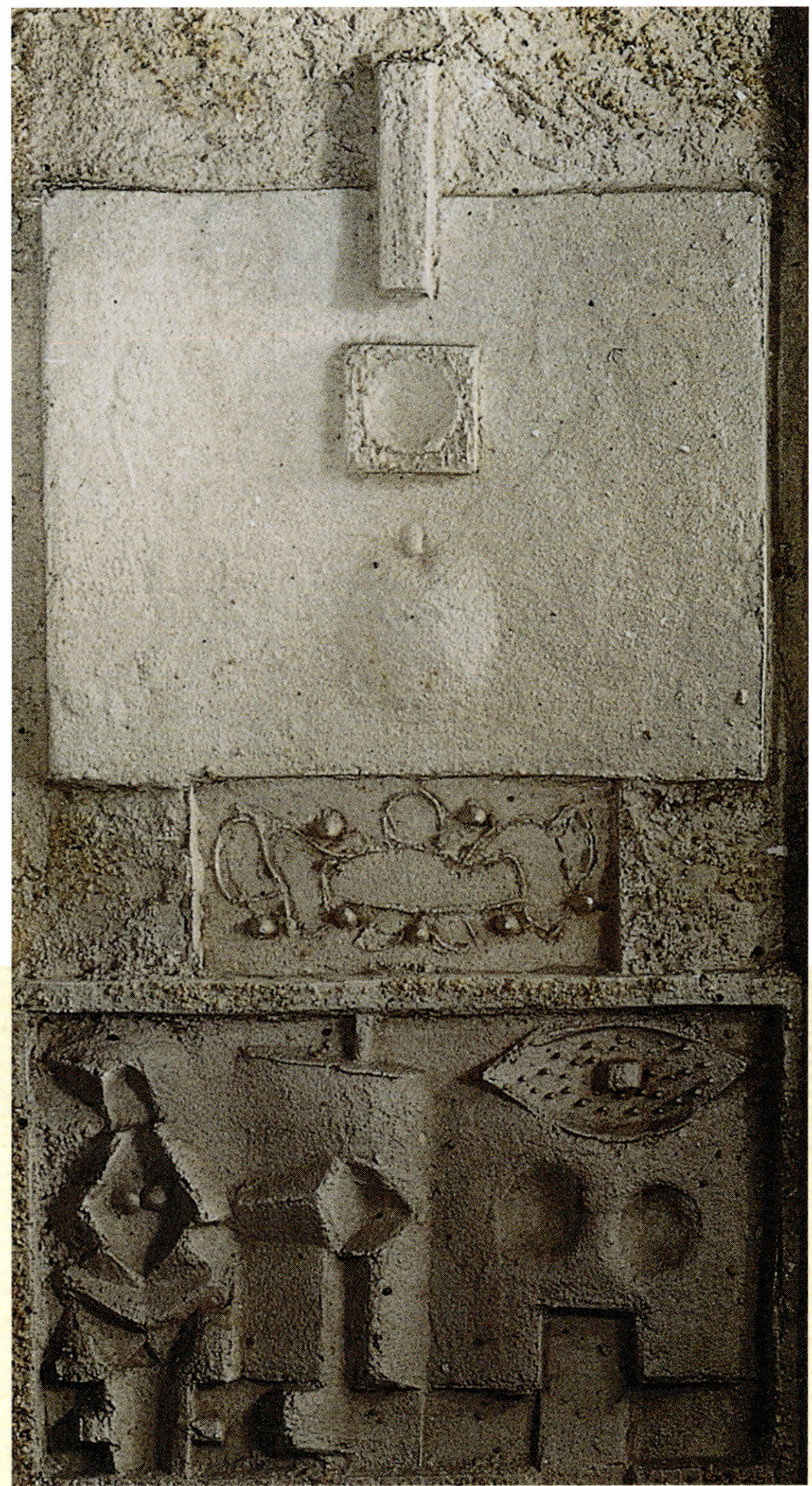

Inspiration from Art

This relief sculpture from sand casting has a subtle textural quality. The artist, Tino Nivola, has been called "the sand man," because he developed this method of working while playing with his children at the beach. To preserve the drawings they made in the sand, he poured plaster over them. From that point on, he perfected this method of sand casting in his studio.

Fig. 9–12 **This relief was created in sand. Think about the objects that the artist could have used to create each different impression.**

Tino Nivola, *Deus*, 1953. Sand and plaster relief sculpture, 64 ¾" x 34 ½" (164 x 88 cm). Collection of Whitney Museum of American Art. Purchase.

Step 2 **Begin to Create**

- Cut off the bottom of a milk carton or other small box. When it is cut, the box should be about 3" deep. **Reinforce the sides of the box by applying a strip of masking tape around the outside.**

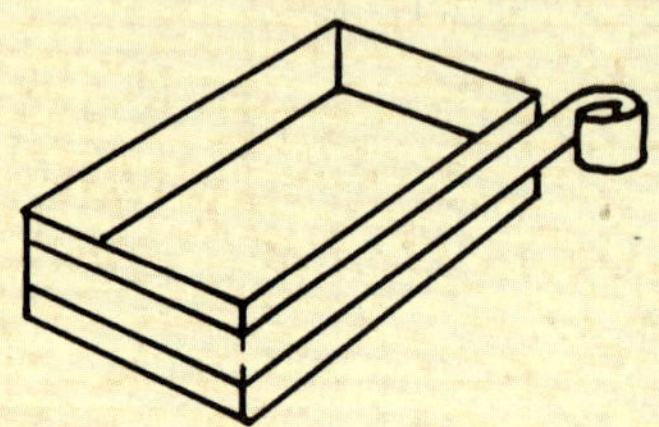

- Place about 1" of fine, damp sand or oil-based clay into the bottom of the container.
- Next, gather one or more textured objects—such as a large seashell, two acorns, or a piece of thick rope—to make impressions into the clay or sand.
- **Press the objects into the clay or sand and lift them straight out again.** This will create a mold, or negative design, for your sculpture: whatever you press into the clay will appear raised up in the final sculpture.
- When your design is ready, mix the plaster.

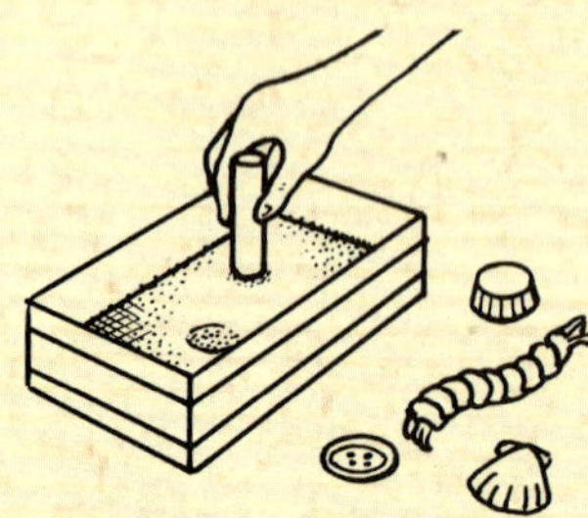

- Slowly pour the plaster into the box. If you are pouring into sand, be careful that the plaster does not wash away the sand. Pour the plaster to a depth of about 1".
- If you would like to hang your small relief sculpture, **press a loop of thick string firmly into the wet plaster before it hardens.**

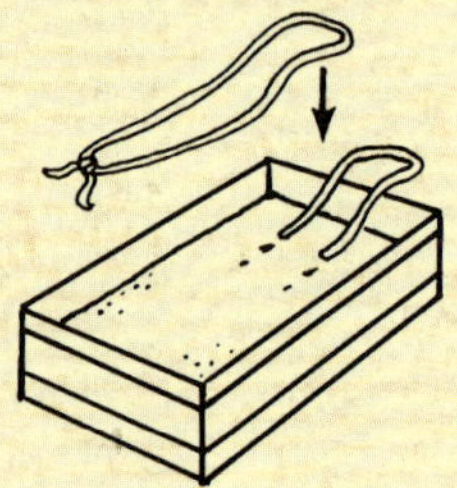

- **After the plaster dries, peel away the box.**

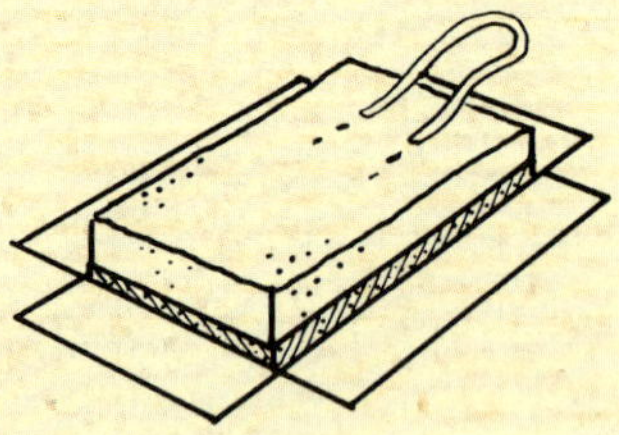

Step 3 **Revise**

Did you remember to:

✓ Use a variety of textured objects?

✓ Arrange the objects' impressions carefully?

✓ Press the objects straight into the sand or clay and lift them straight out again?

Once the plaster has dried, your design is set. It is not possible to change the way the objects are arranged.

Step 4 **Add Finishing Touches**

- Remove the clay, or brush away any sand that sticks to the plaster.
- If you want to keep some of the sand on the sculpture, make sure you shellac it.

Step 5 **Share and Reflect**

- Share your relief with several of your classmates. Compare choice of objects, how deeply they were impressed, and size relationships. Note how different textures were reproduced in the plaster.
- Take turns explaining why you chose the objects you did, and what you found most difficult about the process.

Art Criticism

Describe Tell what you see in this sculpture.

Analyze How did the artist arrange the parts in this relief?

Interpret What do you think this sculpture is about?

Evaluate What do you like best about this sculpture?

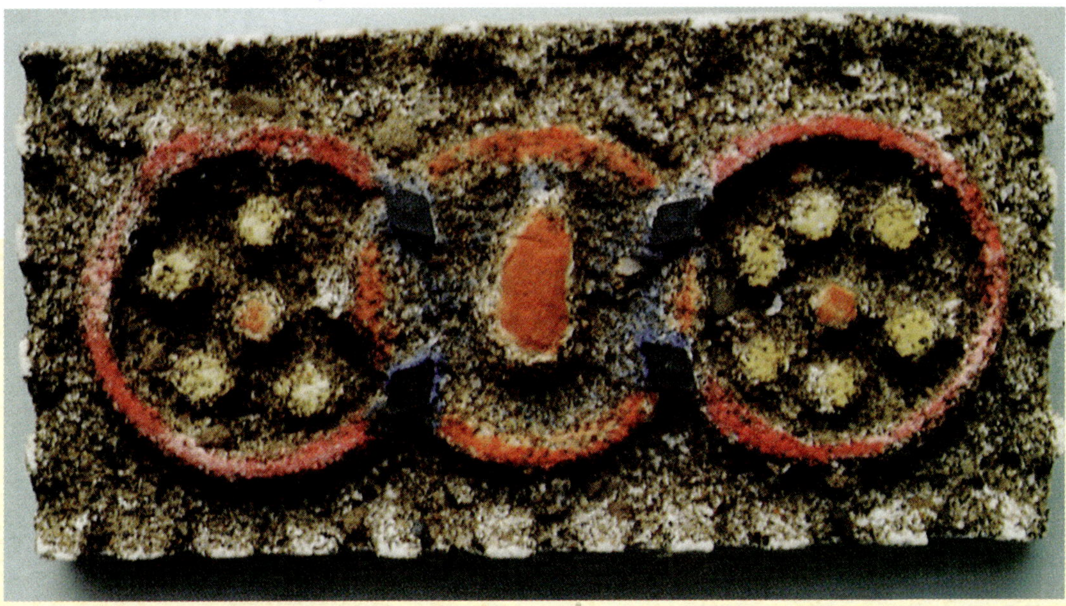

Fig. 9–13 Student artwork

Traditions of Sculpture

Pioneering the Modern Sculpture as an art form has existed since prehistoric times. Some ancient sculpture techniques in stone, wood, and clay are still popular today. In the early 1900s, however, many artists wanted to break with existing styles, to create truly "modern" art. They experimented with new, human-made materials and technology. Other artists used traditional materials, such as wood, plaster, or stone. They explored the texture of these materials. Texture is the feel and look of a surface. Barbara Hepworth was one of the leading artists in this movement. Her *Oval Sculpture Number Two* **(Fig. 9–14)** is an example of how she experimented with the surfaces and textures of plaster.

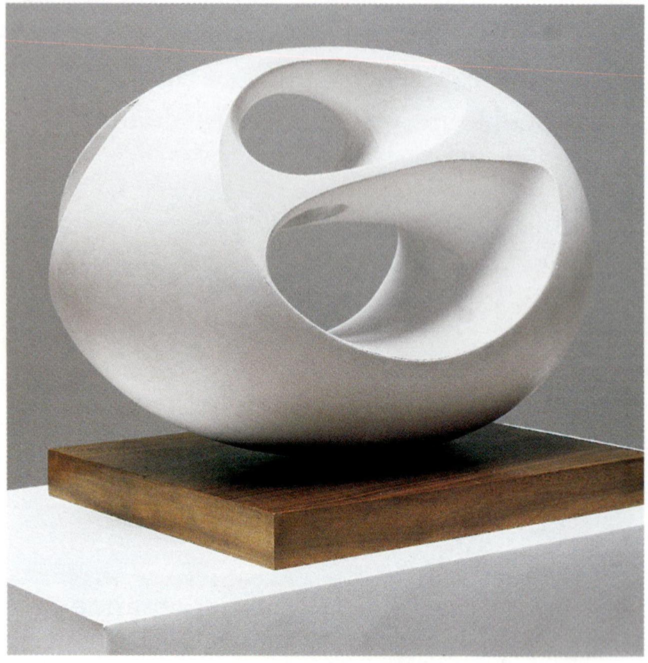

Fig. 9–14 **Hepworth often found inspiration in the natural forms and landscapes of beaches. How does the form of this sculpture look as though it might have been smoothed by sand and ocean waves?**

Barbara Hepworth, *Oval Sculpture Number Two*, 1943. Plaster, 11 ¼" x 16 ¼" x 10" (28.5 x 41.5 x 25.5 cm). The Tate Gallery, London. ©Tate, London 2001. Bowness, Hepworth Estate.

1900s

1943
Hepworth, *Oval Sculpture Number Two*

1947
Jackie Robinson becomes the first African American to play major league baseball.

1955
Chuck Berry releases his first single, becoming a rock and roll pioneer.

1981
Sandra Day O'Connor becomes the first woman named to the Supreme Court.

1992
Koons, *Puppy*

1997
Scottish scientist Ian Wilmut successfully clones an adult mammal.

1999
Dancer, *The Fern Hope Hoop*

New Materials and Places for Art In recent decades, sculptors have looked into using new media and spaces for art. Many artists have started to experiment with materials and surface qualities that are part of everyday life. This has turned the attention of some sculptors, including Jeff Koons (Fig. 9–16), away from the technical skills of carving and casting and toward a focus on ideas.

Sculptor Daniel Dancer is part of a group of pioneering artists whose works are called site-specific sculptures. A site-specific sculpture is a sculpture created for a particular space. It can be temporary or permanent, created indoors or outdoors. In some cases, the artist's purpose is to make viewers more aware of the environment and the textures of natural objects. Dancer works directly with his natural surroundings. For his site-specific sculptures (Fig. 9–15), he first thinks about the site, or location. The site helps determine the form and meaning of the sculpture.

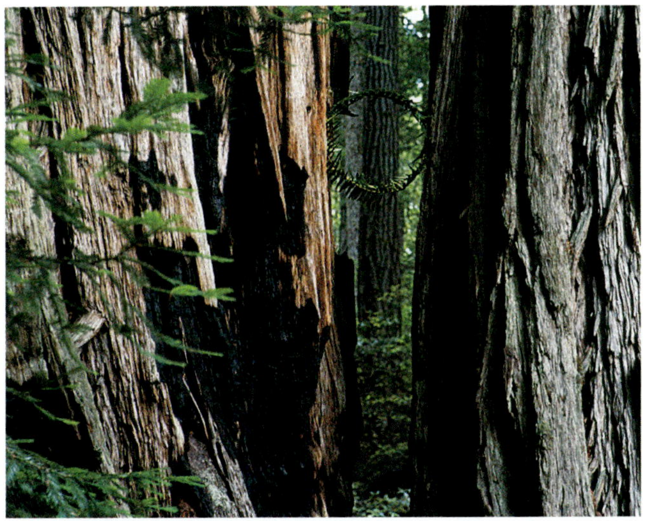

Fig. 9–15 **If you came upon this view while on a walk in the forest, what would be your reaction?**

Daniel Dancer, *The Fern Hope Hoop*, 1999. Fern fronds and redwood tree, hoop: 24" x 24" (61 x 61 cm). Courtesy of the artist.

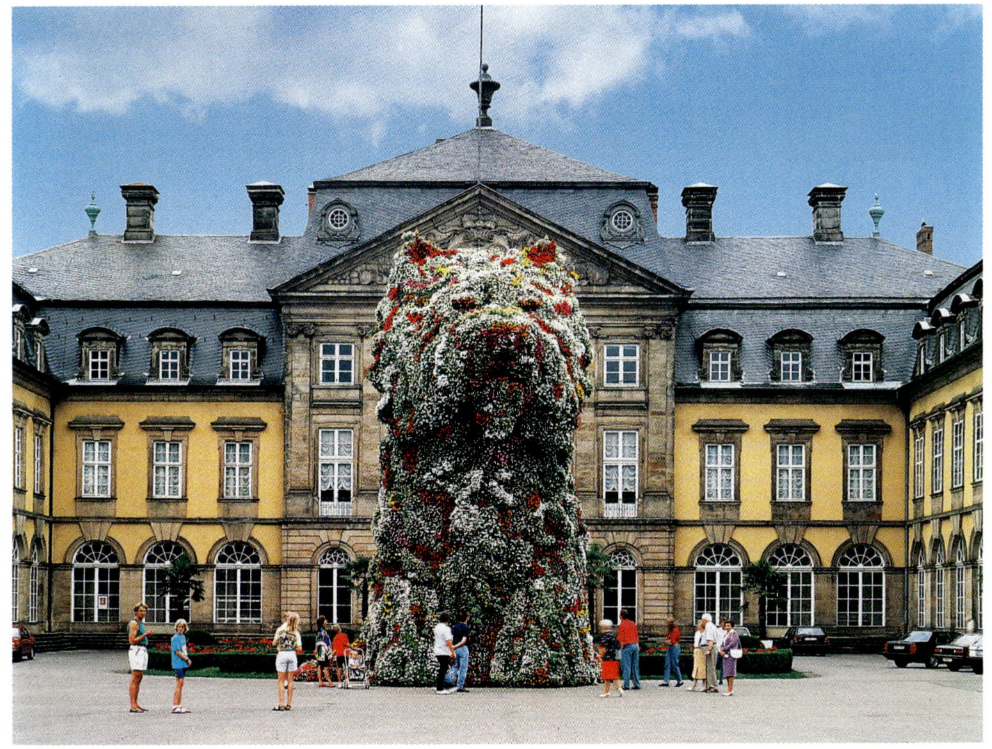

Fig. 9–16 **This 40-foot puppy is made from 17,000 fresh flowering plants. How would you describe its texture?**

Jeff Koons, *Puppy*, 1992. Stainless steel, soil, geotextile fabric, internal irrigation system and live flowering plants. 40' 6" x 40' 6" x 21' 3" (12.3 x 12.3 x 6.5 m). Located at Arolsen Castle, Kassel, Germany. ©Jeff Koons.

Pushing Boundaries Artists today continue to look for new ways of working with materials. They often challenge our understanding of what traditional materials can do. Jesús Moroles pushes the boundaries of traditional sculpture. He takes risks and uses his excellent technical skills to discover new forms and textures in sculpture. To create his large-scale sculptures, he works with traditional hand tools, such as picks, chisels, and mallets. Moroles also uses more modern tools: diamond saws, drills, and grinders. These tools help him cut hard stone and create unusual forms. With these high-tech tools, he can slice, split, chip, grind, or polish the granite to produce sculptures with sharp edges and precise forms. He creates surfaces that are smooth and reflective, or rough and uneven.

Meet Jesús Moroles

Sculptor Jesús Moroles tests the limits of stone, often working on a very large scale. Moroles was born in Corpus Christi, Texas. Growing up, he worked for his uncle, who was a bricklayer. He learned carpentry skills by helping his father redo their home. These early work experiences in carpentry and masonry helped him develop into a mature artist.

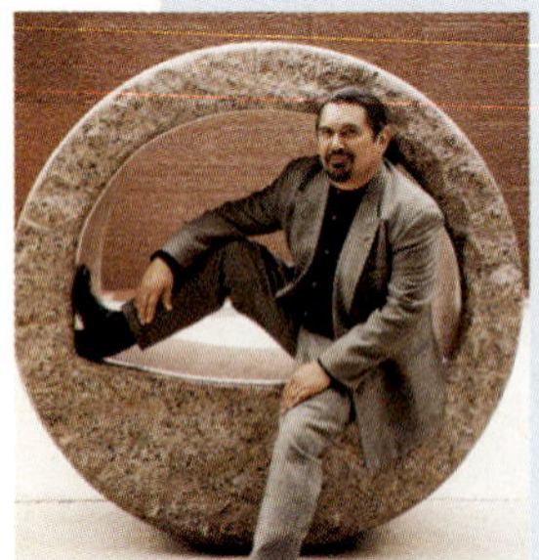

After working for a year in studios in Italy, Moroles came back to the United States in 1981 and purchased his first diamond saw for cutting granite. Since then he has created sculptures, fountains, plazas, and memorials in various locations across the country and around the world. One is a full 120 square feet, and several are over 20 feet tall. Moroles works only in granite, which he calls "the heart and core of the universe."

"I'm trying to just keep going on my own ideas."

— Jesús Moroles (born 1950)

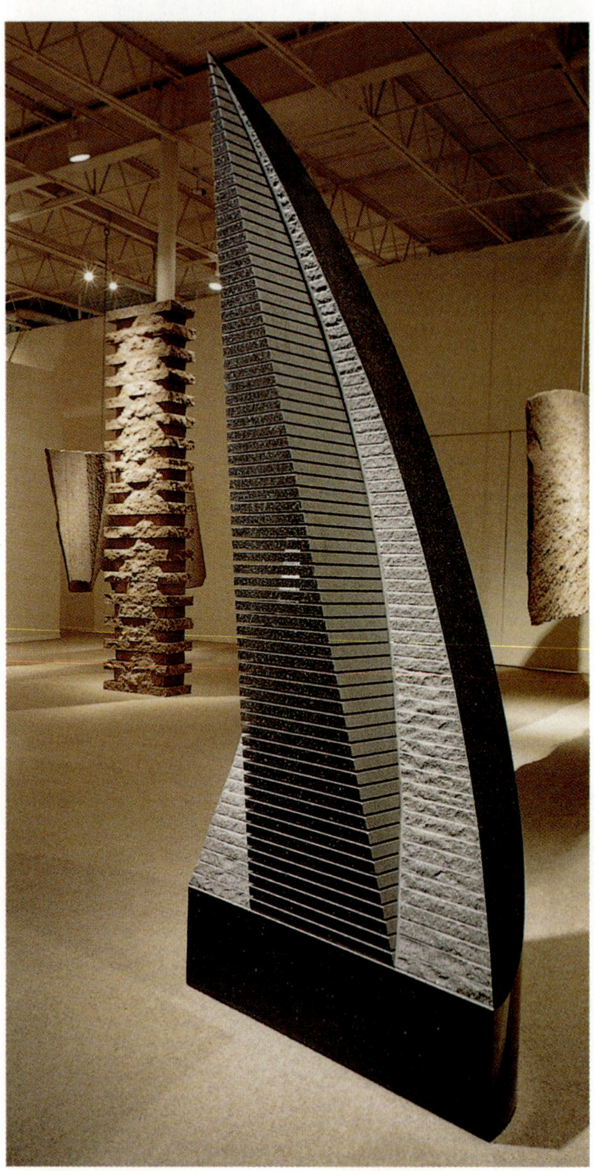

Fig. 9–17 **What different textures exist in this sculpture?**

Jesus Moroles, *Untitled*. Photo: Art Industrial/Rovert Ziebell.

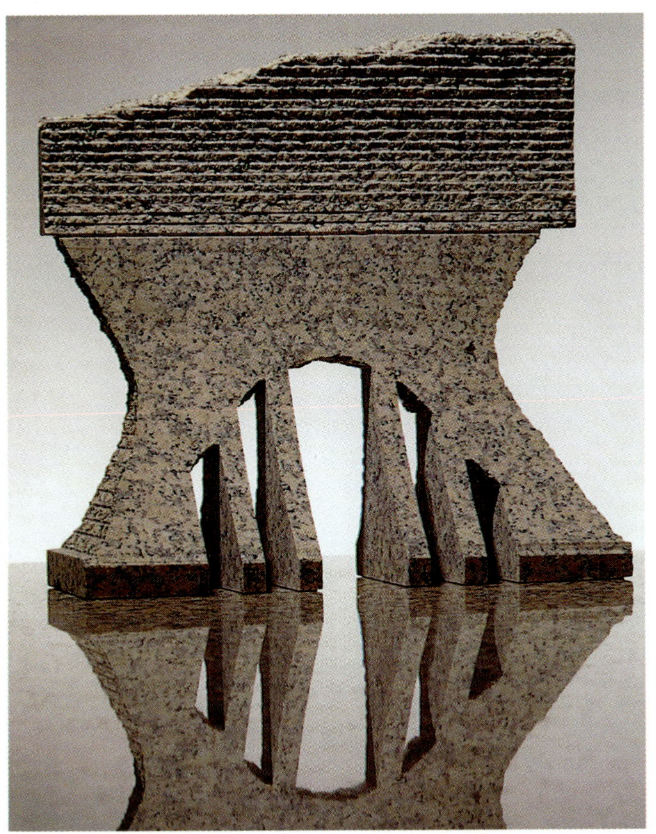

Check Your Understanding

1. Identify two ways that sculptors in recent history have pioneered change in sculpture.

2. Compare and contrast the site-specific sculptures by Dancer and Koons on page 257.

3. Considering the new things happening in sculpture today, what do you think an artist would need to do to be a pioneer in sculpture eighty or ninety years from now?

Fig. 9–18 **How does the title of this artwork relate to its form?**

Jesus Moroles, *Moonring Façade*. Photo: Ann Sherman.

Studio Time

A Challenging Clay Sculpture

Create a clay sculpture that will challenge someone to think about a natural form in a new way.

- Choose a natural form and observe it closely.
- If you've chosen a closed form, such as an acorn, your sculpture could open it up. If you've chosen a flat, open form, such as a leaf, you could close it up.
- Focus on surface and texture.

Reflect on how well your sculpture both reveals and departs from a natural form.

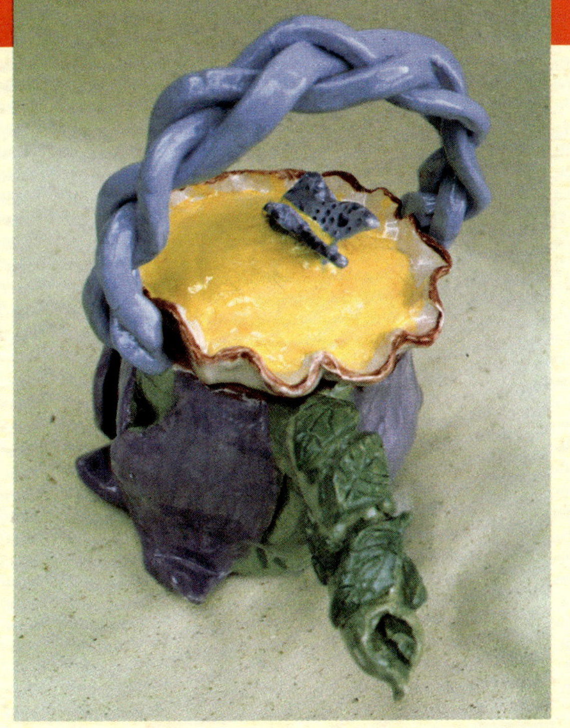

Fig. 9–19 Student artwork

Inventive Forms from Israel

The artistic traditions of Israel and the rest of the Middle East have existed since ancient times, even before the civilizations of Egypt, Greece, and Rome. Ancient Israelite artists became pioneers in many existing art forms, including the art of making glass. They learned to create colorful and complex glass objects and beads **(Figs. 9–20 and 9–21)**.

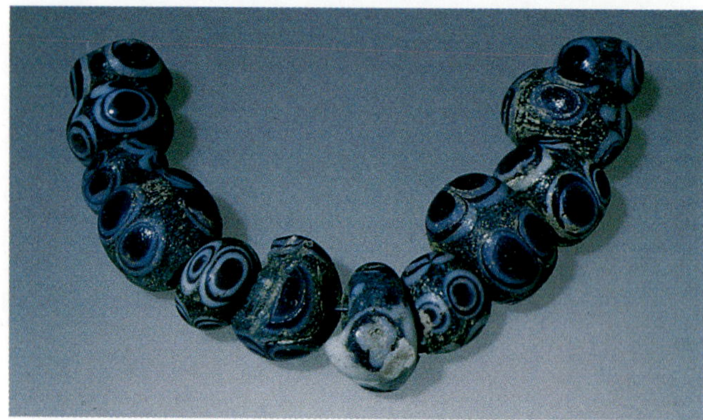

Fig. 9–21 **These are typical of the beads used as trade goods for over 3,000 years. Why might beads such as these, which perhaps no one other than the Israelites knew how to make, be valuable for trade?**

Eastern Mediterranean or Persia, *Composite Eye Beads*, 6th–3rd centuries BC. Translucent bluish-green, deep blue, and opaque white glass, core-formed, trail decorated, and tooled, diameter: ⅛"–½" (9mm–1.3cm). ©The Corning Museum of Glass. Corning, New York.

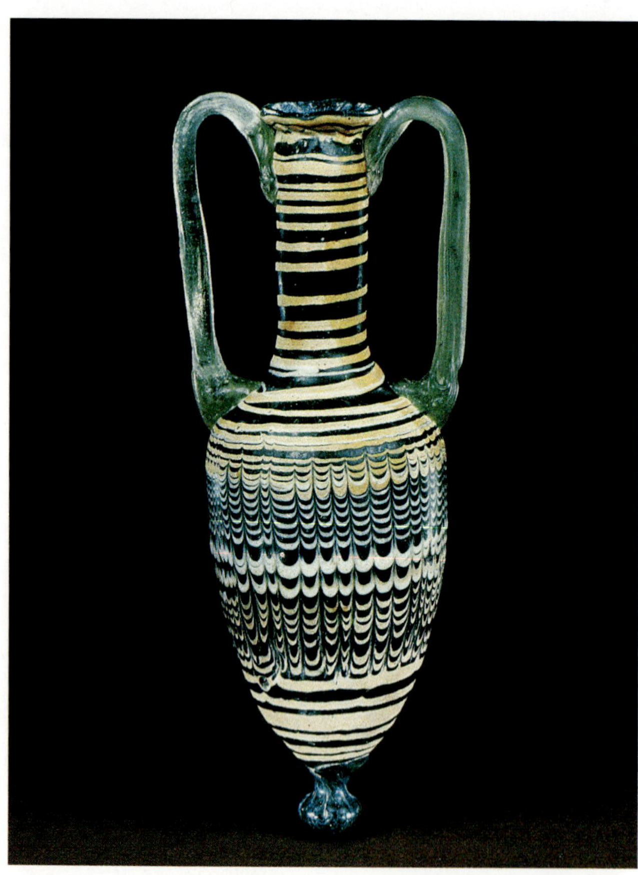

Fig. 9–20 **Glass vessels were produced in Eretz Israel, "the land of Israel," for many centuries before the Greeks and Romans even had a word for glass. How might the surface of this vessel feel?**

Eastern Mediterranean (possibly Cyprus), *Amphoriskos*, 2nd–1st centuries BC. Almost opaque yellow-green glass; core-formed, trail decorated, and tooled, height: 10" (24 cm). ©The Corning Museum of Glass. Corning, New York.

Visual Culture

In this lesson, you learn that textile artists today continue to use traditional materials in their products. Textile artists, like other designers today, also use new, eco-friendly materials in the products they create. Ecodesign is an approach to the design of a product with special consideration for the environmental impact of the product during its life cycle.

Work with your classmates to learn more about the new, natural materials being used in the textile industry today. Compare the environmental impact of natural materials as opposed to manufactured fibers such as nylon and polyester.

Social Studies Connection

The nation of **Israel**, on the eastern shore of the Mediterranean Sea, was founded in 1948. For centuries, however, many cultures have existed in the region. The land has been known as Canaan, Palestine, and the Holy Land (because it is the site of many ancient holy places of the Jewish, Christian, and Muslim religions). Diverse ethnic groups, belief systems, sects, and cultures continue to populate Israel.

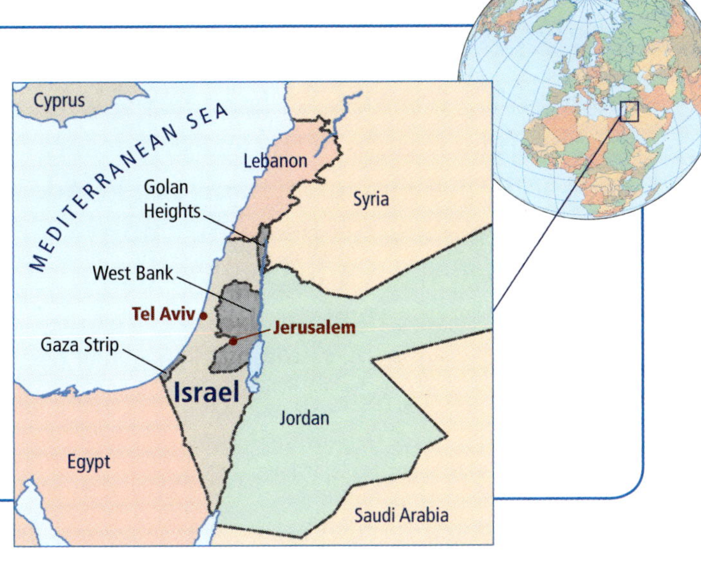

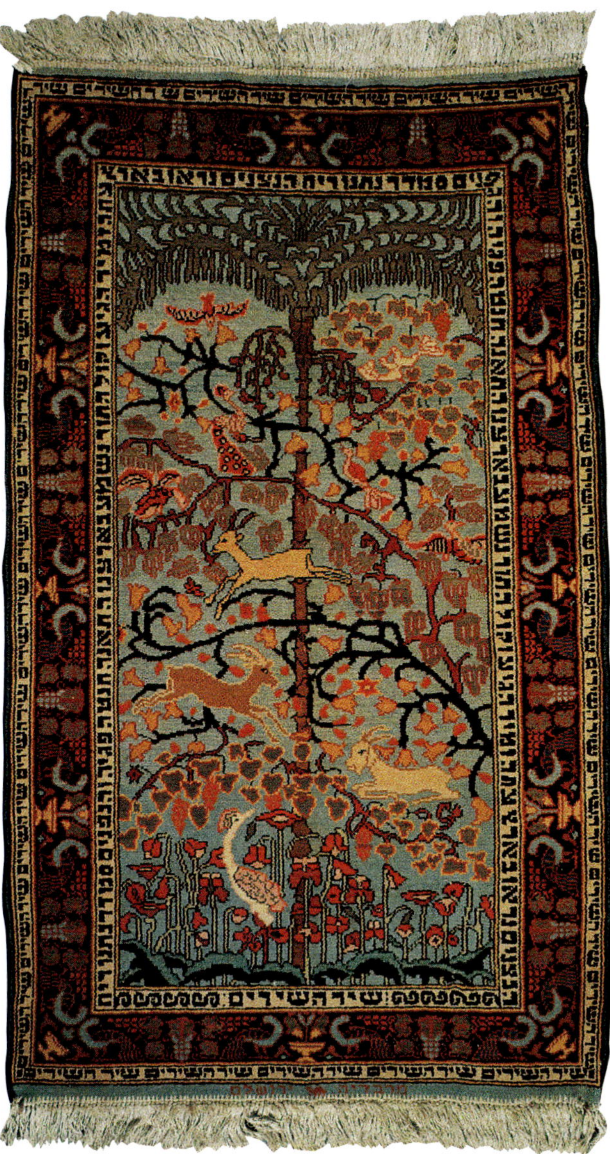

Preserving Traditions In ancient times, Israeli artists were also pioneers in the textile arts. They were masters in the production of fine linen and wool cloth, embroidered fabrics, stitched garments, and carpets. Artists wove colorful designs of plants, flowers, and other natural objects.

Artists today continue the ancient tradition of creating colorful carpets **(Fig. 9–22)**. They use traditional materials, such as silk, wool, goat hair, camel hair, cotton, linen, hemp, and jute. As in the past, the carpets can be found in many Israeli homes and religious buildings.

Fig. 9–22 **Carpets were, and continue to be, valued possessions of Israeli homeowners.**

Israel, Bezalel School, Marvadia Workshop, *"Song of Songs" Carpet*, 1920s. Wool, 68" x 39 ⅓" (173 x 100 cm). The Israel Museum, Jerusalem. Photo ©The Israel Museum, Jeruselum.

Touched by the Desert East Jerusalem and the quiet beauty of the eastern desert made an impression on artist Nomi Wind. She observed how the Bedouin, who are highly skilled at spinning wool by hand, pitched tents of camel wool. For Wind, the raw, stained wool they used seemed to hold traces and smells of the desert. She knew this was the material through which she could best express her ideas about her Middle Eastern heritage.

At first, Wind's interest in creating with wool resulted in wearable art that allowed her to study the material's possibilities. After seeing people wear her art, Wind moved to creating sculptures based on the human form. This led to her present artwork: large, abstract sculptures influenced by the wild, open spaces of the desert. Wind still explores the three-dimensional nature of fibers in her sculptures, adding materials such as stone and iron.

Meet Nomi Wind

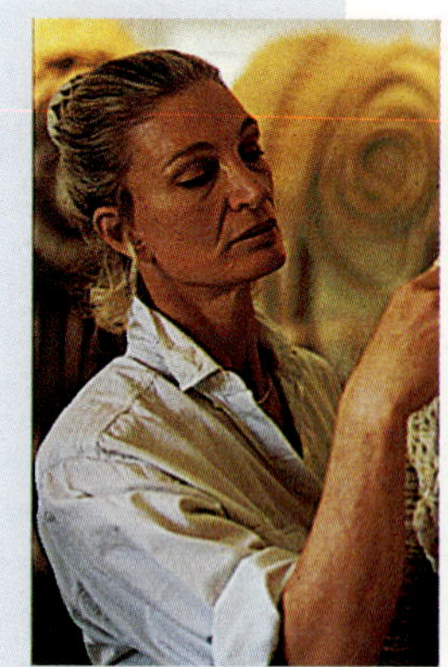

Nomi Wind combines old and new techniques, as well as different cultural traditions, to create her fiber sculptures. Born in West Jerusalem, Wind graduated with a degree in education from Hebrew University. As an Israeli, she was surrounded by the Judaic tradition of women doing needlework. In 1967 in East Jerusalem, she came into contact with Bedouin fiber traditions. These traditions inspired Wind. The Bedouin are a nomadic, desert people. They use camel and goat hair, as well as plant fibers, to make tents and clothing.

"The process of my work [begins] with the use of local materials and the search for expression of my place and my self."

—Nomi Wind (born 1940)

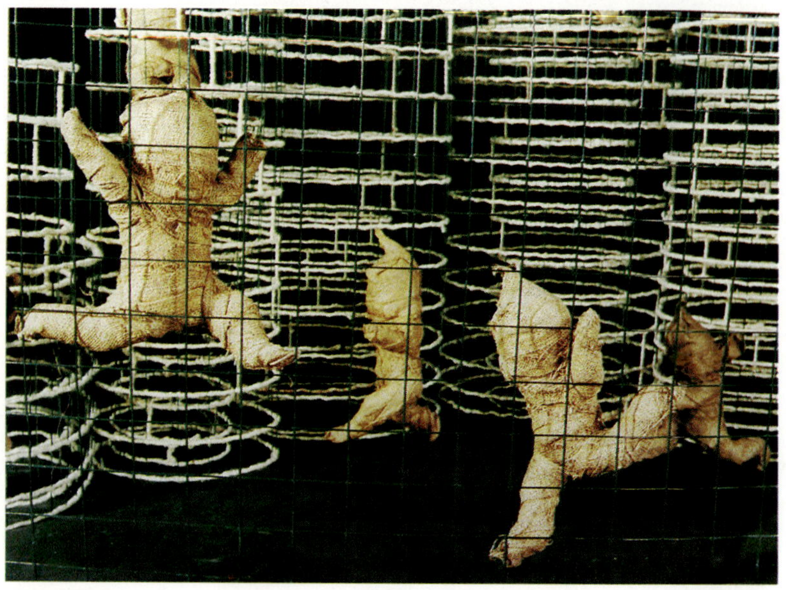

Fig. 9–23 **The artist uses materials other than fiber in constructing her large-scale pieces. How do you think this piece was made?**

Nomi Wind, *Defeated Childhood*, 2000. Handwoven Bedouin sheep's wool and paper, height: approx 72" (183 cm). Courtesy of the artist.

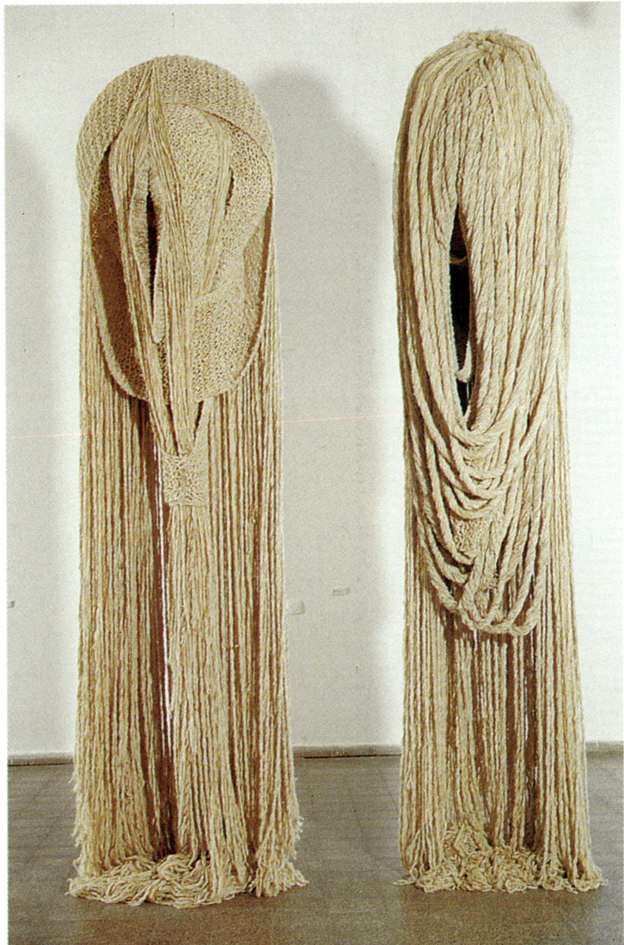

Fig. 9–24 **What reasons might the artist have for titling this sculpture *Women of the Desert*?**

Nomi Wind, *Women of the Desert*, 1992. Handwoven Bedouin sheep's wool, rope, 8' 4" x 15" (255 x 38 cm). Courtesy of the artist.

Check Your Understanding

1. Name two areas in which the Israelites were pioneers of artistic production.
2. Compare and contrast the use of wool in *"Song of Songs" Carpet* with *Women of the Desert*.
3. How is it possible to be a pioneer in weaving if it is an art form that has been practiced for thousands of years?

Studio Time

Experimental Weaving

Be a pioneer, and make an experimental weaving.

- Explore and experiment with traditional weaving techniques, forms, and materials. Combine traditional weaving techniques with other fiber processes, such as knotting and braiding.
- Consider creating a weaving that has a geometric (circular, triangular, or rectangular) or other three-dimensional form.
- Experiment with found materials to create different surface textures and patterns. Try materials like wire, foil, reeds, plastic, ribbons, and beads.

Reflect on the unique qualities of your weaving.

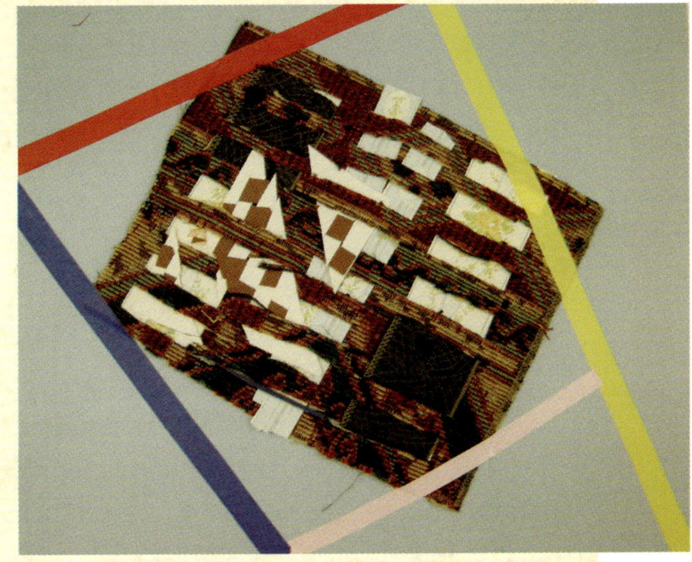

Fig. 9–25 Student artwork

Recycled Art

Studio Background

Isn't the ability to turn trash into art wonderful? Finding new uses for old things can be challenging, but not with some creative imagination. Perhaps you once pretended that an empty milk carton was a train engine, or that a wrapping-paper tube was a telescope. If so, you used your imagination to turn trash into a useful object. Now you just have to turn that object into art!

In this studio exploration, you will create a sculpture from recycled materials. Your challenge is to be inventive with your choice of "junk" materials. Study the materials, and let your imagination pioneer a way to create your artwork. Do the shapes, forms, and textures of the materials suggest an idea or theme? Will your sculpture represent something, such as a bird, or will it be a form with no recognizable subject? Create a sculpture that will show old junk in a new way!

You Will Need

- discarded objects, such as old toys, shoes, kitchen utensils, plastic, metal, and cardboard packaging
- small found materials, such as washers, nuts, bolts, screws, string, pipe cleaners, plastic lids, feathers, and game parts
- white glue
- masking tape
- glue gun

Safety Note: Do not use a glue gun without your teacher present. The tip of a glue gun and the glue itself get very hot and can burn you.

Step 1 **Plan and Practice**

- Look carefully at the materials that are available to you. Consider their sizes and shapes. Feel their textures. Do the materials have interesting holes in them or colored parts?
- Hold materials up against one another, and move them around. Experiment with placement.
- What ideas for a sculpture come to mind?
- You may want to sketch your ideas.

Things to Remember:

✓ Create interesting textures with your objects and materials.

✓ Use the materials' attributes in a way that best conveys your message.

✓ Make sure your sculpture is interesting from all sides.

Inspiration from Art

For their artwork, many sculptors today find ideas and materials in trash cans and junkyards. They turn these found and recycled materials into objects of beauty, usefulness, or humor. Many artists see possibilities in used packaging, old shoes, pieces of jewelry, broken appliances and toys—in anything that sparks an idea.

Artists who work with found and recycled materials are inspired by the surfaces, textures, colors, and forms that they offer. These artists are somewhat like modern archaeologists. They sort through household rubbish and piece together a picture of our society. Sometimes with humor, sometimes with seriousness, they use found materials to challenge our ideas about art and about society.

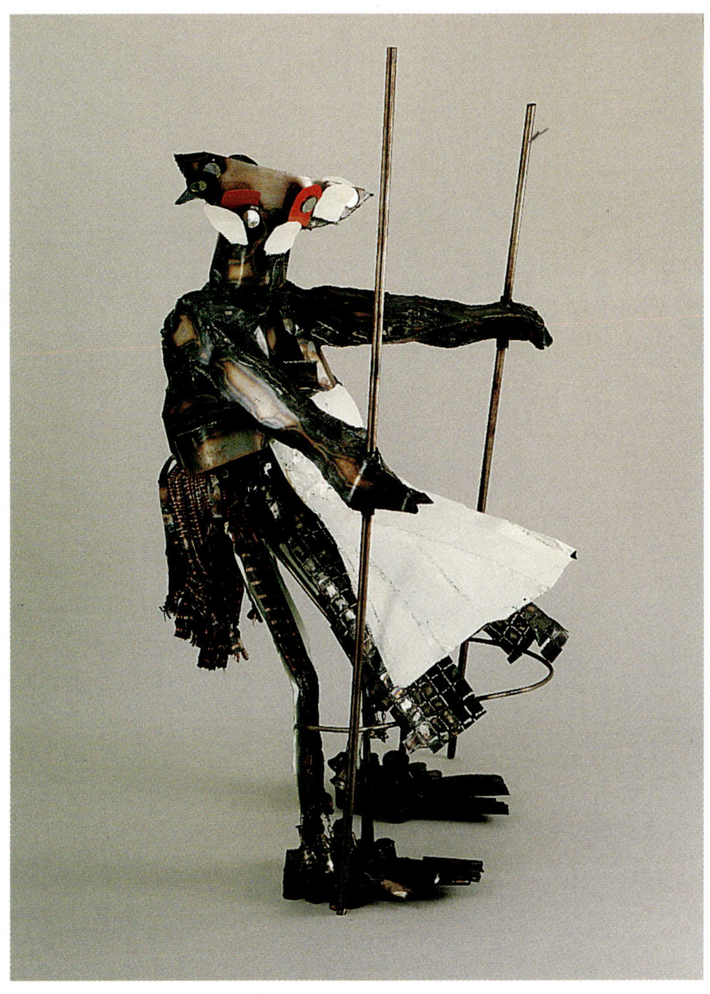

Fig. 9–26 **Camp, a Nigerian sculptor, works with scrap metal and other found materials. Texture, movement, and humor are important elements of her artworks of costumed performers.**

Sokari Douglas Camp, *Masquerader with Boat Headdress*, 1995. Steel and mixed media, height: approx. 78" (200 cm). Courtesy of the artist. Collection of the Museum of African Art, Smithsonian Institution, Washington, DC.

Inspiration from Our World

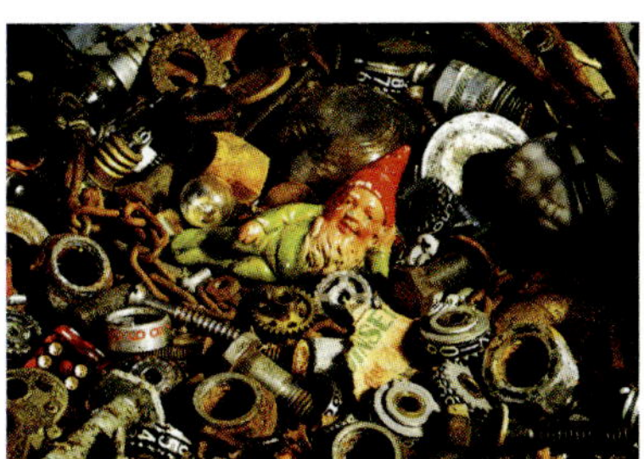

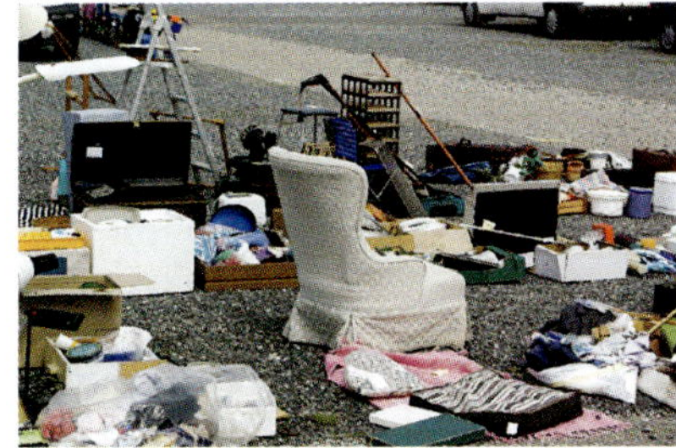

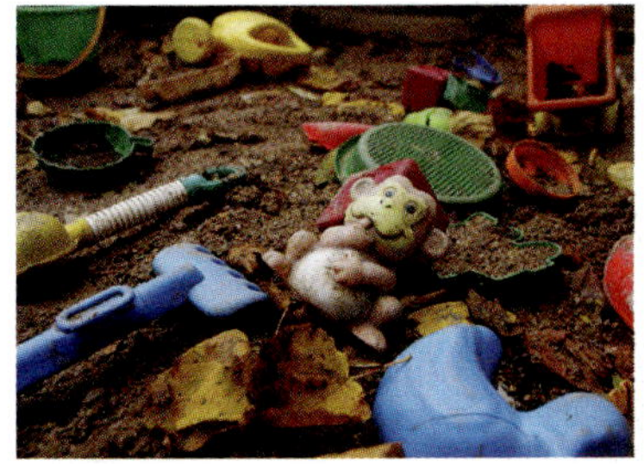

Step 2 **Begin to Create**

- Choose an object to be the main form for your sculpture.
- **Turn the object over in your hands and study it.** Does it remind you of any particular subject, such as an animal or person? Or are you simply drawn to its shape, texture, and color?

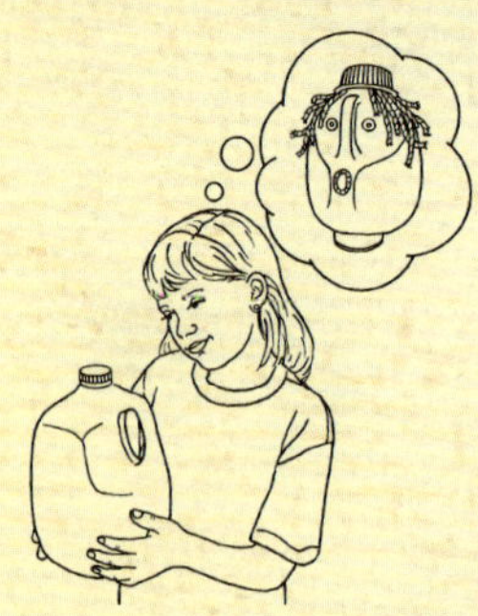

- **Decide which found materials you will add to the main form.**

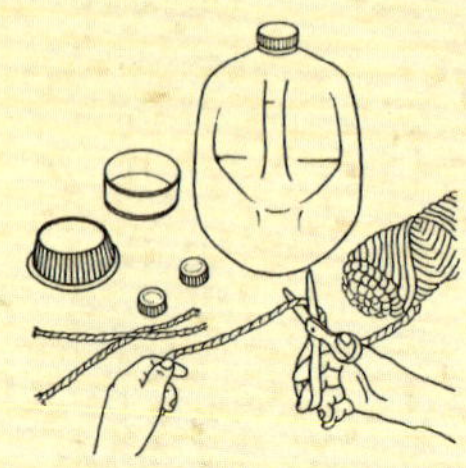

- Will you create limbs or other easily recognizable features? Or will you add materials only to decorate the forms and colors that already exist?
- **Use glue or tape to attach pieces to the main form.**

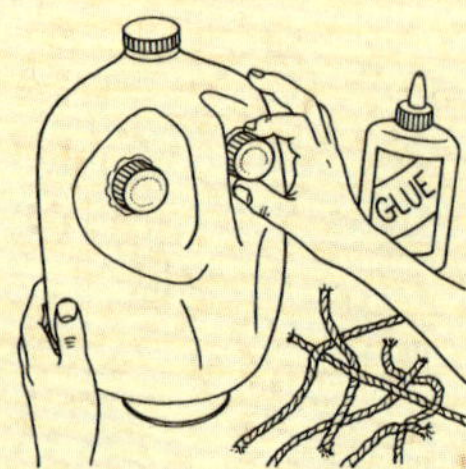

- What kinds of textures can you create?

Step 3 **Revise**

Did you remember to:

- ✓ Create interesting textures with your objects and materials?
- ✓ Use the materials' attributes in a way that best conveys your message?
- ✓ Make sure your sculpture is interesting from all sides?

Adjust your work if necessary. In your sketchbook, make a note of your revisions and why you made them.

Step 4 **Add Finishing Touches**

- Do you need to add more textures or colorful areas?
- Will you paint your finished sculpture to unify it? Does leaving it unpainted make a statement or send a message of some kind?

Step 5 **Share and Reflect**

- Display your sculpture with your classmates' sculptures. Take turns explaining why the features of the forms interested you.
- How did the forms inspire you to create your sculpture?
- What idea or message is important in your artwork?
- How could your sculpture challenge the way people think about discarded materials?

Art Criticism

Describe What recycled materials do you see in this sculpture?

Analyze How has the artist unified the variety of materials used in this sculpture?

Interpret Why do you think this artist titled his sculpture *My Room*?

Evaluate What do you find interesting or pleasing about this artwork?

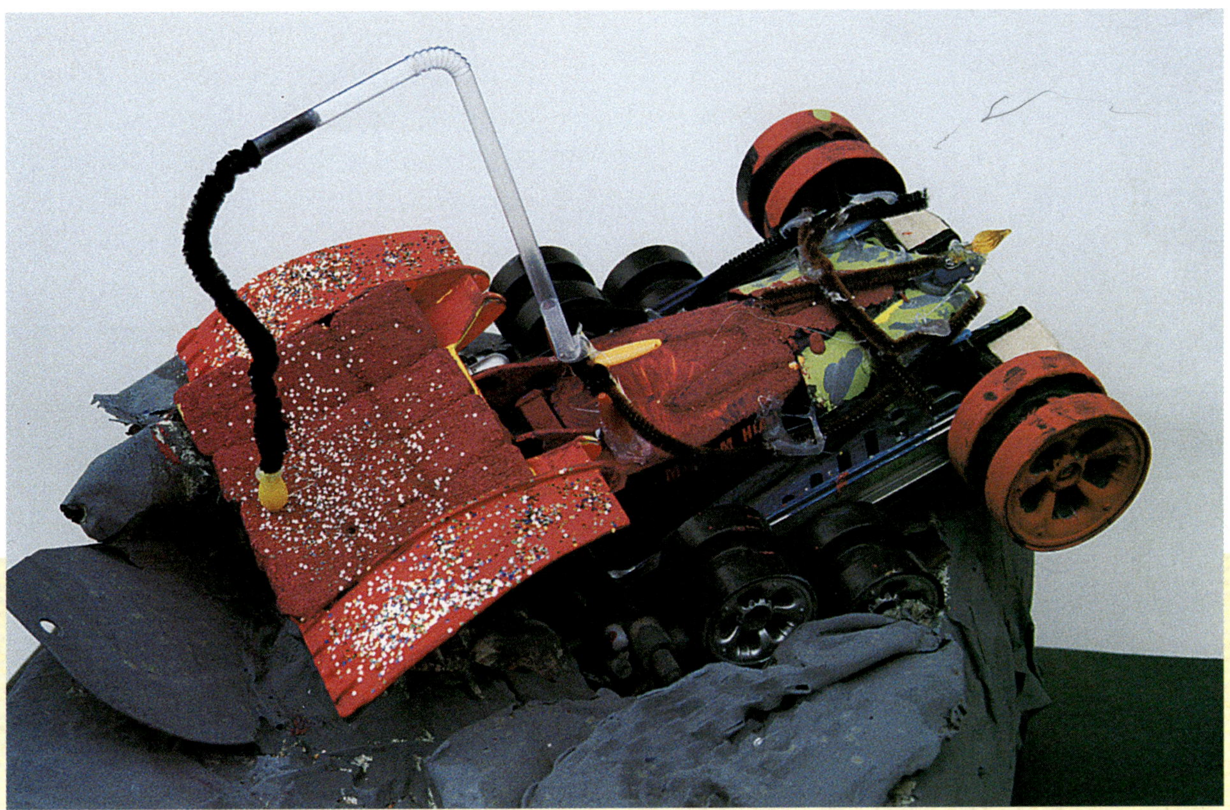

Fig. 9–27 Student artwork

Science

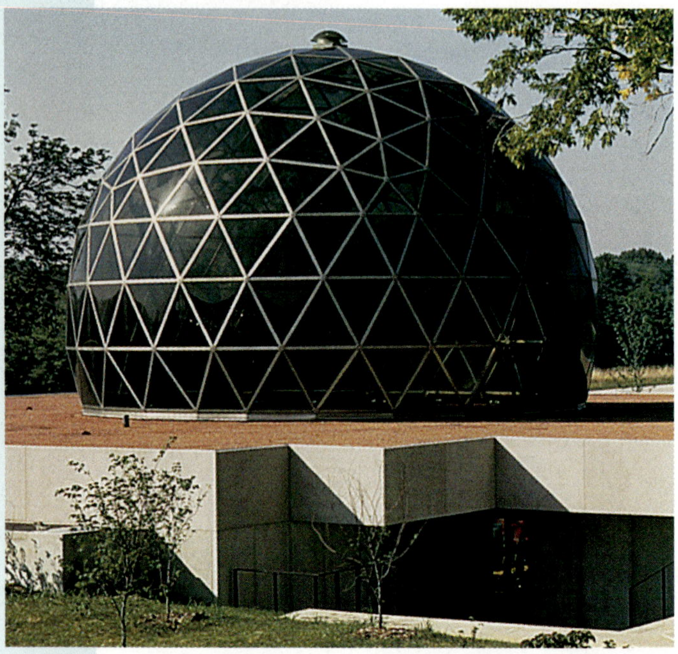

Fig. 9–28 **Fuller once said that he invented objects and waited for people to need them. Why do you think this type of structure never became popular?**

Buckminster Fuller, *Southern Illinois University Chapel*, 1950s. Located in Carbdondale, Illinois. Photo courtesy of Davis Art Images.

Many scientists are pioneers in their field. One well-known pioneering scientist was Buckminster Fuller. In 1947 he patented the geodesic dome. The geodesic dome is a lightweight, domed structure that is formed from many connected triangles. Fuller used advances in technology to help him plan designs that were good for the earth. Since his invention, some homes have been built using this design. In addition to the geodesic dome, his most famous inventions were a doughnut-shaped house and a three-wheeled car.

Dance

The performing arts have had many pioneering artists. One such pioneer was dancer and choreographer Alvin Ailey. His creativity grew from his experiences as a young African American. In 1958, at a time when African Americans were not often accepted in dance schools, he created his own dance company. The Alvin Ailey American Dance Theater changed the world of American dance. Today, his company continues to perform. They also offer dance camps and other outreach programs for young people.

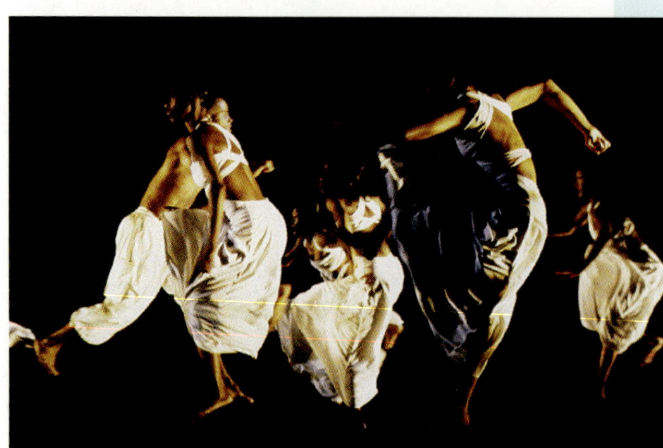

Fig. 9–29

Careers **Fiber Artist**

Fiber artists are artists who work with cloth and thin strands of the materials that cloth is made of. Fiber artists are also called textile artists. They work with many kinds of materials and fibers to create fabrics, wall hangings, sculptures, weavings, quilts, or wearable art. They must understand color theory, drawing, design, and printing processes. They also understand textile science and technology. Contemporary textile artists are pioneering new ideas in their fields. A recent development is the use of computer software that creates complex designs and patterns.

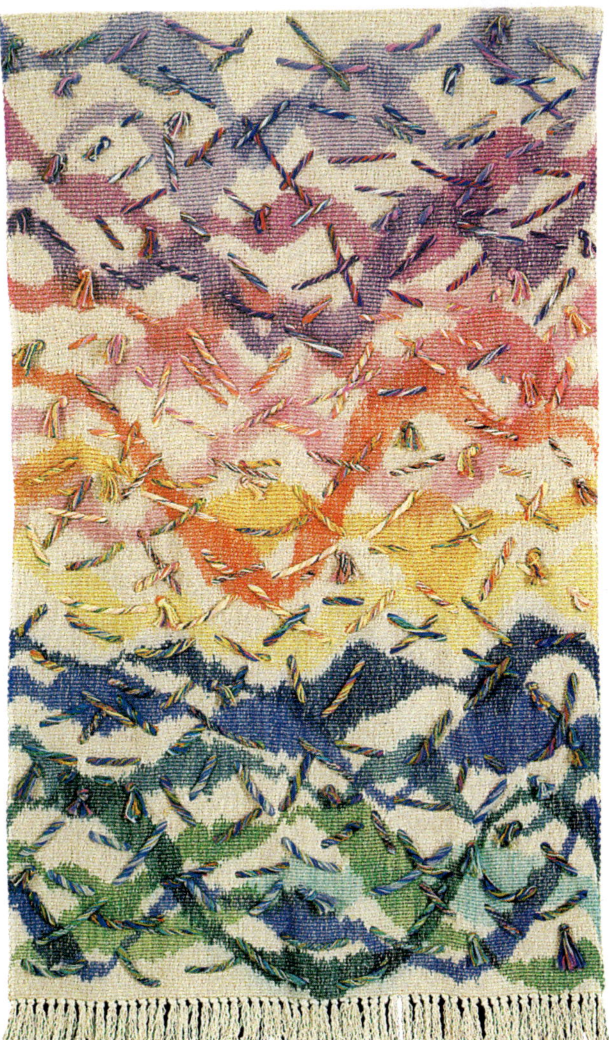

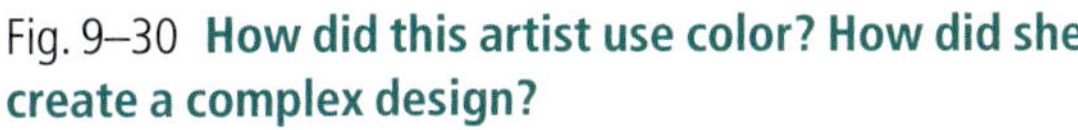

Fig. 9–30 **How did this artist use color? How did she create a complex design?**

Erika Wade, *Duet*, 1991. Warp painted and embroidered cotton, 40" x 62" (102 x 157 cm). Courtesy of the artist.

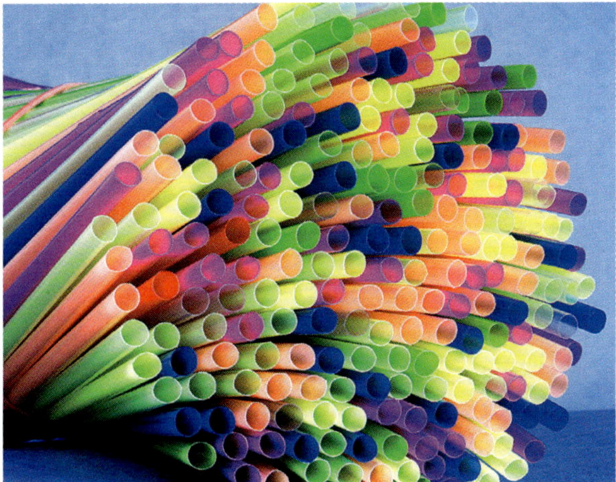

Fig. 9–31

Daily Life

Many artists have used everyday objects in new and inventive ways. What everyday objects do you find beautiful? How could you use creativity to turn these objects into art? By combining objects and presenting them as art, artists challenge us to see things in new ways. Artist Joseph Cornell is known for his inventive use of daily-life objects. He once said: "The question is not what you look at, but what you see." What does this statement mean to you?

Vocabulary Review

Match each art term below with its definition.

petroglyphs
assemblage
site-specific sculpture
casting
relief sculpture

1. a sculpture of combined objects, such as boxes, pieces of wood, and part of old machines
2. a sculpture that is meant to be viewed from one side, like a wall plaque
3. rock carvings created by Native Americans hundreds of years ago
4. a sculpture created for a particular outdoor space
5. the multistep process for creating sculptures in bronze or other materials, such as concrete, plaster, or plastic

Aesthetic Thinking

Digital imaging, animation, video installation, and film are examples of artwork made using technology. How do you decide if technology produces art? How is a traditional photograph similar or different from a digitally-manipulated photograph? How is an animation similar or different from a painting?

Write About Art

Imagine you are an art critic viewing this work shortly after Picasso created it in 1912. In the voice of the critic, write a paragraph evaluating the "new" medium of collage.

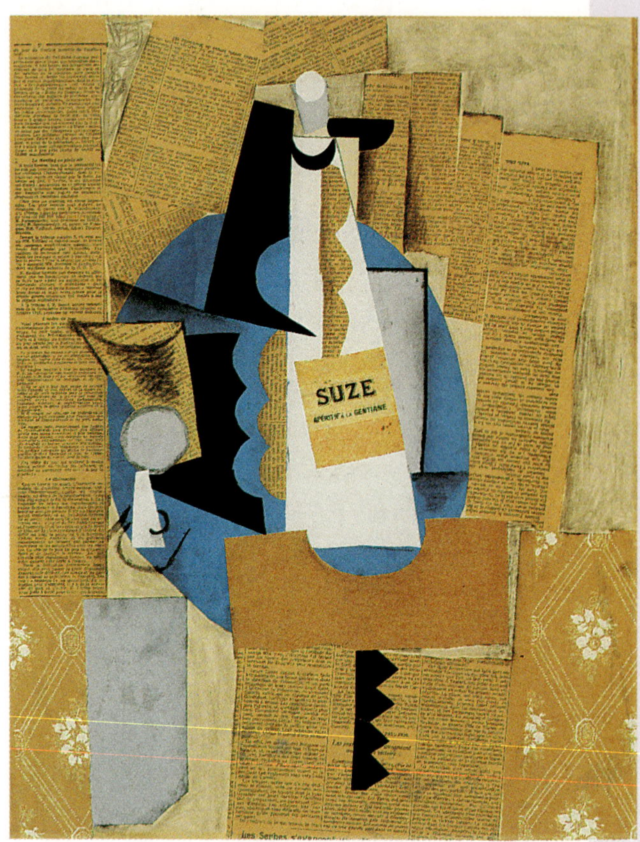

Fig. 9–33 **This is one of the first collages ever made. Soon after this experiment, Picasso made many different collages by using scraps of things he found.**

Pablo Picasso, *Glass and Bottle of Suze*, 1912. Pasted papers, gouache, and charcoal, 25 ¾" x 19 ¾" (65 x 50 cm). Washington University Gallery of Art, Saint Louis. University Purchase, Kende Sale Fund, 1946. ©2001 Estate of Pablo Picasso/Artists Rights Society (ARS), New York.

Art Criticism

Describe What do you see in this painting?

Analyze How does the artist use rhythm to move our eyes through the painting?

Interpret What statement do you think the artist is making about the environment?

Evaluate Would you want to visit the place shown here? Why or why not?

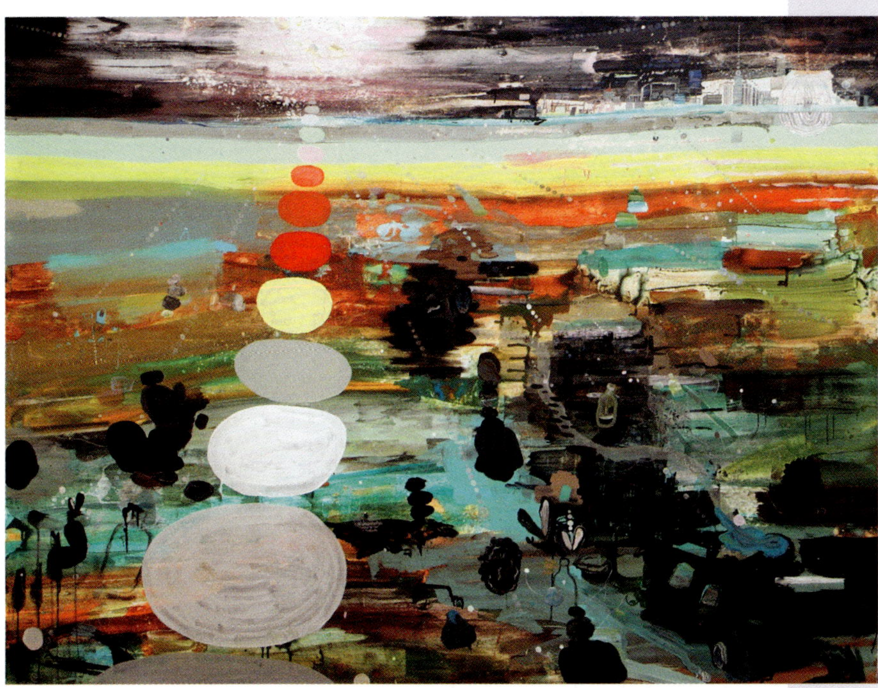

Fig. 9–34 Lisa Sanditz, *Pearl Farm.* Courtesy of the artist and CRG Gallery, NY.

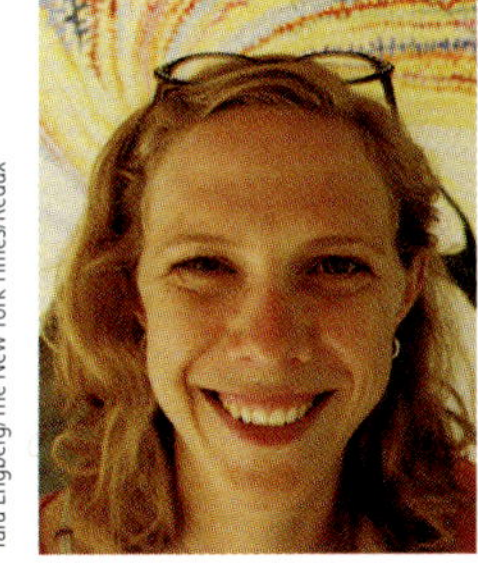

Tara Engberg/The New York Times/Redux

Meet the Artist

Lisa Sanditz was born in St. Louis, Missouri, and now lives in New York. Her large paintings depict modern landscape. In her work, Sanditz explores what happens when civilization intrudes on the natural world. Some of her paintings show actual scenes, while others are imaginary.

"My paintings update the idea of the sublime landscape..."

—Lisa Sanditz (born 1973)

For Your Sketchbook

Look through your sketchbook for evidence of a personal style or a change in the way you work. What have you done consistently? What changes do you see in the way you sketch? In your sketchbook, comment on what you discover.

For Your Portfolio

Use the works in your portfolio to discover where your personal journey in art has taken you. Select four of these works, and use them to explain how you have grown as an artist.

Student Handbook Contents

Studio Safety

Stay safe when you create! No matter what art materials you use, developing safe habits is important. Read labels, follow common safety procedures, and always wash your hands thoroughly after working with art materials.

Avoid breathing dust.

Why? Chalk, pastel, charcoal, and plaster dust can harm your lungs and might trigger an allergic reaction.

What to do? Wear a mask over your nose and mouth if necessary. When carving plaster, keep your work damp and place it in a shallow tray lined with damp newspapers.

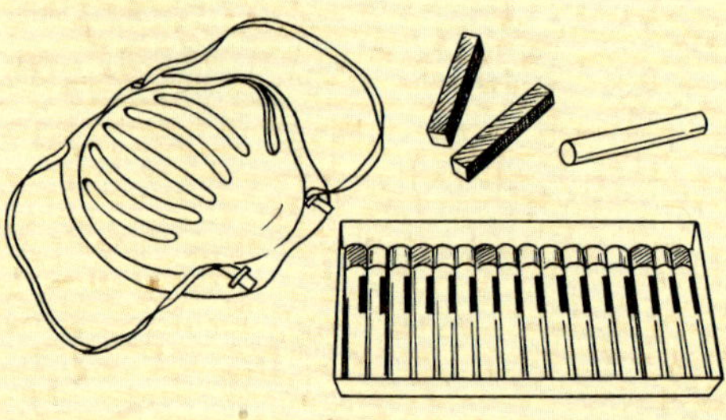

Keep art materials away from your eyes.

Why? Chemicals in paints, solvents, and photo developing solutions can irritate your eyes and skin. Chemicals can also be absorbed through your skin.

What to do? Keep your hands away from your face when you work with art materials. Wear disposable latex or rubber gloves.

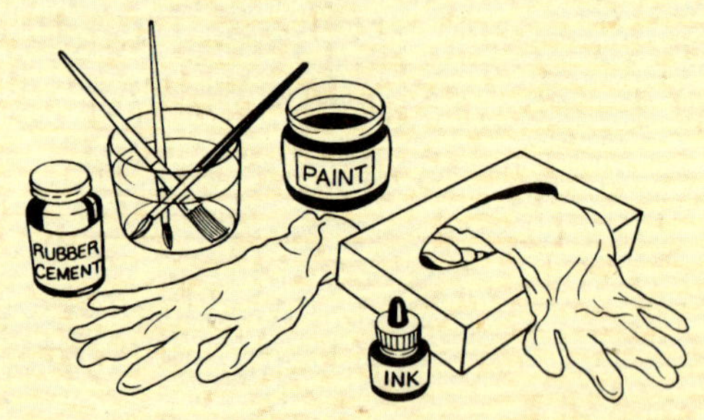

Do not breathe sprays or vapors.

Why? Permanent markers, some paints, some solvents, photo developing solutions, and spray fixatives all give off fumes that can be harmful.

What to do? Do not use permanent markers for any art activity. Use sprays and other chemicals only in areas with active ventilation.

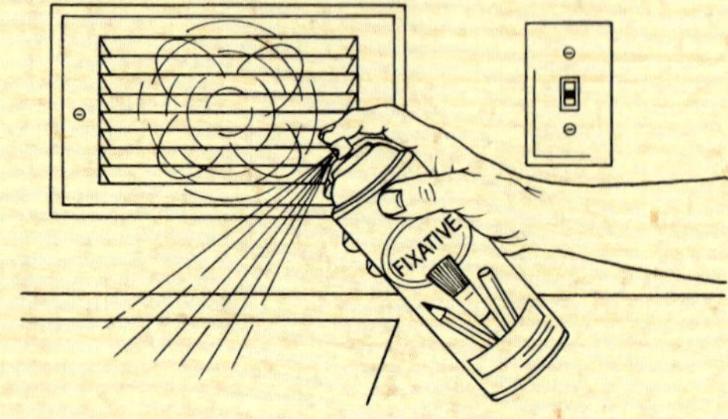

Read labels carefully.

Why? Be sure labels say the materials are *nontoxic*, which means they are *not* poisonous. The word *toxic* or a picture of a small skull and crossbones means the material is poisonous.

What to do? Ask your teacher how to handle the material. Be sure to wash your hands thoroughly after use.

Point scissors and sharp tools away from you.

Why? Scissors, knives, wood or linoleum block cutting tools, clay tools, needles, pins, and tacks are sharp and if mishandled can cause injury.

What to do? Always direct a sharp edge or point away from you and others. When you use the tools, hold your work securely or use a vise. Wear safety goggles. Work slowly.

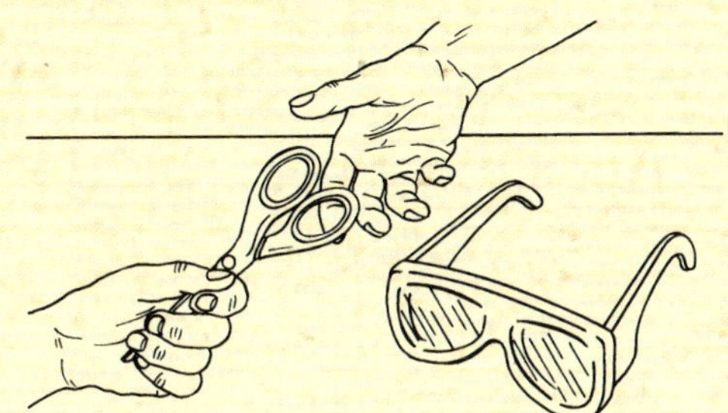

Do not eat or drink in the artroom.

Why? Chemicals from art materials may get into your food or drink. Foods that are part of an edible creation can also become contaminated.

What to do? Always leave the artroom when you want to eat or drink. Create edible artwork in the kitchen using only food preparation tools and materials.

Clean up spills immediately and keep the floor clear of objects.

Why? Liquids are slippery. Liquids and clutter on the floor can cause falls.

What to do? Clean up spills immediately, following your teacher's directions. Keep backpacks, books, and materials in or under your worktable.

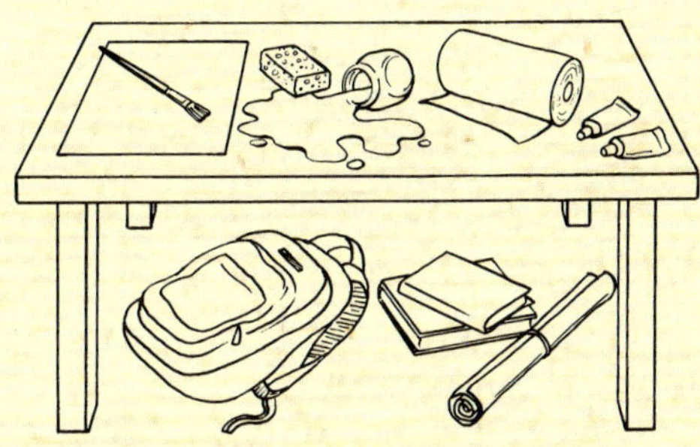

Elements of Art

The *Elements of Art* are the basic building blocks that an artist uses when creating a work of art. Understanding the elements of art can also help you appreciate the artworks of others.

Line

- A mark that has length and direction.
- Outlines shapes and forms or suggests movement.
- *Implied* line is not actually drawn, but suggested by part of an image, such as a path of footprints.
- Line affects the mood of artworks. Thick zigzag lines will give a different "feel" from light, curved lines.

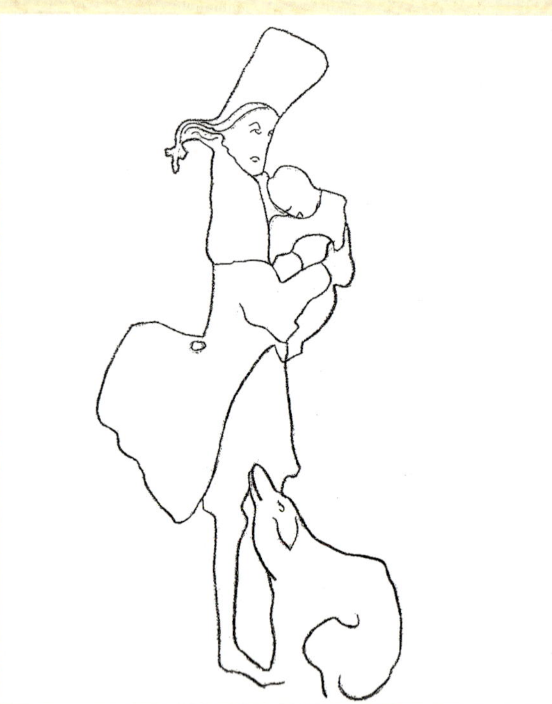

Even a simple outline can convey much information.

Romaine Brooks, *The Soldier at Home*, 1930.

Shape and Form

Shape

- Created when a line encloses a space or color.
- Flat and two-dimensional (2-D).
- Examples: circle, square.
- *Positive* shapes are the main shapes in an artwork.
- *Negative* shapes are the shapes that surround the positive shapes.
- Artists often plan their work so that the viewer's eyes move back and forth between positive and negative shapes.

Form

- Has height, width, and depth.
- Is three-dimensional (3-D).
- Examples: sphere, cube.

Shapes and Forms

- Can be *organic*, meaning irregular, such as leaves or shells.
- Can be *geometric*, meaning precise and regular, such as circles, spheres, triangles, and pyramids.

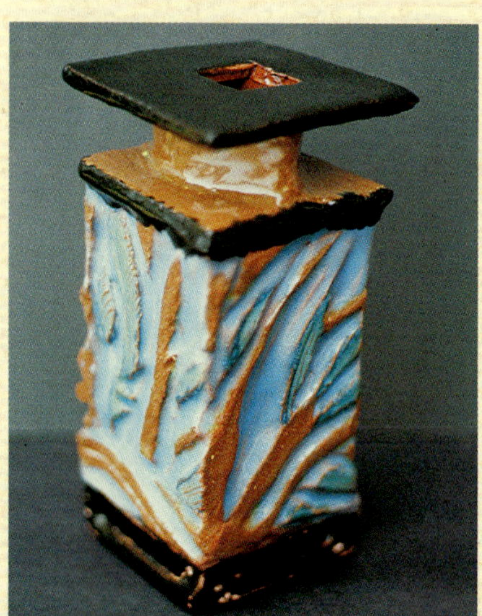

This ceramic work contains geometric shapes and forms.

Student artwork.

Space

- In three-dimensional work, artists use actual space.
- In two-dimensional work, artists create the illusion of space.
- *Positive* space is the space filled by a work.
- *Negative* space is the space that surrounds the work.
- Ways to create the illusion of space or depth include:
  - making closer objects larger, farther objects smaller
  - overlapping objects
  - placing distant objects higher in the picture
  - *linear perspective*, a special technique in which lines meet at a specific point in the picture.

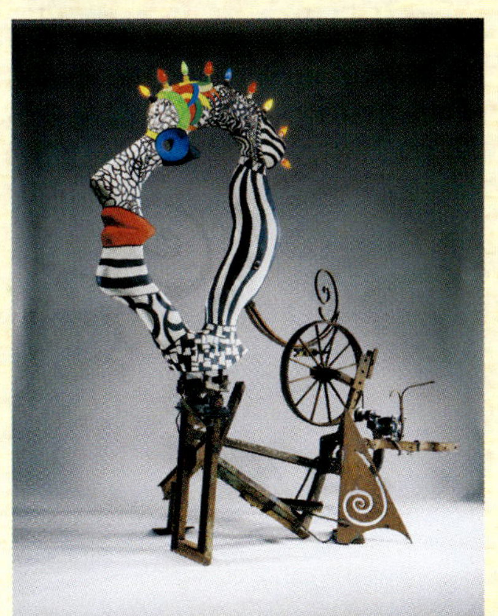

You can see negative space through the open parts of this sculpture.

Nikki de Saint Phalle and Jean Tinguely, *Illumination*, 1988.

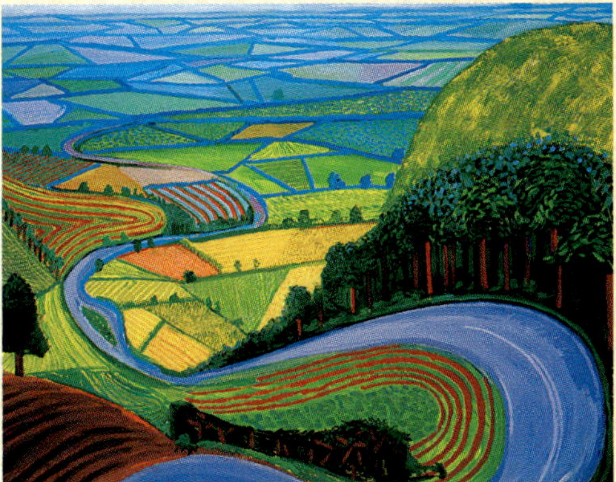

Smaller and smaller fields help create the illusion of space in this painting.

David Hockney, *Garrowby Hill*, 1998.

Texture

- The way a surface feels or seems to feel, such as rough, sticky, prickly.
- *Real* textures are those you can actually feel.
- *Implied* textures are textures that do not feel the way they look, such as soft fur created by painting many fine lines.

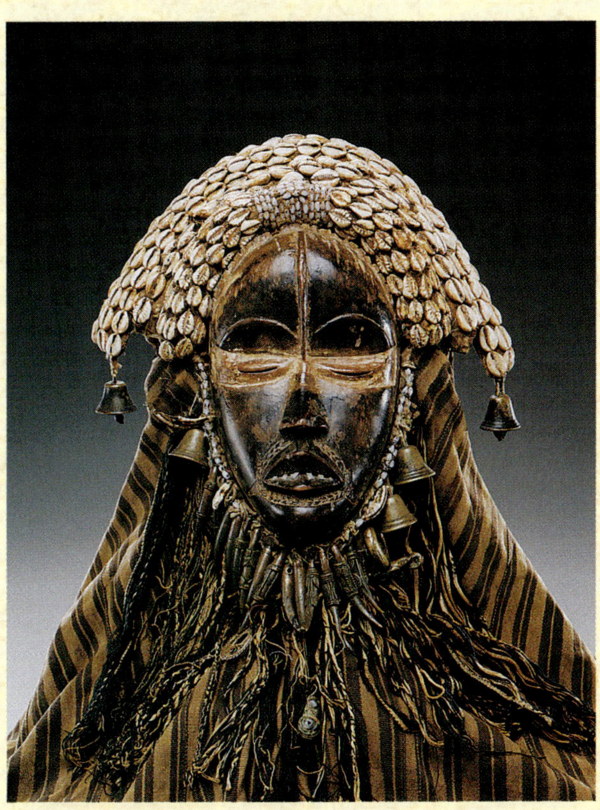

The textures in this mask are real—you could feel them if you touched it.

Africa, Dan Culture (Liberia, Ivory Coast), *Ga-Wree-Wre-Mask*, 20th century.

Color

- The *color spectrum* is created when light passes through a prism.

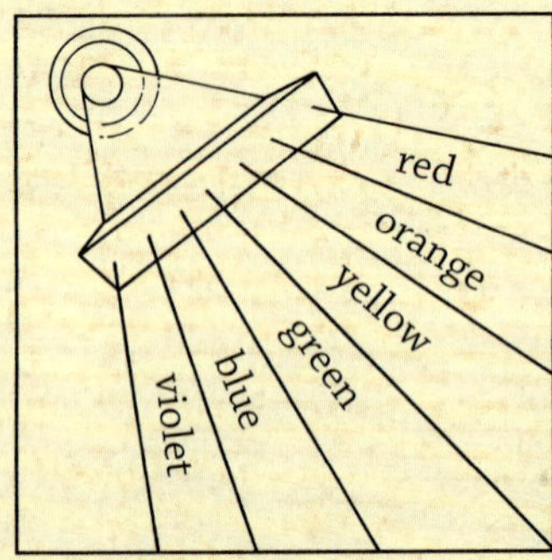

The Spectrum

- Colors of the spectrum are red, orange, yellow, green, blue, indigo, and violet.
- The *primary hues* or colors are red, yellow, and blue. Primary colors cannot be created by mixing other colors.
- The *secondary* colors are orange, green, and violet. Mix two primary colors to create a secondary color.
- To create an *intermediate* color, mix a primary color with the secondary color next to it on the color wheel.
- Use the primary colors, plus black and white, to mix almost every other imaginable color.
- *Intensity* is the brightness or dullness of a color.
- To create dull colors, mix complementary colors, those that are opposite each other on the color wheel.
- A *color scheme* is a specific group of colors an artist works with to create an artwork.

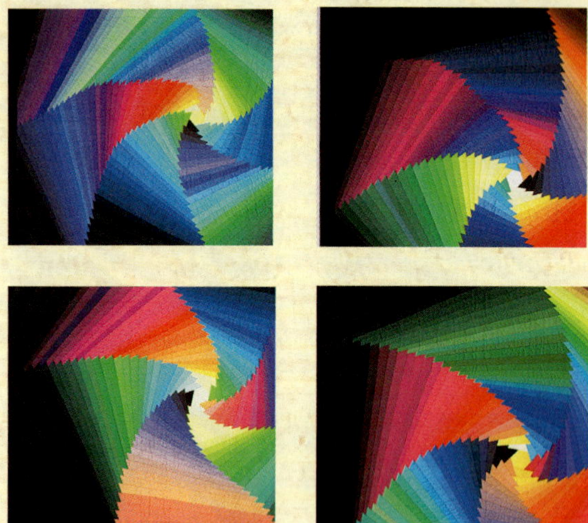

Caryl Bryer Fallert, *Refraction #4–#7*

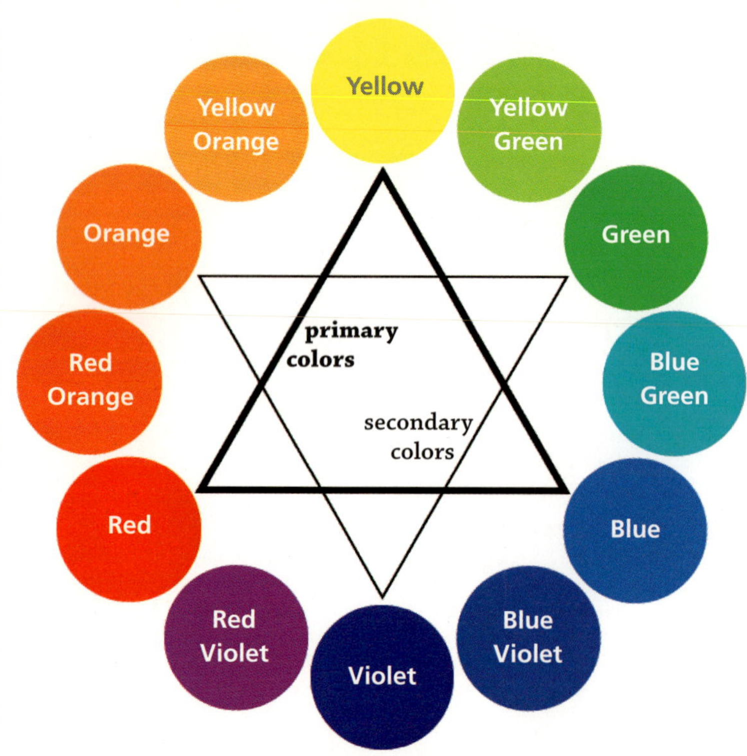

The Color Wheel

Common Color Schemes

- *Warm:* colors that remind people of warm places, things, and feelings.

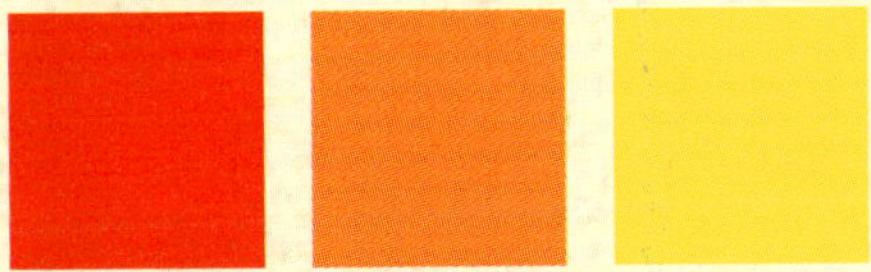

- *Cool:* colors that remind people of cool places, things, and feelings.

- *Neutral:* colors that are not associated with the spectrum.

- *Monochromatic:* the range of values of one color (*monochromatic* means "one color").

- *Analogous:* colors that are next to each other on the color wheel and share a common hue.

- *Split complement:* a color and the two colors on each side of its complement.

- *Triad:* any three colors spaced at an equal distance on the color wheel, such as the primary colors or the secondary colors.

Value

- The lightness or darkness of a color.

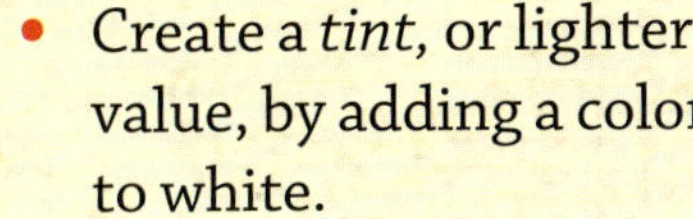

- Create a *tint,* or lighter value, by adding a color to white.

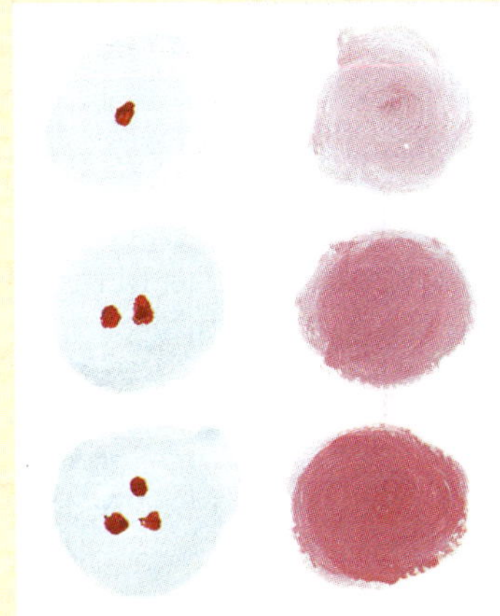

- Create a *shade,* or darker value, by adding black to a color.

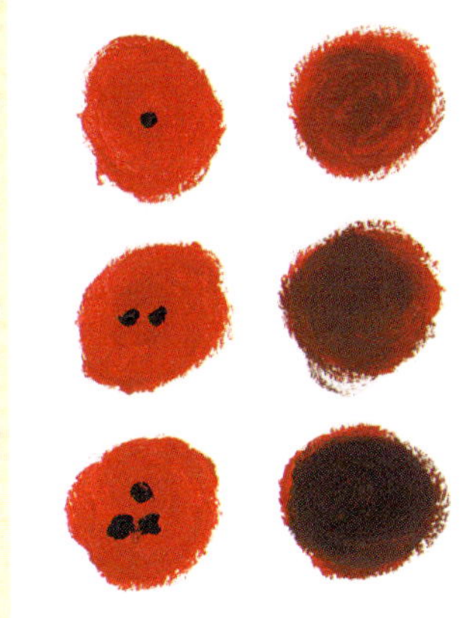

Principles of Design

The principles of design are guidelines that help artists plan relationships among visual elements. These guidelines include balance, emphasis, unity, variety, pattern, proportion, movement and rhythm, and contrast.

Balance

Artists use balance to give the parts of an artwork equal "visual weight" or interest. The three basic types of visual balance are symmetrical, asymmetrical, and radial.

- In **symmetrical balance**, the halves of a design are mirror images of each other, which creates a look of stability and quiet.

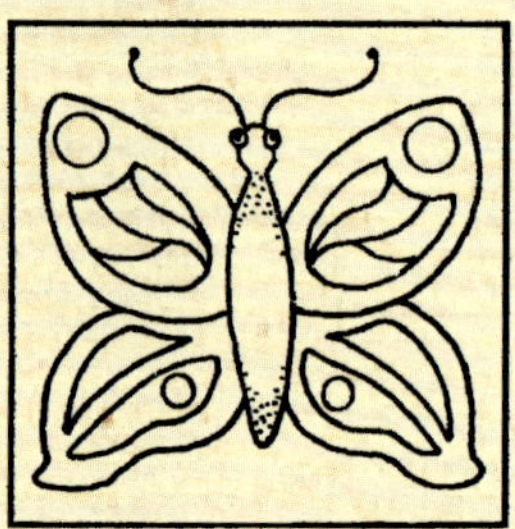

- In **asymmetrical balance**, the halves of a design are visually equal, yet not exactly the same.

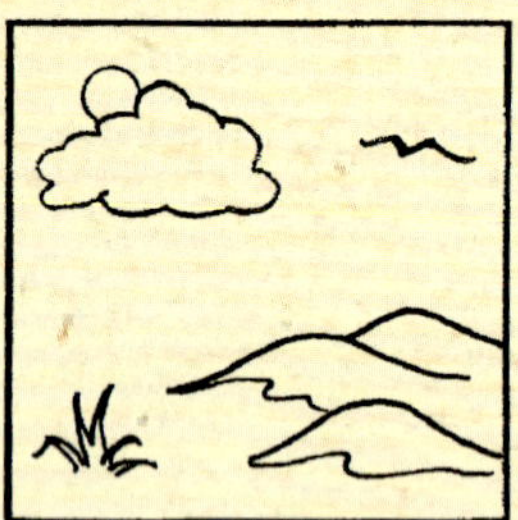

- In **radial balance**, the parts of a design seem to "radiate" from a central point, like the petals of a flower. Designs that show radial balance are often symmetrical.

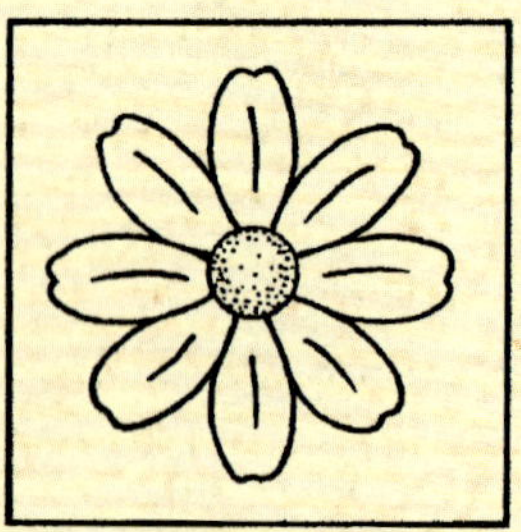

Emphasis

When artists design an artwork, they use emphasis to call attention to the main subject. Emphasis makes objects, shapes, or even white space more noticeable than other elements.

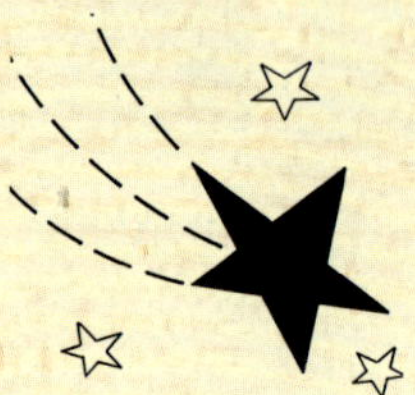

- The **size** of the subject and **where it is placed** are two key factors of emphasis.
- Create emphasis by arranging other elements in the artwork to **lead the viewer's eyes** to the important subject.
- **Group certain objects together** in a design and **use contrasting elements** to create emphasis.

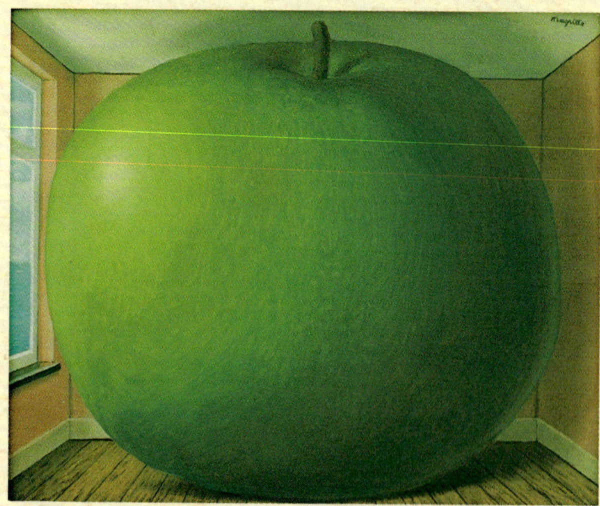

Making the apple unusually large calls your attention to it.

René Magritte, *The Listening Room*, 1958.

Unity

Unity is the feeling that all parts of a design belong together or work as a team. Here are several ways that artists can create unity:

- **repetition:** the use of a shape, color, or other visual element over and over
- **dominance:** the use of a single shape, color, or other visual element as a major part of the design
- **harmony:** the combination of colors, textures, or materials that are similar or related

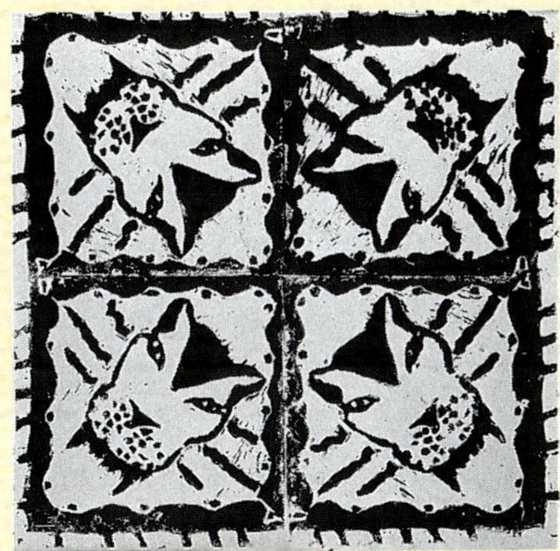

Repeated shapes give this work unity.

Student artwork.

Variety

Variety adds visual interest to a work of art. Artists create variety by combining elements that contrast or are different from one another.

- A painter might draw **varying sizes** of shapes and paint them in contrasting colors.

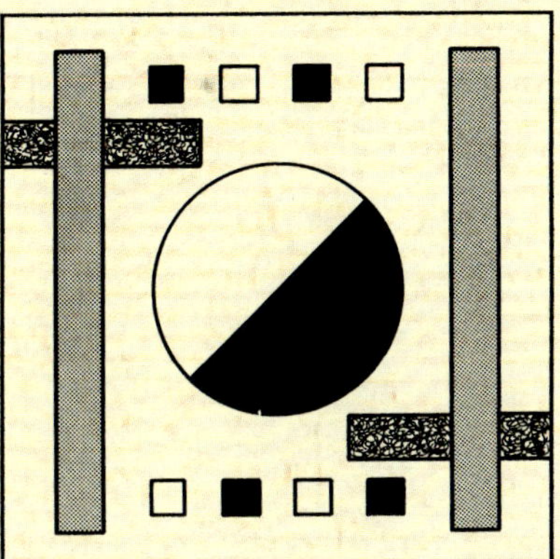

- A sculptor might **combine media** or **vary the texture** of one material.
- Architects create variety when they **use different materials**, such as stone, glass, and concrete, together in one building.

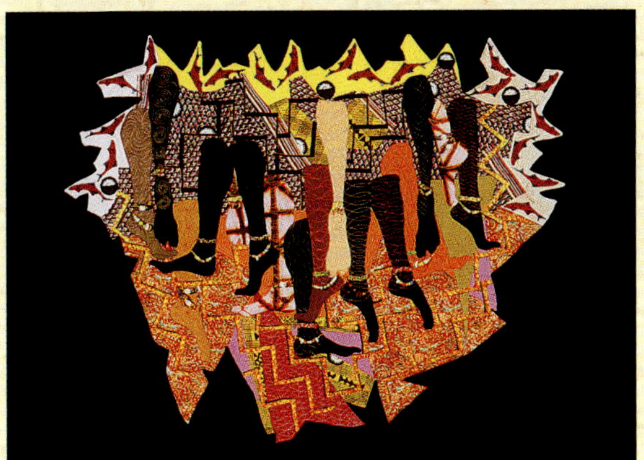

This artist used many different materials to create variety.

Frances Hare, *Sixteen Feet of Dance: A Celebration, A Self-Portrait*, 1996.

Pattern

Artists create pattern by repeating lines, shapes, or colors in a design. Patterns help organize designs and create visual interest. Patterns are either *planned* or *random*.

- In a **planned** pattern, the element repeats in a regular or expected way.
- In a **random** pattern, elements appear scattered throughout the design. Random patterns are usually more exciting than planned ones.

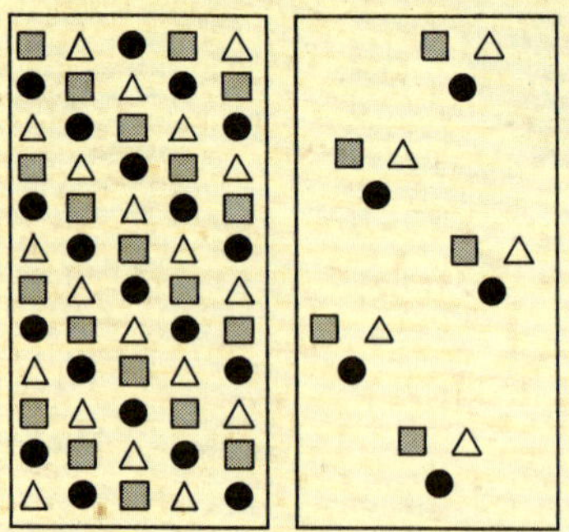

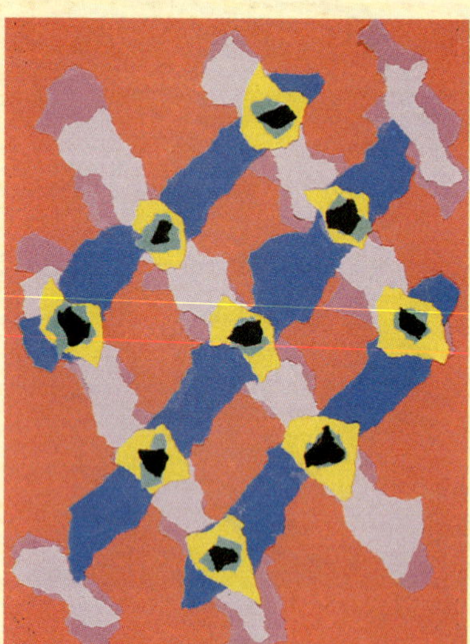

This planned pattern is formed by the color, shape, and position of paper shapes.

Student artwork.

Proportion and Scale

Proportion is the relationship of size, location, or amount of one thing to another.

- In art, **proportion** is mainly associated with the human body. Cartoonists exaggerate human proportions for humorous purposes.

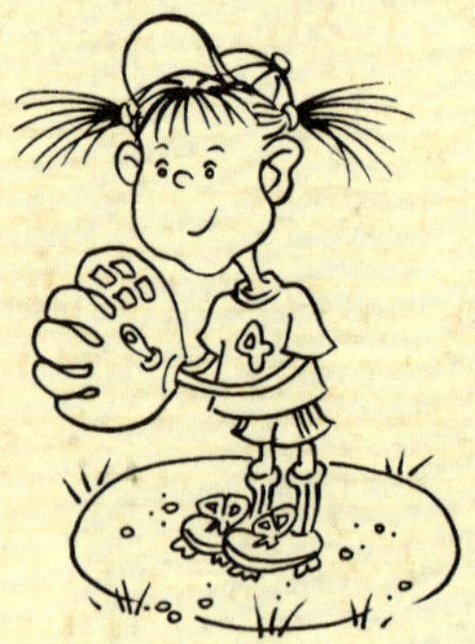

- **Scale** is the size of one object compared to the size of something else.
- Artists sometimes exaggerate the scale of objects in an artwork.

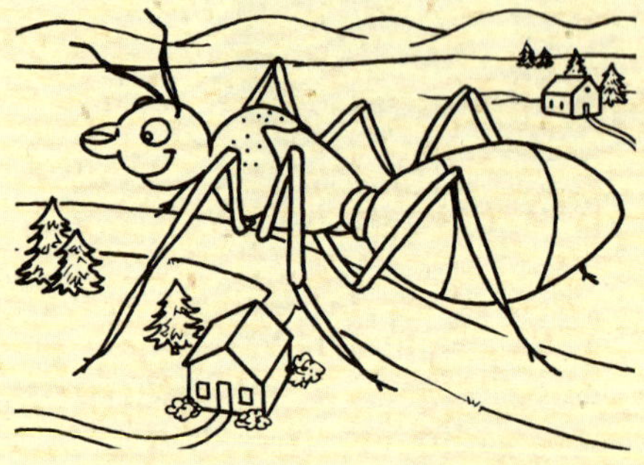

- Drawing an object on a larger scale can make it seem more important or allow the artist to use it in an unexpected way.

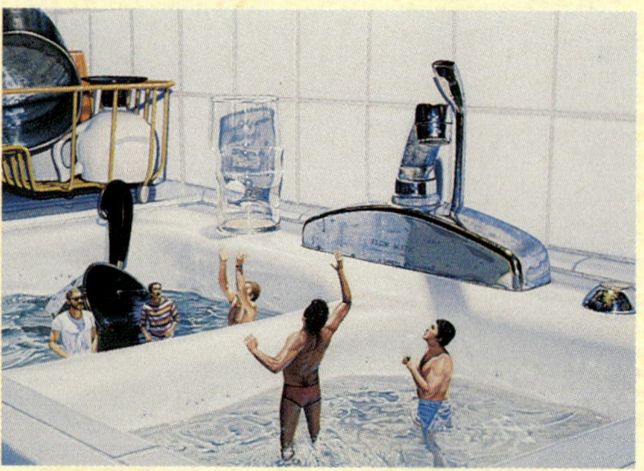

Here, the scale of the sink is greatly enlarged.

Doug Webb, *Kitchenetic Energy*, 1979.

Movement and Rhythm

Artists often use movement to create excitement and energy in their artwork. Rhythm, which is related to both movement and pattern, is created by repeating elements in a particular order.

- Kinetic art, such as mobiles, actually moves, while other forms of art only record the movement of their subjects.

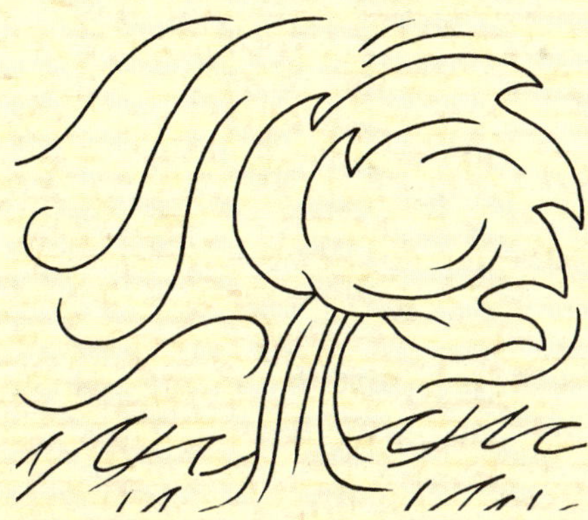

Even simple lines can show rhythmic movement.

- Sometimes movement is added to an artwork to lead the eye to a center of interest or add to a mood.
- Rhythm may be simple and predictable, such as the lines in a sidewalk, or it may be complex and unexpected.
- Artists use rhythm, like pattern, to help organize a design or add visual interest.

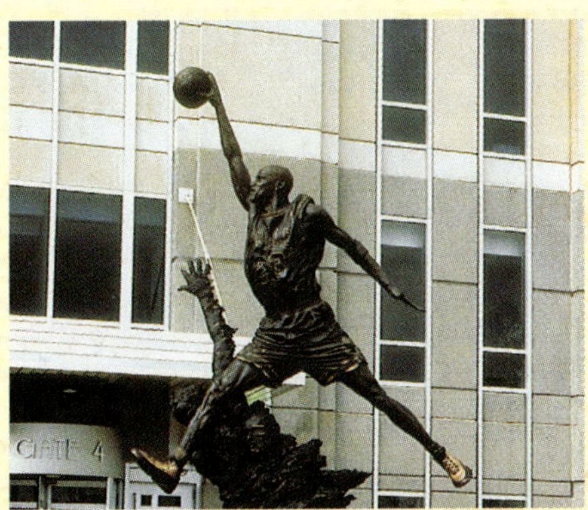

Showing a figure with both feet off the ground helps suggest movement.

Omri Amrany and Julie Rotblatt-Amrany, *The Spirit, Michael Jordan*, 1994.

Contrast

Contrast is a difference between two things. The greater the difference, the greater the contrast.

- The area of greatest contrast captures your attention first.
- Value is one element artists contrast in their work. Contrast in values creates a noticeable difference between light and dark. It adds excitement or drama.
- Artists also create contrast through the use of strong differences in colors, shapes, textures, and lines.
- Some artists use contrast to create a particular mood or feeling.

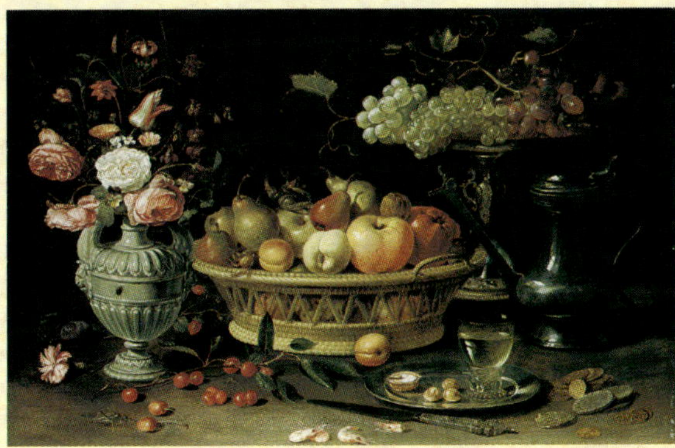

Contrast between bright and dark areas adds drama to this painting.

Clara Peeters, *Still Life with Fruit and Flowers*, after 1620.

New Directions in Design

Design is the act of making a plan for a specific outcome such as a website, an appliance, a building, or a video game. Unlike fine artists, who create for self-expression, designers plan products, structures, and systems for people to use. Designers consider questions such as *How can this object best serve its user? How can its appearance match the way it functions? How can this object use specific materials or the environment for maximum efficiency?*

Information Design

- Information designers and graphic designers consider the different ways to communicate information.
- *Graphic design* is the use of visual art to communicate information.
- Graphic designers use typography (fonts), images, and page layout as part of their overall design.
- They are responsible for creating advertisements, animation, logos, road signs, diagrams in textbooks, book layouts, and websites.

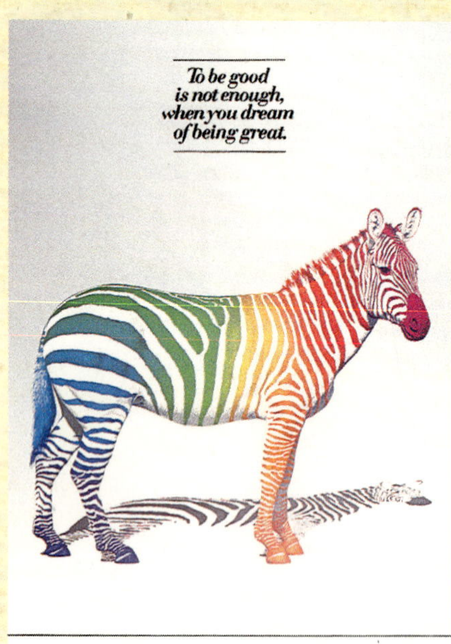

Graphic designers use words and images together to send their messages.

Marvin Mattelson (illustrator), *Subway Poster for School of Visual Arts.*

Object Design

- Object designers create new designs for everyday objects such as automobiles, clothing, furniture, and appliances.
- Many of these objects are intended for mass production. The design of mass-produced consumer products is called *industrial design.*
- Industrial designers are often trained as architects or as visual arts professionals. Many work with a larger creative team to create products that work well, look attractive, and will sell well in a competitive market.

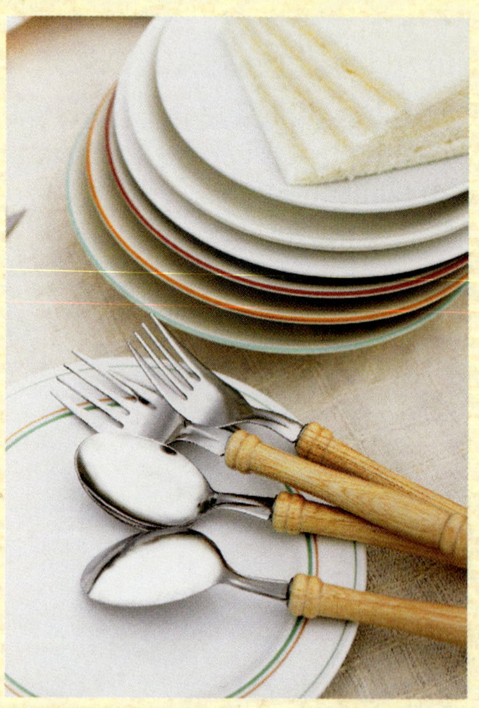

These utensils and plates were designed and then mass-produced.

"Tableware," Bloomimage/Corbis.

Space and Place Design

- Space and place designers plan and determine how a structure—including its interior—interacts with space, objects, and the environment.
- *Architects* design buildings and other structures. They consider the function their structure will serve, how stable and durable it will be, and how its form will communicate ideas.
- *Interior designers* focus on the smaller, more intimate spaces within a building and use a mix of space and objects to create certain moods.
- *Urban planners* work with much larger spaces, so they have much to consider as they design. They focus on how society uses structures and space and the impact society has on both. They also plan the development of open land and the renewal of existing parts of cities.

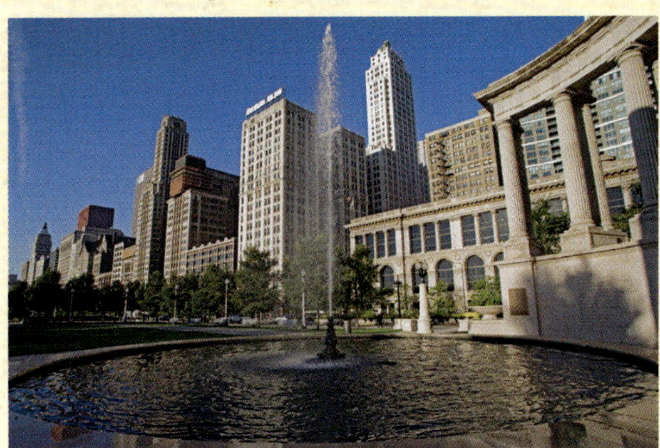

A city's buildings are usually designed by many different architects at various times in history.

Art on File/Corbis.

Experience Design

- Experience designers plan products, processes, services, events, and environments with which people can interact. The results of these designs provide experiences for people.
- Computer-human interface (CHI) designers create products that allow people to physically interact with computers. The computer mouse, the touch screen, and pull-down menus are examples of CHI technology.
- The video games, theme parks, toys, and games you enjoy were all created by experience designers.

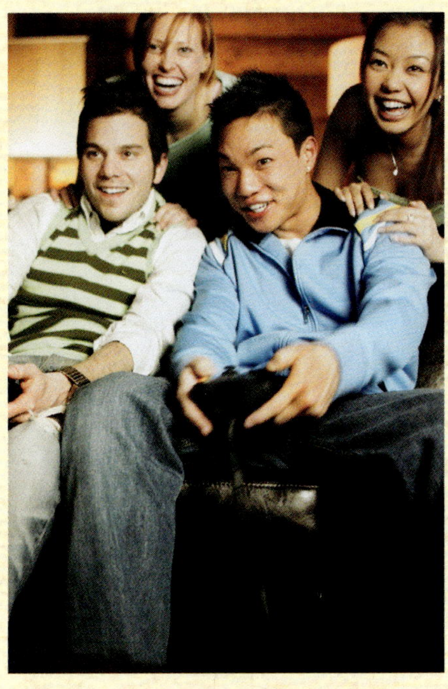

Products that interface with computers should be designed for ease of use.

Brand X/Corbis.

Major Western Art Styles and Movements

For thousands of years, people all over the world have created art. In the following pages, you can observe how artists in western Europe and North America have expressed themselves and how art styles have developed and changed over time.

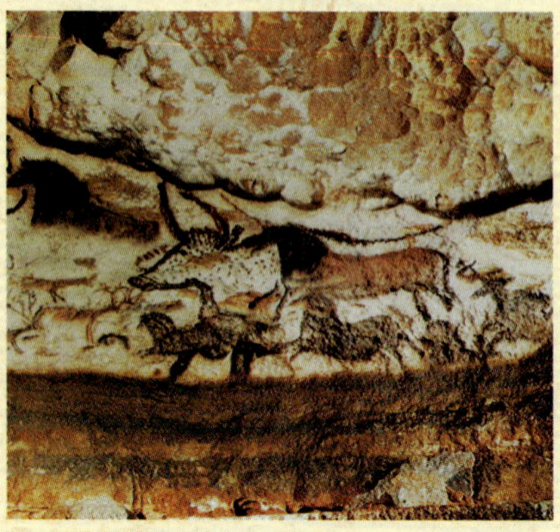

Hall of Bulls, detail, Lascaux, c.15,000–13,000 BC.

Stone Age Art 30,000–2000 BCE

- The earliest known artworks are paintings discovered in caves in Spain, France, and Africa.
- Animals in cave paintings are usually shown in profile with lifelike proportions, details, and actions. People are shown as stick figures with spears.
- Cave paintings may have been used to communicate hope for a successful hunt, to record events, or to educate children.

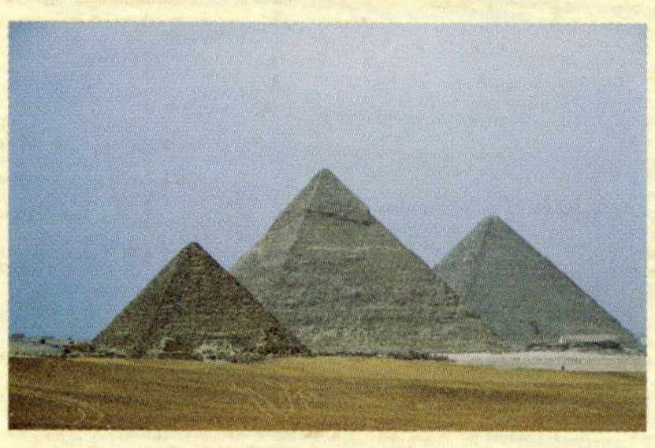

Giza, Egypt, *The Pyramids of Mycerinus, Chefren, and Cheops,* built between 2589 and 2350 BC.

Ancient Egyptian Art 3000–500 BCE

- Pharaohs built pyramid-shaped tombs filled with furniture and jewelry to take with them in the afterlife.
- Wall paintings, relief sculptures, and small models were common art forms.
- Artists worked according to strict rules: head, arms, and lower body in profile, eye and upper torso in front view.

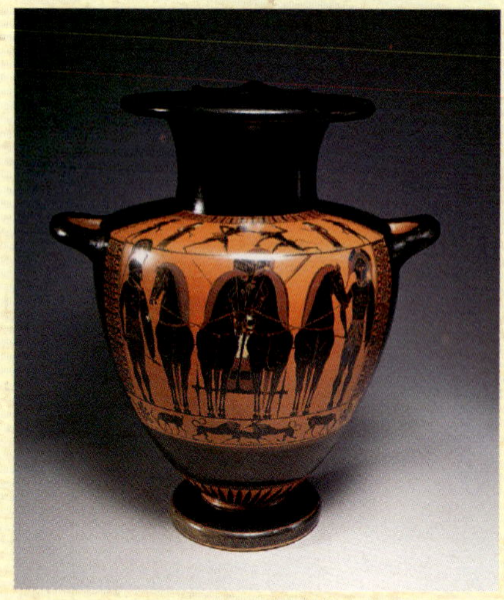

Ancient Greece, Athens, (attributed to the Antimenes painter), *Hydria*, c. 530–510 BC.

Ancient Greek Art 600–150 BCE

- Known for its elegant proportions and perfection of form.
- Mosaic murals were created in many buildings.
- Sculptures were often decorated with paint, gold, and colorful stones.
- Athletes, heroes, myths, and important events were common art subjects.
- Architecture, especially temples and outdoor theaters, featured carved columns and new building techniques.

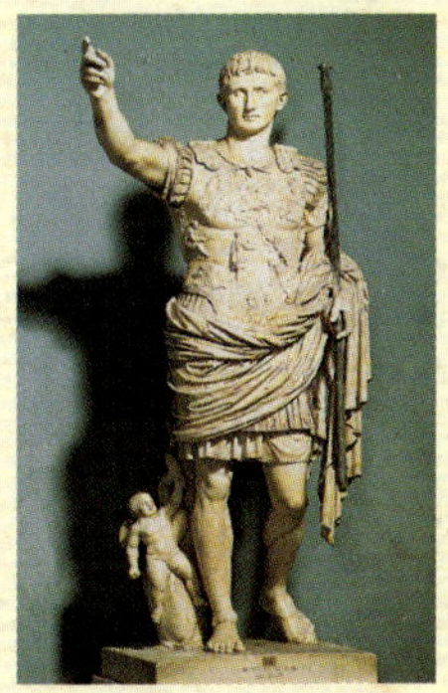

Augustus of Prima Porta, Roman Sculpture, Early first century AD.

Ancient Roman Art 753 BCE–476 CE

- Reflects ideas from Greece, but with a greater interest in naturalistic details
- Emphasized realistic features, showing rulers, ancestors, and peers as they looked in real life.
- Used for practical and political purposes. Exact facial features let people in any part of the vast Roman Empire know what their ruler looked like.

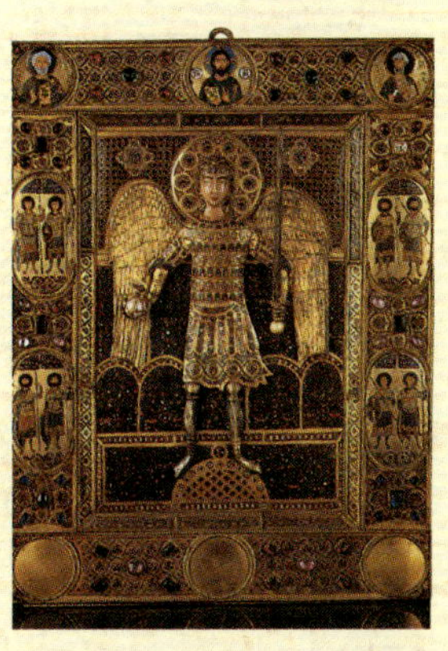

The Archangel Michael with Sword, Byzantine, 11th century.

Byzantine Art 300–1500

- Developed in eastern Roman Empire as a response to the rise of Christianity.
- Rejected Greek and Roman ideals of the perfect human being, physical beauty, and strength.
- Focused on religious themes, using symbols and icons to tell stories about how to live a Christian life.
- Artworks feature a rich use of color and flat, stiff figures.

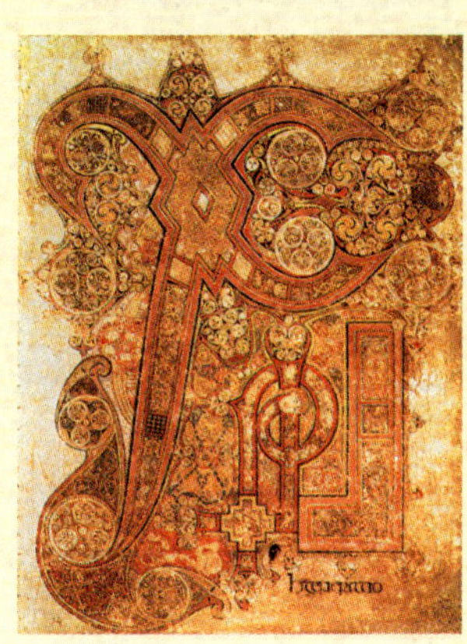

Chi-rho Gospel of St. Matthew, chapter 1 verse 18, Irish (vellum). *Book of Kells*, c. 800.

Medieval Art 400–1400

- Heavily influenced by Christianity, Judaism, and Islam.
- Because many people could not read, art was used to communicate important religious lessons.
- Illustrated scriptures show scenes painted with complex geometric patterns, figures, and fantastic animals. Often, a layer of gold is used to emphasize parts of an image.
- Artworks, in the forms of books and objects of adornment, were small and could be carried easily.

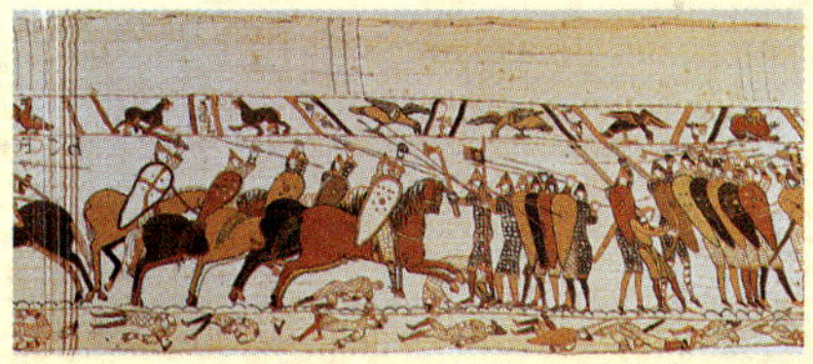

Bayeux Tapestry, 1100 CE.

Romanesque Art 1000–1200

- Developed in western Europe during the Middle Ages.
- Brought back the Greek and Roman tradition of carving large-scale sculptures.
- Cathedrals have thick walls, rounded arches, and sculpted religious scenes.
- Items created for use in worship were often decorated with gold, silver, pearls, and gemstones.

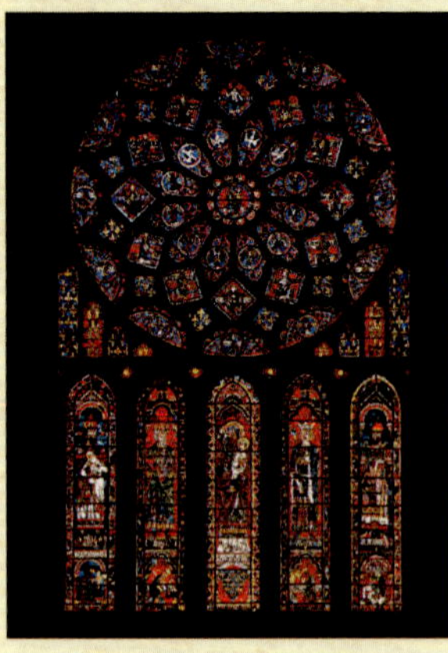

Chartres Cathedral, *North Transept Rose and Lancet Windows,* 13th century.

Gothic Art 1000–1200

- French style that was adopted in parts of Europe and England.
- Art and architecture characterized as vertical, open, delicate, and light.
- Churches used stained-glass windows to let in light.
- Biblical scenes in windows taught churchgoers lessons.

Artists: Giotto di Bondone, Cenni di Pepi Cimabue, Ambrogio Lorenzetti, Simone Martini, Gentile da Fabriano, The Limbourg Brothers (Paul, Jean, and Herman) (painters); Nicola Pisano, Sabina von Steinbach, Claus Sluter (sculptors)

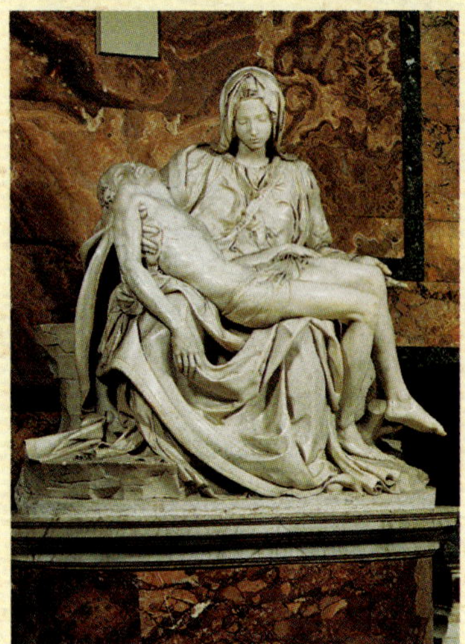

Michelangelo Buonarroti, *Pietà*, 1499.

Renaissance Art 1400–1600

- Began in Italy and gradually spread to the rest of Europe.
- Paintings show realistic textures such as metal, wood, and skin.
- The invention of oil paint allowed artworks to have smooth, glowing surfaces and clear colors.
- Artists focused on light and perspective, and used new techniques to show order, depth, and graceful movements.

Artists: Fra Angelico (painter), Giovanni Bellini (painter), Filippo Brunelleschi (architect), Michelangelo Buonarroti (sculptor), Donatello (sculptor), Jan Van Eyck (painter), Leonardo da Vinci (painter)

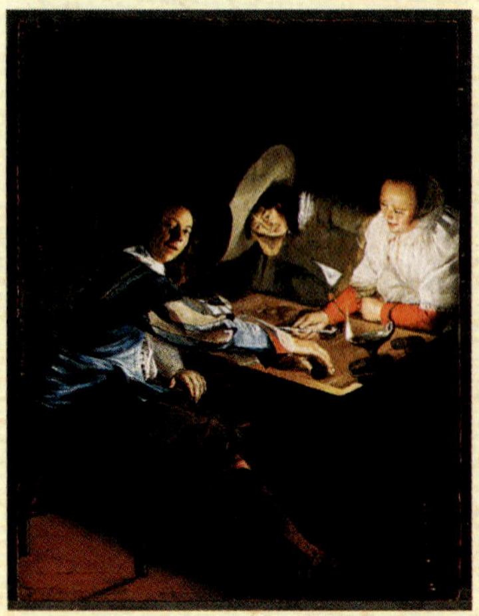

Judith Leyster, *Game of Tric-Trac*, ca.1630.

Baroque Art 1600–1700

- Lively motion, dramatic contrasts in light and shade, and asymmetrical design are typical.
- Artists used rich colors and textures and swirling curves.
- Still lifes, everyday objects and events, portraits, and landscapes were popular subjects.
- Artists shaped metal and stone into fluid forms.

Artists: Michelangelo da Carravaggio, Artemisia Gentileschi, Francisco de Zurbarãn, Bartolomé Murillo, Diego Velásquez, Peter Paul Rubens, Anthony van Dyck, Nicholas Poussin, Claude Lorraine, Frans Hals, Judith Leyster, Jan Vermeer, Jacob van Ruisdael, Clara Peeters, Racel Ruysch, Sibylla Maria Merian (painters); Francesco Borromini, Guarino Guarini, Jakob Prandtauer, Christopher Wren (architects)

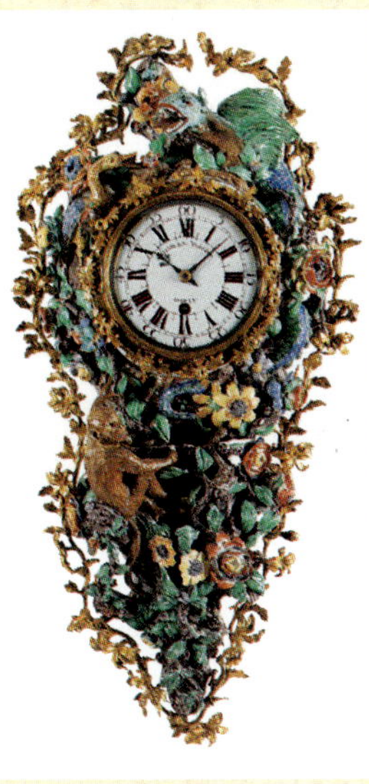

Movement made by Charles Voisin and Chantilly manufactory, *Wall Clock*, c. 1740.

Rococo Art 1700–1800

- Whimsical, decorative variation of Baroque art created for aristocrats in France, Spain, England, and Italy.
- Delicate colors, playful use of lines, and graceful movement show aristocrats at carefree leisure.
- Ordinary household items showed the elegance and charm favored by the upper class.

Artists: Rosalba Carriera, Jean-Baptiste Chardin, William Hogarth, Benjamin West, (painters)

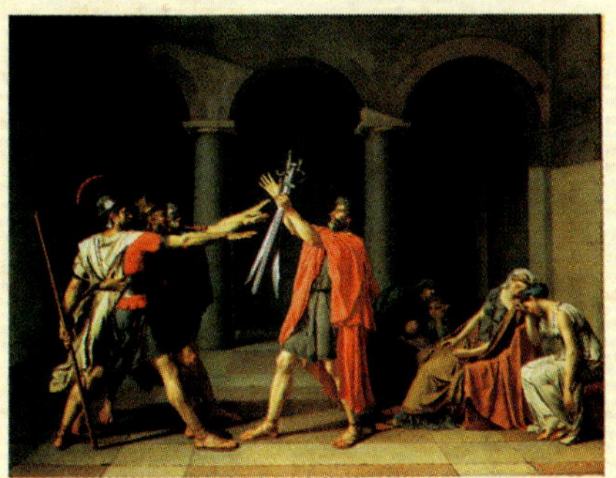

Jacques-Louis David, *Oath of the Horatii*, 1784–1785.

Neoclassicism 1750–1875

- Unearthed classical art at ancient Roman cities Pompeii and Herculaneum inspired the movement.
- Greek and Roman ideals of beauty, courage, sacrifice, and patriotism applied to artworks.
- Formal lines, shapes, proportions, and simple orientation are features of this style.
- In architecture, renewed emphasis on classical arches and columns.

Artists: Antonio Canova (sculptor), Jacques-Louis David (painter), Thomas Jefferson (architect), John Trumbull (painter), Elizabeth Vigée-Librun (painter), Thomas Walter (architect)

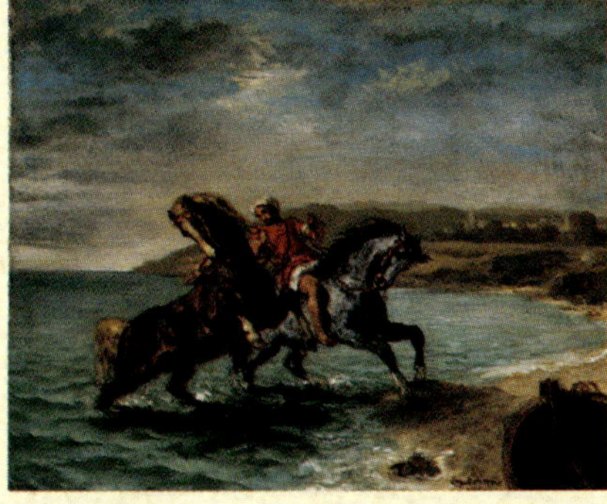

Eugène Delacroix, *Horses Coming Out of the Sea*, 1860.

Romanticism 1815–1875

- Rejected the ordered style of Neoclassical art.
- To show emotion, artists applied color with wild, active brushstrokes.
- Themes included dramatic action, exotic settings, imaginary events, faraway places, or strong feelings.

Artists: Thomas Cole (painter), John Constable (painter), Eugène Delacroix (painter), Sophia Hayden (architect), H.H. Richardson (architect), François Rude (sculptor)

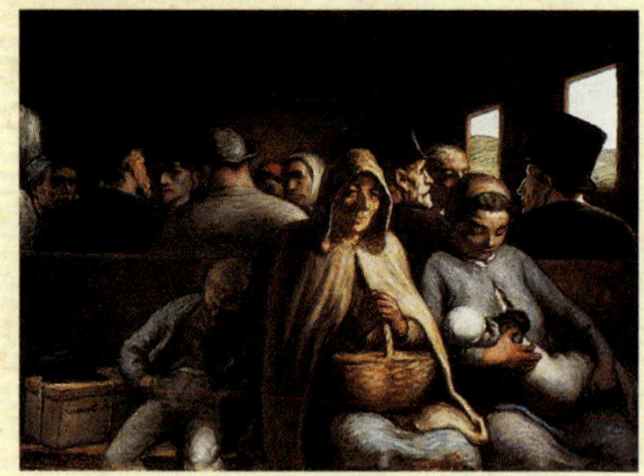

Honoré Daumier, *The Third Class Carriage*, ca. 1863–65.

Realism 1850–

- Rejected Neoclassicism and Romantic styles.
- As subjects, artists chose scenes from real life—rural and city life, people at work, the poor, and political strife
- Realists believed their art recorded simple ways of life that were being destroyed by new technologies.
- Buildings' designs matched their functions.

Artists: Rosa Bonheur (painter/sculptor), Honoré Daumier (painter), Gustave Eiffel (architect), Jean-François Millet (painter), Edouard Manet (painter), Joseph Paxton (architect), John Singer Sargent (painter)

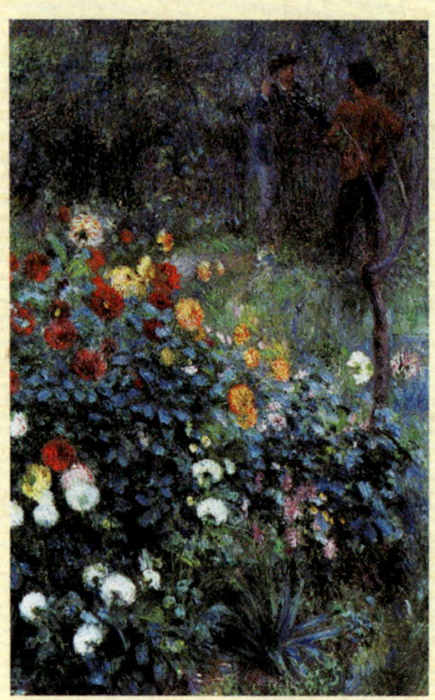

Pierre-Auguste Renoir, *The Garden in the Rue Cortot, Montmarte*, 1876.

Impressionism 1875–

- Began in France; artists created an "impression," capturing a brief moment in time.
- Space and form are suggested by varying the intensity of light and color.
- Paintings are created using short, quick brushstrokes, which cause shapes to merge together.
- Small strokes of color make artworks shimmer and sparkle.

Artists: Daniel Burnham (architect), Mary Cassatt (painter), Edgar Degas (painter/sculptor), Claude Monet (painter), Berthe Morisot (painter), Auguste Rodin (sculptor), Georges Seurat (painter)

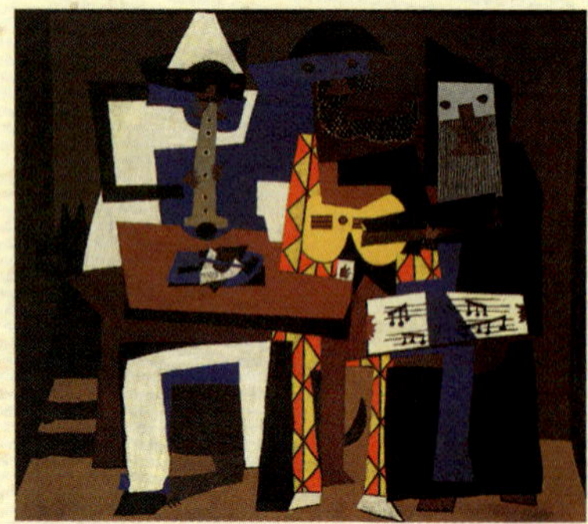

Pablo Picasso, *Three Musicians*, 1921.

Cubism 1907–

- Based on an interest in showing multiple and partial views of objects on the flat surface of a page or canvas.
- Artworks have an abstract, often puzzle-like design with features broken into pieces.
- Another characteristic of this style is the use of hard-edged, geometric forms.

Artists: Georges Braque (painter), Sonia Terk Delaunay (painter), Jacques Lipchitz (sculptor), Georgia O'Keeffe (painter), Pablo Picasso (painter/sculptor)

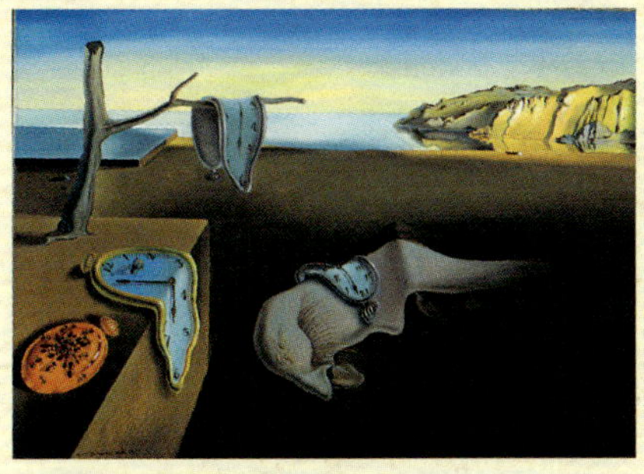

Salvador Dali, *The Persistence of Memory*, 1931.

Surrealism 1924–

- Artists emphasized dream worlds and the subconscious.
- Unrelated objects are often shown realistically in an illogical or unnatural setting.
- Artworks often include visual surprises.

Artists: Marc Chagall, Salvador Dali, René Magritte, Joan Miró, Meret Oppenheim, Henri Rousseau, Kay Sage Tanguy, (painters)

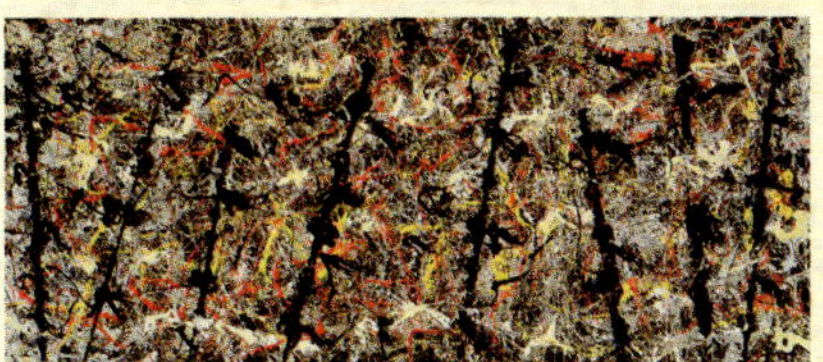

Jackson Pollack, *Blue Poles*, 1952.

Abstract Expressionism 1945–

- Refers to large paintings that are meant to suggest feelings or ideas.
- Artworks are based on emotion and feeling, with little or no recognizable subject matter.
- Artists explore ways of painting. They drip, pour, or splash paint on the canvas.

Artists: Hans Hofmann, Jackson Pollack, Arshile Gorky, Hale Woodruff, Mark Tobey (painters); Louise Nevelson, Nancy Graves, David Smith (sculptors)

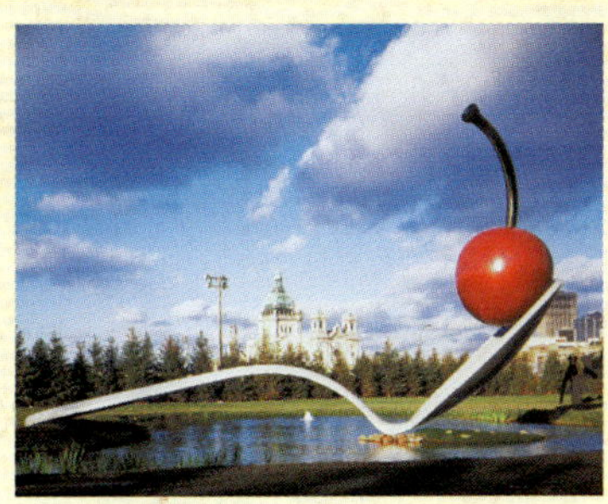

Claes Oldenburg and Coosje van Bruggen, *Spoonbridge and Cherry*, 1988.

Pop Art 1950–

- Everyday objects are used as subject matter.
- Artists draw their ideas from popular and consumer culture: comic strips, hot dogs, movie stars, and so on.
- Artworks often show wit, satire, or humor.

Artists: Roy Lichtenstein, Jasper Johns, Andy Warhol, David Hockney (painters); Claes Oldenburg, George Segal, Duane Hanson (sculptors)

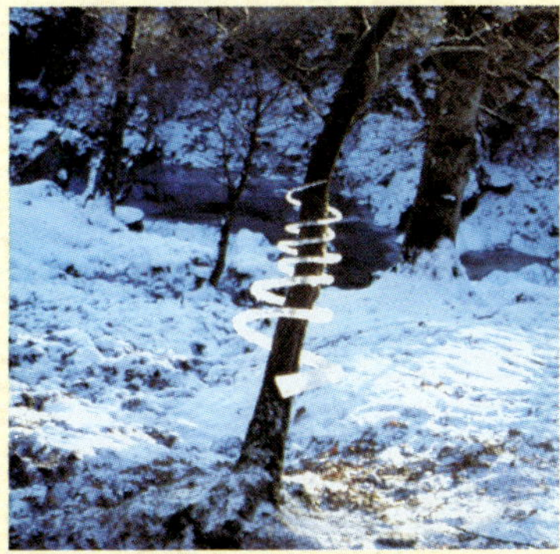

Andy Goldsworthy, *The coldest I have ever known in Britain*, 1995.

Environmental Art/Earthworks 1960–

- Artworks draw attention to environmental issues.
- Movement celebrates the environment.
- Artists often use earth, wind, and water as sculptural media.
- Artworks are often impermanent.

Artists: Robert Smithson, Mary Miss, Christo/Jeanne-Claude, Andy Goldsworthy

Techniques

The following basic art techniques can be used as a guide while drawing and painting.

Contour Drawing

Studio Background

A contour drawing is a drawing that describes the overall shape of an object or figure. It may include some interior details. Contour drawings are usually done slowly.

There are different kinds of contour drawings. In **blind contour drawing** you do not look at the paper while you are drawing.

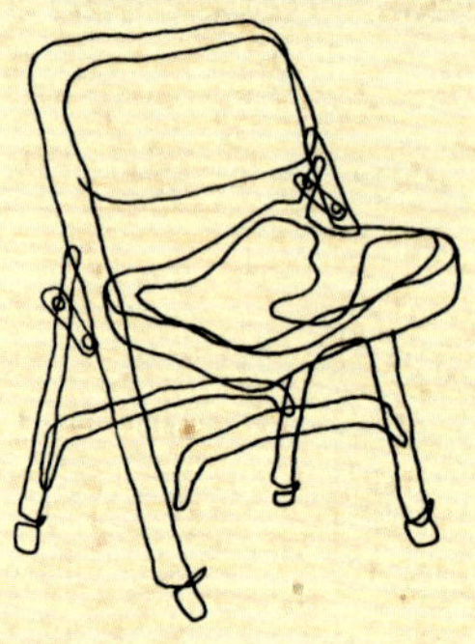

Blind contour drawing

In **modified contour drawing** you use the same technique as blind contour drawing, but you may pause at times to check the position of your drawing tool.

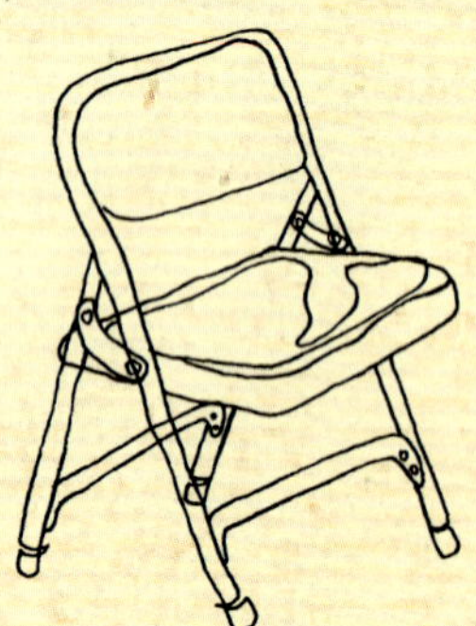

Modified contour drawing

Making a Contour Drawing

- Look only at the object you are drawing, not at your paper.
- First practice drawing the object's outline without letting your drawing tool touch the paper.

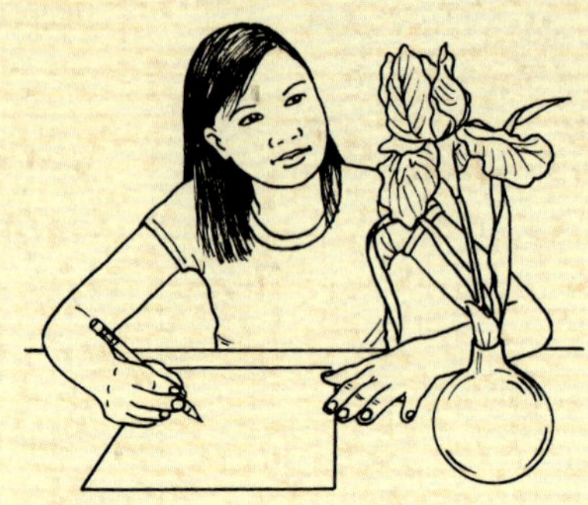

Look only at the object.

- Begin to draw, using a continuous line. Draw slowly.
- Follow the contours of the object, including its wrinkles and folds.
- Do not lift your pencil from the paper until you have finished.

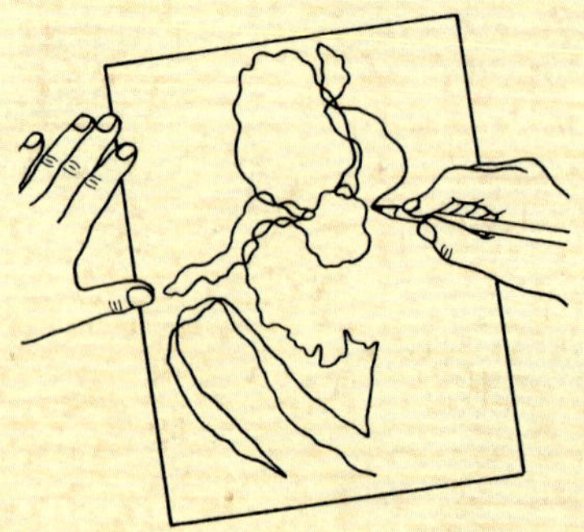

Don't lift your pencil from the paper until you are finished.

Gesture Drawing

Studio Background

Use gesture drawing as a way to quickly capture the main parts of a subject before something moves or changes. When doing a gesture drawing, focus on the action lines of the subject. Most gesture drawings are sketches rather than finished drawings and are completed in a minute or two. Use them to help you plan a painting, sculpture, print, or other work of art.

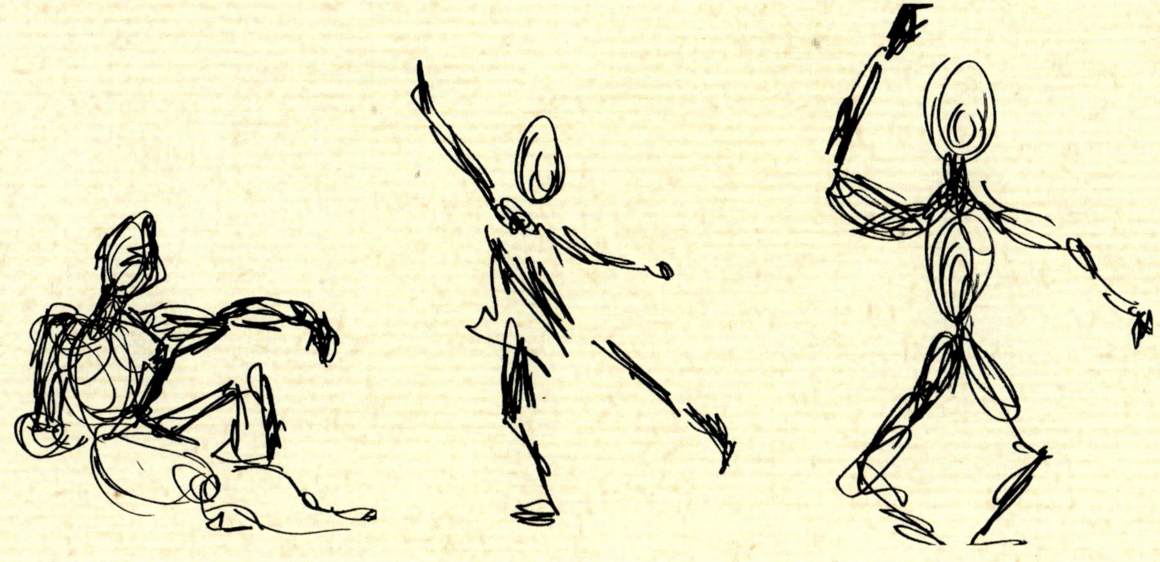

Making a Gesture Drawing

- Practice making gesture drawings using a wide, soft pencil, crayon, or piece of chalk.
- Ask a classmate to strike and hold an action pose, such as dancing, jumping up to catch a ball, or running.

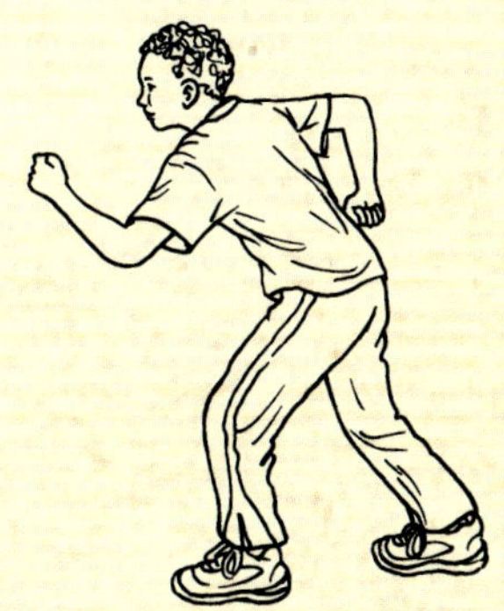

Have a classmate hold a pose.

- Take in the overall action of the scene and position of your subject.
- Make a gesture drawing that captures the form of the pose, but not the details. Draw quickly. You can add details later if you want. Use large, swift strokes to help you capture shapes, angles, and positions.

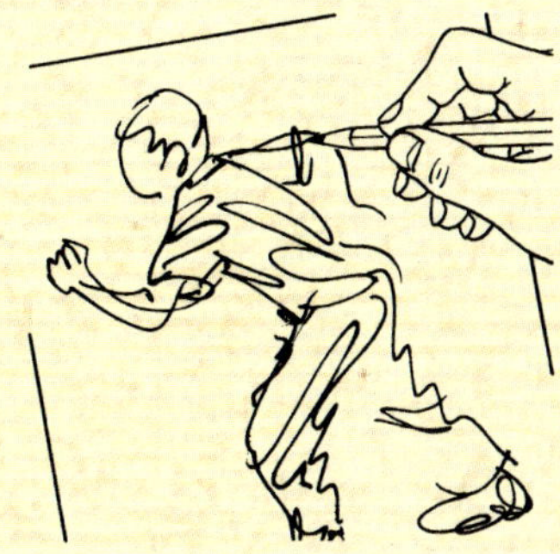

Capture form, not details.

Shading Techniques

Studio Background

Shading is a gradual change in value or tones of color. Drawing techniques such as hatching, stippling, and blending let artists show gradual changes between light and dark areas. In many artworks, the light source determines where an artist places values in an artwork. Artists use shading techniques to create highlights and cast shadows that give clues to the location of the light source.

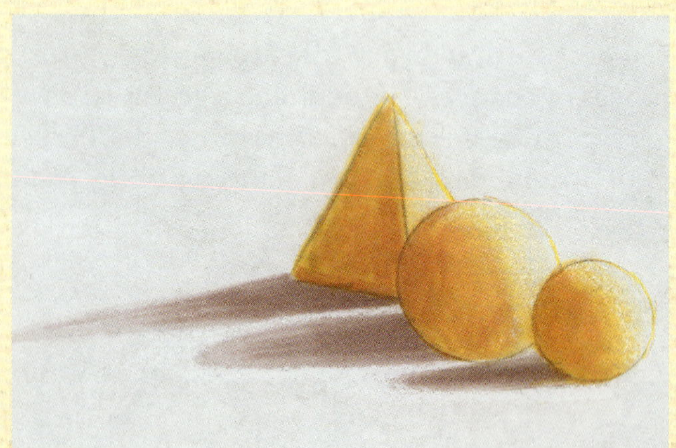

Hatching and Crosshatching

- **Hatched lines** go in one direction and are parallel to one another. Close placement creates dark areas. Use a fine-tipped drawing tool.

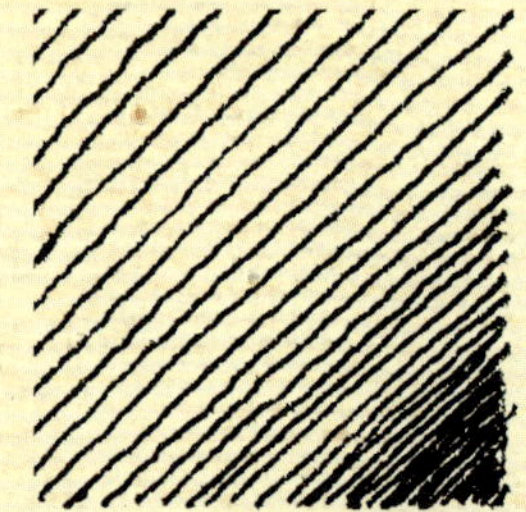

- When **crosshatching**, you start by creating hatched lines and then cross them with another set of lines.

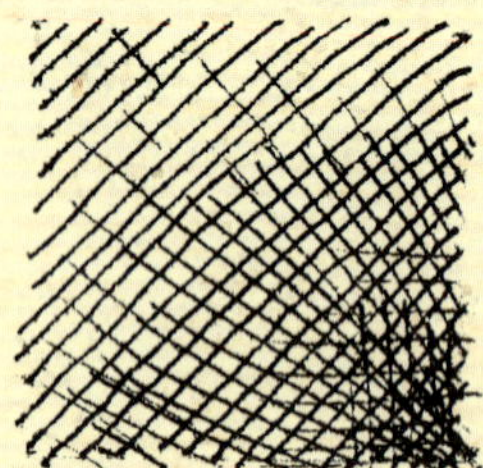

Stippling

- Stippling is the process of making tiny dots. The closer together the dots are, the darker the tone. Use a fine-tipped drawing tool.

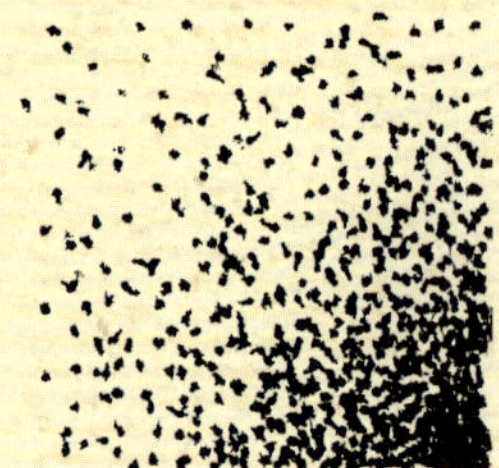

Blending

- For blending, use a soft drawing tool. Draw on paper and then smudge or blend the area with your fingers, a tissue, or a cotton swab.

Perspective

Studio Background

Artists use an assortment of techniques to create **perspective**. These techniques include overlapping, shading and shadow, placement, size, and focus. Some artists invent ways to combine these techniques.

Basic Perspective Techniques

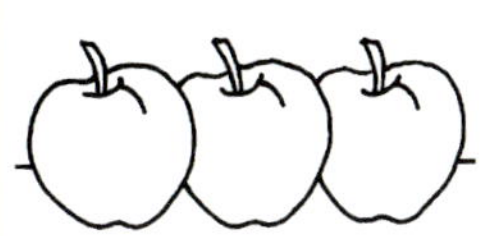

Overlapping

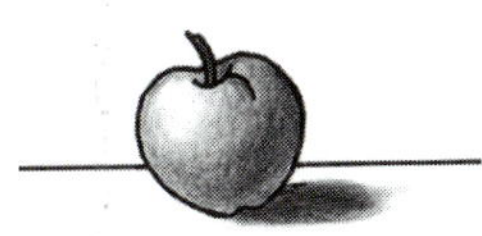

Shading and shadow

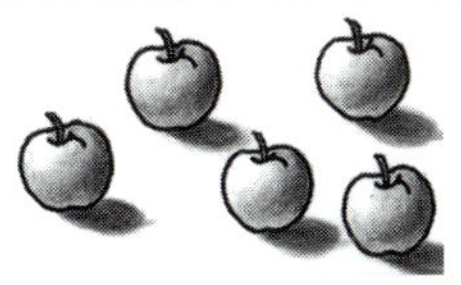

Placement: Objects near top seem more distant

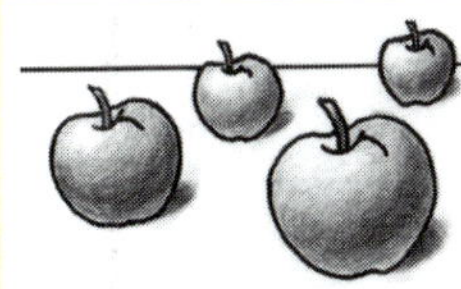

Size: Smaller objects seem more distant

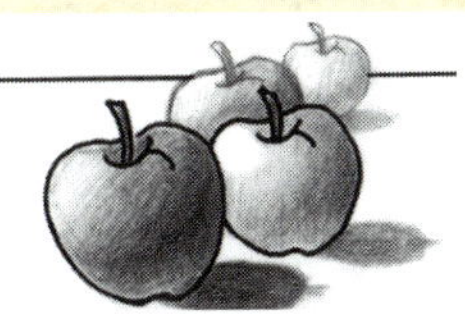

Focus: Sharp detail suggests nearness

Using Linear Perspective

Linear perspective is a system of lines used to create the illusion of three-dimensional space.

One-Point Perspective

- Use a yardstick or ruler to lightly draw a horizon line (HL) across the paper.
- Mark a vanishing point (VP) at the center of your horizon line. Add diagonal guides that recede to the vanishing point.

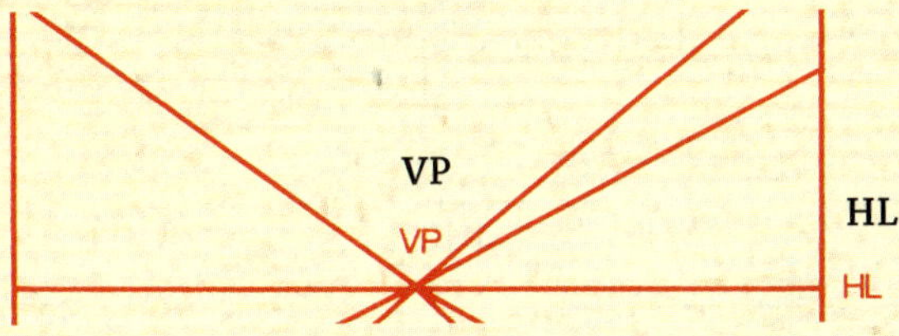

- Draw buildings, houses, or other box-like objects that recede as they approach the vanishing point.
- Vertical lines should be parallel to the side of the paper; horizontal lines should be parallel to the top and bottom of the paper.

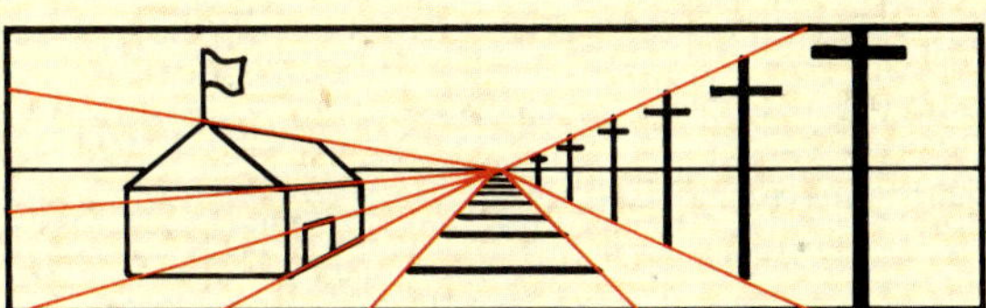

Two-Point Perspective

- Begin your drawing with two vanishing points (VP) on the horizon about the same distance from the edges of the paper.

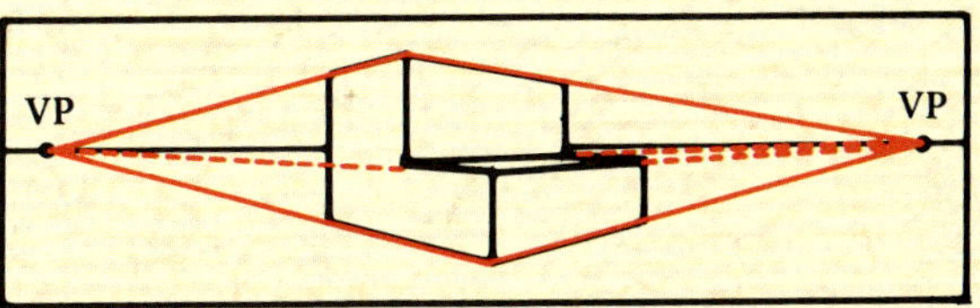

Drawing with Chalk, Crayon, and Pen and Ink

Studio Background

Before they draw, artists think about the medium they will use. Pencils, charcoal, pastels, and crayons are **dry media**. Inks, applied with a pen or brush, are **wet media**. The effects of drawing media can change depending on whether they are used on wet or dry paper. Once artists choose their medium, they experiment with it to find the techniques they like best.

Drawing with Chalk and Crayons

- Colored chalk, or pastels, can be used on wet or dry paper.
- Practice using the tip of the chalk to make solid and dashed lines.

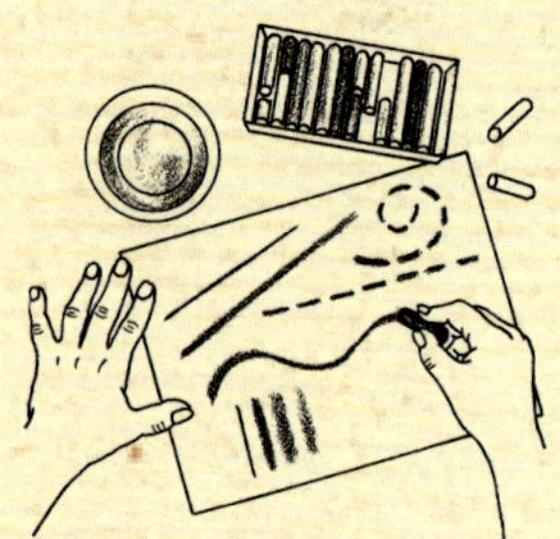

Practice making many kinds of lines.

- To make clean, sharp lines, dip the chalk into water or liquid starch.
- Use the side of the chalk to make wide lines.
- Press harder to make the line darker and more solid. Use less pressure for a lighter, less solid line.

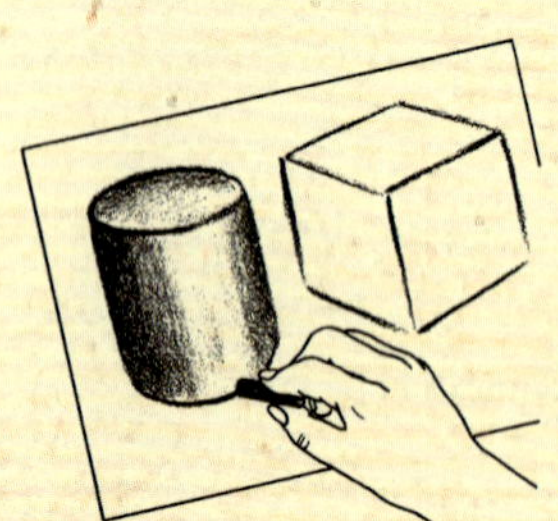

Press hard to make dark lines.

- To mix colors, apply one on top of the other. Use a tissue to blend the colors together.
- Use a kneaded eraser, or putty rubber, to add highlights or small corrections.

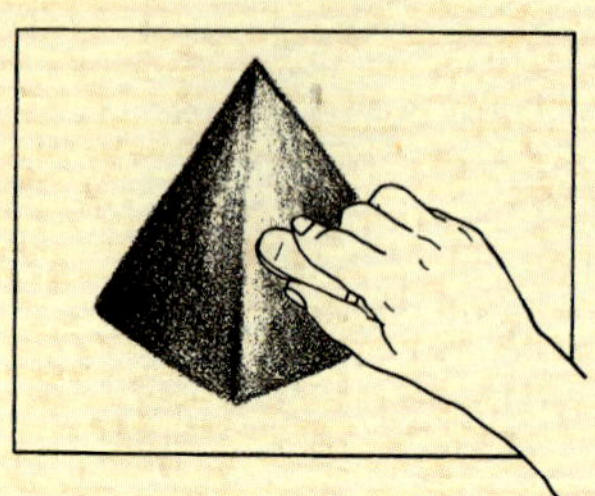

Add highlights with an eraser.

- Practice with crayons in the same way as chalk, but on dry paper only.

Drawing with Pen and Ink

- Ink can be applied with a variety of tools—natural pens like quills, ballpoint pens, nibs, twigs, cotton swabs, or small sponges.

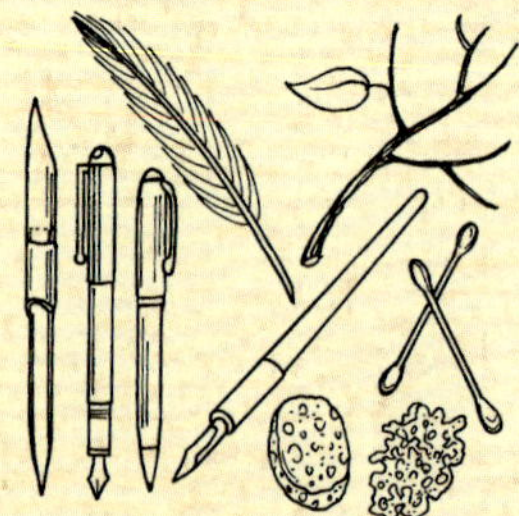

Try a variety of tools.

- Pen and ink can be used on wet or dry paper, but smooth paper gives a more pleasing result.
- Draw your design in pencil first.
- Go over the lines with a pen. Work from one side of the paper to the other so you do not smear the ink.

Brushstrokes

Studio Background

The type of brush and paint you choose, and the brushstrokes you use in your artwork, affect the way your paintings look. The brushstroke techniques below work well with tempera paints, watercolors and thinned acrylic paint.

Making Brushstrokes

- Try different kinds of brushes. Feel how their bristles differ from one another. Certain brushes work best with specific types of paint.

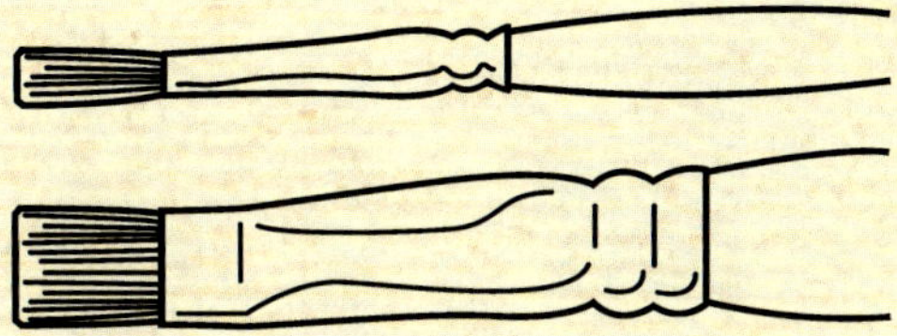

Stiff bristle brush for thick paint

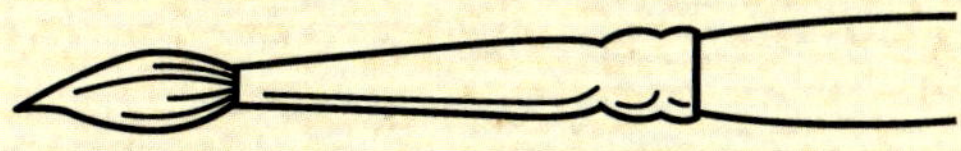

Soft hair-type brush for washes and details

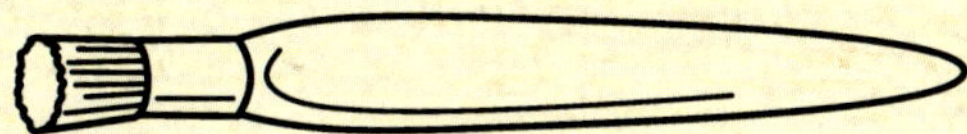

Stiff bristle brush for stencil work

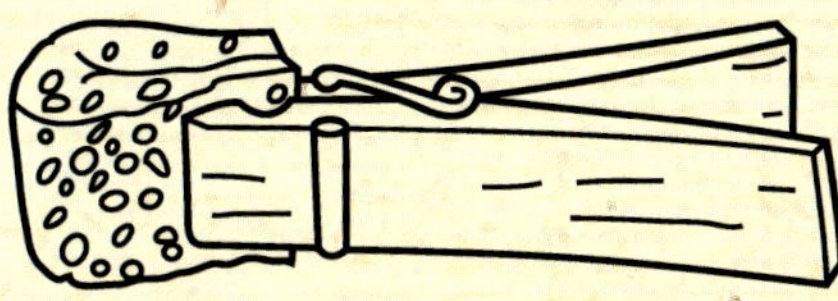

Simple sponge brush

- Choose a soft-hair brush for watercolors or thinner paints. Hold the brush with the bristles pointing down.

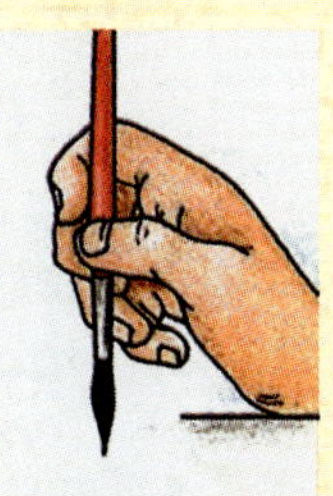

- Press hard for a wide brushstroke. Lift the brush up for a thin stroke. Use one stroke for a shape.

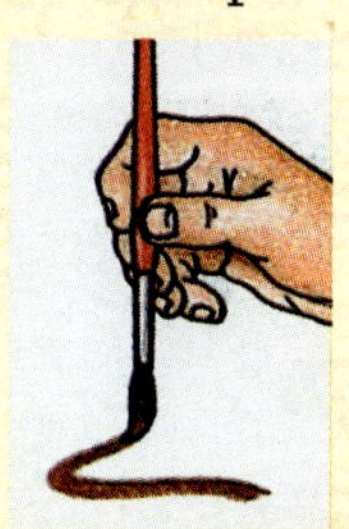
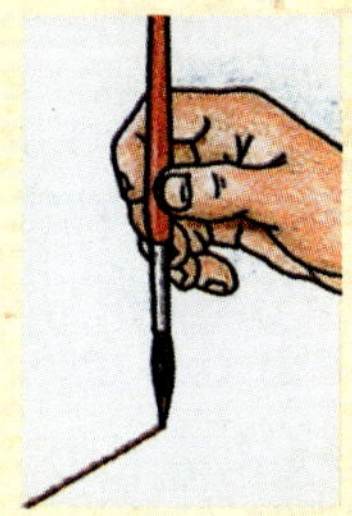
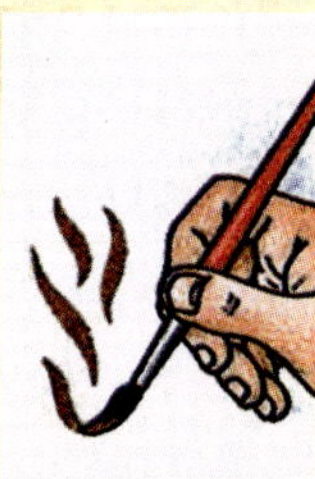

- Practice strokes using different amounts of water in your brush and different amounts of pressure. Observe how the lines change.
- Wash, wipe, and blot your brush before putting it away.

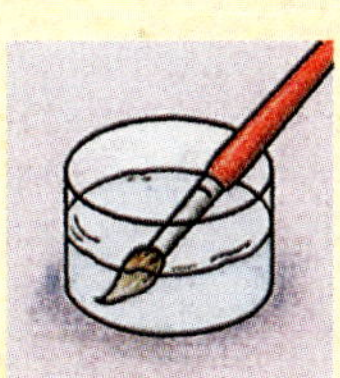
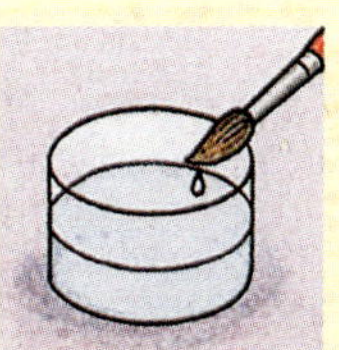

Art Forms and Media

The materials an artist uses to create an artwork are called **media**. Watercolors, pen and ink, pencil, clay, and digital cameras are different kinds of media.

Digital Photography

Studio Background

Instead of using film, digital cameras capture images and movies by changing them into thousands of **pixels**, tiny squares or dots of color, and storing them in the camera's memory. A screen allows you to preview, plan, or review images, hundreds of which can be stored in the camera's memory. You can then either delete these images or download them to a computer to be saved or printed.

Using a Digital Camera

Digital cameras are easy to use. Follow these steps to take pictures and store them in your computer.

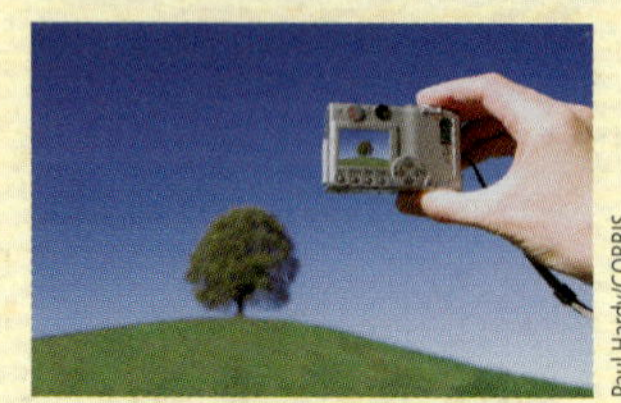
Paul Hardy/CORBIS.

Taking a Picture

- Turn the camera on.
- Your digital camera should be in automatic mode. In this mode, the camera selects all settings.
- To view your subject, look through the viewfinder. If your digital camera does not have one, look at the screen.
- Focus on your subject. Then press the shutter button to take the picture.
- Review the image when it appears on the screen. You may delete it or save it to your camera's memory.

Saving Pictures to Your Computer

- Make sure your camera's software is installed on your computer.
- Connect your camera to the computer using a USB cable.
- Turn the camera on.
- The camera's software should open on your computer.
- Select the images from the camera that you want downloaded to your computer.
- Save or print the images.

Keep In Mind

- Make sure your digital camera has enough power by inserting or replacing the batteries. Keep extra batteries on hand. Digital cameras require a lot of power, so you may need to change the batteries again during use.
- Check that your digital camera has enough memory to record your images and movies. You can either delete images stored in the memory to free up space, or you can use memory cards with higher capacities for image storage.
- Images can be stored in different file formats. The most common file format is JPEG, which does not take up much room in the camera's memory and is processed faster than other file formats. TIFF files use more space in the memory, but they are higher-quality images. RAW files are the least common format and are used mostly by professional photographers because they have editing options.

Multimedia Presentations

Studio Background

A **multimedia presentation** uses a variety of media—text, video, slides, photographs, art, music, and charts—to communicate information about a subject. Presentation software allows you to combine these media to deliver a successful and effective multimedia presentation.

Making a Multimedia Presentation

Gather Your Media

- First, decide what you want to present. If you plan to present your portfolio, gather your artworks. If you plan to present a topic, such as an artist or an art movement, research and record information on that topic.
- Once you know what you will present, think about the kinds of media that you will include. Choose specific artworks from your portfolio. Search your local library or the Internet for audio and video clips, music, or art.

Prepare Your Media

- Scan your artworks so that you can view them on your computer. Save all other media files you might have to your computer.
- Presentation software uses *slides*—individual screens that can contain images, text, sound or animation files—to show information. Use slides to organize your media and information.

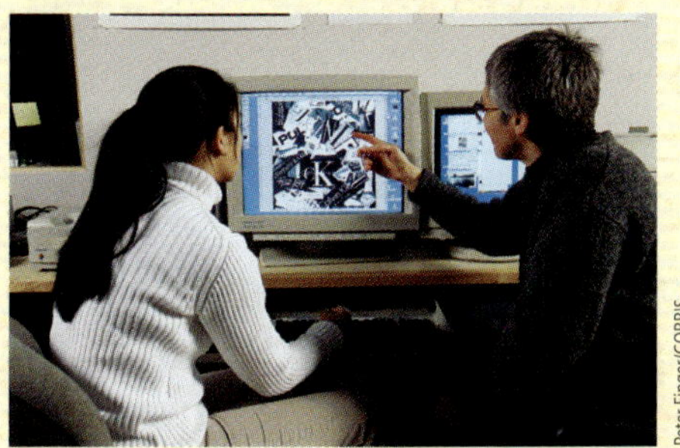

Peter Finger/CORBIS.

Prepare Your Presentation

- Consider *slide transitions*, the movement of one slide to the next. You can choose transitions in which your slides dissolve into each other, push each other off the screen, or open up like blinds. Using many different transitions can be distracting for your audience, so use only one or two kinds of transition throughout your presentation.
- Consider the layout of your slide. Make sure it is readable and visually pleasing. Put the title at the top and important information below it. To keep all your slide layouts consistent, use a *design template*, a model into which you insert your text and files.

Keep In Mind

- The amount of time a slide appears on the screen is very important. Do not change the slides quickly, because your viewers will not get a chance to read or look closely at your artwork or information. Do not keep your slides up for too long, or your viewers may lose interest.
- Electronic media require additional equipment such as projectors that you or your school must provide. If you plan to use your school's equipment, alert your teacher in advance so the equipment will be available on the day of your presentation.

Watercolors

Studio Background

Watercolor paints are transparent, and come in tubes or pans. Start with just a few basic colors, and then mix them to create a wider range.

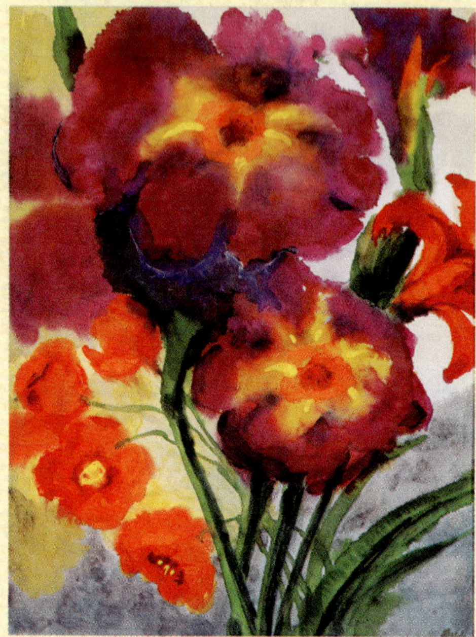

Notice how you can see one color through another in this watercolor painting.

Emile Nolde, *Summer Flowers,* 1930.

Using Watercolors

- To create **sharp edges**, apply wet paint to dry paper.
- To create **soft edges**, apply wet paint to damp paper.
- Paint light colors first, darkest colors last.
- To create a **light value** of a hue, dilute the paint with plenty of water.
- To create a **darker value**, use more pigment and less water.

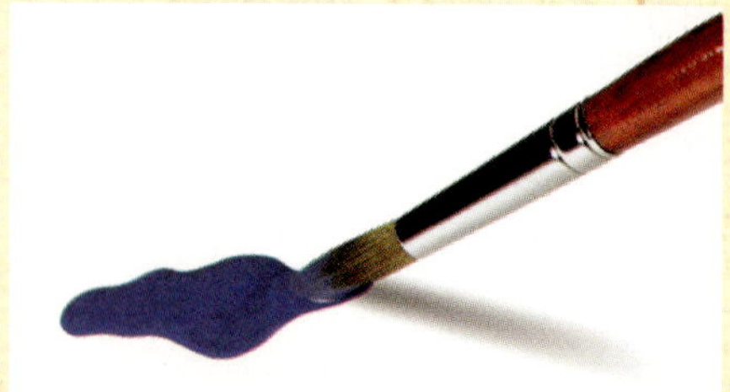

A dark value of blue

- A wash is a thin layer of paint spread over a large area.

A green wash

- You can let a wash dry and then paint over it.
- You can paint over a wash before it has dried.
- To make a white area, do not apply paint. Let the white paper show through.

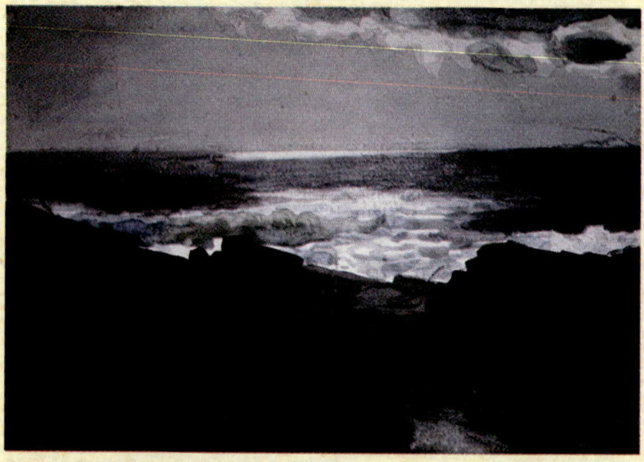

This artist let the white paper show in some areas to create highlights.

Winslow Homer, *Sunshine and Shadow, Prout's Neck,* 1984.

Tempera Paints

Studio Background

Tempera paints come in both liquid and powder form and in brilliant hues. They dry quickly, developing a dull, chalky appearance when dry. They can be layered to produce intense color.

Using Tempera Paints

- Use a stiff bristle brush and short, swift brushstrokes to paint large areas of color first.

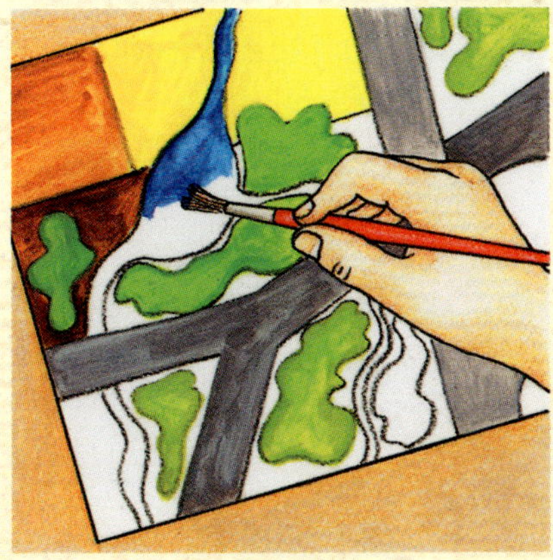

Paint large areas first.

- Allow area to dry before adding small details. Brushing large areas of wet paint over dry paint will cause the paint to run.

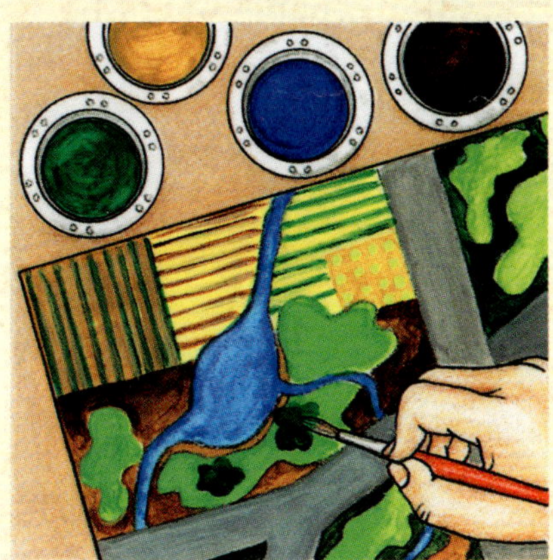

Add small details after the paint dries.

- To mix a **tint**, add small dots of colored paint to white paint.

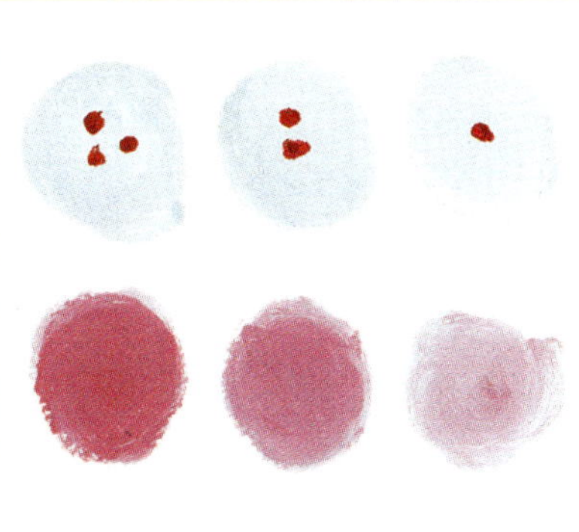

- To mix a **shade**, add small amounts of black to a color.

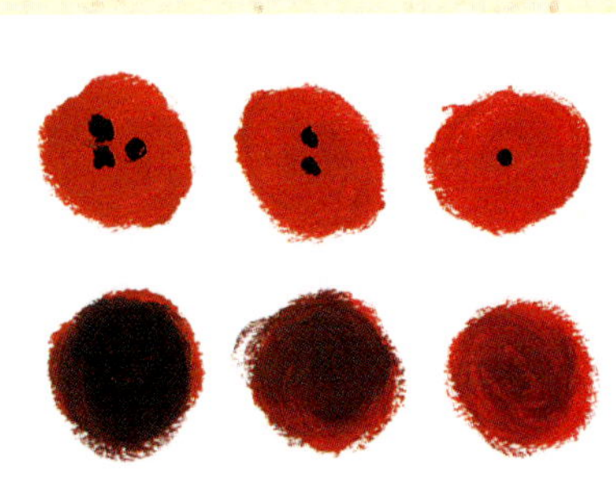

- To mix a new color, add small amounts of a different color to the original color.
- When you change colors, wash, wipe, and blot the brush. Do not dip the brush directly into the bottle.

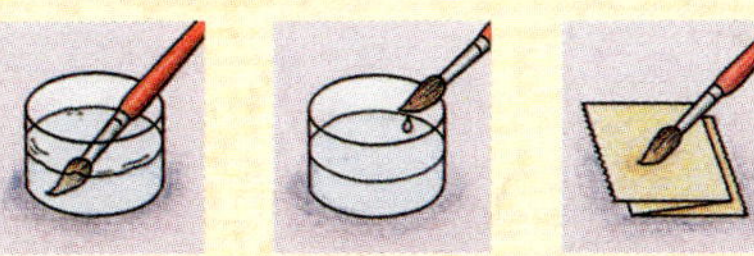

- Once a bottle is opened, use it as quickly as possible. Keep bottles tightly closed. Do not return unused paint to the bottles.

Oil Pastels

Studio Background

Oil pastels are pigments mixed with oil and wax. Unlike chalk pastels, they do not make dust when you use them, but they never dry completely. This means your works will not crack, but they will smudge unless you frame them and cover them with glass or plastic.

Using Oil Pastels

- Use oil pastels to sketch the main shapes and colors.
- Press heavily for a brilliant-colored line. Press lightly to create a fuzzy line.

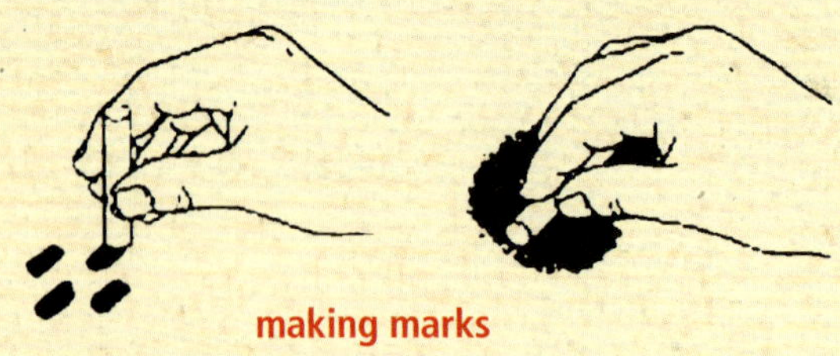

making marks

- Blend colors together using your fingers, a tissue, or cotton swab.

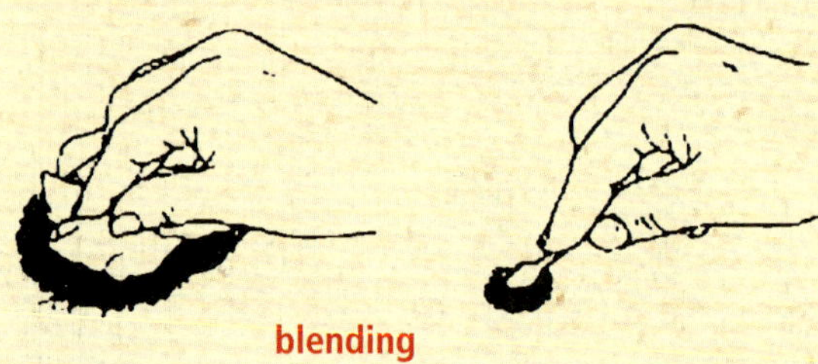

blending

- With your fingers or blending tool, add small swirls or strokes that mimic the details of your subject.
- Change colors of details by blending a new color with the base pastel. Use white or black to make a tint or shade of a color.

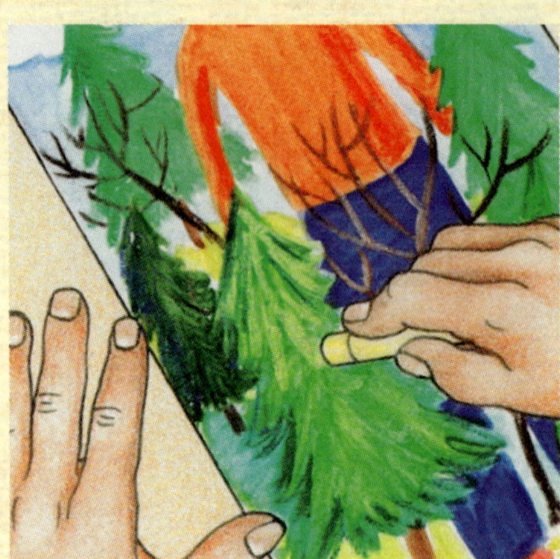

Add one color over another.

- If you are using colored paper or trying a new technique, apply a layer of white first. Scrape away the result if you do not like it, and begin again.

Monoprinting

Studio Background

A monoprint is an edition of only one print. In other forms of printmaking, you can make many prints from the same plate. When you create a monoprint, you can prepare the plate in several ways, but usually the preparations do not survive after the first print.

Making a Monoprint

Method 1

- Roll out a thin, even layer of ink on a smooth, nonabsorbent surface.

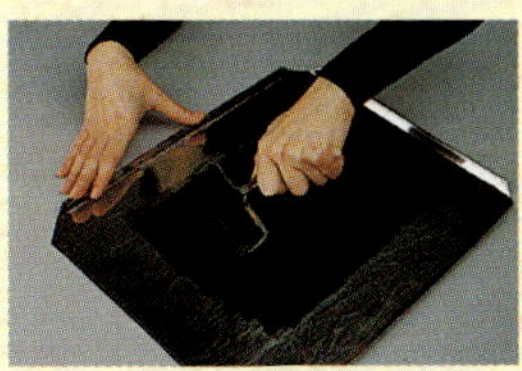

- Draw directly into the ink with a tool such as a toothpick, pencil eraser, cotton swab, facial tissue, or old comb.

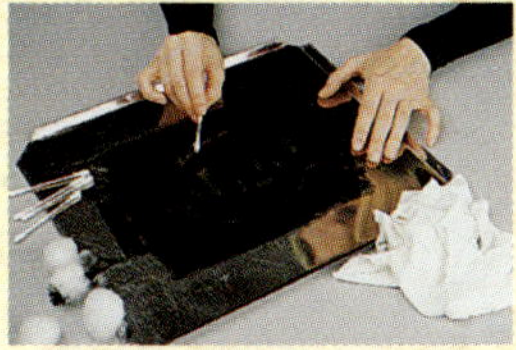

- Place a sheet of paper over the design, and rub it evenly but lightly with your hand.
- Pull the print by lifting the paper away from the surface.

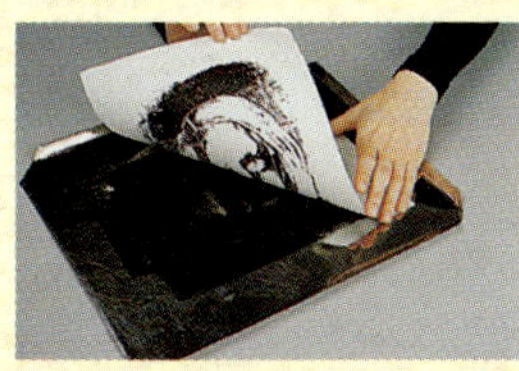

Method 2

- Working quickly, paint an image with tempera paint on a smooth, non-absorbent surface.

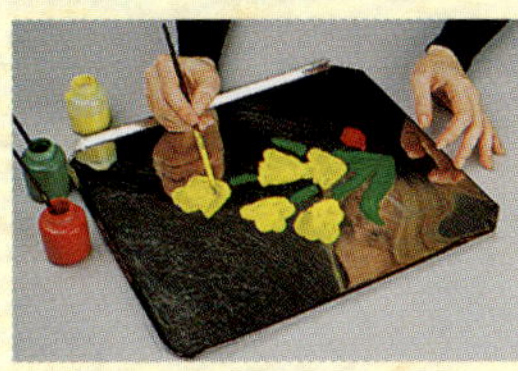

- Place a sheet of paper over the painted image, and rub it evenly but lightly with your hand.

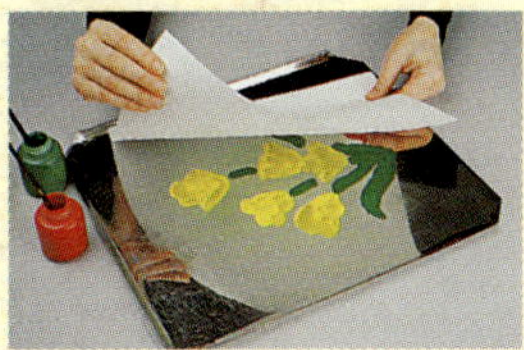

- Pull the print by lifting the paper away from the surface.

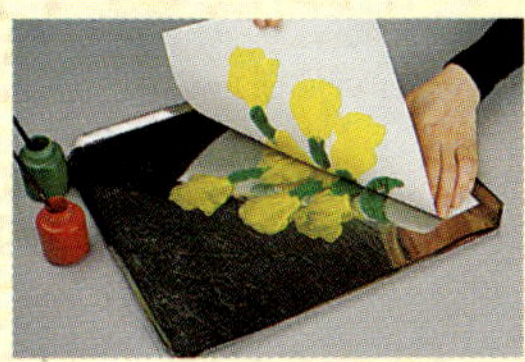

Method 3

- Roll out a thin, even layer of ink on a smooth, non-absorbent surface. Place a sheet of paper over the inked surface, but do not rub it.

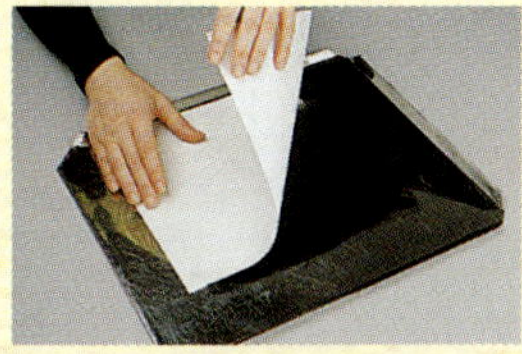

- Using a pencil, draw an image on the paper.

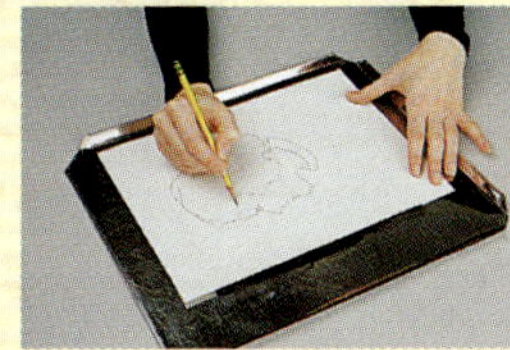

- Pull the print by lifting the paper away from the surface.

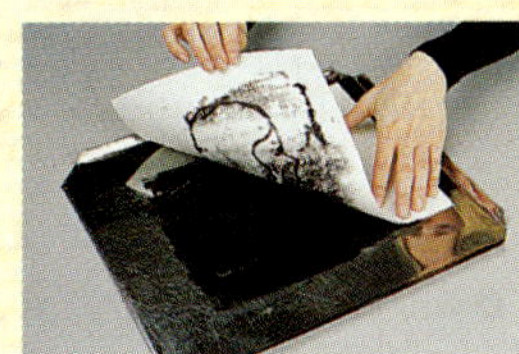

Relief Printmaking

Studio Background

Relief printmaking is one of several basic printmaking processes. A **relief print** is made from a design that is raised from a flat background, usually a wood or linoleum block. Ink is applied to the raised surfaces and then paper or another material is pressed down on the print to leave an image. Printmakers can make many identical prints using this method.

Making a Relief Print

- Create a design on paper.
- Place your design and carbon paper on top of a wood or linoleum block. Alternatively, you can use a dark pencil to black the back of your design.
- Trace over your design to transfer the image to the printing block.

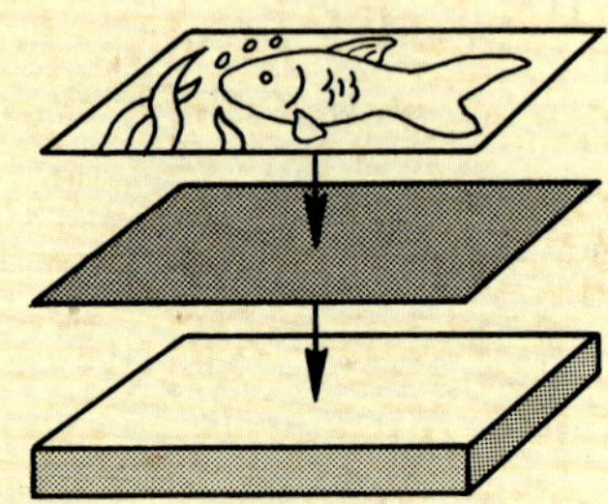

- Use wood-carving or linoleum gouges to carve out areas of your design. These areas will not print.
- Be sure to cut away from your fingers.

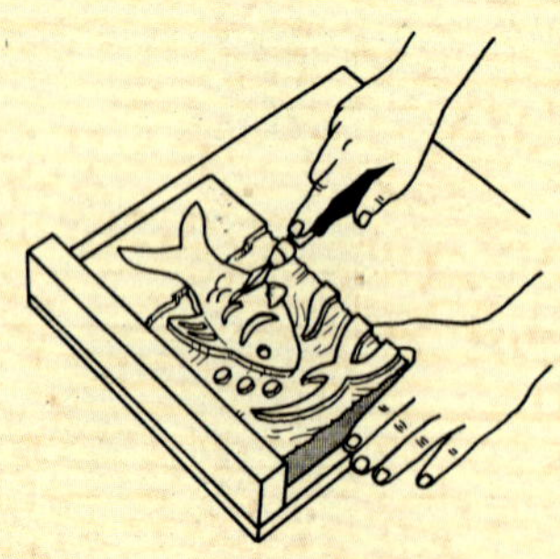

- To keep your block firmly in place, secure it with a bench hook.
- Roll printing ink on a flat surface until it is tacky.
- Roll ink on the printing block surface.
- Place a sheet of paper over your inked block.

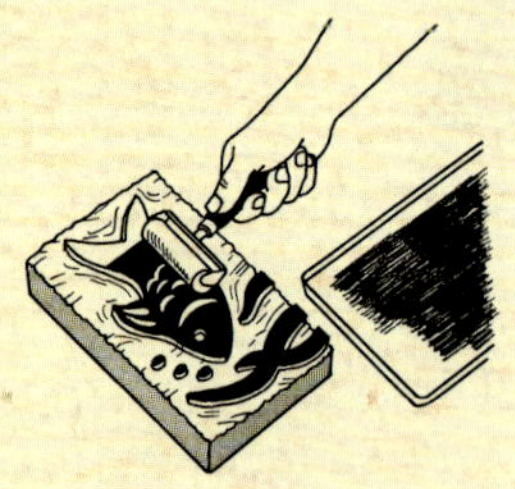

- Rub the back of the paper gently and evenly to transfer ink to the paper.
- Carefully pull the printed paper away.

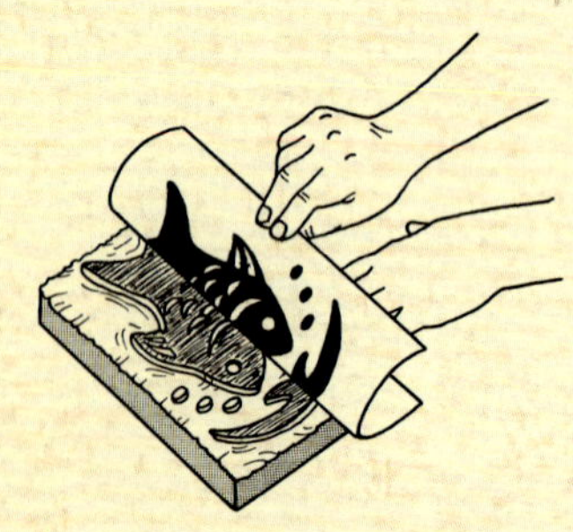

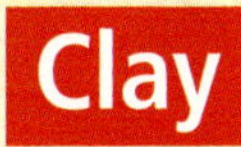

Clay

Studio Background

Clay is earth mixed with oil or water. Oil-based clay is reusable, so it is good to use for planning your artwork or to make molds. Water-based clays harden and your artwork will become permanent when you fire it in a kiln.

Getting Ready to Use Clay

- Protect your desk or work area with a plastic mat or canvas.
- Prepare a *slip*, or liquid clay, to join pieces of clay together. Slip is a creamy mixture of water, clay, and a few drops of vinegar.
- Keep your fingers moist when working with clay. Dip your fingers into water and then spread the water over your palms with your fingers.
- Press or knead the air bubbles out of your clay.

Making a Clay Figure

- Create a five-point star with a ball of clay by pulling out a point for the head, each arm, and each leg.

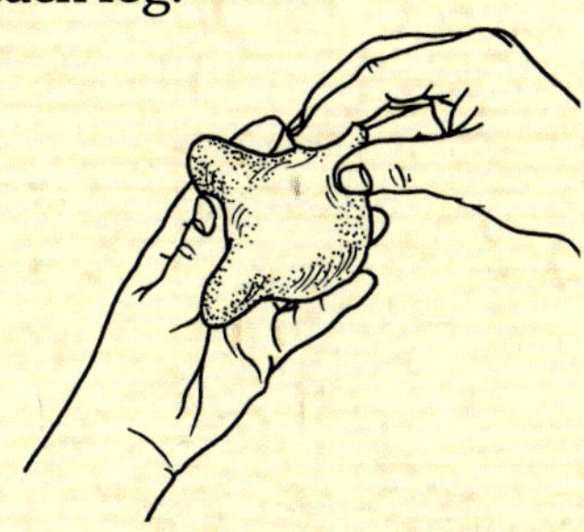

- To shape, pinch and pull the points. Think about the pose of your figure. Twist or bend the shape as needed.

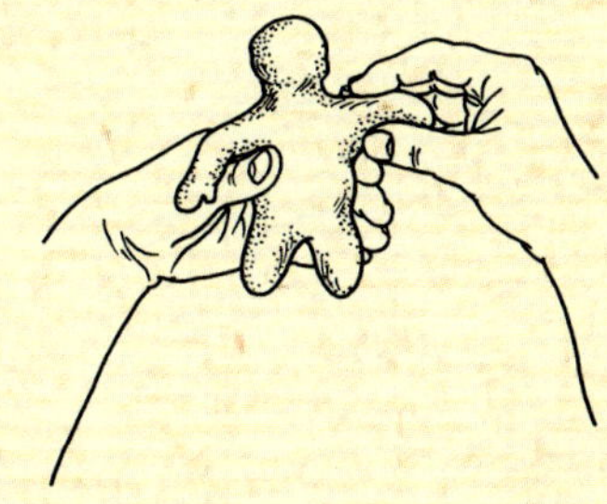

- Add details, such as facial features, hair, and clothing patterns. Press tiny coils or bits of clay into the figure, or press textures onto the surfaces.

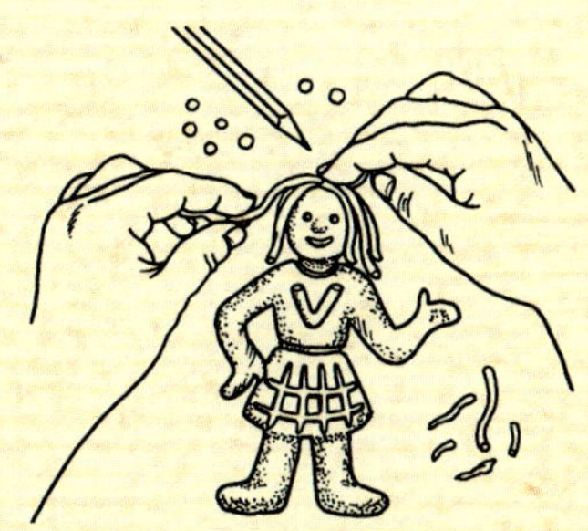

Making a Pinch Pot

- Press your thumb into a ball of clay.
- Slowly turn the pot as you pinch the clay between your thumb and fingers.

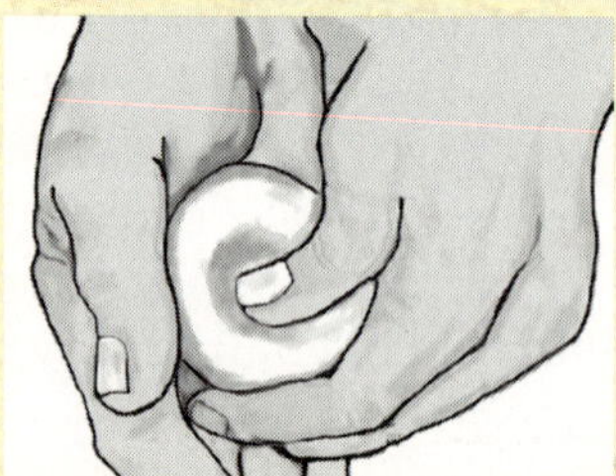

- Continue turning and pinching the pot until the walls are an even thickness all around. Smooth the inside and outside of the pot with a scraper.

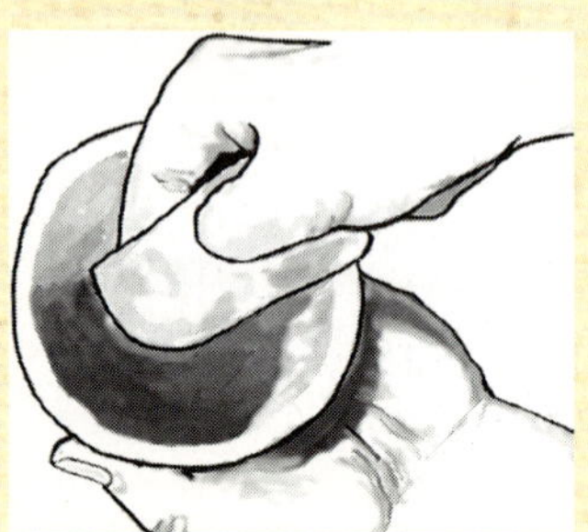

Making Clay Coils

- Roll clay coils to about the thickness of your thumb.

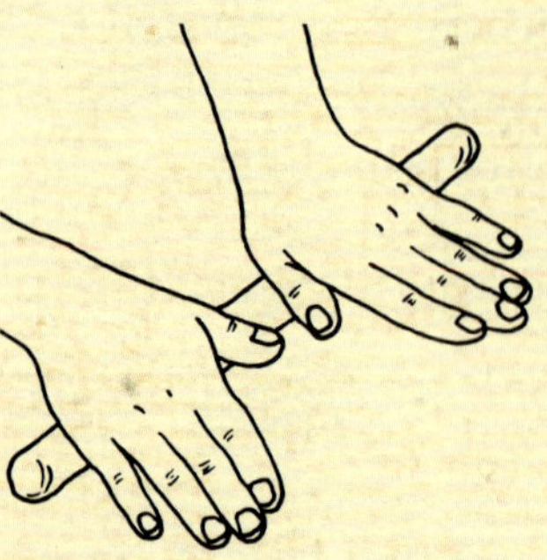

- Form a flat base. Score the edge with a plastic fork. Add slip.

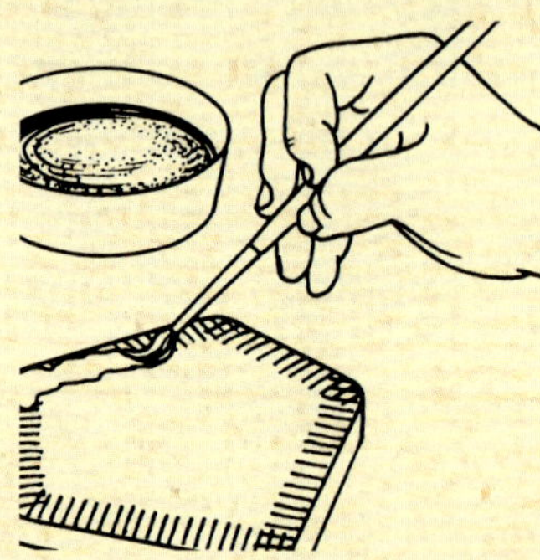

- Bend and press coil to base. Add more coils. Score each new layer and add slip.

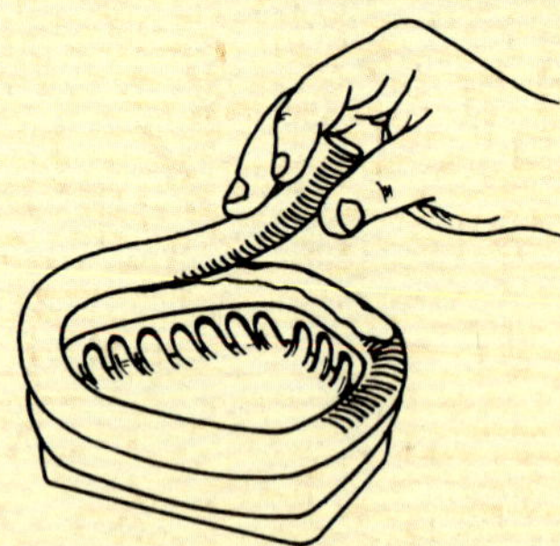

- Smooth coils together with your fingers or a clay tool.

Making a Slab Form

- With a rolling pin, roll clay flat between two sticks of the same thickness.

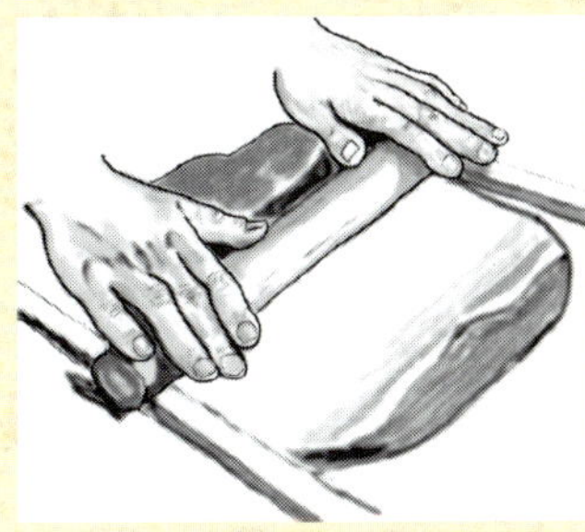

- Cut the slab into shapes that can be joined into a container. Use a plastic fork to score the edges.

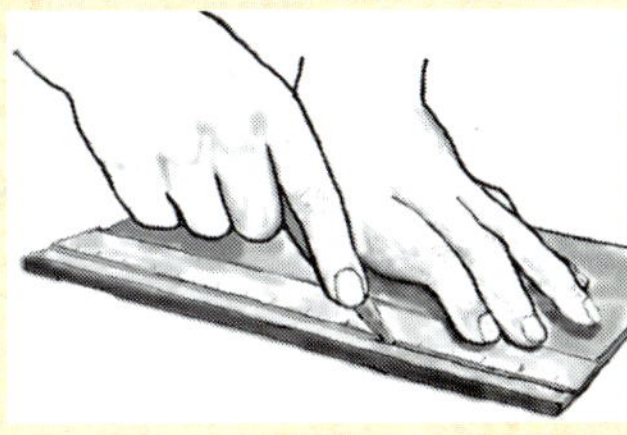

- Use your fingers to apply slip to the edges and join the shapes. Reinforce the inside of the joints with coils.

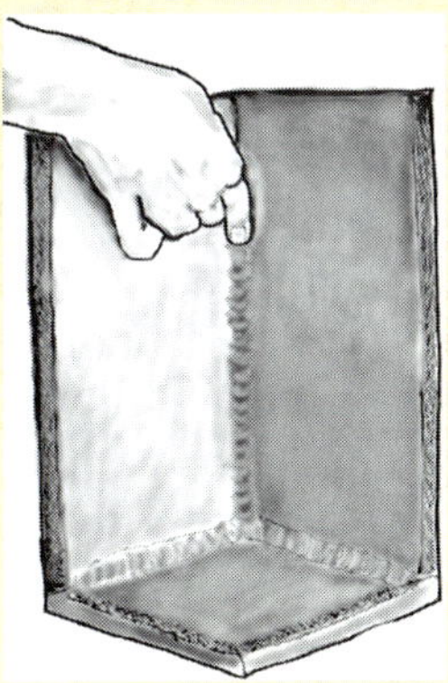

- Pinch the outside edges together and smooth.

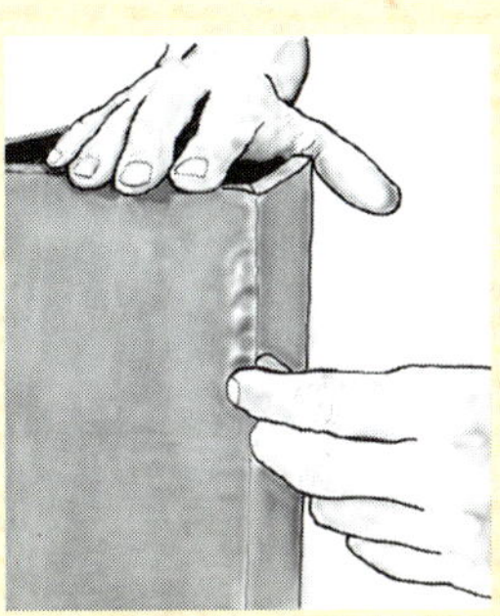

Making a Clay Object With a Press Mold

- Find an appealing form: seashell, plastic bowl, cooking utensil, and so on.
- Roll out a thin, clay slab on a piece of canvas.
- Grasping the edges of the canvas, pick up the slab and invert the clay over the mold.

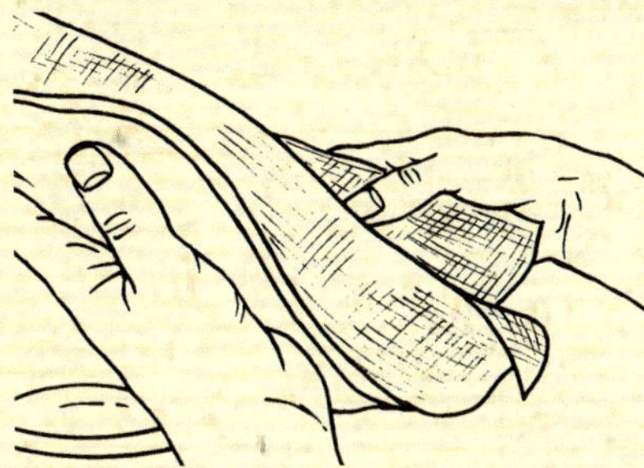

- Using your fingers, gently press the clay into the mold.

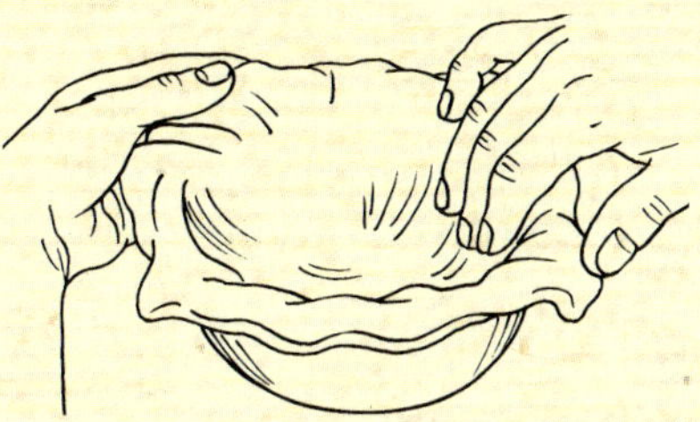

- Smooth surface with a rib tool, and let stiffen till leather-hard.

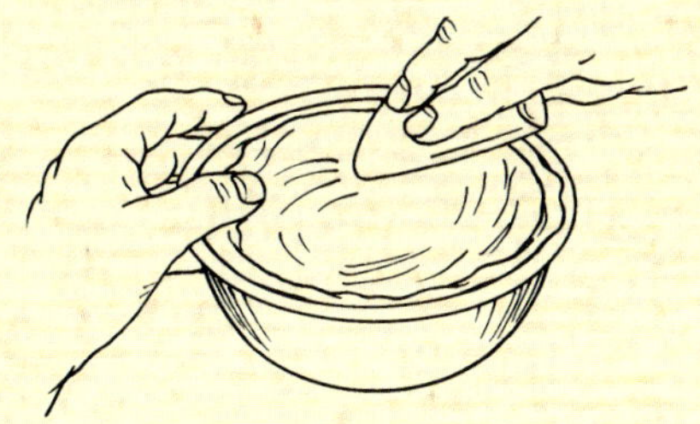

- Turn mold upside down and ease clay out. If clay sticks, let it dry some more.
- Decorate your clay piece.

Papier-Mâché

Studio Background

Papier-mâché comes from French words meaning "chewed paper." This lightweight sculpture material is made from a soupy mixture of wheat paste and paper. The paste-soaked paper is generally applied over an armature, or support. Then the sculpture becomes hard when it dries. When dry, hardened papier-mâché can be painted to be realistic or fantastic.

Using Papier-Mâché

- Begin with an armature , or support, made of wire, folded paper or foil, or recycled objects.

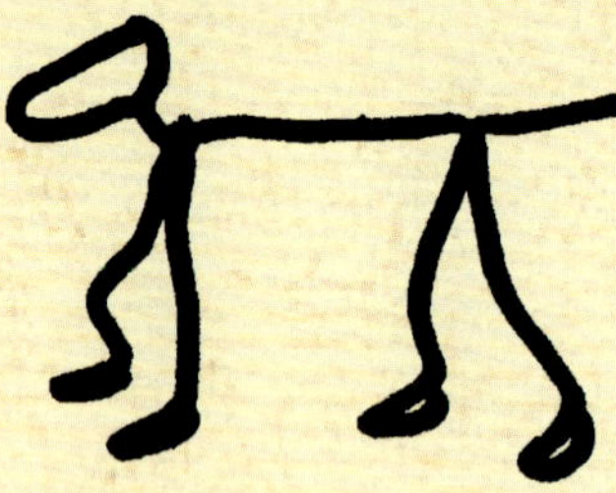

- Add paper with tape to fill out your sculpture's form.

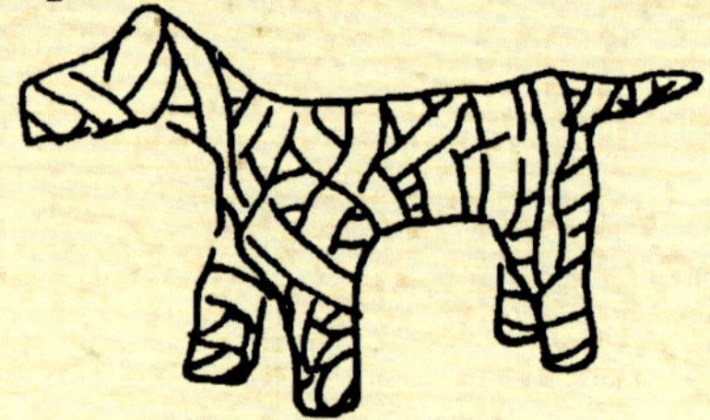

- Tear newspaper or paper towels into strips at least 1" wide.
- Dip the strips into papier-mâché paste. Remove extra paste from the strips with your fingers.

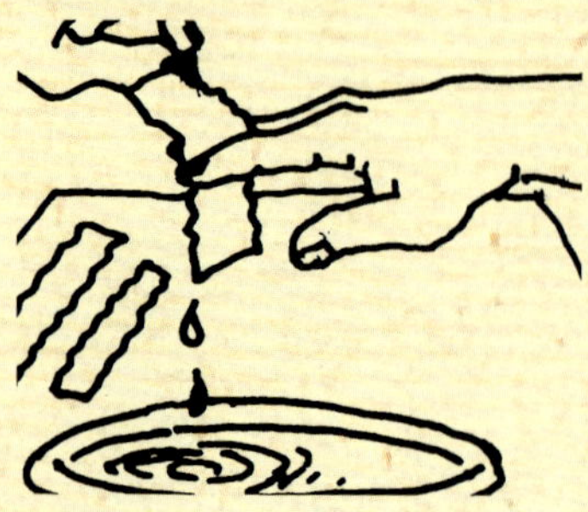

- Place the strips in layers over the support. Use wide strips for large shapes, and thinner strips for smaller shapes. Apply at least two layers.

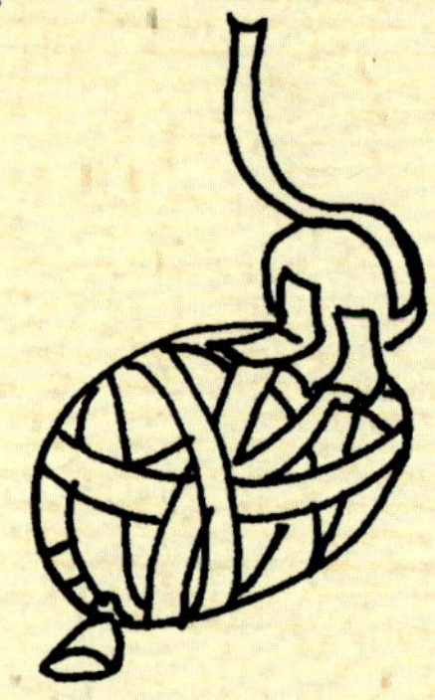

- Use paint and other materials to decorate your dried sculpture.

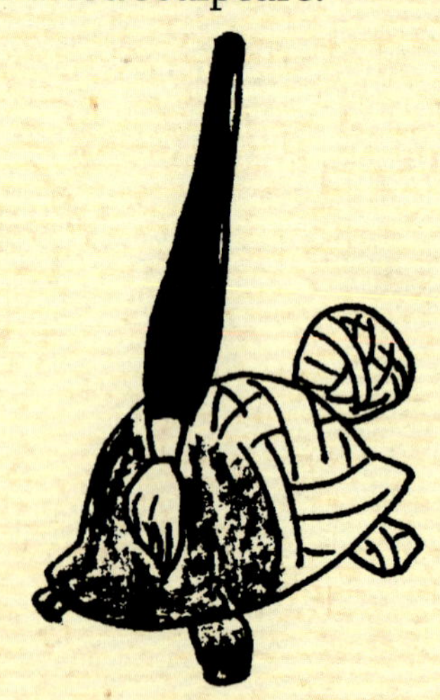

Relief Sculpture

Studio Background

A relief sculpture projects from a background surface. It is not freestanding. Depending on how far the sculpture projects from its background, it can be either *low relief* or *high relief*.

Making Relief Sculptures

Use oil-based or water-based clay to form a slab. Use any of the following techniques to create relief and texture in your sculpture.

- Use clay tools to carve away areas of the clay slab.

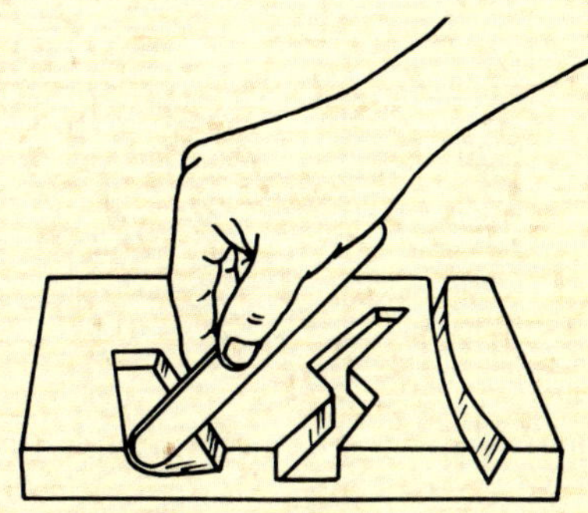

- Press and pull clay to mold lower and higher areas.

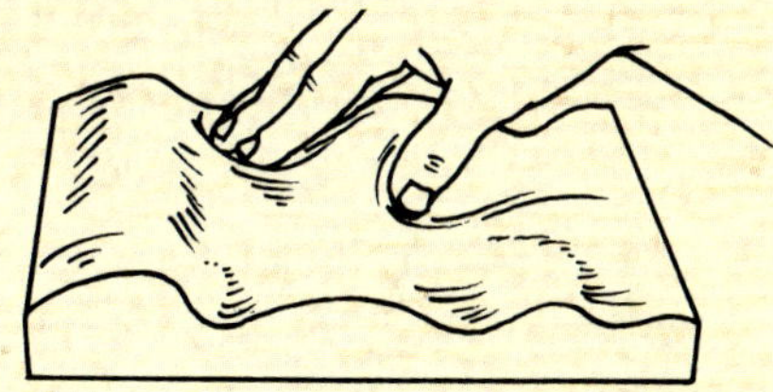

- Press textured objects (seashells, spools, rope, leaves, etc.) into the clay slab.

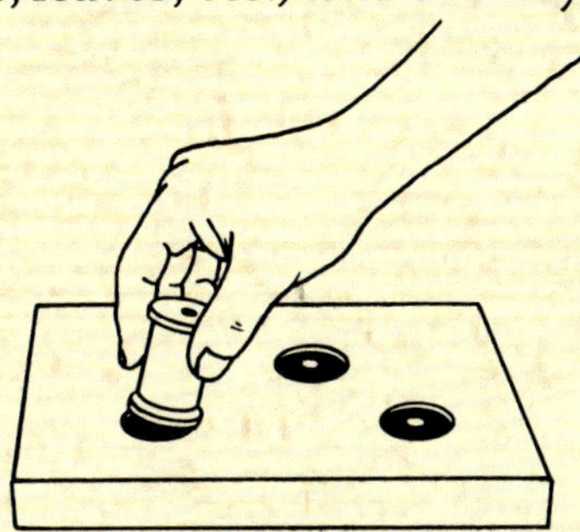

- Attach small coils and clay balls, or scratch lines into the surface to create a variety of textures.

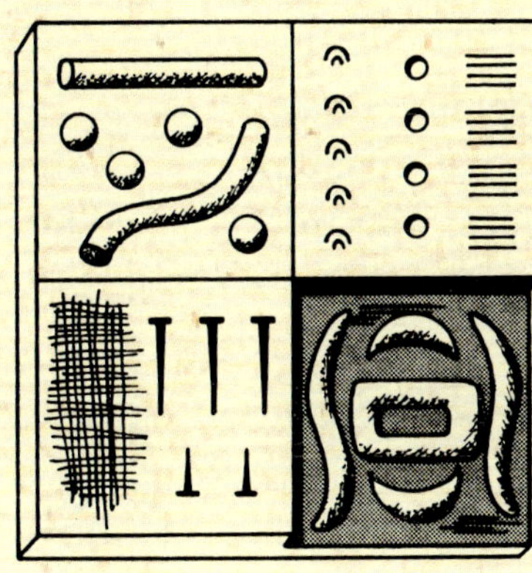

Paper Sculpture

Studio Background

Paper has many purposes in art. Artists draw on paper, of course, but they also use it to create sculptures. The many colors and varieties of paper, as well as paper's ability to be bent, torn, and shaped into forms, make it an exciting medium.

Paper Sculpture Techniques

Gather a variety of paper samples—heavy or light, smooth or rough—and experiment with the techniques shown here. The forms you make can be used to create paper sculptures, or can be added to papier-mâché or other sculptural forms.

1. Make a cut partway across circle; overlap and glue to form a cone.

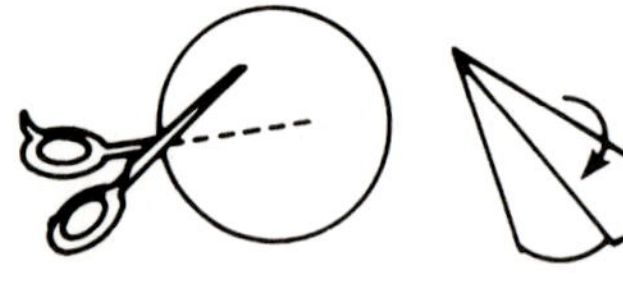

2. Cut tabs at bottom of cone and glue to surface to make it stand or project.

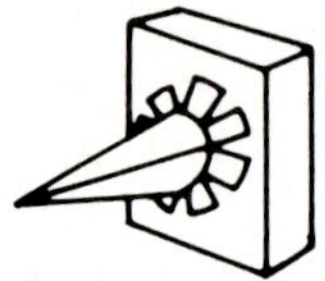

3. Accordion fold, or make folds progressively smaller.

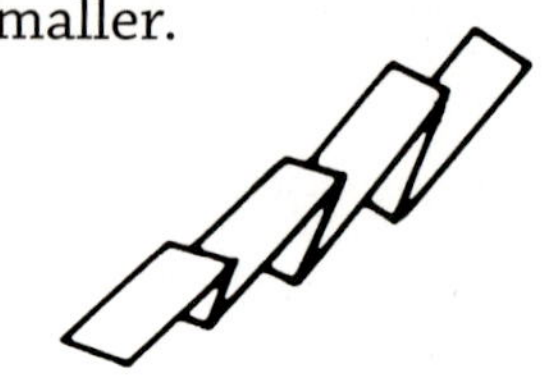

4. Cut triangular or half-circular notches in paper; bend cut pieces upward.

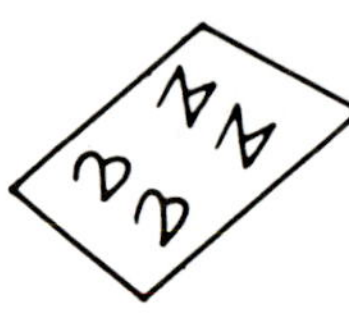

5. Make slots in paper or light cardboard; join pieces by slotting together.

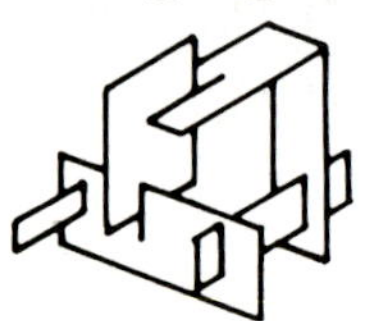

6. Join paper loops by gluing.

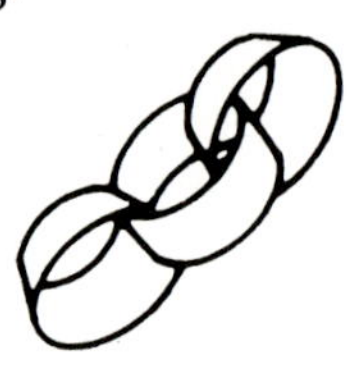

7. Slide scissors blade along strips to form curls.

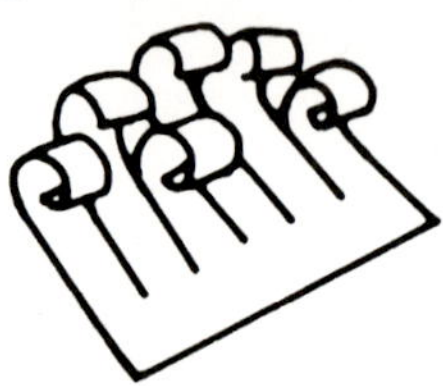

8. Roll paper around pencil to form large curls.

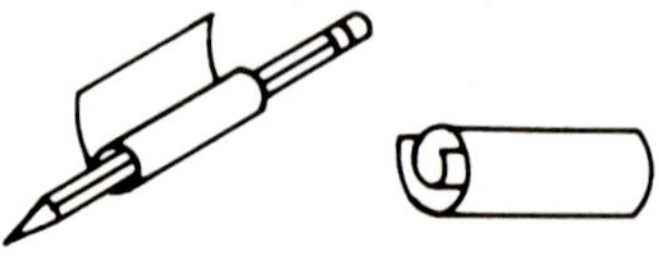

9. Cut crescent shapes; score between points; bend to make forms.

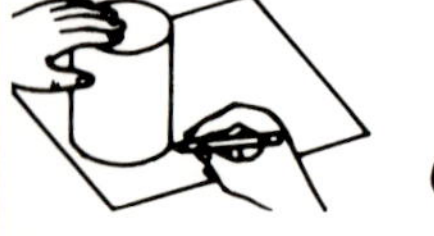

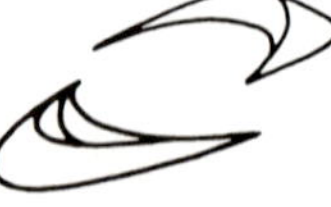

Basic Skills

Whether drawing, painting, making a collage, or sculpting, there are some basic skills that every artist should learn.

Brush Cleaning

Regular and proper brush cleaning is key to ensuring that your brushes last a long time.

- Immediately clean your brush when you change a color or finish a painting. If the brush dries before cleaning, the paint will be difficult to remove and may stain the bristles.
- Most brushes can be cleaned with warm water.
- Try to use most of the paint on the brush before cleaning. Then, wash the brush, wipe excess water on the side of the container, and dry the brush.

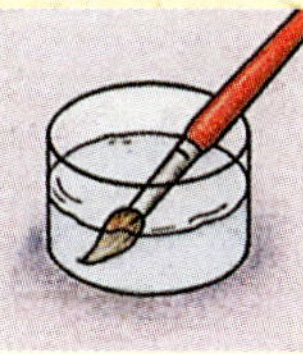

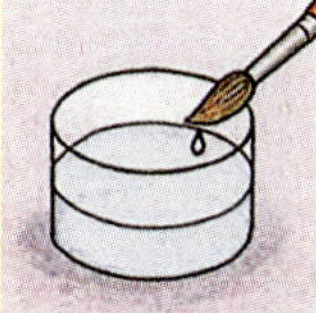

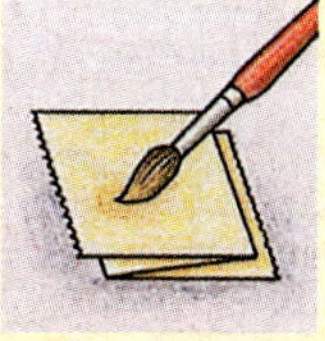

Making a Viewfinder

When drawing or painting, a viewfinder can help focus your vision by isolating parts of an artwork or scene.

- You can make a viewfinder by cutting a square or rectangle in a sheet of paper. Use the viewfinder to plan your artwork.

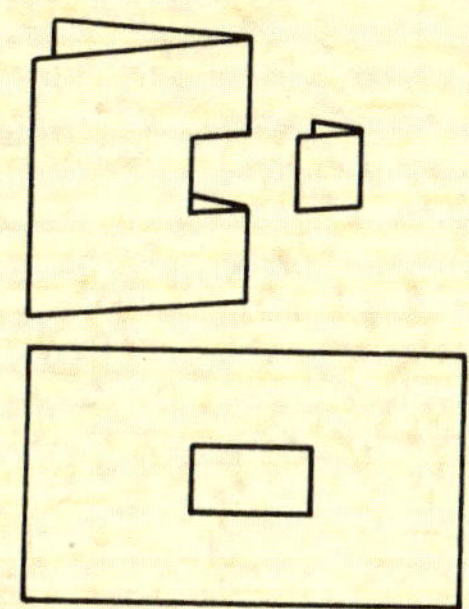

- Look at a scene or subject through a viewfinder to notice shapes formed by the edge of the viewfinder and subject, and to determine which parts of a subject are most interesting.

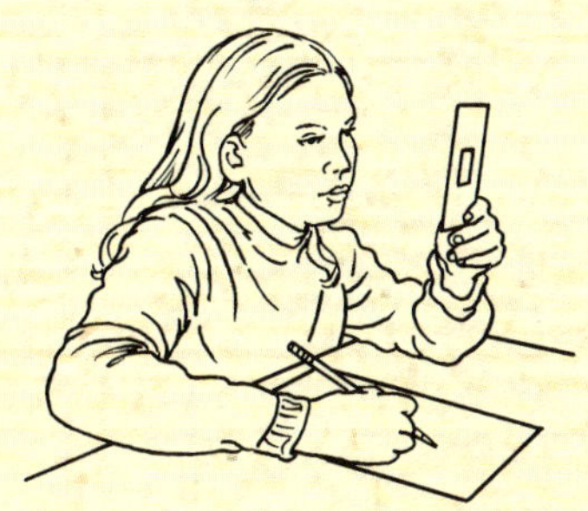

- You can also construct a viewfinder with two L-shaped pieces of paper or cardboard. By sliding these L shapes together or moving them apart, you can see the shape and proportion of the area around your subject.

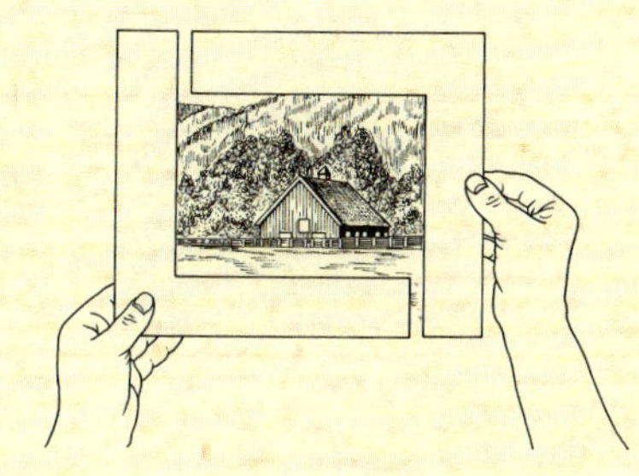

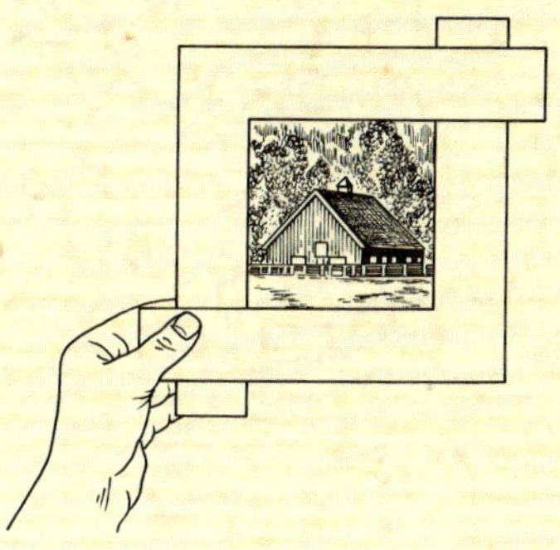

Mixing Paint

- Use tempera paint to mix colors.
- Select a disposable palette.
- Mix colors on a large sheet of paper.
- Clean your brush after each use.

Mixing Primary Colors

Mix Red and Blue

- Paint three circles of red.
- Add one drop of blue paint to the first circle. Use your brush to mix. Add two drops of blue paint to the second circle, and mix. Then add three drops of blue paint to the third circle, and mix.

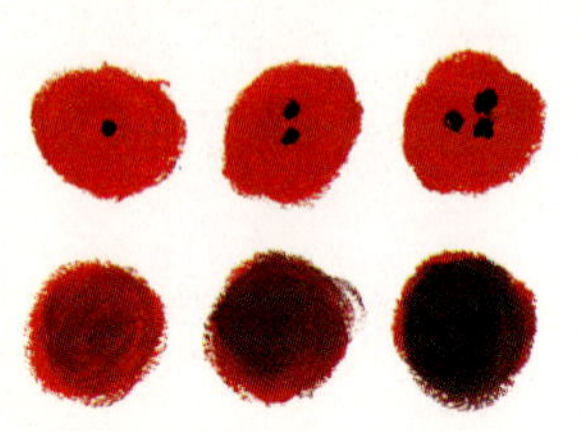

Mix Yellow and Red

- Paint three circles of yellow. Add drops of red, and mix.

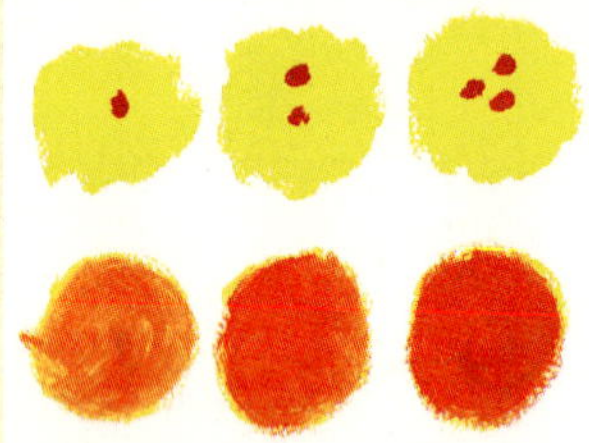

Mix Yellow and Blue

- Paint three more circles of yellow. Add drops of blue, and mix.

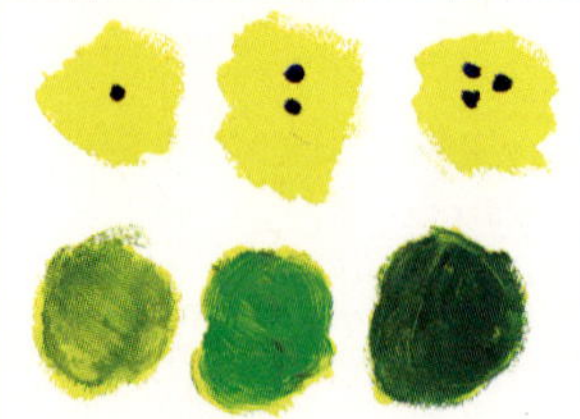

Mixing Tints

- Paint three circles of white. Add drops of a color, and mix.

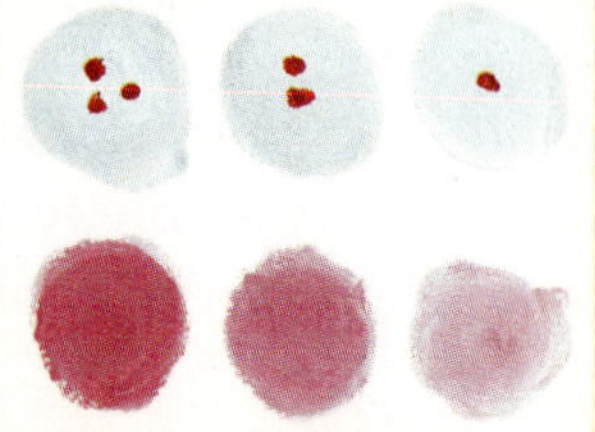

Mixing Shades

- Paint three circles of one color. Add drops of black, and mix.

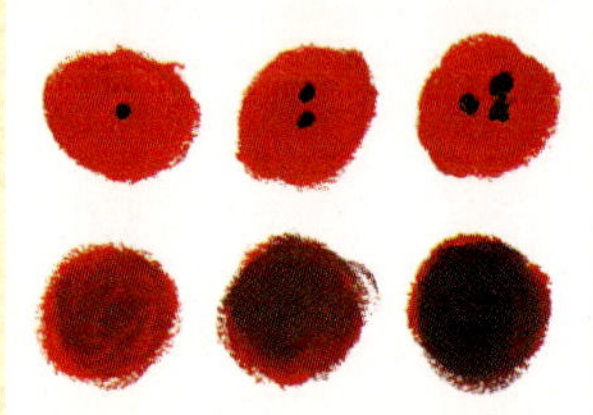

Changing Intensity

- Paint three circles of one color. Leave the first circle alone. Add one drop of the color's complement to the second circle, and mix. Add two drops of the color's complement to the third circle, and mix. Compare intensities.

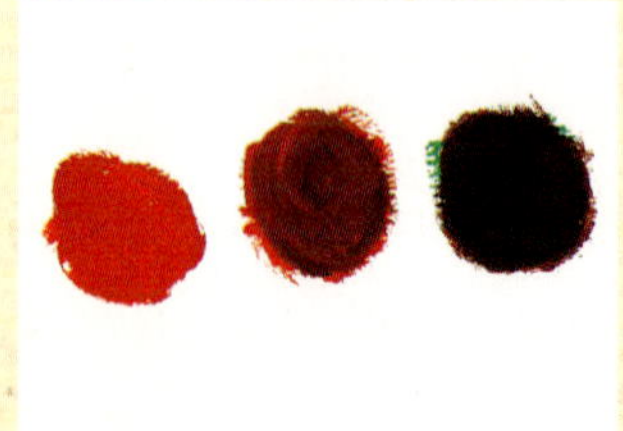

Making a Grid

Grids are networks of squares formed by horizontal and vertical lines. They can be used to recreate or enlarge an existing artwork. The grid lines help transfer the proportions of the original artwork to the copy or enlargement.

- Use a yardstick or ruler to draw horizontal and vertical lines over your artwork.

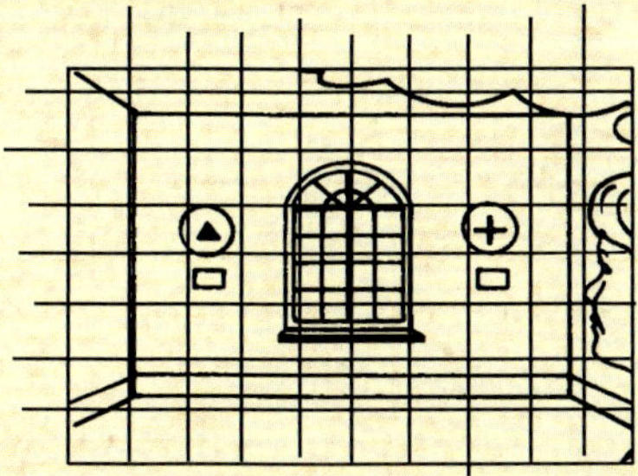

- Draw a second grid on another sheet of paper.
- If you are enlarging the artwork, use a larger sheet of paper for the second grid, and make the squares on this grid proportionally larger than the first grid.
- Carefully copy the contents of each square on the first grid into the corresponding squares on the second grid.

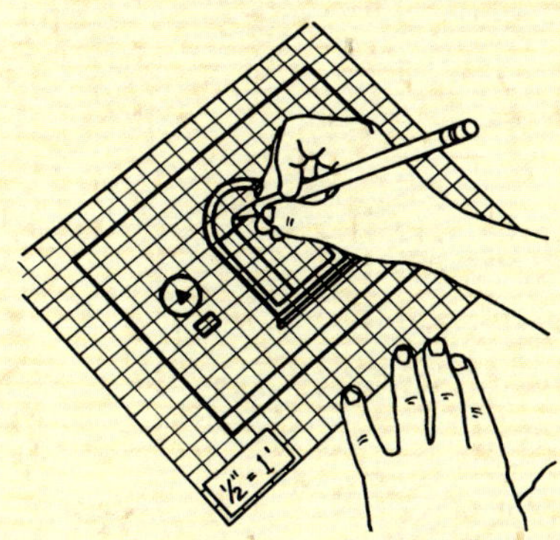

Mounting

Any drawings, prints, photos, or paintings you plan to exhibit should be mounted and accompanied with a label that identifies your work. Follow these steps to mount your work:

- Choose a piece of heavy paper or board that is larger than the artwork you will exhibit. Select a color for your mount that will enhance or match the colors in your artwork.
- Center your artwork on the mount.
- Measure the borders to check that they are even.
- Use a pencil to lightly trace the corners of your artwork.
- Apply glue or double-sided tape to the back of your artwork.
- Position your artwork inside the corner marks.
- Press your artwork onto the mount.
- Print a label that includes your name and other information about the artwork, such as title, date, medium, your grade, and the name of your teacher and school.

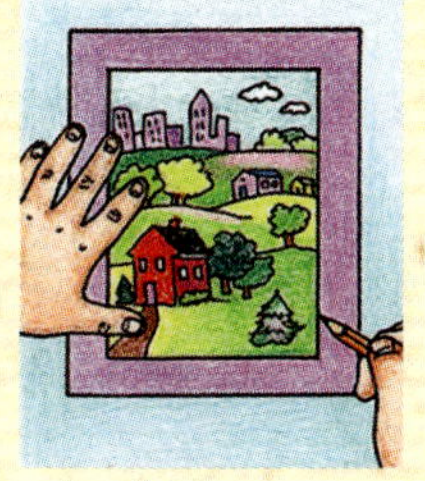
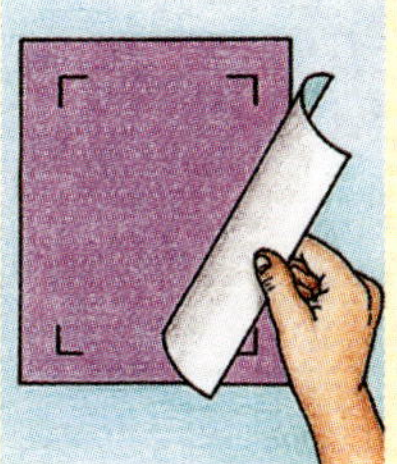
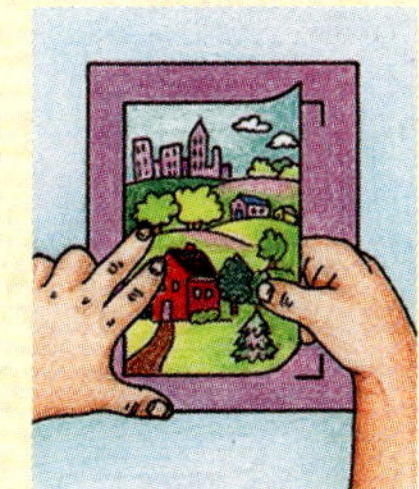
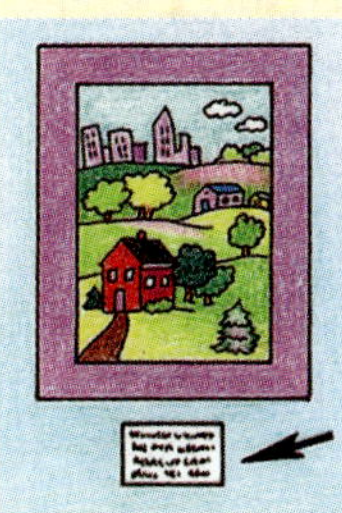

Making a Mat

A **mat** is a colored piece of board or paper that frames an artwork. The purpose of a mat is to enhance and protect an artwork. You can make a mat for an artwork that you want to display in your home or in your school.

- Choose a colored piece of poster or mat board. Be sure to select a color for your mat that will match the colors in your artwork or make the existing colors stand out.
- On the back of your artwork, draw in light pencil a line ¼" from the edges.
- Find the center point of your art. Lightly draw lines dividing your paper into four equal parts.

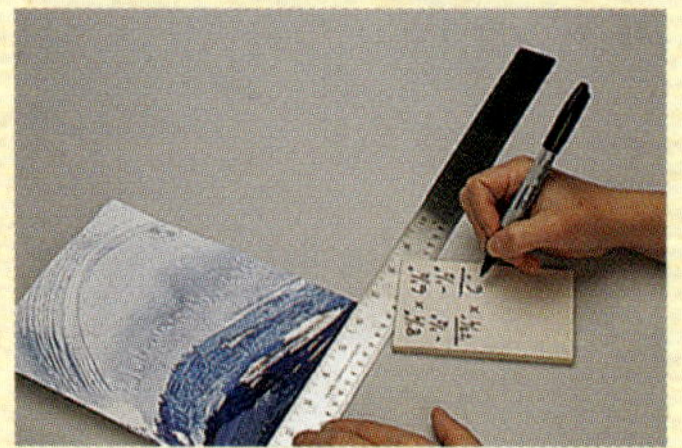

- Cut poster or mat board 6" longer and 6" wider than your artwork.
- To find the center of your mat, on the back, draw a vertical line down the middle of the mat. Then draw a horizontal line across the middle. Where the lines intersect is the center.

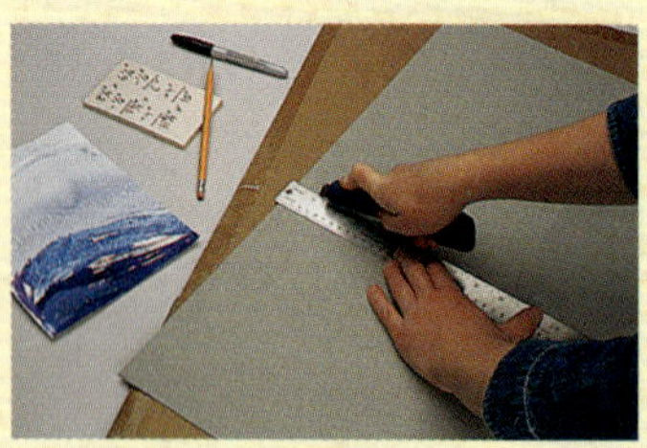

- Place your artwork face down on the back of the mat board. Line up the pencil lines.
- Attach your art to the mat using several small pieces of tape.
- Trace the corners of your artwork.

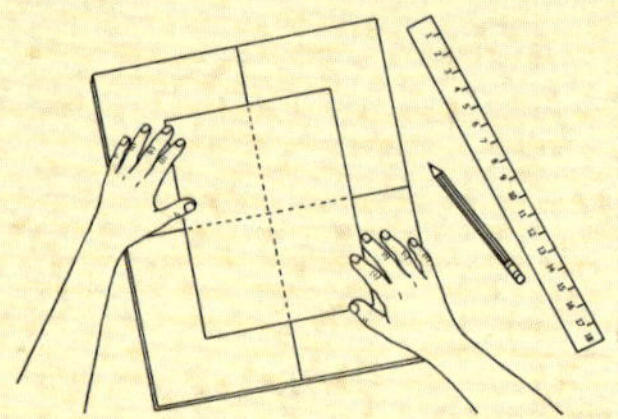

- Locate the four points on your artwork where the ¼" guidelines cross. At each point, press a pin through your artwork, into the mat board, and through to the front of the mat to make pinholes in the mat board. Remove the pins and your artwork.

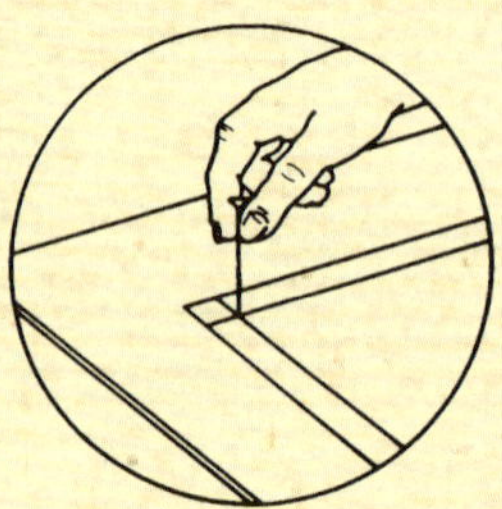

- Place the mat face up on a sheet of cardboard.
- Lay a metal ruler or yardstick between two pinholes and parallel to the mat edge.
- Cut along the edge of the ruler with a sharp mat knife. Repeat, cutting between the other pinholes to create the mat "window."
- Remove the window.
- Place your artwork on the back of the mat over the opening.

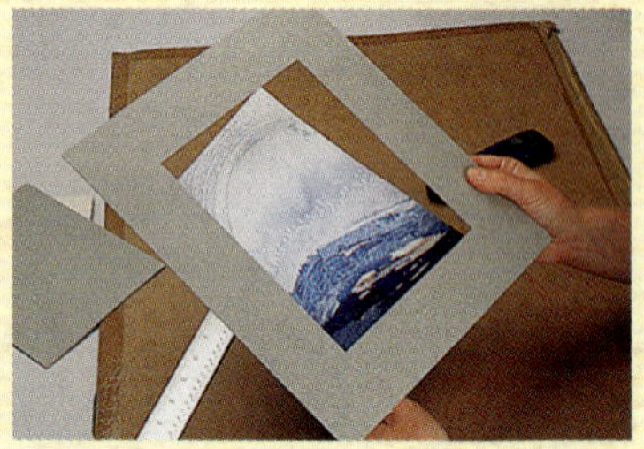

- Secure the artwork to the mat with tape. Check that the artwork is straight. Add more tape if necessary.

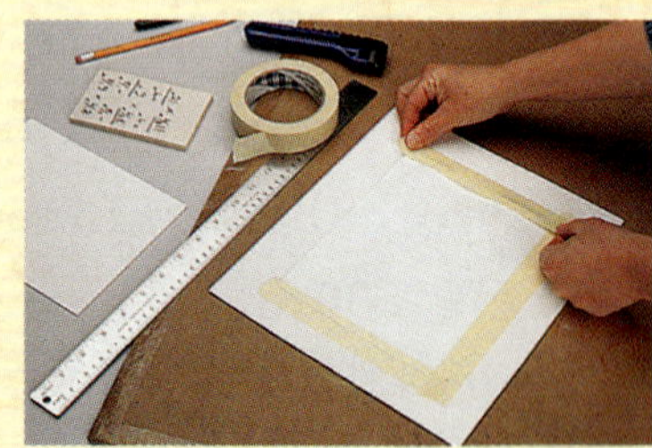

Photographic Credits

An Introduction to Art

Page xviii

Dome of the Rock, late 7th century. Jerusalem, Israel.

Massachusetts Bay Colony, *Bradford Chair*, 1630. Black ash, seat: wood, 46" x 24" x 19" (116.8 x 61 x 48.3 cm). Pilgrim Society, Pilgrim Hall Museum, Plymouth, MA.

China, Qing dynasty, *Wedding Ensemble*, ca. 1860. Silk with embroidery and couched gold threads; robe: 43" x 38" (109 x 97 cm); skirt: 39" x 46" (99 x 117 cm). Pacific Asia Museum Collection, Gift of Dr. and Mrs. Milton Rubini 80.86.1AB. ©Pacific Asia Museum.

Dorothea Lange, *Migrant Mother, Nipomo, California,* 1936. Gelatin silver print. Reproduced from the Collections of the Library of Congress.

Page xix

Paul Klee, *Fish Magic*, 1925. Oil on canvas, mounted on board, 30 ⅜" x 38 ½" (77.3 x 97.8 cm). Philadelphia Museum of Art, The Louise and Walter Arensberg Collection. Photo by Graydon Wood, 1994 Acc # '50-134-112 © 2000 Artists Right Society (ARS), New York / VG Bild- Kunst, Bonn.

Page xx

David Hockney, *Garrowby Hill*, 1998. Oil on canvas, 60" x 72" (152.4 x 182.9 xm). David Hockney No. 1 Trust.

Diego Rivera, *Learning the ABC's (Alfabetizacion)*, 1923–28. Mural, 6 ¾' x 4 9⁄35' (2.06 x 1.33 m). Court of Fiestas, Level 3, West Wall. Secretaria de Educacion Publica, Mexico City, D.F., Mexico Photo Credit: Schalkwijk / Art Resource, NY.

Peter Paul Rubens, *Portrait Study of His Son Nicolas*, 1621. Black, red, and white chalk, 25.2 x 20.3 cm. Inv. 17.650. Graphishe Sammlung Albertina, Vienna, Austria. Erich Lessing / Art Resource, NY.

Page xxi

Mongolian (Casas Grandes style), *Macaw Bowl*, Tardio Period, 1300–1350. Earthenware with polychrome slip painting, 5 ¼" x 8" x 6 ¼" (13.3 x 20.3 x 15.9 cm). Museum of Fine Arts, Houston (Gift of Miss Ima Hogg).

Winold Reiss, *Langston Hughes (1902–1967), Poet*, ca. 1925. Pastel on artist board, 76.3 x 54.9 cm. Gift of W. Tjark Reiss in memory of his father, Winold Reiss. National Portrait Gallery, Smithsonian Institution, Washington, DC / Art Resource, NY.

Anna Mary Robertson Moses, called Grandma Moses, *Summer Party*, 20th century. Oil on masonite, 23 9⁄16" x 15 ¾" (59.9 x 40 cm). The Museum of Fine Arts, Houston; Wintermann Collection of American Art, gift of Mr. and Mrs. David R. Wintermann.

Page xxii

Charles Willson Peale, *The Peale Family*, ca. 1770–73 and 1808. Oil on canvas, 56 ½" x 89 ½" (143.5 x 227.3 cm) Collection of the New York Historical Society (1867.298).

Etruscan, *Chimera of Arezzo*, 6th century BCE. Bronze. Museo Archeologico, Florence, Italy. Scala / Art Resource, New York.

Page xxiii

William H. Johnson, *Soap Box Racing*, ca. 1939–40. Tempera, pen and ink on paper mounted on paperboard, 14 ⅛" x 17 ⅞" (35.9 x 45.5 cm). National Museum of American Art, Smithsonian Institution, Washington, DC / Art Resource, NY.

Page xxiv

China, Tang dynasty, *Tomb Figure of a Saddle Horse*, early 8th century. Earthenware, three- color lead glazes, length: 31 ½" (80.5 cm). Victoria & Albert Museum, London / Art Resource, New York.

Frida Kahlo, *Portrait of Mrs. Christian Hastings*, 1931. Drawing. Fundacion Dolores Olmedo, Mexico City, D. F., Mexico. Photo credit: Schalkwijk/ Art Resource, New York. © Banco de Mexico Trust.

Page xxv

Warren Smith, *Cloak of Heritage*, 1991. Acrylic and collage on canvas, 24" x 36" (61 x 91.4 cm). © 1991 Kevin Warren Smith.

Marsha Burns, *Jacob Lawrence*. Photograph.

Page xxvi

Marc Chagall, *I and the Village*, 1911. Oil on canvas, 75 ⅝" x 5 ⅝". (192 x 151 cm). The Museum of Modern Art, New York/Art Resource, NY. © The Museum of Modern Art/Licensed by SCALA/Art Resource, NY/ARS NY/ADAGP, Paris.

Page xxvii

North American Indian, *Acoma Polychrome Jar*. Museum of Indian Arts and Culture/ Laboratory of Anthropology, Museum of New Mexico. Photograph by Douglas Kahn. (18947/ 12).

Louis Comfort Tiffany, *Dragonfly Lamp*, ca. 1900. Bronze base with color favrile glass, 28" x 22" (71.2 x 55.9 cm). Collection of the New York Historical Society (N84.113).

Page xxviii

Vincent van Gogh, *The Starry Night*, 1889. Oil on canvas, 29" x 36 ¼" (73.7 x 92.1 cm). Acquired through the Lillie P. Bliss Bequest. Museum of Modern Art, New York. © The Museum of Modern Art/Licensed by SCALA /Art Resource, NY.

Page xxix

Claude Monet, *Japanese Footbridge and the Water Lily Pond, Giverny*, 1899. Oil on canvas, 35 ⅛" x 36 ¾" (89.2 x 93.3 cm). Philadelphia Museum of Art: The Mr. and Mrs. Carroll S. Tyson, Jr. Collection.

Cathedral of St. Basil, 1554–1566. Moscow.

Japan, Momoyama period (1568–1615), *Ewer for Use in Tea Ceremony*, early 17th century. Shino-Oribe ware. Stoneware with overglaze enamels, 7 ¾". (19.7 cm) high. The Metropolitan Museum of Art, Purchase, Friends of Asian Art Gifts, 1988 (1988.156ab). Photograph © 2001 The Metropolitan Museum of Art.

Rosa Bonheur, *Ploughing in the Nivernais*, 1849. Oil on canvas, 52 ½" x 102" (133.4 x 259.1 cm). Musee d'Orsay, Paris, France. Photo Credit: Réunion des Musées Nationaux / Art Resource, NY

Thomas Cole, *View on the Catskill, Early Autumn*, 1837. Oil on canvas, 39" x 63" (99 x 160 cm). The Metropolitan Museum of Art, New York, gift in memory of Jonathan Sturges by his children, 1895.

Page xxx

Sakino Hokusai IITSU, *Fukagawa Mannembashi*, from *36 Views of Mt. Fuji*, 1830. Multiple block wood blockprint, 10 ¼" x 15" (26 x 38 cm). Courtesy The Japan Ukiyo-e Museum.

Faith Ringgold, *The Wedding Lover's Quilt No. 1*, 1986. Acrylic on canvas, quilted with pieced border, 77 ½" x 58" (196.9 x 147.3 cm). Private collection. © Faith Ringgold, 1986.

Miriam Schapiro, *Master of Ceremonies*, 1985. Acrylic on fabric on canvas, 90" x 144" (228.6 x 365.8 cm). Collection of Elaine and Stephen Wynn. Courtesy of the Steinbaum Krauss Gallery, New York, New York.

Alberto Giacometti, *Three Men Walking*, 1948–49. Bronze, height: 29 ½" (74.9 cm). Edward E. Ayer Endowment in memory of Charles L. Hutchinson, 1951.256. Photograph courtesy The Art Institute of Chicago. © 2000 Artist Rights Society (ARS), New York/ ADAGP, Paris.

Page xxxi

I. M. Pei, *Addition to the Louvre*, 1988. Glass, steel rods, and cable, I. M. Pei, Paris, France.

Makonde, Tanzania, *Family Group*, 20th century. Wood, 31" (78.7 cm). Gift of Nancy Gray, Collection Bayly Art Museum of the University of Virginia, Charlottesville. (1981.94.75)

Anne Coe, *Migrating Mutants*, 1986. Acrylic on canvas, 61" x 61" (154.9 x 154.9 cm). Horwitch Newman Gallery, Scottsdale, Arizona. Courtesy of the artist.

Page xxxii

Paul Cézanne, S*till Life with Apples and Peaches*, ca. 1905. Oil on canvas, 31 ⅞" x 39 ½" (81 x 100.5 cm). © National Gallery of Art, Washington, Gift of Eugene and Agnes Meyer.

Page xxxiii

Student artwork.

Student Handbook

Page 276

Romaine Brooks, *The Soldier at Home*, 1930. Pencil on paper, 9 9⁄16" x 7 ⅛" (24 x 18 cm). Gift of Romaine Brooks. Smithsonian American Art Museum, Washington, DC/Art Resource, NY.

Page 277

Niki de Saint Phalle and Jean Tinguely, *Illumination*, 1988. Mobile sculpture, mixed media, height: 9' (2.75 m). Courtesy Galerie Bonnier, Genevia. © 2001 Artists Rights Society (ARS), New York/ADAGP, Paris.

David Hockney, *Garrowby Hill*, 1998. Oil on canvas, 60" x 72" (152.4 x 182.9 cm). David Hockney No. 1 Trust.

Page 277

Africa, Dan Culture (Liberia, Ivory Coast), *Ga-Wree-Wre-Mask*, 20th century. Wood, metal, fiber, cowrie shells, glass beads, brass, bone, hand-woven cloth, 47" x 16" x 22" (119.4 x 40.6 x 55.9 cm). Virginia Museum of Fine Arts, Richmond. The Adolph D. and Wilkins C. Williams Fund. Photo: Katherine Wetzel. © Virginia Museum of Fine Arts.

Page 278

Caryl Bryer Fallert, *Refraction #4–#7.* Hand-dyed cotton fabric, machine pieced and quilted, 88" x 88" (224 x 224 cm). Courtesy of the artist.

Page 280

René Magritte, *The Listening Room,* ca. 1958. Oil on canvas 15" x 18" (38 x 46 cm). Kunsthaus, Zürich, donated by Walter Haefner. Photo AKG London. ©2001 C. Herscovici, Brussels/Artists Rights Society (ARS), New York.

Page 281

Frances Hare, *Sixteen Feet of Dance: A Celebration, A Self-Portrait,* 1996. Cotton fabrics, beads, braided cloth, 69" x 56" (175.2 x 152.2 cm). Courtesy the artist.

Page 282

Doug Webb, *Kitchenetic Energy*, 1979. Acrylic on linen, 30" x 40" (76.2 x 101.6 cm). Courtesy of the artist.

Page 283

Omri Amrany & Julie Rotblatt-Amrany, *The Spirit, Michael Jordan*, 1994. Bronze, height (including base): 16' (5 m) United Center, Chicago, Illinois.

Clara Peeters, *Still Life of Fruit and Flowers,* after 1620. ©Ashmolean Museum, University of Oxford.

Page 284

Marvin Mattelson (illustrator), *Subway Poster for School of Visual Arts.* Art Director: Silas H. Rhodes; Designer: William J. Kobasz; Copywriter: Dee Ito.

"Tableware", Bloomimage/CORBIS

Page 285

Art on File/CORBIS

Brand X/CORBIS

Page 286

Lascaux, *Hall of Bulls,* detail, c. 15,000–13,000 BC, Dordogne, France. Color photo Hans Hinz.

Giza, Egypt, *The Pyramids of Mycerinus, Chefren, and Cheops*, built between 2589 and 2350 BC. Limestone. Erich Lessing/Art Resource, NY.

Ancient Greece, Athens (attributed to the Antimenes painter), *Hydria,* c. 530–510 BC. Black-figure earthenware, height: 16 5/8" (42.2 cm). Cleveland Museum of Art. Purchase from the J. H. Wade Fund. 1975.1.

Page 287

Augustus of Prima Porta, Roman Sculpture, Early first century AD. Vatican Museums, Vatican State. Scala/ Art Resource, New York.

The Archangel Michael with Sword, Byzantine, 11th century. Gold, enamel, and precious stone. Framed icon. Tesoro San Marco, Venice. Cameraphoto/Art Resource, New York.

Chi-rho Gospel of St. Matthews, chapter 1, verse 18, Irish (vellum). *Book of Kells*, c. 800. The Board of Trinity College, Dublin, Ireland/Bridgeman Art Library.

Bayeux Tapestry, William preparing his troops for combat with English Army. Musée de la Tapisserie, Bayeux, France. Giraudon/Art Resource, New York.

Page 288

North Transept Rose and Lancet Windows (Melchizedek & Nebuchadnezzar, David & Saul, St. Anne, Solomon & Herod, Aaron & Pharaoh), 13th century. Stained glass, 42' (12.8 m) Diameter. Chartres Cathedral, France. Scala/Art Resource, New York.

Michelangelo Buonarroti, *Pietà*, 1499. Marble, height: 5' 6" (1.7 cm). St. Peter's Basilica, Vatican State. Scala/Art Resource, New York.

Judith Leyster, *Game of Tric-Trac*, c. 1630. Oil on panel, 16" x 12 ¼" (40.7 x 31.1 cm). Worcester Art Museum, Worcester, Massachusetts. Gift of Robert and Mary S. Cushman.

Page 289

Movement made by Charles Voisin and Chantilly manufactory, *Wall Clock*, c. 1740. Soft-paste porcelain, enameled metal, gilt-bronze, and glass, 29 ½" x 14" x 4 3/8" (74.9 x 35.6 x 11.1 cm). The J. Paul Getty Museum, Los Angeles.

Jacques-Louis David, *Oath of the Horatii*, 1784–85. Oil on canvas, 129 11/12" x 167 5/16" (330 x 425 cm). Louvre, Paris, France. Erich Lessing/Art Resource, New York.

Eugène Delacroix, *Horses Coming Out of the Sea*, 1860. Oil on canvas, 20 ¼" x 24 ¼" (5.4 x 61.5 cm). The Phillips Collection, Washington, DC. (0486).

Page 290

Honoré Daumier, *The Third Class Carriage,* ca. 1863–65. Oil on canvas, 25 ¾" x 35 ½" (65.4 x 90.2 cm). National Gallery of Canada, Ottawa. Purchased 1946.

Pierre-Auguste Renoir, *The Garden in the Rue Cortot, Montmarte,* 1876. Oil on canvas, 59 ¾" x 38 3/8" (151.8 x 97.5 cm). Carnegie Museum of Art, Pittsburgh. Acquired through the generosity of Mrs. Alan M. Scaif, 65.35. Photography by Peter Harholdt.

Pablo Picasso, *Three Muscians,* Fontainebleu, summer 1921. Oil on canvas, 6' 7" x 7' 3 ¾" (22.07 x 222.9 cm). The Museum of Modern Art, New York. Mrs. Simon Guggenheim Fund. Photograph ©2000 The Museum of Modern Art, New York. ©2000 Estate of Pablo Picasso/Artists Rights Society (ARS), New York.

Page 291

Salvador Dalì, *The Persistence of Memory,* 1931. Oil on canvas, 9 ½" x 13" (24.1 x 33 cm). The Museum of Modern Art, New York. Given anonymously. Photograph ©2000 The Museum of Modern Art, New York. ©2000 Artists Rights Society (ARS), New York.

Jackson Pollock, *Blue Poles*, 1952. Enamel and aluminum paint with glass on canvas. 6' 10 7/8" x 15' 11 5/8" (212.09 x 488.95 cm). Collection: National Gallery of Australia, Canberra (NGA Acc. No. 74.264). © The Pollock-Krasner Foundation/Artists Rights Society (ARS), New York.

Claes Oldenburg and Coosje van Bruggen, *Spoonbridge and Cherry,* 1988. Aluminum painted with polyurethane enamel and stainless steel, 29'6" x 51'6" x 13'6" (9 x 15.7 x 4.1 m). Minneapolis Sculpture Garden, Walker Art Center, Minneapolis, Photography by Attilio Maranzano. Courtesy of the artists.

Andy Goldsworthy, *The coldest I have ever known in Britain/as early/worked all day/reconstructed icicles around a tree/finished late afternoon/catching sunlight, Glenn Marlin Falls, Dumfriesshire, 28 december 1995,* 1995. Cibachrome print, 23" x 19" (58 x 48.3 cm) square. Galerie Lelong, New York, New York. Courtesy of Private Collector, New York.

Page 300

Emile Nolde, *Summer Flowers,* 1930. Watercolor painting.

Winslow Homer, *Sunshine and Shadow, Prout's Neck,* 1984. Watercolor painting.

Artist Guide

Aboriginal Artists (ab-or-IHDG-in-ul) Australia, pp. 170–171

Alphonse, Inatace (ahl-fahnz, EE-nah-tahss) Haiti, b. 1943, pp. 52–53

Antimenes Painter (ann-TIM-en-eez) Ancient Greece, active 530–510 BCE, p. 76

Apollodorus of Damascus (uh-poll-uh-DOOR-us) Syria, active Greece, 100s CE, p. 30

Arcimboldo, Giuseppe (ar-cheem-BOLE-doh, jyuh-SHE-pee) Italy, ca. 1530–1593, p. 186

Barragán, Luis (bah-rah-GAHN, loo-EES) Mexico, 1902–1988, p. 231

Bazile, Castera (bah-ZEEL, cah-STAIR-uh) Haiti, 1923–1965, p. 51

Beall, Lester US, 1903–1969, p. 163

Bearden, Romare (BEER-den, ro-MAIR) US, 1912–1988, pp. 29, 246

Bezalel School Artists (BAY-zah-lel) Israel, 1900s, p. 261

Biggers, John US, 1924–2001, p. 36

Blomberg, Hugo (blahm-burg) Sweden, b. 1897, p. 66

Boren, Wen (boh-run, wun) Japan, 1502–1575, p. 141

Bosch, Hieronymus (bosh, hee-RAHN-uh-muhs) Netherlands, ca. 1450–1516, p. 210

Braque, Georges (brak, zhorzh) France, 1882–1963, p. 130

Breuer, Marcel (BROY-er, MAR-sel) Hungary/US, 1902–1981, p. 77

Bruegel the Elder, Pieter (BROY-gul, pee-ter) Flanders, ca. 1564–1638, p. 59

Burroughs, Margaret Taylor US, b. 1917, p. 121

Butterfield, Deborah US, b. 1949, p. 126

Caillebotte, Gustave (kye-bott, goohs-tahv) France 1848–1894, pp. 129, 188

Camp, Sokari Douglas (soh-kah-ree) Nigeria, b. 1958, p. 265

Catlett, Elizabeth US, b. 1919, p. 175

Cézanne, Paul (say-zahn, pol) France, 1839–1906, p. 70

Chao Shao-an (chow shau-ahn) China, 1905–1988, pp. 142–143

Chardin, Jean-Baptiste-Siméon (shahr-dan, zhahn bahp-teest sam-ay-ohn) France, 1699–1779, p. 166

Chicago, Judy US, b. 1939, p. 97

Courbet, Gustave (koor-bay, goohs-tahv) France, 1819–1877, p. 150

Dahomey Artists (duh-HOE-mee) African kingdom, pp. 20–22

Dalí, Salvador (dah-LEE, SAHL-vah-door) Spain, 1904–1989, p. 193

Dancer, Daniel US, b. ca. 1945, p. 257

de Saint Phalle, Niki (duh sahn FAHLL, nee-kee) France, 1930–2002, p. 31

Duchamp, Marcel (doo-SHAHM, mar-SEL) France, 1887–1968, p. 246

Eiffel, Alexandre-Gustave (ee-fel, al-ex-andr goo-stahv) France, 1832–1923, p. 235

Escher, M. C. (EH-sher) Germany, 1898–1972, p. 186

Ewen, Phyllis (YOO-wen) US, b. ca. 1945, p. 159

Mark, Mary Ellen US, b. 1940, p. 47

Martinez, Oscar (mar-TEE-nez) US, b. 1950, p. 61

Mayan Artists pre-Columbian Mexico, pp. 230, 238

Mazur, Michael (MAY-zuhr) US, b. 1935, pp. 160, 181

Méndez, Lillian (MAYN-dez) US, b. 1957, pp. 202–203

Metsu, Gabriel (MET-soo, GAH-bree-ell) Netherlands, 1629–1667, p. 46

Ming Dynasty Artists China, 1368–1644, pp. 140–141

Miyake, Issey (mee-YAH-kay, ISS-ee) Japan/US, b. 1938, pp. 62–63

Moran, Thomas US, 1837–1926, p. 118

Morgan, Robert Mark US, b. 1970, p. 90

Moroles, Jesús (moh-ROH-lace, hay-SOOS) US, b. 1950, pp. 258–259

Muhammad, Shaykh (muh-HA-med, shake) Persia, active mid-1500s, p. 8

Nevelson, Louise (NEH-vul-sin) Russia/US, 1899–1988, p. 248

Nivola, Tino (NEE-voh-lah, TEE-noh) Italy/US, 1911–1988, p. 253

Obin, Philomé (oh-bahn, fee-loh-may) Haiti,1892–1986, p. 51

Oleszko, Pat (oh-LESS-koh) US, b. 1947, p. 73

Peeters, Clara (PAY-turs, KLAH-rah) Flanders, 1594–1657, p. 156

Penrose, Roland England, 1900–1984, p. 197

Petyarre, Ada Bird (pet-YAR) Australia, b. 1930, pp. 172–173

Picasso, Pablo (pee-KAHS-soh, PAH-bloh) Spain, 1881–1973, p. 270

Pickersgill, Mrs. Mary (PICK-uhrz-gihl) US, p. 178

Pissarro, Camille (peez-zah-roh, cah-meel) France, 1803–1903, p. 189

Poisson, Louverture (pwah-sohn, loo-vair-toor) Haiti, 1914–1985, p. 50

Powers, Harriet US, 1837–1911, p. 28

Pu Ru China 1896–1963, p. 98

Quick-to-See Smith, Jaune (zhohn) US, b. 1940, pp. 242–245

Raymond, Eleanor US, 1888–1989, p. 241

Renoir, Pierre-Auguste (ren-wahr, p'yare oh-goost) France, p. 68

Rietveld, Gerrit T. (REET-felt, gherr-eet) Holland 1888–1965, p. 89

Rivera, Diego (ree-VARE-ah, dee-AY-go) Mexico, 1886–1957, p. 106

Rockwell, Norman US, 1894–1978, p. 103

Ronibson, René (RON-ib-son, rah-NAY) Australia, active 21st century, p. 171

Rosenquist, James (ROH-zen-kwist) US b. 1933, p. 55

Ruisdael, Jacob van (RIZE-dahl, YAH-kop fahn) Netherlands, ca. 1628–1682, p. 136

Ruscha, Ed (roosh-ah) US, b. 1937, p. 190

Sakkal, Mamoun (Sah-KAHL, Mah-MOON) Syria/US, p. 99

Sanditz, Lisa (SAND-its) US, b. 1973, p. 271

Shahn, Ben US, b. 1898–1969, pp. 103, 120

Shimomura, Roger (shee-moe-MOOR-uh) US, b. 1939, pp. 18–19

Shire, Peter (SHY-ur) US, b. 1947, p. 77

Soleri, Paolo (soh-LARE-ee, POW-loh) Italy, b. 1919, p. 217

Tang Dynasty Artists (tahng) China, 618–906, p. 127

Traylor, Bill (TRAY-ler) US, ca. 1856–1949, p. 181

Turner, J. M. W. England, 1775–1851, p. 137

VanDerZee, James (VAN-dur-zee) US, 1886–1983, p. 47

Varo, Remedios (VAH-roh, reh-MAY-dee-ohs) Spain, 1908–1963, pp. 182–185

Vázquez, Pedro Ramirez (VAHSS-kez, PAY-droh rah-MEE-rez) Mexico, 1900s, p. 230

Venturi, Robert; Brown, Denise Scott and Associates (ven-TOOR-ee) US, b. 1925, b. 1931, p. 227

Wade, Erika US. b. 1953, p. 269

Waddell, Theodore (wah-DELL) US, b. 1941, pp. 122–125

Walkowitz, Abraham (WALK-oh-wits) Russia, active US, 1878–1965, p. 10

Waqialla, Osman (wah-kee-AHL-lah, ohz-MAHN) Sudan, 1925–2007, p. 112–113

Waring, Laura Wheeler US, 1887–1948, p. 68

Webb, Philip England, 1831–1915, p. 226

Wilson, Mary Ellen US, b. ca. 1973, p. 239

Wind, Nomi (NOE-mee) Israel, b. 1940, pp. 262–263

Wolfe, George US, b. ca. 1940 p. 205

Wood, Grant US, 1891–1942, p. 40

Wright, Frank Lloyd US, 1867–1959, pp. 216, 227

Yemadje, Joseph (yeh-MAHD-yeh) Benin, 1900s, p. 22

Yoruba Artists (YOH-roo-bah) Nigeria, Republic of Benin, 1100–present, p. 156

Glossary

appliqué *(ah-plee-kay)* A process of stitching and/or gluing cloth to a background, similar to collage. *(aplicación)*

arabesques *(ah-ruh-BESKS)* Geometric designs and curves, often connected with calligraphic writing. *(arabescos)*

archaeologists Scientists who study past human life by using a series of special methods for digging for objects and remains in the earth. They must first research and locate a place to dig and then carefully preserve and record the items they uncover. *(arqueólogos)*

architect A person who designs the construction of buildings or large structures. *(arquitecto)*

architectural model A small, three-dimensional representation of a building, often made of paper, cardboard, wood, or plastic. Architects usually create such a model during the process of designing a building. *(modelo arquitectónico)*

architecture Buildings and other large structures. Also the art and science of planning and constructing such buildings. *(arquitectura)*

assemblage *(ah-SEM-blij)* A three-dimensional work of art consisting of many pieces joined together. A sculpture made by joining many objects together. *(ensamblaje)*

asymmetrical balance *(ay-sih-MET-trih-kul)* A type of balance in which things on each side of a center line in a composition are different, yet equal in weight or interest. Also called informal balance. *(balance asimétrico)*

banner A piece of cloth with a design or words on it. *(pancarta)*

barrel vault An architectural form made up of a series of connected arches. *(bóveda de cañón)*

bas-relief *(bah ree-LEEF)* Also called low relief. A form of sculpture in which portions of the design stand out slightly from a flat background. *(bajorrelieve)*

blending A shading technique in which the artist rubs from dark areas of a drawing to light areas to create a gradual change in the lightness or darkness of a color. *(mezcla)*

calligraphy *(kah-LIG-rah-fee)* Precise, beautiful handwriting. *(caligrafía)*

cantilever *(kan-tih-LEE-ver)* A structure, such as a beam or roof, that is supported at one end only. *(ménsula)*

casting A multistep process for creating sculptures in bronze, concrete, plaster, plastic, or other materials. Some casting techniques allow an artist to create several sculptures from a single mold. *(vaciado)*

choreographer A person who plans and arranges the different steps and movements of a dance. *(coreógrafo)*

complement The color opposite a color on the color wheel. *(complemento)*

contour drawing A drawing that shows only the edges (contours) of objects. *(contorno)*

contrast A principle of design that refers to differences in elements such as color, texture, value, and shape. Contrasts usually add excitement, drama, and interest to artworks. *(contraste)*

crosshatching Shading effect created by using crossed parallel lines. The lines go in two different directions. The artist makes hatched lines, then crosses those lines with another set of lines. *(sombreado cruzado)*

dynasty *(DIE-nis-tee)* A group of rulers from the same family or related in some other way. *(dinastía)*

ergonomic *(er-goh-NOM-ik)* A design that is built to increase the user's comfort and/or productivity. *(ergonómico)*

expressive color Color that communicates an artist's ideas or feelings. *(color expresivo)*

façade *(fah-SAHD)* The front of a house or building. It also refers to any face of a building given special architectural treatment. *(fachada)*

fiber artist An artist who uses long, thin, thread-like materials to create artwork. *(artista de fibra)*

form An element of design; any three-dimensional object such as a cube, sphere, pyramid, or cylinder. A form can be measured from top to bottom (height), side to side (width) and front to back (depth). Form is also a general term that means the structure or design of a work. *(forma)*

frames A series of connected pictures. This method of linking scenes together led to popular ways of telling stories in the 1900s such as the newspaper comic strip and comic books. *(viñetas)*

function A general term that refers to how the structure or design of a composition works. *(función)*

genre scene *(ZHAHN-ruh)* A scene or subject from everyday life. *(escena costumbrista)*

geodesic dome A lightweight, domed structure that is formed from many connected triangles. *(cúpula geodésica)*

gesture drawing A quick drawing that captures the gestures or movements of the body. *(dibujo gestual)*

graphic designer An artist who plans the lettering and images for books, packages, posters, and other printed materials. *(diseñador gráfico)*

guild A group of skilled craftspeople. Each guild has a specialty, such as working with metal or carving stone. *(gremio)*

hacienda *(ha-SEE-en-duh)* A large agricultural estate that houses hundreds of workers on a plantation. *(hacienda)*

Harlem Renaissance *(HAR-lem ren-eh-SAHNSS)* 1920–1940. A name of a period and a group of artists who lived and worked in Harlem, New York City. They used a variety of art forms to express their lives as African Americans. *(Renacimiento de Harlem)*

hatching This is created by drawing closely spaced, parallel lines. When the lines are close together, they create a dark area. When they are farther apart, they create a lighter area. *(sombreado)*

hieroglyph *(HAHY-er-uh-glif)* A picture or symbol used in writing instead of a word; the system was first used in ancient Egypt. *(símbolo jeroglífico)*

highlights This refers to the area on a form that reflects the most light. *(luces)*

high relief A sculpture that stands sharply off its background. *(alto relieve)*

horizon line A level line where water or land seem to end and the sky begins. It is usually on the eye level of the observer. If the horizon cannot be seen, its location must be imagined. *(línea de horizonte)*

hues Another name for colors; the three primary hues or colors are red, yellow, and blue. Different combinations of these three hues create all other colors. *(tintes)*

incise To cut a shallow line in material such as wood. *(grabar)*

installation art Temporary arrangements of art objects in galleries, museums, or outdoors. *(arte de instalación)*

intensity The brightness or dullness of a color. *(intensidad)*

interpret This is the way we explain or describe the meaning of things such as nature, art, architecture, music, and literature. *(interpretar)*

linear perspective *(lin-EE-er per-SPEK-tiv)* A technique used to show three-dimensional space on a two-dimensional surface. *(perspectiva lineal)*

local color The representation of colors as they appear in the natural world. *(color local)*

low relief This is sculpture that stands out only slightly from its background. *(bajo relieve)*

Luminism *(LOO-min-izm)* A style of painting, popular in the United States in the 1800s, in which artists focused on the realistic depiction of light and its effects. *(luminismo)*

mimes Performers who communicate without using words; they use movements and facial expressions to act out scenes. They do not speak while they are acting. The art form began in ancient Rome. *(mimos)*

monoprint A printing process in which an image is carved into the surface of a plate and transferred from the painted or inked surface onto a sheet of paper. Monoprinting usually involves creating one unique print instead of many. *(monograbado)*

monotype A print that is usually limited to one copy. The plate's surface is not carved. *(monotipo)*

mural A large painting or artwork, usually designed for and created on the wall or ceiling of a public building. *(mural)*

narrative art Art that clearly depicts a story or idea. *(arte narrativo)*

nib the writing point of a calligraphy pen. It comes in various widths. *(plumín)*

pattern A choice of lines, colors or shapes, repeated over and over in a planned way. A pattern is also a model or guide for making something. *(patrón)*

perspective *(per-SPEK-tiv)* Techniques for creating a look of depth on a two-dimensional surface. *(perspectiva)*

petroglyph *(PET-roh-glif)* A line drawing or carving made on a rock or rock surface, often created by prehistoric people. *(petroglifo)*

pictogram A picture that stands for a word or an idea. Also called pictograph. *(pictograma)*

popular culture This is a term used to describe the ideas, people, and things that society likes during a current or past time period. *(cultura popular)*

portrait An artwork that shows a specific person or group of people. *(retrato)*

Post-Modernism A style that reacts against earlier modernist styles, sometimes by using them to extremes. Post-modern architecture often combines some styles from the past with more decoration, line, and/or color. *(Posmodernismo)*

poster A large, printed sheet, usually made of paper or cardboard, that advertises, teaches, or announces something. A poster usually combines pictures and words. *(afiche/cartel)*

primary colors The three colors from which other colors can be made: red, yellow, and blue. *(colores primarios)*

printmaker An artist who uses different techniques to create original prints. *(un grabadista)*

proportion The relation of one object to another in size, amount, or number. Proportion is often used to describe the relationship between one part of the human figure and another. *(proporción)*

prototype An original model from which other similar objects are made. *(prototipo)*

Realists Artists who thought art should be about places and things they saw every day. *(realista)*

relief print A print made by inking the raised surface of a block or plate. *(grabado en relieve)*

relief sculpture A three-dimensional work designed to be viewed from one side, in which surfaces are raised from a background. *(escultura a relieve)*

Romantic A style of art whose themes focus on dramatic action, exotic settings, imaginary events, and strong feelings. *(romántico)*

sabi *(sah-bee)* A traditional rule of Japanese design that refers to the timelessness or simplicity of a design. *(sabi)*

santos (*sahn-toes*) Carved, religious figures, usually made using clay, stone, or wood. *(santos)*

scale The size relationship between two sets of dimensions. For example, if a picture is drawn to scale, all its parts are equally smaller or larger than the parts in the original. *(escala)*

self-portrait Any work of art in which an artist shows himself or herself. *(autorretrato)*

series A group of related artworks, such as a group of sculptures, paintings, or prints. *(serie)*

setting This refers to the time and place in which the artist or writer has events occur in a storytelling painting or sculpture or a written story. (*escenario)*

shade Any dark value of a color, usually made by adding black. *(matiz)*

shading A gradual change from light to dark. Shading is a way of making a picture appear more realistic and three-dimensional. *(sombreado)*

site-specific sculpture A sculpture created for a particular space, usually outdoors. They may be permanent, but site-specific sculptures are often temporary. *(escultura sitial)*

still life Art based on an arrangement of objects that are not alive and cannot move, such as fruit, flowers, or bottles. The items are often symbols for abstract ideas. A book, for example, may be a symbol for knowledge. A still life is usually shown in an indoor setting. *(naturaleza muerta)*

stippling This technique uses patterns of dots to create and make gradual changes in the lightness or darkness of a color. *(punteado)*

subject matter What you see in an artwork, including a topic, idea, or anything recognizable, such as a landscape or a figure. *(asunto)*

Surrealist An artist for whom dreams, fantasy, and the human mind are sources of ideas. *(surrealista)*

symbol Something that stands for something else, especially a letter, figure, or sign that represents a real object or an idea. A red heart shape, for example, is a common symbol for love. *(símbolo)*

symmetry *(SIM-i-tree)* A type of balance that is characterized by the similar placement of parts on opposite sides of an image. *(simetría)*

tapestry *(TAP-iss-tree)* A stitched or woven piece of cloth or fabric, often one that tells a story. *(tapiz)*

texture The way a surface feels (actual texture) or how it may look (implied texture). Texture can be sensed by touch and sight. Textures are described by words such as rough, silky, pebbly. *(textura)*

tint A light value of pure color, usually made by adding a color to white. For example, pink is a tint of red. *(matiz claro)*

value An element of art that means the darkness or lightness of a surface. Value depends on how much light a surface reflects. Tints are light values of pure colors. Shades are dark values of pure colors. Value can also be an important element in works of art in which there is little or no color (drawings, prints, photographs, most sculpture and architecture). *(valor)*

vanishing point In a perspective drawing, one or more points on the horizon where parallel lines that go back in space seem to meet. *(punto de fuga)*

visual rhythm This is created when an artist repeats an element such as a color, line, or shape. *(ritmo visual)*

wabi *(wah-bee)* A traditional rule of Japanese design that refers to the idea of finding beauty in simple, natural things. *(wabi)*

woodcuts Relief prints created by carving into a smooth block of wood, inking the wood, and pressing paper against the ink. *(xilografía)*

Index

Italicized page numbers refer to artworks.

Italicized page numbers refer to artworks.

Italicized page numbers refer to artworks.

N

O

P

Italicized page numbers refer to artworks.

Italicized page numbers refer to artworks.